Clashing Views in

Anthropology

FOURTH EDITION

TAKING SIDES

Clashing Views in

Anthropology

FOURTH EDITION

Selected, Edited, and with Introductions by

Kirk M. Endicott
Dartmouth College

and

Robert L. Welsch
Dartmouth College

Boston   Burr Ridge, IL   Dubuque, IA   New York   San Francisco   St. Louis
Bangkok   Bogotá   Caracas   Kuala Lumpur   Lisbon   London   Madrid   Mexico City
Milan   Montreal   New Delhi   Santiago   Seoul   Singapore   Sydney   Taipei   Toronto

The McGraw·Hill Companies

Higher Education

TAKING SIDES: CLASHING VIEWS IN ANTHROPOLOGY, FOURTH EDITION

Published by McGraw-Hill, a business unit of The McGraw-Hill Companies, Inc., 1221 Avenue of the Americas, New York, NY 10020. Copyright © 2009 by The McGraw-Hill Companies, Inc. All rights reserved. Previous edition(s) 2001–2005. No part of this publication may be reproduced or distributed in any form or by any means, or stored in a database or retrieval system, without the prior written consent of The McGraw-Hill Companies, Inc., including, but not limited to, in any network or other electronic storage or transmission, or broadcast for distance learning.

Some ancillaries, including electronic and print components, may not be available to customers outside the United States.

Taking Sides® is a registered trademark of the McGraw-Hill Companies, Inc.
Taking Sides is published by the **Contemporary Learning Series** group within the McGraw-Hill Higher Education division.

1 2 3 4 5 6 7 8 9 0 DOC/DOC 0 9 8

MHID: 0-07-351522-1
ISBN: 978-0-07-351522-9
ISSN: 1530-0757

Managing Editor: *Larry Loeppke*
Production Manager: *Faye Schilling*
Senior Developmental Editor: *Susan Brusch*
Editorial Assistant: *Nancy Meissner*
Production Service Assistant: *Rita Hingtgen*
Permissions Coordinator: *Lori Church*
Senior Marketing Manager: *Julie Keck*
Marketing Communications Specialist: *Mary Klein*
Marketing Coordinator: *Alice Link*
Project Manager: *Jane Mohr*
Design Specialist: *Tara McDermott*
Senior Administrative Assistant: *DeAnna Dausener*
Cover Graphics: *Kristine Jubeck*

Compositor: Hurix Systems Private Limited
Cover Image: Digital Vision

Library of Congress Cataloging-in-Publication Data
Main entry under title:
Taking sides: clashing views in anthropology/selected, edited, and with introductions by Kirk M. Endicott and Robert L. Welsch.—4th ed.

Includes bibliographical references.
1. Anthropology. I. Endicott, Kirk M., *comp.* II. Welsch, Robert L., *comp.*

306

www.mhhe.com

Preface

Many courses and textbooks present anthropology as a discipline that largely consists of well-established facts. In *Taking Sides: Clashing Views in Anthropology* we present the discipline in quite a different light. Here we focus on active controversies that remain unresolved. These issues represent the kind of arguments and debates that have characterized anthropology for more than a century. They show the varied ways that anthropologists approach the subject of their research and the kinds of anthropological evidence needed to bolster an academic argument.

Generally, we have chosen selections that express strongly worded positions on two sides of an issue. For most issues, several other reasonable positions are also possible, and we have suggested some of these in our introductions and postscripts that accompany each issue.

Taking Sides: Clashing Views in Anthropology is a tool to encourage and develop critical thinking about anthropological research questions, methods, and evidence. We have selected a range of readings and issues to illustrate the kinds of topics that anthropologists study. Another goal of this volume is to provide opportunities for students to explore how anthropologists frame and defend their interpretations of anthropological evidence. We have also chosen issues that raise questions about research methods and the quality or reliability of different kinds of data. All of these complex matters go into shaping the positions that anthropologists debate and defend in their writings. We hope that in discussing these issues students will find opportunities to explore how anthropologists think about the pressing theoretical issues of the day.

Plan of the book   This book is made up of 19 issues that deal with topics that have provoked starkly different positions by different anthropologists. We have divided the volume into five Units reflecting the discipline's four main subfields (Biological Anthropology, Archaeology, Linguistic Anthropology, and Cultural Anthropology) as well as another Unit dealing with Ethics in Anthropology. Each issue begins with an *introduction,* which sets the stage for the debate as argued in the YES and NO selections. Following these two selections is a *postscript* that makes some final observations and points the way to other questions related to the issue. In reading an issue and forming your own opinions, you should remember that there are often alternative perspectives that are not represented in either the YES or NO selections. Most issues have reasonable positions that might appear to be intermediate between the two more extreme viewpoints represented here in the readings. There are also reasonable positions that lie totally outside the scope of the debate presented in these selections, and students should consider all of these possible positions. Each postscript also contains *suggestions for further reading* that will help you find further resources to continue your study of any topic. Students researching any of these issues or related ones for a research paper will find these further readings (as well as their bibliographies) a useful place to begin a more intensive analysis. At the end of the book we have also included a list of all the *contributors to this volume,* which will give you information on the anthropologists and other commentators whose views are debated here. An *Internet References* page accompanies each part opener. This page gives you Internet site addresses (URLs) that are relevant to the issues discussed in that part of the book. Many of these sites contain links to related sites and bibliographies for further study.

Changes to this edition   This edition has been updated to reflect several current and ongoing controversies that can help undergraduates understand the breadth and range of anthropological research within the four fields of the discipline. Seven issues are new to this edition: "Was There a Pre-Clovis Migration to the New World from Europe?" (Issue 3), "Was the Extinction of Pleistocene Megafauna in North America Caused by Climate Change Rather than Over-Hunting?" (Issue 4), "Should Anthropologists and Linguists Be Concerned About Losing Endangered Languages?" (Issue 7), "Should Cultural Anthropology Stop Trying to Model Itself on Sciences?" (Issue 8), "Do Men Dominate Women in All Societies?" (Issue 11), "Is Gay Marriage Natural?" (Issue 12), and "Does the Natural-Supernatural Distinction Exist in All Cultures?" (Issue 13). In addition, we have selected a new pair of readings to address this Issue: "Is Race a Useful Concept for Anthropologists?" (Issue 1).

A word to the instructor   An *Instructor's Resource Guide with Test Questions* (multiple choice and essay) is available through the publisher for the instructor using *Taking Sides* in the classroom. A general guidebook, called *Using Taking Sides in the Classroom,* which discusses methods and techniques for integrating the pro/con approach into any classroom setting, is also available. An online version of *Using Taking Sides in the Classroom* and a correspondence service for Taking Sides adopters can be found at http://www.mhcls.com/usingts/.

   Taking Sides: Clashing Views in Anthropology is only one of many titles in the Taking Sides series. If you are interested in seeing the table of contents for any of the other titles, please visit the Taking Sides Web site at http://www.mhcls.com/takingsides/.

Acknowledgments   We received many helpful comments and suggestions from many friends and colleagues, including Kamyar Abdi, Hoyt Alverson, Colin Calloway, Elizabeth Carpenter, Brian Didier, Dale Eickelman, Rachel Flemming, Jana Fortier, Laura Garzon, Rosemary Gianno, Paul Goldstein, Alberto Gomez, Robert Gordon, Allen Hockley, Judy Hunt, Peter Jenks, Sergei Kan, Steve Kangas, Katherine Keith, Kenneth Korey, Christine Kray, Laura Litton, Lynn MacGillivray, Deborah Martin, Deborah Nichols, Ventura Perez, Lynn Rainville, Kevin Reinhart, John Edward Terrell, Robert Tonkinson, John Watanabe, and Lindsay Whaley. We also want to thank John Cocklin, Lucinda Hall, Francis X. Oscadal, Cindy Shirkey, Reinhart Sonnenberg, and Amy Witzel, members of the Baker-Berry Library Reference Department at Dartmouth College, all of whom helped track down many of the sources and background readings we have used in setting up these issues. We also want to thank our student research assistants Todd Rabkin Golden, Adam Slutsky, Whitney Wilking, and Rachel Yemeni and our Presidential Scholars/student research assistants Eric Goodman, Joseph Hanlon, Tate LeFebre, Lauren Weldon, Russell Herman, and Adam Levine. Ted Knight and Juliana Gribbins at McGraw-Hill offered useful advice, patience, and suggestions. We also want to thank Susan Brusch of McGraw-Hill in Dubuque, Iowa, for her help in making this latest edition a reality. Finally, we wish to thank our wives, Karen L. Endicott and Sarah L. Welsch, for their support and encouragement during the preparation of this volume.

Kirk M. Endicott
Dartmouth College

Robert L. Welsch
Dartmouth College

Contents In Brief

Contents

Archaeologists Bruce Bradley and Dennis Stanford maintain that there is no evidence that the ancestors of the Clovis big-game hunting people of North America originated in Siberia and migrated down an ice-free corridor from Alaska. They argue that Clovis stone tool technology probably developed among the Solutreans of Europe, and that Solutrean hunters traveled across the north Atlantic ice sheet to North America, where they became the ancestors of the Clovis people. Anthropologist Lawrence Guy Straus counters that the Solutrean culture ended at least 5,000 years before the Clovis culture appeared, and that the North Atlantic Ocean would have been an insurmountable barrier to human travel during the last glacial maximum. He argues that the similarities between the Clovis and Solutrean tool technologies are limited and coincidental.

Archaeologists Donald Grayson and David Meltzer argue that the evidence that human predation caused the Pleistocene Megafauna's extinction is circumstantial. They contend that there is little archaeological evidence to support that hypothesis, and they suggest that climate change is a more likely explanation for these extinctions in North America as it seems to be for those in Europe. Archaeologists Stuart Fiedel and Gary Haynes are strong supporters of the overkill hypothesis, which argues that humans overhunted large mammals to extinction in North America. They contend that Grayson and Meltzer have misinterpreted older archaeological evidence and largely ignore more recent data. They maintain that the extinctions took place too fast to have been caused by climate change.

Archaeologists Brian Billman and Banks L. Leonard and bioarchaeologist Patricia Lambert argue that there is evidence of prehistoric cannibalism in the Mesa Verde region of southwestern Colorado. They conclude that the bodies of seven individuals were processed in ways that suggest that they were eaten by other humans. Archaeologists Kurt E. Dongoske and T.J. Ferguson and bioarchaeologist Debra L. Martin object that the analytical framework Billman et al. use assumes that cannibalism took place and does not adequately consider alternative hypotheses.

Psychologist and primate specialist E. S. Savage-Rumbaugh argues that, since the 1960s, attempts to teach chimpanzees and other apes symbol systems similar to human language have resulted in the demonstration of a genuine ability to create new symbolic patterns. Linguist Joel Wallman counters that attempts to teach chimps and other apes sign language or other symbolic systems have demonstrated that apes are very intelligent animals, but up to now these attempts have not shown that apes have any innate capacity for language.

Linguist Ken Hale contends that the loss of endangered languages represents a major tragedy for humanity, because each language that goes extinct reduces the world's linguistic diversity. The pace of extinctions has increased over the past century, mostly because government policies routinely encourage language loss. While linguists have a responsibility for recording and documenting endangered languages, they also have a role to play in influencing government policies that can encourage retention of these minority languages. Linguist Peter Ladefoged accepts the fact that endangered languages are disappearing, but feels that the position taken by Ken Hale and his colleagues is unacceptably paternalistic. He contends that while it is a good thing to study linguistic diversity, the people who speak endangered languages have just as much right to participate in their nation's affairs as anyone else, even if it means their children will learn the metropolitan language, not the endangered language.

distinguishes native communities from dominant Western culture. Hawaiian activist and scholar Haunani-Kay Trask asserts that Keesing's critique is fundamentally flawed because he only uses Western documents—and native peoples have oral traditions, genealogies, and other historical sources that are not reflected in Western historical documents. Anthropologists like Keesing, she maintains, are trying to hold on to their privileged position as experts in the face of growing numbers of educated native scholars.

Sociologist Steven Goldberg contends that in all societies men occupy most high positions in hierarchical organizations and most high-status roles, and they also tend to dominate women in interpersonal relations. This is because men's hormones cause them to compete more strongly than women for status and dominance. Cultural anthropologists Kirk and Karen Endicott argue that among the Batek people of Malaysia gender roles are not rigidly distinguished. Even the headman of the foraging band in which they lived was a woman. Batek women and men have autonomy and similar access to possessions. They contend that Batek social and cultural treatment of the two sexes is remarkably egalitarian.

Anthropologist Linda S. Stone argues that anthropologists have traditionally sought to discover and describe the range of variation among the world's cultures. A definition of marriage that covers this institution in all human societies has been futile. Institutions that resemble marriage in Western countries confer birth rights, sexual access, residence, and other rights, but no set of these rights covers "marriage" in all societies. She views gay marriage in Western Europe, Canada, and Massachusetts as simply another example of the wide variation found in human societies. Anthropologist Peter Wood argues that 150 years of ethnographic studies of kinship have demonstrated that in the vast majority of human societies marriage consists of a union between a man and a woman. Claims by anthropologists that suggest otherwise are misleading by focusing on a handful of exceptional cases in exotic places. Such cases do not demonstrate that gay marriage has ever been an established way of organizing families in non-Western societies. Gay marriage, he argues, is a novel institution, not merely a minor variation among the diverse forms of marriage that have been observed in the ethnographic record.

Cultural anthropologist Roger Ivar Lohmann argues that a supernaturalistic worldview or cosmology is at the heart of virtually all religions. For him the supernatural is a concept that exists everywhere, although it is expressed differently in each society. For him, supernaturalism attributes volition to things that do not have it. He argues that the supernatural is also a part of Western people's daily experience in much the same ways that it is the experience of the Papua New Guineans with whom he worked. Lutheran pastor and anthropological researcher Frederick (Fritz) P. Lampe argues that "supernatural" is a problematic and inappropriate term like the term "primitive." If we accept the term "supernatural," it is all too easy to become ethnocentric and assume that anything supernatural is unreal, and therefore false. He considers a case at the University of Technology in Papua New Guinea to show how use of the term "supernatural" allows us to miss out on how Papua New Guineans actually understand the world in logical, rational, and naturalistic terms that Westerners would generally see as illogical, irrational, and supernaturalistic.

Archaeologists James R. Denbow and Edwin N. Wilmsen argue that the San of the Kalahari Desert in southern Africa have been involved in pastoralism, agriculture, and regional trade networks since at least 800 A.D. They imply that the San, who were hunting and gathering in the twentieth century, were descendants of pastoralists who lost their herds due to subjugation by outsiders, drought, and livestock disease. Cultural anthropologist Richard B. Lee counters that evidence from oral history, archaeology, and ethnohistory shows that the Ju/'hoansi group of San living in the isolated Nyae Nyae-Dobe area of the Kalahari Desert were autonomous hunter-gatherers until the twentieth century. Although they carried on some trade with outsiders before then, it had minimal impact on their culture.

Physician Sangun Suwanlert from Thailand asks whether or not one particular illness he observed in northern Thai villages, called *phii pob*, corresponds to Western diagnostic categories or is restricted to Thailand. He concludes that *phii pob* is indeed a "culture-bound syndrome" that can only occur among people who share rural Thai cultural values and beliefs. Medical anthropologist Robert A. Hahn counters that the very idea of the so-called culture-bound syndrome is flawed. He contends that culture-bound syndromes are reductionist explanations for certain complex illness conditions—that is, explanations that reduce complex phenomena to a single variable.

Indian social researcher Sudhir Kakar analyzes the origins of ethnic conflict from a psychological perspective to argue that ethnic differences are deeply held distinctions that from time to time will inevitably erupt as ethnic conflicts. He maintains that anxiety arises from preconscious fears about cultural differences. In his view, no amount of education or politically correct behavior will eradicate these fears and anxieties about people of differing ethnic backgrounds. American sociologist Anthony Oberschall considers the ethnic conflicts that have recently emerged in Bosnia and contends that primordial ethnic attachments are insufficient to explain the sudden emergence of violence among Bosnian ethnic groups. He adopts a complex explanation for this violence, identifying circumstances in which fears and anxieties were manipulated by politicians for self-serving ends. It was only in the context of these manipulations that ethnic violence could have erupted, concludes Oberschall.

UNIT 5   ETHICS IN ANTHROPOLOGY   317

Assistant professor of justice studies and member of the Pawnee tribe James Riding In argues that holding Native American skeletons in museums and other repositories represents a sacrilege against Native

American dead and, thus, all Indian remains should be reburied. Professor of anthropology and archaeologist Clement W. Meighan believes that archaeologists have a moral and professional obligation to the archaeological data with which they work. Such data are held in the public good and must be protected from destruction.

Anthropologist Terence Turner contends that journalist Patrick Tierney's book *Darkness in El Dorado* accurately depicts how anthropologist Napoleon Chagnon's research among the Yanomami Indians caused conflict between groups and how Chagnon's portrayal of the Yanomami as extremely violent aided gold miners trying to take over Yanomami land. Anthropologists Edward Hagen, Michael Price, and John Tooby counter that Tierney systematically distorts Chagnon's views on Yanomami violence and exaggerates the amount of disruption caused by Chagnon's activities compared to those of others such as missionaries and gold miners.

Postmodernist anthropologist James Clifford argues that the very act of removing objects from their ethnographic contexts distorts the meaning of objects held in museums. Exhibitions misrepresent ethnic communities by omitting important aspects of contemporary life, especially involvement with the colonial or Western world. Anthropologist Denis Dutton asserts that no exhibition can provide a complete context for ethnographic objects, but that does not mean that museum exhibitions are fundamentally flawed.

Correlation Guide

The *Taking Sides* series presents current issues in a debate-style format designed to stimulate student interest and develop critical thinking skills. Each issue is thoughtfully framed with an issue summary, an issue introduction, and a postscript. The pro and con essays—selected for their liveliness and substance—represent the arguments of leading scholars and commentators in their fields.

Taking Sides: Clashing Views in Anthropology, 4/e is an easy-to-use reader that presents issues on important topics such as violence, endangered languages, and male domination. For more information on *Taking Sides* and other *McGraw-Hill Contemporary Learning Series* titles, visit www.mhcls.com.

This convenient guide matches the issues in **Taking Sides: Anthropology, 4/e** with the corresponding chapters in two of our best-selling McGraw-Hill Anthropology textbooks by Kottak and Park.

Taking Sides: Anthropology, 4/e	Anthropology, 12/e by Kottak	Introducing Anthropology, 4/e by Park
Issue 1: Is Race a Useful Concept for Anthropologists?	**Chapter 5:** Human Variation and Adaptation **Chapter 14:** Ethnicity and Race	**Chapter 8:** Human Variation
Issue 2: Are Humans Inherently Violent?	**Chapter 4:** Evolution and Genetics **Chapter 8:** Early Hominins	**Chapter 14:** The Evolution of Our Behaviors
Issue 3: Was There a Pre-Clovis Migration to the New World from Europe?	**Chapter 3:** Ethics and Methods in Physical Anthropology and Archaeology **Chapter 5:** Human Variation and Adaptation **Chapter 10:** The First Farmers	**Chapter 2:** How Anthropology Works **Chapter 8:** Human Variation
Issue 4: Was the Extinction of Pleistocene Megafauna in North America Caused by Climate Change Rather than Over-Hunting?	**Chapter 9:** The Genus Homo **Chapter 10:** The First Farmers	**Chapter 9:** Food **Chapter 14:** The Evolution of Our Behaviors **Chapter 15:** Anthropology in Today's World
Issue 5: Did Prehistoric Native Americans Practice Cannibalism in the American Southwest?	**Chapter 16:** Making a Living	**Chapter 14:** The Evolution of Our Behaviors
Issue 6: Can Apes Learn Language?	**Chapter 6:** The Primates **Chapter 15:** Language and Communication	**Chapter 5:** Our Place in Nature **Chapter 11:** Communication
Issue 7: Should Anthropologists and Linguists Be Concerned About Losing Endangered Languages?	**Chapter 12:** Methods in Cultural Anthropology **Chapter 15:** Language and Communication	**Chapter 11:** Communication

Taking Sides: Anthropology, 4/e	Anthropology, 12/e by Kottak	Introducing Anthropology, 4/e by Park
Issue 8: Should Cultural Anthropology Stop Trying to Model Itself on Sciences?	**Chapter 1:** What is Anthropology? **Chapter 12:** Methods in Cultural Anthropology	**Chapter 2:** How Anthropology Works **Chapter 13:** Culture Change
Issue 9: Was Margaret Mead's Fieldwork on Samoan Adolescents Fundamentally Flawed?	**Chapter 2:** Applying Anthropology	**Chapter 2:** How Anthropology Works **Chapter 13:** Culture Change **Chapter 15:** Anthropology in Today's World
Issue 10: Do Native Peoples Today Invent Their Traditions?	**Chapter 12:** Methods in Cultural Anthropology **Chapter 13:** Culture **Chapter 25:** Cultural Exchange and Survival	**Chapter 4:** Themes of Anthropology
Issue 11: Do Men Dominate Women in All Societies?	**Chapter 18:** Families, Kinship and Descent **Chapter 19:** Marriage **Chapter 20:** Gender	**Chapter 7:** Reproduction **Chapter 10:** Nature of the Group
Issue 12: Is Gay Marriage Natural?	**Chapter 19:** Marriage **Chapter 20:** Gender	**Chapter 7:** Reproduction **Chapter 10:** Nature of the Group
Issue 13: Does the Natural-Supernatural Distinction Exist in All Cultures?	**Chapter 13:** Culture **Chapter 21:** Religion	**Chapter 12:** Maintenance of Order
Issue 14: Are San Hunter-Gatherers Basically Pastoralists Who Have Lost Their Herds?	**Chapter 9:** The Genus Homo **Chapter 10:** The First Farmers	**Chapter 8:** Human Variation **Chapter 9:** Food
Issue 15: Do Some Illnesses Exist Only Among Members of a Particular Culture?	**Chapter 2:** Applying Anthropology **Chapter 5:** Human Variation and Adaptation	**Chapter 8:** Human Variation **Chapter 14:** The Evolution of Our Behaviors **Chapter 15:** Anthropology in Today's World
Issue 16: Is Ethic Conflict Inevitable?	**Chapter 14:** Ethnicity and Race	**Chapter 8:** Human Variation
Issue 17: Should the Remains of Prehistoric Native Americans Be Reburied Rather Than Studied?	**Chapter 3:** Ethics and Methods in Physical Anthropology and Archaeology	**Chapter 2:** How Anthropology Works
Issue 18: Did Napoleon Chagnon's Research Methods and Publications Harm the Yanomami Indians?	**Chapter 3:** Ethics and Methods in Physical Anthropology and Archaeology	**Chapter 1:** Doing Anthropology **Chapter 2:** How Anthropology Works
Issue 19: Do Museums Misrepresent Ethnic Communities Around the World?	**Chapter 3:** Ethics and Methods in Physical Anthropology	**Chapter 15:** Anthropology in Today's World

Introduction

Kirk M. Endicott

Robert L. Welsch

Anthropology is the study of humanity in all its biological, social, cultural, and linguistic diversity. Some of the founders of American anthropology, like Franz Boas, made important contributions to the understanding of human biology, culture, and language. But few such Renaissance men and women can be found today. To master the concepts, methods, and literatures involved in studying the different aspects of human variation, anthropologists have had to specialize. At times it may seem that no two anthropologists actually study the same things, yet they all are working toward a greater understanding of the commonalties and differences that define the human species.

Today, anthropology encompasses four major subdisciplines—biological anthropology, prehistoric archaeology, linguistic anthropology, and cultural anthropology—and several smaller subdisciplines. Controversial issues in each of these subfields are included in the first four parts of this volume.

Biological anthropology, also called *physical anthropology,* concerns the anatomy, physiology, mental capabilities, and genetics of humans and our nearest relatives, the primates. Traditionally, biological anthropologists, like other biologists, have understood human variation in evolutionary terms. Increasingly, as geneticists have introduced new ways of analyzing genetic data encoded in our DNA, biological anthropologists have described and explained human biological variation at the molecular level.

Fundamental questions for biological anthropologists include: How did our species evolve from early non-human primates? When did our species take on attributes that are associated with anatomically modern humans? Where did our species arise? What were the evolutionary forces that contributed to our anatomical and behavioral evolution? How and why did the hominids develop the capacity for culture—socially learned and transmitted patterns of behavior, thought, and feeling? Does our human biology program us to behave in certain ways?

Paleoanthropologists (students of humankind's ancient ancestors) search for and excavate fossil bone fragments of long-dead primates, reconstruct their skeletons, and make inferences about their behavior patterns from bones, teeth, and other clues. They also use sophisticated dating techniques, computer models, and studies of living primates, both in the laboratory and in their natural environments, to create plausible models of human evolution and the relationships among the different branches of the primate order.

Archaeology, which is also referred to as *prehistory,* involves documenting, understanding, and explaining the history of human communities and civilizations that existed before written records. Unlike most historians who can turn to documents and papers to detail the life and times of their subjects, archaeologists must usually find evidence for their reconstructions of the past through excavations of sites where people formerly lived or worked.

One issue at the heart of most archaeological controversies is how we can or should interpret these varied kinds of data to reconstruct the ways of life of earlier times. Recurrent questions include: What is the use and meaning of an artifact? To what extent can we use current lifeways of tribal or foraging groups as analogies for how prehistoric communities lived?

A set of questions that archaeologists continue to ask is when, why, and how people first settled different parts of the world. They also ask why innovations like agriculture developed at particular times and in particular places. Why did some societies develop into complex civilizations, while others remained village-based societies, free of centralized political authority?

A frequent point of debate among archaeologists concerns the dating of archaeological deposits. Accurate dating, even if only relative to other artifacts in a site, is clearly essential for accurate interpretations, although dating alone does not reveal the processes that led to particular changes in the archaeological record. Stratification—the principle that the lower layers of a deposit are older than the upper layers—is still the most reliable basis for relative dating within a site. Now archaeologists also draw on a wide battery of high-tech absolute dating methods—including carbon 14, potassium-argon, and thermoluminescence dating—which have varying degrees of accuracy for different time spans. Dating always requires interpretation because, for example, carbon samples may be contaminated by more recent organic material like tree roots, and scholars do not always agree on the correct interpretation.

Linguistic anthropology includes the study of language and languages, especially non-Western and unwritten languages, as well as the relationship between language and other aspects of culture. Language provides the categories within which culture is expressed. Some anthropologists regard linguistic anthropology as a subdivision of cultural anthropology because language is a part of culture and is the medium by which much of culture is transmitted from one generation to the next. A classic question for linguistic anthropologists has been: Do the categories of a language shape how humans perceive and understand the world? This question was first proposed by linguistic anthropologists Edward Sapir and Benjamin Whorf early in the twentieth century but continues to be one of the central questions of interest to linguistic anthropologists. Another question that linguistic anthropologists have debated for several decades concerns whether chimpanzees and other apes have the innate ability to use symbols in ways that resemble human language. This question is asked in Issue 6, "Can Apes Learn Language?" and is important because if apes are capable of complex symbolic activity, then language and culture are probably not the exclusive capabilities of humans but have their origins in our primate past. A more recent issue for linguistic anthropologists has been how linguists and anthropologists should respond to the fact that many of the world's smaller languages are dying out. Issue 7 addresses this question by asking "Should Anthropologists and Linguists Be Concerned About Losing Endangered Languages?"

Cultural anthropology, which is also called *social anthropology* in Great Britain or sometimes *sociocultural anthropology* in the United States, is concerned with the cultures and societies of living communities. Cultural anthropologists have proposed many different definitions of *culture.* Most emphasize that cultural behavior, thought, and feeling are socially created and learned, rather than generated by biologically transmitted instincts. Anthropologists differ considerably on the relative weight they assign to culture and instincts in explaining human behavior, as some of the issues in this volume show. Because cultures are human creations, they differ from one society to another.

Data for most cultural anthropologists come from observations, informal conversations, and interviews made while living within a study community. The hallmark of cultural anthropology is *fieldwork,* in which the anthropologist lives with another cultural group, learns their language, their customs, and their patterns of interaction. Anthropological fieldwork involves *participant observation*—observing while participating in the life of the community.

As in the other subfields of anthropology, cultural data must be interpreted. Interpretation begins with the creation of the research questions themselves. This reflects what investigators consider as being important to discover and directs their observations and questions in the field. At each step of data collection and analysis, the investigators' theories and interests shape their understanding of other cultures.

Much explanation in cultural anthropology is based on the comparison of cultural features in different societies. Some anthropologists explicitly make cross-cultural comparisons, using statistics to measure the significance of apparent correlations between such things as childrearing practices and adult personalities. Even anthropologists who concentrate on explaining or interpreting features of particular cultures use their knowledge of similar or different features in other societies as a basis for insights.

Like other anthropologists, cultural anthropologists look for uniformities in human behavior as well as variations. Understanding what patterns of human behavior are possible has been at the center of many controversies in cultural anthropology. Questions touched on in this book include: Is gender equality possible? Is violence inevitable? Can small-scale hunting and gathering societies live in contact with more powerful food-producing societies without being dominated by them?

Recently, cultural anthropologists have begun asking questions about possible biases in the ways anthropologists depict and represent other cultures through writing, films, and other media. This movement has been called *post-modern anthropology* or *critical anthropology.* Post-modernists ask, among other things: Do our theories and methods of representation inadvertently portray the people we study as exotic "Others," in exaggerated contrast with Western peoples? This is the question that lies behind Issue 18, "Do Museums Misrepresent Ethnic Communities Around the World?"

Ethics in anthropology   Concerns about the ethics of research have become increasingly important in contemporary anthropology. The American Anthropological Association has developed a Code of Ethics covering both research and teaching (see the American Anthropological Association Web site at http://www.aaanet.org). It recognizes that researchers sometimes have conflicting obligations to the people and animals studied, host countries, the profession, and the public. One basic principle is that researchers should do nothing that could harm or distress the people or animals they study. Cultural anthropologists must be aware of the possibility of harming the living people with whom they work, but similar considerations also affect archaeologists and biological anthropologists because the artifacts of past communities often represent the ancestors of living communities. Here the interests of anthropologists and native peoples may diverge. For example, in Issue 17 we ask, "Should the Remains of Prehistoric Native Americans Be Reburied Rather Than Studied?" Similarly, in Issue 18 we consider the ethical responsibilities of individual field researchers by asking, "Did Napoleon Chagnon's Research Methods and Publications Harm the Yanomami Indians?" Issue 19, "Do Museums Misrepresent Ethnic Communities Around the World?" asks about the ethical obligations museums and anthropologists generally have toward the native peoples in our representations of these peoples and their ancestors.

Some Basic Questions

On the surface, the issues presented in this book are very diverse. Anthropologists from different subfields tend to focus on their own specialized problems and to work with different kinds of evidence. Most of the controversial issues we have chosen for this volume can be read as very narrow, focused debates within a subfield. But many of the issues that confront anthropologists in one subfield arise in other subfields as well. What has attracted us to the issues presented here is that each raises much broader questions that affect the entire discipline. In this section we briefly describe some of the basic questions lying behind specific issues.

Is Anthropology a Science or a Humanity?

Science is a set of ideas and methods intended to describe and explain phenomena in a naturalistic way, seeing individual things and events as the outcome of discoverable causes and as conforming to general laws. Anthropologists taking a scientific approach are concerned with developing broad theories about the processes that lead to observed patterns of variation in human biology, language, and culture. The humanities, on the other hand, are concerned with understanding people's cultural creations in terms of their meanings to their creators and the motivations behind their creation.

Biological anthropology seeks the reasons for human evolution and biological diversity largely in the processes of the natural world, and it uses the methods of the physical sciences for investigating those phenomena. Archaeology, too, uses natural science concepts and methods of investigation, but it also draws on understandings of human behavior that take account of culturally-influenced motivations, values, and meanings. Cultural anthropologists are divided over whether cultural anthropology should model itself on the natural sciences or on the humanities. Some cultural anthropologists try to discover the causes of particular cultural forms occurring at specific places and times, while others try to interpret the meanings (to the people themselves) of cultural forms in other societies in ways that are intelligible to Western readers. Issue 8, "Should Cultural Anthropology Stop Trying to Model Itself on Sciences?", directly addresses the question of whether anthropology is part of the sciences or humanities.

Is Biology or Culture More Important in Shaping Human Behavior?

Most anthropologists accept that both genetically transmitted behavioral tendencies (instincts) and cultural ideas and norms influence human behavior, thought, and emotion. However, anthropologists diverge widely over the amount of weight that they assign to these two influences. *Biological determinists* believe that all human behavior is ultimately determined by the genes, and that culture merely lends distinctive coloration to our genetically driven behaviors. At the other extreme, *cultural determinists* believe that any instincts humans may have are so weak and malleable that cultural learning easily overcomes them. The conflict between supporters of the two extreme views, called the *nature-nurture debate,* has been going on for many years and shows no sign of being resolved soon.

Issue 9, "Was Margaret Mead's Fieldwork on Samoan Adolescents Fundamentally Flawed?", considers the Margaret Mead–Derrick Freeman controversy, which has its roots in the question of whether biology or culture is more important in shaping human behavior. From her research in Samoa, Mead claimed that nurture was most important, while some decades later Freeman concluded from his research in Samoa precisely the opposite. Other issues in this volume deal directly with the nature-nurture question, particularly Issue 2, "Are Humans Inherently Violent?"; Issue 5, "Did Prehistoric Native Americans Practice Cannibalism in the American Southwest?"; Issue 6, "Can Apes Learn Language?"; and Issue 15 "Do Some Illnesses Exist Only Among Members of a Particular Culture?"

Is the Local Development of Culture or Outside Influence More Important in Shaping Cultures?

In trying to explain the form a particular culture takes, different anthropologists place different amounts of emphasis on the local development of culture and on outside influence. Those who favor local development emphasize unique innovations and adaptations to the natural environment, while those favoring outside influences emphasize the borrowing of ideas from neighbors (*diffusion*) and changes forced upon a people by more powerful groups (*acculturation*). Most anthropologists recognize some influence from both sources, but some attribute overriding importance to one or the other.

The debate between proponents of local development of culture and proponents of outside influence plays a major role in two of the issues in this volume: Issue 10, "Do Native Peoples Today Invent Their Traditions?" and Issue 14, "Are San Hunter-Gatherers Basically Pastoralists Who Have Lost Their Herds?"

Some Theoretical Approaches

Anthropologists draw on many theories of widely varying scope and type. We present brief summaries of a number of theoretical approaches used by authors in this book so that you will recognize and understand them when you see them. We have arranged these theories in a rough continuum from most scientific in approach to most humanistic.

Biological evolution   Biological anthropology is based predominantly on the modem theory of biological evolution. This builds upon the ideas that Charles Darwin developed in the mid-nineteenth century. Darwin combined the idea of evolution—the development of species by means of incremental changes in previous species—with the concept of natural selection. Natural selection means that in a variable population those individuals best adapted to the environment are most likely to survive and reproduce, thus passing on their favorable characteristics (called *survival of the fittest*). The modem theory of biological evolution adds an understanding of genetics, including the concepts of *genetic drift* (random variation in gene frequencies) and *gene flow* (transmission of genes between populations). Most biological anthropologists today also subscribe to the notion of *punctuated equilibrium,* which states that evolutionary change takes place in fits and starts, rather than at an even pace.

Virtually all biological anthropologists use the modem theory of evolution, so their disagreements arise not over which theory to use, but over interpretations of evidence and questions of how the theory applies to specific cases.

Sociobiology   Sociobiology is a theory that attempts to use evolutionary principles to explain all behavior of animals, including humans. The best-known practitioner is biologist E. O. Wilson, whose book *Sociobiology: The New Synthesis* (Harvard University Press, 1975) sets out the basic concepts. Sociobiologists believe that human behavior is determined by inherited behavioral tendencies. The genes promoting behaviors that lead to survival and successful reproduction are favored by natural selection and thus tend to become more common in a population over the generations. For sociobiologists such behaviors as selfishness, altruism to close kin, violence, and certain patterns of marriage are evolutionarily and biologically determined. They see individual and cultural ideas as mere rationalizations of innate patterns of behavior. In their view, no culture will persist that goes against the "wisdom of the genes."

Cultural evolution   Drawing on an analogy with biological evolution, nineteenth-century cultural anthropologists developed the idea that complex societies evolve out of simpler ones. The unilineal schemes of such cultural evolutionists as Lewis Henry Morgan, E. B. Tylor, and James G. Fraser postulated that all societies pass through a fixed series of stages, from savagery to civilization. They regarded contemporary simple societies, like the tribal peoples of the Amazon, as "survivals" from earlier stages of cultural evolution.

Unilineal schemes of cultural evolution have now been discredited because they were speculative, ignored differences in patterns of culture change in different places, and were blatantly ethnocentric, regarding all non-Western cultures as inferior to those of Europe. But some archaeologists and cultural anthropologists still espouse more sophisticated versions of cultural evolution regarding at least some aspects of culture change.

Cultural ecology   The theory of cultural ecology was developed by cultural anthropologist Julian Steward in the 1930s as a corrective to the overly simple schemes of cultural evolution. Emphasizing the process of adaptation to the physical environment, he postulated that societies in different environments would develop different practices, though the general trend was toward higher levels of complexity, a process he called *multilinear evolution*. His idea of adaptation, like natural selection, explained why some societies and practices succeeded and were perpetuated, while other less well-adapted ones died out.

Many archaeologists and cultural anthropologists use versions of cultural ecology to explain why certain practices exist in certain environments. Marvin Harris's widely-used theory of *cultural materialism* is a further development of cultural ecology. The basic idea behind all versions of cultural ecology is that societies must fulfill their material needs if they are to survive. Therefore those institutions involved with making a living must be well adapted to the environment, while others, like religions, are less constrained by the environment.

Culture history   One of the founders of American cultural anthropology, Franz Boas, rejected the cultural evolution schemes of the nineteenth century, with their fixed stages of cultural development. He pointed out that all societies had unique histories, depending on local innovations and diffusion of ideas from neighboring societies. Also, change is not always toward greater complexity; civilizations crumble as well as rise. Boas advocated recording the particular events and influences that contributed to the makeup of each culture.

World system theory   The world system theory, which has gained great prominence in the social sciences in recent years, asserts that all societies, large and small, are—and long have been—integrated in a single worldwide political-economic system. This approach emphasizes the connections among societies, especially the influence of politically powerful societies over weak ones, as in colonialism, rather than local development of culture.

Cultural interpretation   Humanist anthropologists emphasize their role as interpreters, not explainers, of culture. They focus on the task of describing other cultures in ways that are intelligible to Western readers, making sense of customs that at first glance seem incomprehensible. The most prominent practitioner of cultural interpretation is Clifford Geertz, who coined the term *thick description* for this process. This approach is used especially for dealing with aspects of culture that are products of human imagination, like art and mythology, but even the institutions involved in physical survival, like families and economic processes, have dimensions of meaning that warrant interpretation.

Feminist anthropology   Feminist anthropology began in the 1970s as an approach meant to correct the lack of coverage of women and women's views in earlier anthropology. It has now developed into a thoroughgoing alternative approach to the study of culture and society. Its basic idea is that gender is a cultural construction affecting the roles and meanings of the sexes in particular societies. The aim of feminist anthropology is both to explain the position of women and to convey the meanings surrounding gender. Feminist anthropologists emphasize that all social relations have a gender dimension.

How Anthropologists Reach Conclusions

None of the issues considered in this volume have been resolved, and several are still the subject of heated, and at times, acrimonious debate. The most heated controversies typically arise from the most extreme points of view. When reading these selections students should bear in mind that only two positions are presented formally, although in the introductions and postscripts we raise questions that should guide you to consider other positions as well. We encourage you to question all of the positions offered before coming to any conclusions of your own. Remember, for more than a century anthropology has prided itself on revealing how our own views of the world are culturally biased. Try to be aware of how your own background, upbringing, ethnicity, religion, likes, and dislikes affect your assessments of the arguments presented here.

In our own teaching we have often used controversial issues as a way to help students understand how anthropologists think about research questions. We have found that five questions often help students focus on the most important points in these selections:

1. Who is the author?
2. What are the author's assumptions?
3. What methods and data does an author use?
4. What are the author's conclusions?
5. How does the author reach his or her conclusions from the data?

For each issue we suggest that you consider what school of thought, what sort of training, and what sort of research experience each author has. We often find it useful to ask why this particular author finds the topic worth writing about. Does one or the other author seem to have any sort of bias?

What assumptions does each author hold? Do both authors hold the same assumptions?

For any anthropological debate, we also find it useful to ask what methods or analytical strategies each author has used to reach the conclusions he or she presents. For some of the issues presented in this book, authors share many of the same assumptions and are generally working with the same evidence, but disagree as to how this evidence should be analyzed. Some authors disagree most profoundly on what kinds of data are most suitable for answering a particular research question. Some even disagree about what kinds of questions anthropologists should be asking.

Finally, we suggest that you consider how the author has come to his or her conclusions from the available data. Would different data make any difference? Would a different kind of evidence be more appropriate? Would different data likely lead to different conclusions? Would different ways of analyzing the data suggest other conclusions?

If you can answer most of these questions about any pair of selections, you will be thinking about these problems anthropologically and will understand how anthropologists approach controversial research questions. After weighing the various possible positions on an issue you will be able to form sound opinions of your own.

Internet References . . .

American Anthropological Association's Statement on "Race"

In 1998 the executive board of the American Anthropological Association issued a Statement on "Race." This statement was compiled by anthropologists from many different research backgrounds and aimed to be general and broad. It does not, however, reflect the consensus of all members of the association.

http://www.aaanet.org/stmts/racepp.htm

Human Origins and Evolution in Africa

Jeanne Sept, an anthropology professor at Indiana University who has done fieldwork on the question of human origins in Africa, created this Web site, which is entitled Human Origins and Evolution in Africa. The site contains much information and provides links to related Web sites.

http://www.indiana.edu/~origins/

Fossil Evidence for Human Evolution in China

The Fossil Evidence for Human Evolution in China Web site was created by the Center for the Study of Chinese Prehistory. This site includes a catalog of Chinese human fossil remains; provides links to other sites dealing with paleontology, human evolution, and Chinese prehistory; and includes other resources that may be useful for gaining a better understanding of China's role in the emergence of humankind.

http://www.chineseprehistory.org

Fossil Hominids: The Evidence for Human Evolution

Created by Jim Foley, this site is entitled Fossil Hominids: The Evidence for Human Evolution, and it provides links to recent articles about human evolution and the question of whether or not Neandertals and early modern humans interbred. A discussion of creationism and the Biblical interpretation of the origins of life is also presented.

http://www.talkorigins.org/faqs/homs/

Biological Anthropology

*B*iological anthropologists, also called physical anthropologists, study the bodies, bones, and genetics of humans and of our nearest relatives, the other primates. Their basic goals are to understand human evolution scientifically and to explain contemporary human diversity. Fundamental questions include: How did our species evolve from early nonhuman primates? When did our species take on attributes that are associated with anatomically modern humans? Where did our species develop as a species, and what were the evolutionary forces that contributed to our anatomical evolution? These questions have traditionally required detailed comparisons of bones from living species and fossilized bones from extinct species. However, increasingly anthropologists asking these kinds of questions are developing new models about evolution from observing and studying living primates either in the laboratory or in their natural environment.

- Is Race a Useful Concept for Anthropologists?
- Are Humans Inherently Violent?

ISSUE 1

Is Race a Useful Concept for Anthropologists?

YES: George W. Gill, from "Does Race Exist? A Proponent's Perspective," *Nova Online* (October 12, 2000)

NO: C. Loring Brace, from "Does Race Exist? An Antagonist's Perspective," *Nova Online* (October 12, 2000)

ISSUE SUMMARY

YES: Biological and forensic anthropologist George Gill argues that the concept of race is useful because races—conceived as populations originating in particular regions—can be distinguished by combinations of external and skeletal features, and the concept of race is especially useful in the forensic task of identifying human skeletons. The notion of race also provides a vocabulary for discussing human biological variation and racism that can be understood by students.

NO: Biological anthropologist C. Loring Brace argues that distinct races cannot be defined because human physical features vary gradually (in clines) and independently from region to region, without sharp discontinuities between physical types. He says races exist in people's perceptions, but not in biological reality.

The European idea of humanity's being divided into physically distinct types—races—developed after the Age of Exploration in the fifteenth and sixteenth centuries. Before the era of rapid transportation and mass population movements, most people were born, lived, and died without seeing anyone who looked appreciably different from themselves. But when European explorers reached Africa, East Asia, and the Americas, they were confronted with people who were very different from them in appearance and in their ways of life. Europeans tried to understand this unforeseen human diversity in terms of the religious worldview of the time. High councils of the Church debated whether particular peoples had souls that missionaries could save. Killing and enslaving colonized peoples was justified by the view that they were inherently inferior beings, not fully human.

By the nineteenth century the idea that populations looked and acted differently because of their different hereditary endowments was widely believed. Scholars viewed different groups as being at different stages of progress on the march to European-style civilization, and they considered those that lagged behind to have been held back by their inferior physical, mental, and moral endowments. The development of cultural evolutionary schemes in the second half of the century, inspired in part by Darwin's theory of the evolution of species, seemed to give a scientific basis for this view. In short, racism and the idea of race developed together.

But anthropology in America developed somewhat differently. One of the founding figures in American anthropology, Franz Boas, challenged the relationship between biological traits and cultural traits. He fought a lifelong battle against racism and the idea that cultural and psychological characteristics could be explained in terms of biology.

Toward the middle of the twentieth century, biological anthropologists tried to refine the concept of race by separating biological differences from cultural ones. They also began to focus on populations, rather than individuals, and on genetic variations, rather than superficial physical differences like head shape. One seemingly intractable problem emerged in the resulting analyses. Different sets of races appeared depending on the number and nature of the specific features considered. No matter how many races were distinguished, there were always some groups that did not fit in.

Here, George W. Gill argues that races should be understood as populations derived from particular geographical regions. Such races can be distinguished not only through their external characteristics, such as skin color, but also by skeletal features. By using a combination of distinctive osteological characteristics, which are found in varying proportions in different geographical races, forensic anthropologists can make highly accurate guesses about the ancestry of persons whose bones they examine. Gill also notes the danger of removing the topic of race from public discourse.

On the other side of the debate, C. Loring Brace contends that race is a meaningless biological concept. He argues that there are no clear-cut boundaries between geographical "races" because human physical features vary gradually and independently from region to region. Brace does not, however, deny that race is a social reality. He recognizes that Americans tend to view physical variations in terms of a concept of race, even though races cannot be scientifically defined and distinguished.

This issue touches on a number of thorny questions for anthropologists, some scientific and some ethical. What sorts of concepts are needed for discussing and analyzing human hereditary differences? Can geographical races be defined in terms of varying proportions of characteristics that together form a distinctive profile? What is the relationship between individuals and racial categories? Does the very idea of classifying humans into clear-cut categories inherently misrepresent the gradual nature of genetic variation and change? Is the term *race* so loaded with racist connotations that it must be replaced by a more neutral term before dispassionate discussion of human hereditary variation can proceed?

YES ↵

George W. Gill

Does Race Exist?
A Proponent's Perspective

Slightly over half of all biological/physical anthropologists today believe in the traditional view that human races are biologically valid and real. Furthermore, they tend to see nothing wrong in defining and naming the different populations of *Homo sapiens*. The other half of the biological anthropology community believes either that the traditional racial categories for humankind are arbitrary and meaningless, or that at a minimum there are better ways to look at human variation than through the "racial lens."

Are there differences in the research concentrations of these two groups of experts? Yes, most decidedly there are. As pointed out in a recent 2000 edition of a popular physical anthropology textbook, forensic anthropologists (those who do skeletal identification for law-enforcement agencies) are overwhelmingly in support of the idea of the basic biological reality of human races, and yet those who work with blood-group data, for instance, tend to reject the biological reality of racial categories.

I happen to be one of those very few forensic physical anthropologists who actually does research on the particular traits used today in forensic racial identification (i.e., "assessing ancestry," as it is generally termed today). Partly this is because for more than a decade now U.S. national and regional forensic anthropology organizations have deemed it necessary to quantitatively test both traditional and new methods for accuracy in legal cases. I volunteered for this task of testing methods and developing new methods in the late 1980s. What have I found? Where do I now stand in the "great race debate?" Can I see truth on one side or the other—or on both sides—in this argument?

Findings

First, I have found that forensic anthropologists attain a high degree of accuracy in determining geographic racial affinities (white, black, American Indian, etc.) by utilizing both new and traditional methods of bone analysis. Many well-conducted studies were reported in the late 1980s and 1990s that test methods objectively for percentage of correct placement. Numerous individual methods involving midfacial measurements, femur traits, and so on are

From *NOVA Online*, October 12, 2000. Copyright © 2000 by George W. Gill. Reprinted by permission.

over 80 percent accurate alone, and in combination produce very high levels of accuracy. No forensic anthropologist would make a racial assessment based upon just *one* of these methods, but in combination they can make very reliable assessments, just as in determining sex or age. In other words, multiple criteria are the key to success in all of these determinations.

I have a respected colleague, the skeletal biologist C. Loring Brace, who is as skilled as any of the leading forensic anthropologists at assessing ancestry from bones, yet he does not subscribe to the concept of race. Neither does Norman Sauer, a board-certified forensic anthropologist. My students ask, "How can this be? They can identify skeletons as to racial origins but do not believe in race!" My answer is that we can often *function* within systems that we do not believe in.

As a middle-aged male, for example, I am not so sure that I believe any longer in the chronological "age" categories that many of my colleagues in skeletal biology use. Certainly parts of the skeletons of some 45-year-old people look older than corresponding portions of the skeletons of some 55-year-olds. If, however, law enforcement calls upon me to provide "age" on a skeleton, I can provide an answer that will be proven sufficiently accurate should the decedent eventually be identified. I may not believe in society's "age" categories, but I can be very effective at "aging" skeletons. The next question, of course, is how "real" is age biologically? My answer is that if one can use biological criteria to assess age with reasonable accuracy, then age has some basis in biological reality even if the particular "social construct" that defines its limits might be imperfect. I find this true not only for age and stature estimations but for sex and race identification.

The "reality of race" therefore depends more on the definition of reality than on the definition of race. If we choose to accept the system of racial taxonomy that physical anthropologists have traditionally established—major races: black, white, etc.—then one can classify human skeletons within it just as well as one can living humans. The bony traits of the nose, mouth, femur, and cranium are just as revealing to a good osteologist as skin color, hair form, nose form, and lips to the perceptive observer of living humanity. I have been able to prove to myself over the years, in actual legal cases, that I am *more* accurate at assessing race from skeletal remains than from looking at living people standing before me. So those of us in forensic anthropology know that the skeleton reflects race, whether "real" or not, just as well if not better than superficial soft tissue does. The idea that race is "only skin deep" is simply not true, as any experienced forensic anthropologist will affirm.

Position on Race

Where I stand today in the "great race debate" after a decade and a half of pertinent skeletal research is clearly more on the side of the reality of race than on the "race denial" side. Yet I do see why many other physical anthropologists are able to ignore or deny the race concept. Blood-factor analysis, for instance, shows many traits that cut across racial boundaries in a purely *clinal* fashion with very few if any "breaks" along racial boundaries. (A cline is a gradient of change, such as from people with a high frequency of blue eyes, as in Scandinavia, to people with a high frequency of brown eyes, as in Africa.)

Morphological characteristics, however, like skin color, hair form, bone traits, eyes, and lips tend to follow geographic boundaries coinciding often with climatic zones. This is not surprising since the selective forces of climate are probably the primary forces of nature that have shaped human races with regard not only to skin color and hair form but also the underlying bony structures of the nose, cheekbones, etc. (For example, more prominent noses humidify air better.) As far as we know, blood-factor frequencies are *not* shaped by these same climatic factors.

So, serologists who work largely with blood factors will tend to see human variation as clinal and races as not a valid construct, while skeletal biologists, particularly forensic anthropologists, will see races as biologically real. The common person on the street who sees only a person's skin color, hair form, and face shape will also tend to see races as biologically real. They are not incorrect. Their perspective is just different from that of the serologist.

So, yes, I see truth on both sides of the race argument.

Those who believe that the concept of race is valid do not discredit the notion of clines, however. Yet those with the clinal perspective who believe that races are not real do try to discredit the evidence of skeletal biology. Why this bias from the "race denial" faction? This bias seems to stem largely from socio-political motivation and not science at all. For the time being at least, the people in "race denial" are in "reality denial" as well. Their motivation (a positive one) is that they have come to believe that the race concept is socially dangerous. In other words, they have convinced themselves that race promotes racism. Therefore, they have pushed the politically correct agenda that human races are not biologically real, no matter what the evidence.

Consequently, at the beginning of the 21st century, even as a majority of biological anthropologists favor the reality of the race perspective, not one introductory textbook of physical anthropology even presents that perspective as a possibility. In a case as flagrant as this, we are not dealing with science but rather with blatant, politically motivated censorship. But, you may ask, are the politically correct actually correct? Is there a relationship between thinking about race and racism?

Race and Racism

Does discussing human variation in a framework of racial biology promote or reduce racism? This is an important question, but one that does not have a simple answer. Most social scientists over the past decade have convinced themselves that it runs the risk of promoting racism in certain quarters. Anthropologists of the 1950s, 1960s, and early 1970s, on the other hand, believed that they were combating racism by openly discussing race and by teaching courses on human races and racism. Which approach has worked best? What do the intellectuals among racial minorities believe? How do students react and respond?

Three years ago, I served on a NOVA-sponsored panel in New York, in which panelists debated the topic "Is There Such a Thing as Race?" Six of us sat on the panel, three proponents of the race concept and three antagonists. All had authored books or papers on race. Loring Brace and I were the two anthropologists "facing off" in the debate. The ethnic composition of the panel was three white and three black scholars. As our conversations developed, I was struck by how similar many of my concerns regarding racism were to those of my two black teammates. Although recognizing that embracing the race concept can have risks attached, we were (and are) more fearful of the form of racism likely to emerge if race is denied and dialogue about it lessened. We fear that the social taboo about the subject of race has served to suppress open discussion about a very important subject in need of dispassionate debate. One of my teammates, an affirmative-action lawyer, is afraid that a denial that races exist also serves to encourage a denial that racism exists. He asks, "How can we combat racism if no one is willing to talk about race?"

Who Will Benefit?

In my experience, minority students almost invariably have been the strongest supporters of a "racial perspective" on human variation in the classroom. The first-ever black student in my human variation class several years ago came to me at the end of the course and said, "Dr. Gill, I really want to thank you for changing my life with this course." He went on to explain that, "My whole life I have wondered about why I am black, and if that is good or bad. Now I know the reasons why I am the way I am and that these traits are useful and good."

A human-variation course with another perspective would probably have accomplished the same for this student if he had ever noticed it. The truth is, innocuous contemporary human-variation classes with their politically correct titles and course descriptions do not attract the attention of minorities or those other students who could most benefit. Furthermore, the politically correct "race denial" perspective in society as a whole suppresses dialogue, allowing ignorance to replace knowledge and suspicion to replace familiarity. This encourages ethnocentrism and racism more than it discourages it.

NO

Does Race Exist? An Antagonist's Perspective

I am going to start this essay with what may seem to many as an outrageous assertion: There is no such thing as a biological entity that warrants the term "race."

The immediate reaction of most literate people is that this is obviously nonsense. The physician will retort, "What do you mean 'there is no such thing as race'? I see it in my practice everyday!" Jane Doe and John Roe will be equally incredulous. Note carefully, however, that my opening declaration did not claim that "there is no such thing as race." What I said is that there is no "biological entity that warrants the term 'race'." "You're splitting hairs," the reader may retort. "Stop playing verbal games and tell us what you really mean!"

And so I shall, but there is another charge that has been thrown my way, which I need to dispel before explaining the basis for my statement. Given the tenor of our times at the dawn of the new millennium, some have suggested that my position is based mainly on the perception of the social inequities that have accompanied the classification of people into "races." My stance, then, has been interpreted as a manifestation of what is being called "political correctness." My answer is that it is really the defenders of the concept of "race" who are unwittingly shaped by the political reality of American history. . . .

But all of this needs explaining. First, it is perfectly true that the long-term residents of the various parts of the world have patterns of features that we can easily identify as characteristic of the areas from which they come. It should be added that they have to have resided in those places for a couple of hundred thousand years before their regional patterns became established. Well, you may ask, why can't we call those regional patterns "races"? In fact, we can and do, but it does not make them coherent biological entities. "Races" defined in such a way are products of our perceptions. "Seeing is believing" will be the retort, and, after all, aren't we seeing reality in those regional differences?

I should point out that this is the same argument that was made against Copernicus and Galileo almost half a millennium ago. To this day, few have actually made the observations and done the calculations that led those Renaissance scholars to challenge the universal perception that the sun sets in the evening to rise again at the dawn. It was just a matter of common sense to believe that the sun revolves around the Earth, just as it was common sense to "know" that the Earth was flat. Our beliefs concerning "race" are based on the same sort of common sense, and they are just as basically wrong.

The Nature of Human Variation

I would suggest that there are very few who, of their own experience, have actually perceived at first hand the nature of human variation. What we know of the characteristics of the various regions of the world we have largely gained vicariously and in misleadingly spotty fashion. Pictures and the television camera tell us that the people of Oslo in Norway, Cairo in Egypt, and Nairobi in Kenya look very different. And when we actually meet natives of those separate places, which can indeed happen, we can see representations of those differences at first hand. But if one were to walk up beside the Nile from Cairo, across the Tropic of Cancer to Khartoum in the Sudan and on to Nairobi, there would be no visible boundary between one people and another. The same thing would be true if one were to walk north from Cairo, through the Caucasus, and on up into Russia, eventually swinging west across the northern end of the Baltic Sea to Scandinavia. The people at any adjacent stops along the way look like one another more than they look like anyone else since, after all, they are related to one another. As a rule, the boy marries the girl next door throughout the whole world, but next door goes on without stop from one region to another.

We realize that in the extremes of our transit—Moscow to Nairobi, perhaps—there is a major but gradual change in skin color from what we euphemistically call white to black, and that this is related to the latitudinal difference in the intensity of the ultraviolet component of sunlight. What we do not see, however, is the myriad other traits that are distributed in a fashion quite unrelated to the intensity of ultraviolet radiation. Where skin color is concerned, all the northern populations of the Old World are lighter than the long-term inhabitants near the equator. Although Europeans and Chinese are obviously different, in skin color they are closer to each other than either is to equatorial Africans. But if we test the distribution of the widely known ABO blood-group system, then Europeans and Africans are closer to each other than either is to Chinese.

Then if we take that scourge sickle-cell anemia, so often thought of as an African disease, we discover that, while it does reach high frequencies in some parts of sub-Saharan Africa, it did not originate there. Its distribution includes southern Italy, the eastern Mediterranean, parts of the Middle East, and over into India. In fact, it represents a kind of adaptation that aids survival in the face of a particular kind of malaria, and wherever that malaria is a prominent threat, sickle-cell anemia tends to occur in higher frequencies. It would appear that the gene that controls that trait was introduced to sub-Saharan Africa by traders from those parts of the Middle East where it had arisen in conjunction with the conditions created by the early development of agriculture.

Every time we plot the distribution of a trait possessing a survival value that is greater under some circumstances than under others, it will have a different pattern of geographical variation, and no two such patterns will coincide. Nose form, tooth size, relative arm and leg length, and a whole series of other traits are distributed each in accordance with its particular controlling selective force. The gradient of the distribution of each is called a "cline" and those clines are completely independent of one another. This is what lies behind the aphorism, "There are no races, there are only clines." Yes, we can recognize people from a given area. What we are seeing, however, is a pattern of features derived from common ancestry in the area in question, and these are largely without different survival value. To the extent that the people in a given region look more like one another than they look like people from other regions, this can be regarded as "family resemblance writ large." And as we have seen, each region grades without break into the one next door.

There is nothing wrong with using geographic labels to designate people. Major continental terms are just fine, and sub-regional refinements such as Western European, Eastern African, Southeast Asian, and so forth carry no unintentional baggage. In contrast, terms such as "Negroid," "Caucasoid," and "Mongoloid" create more problems than they solve. Those very terms reflect a mix of narrow regional, specific ethnic, and descriptive physical components with an assumption that such separate dimensions have some kind of common tie. Biologically, such terms are worse than useless. Their continued use, then, is in social situations where people think they have some meaning.

America and the Race Concept

The role played by America is particularly important in generating and perpetuating the concept of "race." The human inhabitants of the Western Hemisphere largely derive from three very separate regions of the world—Northeast Asia, Northwest Europe, and Western Africa—and none of them has been in the New World long enough to have been shaped by their experiences in the manner of those long-term residents in the various separate regions of the Old World.

It was the American experience of those three separate population components facing one another on a daily basis under conditions of manifest and enforced inequality that created the concept in the first place and endowed it with the assumption that those perceived "races" had very different sets of capabilities. Those thoughts are very influential and have become enshrined in laws and regulations. This is why I can conclude that, while the word "race" has no coherent biological meaning, its continued grip on the public mind is in fact a manifestation of the power of the historical continuity of the American social structure, which is assumed by all to be essentially "correct."

Finally, because of America's enormous influence on the international scene, ideas generated by the idiosyncrasies of American history have gained currency in ways that transcend American intent or control. One of those ideas is the concept of "race," which we have exported to the rest of the world without any realization that this is what we were doing. The adoption of the biologically indefensible American concept of "race" by an admiring world has to be the ultimate manifestation of political correctness.

POSTSCRIPT

Is Race a Useful Concept for Anthropologists?

No one denies that variations in hereditary features between individuals and populations exist. The disagreement between these two biological anthropologists is over whether the concept of race, or subspecies, accurately expresses these variations. Gill argues that combinations of superficial and skeletal characteristics cluster together, making it possible to distinguish geographical populations as separate races. He sees the race concept as particularly useful for forensic anthropologists trying to determine the identity of dead people from their bones alone. Brace counters that distinct races cannot be defined objectively on the basis of biological variations because physical characteristics are not discontinuous between geographical populations; instead, they vary gradually as one goes from region to region. He adds that characteristics vary independently of each other, rather than in clusters.

Both scholars agree, however, that the idea and perception of race is deeply embedded in American culture. The view that races do not exist seems nonsensical to the average American, who has grown up steeped in the idea that humanity is made up of different races. Racial categories are so ingrained in our vocabulary and thought that we identify people by race as readily as by sex or age. We are asked our race on official census forms, and many government policies, such as affirmative action, depend on the reality of race. What is needed, Brace would say, is recognition that this notion of race is a cultural—not biological—construction.

The literature on race, including the concept of race, is enormous. For further reading on the concept of race, a good place to start is the American Anthropological Association's "Statement on 'Race,'" which can be found on the AAA Web site at www.aaanet.org/stmts/racepp.htm. Informative overviews of the concept of race in anthropology include Michael Banton's book *Racial Theories* (Cambridge University Press, 1987), and Eugenia Shanklin's short book *Anthropology and Race* (Wadsworth Publishing Company, 1994). Two landmark books in the development of anthropological views of race are Franz Boas's *Race, Language, and Culture* (The Free Press, 1940) and Ashley Montagu's *Man's Most Dangerous Myth: The Fallacy of Race* (Columbia University Press, 1945). For further discussion of race as a cultural construct, see Jonathan Marks's article "Black, White, Other" (*Natural History*, December 1994). For more on race as biological reality, see Vincent Sarich and Frank Miele's *Race: The Reality of Human Differences* (Westview Press, 2005). Stanley Rhine's *Bone Voyage: A Journey in Forensic Anthropology* (University of New Mexico Press, 1998) is an accessible source on forensic anthropology that includes a discussion on identifying race in human remains.

ISSUE 2

Are Humans Inherently Violent?

YES: Richard Wrangham and Dale Peterson, from *Demonic Males: Apes and the Origins of Human Violence* (Houghton Mifflin Company, 1996)

NO: Robert W. Sussman, from "Exploring Our Basic Human Nature," *Anthro Notes* (Fall 1997)

ISSUE SUMMARY

YES: Biological anthropologist Richard Wrangham and science writer Dale Peterson maintain that male humans and chimpanzees, our closest nonhuman relatives, have an innate tendency to be aggressive and to defend their territory by violence. They state that sexual selection, a type of natural selection, has fostered an instinct for male aggression because males who are good fighters mate more frequently and sire more offspring than weaker and less aggressive ones.

NO: Biological anthropologist Robert W. Sussman rejects the theory that human aggression is an inherited propensity, arguing instead that violence is a product of culture and upbringing. He also rejects the contention that male chimpanzees routinely commit violent acts against other male chimps. Sussman regards the notion that human males are inherently violent as a Western cultural tradition, not a scientifically demonstrated fact.

Human history is rife with wars between groups of all types, from clans to nation-states, and interpersonal violence is common enough that all societies attempt to control it. But is violence a part of human nature, or is violence merely one of many human capabilities that may be either encouraged or discouraged by cultures?

The question of whether or not humans have an instinct for aggression has been around since the formative years of anthropology, and it is still being debated today. Some nineteenth-century scholars interpreted Darwin's concepts of "natural selection" and "survival of the fittest" to mean that the strong would kill off the weak. The strongest and most aggressive individuals, therefore, would have the most offspring, and their strength and instinct for aggression would gradually come to predominate in the population.

Most cultural anthropologists from the 1950s onward rejected the explanation of human aggression in terms of instincts, emphasizing instead the social and cultural causes of violence. They pointed out that the amount of aggression tolerated varies widely from one society to another and that individuals can become aggressive or peaceful depending on how they are raised. They held up such groups as the Semai of Malaysia (see Robert K. Dentan, *The Semai: A Nonviolent People of Malaya* [Holt, Rinehart & Winston, 1968]) as proof that culture could create a people who abhorred all forms of aggression and coercion. Whatever instinct for aggression humans might have, they argued, must be very weak indeed.

The question behind this issue concerns the nature of human nature. Have we a set of innate behavioral predispositions that, when set off by certain stimuli, are very likely to be expressed? Or, are any such predispositions at best weak tendencies that can be shaped or even negated by cultural conditioning? Many apparently innate behaviors in humans turn out to be highly variable in their strength and form. While the sucking instinct of babies operates predictably in all newborns, a hypothesized "mothering instinct" seems quite diverse in expression and variable in strength from one woman to another. The question, then, is whether the hypothesized aggression instinct is a powerful drive that all human males must express in one way or another or a weak and pliable tendency that some males may never act upon.

Richard Wrangham and Dale Peterson argue that human wars and interpersonal violence are driven by inherited behavioral tendencies that have evolved under pressure of sexual selection—natural selection of traits that enhance the reproductive success of one sex. Among both humans and chimpanzees, males who are aggressive use their fighting ability to dominate other males and to prevent them from mating with the available females. Therefore the genes causing aggression are passed on to succeeding generations in greater numbers than the genes causing nonaggressive behavior.

Robert W. Sussman rejects Wrangham and Peterson's assertion that natural selection favors aggressive human males and that aggressiveness is an inherited tendency rather than a result of environment and upbringing. He contends that human hunter-gatherers and most apes are remarkably nonaggressive, as were our earliest human ancestors, the australopithecines. He sees the evidence that chimpanzee males routinely attack other males as weak, and he questions the relevance of chimpanzee behavior for humans.

These selections raise a number of questions with regard to the nature and causes of human aggression. How can we determine whether a person's aggressive act is due to instinct, upbringing, or both? If male aggression in humans is based on instinct, how can scholars explain variations in the amount and type of aggression found in different individuals and cultures? If male aggression is not based on instinct, why is violence between men so widespread? What role did women have in the evolution of an instinct for male violence? To what extent can studies of animal behavior be applied to humans?

YES

**Richard Wrangham
and Dale Peterson**

Demonic Males: Apes and the
Origins of Human Violence

Paradise Lost

The killer ape has long been part of our popular culture: Tarzan had to escape from the bad apes, and King Kong was a murderous gorilla-like monster. But before the Kahama observations [in which males of one chimpanzee group killed the males of a neighboring group], few biologists took the idea seriously. The reason was simple. There was so little evidence of animals killing members of their own species that biologists used to think animals killed each other only when something went wrong—an accident, perhaps, or unnatural crowding in zoos. The idea fit with the theories of animal behavior then preeminent, theories that saw animal behavior as designed by evolution for mutual good. Darwinian natural selection was a filter supposed to eliminate murderous violence. Killer apes, like killers in any animal species, were merely a novelist's fantasy to most scientists before the 1970s.

And so the behavior of people seemed very, very different from that of other animals. Killing, of course, is a typical result of human war, so one had to presume that humans somehow broke the rules of nature. Still, war must have come from somewhere. It could have come, for example, from the evolution of brains that happened to be smart enough to think of using tools as weapons, as Konrad Lorenz argued in his famous book, *On Aggression,* published in 1963.

However it may have originated, more generally war was seen as one of the defining marks of humanity: To fight wars meant to be human and apart from nature. This larger presumption was true even of nonscientific theories, such as the biblical concept of an original sin taking humans out of Eden, or the notion that warfare was an idea implanted by aliens, as Arthur C. Clarke imagined in *2001: A Space Odyssey.* In science, in religion, in fiction, violence and humanity were twinned.

The Kahama killings were therefore both a shock and a stimulus to thought. They undermined the explanations for extreme violence in terms of uniquely human attributes, such as culture, brainpower, or the punishment of an angry god. They made credible the idea that our warring tendencies go back into our prehuman past. They made us a little less special.

And yet science has still not grappled closely with the ultimate questions raised by the Kahama killings: Where does human violence come from, and why? Of course, there have been great advances in the way we think about these things. Most importantly, in the 1970s, the same decade as the Kahama killings, a new evolutionary theory emerged, the selfish-gene theory of natural selection, variously called inclusive fitness theory, sociobiology, or more broadly, behavioral ecology. Sweeping through the halls of academe, it revolutionized Darwinian thinking by its insistence that the ultimate explanation of any individual's behavior considers only how the behavior tends to maximize genetic success: to pass that individual's genes into subsequent generations. The new theory, elegantly popularized in Richard Dawkins's *The Selfish Gene,* is now the conventional wisdom in biological science because it explains animal behavior so well. It accounts easily for selfishness, even killing. And it has come to be applied with increasing confidence to human behavior, though the debate is still hot and unsettled. In any case, the general principle that behavior evolves to serve selfish ends has been widely accepted, and the idea that humans might have been favored by natural selection to hate and to kill their enemies has become entirely, if tragically, reasonable.

Those are the general principles, and yet the specifics are lacking. Most animals are nowhere near as violent as humans, so why did such intensely violent behavior evolve particularly in the human line? Why kill the enemy, rather than simply drive him away? Why rape? Why torture and mutilate? Why do we see these patterns both in ourselves and chimpanzees? Those sorts of questions have barely been asked, much less addressed.

Because chimpanzees and humans are each other's closest relatives, such questions carry extraordinary implications, the more so because the study of early human ancestry, unfolding in a fervor as we approach the century's end, is bringing chimpanzees and humans even closer than we ever imagined. Three dramatic recent discoveries speak to the relationship between chimpanzees and humans, and all three point in the same direction: to a past, around 5 million years ago, when chimpanzee ancestors and human ancestors were indistinguishable.

First, fossils recently dug up in Ethiopia indicate that over 4.5 million years ago there walked across African lands a bipedal ancestor of humans with a head strikingly like a chimpanzee's.

Second, laboratories around the world have over the last decade demonstrated chimpanzees to be genetically closer to us than they are even to gorillas, despite the close physical resemblance between chimpanzees and gorillas.

And third, both in the field and in the laboratory, studies of chimpanzee behavior are producing numerous, increasingly clear parallels with human behavior. It's not just that these apes pat each other on the hand to show affection, or kiss each other, or embrace. Not just that they have menopause, develop lifelong friendships, and grieve for their dead babies by carrying them for days or weeks. Nor is it their ability to do sums like 5 plus 4, or to communicate with hand signs. Nor their tool use, or collaboration, or bartering for sexual favors. Nor even that they hold long-term grudges, deliberately hide their feelings, or bring rivals together to force them to make peace.

No, for us the single most gripping set of facts about chimpanzee behavior is what we have already touched on: the nature of their society. The social world of chimpanzees is a set of individuals who share a communal range; males live forever in the groups where they are born, while females move to neighboring groups at adolescence; and the range is defended, and sometimes extended with aggressive and potentially lethal violence, by groups of males related in a genetically patrilineal kin group.

What makes this social world so extraordinary is comparison. Very few animals live in patrilineal, male-bonded communities wherein females routinely reduce the risks of inbreeding by moving to neighboring groups to mate. And only two animal species are known to do so with a system of intense, male-initiated territorial aggression, including lethal raiding into neighboring communities in search of vulnerable enemies to attack and kill. Out of four thousand mammals and ten million or more other animal species, this suite of behaviors is known only among chimpanzees and humans.

Humans with male-bonded, patrilineal kin groups? Absolutely. *Male bonded* refers to males forming aggressive coalitions with each other in mutual support against others—Hatfields versus McCoys, Montagues versus Capulets, Palestinians versus Israelis, Americans versus Vietcong, Tutsis versus Hutus. Around the world, from the Balkans to the Yanomamö of Venezuela, from Pygmies of Central Africa to the T'ang Dynasty of China, from Australian aborigines to Hawaiian kingdoms, related men routinely fight in defense of their group. This is true even of the villages labeled by anthropologists as "matrilineal" and "matrilocal," where inheritance (from male to male) is figured out according to the mother's line, and where women stay in their natal villages to have children—such villages operate socially as subunits of a larger patrilineal whole. In short, the system of communities defended by related men is a human universal that crosses space and time, so established a pattern that even writers of science fiction rarely think to challenge it.

When it comes to social relationships involving females, chimpanzees and humans are very different. That's unsurprising. Discoveries in animal behavior since the 1960s strongly suggest that animal societies are adapted to their environments in exquisitely detailed ways, and obviously the environments of chimpanzees and humans are a study in contrast. But this just emphasizes our puzzle. Why should male chimpanzees and humans show such similar patterns?

Is it chance? Maybe our human ancestors lived in societies utterly unlike those of chimpanzees. Peaceful matriarchies, for example, somewhat like some of our distant monkey relatives. And then, by a remarkable quirk of evolutionary coincidence, at some time in prehistory human and chimpanzee social behaviors converged on their similar systems for different, unrelated reasons.

Or do they both depend on some other characteristic, like intelligence? Once brains reach a certain level of sophistication, is there some mysterious logic pushing a species toward male coalitionary violence? Perhaps, for instance, only chimpanzees and humans have enough brainpower to realize the advantages of removing the opposition.

Or is there a long-term evolutionary inertia? Perhaps humans have retained an old chimpanzee pattern which, though it was once adaptive, has now acquired a stability and life of its own, resistant even to new environments where other forms of society would be better.

Or are the similarities there, as we believe, because in spite of first appearances, similar evolutionary forces continue to be at work in chimpanzee and human lineages, maintaining and refining a system of intergroup hostility and personal violence that has existed since even before the ancestors of chimpanzees and humans mated for the last time in a drying forest of eastern Africa around 5 million years ago? If so, one must ask, what forces are they? What bred male bonding and lethal raiding in our forebears and keeps it now in chimpanzees and humans? What marks have those ancient evolutionary forces forged onto our twentieth-century psyches? And what do they say about our hopes and fears for the future? . . .

Sexual selection, the evolutionary process that produces sex differences, has a lot to answer for. Without it, males wouldn't possess dangerous bodily weapons and a mindset that sanctions violence. But males who are better fighters can stop other males from mating, and they mate more successfully themselves. Better fighters tend to have more babies. That's the simple, stupid, selfish logic of sexual selection. So, what about us? Is sexual selection ultimately the reason why men brawl in barrooms, form urban gangs, plot guerrilla attacks, and go to war? Has it indeed designed men to be especially aggressive?

Until we have carefully examined the evidence, our answer should be: not necessarily. Because the social, environmental, genetic, and historical circumstances for any single species are so extremely complex, we can't assume a priori that sexual selection has acted in any particular way for any single species. Among the 10 million or more animal species on earth, you can find interesting exceptions to almost every rule. On the one hand, you can find species like spotted hyenas, where such extraordinary ferocity has evolved among females that it outshines even the stark sexual aggression shown by males. And on the other, you will discover the pacifists. . . .

So there is no particular reason to think that human aggression is all cultural, or that our ancestors were as pacific as muriquis [nonaggressive monkeys of South America]. The only way to find out whether sexual selection has shaped human males for aggression is to leave the theory and go back to the evidence. There are two places to look for an answer. We can look at our bodies, and we can think about our minds. The easier part is our bodies.

∾☉∾

A biologist from Mars looking at a preserved human male laid out on a slab might find it hard to imagine our species as dangerous. Lined up next to male specimens from the other apes, or from virtually any other mammal species, human males don't look as if they are designed to fight at all. They are rather slender, their bones are light, and they appear to have no bodily weapons. People don't think of humans in the same way that they think of dangerous animals.

That first impression is misleading, however. Humans are indeed designed to fight, although in a different way from most of the other primates.

Here's one clue. Men are a little larger and more heavily muscled than women. For other primate species, larger male size links strongly to male aggression. But with humans, that apparent evidence seems to conflict with the absence of fighting canine teeth. Could it be that humans break the general rule linking larger males to an evolved design for aggression?

Consider our teeth. The upper canines of most primates are longer and sharper than any other tooth. These long teeth are obvious weapons, bright daggers ground to a razor-sharp edge against a special honing surface on a premolar tooth in the lower jaw. Baboons, for example, have canines five to six centimeters long. Male baboons trying to impress each other grind their canines noisily, occasionally showing off their teeth in huge, gaping yawns. When male baboons make those display yawns, they are acting like cowboys twirling their revolvers.

By comparison, human canines seem tiny. They barely extend beyond the other teeth, and in males they are no longer than in females. Those canines may help us bite an apple, we love to imagine them elongated for the Halloween scare, and we unconsciously display them when we sneer, but our canines virtually never help us fight. In fact, the fossil record indicates that ever since the transition from rainforest ape to woodland ape, our ancestors' canines have been markedly smaller than they are in chimpanzees. In the woodlands, those teeth quickly became muriqui-like in appearance—one reason why some people wonder if woodland apes were as pacific as modern muriquis are.

But we should not allow ourselves to become misled by the evidence of canine teeth. The importance of a species' canines depends entirely on how it fights. . . .

Apes can fight with their fists because they have adapted to hanging from their arms, which means that their arms can swing all around their shoulders, the shoulder joint being a flexible multidirectional joint. So chimpanzees and gorillas often hit with their fists when they fight, and they can keep most canine-flashing opponents at bay because their arms are long. If chimpanzees and gorillas find punching effective, then surely the woodland apes, who were standing up high on hind legs, would have fought even better with their arms.

Fists can also grasp invented weapons. Chimpanzees today are close to using hand-held weapons. Throughout the continent, wild chimpanzees will tear off and throw great branches when they are angry or threatened, or they will pick up and throw rocks. Humphrey, when he was the alpha male at Gombe, almost killed me once by sending a melon-size rock whistling less than half a meter from my head. They also hit with big sticks. A celebrated film taken in Guinea shows wild chimpanzees pounding meter-long clubs down on the back of a leopard. (Scientists were able to get that film because the leopard was a stuffed one, placed there by a curious researcher. The chimpanzees were lucky to find a leopard so slow to fight back.) Chimpanzees in West Africa already have a primitive stone tool technology, and there could well be a community of chimpanzees today, waiting to be discovered, who are already using heavy sticks as clubs against each other. Certainly we can reasonably imagine that the woodland apes did some of these things.

. . . The shoulders of boys and girls are equally broad until adolescence; but at puberty, shoulder cartilage cells respond to testosterone, the male sex hormone newly produced by the testes, by growing. (In an equivalent way, pubertal girls get wider hips when their hip cartilage cells respond to estrogen, the female sex hormone.) The result is a sudden acceleration of shoulder width for boys around the age of fourteen, associated with relative enlargement of the upper arm muscles. In other words, the shoulders and arms of male humans—like the neck muscles of a red deer, the clasping hands of a xenopus frog, or the canine teeth of many other primates—look like the result of sexual selection for fighting. All these examples of male weaponry respond to testosterone by growing. They are specialized features that enlarge for the specific purpose of promoting fighting ability in competition against other males. Small wonder, then, that men show off to each other before fights by hunching their shoulders, expanding their muscles, and otherwise displaying their upper-body strength. . . .

If the bipedal woodland apes fought with fists and sometimes with weapons, those species should have had especially broad shoulders and well-muscled arms, like modern men. We haven't enough fossils yet to know if that's true. Indeed, it is not yet absolutely certain that male woodland apes were larger than females, though most of the current fossil evidence suggests so. If they were, we can confidently imagine that the males were designed for aggression. Perhaps the early development of club-style weapons might also explain why the skulls of our ancestors became strikingly thicker, particularly with *Homo erectus* at 1.6 to 1.8 million years ago. That's a guess, but it's clear in any case that our present bodies carry the same legacy of sexual selection as other mammals whose males fight with their upper bodies. The broad shoulders and powerful, arching torso we so admire in Michelangelo's *David* are the human equivalent of antlers. The mark of Cain appears in our shoulders and arms, not in our teeth.

✺

What about our minds? Has sexual selection shaped our psyches also, in order to make us better fighters? Can sexual selection explain why men are so quick to bristle at insults, and, under the right circumstances, will readily kill? Can our evolutionary past account for modern war?

Inquiry about mental processes is difficult enough when we deal just with humans. Comparison with other species is harder still. The supposed problem is that animals fight with their hearts, so people say, whereas humans fight with their minds. Animal aggression is supposed to happen by instinct, or by emotion, and without reason. Wave a red rag in a bull's face and the bull charges thoughtlessly—that's the model. Human wars, on the other hand, seem to emerge, so Karl von Clausewitz declared, as "the continuation of policy with the admixture of other means." According to historian Michael Howard, human wars "begin with conscious and reasoned decisions based on the calculation, made by both parties, that they can achieve more by going to war than by remaining at peace." The principle seems as true for the measured deliberations on the top floor of the Pentagon as for the whispered councils among the Yanomamö, and it suggests a wholly different set of psychological processes from the supposedly rigid, instinctual, emotional drives of animals. The fact that we possess consciousness and reasoning ability, this theory says, takes us across a chasm into a new world, where the old instincts are no longer important. If there is no connection between these two systems, the rules for each cannot be the same. In other words, aggression based on "conscious and reasoned decisions" can no longer be explained in terms of such evolutionary forces as sexual selection.

The argument sounds fair enough, but it depends on oversimplified thinking, a false distinction between animals acting by emotion (or instinct) and humans acting by reason. Animal behavior is not purely emotional. Nor is human decision-making purely rational. In both cases, the event is a mixture. And new evidence suggests that even though we humans reason much more (analyze past and present context, consider a potential future, and so on) than nonhuman animals, our essential process for making a decision still relies on emotion. . . .

People have always accepted that animals act from emotions; humans . . . can never act without them. Suddenly the apparent chasm between the mental processes of chimpanzees and our species is reduced to a comprehensible difference. Humans can reason better, but reason and emotion are linked in parallel ways for both chimpanzees and humans. For both species, emotion sits in the driver's seat, and reason (or calculation) paves the road.

We are now ready to ask what causes aggression. If emotion is the ultimate arbiter of action for both species, then what kinds of emotions underlie violence for both? Clearly there are many. But one stands out. From the raids of chimpanzees at Gombe to wars among human nations, the same emotion looks extraordinarily important, one that we take for granted and describe most simply but that nonetheless takes us deeply back to our animal origins: pride.

Male chimpanzees compete much more aggressively for dominance than females do. If a lower-ranking male refuses to acknowledge his superior with one of the appropriate conventions, such as a soft grunt, the superior will become predictably angry. But females can let such insults pass. Females are certainly capable of being aggressive to each other, and they can be as politically adept as males in using coalitions to achieve a goal. But female chimpanzees act as if they just don't care about their status as much as males do.

By contrast, we exaggerate only barely in saying that a male chimpanzee in his prime organizes his whole life around issues of rank. His attempts to achieve and then maintain alpha status are cunning, persistent, energetic, and time-consuming. They affect whom he travels with, whom he grooms, where he glances, how often he scratches, where he goes, and what time he gets up in the morning. . . .

Eighteenth-century Englishmen used less dramatic tactics than wild chimpanzees, but that acute observer Samuel Johnson thought rank concerns were as pervasive: "No two people can be half an hour together, but one shall acquire an evident superiority over the other." Pride obviously serves as a stimulus for much interpersonal aggression in humans, and we can hypothesize confidently that this emotion evolved during countless generations in which males who achieved high status were able to turn their social success into extra reproduction. Male pride, the source of many a conflict, is reasonably seen as a mental equivalent of broad shoulders. Pride is another legacy of sexual selection. . . .

⋯◈⋯

Our ape ancestors have passed to us a legacy, defined by the power of natural selection and written in the molecular chemistry of DNA. For the most part it is a wonderful inheritance, but one small edge contains destructive elements; and now that we have the weapons of mass destruction, that edge promotes the potential of our own demise. People have long known such things intuitively and so have built civilizations with laws and justice, diplomacy and mediation, ideally keeping always a step ahead of the old demonic principles. And we might hope that men will eventually realize that violence doesn't pay.

The problem is that males are demonic at unconscious and irrational levels. The motivation of a male chimpanzee who challenges another's rank is not that he foresees more matings or better food or a longer life. Those rewards explain why sexual selection has favored the desire for power, but the immediate reason he vies for status is simpler, deeper, and less subject to the vagaries of context. It is simply to dominate his peers. Unconscious of the evolutionary rationale that placed this prideful goal in his temperament, he devises strategies to achieve it that can be complex, original, and maybe conscious. In the same way, the motivation of male chimpanzees on a border patrol is not to gain land or win females. The temperamental goal is to intimidate the opposition, to beat them to a pulp, to erode their ability to challenge. Winning has become an end in itself.

It looks the same with men.

Robert W. Sussman

➡ **NO**

Exploring Our Basic Human Nature

Are human beings forever doomed to be violent? Is aggression fixed within our genetic code, an inborn action pattern that threatens to destroy us? Or, as asked by Richard Wrangham and Dale Peterson in their recent book, *Demonic Males: Apes and the Origins of Human Violence,* can we get beyond our genes, beyond our essential "human nature"?

Wrangham and Peterson's belief in the importance of violence in the evolution and nature of humans is based on new primate research that they assert demonstrates the continuity of aggression from our great ape ancestors. The authors argue that 20–25 years ago most scholars believed human aggression was unique. Research at that time had shown great apes to be basically nonaggressive gentle creatures. Furthermore, the separation of humans from our ape ancestors was thought to have occurred 15–20 million years ago (Mya). Although Raymond Dart, Sherwood Washburn, Robert Ardrey, E.O. Wilson and others had argued through much of the 20th century that hunting, killing, and extreme aggressive behaviors were biological traits inherited from our earliest hominid hunting ancestors, many anthropologists still believed that patterns of aggression were environmentally determined and culturally learned behaviors, not inherited characteristics.

Demonic Males discusses new evidence that killer instincts are not unique to humans, but rather shared with our nearest relative, the common chimpanzee. The authors argue that it is this inherited propensity for killing that allows hominids and chimps to be such good hunters.

According to Wrangham and Peterson, the split between humans and the common chimpanzee was only 6–8 Mya. Furthermore, humans may have split from the chimpanzee-bonobo line after gorillas, with bonobos *(pygmy chimps)* separating from chimps only 2.5 Mya. Because chimpanzees may be the modern ancestor of all these forms, and because the earliest australopithecines were quite chimpanzee-like, Wrangham speculates (in a separate article) that "chimpanzees are a conservative species and an amazingly good model for the ancestor of hominids" (1995, reprinted in Sussman 1997:106). If modern chimpanzees and modern humans share certain behavioral traits, these traits have "long evolutionary roots" and are likely to be fixed, biologically inherited parts of our basic human nature and not culturally determined.

Wrangham argues that chimpanzees are almost on the brink of humanness:

> Nut-smashing, root-eating, savannah-using chimpanzees, resembling our ancestors, and capable by the way of extensive bipedalism. Using ant-wands, and sandals, and bowls, meat-sharing, hunting cooperatively. Strange paradox . . . a species trembling on the verge of hominization, but so conservative that it has stayed on that edge. . . . (1997:107).

Wrangham and Peterson (1996:24) claim that only two animal species, chimpanzees and humans, live in patrilineal, male-bonded communities "with intense, male initiated territorial aggression, including lethal raiding into neighboring communities in search of vulnerable enemies to attack and kill." Wrangham asks:

> Does this mean chimpanzees are naturally violent? Ten years ago it wasn't clear. . . . In this cultural species, it may turn out that one of the least variable of all chimpanzee behaviors is the intense competition between males, the violent aggression they use against strangers, and their willingness to maim and kill those that frustrate their goals. . . . As the picture of chimpanzee society settles into focus, it now includes infanticide, rape and regular battering of females by males (1997:108).

Since humans and chimpanzees share these violent urges, the implication is that human violence has long evolutionary roots. "We are apes of nature, cursed over six million years or more with a rare inheritance, a Dostoyevskyan demon . . . The coincidence of demonic aggression in ourselves and our closest kin bespeaks its antiquity" (1997:108–109).

Intellectual Antecedents

From the beginning of Western thought, the theme of human depravity runs deep, related to the idea of humankind's fall from grace and the emergence of original sin. This view continues to pervade modern "scientific" interpretations of the evolution of human behavior. Recognition of the close evolutionary relationship between humans and apes, from the time of Darwin's *Descent of Man* (1874) on, has encouraged theories that look to modern apes for evidence of parallel behaviors reflecting this relationship.

By the early 1950s, large numbers of australopithecine fossils and the discovery that the large-brained "fossil" ancestor from Piltdown, in England, was a fraud, led to the realization that our earliest ancestors were more like apes than like modern humans. Accordingly, our earliest ancestors must have behaved much like other non-human primates. This, in turn, led to a great interest in using primate behavior to understand human evolution and the evolutionary basis of human nature. The subdiscipline of primatology was born.

Raymond Dart, discoverer of the first australopithecine fossil some thirty years earlier, was also developing a different view of our earliest ancestors.

At first Dart believed that australopithecines were scavengers barely eking out an existence in the harsh savanna environment. But from the fragmented and damaged bones found with the australopithecines, together with dents and holes in these early hominid skulls, Dart eventually concluded that this species had used bone, tooth and antler tools to kill, butcher and eat their prey, as well as to kill one another. This hunting hypothesis (Cartmill 1997:511) "was linked from the beginning with a bleak, pessimistic view of human beings and their ancestors as instinctively bloodthirsty and savage." To Dart, the australopithecines were:

> confirmed killers: carnivorous creatures that seized living quarries by violence, battered them to death, tore apart their broken bodies, dismembered them limb from limb, slaking their ravenous thirst with the hot blood of victims and greedily devouring livid writhing flesh (1953:209).

Cartmill, in a recent book (1993), shows that this interpretation of early human morality is reminiscent of earlier Greek and Christian views. Dart's (1953) own treatise begins with a 17th century quote from the Calvinist R. Baxter: "of all the beasts, the man-beast is the worst/ to others and himself the cruellest foe."

Between 1961–1976, Dart's view was picked up and extensively popularized by the playwright Robert Ardrey (*The Territorial Imperative, African Genesis*). Ardrey believed it was the human competitive and killer instinct, acted out in warfare, that made humans what they are today. "It is war and the instinct for territory that has led to the great accomplishments of Western Man. Dreams may have inspired our love of freedom, but only war and weapons have made it ours" (1961:324).

Man the Hunter

In the 1968 volume *Man the Hunter,* Sherwood Washburn and Chet Lancaster presented a theory of "The evolution of hunting," emphasizing that it is this behavior that shaped human nature and separated early humans from their primate relatives.

> To assert the biological unity of mankind is to affirm the importance of the hunting way of life. . . . However much conditions and customs may have varied locally, the main selection pressures that forged the species were the same. The biology, psychology and customs that separate us from the apes . . . we owe to the hunters of time past . . . for those who would understand the origins and nature of human behavior there is no choice but to try to understand "Man the Hunter" (1968:303).

Rather than amassing evidence from modern hunters and gatherers to prove their theory, Washburn and Lancaster (1968:299) use the 19th-century concept of cultural "survivals": behaviors that persist as evidence of an earlier time but are no longer useful in society.

Men enjoy hunting and killing, and these activities are continued in sports even when they are no longer economically necessary. If a behavior is important to the survival of a species . . . then it must be both easily learned and pleasurable (Washburn & Lancaster, p. 299).

Man the Dancer

Using a similar logic for the survival of ancient "learned and pleasurable" behaviors, perhaps it could easily have been our propensity for dancing rather than our desire to hunt that can explain much of human behavior. After all, men and women love to dance; it is a behavior found in all cultures but has even less obvious function today than hunting. Our love of movement and dance might explain, for example, our propensity for face-to-face sex, and even the evolution of bipedalism and the movement of humans out of trees and onto the ground.

Could the first tool have been a stick to beat a dance drum, and the ancient Laetoli footprints evidence of two individuals going out to dance the "Afarensis shuffle"? Although it takes only two to tango, a variety of social interactions and systems might have been encouraged by the complex social dances known in human societies around the globe.

Sociobiology and E.O. Wilson

In the mid-1970s, E.O. Wilson and others described a number of traits as genetically based and therefore human universals, including territoriality, male–female bonds, male dominance over females, and extended maternal care leading to matrilineality. Wilson argued that the genetic basis of these traits was indicated by their relative constancy among our primate relatives and by their persistence throughout human evolution and in human societies. Elsewhere, I have shown that these characteristics are neither general primate traits nor human universals (Sussman 1995). Wilson, however, argued that these were a product of our evolutionary hunting past.

For at least a million years—probably more—Man engaged in a hunting way of life, giving up the practice a mere 10,000 years ago. . . . Our innate social responses have been fashioned through this life style. With caution, we can compare the most widespread hunter-gatherer qualities with similar behavior displayed by some of the non-human primates that are closely related to Man. Where the same pattern of traits occurs in . . . most or all of those primates—we can conclude that it has been subject to little evolution. (Wilson 1976, in Sussman 1997:65–66).

Wilson's theory of sociobiology, the evolution of social behavior, argued that:

1. the goal of living organisms is to pass on one's genes at the expense of all others;
2. an organism should only cooperate with others if:

   (a) they carry some of his/her own genes (kin selection) or
   (b) if at some later date the others might aid you (reciprocal altruism).

To sociobiologists, evolutionary morality is based on an unconscious need to multiply our own genes, to build group cohesion in order to win wars. We should not look down on our warlike, cruel nature but rather understand its success when coupled with "making nice" with *some* other individuals or groups. The genetically driven "making nice" is the basis of human ethics and morality.

> Throughout recorded history the conduct of war has been common . . . some of the noblest traits of mankind, including team play, altruism, patriotism, bravery . . . and so forth are the genetic product of warfare (Wilson 1975:572–3).

The evidence for any of these universals or for the tenets of sociobiology is as weak as was the evidence for Dart's, Ardrey's and Washburn and Lancaster's theories of innate aggression. Not only are modern gatherer-hunters and most apes remarkably non-aggressive, but in the 1970s and 1980s studies of fossil bones and artifacts have shown that early humans were not hunters, and that weapons were a later addition to the human repertoire. In fact, C.K. Brain (1981) showed that the holes and dents in Dart's australopithecine skulls matched perfectly with fangs of leopards or with impressions of rocks pressing against the buried fossils. Australopithecines apparently were the hunted, not the hunters (Cartmill, 1993, 1997).

Beyond Our Genes

Wrangham and Peterson's book goes beyond the assertion of human inborn aggression and propensity towards violence. The authors ask the critical question: Are we doomed to be violent forever because this pattern is fixed within our genetic code or can we go beyond our past?—get out of our genes, so to speak.

The authors believe that we can look to the bonobo or pygmy chimpanzee as one potential savior, metaphorically speaking.

Bonobos, although even more closely related to the common chimpanzee than humans, have become a peace-loving, love-making alternative to chimpanzee-human violence. How did this happen? In chimpanzees and humans, females of the species select partners that are violent . . . "while men have evolved to be demonic males, it seems likely that women have evolved to prefer demonic males . . . as long as demonic males are the most successful reproducers, any female who mates with them is provided with sons who themselves will likely be good reproducers" (Wrangham and Peterson 1996:239). However, among pygmy chimpanzees females form alliances and have chosen to mate with less aggressive males. So, after all, it is not violent males that have caused humans and chimpanzees to be their inborn, immoral, dehumanized selves, it is rather, poor choices by human and chimpanzee females.

Like Dart, Washburn, and Wilson before them, Wrangham and Peterson believe that killing and violence is inherited from our ancient relatives of the past. However, unlike these earlier theorists, Wrangham and Peterson argue this is not a trait unique to hominids, nor is it a by-product of hunting. In fact, it is just this violent nature and a natural "blood lust" that makes both humans and chimpanzees such good hunters. It is the bonobos that help the authors come to this conclusion. Because bonobos have lost the desire to kill, they also have lost the desire to hunt.

> . . . do bonobos tell us that the suppression of personal violence carried with it the suppression of predatory aggression? The strongest hypothesis at the moment is that bonobos came from a chimpanzee-like ancestor that hunted monkeys and hunted one another. As they evolved into bonobos, males lost their demonism, becoming less aggressive to each other. In so doing they lost their lust for hunting monkeys, too . . . Murder and hunting may be more closely tied together than we are used to thinking (Wrangham and Peterson 1996:219).

The Selfish Gene Theory

Like Ardrey, Wrangham and Peterson believe that blood lust ties killing and hunting tightly together but it is the killing that drives hunting in the latter's argument. This lust to kill is based upon the sociobiological tenet of the selfish gene. "The general principle that behavior evolves to serve selfish ends has been widely accepted; and the idea that humans might have been favored by natural selection to hate and to kill their enemies has become entirely, if tragically, reasonable" (Wrangham and Peterson 1996:23).

As with many of the new sociobiological or evolutionary anthropology theories, I find problems with both the theory itself and with the evidence used to support it. Two arguments that humans and chimpanzees share biologically fixed behaviors are: (1) they are more closely related to each other than chimpanzees are to gorillas; (2) chimpanzees are a good model for our earliest ancestor and retain conservative traits that should be shared by both.

The first of these statements is still hotly debated and, using various genetic evidence, the chimp-gorilla-human triage is so close that it is difficult to tell exact divergence time or pattern among the three. The second statement is just not true. Chimpanzees have been evolving for as long as humans and gorillas, and there is no reason to believe ancestral chimps were similar to present-day chimps. The fossil evidence for the last 5–8 million years is extremely sparse, and it is likely that many forms of apes have become extinct just as have many hominids.

Furthermore, even if the chimpanzee were a good model for the ancestral hominid, and was a conservative representative of this phylogenetic group, this would not mean that humans would necessarily share specific behavioral traits. As even Wrangham and Peterson emphasize, chimps, gorillas, and bonobos all behave very differently from one another in their social behavior and in their willingness to kill conspecifics.

Evidence Against "Demonic Males"

The proof of the "Demonic Male" theory does not rest on any theoretical grounds but must rest solely on the evidence that violence and killing in chimpanzees and in humans are behaviors that are similar in pattern; have ancient, shared evolutionary roots; and are inherited. Besides killing of conspecifics, Wrangham "includes infanticide, rape, and regular battering of females by males" as a part of this inherited legacy of violent behaviors shared by humans and chimpanzees (1997:108).

Wrangham and Peterson state: "That chimpanzees and humans kill members of neighboring groups of their own species is . . . a startling exception to the normal rule for animals" (1996:63). "Fighting adults of almost all species normally stop at winning: They don't go on to kill" (1996:155). However, as Wrangham points out there are exceptions, such as lions, wolves, spotted hyenas, and I would add a number of other predators. In fact, most species do not have the weapons to kill one another as adults.

Just how common is conspecific killing in chimpanzees? This is where the real controversy may lie. Jane Goodall described the chimpanzee as a peaceful, non-aggressive species during the first 24 years of study at Gombe (1950-1974). During one year of concentrated study, Goodall observed 284 agonistic encounters: of these 66% were due to competition for introduced bananas, and only 34% "could be regarded as attacks occurring in 'normal' aggressive contexts" (1968:278). Only 10 percent of the 284 attacks were classified as 'violent', and "even attacks that appeared punishing to me often resulted in no discernable injury. . . . Other attacks consisted merely of brief pounding, hitting or rolling of the individual, after which the aggressor often touched or embraced the other immediately (1968:277).

Chimpanzee aggression before 1974 was considered no different from patterns of aggression seen in many other primate species. In fact, Goodall explains in her 1986 monograph, *The Chimpanzees of Gombe,* that she uses data mainly from after 1975 because the earlier years present a "very different picture of the Gombe chimpanzees" as being "far more peaceable than humans" (1986:3). Other early naturalists' descriptions of chimpanzee behavior were consistent with those of Goodall and confirmed her observations. Even different communities were observed to come together with peaceful, ritualized displays of greeting (Reynolds and Reynolds 1965; Suguyama 1972; Goodall 1968).

Then, between 1974 and 1977, five adult males from one subgroup were attacked and disappeared from the area, presumably dead. Why after 24 years did the patterns of aggression change? Was it because the stronger group saw the weakness of the other and decided to improve their genetic fitness? But surely there were stronger and weaker animals and subgroups before this time. Perhaps we can look to Goodall's own perturbations for an answer. In 1965, Goodall began to provide "restrictive human-controlled feeding." A few years later she realized that

> the constant feeding was having a marked effect on the behavior of the chimps. They were beginning to move about in large groups more often than they had ever done in the old days. Worst of all, the adult males were becoming increasingly aggressive. When we first offered the chimps bananas the males seldom fought over their food;. . . . now . . . there was a great deal more fighting than ever before. . . . (Goodall 1971:143).

The possibility that human interference was a main cause of the unusual behavior of the Gombe chimps was the subject of an excellent, but generally ignored book by Margaret Power (1991). Wrangham and Peterson (1996:19) footnote this book, but as with many other controversies, they essentially ignore its findings, stating that yes, chimpanzee violence might have been unnatural behavior if it weren't for the evidence of similar behavior occurring since 1977 and "elsewhere in Africa" (1996:19).

Further Evidence

What is this evidence from elsewhere in Africa? Wrangham and Peterson provide only four brief examples, none of which is very convincing:

(1) Between 1979–1982, the Gombe group extended its range to the south and conflict with a southern group, Kalande, was suspected. In 1982, a "raiding" party of males reached Goodall's camp. The authors state: "Some of these raids may have been lethal" (1996:19). However, Goodall describes this "raid" as follows: One female "was chased by a Kalande male and mildly attacked. . . . Her four-year-old son . . . encountered a second male—but was only sniffed" (1986:516). Although Wrangham and Peterson imply that these encounters were similar to those between 1974–77, no violence was actually witnessed. The authors also refer to the discovery of the dead body of Humphrey; what they do not mention is Humphrey's age of 35 and that wild chimps rarely live past 33 years!

(2) From 1970 to 1982, six adult males from one community in the Japanese study site of Mahale disappeared, one by one over this 12 year period. None of the animals were observed being attacked or killed, and one was sighted later roaming as a solitary male (Nishida et al., 1985:287–289).

(3) In another site in West Africa, Wrangham and Peterson report that Boesch and Boesch believe "that violent aggression among the chimpanzees is as important as it is in Gombe" (1986:20). However, in the paper referred to, the Boesches simply state that encounters by neighboring chimpanzee communities are more common in their site than in Gombe (one per month vs. 1 every 4 months). There is no mention of violence during these encounters.

(4) At a site that Wrangham began studying in 1984, an adult male was found dead in 1991. Wrangham states: "In the second week of August, Ruizoni was killed. No human saw the big fight" (Wrangham & Peterson 1996:20). Wrangham gives us no indication of what has occurred at this site over the last 6 years.

In fact, this is the total amount of evidence of warfare and male-male killing among chimpanzees after 37 years of research!! The data for infanticide and rape among chimpanzees is even less impressive. In fact, data are so sparse for these behaviors among chimps that Wrangham and Peterson are forced to use examples from the other great apes, gorillas and orangutans. However, just as for killing among chimpanzees, both the evidence and the interpretations are suspect and controversial.

Can We Escape Our Genes?

What if Wrangham and Peterson are correct and we and our chimp cousins are inherently sinners? Are we doomed to be violent forever because this pattern is fixed within our genetic code?

After 5 million years of human evolution and 120,000 or so years of *Homo sapiens* existence, is there a way to rid ourselves of our inborn evils?

> What does it do for us, then, to know the behavior of our closest relatives? Chimpanzees and bonobos are an extraordinary pair. One, I suggest shows us some of the worst aspects of our past and our present; the other shows an escape from it. . . . Denial of our demons won't make them go away. But even if we're driven to accepting the evidence of a grisly past, we're not forced into thinking it condemns us to an unchanged future (Wrangham 1997:110).

In other words, we can learn how to behave by watching bonobos. But, if we can change our inherited behavior so simply, why haven't we been able to do this before *Demonic Males* enlightened us? Surely, there are variations in the amounts of violence in different human cultures and individuals. If we have the capacity and plasticity to change by learning from example, then our behavior is determined by socialization practices and by our cultural histories and not by our nature! This is true whether the examples come from benevolent bonobos or conscientious objectors.

Conclusion

The theory presented by Wrangham and Peterson, although it also includes chimpanzees as our murdering cousins, is very similar to "man the hunter" theories proposed in the past. It also does not differ greatly from early European and Christian beliefs about human ethics and morality. We are forced to ask:

Are these theories generated by good scientific fact, or are they just "good to think" because they reflect, reinforce, and reiterate our traditional cultural beliefs, our morality and our ethics? Is the theory generated by the data, or are the data manipulated to fit preconceived notions of human morality and ethics?

Since the data in support of these theories have been weak, and yet the stories created have been extremely similar, I am forced to believe that "Man the Hunter" is a myth, that humans are not necessarily prone to violence and aggression, but that this belief will continue to reappear in future writings on human nature. Meanwhile, primatologists must continue their field research, marshaling the actual evidence needed to answer many of the questions raised in Wrangham and Peterson's volume.

References

Ardrey, Robert. 1961. *African Genesis: A Personal Investigation into Animal Origins and Nature of Man.* Atheneum.

——. *The Territorial Imperative*. Atheneum, 1966.

Brain, C.K. 1981. *The Hunted or the Hunter? An Introduction to African Cave Taphonomy*. Univ. of Chicago.

Dart, Raymond. 1953. "The Predatory Transition from Ape to Man." *International Anthropological and Linguistic Review* 1:201–217.

Darwin, Charles. 1874. *The Descent of Man and Selection in Relation to Sex*. 2nd ed. The Henneberry Co.

Cartmill, Matt 1997. "Hunting Hypothesis of Human Origins." In *History of Physical Anthropology: An Encyclopedia*, ed. F. Spencer, pp. 508–512. Garland.

——. 1993. *A View to a Death in the Morning: Hunting and Nature Through History*. Harvard Univ.

Goodall, Jane. 1986. *The Chimpanzees of Gombe: Patterns of Behavior*. Belknap.

——. 1971. *In the Shadow of Man*. Houghton Mifflin.

Goodall, Jane. 1968. "The Behavior of Free-Living Chimpanzees in the Gombe Stream Reserve." *Animal Behavior Monographs* 1:165–311.

Nishida, T., Hiraiwa-Hasegawa, M., and Takahtat, Y. "Group Extinction and Female Transfer in Wild Chimpanzees in the Mahali Nation Park, Tanzania." *Zeitschrift für Tierpsychologie* 67:281–301.

Power, Margaret. 1991. *The Egalitarian Human and Chimpanzee: An Anthropological View of Social Organization*. Cambridge University.

Reynolds, V. and Reynolds, F. 1965. "Chimpanzees of Budongo Forest." In *Primate Behavior: Field Studies of Monkeys and Apes*, ed. I. DeVore, pp. 368–424. Holt, Rinehart, and Winston.

Suguyama, Y. 1972. "Social Characteristics and Socialization of Wild Chimpanzees." In *Primate Socialization*, ed. F.E. Poirier, pp. 145–163. Random House.

Sussman, R.W., ed. 1997. *The Biological Basis of Human Behavior*. Simon and Schuster.

Sussman, R.W. 1995. "The Nature of Human Universals." *Reviews in Anthropology* 24:1–11.

Washburn, S.L. and Lancaster, C. K. 1968. "The Evolution of Hunting." In *Man the Hunter*, eds. R. B. Lee and I. DeVore, pp. 293–303. Aldine.

Wilson, E. O. 1997. "Sociobiology: A New Approach to Understanding the Basis of Human Nature." *New Scientist* 70(1976):342–345. (Reprinted in R.W. Sussman, 1997.)

——. 1975. Sociobiology: *The New Synthesis*. Cambridge: Harvard University.

Wrangham, R.W. 1995. "Ape, Culture, and Missing Links." *Symbols* (Spring):2–9, 20. (Reprinted in R. W. Sussman, 1997.)

Wrangham, Richard and Peterson, Dale. 1996. *Demonic Males: Apes and the Origins of Human Violence*. Houghton Mifflin.

POSTSCRIPT

Are Humans Inherently Violent?

Wrangham and Peterson's argument that human males have an innate tendency toward aggressive behavior is a classic sociobiological explanation. Sociobiological explanations consist of two basic assertions: (1) that all human behavior is ultimately driven by instincts, and (2) that those instincts result from natural selection favoring the behaviors they cause. Sociobiology, which has become very popular in recent years, began in biology and ethology (the study of animal behavior) and spread to the social sciences, including psychology, where it is called "evolutionary psychology." Its popularity is probably due to its attempt to explain many confusing variations in behavior by using a few simple, scientific principles. Any human social behavior—from selfishness to altruism—can be explained by sociobiology. It's all in the genes. Why are human males aggressive? Sociobiology would say it is because natural selection favored our more aggressive ancestors, allowing them to have more children than less aggressive individuals, thus ensuring that the tendency for male aggression increased in our species.

To learn more about sociobiology in general, the best starting point is probably E. O. Wilson's seminal book *Sociobiology: The New Synthesis* (Harvard University Press, 1975). Works explaining the human propensity for violence in terms of instincts include—besides Wrangham and Peterson's book *Demonic Males* (Houghton Mifflin, 1996)—Konrad Lorenz's classic book *On Aggression* (Harcourt, Brace & World, 1967), Martin Daly and Margo Wilson's book *Homicide* (A de Gruyter, 1988), and Michael Ghiglieri's book *The Dark Side of Man: Tracing the Origins of Male Violence* (Perseus Books, 1999). Carrying sociobiological reasoning a step further, Randy Thornhill and Craig T. Palmer argue in their book *A Natural History of Rape: Biological Bases of Sexual Coercion* (MIT Press, 2000) that human males have an instinct for rape because in the evolution of hominids rape was an effective way for males to pass on their genes.

Sussman's argument that human violence is basically a product of social and cultural conditions comes from the tradition of cultural anthropology. He challenges Wrangham and Peterson's assumptions that human behaviors are driven by instincts. Sussman says that the behaviors that Wrangham and Peterson, following E. O. Wilson, attribute to instinct, such as territoriality and male dominance over females, are not in fact universal among humans and lower primates. He also rejects Wrangham and Peterson's contention that an instinct exists if a behavior is universal to the human species, is easy to learn, and is pleasurable to perform. By these criteria, Sussman says, dancing must also be caused by an instinct to dance. Presumably a long list of similar activities, such as playing games and telling jokes, must also have their governing instincts. Sussman also rejects Wrangham and Peterson's contention that aggressive males would have been favored by natural (sexual) selection during hominid evolution. If this were so, he implies, why aren't all males equally aggressive today? How could the genes for nonaggressive behavior have survived countless generations of selection against them? Further, Sussman ridicules the notion that female hominids (or chimpanzees) would deliberately select aggressive males to father their offspring.

Important works challenging the sociobiological explanation of human violence include Ashley Montagu's book *The Nature of Human Aggression* (Oxford University Press, 1976), Richard Lewontin, Leon Kamin, and Stephen Rose's book *Not in Our Genes: Biology, Ideology, and Human Nature* (Pantheon Books, 1984), Kenneth Bock's book *Human Nature and History: A Response to Sociobiology* (Columbia University Press, 1980), and Matt Cartmill's book *A View to a Death in the Morning: Hunting and Nature Through History* (Harvard University Press, 1993). For descriptions and analyses of societies in which aggression is minimized, see Leslie E. Sponsel and Thomas A. Gregor's edited volume *The Anthropology of Peace and Nonviolence* (L. Rienner, 1994) and Signe Howell and Roy Willis's volume *Societies at Peace: Anthropological Perspectives* (Routledge, 1989).

Internet References . . .

Archaeology Magazine

This is the Web site of *Archaeology* magazine. This site has a searchable database with links to various articles about recent issues in archaeology, including a number of articles on the goddess cult in Europe.

```
http://www.archaeology.org
```

Center for the Study of the First Americans

The Center for the Study of the First Americans works to promote interdisciplinary scholarly dialogue and to stimulate public interest concerning the colonization of the Americas. This Web site provides articles that describe several theories on how the Americas were first colonized.

```
http://www.centerfirstamericans.com/cat.html?c=4
```

Earliest Americans Theme Study

This Web site by the National Park Service covers a wide range of issues involving early Paleoindian inhabitants of the United States. It addresses a variety of issues and topics that students may find useful for further research and offers citations of other articles and sources. The focus is on the Southeastern United States.

```
http://www.nps.gov/history/seac/outline/
  02-paleoindian/se_paleo/01-intro.htm
```

```
http://www.nps.gov/history/seac/outline/
```

Archaeology

*A*rchaeologists are prehistorians concerned with questions about the unrecorded history of human communities and civilizations. Like other historians, archaeologists seek evidence about how people lived, what they subsisted on, and the kinds of social institutions they established. But, unlike most historians who can turn to documents and papers to detail the lives and times of their subjects, archaeologists must find evidence in excavations. Over the past century, archaeologists have developed specialized methods for excavating and analyzing artifacts, stone tools, animal bones, shells, pollen, and carbon from old fires to determine a great deal about the environment, vegetation, subsistence patterns, living arrangements, and also when sites were occupied. At issue is how these varied kinds of data from ancient sources can be interpreted to reconstruct the lifeways of earlier times. A traditional set of questions that archaeologists ask is when, why, and how did people first settle different parts of the world, such as the Americas. They also ask questions about the meaning and significance of certain kinds of artifacts, such as the goddess figures of ancient Europe and the Middle East. Archaeologists also ask questions about why complex civilizations rose and fell.

- Was There a Pre-Clovis Migration to the New World from Europe?
- Was the Extinction of Pleistocene Megafauna in North America Caused by Climate Change Rather Than Over-Hunting?
- Did Prehistoric Native Americans Practice Cannibalism in the American Southwest?

ISSUE 3

Was There a Pre-Clovis Migration to the New World from Europe?

YES: Bruce Bradley and Dennis Stanford, from "The North Atlantic Ice-Edge Corridor: A Possible Palaeolithic Route to the New World," *World Archaeology* (December 2004)

NO: Lawrence Guy Straus, from "Solutrean Settlement of North America? A Review of Reality," *American Antiquity* (April 2000)

ISSUE SUMMARY

YES: Archaeologists Bruce Bradley and Dennis Stanford maintain that there is no evidence that the ancestors of the Clovis big-game hunting people of North America originated in Siberia and migrated down an ice-free corridor from Alaska. They argue that Clovis stone tool technology probably developed among the Solutreans of Europe, and that Solutrean hunters traveled across the north Atlantic ice sheet to North America, where they became the ancestors of the Clovis people.

NO: Archaeologist Lawrence Guy Straus counters that the Solutrean culture ended at least 5,000 years before the Clovis culture appeared, and that the North Atlantic Ocean would have been an insurmountable barrier to human travel during the last glacial maximum. He argues that the similarities between the Clovis and Solutrean tool technologies are limited and coincidental.

Archaeologists have long wondered when and how human beings first arrived in the Americas. The conventional view has been that the first humans arrived from Asia over a land bridge across the Bering Strait that connected Siberia and Alaska during the last Ice Age, when the sea level was lower. The ice sheet covering northern North America would have presented an impenetrable barrier to human passage until the end of the Ice Age, when a narrow ice-free corridor to the south opened up about 14,500 years ago. Big-game hunters then followed mammoths and other megafauna into the Great Plains (see Issue 4). From there they spread rapidly throughout North and South America.

In the early 1930s, archaeologists discovered a site near Clovis, New Mexico that contained large stone points with a distinctive thinning at the base (called "fluting"). Similar points were later found at other sites throughout what is now the United States and in Canada and Central America, some of them in conjunction with bones of now-extinct animals. Archaeologists called the complex of tools the "Clovis culture." Carbon-14 dating suggests that this culture first appeared about 11,500 years ago. Until the 1980s the orthodox view in American archaeology was that the Clovis people were the immediate descendants of the first immigrants into the Americas and the ancestors of the native peoples of North and South America.

In recent decades, however, archaeologists have found and excavated a small number of North and South American sites that may predate the Clovis culture. The best-known such site Monte Verde in south-central Chile has been carbon-14 dated at about 12,500 years ago, one thousand years earlier than the earliest Clovis sites!

A further challenge to the theory that the Clovis people were direct descendants of the first immigrants to the Americas and the sole ancestors of the native peoples of the Americas comes from the recent discovery of ancient human remains that do not resemble contemporary Native Americans. The skeletal remains have been compared to Australian Aborigines, Africans, south Asians, Ainu of Japan, Polynesians, and Europeans. The implication is that there may have been a number of migrations into the Americas from different points of origin.

The discovery of apparently pre-Clovis cultures in the Americas has once again thrown open the questions of who the first immigrants to the Americas were, where they came from, and how they got here. If they came before the ice-free corridor opened up, they must somehow have circumvented the vast ice sheet that covered northern North America. One possibility is that immigrants from Asia came down the west coast of Alaska and British Columbia in boats, stopping at ice-free islands and beaches and living mostly off the resources of the sea. Another possibility, represented by Bradley and Stanford's article, is that early Europeans made their way across the North Atlantic in small boats, living off fish and sea mammals and camping on the edge of the ice sheet. Bradley and Stanford argue that those migrants brought the Solutrean stone tool tradition, which developed into the Clovis culture in North America. Straus, on the other hand, points out that there is a gap of about five thousand years between the last Solutrean tool makers in Europe and the first Clovis tool makers in America, and that the pre-Clovis tools found so far in North America bear little resemblance to Solutrean tools. He also questions whether people could have crossed the stormy and ice-clogged Atlantic Ocean in primitive boats.

As you read these selections, ask yourself what kinds of evidence would be needed to resolve this question. Do the authors agree on the processes by which stone tool traditions arise and evolve? How many and what kinds of similarities must exist between two tool traditions to show that they are historically connected rather than independently invented?

YES

**Bruce Bradley and
Dennis Stanford**

The North Atlantic Ice-Edge Corridor:
A Possible Palaeolithic Route
to the New World

Introduction

Because of the fully modern anatomical features of Native Americans, early twentieth-century anthropologists staunchly denied the possibility that humans were present in the Americas before about 4000 BC. By contrast, a dedicated group of amateur archaeologists, erroneously believing that simple crude stone tools were comparable in age to the early Palaeolithic tools of Europe, advocated a more ancient occupation. The resolution of these debates came in 1926 with the documentation of a direct association between projectile points and extinct Pleistocene bison at a site near Folsom, New Mexico. A few years later, another distinctive type of fluted spear point was found in direct association with mammoth bones near Clovis, New Mexico. Although these early discoveries were not directly dated, the associations with extinct animals confirmed that the North American continent was populated by the end of the Pleistocene. Since their initial discovery, fluted Clovis-like points have been found from the Atlantic to the Pacific coast and from southern Canada to Central America.

After the late Pleistocene human presence in North America was established, archaeologists sought to explain the origin of the unique Clovis technology. It was thought that the ancestors of Clovis people must have come from Asia by crossing a land bridge, known as Beringia, that connected Siberia and Alaska. This land bridge formed when Ice Age sea levels dropped during the build up of the continental glaciers. The hypothesis continued that, after early populations arrived in Alaska, the glaciers began to melt, creating an 'ice-free corridor' between the Arctic and the rest of the Americas. Using the corridor as a migration route, Clovis people spread southward.

This theory seems eminently logical as Siberia is only a short distance from Alaska, and North American Indians share many physical traits with north-eastern Asians. Thus, practically all scholars accept the proposition that the bearers of Clovis culture must have come from north-eastern Asia and were the ancestors of modern Native Americans. Alternative routes were not considered since they would have required the use of watercraft, and it is inconceivable that Palaeolithic people had either the technical skills or the material culture to have crossed an Ice Age sea.

We must remember that these ideas on New World origins are based on informed speculation and are not supported by archaeological evidence. Through time and repetition, and in the absence of any clear alternatives, the theory has become dogma, and ultimately ideology, appearing in all textbook and popular publications. Over the past fifty years, archaeologists have expended a great deal of effort and resources trying to find evidence of Clovis ancestors in Alaska and north-eastern Siberia. In addition, anybody who suggested that there might be an alternative theory relative to either place or time of origin has been immediately discounted. The profession has come full circle, with the time of origin simply moved from 4000 years ago to the end of the Pleistocene, and the only acceptable place of origin being north-east Asia. However, there is a lack of data supporting an Asian connection and the origin of Clovis culture and technology still remains a mystery.

The Clovis Baseline

Although it is well established that Clovis people were in North America by 11,500 14 C BP [carbon: 14 years before present] years ago, there is very little evidence regarding early colonization. New dating techniques have placed many sites in a chronological context, but most Clovis sites are surface manifestations and cannot be directly dated. This is especially true in eastern North America where preservation of organic remains is poor. Nevertheless, it has been possible to document a basic assemblage of stone tool types and technologies that are readily identifiable as Clovis or at least related to Clovis.

Although there is some variability in tools and technologies, especially in relation to site function, the basic Clovis tool-kit is surprisingly consistent across diverse environments, ranging from the sub-tropics to the sub-arctic. This broad geographic distribution suggests that the tool-kit was designed for effective exploitation of almost any environment. As more sites are found our understanding of this early culture grows, and scholars are recognizing its complexity. Nevertheless, regardless of either time or space, Clovis artefacts retain an amazing technological consistency.

Clovis flint knappers used two basic flaked-stone technologies: bifacial thinning and large blade production. Both of these technologies are characterized by complex reduction strategies and specific sequences of flake and blade removal. Although space does not permit detailed description of these highly sophisticated technologies, we can summarize their salient characteristics.

Biface thinning was accomplished by highly organized reduction sequences and the application of a very difficult technique known as overshot flaking. When using this method flakes are struck that cross the entire width of the biface, many times removing a small portion of the edge opposite the striking platform. . . .

Along with controlled percussion thinning, most Clovis bifaces are basally thinned, with distinctive, well-controlled flakes called flutes. It is fluting that caught the attention of archaeologists because of its rarity in biface industries around the world. Flutes are negative flake scars desired as an end product on the finished artefacts. Inordinate attention has been placed on this interesting technological innovation, to the near exclusion of other traits. But is fluting really so special? In terms of Clovis biface technology, it is evident that fluting was done throughout the flaking sequence and is not technically different from other thinning flake removals; it just originates from the base of the preform rather than the side. Its distinctiveness comes from the intentional retention of the flake scar on finished pieces. . . .

Large blade production is typical of Clovis assemblages, and is especially common at habitation sites located on abundant sources of good flaking stone in south-eastern North America. Interestingly, blades and blade tools are much less common in the kill/processing sites that dominate the Rocky Mountain and Plains records. As with the bifaces, it is the details of blade production that are of special interest. The most frequent blade production technology resulted in large wedge-shaped cores. These cores have a single acute-angle platform, a single blade production face and a flat back (either cortical or prepared). The reduction sequence of this technology has yet to be completely reconstructed.

Retouched Clovis tools were made both from blades and from large biface thinning flakes. The former are most common at the large settlements, such as Gault in Texas and the latter at most large game kill/processing sites. Formal retouched tool types are limited in number, with side and end scrapers, biface knives, small gravers and weapon points being most prevalent. The number of formal tool forms increases with the size of assemblages and especially at habitation sites, where end scrapers, borers, adzes and backed pieces occur. Conspicuously lacking or rare are burins.

Among specific Clovis behaviours relative to lithic artefacts were caching large bifaces and a preference for exotic raw materials tools. Although they rarely resorted to heat-treating intractable tool-stone, Clovis flint knappers would occasionally heat raw material to improve its flaking quality. Recently recognized additions to Clovis lithic assemblage are small limestone slabs and pebbles. They mainly exhibit geometric designs, but at least two may have animal depictions. . . .

Although rare and poorly represented, bone and ivory artefacts, including sagaie (single bevelled points), bi-bevelled rods, awls, a shaft straightener, two barbed harpoons, a billet, an eyed needle and several dart throwing board hooks, have been found in Clovis assemblages. Most of these items have been recovered from sites with exceptional preservation and their rarity results from preservation problems rather than their uniqueness in Clovis assemblages.

So what are the implications for seeking a Clovis progenitor? It is our opinion that the well-developed Clovis bone and lithic technologies did not spring up overnight and there should be archaeological evidence of a transitional technology. Thus, we believe that a developmental Clovis assemblage should minimally include a formal tool assemblage with biface thinning, large blades, large bifaces, thin bifacial projectile points, end and side scrapers and a range of bone and ivory tools, including simple sagaies, awls and needles. In addition, we expect to see detailed similarities in specific manufacturing techniques, including overshot flaking, basal thinning of projectile points and pressure flaking.

What Evidence of Asian Origins?

The Ushki site on the Kamchatka Peninsula, was once thought to have been occupied over 14,000 years ago and was considered by many to be the origin point for the first Americans. Unfortunately, a recent re-evaluation of the site has demonstrated that its earliest occupation occurred only 10,700 years ago, much too late to figure in a first Americans scenario. As a result, one has to look over a thousand kilometres west of the Bering Strait to find technologies older than Clovis or to even find artefacts that are remotely similar. The bottom line is that there are no pre-12,000-year-old sites in Beringia that contain a lithic technology that remotely resembles anything we would be expecting as a precursor to Clovis. . . .

With the conviction that Clovis culture originated in north-eastern Asia, American archaeologists have focused their attention on Alaska. However, after over seventy years of research, there is no evidence of an early lithic technology related to Clovis in Alaska, in spite of concerted efforts to find it. So far, the oldest Alaskan lithic assemblages contain Asian microblades and wedge-shaped microblade cores. These eastern Beringian industries used inset technologies that have little in common with Clovis technology; moreover, they are contemporary with Clovis and persist into later Holocene times. . . .

As in Alaska, years of concentrated research in the ice-free corridor of Canada have failed to find unequivocal archaeological evidence of the passage of either Clovis or any other people through the corridor in the late Pleistocene. The few fluted projectile points found in the area appear to be related to weapon tips found in Alaska, and the few radiocarbon assays indicate a post-Clovis age. . . .

Thus, it is clear to us that there is no archaeological evidence that Clovis ancestors came out of Siberia by crossing the land bridge or that they passed down an ice-free corridor linking north-east Asia to America. When the ice-free corridor finally became habitable, it appears that the first people to move through it came from the south rather than the north. This should not be surprising because the gateway became biologically viable much sooner in the south than the north and we now know there was a resident Clovis-related population poised to move northward. Although there is no doubt that later people of Asian ancestry did indeed populate the territory of the former ice-free corridor, we reject the standard New World origins hypothesis.

Asian Alternatives?

Given the relative unlikelihood of a pre-Clovis terrestrial trek down the ice-free corridor, early immigrants must have used alternative routes to the

New World. Fladmark and Dixon have proposed that people using watercraft established a foothold in the Americas while exploiting the coastal environments of the Pacific Rim and continental shelf, which were ice-free by 13,000 years ago. This proposal is supported by recent reconstructions of former environments and ecosystems verifying that Pleistocene animals flourished along the Ice Age coastline. In addition, artefacts have been found in off-shore island sites, and drowned terrestrial and intertidal deposits. To date, these discoveries are too young to be ancestral Clovis, nor are the artefacts technologically related. Nevertheless, these discoveries indicate that early inhabitants had maritime capabilities and were utilizing the now-inundated continental shelf. . . .

Unfortunately, direct archaeological evidence of ancient watercraft is problematic at best. Materials used in early boat construction were perishable and would not readily survive in most environments. In addition, such craft are usually stored near water and would have suffered degradation through erosion by the tides of rapidly rising sea levels associated with deglaciation. This situation applies to many coastal habitation sites as well. . . .

Regardless of how issues of the antiquity and use of watercraft are resolved, and even though it is clear that Asian cultures contemporary with Clovis moved into the Americas, technological evidence for a pre-Clovis Asian ancestor is still totally absent. . . .

A European Alternative?

Over the years, scholars have observed significant similarities between Clovis and the older Upper Palaeolithic Solutrean technologies of south-western Europe. Jelinek identified the Solutrean culture in the Vasco-Cantabrian region of northern Spain as having the most striking resemblance to Clovis tools and technology. He noted a great many correspondences, including bifacially flaked lanceolate projectile points with concave bases and basal/edge grinding, a blade industry, small end scrapers with graver tips, large side scrapers made on flakes, cylindrical bevel-based bone points (sagaie) and a relative scarcity of burins. Yet he concluded that a direct historical relationship between Clovis and Solutrean was unlikely because Solutrean is more than 6,000 years older than Clovis, and the crossing of the glacial Atlantic Ocean would have been a major obstacle. More recently, Straus reaffirmed these concerns and attributed the similarities to independent invention. Although these observations are valid and must be resolved, neither author supported his opinions with archaeological or theoretical data demonstrating why this extraordinary convergence occurred. We suggest that the lack of evidence from Siberia and a new appreciation of the antiquity of watercraft warrant re-evaluation of the Solutrean hypothesis.

A Solutrean Solution?

Solutrean is the only Old World archaeological culture that meets our criteria for an ancestral Clovis candidate. It is older than Clovis, its technology is amazingly similar to Clovis down to minute details of typology and manufacture technology, and the two cultures share many unique behaviours. Indeed, the degree of similarity is astounding.

Solutrean sites are primarily found in south-western France, especially in the Aquitaine, and in Cantabria and Asturias in northern Spain. A variant also occurs in Portugal and on the Mediterranean coast. Solutrean sites date between 22,000 and 16,500 BP, the period of the Last Glacial Maximum (LGM) when continental glaciers covered much of Europe. . . .

The most impressive similarity is the basically identical manufacturing technology of thin bifaces using an overshot flaking method. Although we have studied many biface-thinning technologies, the only deliberate and systematic use of this technique occurs in Solutrean and Clovis. The complexity and difficulty of this technique and its rarity argue against it being independently developed. In addition, Solutrean is credited with introducing pressure flaking, intentional pre-treatment of stone by controlled heating to improve flaking quality, basal thinning and intentional margin grinding, possibly to dull edges for hafting. Individually these techniques may have been developed in different places and times, but a duplication of the complete comprehensive technological system seems unlikely to have occurred without a historical connection.

Large Solutrean bifaces, called laurel leafs, are bipointed, thin (width to thickness ratio greater than 5 to 1), have their widest dimension approximately $\frac{1}{3}$ of the distance from the base to the tip, and exhibit heavy lower lateral margin grinding. This also describes Clovis points except they usually have indented bases with distinctive flutes. Some Solutrean projectile points, mainly in northern Spain, are shaped like Clovis weapon tips. The main difference is that just under half of the Solutrean indented base points are primarily unifacially flaked.

At least one method of producing large blades is shared by Solutrean and Clovis flint knappers. This includes specific pre-core shaping, the way the core face is set up, and blade detachment techniques. This Solutrean blade technology is more like Clovis than it is like any other European blade core technology used either before or after Solutrean.

Many other Solutrean chipped-stone tool types resemble Clovis tools made on blades and over-shot flakes, among them distinctive end scrapers, retouched biface flakes, strangulated blades, borers and multiple gravers. Burins are rare in both Solutrean and Clovis assemblages, but occasionally appear. Backed blade tools are also rare in Clovis, but as more campsites are excavated they are becoming more common, although some Solutrean tools, such as the distinctive shouldered points and 'willow leaves', are not present in Clovis. However, all Clovis tool types including fluted bifaces occur in Solutrean assemblages. By contrast, only a few ubiquitous flaked tool types are shared between Clovis and any Siberian technology. . . .

The similarity between Solutrean and Clovis is also evident in the bone, antler and ivory tools, especially projectile points (sagaie). Bone shaft wrenches occur in both assemblages, and an eyed ivory needle has been found in Florida. Stones engraved with geometric and zoomorphic designs have been found in both cultures.

Figure 1

Clovis and Solutrean tools. a–k: Clovis; l–v: Solutrean; a, m–n: end scrapers on blades; b, o: borers; c: retouched bladelet; d: retouched blade; p: shouldered point; e, f, r: notches; g, s: burins; h–j, t–v: gravers. (a: Gault Site; b, c, j: Bostrum site; d, e: Simon Cache; f, g, i: Murray Springs; h: Blackwater Draw Locality 1; k: Fenn Cache; l: Solutré; m, q: Fourneau-du-Diable; n, r, s, t, u: Laugerie-Haute Ouest; o: Oulen; p: La Placard; v: La Riera.)

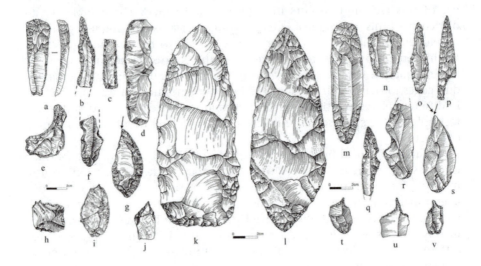

How much similarity is necessary before an interpretation of convergence gives way to an historical relationship? When a single artefact similar to Clovis discovered in Siberia, no matter how remote in time and space or even if out of context and misidentified, rates publication in *Science,* we believe that scholars should seriously consider the ramifications of the overwhelming number of unique technological and cultural similarities shared between Solutrean and Clovis. If a Solutrean assemblage were found in Siberia, everyone would consider the question of Clovis origins resolved.

Crossing the Water

During the LGM, the Polar Front was pushed to latitudes as far south as Portugal, turning the Iberian peninsula into a steppe-tundra environment with lowered temperatures, shortening growing seasons and reducing the extent and quality of natural grasslands. Game animals may have abandoned or become rare in the interior regions of Western Europe, forcing both animal and human populations into more favourable areas along the rivers and the coastlines of south-western Europe. In northern Spain, the Solutrean population lived in a narrow strip of coastal plain and foothills wedged between mountains with glaciers and heavy snow pack and an ice-covered ocean for much of the year. Although hunting was probably seasonally effective in the nearby mountains, people augmented their food supply by turning to alternative food resources, including hunting and fishing along the river estuaries and beaches.

The perennial Arctic ice formed much further south during the LGM, covering major portions of the North Atlantic and connecting Europe and North America with an ice bridge. This pushed the active young ice-edge margin and the animals adapted to sub-Arctic waters southward. The ice margin is

Figure 2

Early indented base projectile points. a: unifacial Clovis point, Delmarva Peninsula, Maryland; b: Page-Ladson point, Page-Ladson site, Florida; c: Page-Ladson point, Delmarva Peninsula, Maryland; d, e: Cactus Hill points, Cactus Hill, Virginia; f, g, h: Solutrean points, Las Caldas, Spain.

a region with intense biological productivity, providing a major food source for much of the marine food chain. . . .

These conditions resulted in a major annual influx of migratory sea mammals, birds and fishes into the Bay of Biscay from early fall through spring. By comparison, over 4 million harp seals were counted in the western rookery during the most recent census, an amazing figure considering the reduced productivity of food along the Canadian coast and the impact of major long-term hunting fishing pressures. A Solutrean hunter must have been awe-struck when he watched for the first time a pristine seal colony stretching for as far as he could see, basking on an ice floe as it drifted towards the shore. . . .

Solutrean artists left evidence in their rock art depicting sea mammals, deep-water fish and great auks that they were giving these resources serious thought. With their talent for innovation and several thousand years to observe the environment, Solutreans would have learned to target these resources.

Faunal collections from Solutrean sites in northern Spain contain abundant evidence that people were utilizing coastal and estuarian resources, and there was an increasing dependence on marine resources through time.

Figure 3

The North Atlantic region at the Last Glacial Maximum.

Even though the sea coast was farther away than today, people were transporting substantial quantities of limpets up to 10km from the shore to La Reira Cave. Based on this evidence, Straus suggested that, since many pleniglacial coastal sites are under the sea, marine resources may have been even more significant as dietary supplements than the present evidence would indicate. . . .

Although upland hunting sites were periodically used to stage ibex and red deer hunts, the marine resources would have been available year around. Sea mammal hunting on winter sea ice, hunting leads and ice edge in the late spring and summer would have provided food and fuel throughout the year. Sea birds such as the great auk and fish were seasonally abundant and would have augmented the Solutrean larder.

In the process of adapting to a coastal marine economy, tool-kits would have been elaborated to exploit the sea more efficiently; waterproof clothing, nets, harpoon gear and watercraft were necessary to exploit the marine resources and would have been useful on inland rivers during the LGM. It would not have taken long for the people to recognize the signs of impending storms and changing weather conditions. Nor would it have taken long to understand various sea-ice types, dangers and advantages. Hunters would learn that ice leads are not only excellent hunting locations, but provide havens during storms as the surrounding ice greatly reduces wave formation. Large ice floes are also good hunting locations and provide pullout 'islands' for camping or temporarily sitting out a storm in an overturned, well-secured skin boat.

Survival along the ice edge is possible with only a few skills and a little knowledge, particularly when following the harp and grey seal migrations. These seals feed along the northward receding ice edge during the summer, and move south in the fall as the winter ice begins to form. Successful hunting of these animals alone would provide all the resources necessary to sustain human life. Beyond a food source, seals provide oil for heating and cooking, and there is melting ice for fresh water, all of which can be accomplished with a single flame burning in a basin chipped into the ice. Seal body parts contribute soft tissue and bone for the manufacture of tools, waterproof garments, ropes and lashing, and covers and repair patches for tents and boats. There are many documented tales of groups of hunters set adrift on ice islands surviving for months, and being swept across the sea when the floe was trapped in an oceanic gyre. . . .

Solutrean hunters probably developed their techniques for exploiting the marine environment during a colder climatic period when the annual ice regularly formed in the Bay of Biscay. Once this tradition was established, there would have been increasing reliance on the use of ice-edge resources. Inevitably, this cool climate phase began to collapse, with slow warming and the distance between land's end and the ice-edge habitat continually increasing: good for seals, bad for seal hunters, especially if they did not have boats. Thus, in order to maintain the ice-edge economy, the hunters had to travel further and further out to sea to find the seals. These hunts likely became major extended treks with entire kin groups participating in the events. Inevitably, a group following the European seals on their northward migration would have ended up at the western end of the gyre, not knowing until too late that they were hunting Canadian seals heading southward to rookeries along the Atlantic coast of North America. Once they understood the seal migration patterns, the hunters could work the pattern back and forth. The entire distance along the ice bridge would have been around 2500km, shorter than the Thule Inuit migrations from Alaska to Greenland. Some families eventually established camps along the Western Atlantic seaboard and did not return to Europe.

The Missing Links

In recent years, three sites in eastern North America—Meadowcroft rock shelter in Pennsylvania, Cactus Hill in Virginia and Page-Ladson in Florida—have yielded stratified deposits with pre-Clovis radiocarbon dates associated with undeniable artefacts. Although the number of artefacts from these sites is small, most of the technological characteristics we propose for the developmental Clovis technology are present. These include thinned bifaces, indented base projectile points (that are pressure thinned, without true flutes), blades and bladelettes, backed blades and overshot flaking.

The early dates from Meadowcroft have been vociferously challenged, but microstratigraphic research has concluded that there are no geochemical reasons to reject the dates. Likewise, the radiocarbon dates from pre-Clovis features at Cactus Hill suggesting occupations between 15,000 and 18,000 14 C BP have come under scrutiny, but Wagner and McAvoy have adequately resolved these issues. At the Page-Ladson site, two points of a Suwannee variety, now redefined as Page-Ladson, were recovered from a displaced context, but are probably associated with artefacts and mastodon remains dated to nearly 14,345 C BP.

The oldest radiocarbon dates for a Clovis site are from the south east, whereas the youngest dates are from the west. There is a clear overlapping of declining radiocarbon ages from Solutrean, Cactus Hill, Meadowcroft, Page-Ladson and the earliest Clovis in the East and western Clovis. We therefore suggest that the pre-Clovis technologies are transitional between Solutrean and Clovis as, not only do they fill the time gap, they are also conveniently located near the Atlantic Coasts of Europe and North America.

Conclusion

Although there have been numerous efforts to find the origin of Clovis culture in Alaska and north-eastern Siberia, little new evidence has been encountered during the past seven decades. In fact, the more remains we find, the less they look like Clovis. The better our dating has become, the younger the sites turn out to be. It now seems that the materials most closely resembling Paleoindian in the north probably originated from groups travelling up through the opening ice-free corridor, rather than the other way around.

We contend that the overwhelming and diverse number of similarities between Solutrean and Pre-Clovis/Clovis mediate against the simple explanation of convergence. The location, dating and technology represented by the Cactus Hill, Meadowcroft and Page-Ladson sites provide the 'missing' chronological and technological links between Solutrean and Clovis. The hypothesis that a Solutrean Palaeolithic maritime tradition ultimately gave rise to Clovis technology is supported by abundant archaeological evidence that would be considered conclusive were it not for the intervening ocean. None of the competing hypotheses for Clovis origins are supported by archaeological data. Therefore, we argue that the hypothesis that a Solutrean Palaeolithic maritime tradition gave rise to pre-Clovis and Clovis technologies should be elevated from moribund speculation to a highly viable research goal.

Lawrence Guy Straus **NO**

Solutrean Settlement of North America? A Review of Reality

Recent popular—albeit influential—writings on the peopling of the New World in the wake of Kennewick Man, cite some prominent Paleoindian authorities (notably Dennis Stanford and Bruce Bradley) as suggesting a European origin for at least one episode of settlement of North America during the late Upper Pleistocene. . . .

Although I have tried to set the factual record straight, my attempts to publish letters to the editors of *The New Yorker* and *Newsweek* have been rebuffed. As an Old World prehistorian who lives and teaches in the United States, I feel an obligation to clarify the factual archeological record, especially since the issue has been overtly linked to the supposed "caucasoid" appearance of certain Paleoindian skeletal remains, with all the implications that would carry for public policy and the practice of both biological anthropology and archaeology in the United States (and presumably Canada). I am concerned that scientific debate must not be conducted *primarily* in the news media, where standards of argument and proof are very different than in academic discourse, but where the ramifications may be most serious, given mass dissemination and easy misunderstanding.

According to the Stanford-Bradley hypothesis as interpreted by reporters, a European peopling of America would supposedly have taken place by crossing the ice-laden northernmost Atlantic on foot or by boat. Specifically, similarities are claimed between certain lithic and osseous artifacts of the Solutrean "culture" of southern France and Iberia and some items typical of the Clovis "tradition" in the eastern three-quarters of the United States. These putative resemblances are then translated into an hypothesis of migration, "explaining" Clovis with reference to the Solutrean. This is in fact an old theory, having been proposed by Emerson Greenman in 1960. Seductive though such hyper-migrationist ideas apparently still seem to be in the archaeology of 2000, they are no more based in reality than they were 40 years ago. As a specialist in the Upper Paleolithic of western Europe in general and in the Solutrean in particular, I propose to set the record straight on the Solutrean and to show that the appearance of bifacial foliate "points" and bone "rods" in Clovis is merely one more instance of widespread technological convergence or parallelism in prehistory. Rather than requiring the presence of "sophisticated" paleo-European immigrants to develop the Clovis technology, it was the work of Native Americans, undoubtedly of trans-Beringian Asian origin.

Chronology

Stanford, in his Web page, states that the Solutrean is "not that much older" than Clovis. However, even the oldest bifacial foliate point (unfluted and straight-based) from the supposed "pre-Clovis" context in Meadowcroft Rockshelter is bracketed by radiocarbon dates of 11,300 and 18,800 B.P.[1]—and that is taking these controversial dates at face value. The Clovis techno-complex has now been carefully dated between 11,200–10,900 B.P.

The Solutrean of France, Spain, and Portugal is now dated by over 80 credible radiocarbon dates (both conventional and AMS). In France, the distinctive Solutrean lithic technology (i.e., bifacial and unifacial leaf-shaped, shouldered and stemmed points made on flakes and blades) lasted a short time, from about 20,500 B.P. to about 18,500 B.P., when it was replaced by the flake-based Badegoulian (aka Magdalenian 0+1) technology in the southwest and by the derivative Salpêtrian industry in the southeast. In Cantabrian (Atlantic) Spain, the dates for the Solutrean range from about 20,500 to 17,000 B.P., after which it was gradually replaced by backed bladelet-rich assemblages labeled "early Magdalenian." In Mediterranean Spain (Catalonia, Levante and Andalusia), the Solutrean dates between about 21,000 and 16,500 B.P. and is followed by an early Magdalenian or "Badegoulian". In Portugal, recent research, principally by J. Zilhao, shows that Solutrean technology developed as early as 21,000 B.P. and was replaced at some time between 17,000–16,500 B.P. by a bladelet-rich "early Magdalenian." In short, the *latest* Solutrean stone points are more than *5,000 radibcarbon years older* than the oldest Clovis points.

Geographic Distribution

The Solutrean techno-complex coincided with (and clearly represented a behavioral adaptation to) the Last Glacial Maximum, centered on 18,000 B.P. Prior to ca. 25,000–22,000 B.P., northwestern Europe (i.e., northern France, southern England and Wales, Belgium and Germany) was occupied by humans making backed and/or tanged lithic projectile points associated with the Gravettian technological tradition. With the onset of the extreme cold and, especially, the aridity of the Last Glacial Maximum (LGM), the human geographic range gradually contracted, resulting in the total (or near-total) abandonment of these previously occupied regions. They were not to be reoccupied until the Late Glacial. Specifically, although there *may* have been some ephemeral "visits" to or "explorations" of northern France, Belgium and southern Germany by around 16,000 B.P. or slightly earlier, actual resettlement of the Paris Basin, the Belgian Meuse Basin, southern England, and Germany only occurred between 13,000–12,500 B.P. This recolonization came during the distinct warming trend that was well underway by ca. 13,000 B.P. Culturally, this period corresponds to the late Magdalenian, materially defined by the frequent presence of antler harpoons, whereas the earlier Late Glacial corresponds to the "early Magdalenian," often rich in antler spear points and backed bladelets, but with no foliate or tanged lithic projectiles.

But during the LGM (i.e., during the Solutrean), the human occupation in western Europe was restricted to several refugia in southwest and southeast France and (mainly) to the lowland peripheries of the Iberian Peninsula (Vasco-Cantabrian, eastern and southern Mediterranean Spain, and Portugal). The very northernmost Solutrean site, Saint-Sulpice-de-Favières, is south of Paris at ca. 48°30' N. Although this site is undated, the absence of shouldered points and the presence of many large bifacial laurel leaf points and blanks at this specialized lithic quarry-workshop camp might suggest repeated brief visits at a relatively early Solutrean date, before the height of the LGM. Otherwise, the northern frontier of Solutrean settlement seems to have corresponded to the Loire River valley, at ca. 47°30' N, where there is a cluster of sites, notably Fritsch, Fressignes, and Tannerie, with radiocarbon dates between 19,000–18,000 B.P. In sum, there were simply *no people* living in (or even visiting with any degree of frequency) the regions north of Paris during the period from about 22,000–16,000 B.P., which is when the peopling of the New World now seems to have occurred. And there were certainly no people even in the southern part of England until ca. 12,500 B.P., so humans could not have crossed on pack ice between the British Isles and the Maritime Provinces. On the other hand, the distance from Portugal to Virginia is *5,000 km* straight across the open mid-North Atlantic Ocean.

Technology

Despite a few superficial similarities—which can easily be attributed to independent invention—there are vast differences between the Solutrean and Clovis technologies.

The technological traditions of the Franco-Iberian Solutrean were firmly rooted in those of the Gravettian (middle Upper Paleolithic) of western Europe. Depending on the local availability and quality of lithic raw materials, as well as on site function, blanks used for making stone implements were flakes, blades, and bladelets ("micro-blades" in American terminology), although the Solutrean leaf, shouldered, and stemmed points were usually made on blades often produced from diverse specific forms of prismatic cores. The hallmark of Solutrean lithic technology is indeed its projectile component, consisting of both a variety of single-element tips (of widely varying sizes and weights, including many "laurel leaves" that may actually have been used as knives) *and* (especially in later Solutrean contexts) backed bladelets that were used multiply as barbs and/or tips of projectiles, whose other elements were basally beveled antler points. Modern-quality Solutrean excavations (using fine-screening techniques) are yielding backed bladelets in quantities up to 40 percent of the total retouched tool fraction, although 5–20 percent is a more common range of proportions.

The classic Solutrean stone points include unifacial and bifacial pieces, often worked by invasive percussion (and sometimes pressure) flaking, with occasional evidence of heat treatment. The finest pieces are finished with ribbon removals that sometimes overshoot the opposite edge. But most pieces are far less sophisticated. (Overshot flakes are common whenever facially working techniques were used, as they were in many times and places in the prehistory of the world.) The Solutrean bifaces come in a variety of forms: long, narrow "willow leaves," classic bipointed, convex-sided "laurel leaves," rhomboidally shaped pieces, different classes of asymmetrical bifaces, pieces with a slight central tang, ones with a rounded base, others with a straight base, and bifaces (and some unifaces) with a concave base. *Bases are never fluted.* There also exist a variety of shouldered points, which are integral components of the Solutrean arsenal: these include both fully and partially invasively retouched (mostly unifacial) pieces in a variety of standardized forms, as well as pieces whose tang has been formed by abrupt retouch and which are otherwise (marginally) retouched. Finally there are true stemmed points in various forms and sizes that resemble (and may actually have been) "arrowheads".

One of the most distinctive aspects of this wide array of Solutrean projectiles is their regionally-specific character; while standard "laurel leaves" are fairly ubiquitous, many others have very limited geographic distributions. Notably, the true stemmed points are found in Mediterranean Spain (from Catalonia to Cádiz) and in southern Portugal. The basally concave points are mainly found in the eastern half of Asturias and in Cantabria, with a handful of outliers (exchange items, curiosities?) that have been found in the adjacent Basque Country and French Pyrenean foreland. (The concavities are slight–rarely deep, as in many Clovis points. According to Collins, "complete, pristine [Clovis] points generally exceed 100 mm in length," whereas the average length of whole Solutrean concave base points is 634 mm.) There are different shouldered point types peculiar respectively to Asturias-Cantabria, Dordogne-Charentes, Gascogne, Girona, and, more generally, the Mediterranean regions. This regional point style phenomenon is suggestive of an increase in territorialism associated with a compressed, circumscribed area of human occupation during the Last Glacial Maximum in southwestern Europe.

But Solutrean lithic technology is far more than just projectile elements. There are many different kinds of endscrapers, perforators, knives, and true burins (i.e., pieces from which one or more lateral spalls have been struck by the burination technique). This diversity of lithic tools and production strategies is accompanied by an organic technology that includes a couple of major Solutrean innovations: the eyed bone needle and the antler spearthrower—in addition to a wealth of beveled antler points and possible foreshafts (or even self-barbed point). Antler and bone artifacts, while not as common as in the subsequent Magdalenian, are not at all rare in the Solutrean. They are in Clovis.

Most significantly, Solutrean technology is thus very different from both the well-known Clovis and much less-understood pre-Clovis industries of North America, both in its specific artifact forms (e.g., true burins, backed bladelets) and in its diversity of projectile types, as well as other lithic and organic implements and fabrication techniques.

Insofar as it is formally described, Clovis technology can be character-ized as follows: bifaces (some of which are concave base, *fluted* projectile points, others probably knives) and unifaces, both made either on flakes or blades depending on local raw material availability; a limited variety of other lithic tools including end- and sidescrapers, gravers, but very few true burins; rare ivory and bone points or foreshafts, *one* example of a bone shaft wrench. Microblades, tanged and shouldered points—all common in various Solutrean assemblages—are absent in the far more limited technological repertoire of Clovis. While there are superficial similarities (e.g., some concave base foliate projectile points, some organic points or foreshafts with anti-skid engraved lines on basal bevels), these are most parsimoniously explainable as indepen-dent developments—similar solutions to similar functional problems, given limited available lithic and osseous materials and manufacturing techniques. The fact that red ochre was used by people in both techno-complexes—as cited by Stanford—is meaningless, as such pigment use is virtually a cultural universal among *Homo sapiens* foragers worldwide.

Subsistence: Marine Resource Exploitation?

The transatlantic migration hypothesis would require that people in western Europe during the Last Glacial Maximum have a highly specialized maritime adaptation.

At La Riera Cave, a two-hour walk from the pleniglacial shore of the Cantabrian Sea during the Solutrean, we documented evidence of significant marine mollusc collection and minor fishing (of salmon and trout, which are anadromous to varying degrees and could have been taken at the shore or in nearby estuaries or freshwater streams). Similar evidence exists at other Solutrean sites in the region (e.g., Cova Rosa, Altamira), and presages a major boom in aquatic resource exploitation during the Magdalenian. However, there is no evidence in Cantabrian Spain (or elsewhere) for Solutrean pre-dation on deep sea fish or marine mammals. (There is *one* rear first phalanx of a common seal in the Solutrean collection from Obermaier's 1924–25 excavations at Altamira that could well represent a scavenged animal. No additional seal remains were found in the recent Altamira excavations of González Echegaray and Freeman.) Humans were certainly acquainted with the seacoast, as attested by the penguin drawings and seal engravings of possible Solutrean age in Cosquer Cave, coastal southeast France, as well as fish and seal images in a number of other caves, such as Candamo in Asturias, La Pileta and Ardales in Andalusia, attributable for stylistic and archaeological reasons to the Solutrean. However, there are no representations of boats and no evidence whatsoever either of seafaring or of the ability to make a living mainly or solely from the ocean during the Solutrean. For Vasco-Cantabria and Aquitaine, at least, this is not surprising, as the Bay of Biscay, with its very steep thermal gradient, due to the clash of polar and latitudinally depressed Gulf Stream waters off the coast of Galicia, was a cold, windy and intensely stormy sea during the Last Glacial Maximum. In sum, there is simply no empirical support for assertions that Solutrean people could have survived on pack ice or navigated across the open Atlantic. The Solutrean was essentially a terrestrial adaptation, despite the peri-coastal distribution of many of its Iberian sites.

Depending on the region, hunter-gatherers during the Solutrean subsisted in largely treeless grasslands and heaths, mainly hunting medium to large terrestrial ungulate game: principally reindeer and horse in France, red deer and ibex in Iberia, with smaller numbers of bison, chamois and other mammals in all regions. There are trace quantities of mammoth remains in a few Solutrean sites of southwest France and Cantabrian Spain, but these are mainly pieces of worked ivory that could have been scavenged. The mammoth was already a rare creature on the landscape by this time in southwest Europe. There is no evidence for any degree of Solutrean mammoth hunting (specialized or not), in contrast to at least several classic Clovis sites.

Whereas Clovis pyrotechnology is said not to have included the use of stones to bank heat or to roast, such techniques are common in the Solutrean.

Art & Ornamentation

A major distinction between the Solutrean and Clovis lies in the area of artistic and decorative activity.

Although not as reknowned for works of portable or rock art and ornamentation as its successor the Magdalenian, the Solutrean is in fact better endowed with such images and artifacts than had been widely recognized until recently. Direct AMS dating of some of the charcoal drawings in Cosquer Cave prove that they were executed about 18,000–19,000 B.P., and new dates from La Pileta and Nerja in Andalusía yield ages of ca. 20,000 B.P. There are strong stratigraphic and/or indirect (but closely associated) radiocarbon arguments for attributing cave art in a number of other sites in France and Spain (e.g., Le Placard, Cougnac, Tête de Lion, Les Escabasses, Peña de Candamo, El Buxú) to the Solutrean. Even some of the spectacular limestone bas relief or deeply engraved friezes in Southwest France (e.g., Roc de Sers, Fourneau du Diable, Isturitz) are be [sic] attributable to this period.

Of the over 5,000 engraved and painted limestone or slabs from Parpalló Cave in Valencia, more than half are from Solutrean levels. By comparison with the Parpalló portable art objects, other rock art sites (notably the open-air figures of the Côa Valley in northeast Portugal, together with similar manifestations in nearby areas of Spain, as well as Portugal's only cave art site, Escoural) have been attributed to the Solutrean. Engraved stone slabs have been found in other Solutrean deposits, and engraved and "tick-marked" bones and ivory lamellae, perforated animal teeth and shells are common.

In short, one of the defining cultural characteristics of the Solutrean, along with the foliate and tanged points, is a wealth of both wall and portable art and ornamentation typical of neither Clovis nor "pre-Clovis." The facts that bones *are* well-preserved in many Clovis sites and that Solutrean rock art includes *open-air* examples (not just caves), are arguments against this distinction being merely one of differential preservation between the two cultural phenomena.

Discussion and Conclusions

The Solutrean represents the material evidence of the cultural adaptations of human groups surviving in the refugia of southwest Europe during the Last Glacial Maximum. This was a time of inventiveness and ingenuity under environmental and resource stress. The creativity of the Solutrean extended beyond the "arms race" that is attested by the plethora of lithic and antler point sizes and types (and even backed micro-blade elements) and by the invention of the spearthrower. It included new strategies for specialized, land-based, herd game hunting (including the swift, wary, cliff-dwelling ibex), supplemented by the use of littoral and riverine (but *not* oceanic) food resources. It also was characterized by a wealth of artistic and "marking" activities, no doubt related to social and ideological developments that helped humans to cope with hard times.

Significantly, Solutrean hunter-gatherers did not extend their range anywhere far enough north to put them in a geographic position to ever cross the North Atlantic to America (either on ice floes or in boats). Nor is there any evidence that they were skilled seafarers or marine mammal hunters.

Located 5,000 km from the U.S. eastern seaboard, the Solutrean techno-complex ended 5,000 radiocarbon years (over 200 human generations!) before the appearance of Clovis. Far more diverse in its lithic and organic technologies than Clovis, and characterized by an artistic tradition that is absent from Clovis, what the Solutrean would mainly seem to "share" with Clovis are concave base, bifacially-worked points. Yet such pieces in the Solutrean are found only at a handful of sites in a small area of northern Spain—not in France or in the rest of Iberia. Nor are the Solutrean points fluted, a feature which is absolutely diagnostic of Clovis points. Shouldered and stemmed points, as well as micro-blades, all so common in the Solutrean, are completely absent from the Clovis lithic repertory. And beveled antler points (or foreshafts), common in the Solutrean, are very rare in Clovis.

Thus, the most parsimonious explanation for the (superficial) similarities between the Solutrean and Clovis is the well-known (but under-acknowledged) phenomenon of technological convergence or parallelism. In short, there are only a limited number of ways in which to make a projectile point (or knife) out of stone. Invasive retouch (by pressure flaking or by hard or soft, direct or indirect percussion), including ribbon removals with overshooting for bifacial thinning, is among them. As has long been known, the prehistory of the world is replete with examples of bifacial foliate points. Just within Europe (not to mention Africa and Siberia), bifacial foliates reoccurred in the Middle and Upper Paleolithic (as well as in the Chalcolithic and Bronze Age) in different regions. It is a technological practice that has been invented and reinvented time and time again to fulfill a set of specific purposes, namely the killing and/or butchering of animals. Such convergence is recognized today in Europe, since bifaces span such vast distances of space and time that the search for "genetic" relationships is now seen to be a futile exercise. Similarly there are only limited numbers of effective hafting treatments possible for large lithic points; the basal concavity is one of them, independently invented not only in Clovis and in the Cantabro-Asturian Solutrean, but also in other prehistoric traditions (e.g., in Russia). One or two technical attributes are insufficient to establish a *cultural* link or long-distance interconnection.

While basal thinning has been used in various regions since Middle Paleolithic times, fluting is apparently a peculiar, specific and difficult-to-master technique for basal thinning that seems to have been a genuinely Native American invention. There is simply nothing like this form of basal thinning among the concave base Solutrean points made 9,000–5,000 years earlier. Credit should be given where credit is due: Native Americans, descended from diverse Asian populations, were the makers of Clovis and "pre-Clovis" lithics. The Solutrean of southwestern Europe was another story altogether. It seems to me particularly irresponsible–in the absence of any credible scientific evidence for prehistoric European settlement of the New World–for some professional archeologists to be suggesting that Native Americans are not the descendents of the first colonizers of this land.

Note

1. All dates given here are approximations based on generally large numbers of uncalibrated radiocarbon determinations. See the cited publications for exact dates.

POSTSCRIPT

Was There a Pre-Clovis Migration to the New World from Europe?

In their article, Bradley and Stanford maintain that the Clovis stone tool tradition of North America was derived from the Solutrean tool tradition of southern Europe. They hypothesize that some Solutrean people who had adapted to hunting and fishing on the edge of the ice sheet crossed the Atlantic in boats, and their descendants developed the Clovis culture in North America. Straus, however, regards it as unlikely that Solutreans could have crossed the Atlantic in boats during the last glacial maximum, and he considers the similarities between the Solutrean and Clovis tool traditions to be superficial and coincidental.

Archaeologists are continuing to pursue the answers to the questions of when the first humans reached the Americas, where they came from, and how they got here. They are concentrating their attention on the presumed pre-Clovis sites—such as Monte Verde in Chile, Meadowcroft Rockshelter in Pennsylvania, the Topper site in South Carolina, and Cactus Hill in Virginia. They focus especially on issues of dating and the question of how the artifacts in those sites relate to those of the later Clovis culture. Proponents of the theory that the first immigrants came down the west coast of North America in boats are looking for evidence of early human presence on islands and coastal areas. A major problem is that most of the places where such people would have camped or settled are now under water. Still, promising sites on islands include On Your Knees Cave off the Alaska coast, Daisy Cave off the California coast, and Cedros Island off the coast of Baja California. Recently a team of geoarchaeologists from Liverpool John Moores University in Britain caused a controversy when they claimed that apparently human footprints preserved in volcanic ash in Puebla, Mexico were 40,000 years old (see Robert Adler, "The First Americans," *New Scientist*, April 2006).

Other scholars are pursuing other lines of evidence. Biological anthropologists continue to study the bones of the oldest humans in the Americas, including Kennewick Man, whose bones have only recently been made available for study after a long legal battle between scientists and the Umatilla Indians, who wanted to rebury the bones (see Issue 17). Some geneticists are studying the DNA of Native Americans to try to determine which Old World populations are their closest relations, whether they are descended from one or more founding populations, and how long they have been in the Americas. Some linguists are using the similarities and differences among the languages of indigenous Americans to work out whether the languages come from one or several sources and how long they have been evolving in the Americas.

So far the results of these studies are inconclusive, as different scholars have reached different conclusions, but the genetic and linguistic studies generally suggest pre-Clovis entry of humans into the Americas.

For more on the Solutrean-Clovis controversy see Lawrence Straus, David J. Meltzer, and Ted Goebel, "Ice Age Atlantis?: Exploring the Solutrean-Clovis 'Connection,'" *World Archaeology* (vol. 37, no. 4, 2005) and Bruce A. Bradley and Dennis Stanford, "The Solutrean-Clovis Connection: Reply to Straus, Meltzer and Goebel," *World Archaeology* (vol. 38, no. 4, 2006). For discussions of some of the important pre-Clovis sites and their implications for our understanding of the arrival of humans in the Americas, see James Adovasio and Jake Page, *The First Americans: In Pursuit of Archaeology's Greatest Mystery* (Random House, 2002), which discusses Meadowcroft Rockshelter, and Tom D. Dillehay, *The Settlement of the Americas: A New Prehistory* (Basic Books, 2000), which discusses Monte Verde. For more on the possibility that the first immigrants to the Americas came down the west coast in boats, see E. James Dixon's book *Bones, Boats and Bison: Archaeology and the First Colonization of Western North America* (University of New Mexico Press, 1999). For a discussion of Kennewick Man and his significance, see James C. Chatters, *Ancient Encounters: Kennewick Man and the First Americans* (Simon and Schuster, 2001). Popular accounts of the controversies surrounding the initial migration into the Americas include Sharon Begley and Andrew Murr, "The First Americans" (*Newsweek*, April 26, 1999); Evan Hadringham, "America's First Immigrants" (*Smithsonian*, November 2004); and Michael D. Lemonick and Andrea Dorfman, "Who Were the First Americans?" (*Time*, March 13, 2006).

ISSUE 4

Was the Extinction of Pleistocene Megafauna in North America Caused by Climate Change Rather than Over-Hunting?

YES: Donald K. Grayson and David J. Meltzer, from "A Requiem for North American Overkill," *Journal of Archaeological Science* (May 2003)

NO: Stuart Fiedel and Gary Haynes, from "A Premature Burial: Comments on Grayson and Meltzer's 'Requiem for Overkill,'" *Journal of Archaeological Science* (January 2004)

ISSUE SUMMARY

YES: Archaeologists Donald Grayson and David Meltzer argue that the evidence that human predation caused the Pleistocene megafauna's extinction is circumstantial. They contend that there is little archaeological evidence to support that hypothesis, and they suggest that climate change is a more likely explanation for these extinctions in North America, as it seems to be for those in Europe.

NO: Archaeologists Stuart Fiedel and Gary Haynes are strong supporters of the overkill hypothesis, which argues that humans over-hunted large mammals to extinction in North America. They contend that Grayson and Meltzer have misinterpreted older archaeological evidence and largely ignore more recent data. They maintain that the extinctions took place too fast to have been caused by climate change.

Between 10,000 and 30,000 years ago the first wave of settlers swept into the New World. The exact date of this immigration is uncertain. During this period the global climate was changing. The cool, dry conditions of the last ice age (the Pleistocene) were gradually giving way to the warmer and wetter conditions of the Holocene (the geological period in which we currently live).

At the same time that humans were first arriving in the New World and glacial ice was retreating as the earth's climate warmed, the large mammals that were characteristic of the Pleistocene, such as the mastodon and wooly mammoth went extinct. These Pleistocene megafauna (literally, "huge animals") were well adapted to the cool, dry conditions of the last ice age. Their large size and thick fur would have helped them conserve their body heat. But they had never had to deal with human predators until people started migrating to the New World from Asia. The question is: did the warming climate or human hunters cause their extinction?

After the ice age ended megafauna had also gone extinct in Eurasia and Australia, but it was the archaeologist Paul Martin who first attempted to address this question systematically for the North American context. In the 1930s archaeologists had found a distinctive type of flint projectile point at Clovis, New Mexico, associated with bones from one of these large mammals. The assumption was that people who had made and used these tools were the first immigrants to the New World from Asia and that they lived at least partly by hunting mastodons and mammoths. Some years later Martin reasoned that because these large mammals had not been exposed to human predation before, perhaps humans had been responsible for their decline and ultimate extinction. After all, in the nineteenth century Americans had seen the American bison hunted to the brink of extinction. Could human predation not also have sealed the fate of the megafauna? Martin called this explanation the "overkill hypothesis."

Martin used computer modeling as well as the archaeological record to make his case. But like any computer simulation, Martin's model is only as good as its assumptions and premises. Grayson and Meltzer challenged those assumptions and the archaeological evidence.

Donald Grayson and David Meltzer contend that the archaeological data actually *contradicts* the overkill hypothesis. They are especially skeptical that the lack of sites where humans killed megafauna is evidence in support of Martin's model. Martin had suggested that there were few such archaeological remains because the megafauna were killed off so quickly. Meltzer and Grayson argue that Martin's interpretation of the "negative evidence" removes his proposal from the realm of theory, since it cannot be tested. In place of the overkill hypothesis, Grayson and Meltzer suggest that the best explanation for the extinctions is drastic climate change.

Stuart Fiedel and Gary Haynes argue in support of the overkill model. They contend that Grayson and Meltzer have ignored most of the evidence—both archaeological and climatological—that supports the overkill hypothesis. In particular, the rapid extinction of these large mammals over a period of about 400 years suggests to them that climate change could not have played as central a role as Grayson and Meltzer suggest. They also argue that the Pleistocene extinctions were contemporaneous with the arrival of the first humans but predated the Pleistocene-Holocene warming period by as much as 1000 years.

This debate has raised a number of questions important to prehistoric and contemporary societies. Can small-scale societies (e.g., hunter-gatherers) have impacts on their environment? How important is the impact of climate change on natural species? Can both the overkill and the climatological hypotheses be synthesized? Are human beings wasteful? What implications does the overkill hypothesis have for the traditional image of Native Americans?

YES

**Donald K. Grayson and
David J. Meltzer**

A Requiem for North American Overkill

Introduction

Toward the end of the Pleistocene, some 35 genera of primarily large mammals became extinct in North America, either in the sense that they no longer exist anywhere in the world (29 genera), or that they ceased to exist here while living on elsewhere (six genera). More than 40 years ago, Paul S. Martin began to develop what has become the most visible explanation for these losses: the extinctions, he argues, were due entirely to the impacts of human hunting.

Few speculations about the prehistoric past have achieved as much celebrity as this one. Hardly a textbook or popular scientific treatment of New World archaeology, ecology, and environmental history misses the opportunity to discuss it, with many understandably keen to use this apparent illustration of human destructiveness to teach a well-intentioned lesson in conservation. Yet despite this popularity, Martin's position gains virtually no support from the North American late Pleistocene archaeological and paleontological records. As a result, it gains almost no support from the scientists who specialize in these records. Here, we provide a brief historical background to Martin's argument, and then turn to the empirical record that shows it to be incorrect.

The Heart of the Argument

In developing what has become known as the 'overkill hypothesis', Martin was tackling a problem that has intrigued scholars ever since the former existence of such now-extinct mammals as mammoth and ground sloths became known, a process of recognition that began as the 18th century came to an end. Martin's particular approach to explaining the extinctions, however, became popular only after 1860, the year it was demonstrated in Europe that people had walked the earth with such beasts as the woolly rhinoceros, woolly mammoth, and 'Irish elk'. Soon after that acceptance occurred, it became so routine to attribute European extinctions to human hunting that, by 1872, this argument was being referred to as 'the favorite hypothesis'.

From *Journal of Archaeological Science*, vol. 30, 2003, pp. 585–593, 5 pages. Copyright © 2003. Reprinted with permission from Elsevier.

While the intellectual roots of the overkill approach to explaining Pleistocene extinctions lie in 19th-century western Europe, our current understanding of the archaeology, vertebrate paleontology, and late Pleistocene climate history of that region is such as to leave the hypothesis no strong adherents there. Instead, it lives on elsewhere, most notably in Australia and North America. The situation in Australia is in considerable flux, and we therefore do not comment on it but instead focus on North America, the area we know best.

In North America, the contemporaneity of humans and extinct Pleistocene mammals was not demonstrated until the early 1930s, at Clovis, NM, where the evidence suggested that people had hunted the animals involved. A series of similar sites were discovered during the decades that followed. That several of those sites on the North American Plains and in the southwest contained the remains of mammoth clearly warranted the inference that Clovis groups at least occasionally hunted this animal. This reasonable observation was then transformed into the generalization that Clovis groups were specialized big-game hunters, even though there was (and is) no evidence for such specialization. Once that had occurred, a number of scholars found it reasonable to attribute North American Pleistocene extinctions at least in part to human hunting.

The contemporary North American version of the overkill hypothesis is due almost entirely to Martin, who has developed the hypothesis in sufficient detail to make it convincing to many, although its most vocal adherents are primarily those whose expertise lies outside the place and time period involved. Martin's hypothesis has changed somewhat over the years, but it has always included four major premises:

1. It has been well established through archaeological and paleontological research that the prehistoric human colonization of islands was followed by often massive vertebrate extinctions.
2. The archaeological phenomenon known as Clovis, marked by well made and distinctive fluted points and well dated to about 11,000 radiocarbon years ago, is extremely likely to have been created by the first peoples to have entered North America south of glacial ice, and represents the first peoples known to have hunted large-mammals in this huge area.
3. Clovis peoples preyed on a diverse variety of now-extinct mammals.
4. The late Pleistocene North American mammal extinctions occurred at or near 11,000 radiocarbon years ago.

From these key premises, Martin concludes that Clovis hunters caused these extinctions. Direct human predation, he argues, removed the herbivore contingent, while the loss of the herbivores led to the extinction of such carnivores as the saber-tooth and scimitar cats and the giant short-faced bear.

As we have noted, the overkill hypothesis was born in 19th-century Europe, only to be rejected as our understanding of western European archaeology, vertebrate paleontology, and climate history became sufficiently well refined to make it clear that the comings and goings of large mammals in this region were tightly linked to climate change. The North American situation is quite different. Here, the late Pleistocene climate record is strong, but our understanding of the archaeology and paleontology of this period is not. We do, however, know enough to examine Martin's critical premises in detail, and, in doing so, to find his argument significantly wanting.

Island Extinctions

To establish that prehistoric humans not only could have caused extinction, but did so on multiple occasions, Martin turns to island settings. There is good reason for this, since it is extremely well documented that on island after island in nearly all parts of the world, prehistoric human colonization was quickly followed by vertebrate extinction.

The most famous example of this phenomenon is certainly provided by New Zealand, where some 11 species of moas—large, flightless birds that ranged in estimated weight from 20 to over 200 kg—succumbed within a few hundred years of permanent human colonization some 900 years ago. All agree that these extinctions resulted from human activities. At least 25 other species of smaller vertebrates—lizards, frogs, birds, and at least one species of bat—were lost with the moas, and the list of species lost will surely grow as our knowledge of the recent biotic history of New Zealand grows.

While New Zealand may provide the most famous example of human-caused vertebrate extinction in a prehistoric island setting, nearly every island whose archaeology and paleontology is well known illustrates the same phenomenon. In the Mediterranean, only two species of mammals—both shrews—remain of the mammals that were present just prior to the human arrival. On Mangaia, in the Cook Islands, 13 of 17 species of landbirds known archaeologically did not survive to be described in writing. In the West Indies, multiple species of hutias, rodents that had long been present in the region, became extinct after people arrived. No matter where we look, as long as terrestrial vertebrates were present, the outcome is the same.

In no case is the precise cause or causes of these extinctions known. This is because in all known cases, human colonization was associated with multiple possible impacts on the species that were lost. In New Zealand, for instance, people not only hunted moas, but they also set fires that quickly destroyed massive expanses of forest and introduced competitors and predators in the form of rats and dogs. Some combination of hunting, introduced species (including pathogens), and anthropogenic vegetational change caused the losses that are so well documented there. We cannot, however, say what that combination was. The same is true for all known prehistoric, human-caused island extinctions. Because this is the case, none of these extinctions can be securely attributed to hunting alone, although this may certainly have occurred.

The magnitude of prehistoric human-caused vertebrate extinctions on islands came as a surprise when it first began to be described in detail by such scientists as Storrs Olson, Helen James, and David Steadman during the 1980s. Nonetheless, it has long been known that island faunas are in general prone to extinction, and the reasons for this are well understood. Island vertebrates are vulnerable because their populations are small, because they are confined to well-delineated areas of land that may undergo rapid environmental change, because they may have lost (and in some cases have clearly lost) the behavioral mechanisms needed to cope with introduced predators, pathogens, and competitors, and because there is no ready source of conspecific individuals to replenish dwindling populations. Island faunas are, as Paulay has noted, "among the most vulnerable in the world".

Martin's first premise is, then, depressingly true. The initial human colonization of island after island was followed by vertebrate extinction. That this premise is true, however, does not mean that it is relevant to continental extinctions. After all, the factors that make islands prone to vertebrate extinction—small population sizes of resident vertebrates, the lack of a ready source of conspecific colonizers, and so on—do not apply to the continental setting.

What might make some of the lessons learned from the biotic history of islands applicable to the North American setting is evidence that Clovis-aged peoples caused massive environmental disruption of the sort routinely seen in island settings. Of this, however, there is absolutely no evidence. In addition, Martin's hypothesis relies on hunting and hunting alone, and island extinctions resulted not from hunting but from 'the manifold impacts of human colonization', as Holdaway has so aptly put it for New Zealand.

Clovis First

Clovis dates to within a few hundred radiocarbon years of either side of 11,000 years ago. Until recently, most archaeologists accepted Clovis as the archaeological manifestation of the first people to have occupied the Americas south of glacial ice. With the recent and fairly general acceptance of the validity of the 12,500-year-old human occupation at the southern Chilean site of Monte Verde, this view has largely crumbled. Given that there is no reason to doubt that people entered the Americas via the Bering Land Bridge, it follows that they must have been in North America long before they reached southern South America. Nonetheless, it remains true that Clovis is the earliest well-accepted archaeological phenomenon known from North America. Clovis also provides the earliest secure North American evidence that people did, in fact, encounter now-extinct large mammals.

Clovis Hunters

If Martin is correct in blaming Clovis hunters for late Pleistocene mammal extinctions in North America, it would seem to follow that these people must have hunted all of the animals whose extinction they are argued to have caused.

How many of those genera can be shown to have been human prey during Clovis times? The answer is two—mammoth and mastodon—and there are only 14 sites that securely document this relationship. As has long been known, this is not a sampling fluke. There are more late Pleistocene occurrences of horse than there are of mammoth or mastodon, and nearly as many for camel as for mastodon, yet there are no demonstrable kill sites for horse or camel or for any of the remaining genera. This is not for want of looking. Given the high archaeological visibility of the remains of extinct Pleistocene mammals, and their great interest to archaeologists and Quaternary paleontologists alike, if such sites were out there, they would surely be found. Indeed, there is a strong bias in the Clovis archaeological record toward just such sites.

The rarity of megafaunal kill sites is such an evident feature of the late Pleistocene archaeological and paleontological records of North America that Martin has had to address it. After all, other parts of the world—Late Pleistocene Europe, for example—are littered with sites that document human predation on large mammals.

Martin has attempted to account for the virtual absence of kill sites in an extraordinary way. He argues that it all happened so fast that we should not expect to find empirical evidence of that process. That is, he has been forced to argue that "much evidence of killing or processing of the extinct fauna is not predicted" by his position. It is a rare hypothesis that predicts a lack of supporting evidence, but we have one here, and we have it only because evidence for it is, in fact, lacking. Martin argues quite differently for New Zealand, where he calls on the abundance of archaeological sites containing moa remains to bolster his position that human hunting played a role in the extinction of these animals.

The Extinctions Occurred 11,000 Years Ago

Obviously, if Clovis-age hunters caused the extinctions, either directly (the herbivores) or indirectly (the carnivores) of some 35 genera of mammals, those extinctions must have occurred at or soon after Clovis times. However, of the 35 genera involved, only 15 can be shown to have lasted beyond 12,000 years ago. This leaves open the possibility that many of the remaining genera became extinct well before Clovis times. In western Europe, late Pleistocene extinctions were scattered in time and space, and there is little in the North American record to suggest that the same thing did not happen here.

This possibility causes difficulties for the overkill position. Martin and Steadman, for instance, have suggested that the Aztlan rabbit might have been 'large enough' to have been hunted to extinction by Clovis-age peoples. This genus, however, cannot be shown to have survived the last glacial maximum some 18,000 years ago. Clovis hunters are thus asserted to have driven the extinction of a very small animal that, as far as we can tell, predated Clovis by at least 7000 years.

But let us assume that as the years go by, more of the mammals will be shown to have become extinct during or soon after Clovis times. How unique would this make the North American extinctions?

The answer is 'not very'. The Northern Hemisphere, in general, saw substantial large mammal extinctions at the end of the Pleistocene. In Ireland, the latest radiocarbon date for the giant deer (sometimes called the 'Irish Elk') falls at 10,610 years ago; the latest date for reindeer falls at 10,250 years ago. In southwestern France, reindeer, mammoth, saiga, and the giant deer (among others) disappeared at about the same time that Clovis appeared in North America. In the southern Jura and northern French Alps, reindeer disappeared sometime between 12,000 and 11,000 years ago. In the Taimyr Peninsula of northern Siberia, mammoth disappeared from the mainland shortly after 10,000 years ago, although they persisted well into the Holocene on Wrangel Island. While all this was happening, Harrington's mountain goat and the Shasta ground sloth disappeared from the American Southwest, caribou (North American reindeer) retreat from their late Pleistocene ranges in the American midwest and southeast, and mammoth and mastodon (among others) are lost from the American landscape. Genetic data even suggest that cheetahs in Africa and cougars in North America may have undergone severe population declines as the Pleistocene ended.

Human hunting had nothing to do with the Eurasian losses. Martin cannot blame human hunters for the disappearance of reindeer and giant deer in Ireland since there were no people in Ireland at the time. In France, reindeer were an important part of the human diet for tens of thousands of years but were not lost until the Pleistocene ended. There were no Clovis hunters in Siberia, yet large mammal extinctions occurred here anyway. Large mammal extinctions occurred at the end of the Pleistocene with or without Clovis, with or without the presence of human predators.

The End of North American Overkill

Martin has recently noted that "archaeologists have always washed their hands of human complicity in large [mammal] extinction" in North America, and he is right. He might also have added that vertebrate paleontologists who specialize in late Pleistocene North America have also cleansed themselves of this notion. The reason is straightforward. There is no evidence for it and much against it. While Martin claims that a lack of evidence provides strong support for his position, others have different expectations of the empirical record.

Given that archaeologists and paleontologists have washed their hands of North American overkill, who accepts it and what explains its popularity? As we have mentioned, those who praise overkill are, by far and large, scientists who are not familiar with the details of the North American late Pleistocene. . . .

Our point is simple. The North American version of the overkill hypothesis lives on not because of archaeologists and paleontologists who are expert in the area, but because it keeps getting repeated by those who are not. As to why it remains popular in those circles, there are likely several reasons, but one seems especially compelling.

The first detailed development of the overkill hypothesis came in 1967, the same year that the Environmental Defense Fund was launched. Five years earlier, Rachel Carson's *Silent Spring* had appeared; a year later, in 1968, Paul Ehrlich produced *The Population Bomb*. By 1970, the US National Environmental Policy Act had been passed and Earth Day created. We are not suggesting that the overkill argument emerged as an integral part of the environmental movement; after all, Martin first raised the idea a decade earlier, and overkill models emerged in mid-19th century England in a very different historical context. Instead, we suggest that the overkill argument captured the popular imagination during a time of intense concern over our species' destructive behavior toward life on earth. It retains that grasp today.

It is easy to show that overkill's continued popularity is closely related to the political uses to which it can be put. Take, for instance, Peter Ward's recent discussion of the matter. Ward—a superb paleontologist whose scientific research focuses on fossils that are between about 300 million and 60 million years old—is convinced by Martin's arguments, concluding that "the ravages of hungry people surely were involved in the destruction of many species now extinct". In this conclusion, he finds "tragic validity for times approaching": "the Snake River salmon is virtually extinct . . . king crab fishing in Alaska has been essentially terminated because the stocks are gone; the great shellfish fisheries of Puget Sound have been halted because the oysters and mussels are too poisoned by industrial wastes to eat". For Ward, the overkill position is inextricably linked to modern times and to the homily of ecological ruin.

Ward is not alone in taking this approach. In *The Third Chimpanzee*, ecologist Jared Diamond enthuses over Martin's argument and ends the chapter with a brief discussion of "the blitzkriegs by which modern European hunters nearly exterminated bison, whales, seals, and many other large animals". The next chapter begins with a discussion of "the risk of a nuclear holocaust".

For these discussions, and others like them, overkill provides powerful political capital. That we may agree with the political goals of these authors is immaterial. Our concern here is that both science and environmental concerns are being done a disservice by relying on claims that have virtually no empirical support. We are not suggesting that those who use overkill in this way do so in disregard of the facts against it. We do believe, however, that they are insufficiently familiar with the archaeological and paleontological records bearing on overkill, and so cannot properly judge Martin's claims of its explanatory power.

In fact, Martin's recent writings suggest to us that he is no longer trying to approach this issue within a scientific framework. As we have noted, he explicitly maintains that the North American overkill position does not require supporting evidence. He is unconcerned that archaeologists 'wash their hands' of his ideas. He criticizes the search for pre-Clovis sites in the New World as "something less than serious science, akin to the ever popular search for 'Big Foot' or the 'Loch Ness Monster'". As one of us has observed elsewhere, Martin's position has become a faith-based policy statement rather than a scientific statement about the past, an overkill credo rather than an overkill hypothesis.

By emphasizing the nature of the problem and by focusing research on the latest Pleistocene archaeology and paleontology of North America, Martin's arguments have led to a good deal of productive science. Now, however, it has become quite clear that things did not happen the way that Martin has envisaged. Martin's arguments drawn from islands are not relevant to continental settings, especially given that in every known instance, island extinctions were accompanied by massive habitat disruption. Northern Hemisphere mammal communities saw substantial extinctions at the end of the Pleistocene, with or without Clovis and even with or without a human presence. There are no kill sites for 26 of the 28 genera of North American herbivores and only 14 sites for the remaining two. It remains fully possible that the North American extinctions were not confined to the very end of this period, but were scattered across thousands of years, as occurred in Europe. Unless we can somehow accept that the very absence of evidence demonstrates that overkill occurred, it is time to focus on understanding what really did happen.

Unfortunately, what did happen is not at all clear. Although a number of climate-based hypotheses have been forwarded for North America, none have gained widespread acceptance, since none connect particular climate variables with particular organisms in powerful ways. Doing so is likely to be a daunting task, since it is very likely that an adequate explanation will have to be built by treating each organism on its own. Nonetheless, experience in other parts of the world shows that it can be done. It is clearly time to begin the task in a North American context.

Stuart Fiedel and
Gary Haynes

 NO

A Premature Burial: Comments on Grayson and Meltzer's "Requiem for Overkill"

In a recent JAS article ("A requiem for North American overkill"), Donald Grayson and David Meltzer attack Paul Martin's "overkill" hypothesis that humans caused America's Terminal Pleistocene megafaunal extinctions. This is one of three similar recent articles by these authors in which, by scrupulous evaluation of the archaeological record, they have reduced the list of unambiguous instances of human interactions with now-extinct mammals in North America to 14 proboscidean kill sites. We applaud their informed skepticism about the evidence, especially since one of us (Haynes) wrote a set of strict standards that Grayson and Meltzer used in their analyses. . . .

Although their critical assessment of the Late Pleistocene archaeological record is laudable, Grayson and Meltzer unfortunately make numerous mistakes, indulge in unwarranted ad hominem rhetoric, and thus grossly misrepresent the overkill debate. In this comment, we first briefly address those aspects of their papers that represent mere theatrical posturing, and then we turn our attention to their more serious errors of fact and interpretation.

First, the theater. A phrase repeated or paraphrased in each of the articles is that overkill is "a faith-based policy statement rather than a scientific statement about the past, an overkill credo rather than an overkill hypothesis". By thus denying the very scientific legitimacy of the overkill hypothesis, Grayson and Meltzer seek to preclude any further serious engagement with its advocates. Science is not advanced by such dogmatic dismissal of competing hypotheses. Also theatrical but unfounded are three points Grayson and Meltzer chose to emphasize in their article summary: (1) overkill has been rejected for western Europe (it has decidedly not been rejected by knowledgeable experts, such as A.J. Stuart and colleagues, (2) Paul Martin is the only reason overkill is still discussed for North America and Australia (also wrong—see, for example, the recent work of Alroy Flannery, and O'Connell, and (3) "there is virtually no evidence" to support overkill, which, as we show in this reply, is absolutely wrong. In fact, we think there is far more support for overkill than for climate change as the principal cause of the extinctions.

From *Journal of Archaeological Science*, vol. 31, 2004, pp. 121–131, 5 pages. Copyright © 2004. Reprinted with permission from Elsevier.

Is There No Evidence of Overkill?

It seems as though it should be simple enough to test the overkill hypothesis. If, as hypothesized, Paleoindian hunters killed thousands of giant mammals, there ought to be lots of kill sites with unambiguous evidence of hunting and butchering (e.g., broken, cut, and burned bones, semi-disarticulated skeletons at hearth areas, associated stone tools). But in reality, such sites are very rare. Martin has responded to archaeologists' disappointment over the scarcity of megafaunal kill sites by stating that,

> Sufficiently rapid rates of killing could terminate a prey population before appreciable evidence could be buried. Poor paleontological visibility would be inevitable. In these terms the scarcity of known kill sites on a landmass which suffered severe megafaunal losses ceases to be paradoxical and becomes a predictable consequence of the special circumstances which distinguish *invasion* from cultural development within a continent. Perhaps what is remarkable in America is not that so few, but that *any* kill sites of extinct mammals have been found.

In short, the absence of kill sites is just as expectable as their presence. Thus, the overkill hypothesis seems immune from any simple and conclusive archaeological testing. For this reason, Grayson and Meltzer condemn Martin's theory as unscientific, driven by ideology not evidence. They also contend that the circumstantial evidence used by Martin to support a global overkill model is weak or nonexistent.

Grayson and Meltzer present their opinions ex cathedra; trust us, they advise the reader, because we are experts on Pleistocene North America, whereas overkill advocates such as Martin, John Alroy, and Tim Flannery are not. To the extent that they attempt to substantiate their opinions with actual evidence, they provide outmoded data and interpretations and ignore or deliberately omit the most recent chronological, archaeological and climatic data.

While Grayson and Meltzer mostly restrict their "requiem" to North America, which is the region of their self-proclaimed exclusive authority, they also deign to pronounce upon evidence from other parts of the world and in so doing reveal deficiencies in their knowledge. We are glad to provide a less biased overview of the recent literature, which tends to contradict their case. Regarding the European record, in which extinctions cluster at 40–20,000 and 14–10,000 rcbp, they write that "Human hunting had nothing to do with the Eurasian losses" of several megafaunal species, extinctions which were "scattered in time and space". Although they cite A.J. Stuart's recent informed assessment of the European record in support of their assertion that overkill is today rejected by European scientists, in fact, Stuart concludes that "the staggered pattern probably results from the interplay of climatic change and overkill by human hunters." . . .

Grayson and Meltzer strangely omit from their discussion the ca. 150 radiocarbon dates run on bones of megafauna by Tom Stafford, Russ Graham and Holmes Semken. Although there has been a delay in the formal publication of those dates, oral presentations have been given in several public venues.

A brief summary of the new dates was published in *Quaternary Times*, the newsletter of AMQUA, in June 1999. Indeed, Grayson demonstrates an awareness of the new dates for proboscidean extinction. Although they do not cite the new dates, presumably Grayson and Meltzer allude to them when they assert that "to date, of the 35 genera involved, only 15 can be shown to have survived beyond 12,000 years ago. As a result, it is possible, though certainly not demonstrated, that a significant number of the losses predated the Clovis arrival". This is misleading sophistry, as it leaves the false impression that the extinctions of the 15 well-dated genera (17, actually) might have occurred sporadically over the millennium between 12,000 rcbp and Clovis expansion at 11,000 rcbp [or were even "scattered across thousands of years, as occurred in Europe"]. In fact, the 17 genera all disappear abruptly and simultaneously at 10,800–11,400 rcbp. Grayson and Meltzer do not acknowledge that these dates fatally undermine their arguments for gradual climate change as the cause of the extinctions. As they have recognized, demonstration that the extinctions were synchronous "requires that we attribute to the extinction 'event' . . . speed and taxonomic breadth. . . . Once that is done, explanations of the extinctions must be structured to account for these assumed properties, whether those explanations focus on people, climate . . . or disease." . . .

The abruptness and synchroneity of the extinction event are also clearly manifest in stratigraphic sequences on both site-specific and regional scales. As Vance Haynes has emphasized in the Southwest, megafauna (mammoth, horse, camel) fossils are found below the ubiquitous "black mats" (spring-laid organic layers), and never above them. These layers demarcate the Terminal Pleistocene extinction event as clearly as the K-T boundary marks the dinosaur extinction. The mats typically date to ca. 10,700 rcbp, early in the Younger Dryas chron. It should also be noted that, at locations frequented by megafauna throughout the late Pleistocene, their dung disappears at 11,000 rcbp or soon thereafter. . . .

Is There Evidence for Climate Change as the Cause of Extinctions?

Grayson and Meltzer advocate a vague theory of climate change in place of overkill, while candidly admitting that for now, "none (of the climate change hypotheses) connect particular climate variables with particular organisms in powerful ways".

Climate change has always been the main theoretical alternative to human predation. Grayson and Meltzer offer no new refinements to the climate model, and seem unaware of recent developments in the study of latest Pleistocene climates. It must be emphasized that a drastic revision of the climatic hypothesis has occurred recently, which they do not acknowledge. Formerly, the demise of megafauna was attributed to dramatic yet rather gradual changes in temperature and vegetation that occurred during the transition from the Pleistocene to the Holocene. But we now understand that the Holocene warming was delayed in the northern hemisphere by the 1100- or 1300-year Younger Dryas. This near-glacial cold interval ended abruptly, in only a few decades, with a sudden warming at 11,570 cal BP (10,000 rcbp) that occurred more than 1000 years after the crash of the megamammals; so, obviously, neither the concomitant temperature, climate, nor vegetation changes can have played an immediate causal role in the extinction. For this reason, Russell Graham, one of the foremost and best-informed proponents of climatic causation, now cites the Younger Dryas *onset* as the straw that broke the collective backs of the megafauna. . . .

In view of the new paleoclimate data, to make any case for climate as the killer, one would now have to show that the *Ice Age* (!) megafauna, having survived for 2 million years in climates often much colder than the present, were fatally stressed by rapid *cooling*, not warming. The Younger Dryas never got as cold, for a sustained period, as the many typical full glacial episodes that preceded it. True, the Younger Dryas caused the congregation of plants into anomalous communities with no precise modern analogues, and in some areas of North America, annual temperature extremes during the Younger Dryas were unprecedented in the previous 10,000 years (although conditions during numerous earlier stadial events were probably quite similar. However, except for an insignificant species of southeastern spruce—not demonstrably critical to the diet of any megamammal—no Terminal Pleistocene plant extinctions are recorded. Available dietary evidence (e.g., Columbian mammoth and ground sloth dung shows that megafauna were not overly picky eaters. They would not have been challenged by a shift in relative percentages of local plant species; and in response to geographic retraction, expansion, or translocation of plant communities on a decadal scale, these big animals were perfectly capable—as are modern proboscideans—of moving hundreds of miles ([There is] evidence of mastodon migration between Florida and Georgia). . . .

Apart from reduction in numbers and migration into hospitable refugia, another way that animal species may react to environmental stresses over time is reduction in body size, presumably the mechanism by which *Bison antiquus* was transformed into *B. bison* in the mid-Holocene (although an interesting alternative possibility is that an immigrant bison species from eastern Beringia replaced *B. antiquus* about 10,000 rcbp—in which case we could add giant bison, often hunted by Clovis Paleoindians (e.g., at Murray Springs and Jake Bluff to the list of extinct megafauna). . . . If climate alone wiped out giant mammals, we might expect smaller collateral or descendant forms of those genera to have survived to the present: monkey-sized ground sloths, little ponies, or tapir-sized proboscideans. Sadly, this did not happen on the American mainland. . . .

For now, as Grayson and Meltzer admit, there is no testable climate change hypothesis. If climate change is to be taken seriously as the sole cause of extinction, its advocates must show that the challenges posed to American fauna by the Bølling–Allerød warming (14,700 cal BP) and Younger Dryas cooling (12,900 cal BP) were unique and more severe than in any past episodes. But the GRIP and GISP2 ice core records of past climates show that the Terminal Pleistocene changes were not unique in either their abruptness or severity. . . .

The Younger Dryas episode is unique in its faunal consequences only because its onset coincided with the arrival of human hunters.

Why are There So Few Killsites If Overkill is the Better Explanation for the Extinctions?

To summarize the argument to this point, it is clear that, at the very least, a purely circumstantial case can be made that humans played some role in Terminal Pleistocene extinctions in the Americas. One simply cannot ignore the fact that rapid human expansion is coeval with unprecedented faunal collapse. Plus, the "smoking spear" is there to see for anyone without conceptual blinders. In the very brief interval of Clovis hunting of megamammals, humans left behind at least 14 unambiguous kill and butchery sites in North America, by Grayson and Meltzer's own conservative estimate, and possibly many more than that according to other authorities. In view of the extremely narrow time interval, this is a phenomenally rich record.

With respect to the scarcity of non-proboscidean killsites, the taphonomic probability is extremely low that natural processes ever would preserve upland sites containing the butchered carcasses of horses, camels, ground sloths, and smaller megafaunal taxa. One of us (Haynes) can speak with authority on this matter, having devoted 25 years to neotaphonomic studies of large-mammal skeletons in Africa, Australia, and North America. Haynes has spent much of his professional career comparing fossil sites with the modern death sites of hundreds of African elephants and other large mammals that died as a result of non-cultural processes such as die-offs or carnivore predation, as well as government-sponsored killing operations. Even in protected situations such as permanent waterholes where burial may be rapid, very (very!) few modern mammal skeletons are preserved whole or meaningfully associated with evidence about the condition of their death, whether it was cultural or non-cultural. In general, modern death sites containing bones are very rarely preserved—in fact, depending on the local conditions, the proportion of large-mammal death sites (cultural or non-cultural) that will be preserved may be as low as 0.01% or less of total numbers being killed or dying naturally.

Grayson and Meltzer show that 25 of the extinct North American genera are represented by fewer than 50 FAUNMAP occurrences dated to the last millennia of the Pleistocene. Given likely human kill rates and preservation factors, there is an infinitesimal probability that even one of these few cases would be a provable kill site. It is thus remarkable that, for eight of these genera, there should be even ambiguous human involvement.

So there actually *is* empirical evidence, from analogous modern cases, that overkill would leave few fossil remains behind to indicate the very processes involved in the extinctions. Why then is the osseous evidence of human predation on non-proboscidean taxa so much more abundant in European archaeological sites? One reason is that almost none of these are actual kill sites; the bones occur in camps and settlements, often rockshelters that were occupied for long periods and repeatedly, where occupational debris is thick and abundant. North American Paleoindians, in contrast, rarely occupied rockshelters. Another reason is that hominid predation has a history of some 500,000 years in Europe, as against the few hundred years of Clovis megafauna hunting. The "scores" of bone-bearing archaeological sites in Europe must be only a small remnant of the tens of thousands of original occupational loci, the overwhelming majority of which were not preserved.

It is important to observe that, while there are at least two good Terminal Pleistocene kill sites east of the Plains (the Kimmswick mastodon in Missouri and, probably, the Wacissa River bison in Florida), we know of none involving any large mammal from the entire subsequent 12,500-year span of the Holocene. If archaeologists in eastern North America have not yet stumbled upon the remains of any butchered carcasses of elk, deer, bear, or woodland bison of Holocene age—*12,500 years with no discoveries*—what is the likelihood of finding a butchered Terminal Pleistocene ground sloth, stag-moose, horse, or musk-ox? Should we infer that Clovis hunters never preyed upon those animals? Faunal preservation in the east is generally poor; the common assumption that eastern Paleoindians focused almost exclusively upon caribou hunting is based upon a total of seven minute fragments of cervid bone from three early Paleoindian sites (Udora, Whipple and Bull Brook). This sparse evidence does not allow confident reconstruction of early Paleoindian hunting behaviors in the east.

Although we contend that human predation was instrumental in the collapse of American megafauna, we are not saying that Martin's original model was correct on all the particulars of the process. Available archaeological and ecological data suggest that, in several respects, the simulation models of overkill presented by Mosimann and Martin (blitzkrieg at the front of the wave of advance) and more recently by Alroy are rather unrealistic and require modifications of details:

1. Human populations of the Clovis era never approached 500,000–1 million or more; probably, there were no more than 50,000 people in North America at 12,900 cal BP.
2. Extinction of most species in North America probably was complete within about 400 years after human entry; thus, overkill had to be accomplished by many fewer people, and over a much shorter time, than Martin or Alroy postulates.
3. Humans probably did not advance in a wavefront across the continent; rather, exploratory stations (marshaling camps, staging areas) were established at favorable loci, such as game refugia, lakes and river confluences, and bands "leapfrogged" from one amenable spot to the next. Thus, the dragnet effect that Martin imagined, squeezing surviving megafauna into an ever-smaller safe haven ahead of the wavefront, is improbable. Some other circumscription factor—imperative access to potable water under drought conditions, perhaps—would have prevented the animals' escape from human hunting.
4. Clovis hunters may have either specialized in predation on mammoths, in which case collapse of this keystone species could have set in train a cascading collapse of Late-glacial ecosystems; or Clovis hunting may have been more generalized, in which case low levels of additional predation pressure may have had wider synchronous effects on many genera. A more diverse dietary base would also

mean that hunters did not have to curtail hunting in any one region as the numbers of available mammoths dwindled.

5. Various simulations show that a very small increase in predation loss due to humans (less than 5%) can wreak havoc upon animal populations. This is not the non-stop killing spree that overkill opponents often caricature.

6. We cannot ascertain the precise density of large mammal populations of the Late Pleistocene. We do not think there were vast herds or high-density populations. Some critics of overkill have wondered how Paleoindians armed only with spears ever could have wiped out large numbers of megafauna, when 18–19th century hunters with rifles took so long even to put a dent in American bison populations. The great herds of bison witnessed in the Contact period may have been a brief anomaly, reflecting both Little Ice Age climatic change and the decimation of Native American populations by European diseases after AD 1550. Was Terminal Pleistocene North America really comparable to the Serengeti? Or to a densely stocked cattle ranch? Or, were there pockets of animals in scattered clearings and river bottoms amid the taiga-like forests covering much of the continent? Patchy distribution of small prey populations makes overkill more imaginable, given very low-density, mobile human populations.

7. Before arrival of human hunters, the size of megaherbivore populations may have been limited more stringently by native carnivores rather than by food supply. Several authors have suggested that interactions between humans and indigenous animal predators (dire wolf, short-faced bear, sabertooth cats, lions, cheetahs) may have played some role in rapid megafauna extinction. These could have entailed either human eradication of direct competitors, as argued by Whitney-Smith, or disruption and dislocation of longstanding prey-predator relationships. Either way, modeling suggests that the consequent collapse of both herbivore and carnivore populations can be dramatic and very rapid.

8. It may never be possible to unambiguously extricate the relative causative roles of abrupt climate oscillations between 14,700 and 11,570 cal BP and of contemporaneous human hunting after 13,400 cal BP in instigating the megamammal collapse. Thus, North America cannot serve as the best laboratory-like example of a pure overkill process. Then again, climate is always changing, so there will probably always be some minor effect that can be temporally associated with any instance of extinction.

It seems that for Grayson and Meltzer, their intellectual problem with overkill may ultimately be an issue of scale. They have no qualms about accepting the central role played by humans in the demise of island faunas (e.g., the extinction of the moas within 150 years after humans arrived on New Zealand. We agree with them that, even in these cases, pure predation need not be the sole human impact. Species that accompany humans (e.g., dogs, rats, pigs) and pathogens played a role in island extinctions, as did anthropogenic transformation of the vegetation by felling and burning.

We are willing to entertain and investigate the possibility that the American case also may have entailed similar factors in addition to hunting per se (e.g., introduction of dogs accompanying the first Paleoindian migrants; possible spread of canine distemper or other zoonotic diseases, perhaps initially to carnivores; landscapes altered by burning in Central and South America and perhaps the Northeast, ca. 11,000 rcbp. However, for some intuitive reason, which they do not clarify by quantitative modeling, Grayson and Meltzer are incredulous that these processes could have operated at the scale of an entire continent. We wonder if they would classify Australia, at about 7 million km^2, as an island or a continent. As noted above, extinction of megamarsupials, giant reptiles and giant birds appears coincident with the rapid expansion of humans across the entire land mass around 48,000 BP. Sure, America is big, but within 500 years or less after their arrival, Paleoindians had explored the whole of America south of the ice sheets, depositing their distinctive and remarkably uniform tools in Washington State, Nova Scotia, Florida, Sonora, and from Panama to Tierra del Fuego by ca. 12,900 cal BP. Really, a continent is ultimately just a gigantic island. Animals could retreat from human predators for a while, but not indefinitely.

In the end, we do not understand why Meltzer and Grayson have elected to launch their concerted assault upon Martin's theory just at this moment. Within the last decade, paleoclimate studies, focused on ice cores and lake bed sediments, have achieved an unprecedented decadal precision in chronology, and ingenious use of proxy measurements now allows accurate estimates of temperature and precipitation at a micro-scale. Surely, anyone seriously proposing "climate" as the critical factor in megamammal extinctions should avail themselves of the new data. Yet, Grayson and Meltzer do not. Exciting new Paleoindian sites, some with relevant faunal data, are being reported every year from North and South America. Apart from their dogged defense of the ambiguous Monte Verde site, Grayson and Meltzer do not concern themselves with the rapidly accumulating South American evidence. Their failure to make any use of the new radiocarbon evidence of Stafford et al. has already been noted. . . .

The best explanation for American megafaunal extinctions right now is some form of human predation. As at least one leading archaeologist has recognized, "The right questions probably isn't whether people were involved, but how?". We have begun to outline realistic scenarios entailing human hunting in a time of dramatic climate oscillations. At the same time, we are eager to employ the latest evidence from many Quaternary subdisciplines to test a plausible competing hypothesis of extinction triggered solely by climate change, but none has been put forward.

If Meltzer and Grayson have a compelling new climate change hypothesis to offer, it behooves them to set it out, in adequate detail, for scientific assessment. Instead, they have published an indefensibly abusive and unsubstantiated ad hominem attack on Paul Martin's research. If they or anyone else ever does present a climate change hypothesis that purports to fit the rapidly expanding body of evidence, then we can all proceed to do real science. Until then, in the words of Monty Python, "This isn't an argument—it's just contradiction."

POSTSCRIPT

Was the Extinction of Pleistocene Megafauna in North America Caused by Climate Change Rather than Over-Hunting?

$\mathbf{A}$t the heart of the debate about the extinction of Pleistocene megafauna is the question of whether or not correlation is the same as causation. Both the overkill hypothesis and the climate change hypothesis are plausible models, and there is evidence in support of both of their models. But the evidence is not unambiguous for either model.

Grayson and Meltzer argue that the drastic climate change would have driven the megafauna—which were adapted to the cool, dry Pleistocene climate—to extinction. Their main evidence is that the beginning of the Holocene and its warmer climate coincided with the extinctions. They also argue that there is little archaeological evidence that links humans and megafauna and that it makes no sense to use this absence of megafauna kill sites to support the overkill hypothesis. Fiedel and Haynes oppose this view, citing Martin's original argument as a justification for the lack of archaeological data. These scholars argue that the overkill hypothesis *expects* or *predicts* limited archaeological data because humans hunted the animals to extinction so fast. Fiedel and Haynes likewise contend that the end of the Pleistocene did not coincide with the extinction of the megafauna, but that the main warming phase happened much later.

For further reading on Martin's original formulation of the overkill hypothesis, refer to his article "Prehistoric Overkill" in his volume (edited with Henry Wright) *Pleistocene Extinctions: The Search for a Cause* (Yale University Press, 1967). This idea was repeated in his later works, most notably in his article coauthored with D. W. Steadman: "Prehistoric Extinctions on Islands and Continents," in the volume *Extinctions in Near Time* (Plenum Press, 1999). For a more updated overkill simulation see John Alroy's "A Multispecies Overkill Simulation of the End-Pleistocene Megafaunal Mass Extinction" (*Science* 292:1893–1896, 2001).

Grayson has written many papers dealing with late Pleistocene extinctions, climate change, and the overkill hypothesis, including "Reassessing Overkill: Early Americans and Pleistocene Mammals" in *Bulletin of the Florida State Museum of Natural History* (29:1439–1449, 2001) and "Late Pleistocene Extinctions in North America," *Journal of World Prehistory* (5:193–232, 1991).

For less quantitative and more agency-based models, see David and Gary Webster's use of optimal foraging theory in their article "Optimal

Hunting and Pleistocene Extinction" (*Human Ecology* 12:275–289, 1984). Shephard Krech III provides a less technical overview of this debate and a good synthesis of the overkill and climatological theses in his recent and controversial book *The Ecological Indian: Myth and History* (W. W. Norton & Company, 1999).

ISSUE 5

Did Prehistoric Native Americans Practice Cannibalism in the American Southwest?

YES: Brian R. Billman, Patricia M. Lambert, and Banks L. Leonard, from "Cannibalism, Warfare, and Drought in the Mesa Verde Region During the Twelfth Century A.D.," *American Antiquity* (January 2000)

NO: Kurt E. Dongoske, Debra L. Martin, and T.J. Ferguson, from "Critique of the Claim of Cannibalism at Cowboy Wash," *American Antiquity* (January 2000)

ISSUE SUMMARY

YES: Archaeologists Brian Billman and Banks L. Leonard and bio-archaeologist Patricia Lambert argue that there is evidence of pre-historic cannibalism in the Mesa Verde region of southwestern Colorado. From their analysis of human skeletal remains and associated assemblages at Cowboy Wash, they conclude that the bodies of seven individuals were processed in ways that suggest that they were eaten by other humans.

NO: Archaeologists Kurt E. Dongoske and T.J. Ferguson and bioar-chaeologist Debra L. Martin object that the analytical framework Billman et al. use assumes that cannibalism took place and does not adequately consider alternative hypotheses. Although Dongoske et al. feel that cannibalism was possible at Cowboy Wash, they contend that other interpretations of the same data are equally viable.

T he idea that "primitive" people are prone to cannibalism has a long history in Western thought. During the Age of Exploration, European explorers eagerly sought and readily accepted reports that the tribal people they encountered were cannibals, and they used such claims as a justification for conquering, converting, enslaving, or exterminating them. Many societies around the world—including contemporary Pueblo peoples of the American Southwest—regard cannibalism as a sign of utter depravity and attribute it to enemy groups, despised minorities (such as Jews in medieval Europe), witches, or monsters. Until recently most cultural anthropologists believed that some tribal peoples had practiced cannibalism for various reasons, ranging from revenge against enemies to reverence for deceased relatives, but these practices ceased soon after European contact. Thus, cultural anthropologist William Arens caused a major sensation in 1979 when he wrote in his book *The Man-Eating Myth: Anthropology and Anthropophagy* (Oxford University Press) that he was highly skeptical that any people had ever practiced cannibalism as a socially approved institution. Most evidence of cannibalism, he said, was circumstantial or based on second- or third-hand reports, often reports in which members of one group accused a neighboring, enemy group of the horrible deed.

Many archaeologists believe that some prehistoric peoples practiced cannibalism, and they have tried to specify the kinds of evidence that would indicate cannibalism in the archaeological record. Although archaeologists deal with hard evidence, such as bones and stone tools, that evidence must be interpreted. They try to imagine the most likely sequence of human behaviors and other events that could have produced the assemblage of bones and artifacts actually found, the process termed "taphonomy." Archaeologists have often invoked cannibalism when they find human bones that were apparently treated in the same fashion as the bones of game animals found at the same site. Biological anthropologist Christie Turner and others have developed lists of characteristics of bones and their context that they believe unequivocally indicate cannibalism, at least when found in combination. These include such features as cut marks on bones, split open long bones (as if the marrow was extracted), and burned bones (as if the flesh was cooked). Using these criteria, Turner has concluded that at least 38 archaeological sites in the American Southwest show evidence of cannibalism. Other archaeologists and biological anthropologists have objected that the evidence is inconclusive, as the same combination of characteristics could be due to other causes, such as revenge massacres, secondary burial practices, or deliberate mutilation of the bodies of suspected witches.

In the first selection, Billman, Lambert, and Leonard argue that a massacre and episode of cannibalism is the most plausible explanation for the assemblage of bone fragments and artifacts found at site 5MT10010 at Cowboy Wash. They examine cut marks on the bones, patterns of fractures, traces of blood on stone tools, and a coprolite (fossilized piece of excrement) for evidence supporting their hypothesis. They also point to indications that the site was abandoned immediately after the apparent episode of cannibalism. They go on to suggest that the attack and cannibalism were due to extreme drought and food shortages, which caused some groups to attempt to eliminate or drive off other groups that were competing for the limited resources.

In response, Dongoske, Martin, and Ferguson criticize Billman et al. for prematurely concluding that cannibalism took place at Cowboy Wash and for only adducing evidence that supports that conclusion. They point out that Billman et al.'s explanation ignores about 75 percent of the bone fragments found at the site, and they offer alternative possible explanations for the bone fragmentation, bone burning, blood traces on stone tools, and the coprolite containing human proteins.

YES ⤶ Brian R. Billman, Patricia M. Lambert, and Banks L. Leonard

Cannibalism, Warfare, and Drought in the Mesa Verde Region During the Twelfth Century A.D.

Around A.D. 1150, a violent sequence of events took place at a small Puebloan habitation site (5MT10010) in southwestern Colorado. Seven individuals— men, women, and children—were systematically dismembered and defleshed. Body parts of at least three individuals were placed on a fire and roasted. After processing and discarding these remains, the perpetrators walked away, leaving human remains and tools scattered on the floors of two pithouses.

The possible existence of cannibalism has emerged as one of the most controversial issues in southwestern archaeology. Disarticulated, broken, and cut-marked human bone assemblages have been reported in the northern Southwest for nearly 100 years. Many investigators have proposed that at least some of those assemblages resulted from cannibalism. Turner and Turner have reviewed data from 40 sites in the American Southwest with disarticulated assemblages, and concluded that 32 sites meet their proposed criteria for the presence of cannibalism. Explanations for the occurrence of cannibalistic behavior in the American Southwest include starvation, pathological acts by deranged individuals, or social control. In contrast, others have proposed that these assemblages may have resulted from extreme violence or mutilation of the dead, the disturbance of secondary burials, or the destruction of witches.

Resolution of this controversial issue requires investigations at three scales of analysis. At the site level, fine-grained analyses of the condition and distribution of human remains and associated artifacts and ecofacts are required to reconstruct the formation processes that created and modified the assemblages. Next, settlement pattern data drawn from local surveys and the excavation of nearby contemporary sites are needed to examine the social context of the occurrences at the community level. Finally, regional analysis of the spatial and temporal distribution of similar assemblages is required to understand the historical development of the phenomenon. Both fine-grained studies of individual assemblages and reviews of their regional occurrence have been conducted. However, information on the local social context of these finds has been lacking, even though such data are essential for bridging the gap between site-specific and regional scales.

From *American Antiquity* by Brian R. Billman, Patricia M. Lambert, and Banks L. Leonard, pp. 179–187. Copyright © 2000 by Society for American Archaeology. Reprinted by permission.

In this paper, we examine this issue by presenting the results of our investigation of 5MT10010 (a small Early Pueblo III habitation site in south-western Colorado), the local settlement context of that site, and distribution of similar possible incidences of cannibalism in the Mesa Verde region. The results of our analysis of the battered, broken remains of seven individuals and associated artifacts recovered from the site implicate humans in the disarticulation and reduction of those bodies. Evidence of cooking of the human remains, blood residue found on associated tools, and analysis of an associated coprolite [piece of excrement] support our interpretation that people prepared and consumed human body parts. Local settlement pattern data indicate that 5MT10010 was part of a small community that may have been extinguished in a single, violent episode of raiding and cannibalism. Further, our review of well-documented cases of disarticulated and modified human remains in the Mesa Verde region points to a sharp increase in cannibalism around A.D. 1150, a time of drought and the collapse of the Chaco system. We propose that, faced with severe environmental stress, food scarcity, and sociopolitical upheaval in the mid A.D. 1100s, certain groups in the Mesa Verde region used violence to terrorize or even eliminate neighboring villages, and that cannibalism was part of this pattern of violence. This apparent outbreak of cannibalism subsided as rapidly as it began. No possible cases of cannibalism postdating A.D. 1200 have been reported in the Mesa Verde region, and few cases have been documented anywhere in the American Southwest after that date.

Numerous cases of cannibalism have been documented over the last 200 years in many different cultures throughout the world. Reasons for the occurrence of this practice range from ancestor worship, starvation, deviant acts by deranged individuals, or political terrorism. Although cannibalism apparently holds a macabre fascination with a wide segment of contemporary European and North American society—note the amount of media attention garnered by this issue in recent years—the occurrence of cannibalism in the American Southwest prior to European contact is not necessarily an issue of great importance in anthropology. However, the documentation of an outbreak of cannibalism and violence in the Mesa Verde region in the mid A.D. 1100s and the subsequent suppression of that behavior does raise questions of profound anthropological importance. Under what circumstances do groups of individuals turn to terroristic, violent, or genocidal [behavior]; and under what circumstances do they turn away from it? In this paper we hope to move the debate from the issue of whether or not cannibalism occurred in the prehistoric Southwest to questions of broader anthropological significance. . . .

The Osteological Evidence for Cannibalism at 5MT10010

The osteological evidence for cannibalism at 5MT10010 is essentially the same as that described for an increasing number of sites in the American Southwest and elsewhere in the world. Turner and Turner summarize the taphonomic features used to identify cannibalism in the archaeological record to include "breakage, cutting, anvil or hammerstone abrasions, burning, missing vertebrae, and fragment polishing." . . . Other common characteristics of these assemblages, as summarized by Turner, include occurrence during "a single, short-term depositional episode, . . . good to excellent bone preservation, . . . nearly complete disarticulation of elements, . . . almost universal breakage of the head, face, long bones, [animal] gnawing on fewer than 5 percent of all specimens . . . ," and a high ratio of breakage to burning and cut marks. In addition, Villa notes the lack of evidence for even the most basic attempt at formal burial as an important criterion for distinguishing cannibalistic activities. . . . Collectively, these criteria indicate that human remains were treated like those of food animals found in archaeological contexts.

The evidence from 5MT10010 is consistent with these criteria. First, these remains were not intentionally buried, nor is there any indication that they were accorded respectful treatment. The treatment of the disarticulated remains at 5MT10010 was dramatically different from the treatment of most of the Puebloan period human remains recovered during the UMUILAP [Ute Mountain Ute Irrigated Lands Archaeological Project]. As elsewhere in the northern Southwest, individuals were interred in a flexed position with vessels and other burial goods, indicating concerned treatment of the dead. Although valuable artifacts were present in the pithouses at 5MT10010, their distribution did not correlate with that of the human remains, and they did not obviously constitute burial goods. . . . The mutilation and haphazard distribution of body parts preclude any notion of respectful treatment of the dead in pithouses at 5MT10010.

Second, evidence of perimortem dismemberment and bone breakage was abundant at 5MT10010, and included the disarticulation of bones at joints and heavy fracturing of skeletal elements. Almost no skeletal elements remained articulated, and perimortem breakage was apparent in many, including the cranial vault bones, ribs, marrow-rich long bones, and fat-laden vertebrae. According to Turner and Turner, the underrepresentation of vertebrae in particular may be attributable to their having been "smashed to extract their oily content by boiling."

Direct evidence of the use of tools to process the remains provides a third critical line of evidence. Following criteria detailed in White, marks identified as evidence for tool use included cut marks from sharp-edged knives, and chop marks, percussion pits, and percussion striae from chopping tools and hammerstones. In the 5MT10010 assemblage, cut marks were particularly apparent on the ribs, clavicles, humeri, and femora in proximity to sites of major muscle and connective tissue attachment, and provide evidence that bodies were processed while still covered with flesh. . . .

Notably, no canine puncture marks or other signs of carnivore involvement were observed in these remains, despite the presence of such damage on human remains from other sites in Cowboy Wash. In other words, carnivores were around and scavenged human corpses when they could, but they obviously did not have access to the bodies (at least, while fleshed) in this case. Their condition therefore cannot reasonably be attributed to the activities of nonhuman scavengers.

Up to this point, a reasonable argument could still be made for mutilation without intent to consume the remains. However, the light color and excellent surface condition of the bones in this assemblage suggests that the flesh was removed from the bones, perhaps through stewing or boiling, rather than left to rot away over time. Even more compelling osteological evidence for the consumption of human remains at 5MT10010, however, is the distinct pattern of burning. Many, if not most, of the burned bones in this assemblage were exposed to fire while still covered with flesh, as the patchy distribution of scorch marks favoring exposed broken ends and thinly fleshed expanses clearly indicates. The absence of burn marks on the internal surfaces of many fire-affected cranial and limb elements further indicates that a second phase of disarticulation and breakage took place after rather than before cooking. It is difficult to argue that disposal was the ultimate goal of fire processing. None of the three pithouses was burned, nor were any of the bones from these structures calcined, as usually occurs with at least a portion of the skeleton in cremation. Rather, the browning and occasional blackening apparent in some of these remains is more consistent with limited, controlled exposure to fire for purposes of cooking the flesh. . . .

Although these lines of evidence indicate that seven people at 5MT10010 were mutilated and processed as though for consumption, the actual cause of death of each individual is obscured by subsequent activities. No projectiles or other weapons were found in association with the remains. Any one of a number of observed blows could have caused death. Establishing if any of the traumatic injuries was the cause of death was not possible. . . .

Cannibalism at 5MT10010: The Evidence from Ancient Feces

Although various lines of osteological evidence demonstrate that human body parts were butchered and cooked in the same manner that people prepared food animals for consumption, the bones from 5MT10010 do not document the actual ingestion of human flesh. The only scientific evidence that has the potential to bridge the gap between preparation and consumption is preserved human waste. Such evidence was previously lacking in contexts from which "cannibalized" human remains have been recovered. Thus, the human coprolite found in the hearth of Feature 15 provided a rare opportunity to establish such a link.

Analyses of the coprolite detected absolutely no macroscopic plant remains and found that starch granules and phytoliths were virtually absent. The absence of starch granules is a strong indication that maize kernels were not present in the meal or meals represented in the coprolite. The absence of macroscopic plant remains is extremely unusual for an Anasazi coprolite. The only pollen present was from Cheno-am, low-spine Compositae, and trace amounts of Poaceae, all of which could have derived from windblown, ambient pollen during spring. Characteristics of texture, color, and odor in a reconstituted sample of the coprolite indicated that the meal or meals it represented were probably entirely composed of meat. The size and shape of the coprolite demonstrate that it was of human origin.

Analysis of the coprolite by ELISA (enzyme immunosorbent assay) revealed the presence of human myoglobin in the coprolite. . . . Myoglobin is an oxygen-carrying molecule that transports oxygen from the surface of the muscle to the energy generating apparatus within the muscle. Myoglobin is found only in skeletal muscles and cardiac muscle cells. Importantly, it is not found in the smooth muscles of the digestive system, in blood, or in vascular tissue. Control tests were conducted to determine if human myoglobin is present in normal individuals (25 samples), individuals with blood in their stools (10 samples), or individuals that had consumed cooked beef within 24 hours (4 samples). None of these samples tested positive for human myoglobin. The stool samples from people who had eaten beef did test positive for bovine myoglobin, which demonstrates that myoglobin can survive the process of cooking and digestion and can be detected in human fecal material. In sum, results of the analysis of the human coprolite are consistent with osteological and artifactual evidence of cannibalism at 5MT10010 and demonstrate that human flesh was not only processed but also consumed at the site. This is the first direct evidence of the consumption of human flesh in the prehistoric Southwest.

Cannibalism on the Southern Piedmont of Ute Mountain

If we are to understand the butchering and consumption of human remains at 5MT10010, we must first understand the local social context of those acts. Fortunately, we are in a unique position to reconstruct the social history and organization of the community associated with the site. After several years of archaeological investigations conducted in the area, the Puebloan occupation of the southern piedmont of Ute Mountain is well documented. . . .

Investigations indicate that during the Puebloan era there were five separate occupations of the southern piedmont between A.D. 600 and 1280. During that period, the piedmont was abandoned more than it was occupied (approximately 380 years of abandonment and 300 years of occupation), a fact that attests to the marginal nature of the area. . . .

The focus of this paper is the occupation between A.D. 1075 and the early A.D. 1150s. At the start of that period, the pattern of settlement on the southern piedmont changed dramatically. In contrast to the dispersed pattern of occupation in late Basketmaker III (A.D. 600–725) and middle-to-late Pueblo II (A.D. 1050–1075), there was a significant influx of population and three communities were founded. The formation of these communities represents a third attempted colonization of the southern piedmont and a new colonization strategy. In this period, horticulturalists attempted to colonize the piedmont by establishing communities in the most productive areas of floodwater agriculture. Establishing integrated communities may have provided a means of sharing risk among households. . . .

The pattern of abandonment at these three sites . . . is remarkably similar to that of 5MT10010. The processing of human remains appears to have occurred at abandonment. Numerous artifacts, including whole ceramic vessels, ground and flaked stone tools, a rabbit blanket, a woven mat, and baskets, were left in the pithouses. Blood residue analysis indicates that some of the stone tools left behind at abandonment were used to butcher human remains. Like 5MT10010, contexts associated with the final use of the three sites—*in situ* hearth deposits, floors, and single event trash dumps near the time of abandonment—contained almost no cultivated plant remains. . . .

In summary, all of the excavated sites, and perhaps the entire early Pueblo III Cowboy Wash community, were abandoned suddenly just after the processing and consumption of humans. Community residents left behind large quantities of high-quality, valuable artifacts, many of which were light-weight and easily transportable. A significant portion of the community appears to be represented in the total assemblage of butchered human remains. Finally, the occurrence of cannibalism on the southern piedmont of Ute Mountain was temporally limited. Despite the excavation of 71 sites, including 29 habitation sites from all of the episodes of Puebloan occupation of the piedmont, only one other possible incident of cannibalism has been found that does not clearly date to around A.D. 1150. . . .

The abandonment of the Cowboy Wash community around A.D. 1150 corresponds to a period of extreme drought from A.D. 1145 to 1193. Based on tree ring data, Burns has proposed that this was the second worst prolonged shortfall of corn yields in the period from A.D. 652 to 1968. Ethnobotanical evidence from the four sites likewise confirms that crop yields were probably very low and that stored domesticated foods probably were severely diminished at abandonment. The correlation of this outbreak of cannibalism at Cowboy Wash with the second worst regional drought in the tree-ring record surely is more than mere coincidence.

Cannibalism in the Mesa Verde Region

If the events at Cowboy Wash were isolated occurrences in the northern Southwest, it would be easy to dismiss them as the pathological acts of a small group of demented individuals or a rare case of starvation induced cannibalism. However, these sites are but four of 32 sites in the northern Southwest that have yielded similar assemblages of cut, battered, disarticulated, and partially burned human remains. In order to place the Cowboy Wash sites in the context of the prehistory of the Mesa Verde region, a subset of Turner's 32 possible cannibalism sites was reviewed. This review was limited to sites in the Mesa Verde region that are well documented and well dated, thus reducing the number of sites from 32 to 18.

Our review of primary sources on those 18 sites revealed two interesting patterns relevant to understanding the events that occurred at the abandonment of the Cowboy Wash sites. First, there is a cluster of occurrences of cannibalism in the Mesa Verde region around A.D. 1150, the time of abandonment of the Cowboy Wash sites. . . . What these data suggest is that half of the well-documented, well-dated disarticulated assemblages from the 1,300-year Puebloan occupation of the Mesa Verde region occurred during a 25-year period between A.D. 1150 and 1175. The other nine sites date to between A.D. 850 and 1125. Although there apparently was a severe outbreak of cannibalism between A.D. 1150 and 1175, cannibalism may have occurred periodically for several hundred years prior to that outbreak. In other words, these data suggest that, although occurrences were rare prior to A.D. 1150, there may have been an existing local precedent for cannibalism in the Mesa Verde region.

The second pattern revealed by the review of literature relates to the types of sites where cannibalized assemblages were found. In the Southwest, sites with these kinds of human remains can be divided into three distinct types: isolated assemblages found away from habitation sites, habitation sites with dumped secondary deposits, and habitation sites with *in situ* floor deposits. Isolated assemblages have been reported from a few locations in the Southwest, including one of the 18 sites in the Mesa Verde region.

At sites with secondary deposits, butchered human remains are located in pits, trash deposits, or the fill of abandoned rooms, but not on the floors or other use surfaces of structures. This pattern suggests that human bodies were processed at the site, after which the butchering areas were cleaned and the remains dumped elsewhere on the site with no effort at formal burial. Of the 18 Mesa Verde sites, only 5MTUMR2346 in Mancos Canyon may fit this pattern. . . .

As the name suggests, sites with *in situ* floor deposits have scatters of human remains on the floors of structures. Human remains were deposited at the time of abandonment and apparently resulted from the *in situ* processing of human beings. Numerous artifacts were left behind in association with the human remains, including butchering tools, personal ornaments, and typical domestic artifacts such as metates, manos, and whole ceramic vessels. Eight of the nine sites dating between A.D. 1125 and 1175 have these characteristics. In contrast to the secondary deposit sites, assemblages at these sites appear to have resulted from a single, intense episode of cannibalism, rather than several episodes spread over the duration of the occupation of the site.

Explaining Cannibalism in the American Southwest

Many explanations have been offered for these assemblages of broken, battered, and sometimes partially burned human remains. Andrew Darling and others have proposed that disarticulated remains found at prehistoric Puebloan sites were the result of executions of individuals, families, or even villages suspected of practicing witchcraft and cannibalism. Based on a review of ethnographic literature on historic pueblos, Darling argues that witchcraft was so closely associated with acts of human sacrifice and cannibalism in Puebloan traditions that the concepts of witch and cannibal became virtually synonymous. Further, he notes that the physical destruction of witches played a large role in ridding the community of evil influences and preventing sickness. His reconstructed model of witch execution involves a trial of the suspect followed by death, dismemberment, defleshing, and burning.

Darling's argument has several shortcomings, as do similar reconstructions. First, Darling unintentionally provides evidence for the existence of cannibalism, albeit couched in terms of witchcraft. Many of his accounts specifically mention cannibalism or suspected cannibals, suggesting that the practice existed even if it was not socially sanctioned. Second, his argument is limited by a lack of historic or ethnographic evidence of dismemberment, defleshing, and burning of witches. His compiled research on 24 Zuni witch trials suggests that witch executions might have occurred in the historic period, but he does not present accounts of what happens to the bodies of witches after execution. Perhaps because of this lack of historical evidence, Darling is unable to propose a set of material correlates for distinguishing cannibalism from witch execution in the archaeological record. Instead he offers a hypothetical reconstruction of the disposal of bodies that follows exactly the same steps as cannibalism except for the final consumption of flesh.

One possible distinguishing trait between witch destruction and cannibalism is the degree of burning of the bodies of suspected witches. Darling emphasizes the importance of burning for purification. However, at 5MT10010 and similar sites, many bones show no signs of direct fire exposure and those that do generally exhibit a patchy distribution of browning and occasional blackening more consistent with cooking than with incineration.

In contrast, Turner and Turner have argued that these assemblages are clearly the remains of cannibalism, a finding that has been supported by our analysis and independent analyses such as White, Dice, and Minturn. . . .

A third possible explanation for the occurrence of these disarticulated human remains in the region is hunger-induced cannibalism, as is documented in France and Germany during the Middle Ages, during Euroamerican expeditions to the Canadian Arctic, during the settlement of the western American frontier, and during World War II when Japanese troops on the Kokoda trail of New Guinea were isolated from supplies. Indeed, the low incidence of cultigens at the Cowboy Wash sites and the date of their abandonment in a period of regional drought are consistent with simple food shortage as an explanation.

Several aspects of the evidence at sites like 5MT10010 do not resemble historic accounts of simple, hunger-induced cannibalism. First, such incidents typically occurred within groups that were trapped by severe winter conditions, held prisoner, or cut off during military campaigns. In those cases, escape was impossible, and all other food resources were depleted or unreachable. The Cowboy Wash area is low in elevation and lacks insurmountable barriers to movement even in winter. Thus, dispersal from the sites to other areas may have been possible. Numerous instances of population movement at both local and regional levels are known for prehistoric and historic Puebloan groups, and immigration clearly was an important strategy for coping with environmental and social stress.

Second, all of the people in these assemblages appear to have been processed, if not consumed, in one incident. There is no evidence that people were consumed slowly over a period of weeks or months as individuals gradually succumbed to hunger, disease, or ongoing military action.

Finally, as previously noted, the demographic profile of the Cowboy Wash assemblage differs in important respects from natural death profiles. Infants and young children—the age group most susceptible to malnutrition and disease—are present but are significantly underrepresented. Older children and adolescents, on the other hand, are more common than in natural death profiles from the region.

Osteological data from the other Puebloan habitation sites excavated during the UMUILAP shed light on the social context of events at 5MT10010. Traumatic injuries likely to have resulted from interpersonal conflict were common in the individuals recovered during the course of the UMUILAP. . . .

These data are evidence that the cannibalistic events that culminated in the abandonment of the southern piedmont took place in a climate of violence. The death of many of the inhabitants of Cowboy Wash in a single incident and the apparent sudden and complete abandonment of the community following that incident is consistent with a successful attack by an outside group. Because the Cowboy Wash community was relatively small and isolated compared to other communities in the region, it was vulnerable to attack. Further, the presence of large quantities of Chuskan ceramics demonstrates that the community either consisted of Chuskan immigrants or had closer ties with groups outside the Mesa Verde region than with groups within the region. Such a situation would have made the community more susceptible to aggression by other local groups.

Whereas the present data strongly suggest that site inhabitants were the victims in Cowboy Wash, and perhaps in the majority of cases in the Mesa Verde region, the identity of the perpetrators is less clear. Although it seems likely that another Anasazi group or groups were involved, the data are insufficient on this point. . . .

The outbreak of violence around A.D. 1150 may have been caused by severe drought and possibly the social and ideological breakdown that followed the abandonment of Chaco Canyon and the collapse of the Chaco system. The reshuffling of the population in the San Juan basin and Mesa Verde region introduced outsiders into new areas, perhaps upsetting local intercommunity alliances that had maintained peace. The search for diminishing resources in the face of drought also would have heightened competition and increased psychological stress. Violence, raiding, and warfare have been documented as one response to environmental stress and resource scarcity in the American Southwest and elsewhere in the world. Mutilation and consumption of individuals killed in conflict is a potential strategy for instilling fear in opposing groups. In the mid A.D. 1100s, certain groups in the Mesa Verde region may have used just such a practice to terrorize, intimidate, or even eliminate neighboring villages, especially those composed of recent immigrants to the region or whose primary alliances were with groups outside the region. In that time of severe drought, human flesh also could have constituted an important spoil of war.

Whatever the root cause, the outbreak of cannibalism apparently stopped as suddenly as it began. Tree-ring and regional settlement pattern data indicate that by the end of A.D. 1100s, much of the Mesa Verde region was abandoned, possibly due to the worsening environmental and social conditions. When climatic conditions improved in the early A.D. 1200s, the area was reoccupied by Puebloan groups until the final abandonment of the region around A.D. 1280. Although osteological evidence from Cowboy Wash and archaeological data from elsewhere in the northern southwest demonstrate that lethal violence continued in late Pueblo III times, no incidents of cannibalism have been reported in the Mesa Verde region after A.D. 1200. The occurrence of an even more severe drought in the Mesa Verde region in the late A.D. 1200s may not have resulted in any incidents of cannibalism. Beyond the Mesa Verde region, only two cases of disarticulated, modified human remains associated with Puebloan sites has been documented in the entire northern Southwest after A.D. 1200. The reason for the sudden demise of this one- or two-generation outbreak of cannibalism and violence remains even more mysterious than its origins. . . .

Kurt E. Dongoske, Debra L. Martin, and T. J. Ferguson

➡ **NO**

Critique of the Claim of Cannibalism at Cowboy Wash

The article by Billman et al. contributes to a growing body of data that demonstrates the complex variability of the Pueblo world during the twelfth century. Although the article's title promises a comprehensive review of major cultural and environmental processes (drought, warfare, cannibalism, regional interactions), relatively little theory regarding these processes informs their research design, and much of their interpretation is based on weak inferences. The empirical data they present are not used to test alternative hypotheses or rigorously examine expectations derived from modeling. Dynamic aspects of cultural patterns relating to migration, settlement, environment, abandonment, mortuary behaviors, conflict and group identity are implicated in their research but are not adequately contextualized.

The conclusion that cannibalism occurred at Cowboy Wash is founded, like the majority of other recent claims of cannibalism, on the assumption that perimortem modification of human bone (i.e., breakage, cutmarks, percussion striae, burning, missing vertebrae, and fragment end "polishing") in *every case* is due to cannibalism. Billman et al. draw primarily on Turner's accounts of alleged cannibalism in the Southwest for their methodology. The authors argue that if human bones are processed and deposited in a manner thought to be similar to the bones of game animals, then the only possible conclusion is that human flesh was consumed. At Cowboy Wash, the claim for cannibalism is specifically said to be based on 1) human involvement in the disarticulation and reduction of seven bodies, 2) evidence of cooking of the human remains, 3) blood residue found on associated tools, and 4) analysis of a coprolite.

Our response to the study by Billman et al. is intended to provide a critical yet constructive commentary, propose fresh ways of thinking about what assemblages of disarticulated and broken bones might mean, and reformulate how research questions are being asked. We believe that the research approach used in the Cowboy Wash study, and other studies that narrow the focus to cannibalism, is ultimately too limited to address the full range of variability that exists in disarticulated and broken bone assemblages. In many ways, this approach lacks a rigorous scientific approach that uses hypothesis testing and strong inferences to deduce patterns and interpretations about complex human behaviors. There is a tendency to assume that there is just one means to an end, and to force data to fit preconceived notions about past cultural and formation processes.

From *American Antiquity* by Kurt E. Dongoske, Debra L. Martin, and T.J. Ferguson, pp. 145–146, 164–173. Copyright © 2000 by Society for American Archaeology. Reprinted by permission.

In our comments, we seek to generate a dialogue regarding the method and theory used to study disarticulated bone assemblages and conflict in the American Southwest. In so doing, we consider the variation and ambiguities in the data, and suggest avenues for a more rigorous approach in future research. We begin with a few general comments, and then specifically address the four lines of evidence advanced by Billman et al. as support for their interpretation that people prepared and consumed human body parts.

General Comments about Cowboy Wash Archaeology and the Study of Cannibalism

The article by Billman et al. is essentially a site report that focuses on the categories of data the authors think support their conclusion. Cannibalism is invoked in the title and sets the tone for the study. In pre-emptive strikes, the authors provide what we think is superficial denouncement of alternative hypotheses such as witch execution, secondary burial, ritualized dismemberment, and massacre. As archaeologists, we can generate any number of interesting and even fantastical hypotheses, but because we work with a particular kind of empirical data, these hypotheses need to be framed in such a way that evidence can be used to either reject or fail to reject them. In contrast, the Cowboy Wash study essentially asserts that cannibalism has been found and presents the data in particular ways that bolster rather than test that assertion.

As anthropologists, we are concerned with the indiscriminate use of the word cannibalism. Cannibalism has many meanings, all of which have loaded cultural connotations, and carries some very heavy historical and emotional baggage. The word was concocted by Columbus to label the people he first encountered (the Tainos). He referred to all of the groups on the islands as "caribes," who he believed were flesh-eaters, and this term helped to ideologically pave the way for the eventual campaign of conquest, Christianization, and genocide that followed. Any characterization of Indians as "cannibals" dredges up a long history of oppression and racism, and we have to realize that this may generate ill-will and negative emotions about archaeology in many descendant communities.

The anthropological discourse on cannibalism has been used in the past to establish differences and construct racial boundaries dividing "civilized" people from the "other." Anthropological accounts of cannibalism are part of a "we/they" dichotomy that legitimizes treating the "other" as inferior. This has implications for how archaeological studies are used in a larger social context. As Kilgour has observed, cannibalism is gaining force as a symbol associated with the tools of oppression used by a guilty imperial past and fears about the present. Much of the anthropological literature on cannibalism is a meta-myth used as a means of boundary definition in the construction of Western identity. Historically, the conceptualization of cannibalism has been used both as a foil for emerging Western identity and as a legitimization of cultural appropriation.

We raise this point not out of an attempt to be politically correct but to simply draw attention to the larger discourse in which our archaeological findings are used. Archaeologists need to think about the broad social and cultural implications of their research. With respect to cannibalism, this does not mean that it is a forbidden subject for investigation but that its investigation must meet the most rigorous scientific standards possible. Since much rides on claims of cannibalism, the standards of proof must be high. Our work will be appropriated by the popular press so our research must be unassailable, and we must be precise in what we mean when we use the term cannibalism.

In the literature that documents cultures where cannibalism is said to have been practiced, a wide range of behaviors fall into that category. These include exocannibalism (eating those outside your group), endocannibalism (eating those within your group), ceremonial cannibalism (eating small token amounts), ritualized cannibalism (more ritual than gastronomical), vengeance cannibalism (more symbolic than gastronomic), and psychopathic cannibalism (Jeffrey Dahmer comes to mind). Some may argue that it would be too difficult to tease apart these various kinds of behaviors from the present data. However, we believe that a discussion of the variability in the possible motivations for cannibalism would be useful and necessary to generate more complex and multifaceted theories.

Arens has challenged virtually all ethnographic and historical accounts of cannibalism as a cultural practice (as opposed to survival cannibalism, e.g., a plane crash in the Andes), claiming they rest upon embarrassing and unsupported empirical grounds. According to Arens, ethnographic investigations of cannibalism have tended to document the existence of cannibalism after the cessation of the presumed activity, rather than observing and describing it in the present tense. Arens argues that the good anthropology involves the description of custom prior to its interpretation. Arens' thesis is controversial, of course, and has been challenged by many critics who question the methods and data used in his historical analysis.

We think archaeology has a vital role to play in the investigation of cannibalism. As White has pointed out, "Cannibalism is a globally claimed but sparsely documented human behavior. Its spatial and temporal dimensions, situational contexts, and archaeological signatures are poorly understood." Given the absence of uncontested ethnographic documentation of cannibalistic behavior, we think that archaeology may offer the best, and perhaps only, means to scientifically verify the occurrence of anthropophagy as a cultural practice. Like Arens, we do not argue that customary cannibalism did not exist in the past, only that the current evidence for it is weak. If it existed in the past, there should be incontrovertible archaeological evidence of its existence. . . .

Osteology and Taphonomy: Evidence for Cannibalism?

We have methodological concerns about the use of taphonomy in the Cowboy Wash study. Our experience with disarticulated and broken bones is that stratigraphy and depositional history is crucial for understanding these bone assemblages. Bone by bone placement vis-à-vis other artifacts in horizontal and stratigraphic profile are key elements in unraveling the sequence and ordering of the various processes that effected where the bones ended up, how they came to be broken and burned, and what kinds of processes mimic each other. Taphonomic analysis is difficult and complex, particularly when assemblages have had multiple steps involved in their modification and interment. The categories of bone changes used by Billman and colleagues are very narrowly conceived (i.e., breakage, tool marks, burning). Accounting for the presence and absence of these observations artificially reduces them in scope and meaning.

For example, to understand how a bone came to have a spiral fracture, it is crucial to know its placement, impact, size of area affected, and relationship to other indicators such as percussion pits, adherent flakes, incipient fracture lines, conchoidal scars, percussive striae, flaking, and peeling. In other words, not all spiral fractures are created equal. These variables can provide crucial data about how the bone came to be broken with a high degree of specificity and this can define a number of taphonomic processes at work. Burning is likewise a very broad, diverse, and problematic category to describe as simply a present or absent phenomenon because there are literally a dozen or so factors involved in how burning affects bone surfaces. Burning is extremely difficult to detect and differentiate when it alters the bone slightly and mimics normal weathering. Dry or wet bone, high or low heat, and short or long exposure all differentially affect bone surfaces. In short, these categories of bone changes are complex, multifaceted, and important to document using as fine-grained analysis as possible. The behaviors that led to the events examined by the authors are obviously complex and possibly not singular.

We are disappointed that the reporting of osteology and taphonomy in the Cowboy Wash study does not present the data in the detail needed to meaningfully compare this assemblage with other assemblages. White recommends procedures for the recovery and analysis of broken and scattered human bone from archaeological and forensic contexts. He identifies 17 variables of bone modification that are relevant to claims of cannibalism. Only 4 variables (perimortem breaks, cut marks, chop marks, burning) are reported in the Cowboy Wash study, thus masking the variability that is essential to understanding human behavior and formation processes.

Furthermore, the Cowboy Wash study does not adequately account for all the bone specimens (individual pieces of bone). For instance, the Feature 3 assemblage contained 1,150 bone specimens, yet only 287 minimum number of elements (MNE) are tabulated; the Feature 13 assemblage contained 479 bone specimens, yet only 86 MNE are tabulated. How conjoinable bones were handled in the analysis is not adequately described. Presumably the remaining bones in the assemblages were unidentifiable but these are not accounted for in the tables. As White demonstrates, indeterminate bones can be grouped into meaningful categories, including indeterminate cranial fragments, various types of indeterminate long bones, and completely indeterminate bone groups. Understanding the human modification of these indeterminate categories of bone is essential to unraveling the taphonomic processes of the assemblage.

As far as we can determine, in the Cowboy Wash study these indeterminate bones apparently constitute about 75 percent of the total assemblage. . . .

For too long, skeletal and mortuary analyses in the Southwest have focused on normative assumptions. This practice has greatly hampered our ability to see the abundance of variability in mortuary behavior both within and among sites and regions. There have not been any good studies of what the "rules" were for disposal of the dead in Ancestral Pueblo communities. Even the ethnohistoric information on preparation and disposal of the dead is not well known. It is possible that in the ancient Southwest there were cultural norms about the proper curation of some bones in some contexts at some sites that involved bone reduction, modification, and secondary burial. Why not? We simply do not know at this point what constitutes normal mortuary behavior. Therefore, it is difficult to consider all of the disarticulated remains that have been recovered over the years to be abnormal and the result of cannibalism or even violence. And it is even more problematic to lump all of the disarticulated remains together under a single cause.

We provide one cautionary example here. There were three disarticulated bone assemblages from the La Plata Highway project examined by a team of osteologists (led by Martin) in conjunction with archaeologists at the Museum of New Mexico. Turner and Turner also analyzed these remains but mistakenly concluded that all of the bone deposits were the result of cannibalism. A detailed taphonomic analysis conducted by Akins demonstrated quite conclusively that one of the assemblages was due to carnivore damage and recent (trenching) damage, one was due to ancient movement of remains and secondary burial, and one was likely due to some human activity involving dismemberment and intentional arrangement. The La Plata study demonstrates that three seemingly similar bone assemblages upon closer inspection using a more fine-grained taphonomic and contextualized analysis are actually dissimilar, and the products of several very different processes.

Evidence for Cooking Human Remains?

Billman et al. assert that "evidence of cooking of human remains" supports their interpretation of cannibalism. The only direct evidence that might indicate cooking is burned bones, and, in fact, Billman et al. assert these burned bones indicate parts of two individuals were "roasted." This raises a question about how the body parts of the other five individuals were cooked. . . .

There are other questions about the patterning of burned bones in the site assemblage. Billman et al. state that, "Many, if not most, of the burned bones in this assemblage were exposed to fire while still covered with flesh, as the patchy distribution of scorch marks favoring exposed broken ends and thinly fleshed expanses clearly indicates." As discussed above, the tabulation of burning as a presence/absence variable makes this difficult to evaluate. The elements tabulated for the two bone assemblages also exhibit different patterns of burning that remained unexplained with respect to possible consumption. Billman et al. add that the burning patterns indicate "a second phase of disarticulation and breakage took place after rather than before burning," yet the explanation of this postburning breakage is not adequately addressed. While these patterns are certainly intriguing, we do not think in and of themselves they are evidence of cooking. The behaviors that would produce these patterns are not described, and an alternate explanation (as offered below) is possible.

Indirect evidence of cooking might include breakage of marrow-rich long bones and breakage of bones into small pieces that could fit into stew pots. In this regard, however, no "pot polishing" was observed in the assemblage. Billman et al. state that the pale color of bones "could" have resulted from processing for fat extraction and "may" provide a line of evidence for stewing. They suggest that the reduction strategy "may" have served the specific purpose of producing pot-sized fragments. Billman et al. assert that "the remains resembled refuse from animal foods consumed by Cowboy Wash inhabitants" but do not present the comparative data needed to assess this claim. All in all, we find the evidence for cooking to be suggestive but equivocal.

Blood Residue Analysis: Evidence for Cannibalism?

Billman et al. contend that the identification of human blood on two sharp lithic flakes is supporting evidence that these tools were used in the process of defleshing human remains. We believe that this is circumstantial evidence and does not corroborate a conclusion that human remains were processed for consumption. An alternative explanation for the appearance of human blood residue on lithic flakes, as any flintknapper can attest to, is the frequency that one experiences cuts on the hands during the knapping process. Therefore, it would not be unreasonable to expect blood residue on these artifacts as a result of a prehistoric "accident" in tool manufacture or resharpening. An equally valid alternative explanation is that these artifacts could contain human blood residue as a result of low-level contamination produced during the handling of the artifacts during excavation. Thus, Billman et al.'s conclusion that the blood residue analysis indicates that some of the identified tool kits were used to butcher the human remains is at best premature, but more probably an unreliable conjectural conclusion. . . .

Fecal Evidence for Cannibalism?

The article presents the analysis of fecal material as the "smoking gun" proving cannibalism. This is hard to accept based solely on three paragraphs of discussion. We are left with the perception that the authors are asking us to "trust" their conclusion, without offering us an in-depth discussion of the analytical process used to derive the data used in their conclusion. We note that the techniques used to analyze the fecal data offered as conclusive evidence for cannibalism are as yet unsupported, unverified, and unreplicated by other scientists in different laboratories. The mere citation of a letter on file from a microbiologist is not satisfactory.

While the actualistic studies reported by Billman et al. indicate that bovine myoglobin can survive cooking and digestion for 24 hours, blood proteins are known to degrade with time. Whether or not human myoglobin survives in analytically traceable amounts for 800 years or more has yet to be determined. With ELISA, problems with degradation of blood proteins may result in antigen binding that produce nonspecific results.

While ELISA is a standard technique for these kinds of assays, we need to know that the small coprolite retrieved was never directly handled by any humans because this could contaminate the material by introducing foreign proteins (found in abundance on everyone's hands). This sort of contamination is known to affect immunological methods in molecular paleontology.

Because the fecal data are so sketchy, the authors out of necessity focused on Reinhard's process of elimination method in which the absence of macroscopic plant remains suggests that the coprolite did contain meat. This line of reasoning using negative evidence is weak and unconvincing. We do not accept the authors' conclusion that the fecal data ". . . is the first direct evidence of the consumption of human flesh in the prehistoric southwest." We have to ask the question: Isn't anyone else bothered by the fact that there were virtually *no* plant remains in the fecal material? Is this even possible in humans? Although Reinhard says this is surely a human piece of feces, we would like other scientists (faunal specialists) to verify that this is not in fact a carnivore coprolite.

We are not microbiologists, and therefore before accepting the claim that the coprolite contains human myoglobin, we await peer review and publication of the fecal study by *Science* or another scientific journal specializing in biomolecular research. As presented in the Cowboy Wash study, the fecal evidence is suggestive but not convincing. More work pursuing this line of evidence is warranted in future studies.

Aspects of Archaeological Context

In part, a mode of "abandonment" described as "catastrophic" is used as a line of evidence supporting the claim of cannibalism. In the Feature 3 pithouse, the inference of rapid abandonment is based on *in situ* artifacts and disarticulated human remains found on the floor and in the southern chamber. However, the bone pile in the southern chamber is reported to "lay on top of a layer of trash that was deposited well before abandonment." At the same time, Billman et al. infer that "evidently the bone in this pile was dumped down the ventilator shaft from the ground surface at the time of site abandonment." Apparently, the authors think the trash in the southern chamber was either dumped down the ventilator shaft or dragged into the chamber during the occupation of the pithouse. Whether or not this pattern of trash deposition would foul the air drawn down the ventilator shaft is not addressed by the authors, yet this is a relevant issue to their reconstruction of the occupational history of the structure. We have questions but no answers as to what this means in terms of their argument. Trash deposition in a occupied structure seems to be an anomaly. . . .

Finally, Billman et al. suggest there was a "ritual" placement of scapulae on either side of the deflector in the Feature 3 pithouse. This sort of ritual behavior seems somewhat contradictory to the dominant theme of the paper that violent cannibalism was a form of disrespect. After a brief mention of the possible ritual placement of human remains, the authors never return to considering what this means in terms of their interpretation of cannibalism, or in terms of distinguishing between different kinds of cannibalism.

Alternative Explanations

One can easily develop alternative explanations for the disarticulated and broken bones found at Cowboy Wash. In their discussion of disarticulated, butchered, burned, and commingled human remains recovered from two puebloan sites in northwestern New Mexico, Oglivie and Hilton offer warfare and secondary mortuary practices as alternative explanations to cannibalism. In their discussion, Oglivie and Hilton cite Willey's Crow Creek Massacre as an example of prehistoric warfare that resulted in the disarticulated and butchered human remains in the archaeological record. This mass interment contained the modified remains of at least 486 men, women, and children from the Plains site in South Dakota. The osteological evidence of warfare consisted of mutilations including scalping, blows to the head, evulsions, decapitation, burning, and dismemberment. Interestingly, Willey noted that the bone damage patterns resulting from warfare mimicked those patterns seen in butchered faunal assemblages.

For the sake of argument, we offer the following alternative hypothesis that accounts for the osteological data. The small community was attacked by unknown perpetrators. Many of the community members escaped but some were captured and killed. As was done in Kosovo and Rwanda in recent times, individuals were hacked repeatedly. Some bodies fell near fires or in fires and were subjected to burning. Perpetrators ransacked the site and took what they wanted. The perpetrators left. Carnivores dragged off key pieces of the bodies. Later, the survivors returned and gathered up all remaining body parts and deposited them in two pitstructures as a form of burial and last rites, and quickly relinquished use of the site for habitation.

Breakage associated with violent death, ritualized dismemberment, and movement of cadavers in varying states of decomposition by carnivores or humans can account for all the bone damage reported by Billman et al.. What we thus have are plausible but mutually exclusive explanations for the same archaeological assemblage. As scientists, we think the fact that one or the other of the hypotheses can't be proven false with the existing data indicates we simply don't yet know enough about the phenomena. The need for more study is indicated before conclusions about cannibalism are made.

Theoretical Considerations

In writing about what he considered to be an incident of cannibalism in the Mesa Verde region, White cautioned that "Just as no person characterizes all

American pioneers of the last century as cannibals on the basis of cannibalism of the Donner Party, no person should characterize all Anasazi as cannibals." Yet this is essentially what Billman et al. do in developing a theoretical perspective on the purported "outbreak of cannibalism" they say characterized the twelfth century in the Mesa Verde region.

In offering an explanation for cannibalism, Billman et al. leap from 5MT10010 to all of Cowboy Wash and the Mesa Verde region. They assert there are similarities in processing of disarticulated human remains throughout the region but no data describing these similarities are presented or analyzed. In considering the regional context, Billman et al. refer to 18 "*possible* cannibalism sites" and then in the next paragraph promptly describe these sites as a "severe outbreak of cannibalism." Why the authors move from discussion of "possible" cannibalism sites to writing about them as if they were all confirmed incidents of cannibalism begs explanation. These things bring to mind Arens' admonition that we need to describe a custom prior to its interpretation.

Billman et al. speculate that "correlation of this outbreak of cannibalism at Cowboy Wash with the second worst drought in the tree-ring record surely is more than mere coincidence." However, only half of the disarticulated assemblages in the Mesa Verde region temporally coincide with the Cowboy Wash sites, so the authors conclude that cannibalism may have occurred periodically for several hundred years prior to the Cowboy Wash "outbreak." At the same time, they suggest cannibalism occurred over two centuries, they claim that cannibalism never became a multigenerational or institutionalized practice. They seem to want it both ways—a phenomenon spanning centuries and an "outbreak" concomitant with people leaving the sites they dug.

While Billman et al. suggest the low incidence of cultigens and the abandonment of the Cowboy Wash sites in a period of drought are consistent with hunger-induced cannibalism, they note that other aspects of the situation are not, i.e., the Cowboy Wash residents were free to migrate to other areas, and the incidence of purported cannibalism occurred in one brief episode rather than over a long period, as is found in historical cases of starvation cannibalism. A climatic explanation for cannibalism as a way to obtain a source of food in hard times ultimately fails because the purported behavior apparently occurred in both good and bad climatic regimes.

Billman et al. then suggest that cannibalism is related to terrorism used to control scarce resources in a time characterized by severe drought and, possibly, a social and ideological breakdown that accompanied the collapse of the Chaco regional system. Again, however, the occurrence of disarticulated and broken bone assemblages over a period of 200 years seems to argue against this as an explanation. Turner and Turner's thesis that cannibalism was a terroristic behavior introduced by cannibal warriors from Mexico led by a psychopath like Charles Manson does not seem to apply to Cowboy Wash because a lack of Chacoan outliers seems to indicate the area did not directly participate in the Chacoan system. Furthermore, the violence at Cowboy Wash occurred after the occupation of Chaco, and no mechanism for diffusion of this form of social behavior is offered.

A smorgasbord of theoretical variables and explanations is offered in the Cowboy Wash study to explain mutilation and consumption of human beings. In the end, however, this pastiche of notions is unsatisfying, and the authors acknowledge they haven't really explained cannibalism by beginning their concluding paragraph with the statement, "Whatever the root cause . . ." The study ends by noting that the weather in the Mesa Verde region improved, and while lethal violence continued elsewhere in the northern Southwest, there are no more incidents of cannibalism in Mesa Verde, even though a more severe drought occurred. The authors conclude, "The reason for the sudden demise of this one- or two-generation outbreak of cannibalism and violence remains even more mysterious than its origins."

Unless and until archaeologists can offer a theory that accounts for cannibalism over many generations, and during varying climatic regimes, we do not think cannibalism is the best or only explanation for assemblages with disarticulated and broken bones. We are also concerned about a theory that only explains a portion of the total variability in disarticulated assemblages. Turner and Turner list 76 sites with disarticulated and broken bones, only 38 of which are reputed to evidence cannibalism. What about the other half of the variability? We think we need a model that explains the full range of variability, not just a portion of it.

Given the relative rarity of sites with assemblages of disarticulated and commingled human remains, and the long time span that applies to these assemblages, we think it is probable that there are multiple explanations for their occurrence. As White concluded, "It is premature to offer comprehensive regional explanations for the assemblages . . . and there is no reason to conclude that the reasons behind them will not be multiple and independent." Assemblages of disarticulated and commingled human remains in the northern Southwest are phenomena that span at least 800 years and tens of thousands of square kilometers of space. These assemblages occur in a variety of archaeological contexts, including rock shelters, crypts, open sites, pit structures, kivas, and pueblo rooms. Patterns of perimortem modification of the human remains in these assemblages vary, and there are thus a number of different possible explanations to account for their presence in archaeological sites.

In the final analysis, we think the statement that the entire early Pueblo III Cowboy Wash community was perhaps "abandoned suddenly after the processing and consumption of humans" remains a supposition rather than a demonstrated fact. If nothing else, the Cowboy Wash study indicates that the theory of cannibalism in the Southwest is weak and in need of further development.

POSTSCRIPT

Did Prehistoric Native Americans Practice Cannibalism in the American Southwest?

Billman, Lambert, and Leonard see the evidence that cannibalism took place at site 5MT10010 at Cowboy Wash as so compelling that they quickly dismiss all alternative possible explanations of the assemblage. They regard the presence of human myoglobin in a coprolite (piece of excrement) as conclusive proof that humans ate other humans there. Dongoske, Martin, and Ferguson respond that the evidence lends itself to several possible interpretations, of which cannibalism is only one. In their view, Billman et al.'s classification of the cut marks on the bones, for example, is too crude to distinguish whether the bodies were dismembered for food or as part of some mortuary practice. They also argue that the coprolite should be tested by other independent labs, and they ask whether it might have been produced by a carnivorous animal, rather than a human being.

This controversy centers on one of the fundamental problems in archaeology, namely that the physical remains in archaeological sites do not speak for themselves. They must be interpreted. The analyst must engage in a process of deduction that goes from the physical evidence to an account of the probable human actions and natural processes that produced the existing pattern of remains. More adventurous scholars then go on to speculate about *why* the people carried out those actions. Some archaeologists believe that physical remains are a better route to the "truth" about a culture than what living people say they do and believe. In a famous study, archaeologist William Rathje and his colleagues at the University of Arizona showed, by analyzing people's garbage, that middle class suburbanites in Tucson, Arizona, inaccurately describe their patterns of consumption to researchers, for example, by understating the amount of beer they consume at home. On the question of whether the ancestors of the Pueblo Indians practiced cannibalism, bioarchaeologist Christy Turner has been quoted as saying that "we can't trust the ethnographic record. When the Spanish arrived, they dictated to the Puebloans what they should and shouldn't do" (Constance Holden, "Witches or *Cannibals*," *Science*, January 29, 1999). Archaeologists of this persuasion seem to see the actions and statements of living peoples as merely obscuring what really happened. Similarly, some argue that we should not depend too much on the "ethnographic analogy"—the reconstruction of behavior at an archaeological site by comparison with the documented behavior of recent societies of a similar type in a similar environment—as this precludes our recognition of prehistoric behaviors that were completely different from recent ones. This consideration is particularly important when dealing with our prehuman ancestors, who might or might not have behaved like fully modern humans. Thus, even if we believe that most if not all people today view a practice such as cannibalism with horror and disgust, how can we know that people in prehistoric times didn't see it as perfectly normal and reasonable?

Other archaeologists, however, view archaeological remains as inherently ambiguous, contending that we can seldom know for certain the nature of the human actions that produced an assemblage of material remains, much less the reasons for and meanings of those actions. They argue, therefore, that we must consider clues from the ethnographic record, ethnohistorical records, and the cultures of the still-living descendants of the people who produced the remains. For those archaeologists, the attitude of modern and historically documented Pueblo Indians toward cannibalism *is* relevant to the interpretation of Anasazi remains, as it helps to assess the likelihood of the various actions that could have produced the remains, including cannibalism, mortuary practices, and witch execution. They argue that those who ignore the influence of the cultures of the producers are in danger of interpreting the evidence on the basis of their own unexamined cultural assumptions, including assumptions about human nature. For them the question of whether cannibalism was actually widely practiced during historical times, or whether it was falsely attributed to tribal peoples by European explorers, is relevant to the interpretation of archaeological evidence, as it gives an idea of how common it would have been prehistorically.

The literature on the issue of prehistoric cannibalism is growing rapidly. Useful overviews of the question of whether cannibalism occurred in the American Southwest include Stephen Plog's article "Social Conflict, Social Structure and Processes of Culture Change" (*American Antiquity* 68(1), 2003) and Randall H. McGuire's article "Stories of Power, Powerful Tales: A Commentary on Ancient Pueblo Violence" (*The Dynamics of Power*, Maria O'Donovan, ed., Center for Archaeological Investigations, Southern Illinois University, Occasional Paper No. 30, 2002). Important works supporting the occurrence of cannibalism in the American Southwest include Tim White's book *Prehistoric Cannibalism at Mancos* (Princeton University Press, 1992), a detailed analysis of the evidence from one site; Christy and Jacqueline Turner's book *Man Corn: Cannibalism and Violence in the Prehistoric American Southwest* (University of Utah Press, 1999), which summarizes evidence for the region as a whole; and Sharon Hurlbut's article "The Taphonomy of Cannibalism: A Review of Anthropogenic Bone Modification in the American Southwest" (*International Journal of Osteoarchaeology* volume 10, 2000), which includes a comparison of a variety of postmortem bone modifications found worldwide. Billman et al. offer their rebuttal of Dongoske et al. in P.M. Lambert et al.'s article "Response to Critique of the Claim of Cannibalism at Cowboy Wash" (*American Antiquity* 65, 2000). Tim White reports on recent research in Europe, claiming that cannibalism was practiced by *Homo antecessor* about 800,000 years ago and by Neanderthals about 100,000 years ago in his article "Once Were Cannibals" (*Scientific American*, special edition, July 2003).

Internet References . . .

The Chimpanzee and Human Communication Institute Home Page

The Chimpanzee and Human Communication Institute provides information on this site about current research on teaching American Sign Language to chimpanzees. The site includes information about experiments with chimps as well as links to other sites dealing with the question of whether apes can learn a language.

```
http://www.cwu.edu/~cwuchci/
```

Endangered Languages

This Web site has general information about endangered languages as well as links to other sites with more detailed information about specific groups of languages.

```
http://www.nvtc.gov/lotw/months/november/
endangered.html
```

Ethnologue

This site produced by the Summer Institute of Linguistics gives information about 6,900 known languages in the world. Many of these are endangered and only about half of these have been well studied.

```
http://www.ethnologue.com/web.asp
```

Linguistic Anthropology

*L*inguistic anthropologists study languages, particularly non-Western and unwritten languages. They also investigate the complex relationship between language and other aspects of culture. Language provides the categories within which culture is expressed and is the medium by which much of culture is transmitted from one generation to the next. Here we consider two classic questions that have confronted linguistic anthropologists for several decades. The first concerns whether chimpanzees and other apes have the innate ability to use symbols in ways that resemble human language. This question is important because if apes are capable of complex symbolic activity, then language and culture are probably not the exclusive capabilities of humans but have their origins in our primate past. The second question concerns what, if anything, scholars should do about the fact that many minority languages around the world are dying out as their last surviving speakers pass away. The problem is less about whether anything should be done about the elderly speakers themselves, than about what could or should be done to encourage young people to learn the languages of their parents or grandparents.

- Can Apes Learn Language?
- Should Anthropologists and Linguists Be Concerned about Losing Endangered Languages?

ISSUE 6

Can Apes Learn Language?

YES: E. S. Savage-Rumbaugh, from "Language Training of Apes," in Steve Jones, Robert Martin, and David Pilbeam, eds., *The Cambridge Encyclopedia of Human Evolution* (Cambridge University Press, 1999)

NO: Joel Wallman, from *Aping Language* (Cambridge University Press, 1992)

ISSUE SUMMARY

YES: Psychologist and primate specialist E. S. Savage-Rumbaugh argues that, since the 1960s, attempts to teach chimpanzees and other apes symbol systems similar to human language have resulted in the demonstration of a genuine ability to create new symbolic patterns.

NO: Linguist Joel Wallman counters that attempts to teach chimps and other apes sign language or other symbolic systems have demonstrated that apes are very intelligent animals, but up to now these attempts have not shown that apes have any innate capacity for language.

For more than a century anthropologists have generally assumed that humankind's ability to make tools and use language are two characteristics that distinguish humans from other animals. In the 1960s and 1970s Jane Goodall and other primatologists convincingly demonstrated that chimpanzees, our nearest biological relatives, made simple tools, thus narrowing the gap between apes and humans. Beginning in the 1940s a series of other scientists have worked with gorillas, chimps, and most recently the bonobo (or pygmy chimp), attempting to teach these apes simple forms of human-like language.

In the 1950s psychologist B. F. Skinner argued that human children learn natural language through conditioning, such that positive responses to utterances from proud parents and other adults essentially train children to recognize both grammatical patterns and vocabulary. But in the 1960s linguist Noam Chomsky disproved Skinner's theory, showing that human language is so highly complex that it must require some innate biological capability, which he called a "language acquisition device." In several respects, all of the ape-language experiments since then have sought to understand when this biological capacity for language learning evolved in primates.

The early years of the ape-language projects encountered one major difficulty. Try as they might, trainers could not get apes to vocalize human words reliably. This difficulty was a consequence of the fact that a chimp's vocal apparatus simply does not allow the possibility of human utterances.

Since Chomsky's studies of human language, linguists have generally accepted that the manipulation of symbols in systematic grammatical ways, rather than the ability to make utterances, is the most important and complex aspect of human language. Thus, if apes could manipulate symbols in linguistic ways, researchers hoped they could demonstrate that the ability to acquire language is a biological trait shared by at least certain species of the apes and humans.

If true, the ability to learn and use language, the last barrier that separates human beings from our nonhuman primate relatives, has fallen away. This view has its supporters and detractors, many of whom—largely on political or religious grounds—would either like to see humans as just another of the great apes or prefer to view human beings as unique in the animal kingdom. But at issue is whether or not the long series of ape-language projects has demonstrated that apes can learn to manipulate signs and symbols.

E. S. Savage-Rumbaugh and her husband Duane Rumbaugh have been among the most innovative researchers in their field at the intersection of anthropology, linguistics, and cognitive psychology. They argue that of all the great apes a certain species of pygmy chimps, the bonobo, is biologically closest to *Homo sapiens*. Their recent work with a bonobo named Kanzi has been among the most successful of these ape-language projects. After tracing the history of these projects, Savage-Rumbaugh concludes that Kanzi's ability to use symbols closely resembles similar abilities observed among young human children.

Joel Wallman interprets the evidence very differently from Savage-Rumbaugh. He acknowledges that the various gorillas, chimps, and bonobos are clever animals, which have learned to respond to their trainers. But he argues that these animals have not learned anything resembling human language. However, chimps and bonobos are clever animals, and while they do not have full linguistic abilities, their abilities to use mental abstractions suggest that at least modest versions of these mental processes arose before our branch of the hominoid lineage split off from the lineage of the great apes.

These selections raise a number of questions about the similarities and differences between apes and humans. What kind of linguistic ability do these ape learners exhibit? Do their symbolic strings genuinely parallel early childhood language acquisition? Most importantly, do these ape-language studies show that apes and human beings genuinely share a common ability for language? What are the minimal features that make up any natural language?

YES

E. S. Savage-Rumbaugh

Language Training of Apes

Can apes learn to communicate with human beings? Scientists have been attempting to answer this question since the late 1960s when it was first reported that a young chimpanzee named Washoe in Reno, Nevada had been taught to produce hand signs similar to those used by deaf humans.

Washoe was reared much like a human child. People made signs to her throughout the day and she was given freedom to move about the caravan where she lived. She could even go outdoors to play. She was taught how to make different signs by teachers who moved her hands through the motions of each sign while showing her the object she was learning to 'name'. If she began to make a portion of the hand movement on her own she was quickly rewarded, either with food or with something appropriate to the sign. For example, if she was being taught the sign for 'tickle' her reward was a tickling game.

This training method was termed 'moulding' because it involved the physical placement of Washoe's hands. Little by little, Washoe became able to produce more and more signs on her own. As she grew older, she occasionally even learned to make new signs without moulding. Once Washoe had learned several signs she quickly began to link them together to produce strings of signs such as 'you me out'. Such sequences appeared to her teachers to be simple sentences.

Many biologists were sceptical of the claims made for Washoe. While they agreed that Washoe was able to produce different gestures, they doubted that such signs really served as names. Perhaps, to Washoe, the gestures were just tricks to be used to get the experimenter to give her things she wanted; even though Washoe knew how and when to make signs, she really did not know what words meant in the sense that people do.

The disagreement was more than a scholarly debate among scientists. Decades of previous work had demonstrated that many animals could learn to do complex things to obtain food, without understanding what they were doing. For example, pigeons had been taught to bat a ball back and forth in what looked like a game of ping pong. They were also taught to peck keys with such words as 'Please', 'Thank you', 'Red' and 'Green' printed on them. They did this in a way that made it appear that they were communicating, but they were not; they had simply learned to peck each key when a special signal was given.

From *The Cambridge Encyclopedia of Human Evolution*, 1999, pp. 138–141. Copyright © 1999 by Cambridge University Press. Reprinted by permission.

This type of learning is called *conditioned discrimination* learning, a term that simply means that an animal can learn to make one set of responses in one group of circumstances and another in different circumstances. Although some aspects of human language can be explained in this way, such as 'Hello', 'Goodbye', 'Please' and 'Thank you', most cannot. Human beings learn more than what to say when: they learn what words stand for.

If Washoe had simply signed 'drink' when someone held up a bottle of soda, there would be little reason to conclude that she was doing anything different from other animals. If, however, Washoe used the sign 'drink' to represent any liquid beverage, then she was doing something very different— something that everyone had previously thought only humans could do.

It was difficult to determine which of these possibilities charcterised her behaviour, as the question of how to distinguish between the 'conditioned response' and a 'word' had not arisen. Before Washoe, the only organisms that used words were human beings, and to determine if a person knew what a word stood for was easy: one simply asked. This was impossible with Washoe, because her use of symbols was not advanced enough to allow her to comprehend complex questions. One- and two-year-old children are also unable to answer questions such as these. However, because children are able to answer such questions later on, the issue of determining how and when a child knows that words have meanings had not until then been seen as critical.

Teaching Syntax

Several scientists attempted to solve this problem by focusing on sentences instead of words. Linguists argue that the essence of human language lies not in learning to use individual words, but rather in an ability to form a large number of word combinations that follow the same set of specific rules. These rules are seen as a genetic endowment unique to humans. If it could be shown that apes learn syntactical rules, then it must be true that they were using symbols to represent things, not just perform tricks.

Three psychologists in the 1970s each used a different method in an attempt to teach apes syntax. One group followed the method used with Washoe and began teaching another chimpanzee, Nim, sign language. Another opted for the use of plastic symbols with the chimpanzee Sarah. Still another used geometric symbols, linked to a computer keyboard, with a chimpanzee named Lana. Both Lana and Sarah were taught a simple syntax, which required them to fill in one blank at a time in a string of words. The number of blanks was slowly increased until the chimpanzee was forming a complete 'sentence'. Nim was asked to produce syntactically correct strings by making signs along with his teacher.

Without help from his teachers, Nim was unable to form sentences that displayed the kind of syntactical rules used by humans. Nim's sign usage could best be interpreted as a series of 'conditioned discriminations' similar to, albeit more complex than, behaviours seen in many less-intelligent animals. This work suggested that Nim, like circus animals but unlike human children, was using words only to obtain rewards.

However, the other attempts to teach sentences to apes arrived at a different conclusion, perhaps because a different training method was used. Both Sarah and Lana learned to fill in the blanks in sentences in ways that suggested they had learned the rules that govern simple sentence construction. Moreover, 6 per cent of Lana's sentences were 'novel' in that they differed from the ones that she had been taught. Many of these sentences, such as 'Please you move coke in cup into room', followed syntactical rules and were appropriate and meaningful communications. Other sentences followed the syntactical rules that Lana had learned, but did not make sense; for example, 'Question you give beancake shut-open'. Thus, apes appeared to be able to learn rules for sentence construction, but they did not generalise these rules in a way that suggested full comprehension of the words.

By 1980, Washoe had matured and given birth. At this time there was great interest in whether or not she would teach her offspring to sign. Unfortunately, her infant died. However, another infant was obtained and given to Washoe. This infant, Loulis, began to imitate many of the hand gestures that Washoe used, though the imitations were often quite imprecise. Washoe made few explicit attempts to mould Loulis's hands. Although Loulis began to make signs, it was not easy to determine why he was making them or what, if anything, he meant. Loulis has not yet received any tests like those that were given to Washoe to determine if he can make the correct sign when shown an object. It is clear that he learned to imitate Washoe, but it is not clear that he learned what the signs meant.

The question of whether or not apes understand words caused many developmental psychologists to study earlier and earlier aspects of language acquisition in children. Their work gave, for the first time, a detailed insight into how children use words during the 'one-word' stage of language learning and showed that children usually learn to understand words before they begin to use them. At the same time, there was a new approach to the investigation of ape language. Instead of teaching names by pairing an object with its sign or symbol and rewarding correct responses, there was a new emphasis on the communicative aspect of symbols. For example, to teach a symbol such as 'key', a desirable item was locked in a box that was given to the chimpanzee. When the chimpanzee failed to open it, he was shown how to ask for and how to use a key. On other occasions, the chimpanzee was asked to retrieve a key for the teacher, so that she might open the box.

This new approach was first used with two chimpanzees named Sherman and Austin. It resulted in a clearer symbolic use of words than that found in animals trained by other methods. In addition, because these chimpanzees were taught comprehension skills, they were able to communicate with one another and not just with the experimenters. Sherman and Austin could use their symbols to tell each other things that could not be conveyed by simple glances or by pointing. For example, they could describe foods they had seen in another room, or the types of tools they needed to solve a problem. Although other apes had been reported to sign in each other's presence, there was no evidence that they were intentionally signing to each other or that they responded to each other's signs.

Most important, Sherman and Austin began to show an aspect of symbol usage that they had not been taught; they used symbols to say what they were going to do *before* they did it. Symbol use by other apes had not included descriptions of intended actions; rather, communications had been begun by a teacher, or limited to simple requests.

Sherman and Austin also began to use symbols to share information about objects that were not present and they passed a particularly demanding test, which required them to look at symbols and answer questions that could be answered only if they knew what each symbol represented. For example, they could look at printed lexigram symbol such as 'key', 'lever', 'stick', 'wrench', 'apple', 'banana', 'pineapple' and 'juice', and state whether each lexigram belonged to the class of 'food' words or 'tool' words. They could do this without ever being told whether these lexigram symbols should be classified as foods or tools. These findings were important, because they revealed that by using symbols an ape can describe what it is about to do.

How Similar Is Ape Language to Human Language?

Even though it was generally agreed that apes could do something far more complex than most other animals, there still remained much disagreement as to whether ape's symbols were identical to human symbols. This uncertainty arose for two reasons: apes did not acquire words in the same manner as children—that is, by observing others use them; and apes did not appear to use true syntactical rules to construct multiple-word utterances.

The first of these differences between ape and child has recently been challenged by a young pygmy chimpanzee or bonobo named Kanzi. Most previous studies had focused on common chimpanzees because pygmy chimpanzees are very rare (they are in great danger of having their habitat destroyed in the coming decade and have no protected parks).

In contrast to other apes, Kanzi learned symbols simply by observing human beings point to them while speaking to him. He did not need to have his arms placed in position, or to be rewarded for using a correct symbol. More important, he did not need to be taught to comprehend symbols or taught that symbols could be used for absent objects as well as those present. Kanzi spontaneously used symbols to announce his actions or intentions and, if his meaning was ambiguous, he often invented gestures to clarify it, as young children do.

Kanzi learned words by listening to speech. He first comprehended certain spoken words, then learned to read the lexigram symbols. This was possible because his caretakers pointed to these symbols as they spoke. For example, Kanzi learned 'strawberries' as he heard people mention the word when they ran across wild strawberries growing in the woods. He soon became able to lead people to strawberries whenever they asked him to do so. He similarly learned the spoken names of many other foods that grew outdoors, such as wild grapes, honeysuckle, privet berries, blackberries and mushrooms, and could take people to any of these foods upon spoken request.

Unlike previous apes reared as human children, Kanzi was reared in a semi-natural woodland. Although he could not produce speech, he understood much of what was said to him. He could appropriately carry out novel spoken requests such as 'Will you take some hamburger to Austin?', 'Can you show your new toy to Kelly?' and 'Would you give Panzee some of your melon?'. There appeared to be no limit to the number of sentences that Kanzi could understand as long as the words in the sentences were in his vocabulary.

During the first 3 or 4 years of his life, Kanzi's comprehension of spoken sentences was limited to things that he heard often. However, when he was 5 years old, he began to respond to novel sentences upon first hearing them. For example, the first time he heard someone talk about throwing a ball in the river, he suddenly turned and threw his ball right in the water, even though he had never done this before. Similarly, when someone suggested, for fun, that he might then try to throw a potato at a turtle that was nearby, he found a potato and tossed it at the turtle. To be certain that Kanzi was not being somehow 'cued' inadvertently by people, he was tested with headphones. In this test he had to listen to a word and point to a picture of the word that he heard. Kanzi did this easily, the first time he took the test.

About this time, Kanzi also began to combine symbols. Unlike other apes, he did not combine symbols ungrammatically to get the experimenter to give something that was purposefully being held back. Kanzi's combinations had a primitive English word order and conveyed novel information. For example, he formed utterances such as 'Ball go group room' to say that he wanted to play with a specific ball—the one he had seen in the group room on the previous day. Because the experimenter was not attempting to get Kanzi to say this, and was indeed far from the group room, such a sentence conveyed something that only Kanzi—not the experimenter—knew before Kanzi spoke.

Thus Kanzi's combinations differed from those of other apes in that they often referred to things or events that were absent and were known only to Kanzi, they contained a primitive grammar and were not imitations of the experimenter. Nor did the experimenter ask rhetorical questions such as 'What is this?' to elicit them, Kanzi's combinations include sentences such as 'Tickle bite', 'Keep-way balloon' and 'Coke chase'. As almost nothing is yet known of how pygmy chimpanzees communicate, they could use a form of simple language in the wild. Kanzi understands spoken English words, so the ability that is reflected in language comprehension is probably an older evolutionary adaptation than is the ability to talk.

Studying ape language presents a serious challenge to the long-held view that only humans can talk and think. Certainly, there is now no doubt that apes communicate in much more complex and abstract ways than dogs, cats and other familiar animals. Similarly, apes that have learned some language skills are also able to do some remarkable non-linguistic tasks. For example, they can recognise themselves on television and even determine whether an image is taped or live. They can also play video games, using a joystick to catch and trap a video villain.

Scientists have only just begun to discover ways of tapping the hidden talents for language and communication of our closest relatives. Sharing 98 per cent of their DNA with human beings, it has long been wondered why African apes seem so much like us at a biological level, but so different when it comes to behaviour. Ape-language studies continue to reveal that apes are more like us than we ever imagined.

Joel Wallman

Aping Language

Experiments carried out over the past two decades . . . attempted to impart a language, either natural or invented, to an ape. The debate engendered by these projects has been of interest—consuming for some, passing for others—to all of those whose concerns include the enduring questions of human nature, among them anthropologists, psychologists, linguists, biologists, and philosophers.

An adequate treatment of the linguistic capabilities of apes entails consideration of a number of related issues, each of which is an interesting problem in its own right. Continuities in primate mentality, the relationship between language and thought in the individual and in the species, and the origin of language . . . are themes that . . . recur throughout this [debate].

. . . [N]one of the ape-language projects succeeded, despite employing years of tutelage far more intense than that experienced by most children, in implanting in an ape a capacity for language equal to that of a young child, let alone an adult. . . .

Why the Ape-Language Controversy Is a Controversy

All scientific arguments have in common at least these elements: (1) a minimum of two positions regarding the subject in dispute, positions generally held to be irreconcilable, and (2) an intensification of the normal emotional investment of the scientist in his or her position, due in some measure to the contending itself but perhaps also related to the ideological significance of the subject within the larger society. If, in addition, the argument includes suggestions of fraudulent or quasi-fraudulent procedures, the disagreement becomes a controversy. To the extent that this is an accurate characterization of scientific controversies, the ape-language debate is an exemplary one.

The radical opposition of opinion about the achievement of the various ape-language projects is well conveyed by the following quotations:

> [Washoe] learned a natural human language and her early utterances were highly similar to, perhaps indistinguishable from, the early utterances of human children. (Gardner and Gardner 1978, p. 73)

The evidence we have makes it clear that even the brightest ape can acquire not even so much as the weak grammatical system exhibited by very young children. (Premack and Premack 1983, p. 115)

On measures of sign performance (form), sign order (structure), semantic relations (meaning), sign acts (function) and sign acquisition (development), apes appear to be very similar to 2 to 3 year old human children learning sign . . . Apes also appear to be very similar to 2 to 3 year old human children learning to speak. (Miles 1978, p. 114)

[The experimental chimpanzees] show, after years of training and exposure to signing, not the slightest trace of homological development parallel to that of human children. (Leiber 1984, p. 84)

After years of gentle teaching Koko has learned to use American Sign Language—the very same sign language used by the deaf. With her new-found vocabulary, Koko is now providing us with an astounding wealth of knowledge about the way animals view the world. (Patterson 1985a, p. 1) . . .

There are several sources of the stridency of the debate.

. . . [L]anguage, at least in the European intellectual tradition, is the quintessential human attribute, at once evidence and source of most that is transcendent in us, distinguishing ours from the merely mechanical nature of the beast. Language is regarded as the *sine qua non* of culture, and its presence in our species is the most salient behavioral difference between us and the other hominoids—with the relinquishing of tool use and, more recently, tool making (Goodall 1971; Beck 1980) as uniquely human capabilities, the significance of language as a separator has grown. And resistance to losing our quintessential attributes is, arguably, itself one of those uniquely human traits. Hence, some ape partisans (Linden 1974; Gysens-Gosselin 1979) have argued, the prevalent reluctance to accord the talking apes their due. An occasional variant of this interpretation is the accusation that those who refuse to recognize ape language are insufficiently committed to the Darwinian perspective or, worse, are anti-Darwinian. Thus Linden (1987) depicts those who question the likelihood of ape–human linguistic continuities as latter-day Wilberforces, averse to investigating "creatures who threaten to paralyze us by shedding light on the true nature and origins of our abilities" (p. 8).

A countervailing vector of our ideology, perhaps peculiar to our culture but possibly pancultural, consists of careless anthropomorphic projection and an irrepressively attractive vision of communication between our own and other species. In fact, it seems correct to observe that, at least until recently in the debate and probably up to the present, the majority opinion, both lay and scientific, regarding the linguistic capabilities of the apes has been positive. People seem not only accepting but positively desirous of the possibility of ape language.

Even if language did not have the sacrosanct status it does in our conception of human nature, the question of its presence in other species would still promote argument, for we are lacking any universally accepted, unassailable diagnostic criteria for language. There is no shortage of candidates for the indispensable attribute of language. For Katz (1976) and Limber (1977), the projective capability is crucial, the provision of language for the articulation of any conceivable new proposition through a novel combination of words. Savage-Rumbaugh (1981) holds the referential nature of individual symbols to be the essence of language, while Premack (1984) and Marshall (1971) see the capacity for representation of real-world situations to be paramount, and so on. The property most commonly invoked as definitive of language is its predication on a system of abstract rules for the production and interpretation of utterances—in other words, grammar. Hockett's (1959, 1960, 1963; Hockett and Altmann 1968) famous list of so-called design features of language—including rapid fading, duality of patterning, and displacement—has provided a useful orientation for those trying to capture the differences between human and nonhuman natural systems of communication. What is wanting, nonetheless, is consensus on what the necessary and sufficient, as distinguished from inessential, property or properties of language are and hence on how we might unequivocally identify language in another species.

This problem of defining features is more severe where the language of the young child is concerned, and it is the child's language that is taken by most parties to the debate to be the proper material for comparison with the apes. If the young child is not, in fact, capable of linguistically encoding anything she can think of, if her production and understanding of utterances do not suggest abstract grammatical constituents and processes, then can it be said that the child has language? Limber (1977) and Lightfoot (1982), at least, would say no.

This is a defensible position, its major problem found in the fact that the young child's language, which may not yet be language, will eventually become language. How is this discontinuity in development to be bridged? The difficulty is not the existence of a discontinuity per se—there are a number of others in human development. The physiological transition from prepubescence to pubescence, for example, poses a similar problem—the two developmental phases are identifiably distinct, yet there are no two adjacent points in time about which it could be said that the child was prepubescent in the first but pubescent in the second.

What makes the transition from "nonlanguage" (. . . early language) to language more problematic is that, unlike the case of puberty, in which the first phase is defined largely by the absence of characteristics of the later one, early language has its own, very salient features. Moreover, there are some striking functional and possibly structural similarities between these features and those of adult language. . . . And, contrary to those who would deny language to the young child, there is extensive evidence for grammatical structure in the earliest word combinations (Bloom 1970; Brown 1973), and, some have suggested (De Laguna 1927; McNeill 1970), in single-word utterances as well. (The proper characterization of this structure, however, is the subject of ongoing debate in developmental psycholinguistics—in fact, this may be the dominant concern of the field. . . .

Language, in summary, is central to our self-definition as a species, even though we have yet to derive an adequate definition of language itself, one that includes the essential but excludes the merely contingent.

Behaviorist Roots of the Ape-Language Experiments

There is an additional source of the contention surrounding the ape-language question. The issues in the debate tend to resonate along the long-standing cleavage within the behavioral sciences between those who advocate study of cognition and/or innately determined behavior, on the one hand, and those, on the other, who are behaviorist in method and theory.

Behaviorism, or stimulus–response psychology, came into being in the early decades of this century as an avowed antidote to the introspectionist trend in turn-of-the-century psychological investigation. Knowledge, thought, intention, affect, and all other unobservable mental phenomena were banished in favor of overt behavior as the only proper subject of a scientific psychology. To explain the behavior of animals, behaviorism, like the eighteenth-century empiricism from which it descends, posits a bare minimum of cognitive apparatus: (1) perception, (2) a capacity to represent in durable format the results of perception, and (3) the ability to form associations among those representations. In the behaviorist paradigm, the acquisition and strengthening of such associations constitute learning.

An association may be formed between a perceptual stimulus and an inborn response if that stimulus consistently accompanies another one that is innately connected to the response, as in the celebrated conjunction of the ticking of a metronome, food, and salivation in Pavlov's dogs. Or an animal may form an association between one of its own actions and a subsequent stimulus, as when a pigeon comes reliably to peck a button because its activation results in the dispensing of food. In this process, an association is created between an action and a following stimulus that "reinforces" that action. To qualify as a reinforcing stimulus, a consequence need not be one that we would regard a priori as satisfying or pleasant—in fact, any stimulus that increases the probability of the organism emitting the behavior that preceded it is, by definition, reinforcing.

In the behaviorist conception, all behavior is determined either by current stimuli or by past consequences. Language is verbal behavior; words function both as responses to stimuli and as stimuli themselves, eliciting further responses. Thus a sentence can be interpreted as a chain of stimulus–response events, each word a response to the preceding one and also a stimulus evoking the next, with the first word elicited by an environmental stimulus or an internal one, a "private event." Or, in some formulations, the entire sentence is regarded as one complex response to a stimulus.

The orthodox behaviorist account of learning has little use for traditional distinctions among types of behavior. Nor are species differences in behavioral mechanisms acknowledged. Although sometimes touted as such, the latter attitude is not an appreciation of evolutionary continuity, with the selectively and historically wrought similarities and divergences in behavior that such a theoretical affirmation entails. Rather, it reflects a commitment to cross-species *homogeneity*, a rejection of the notion that there are important differences across species in the processes that underlie the development and causation of behavior. . . .

Like other contemporary adherents of behaviorism, the ape-language experimenters embraced the various concessions to reality that the most primitive versions of behaviorism were forced to make over the years. The Gardners, for example, acknowledge that some parts of the innate behavioral repertoire of a species are more plastic and hence more readily conditioned than others, and also that species differ in their intrinsic propensities for various behaviors. Thus the chimpanzee's inborn motivation to communicate obviates conditioning as laborious as another behavior might require. That language acquisition in the chimpanzee and in the child are similarly dependent on extensive molding, shaping, and imitation, however, is an assumption that is fundamental to their research, and fundamentally erroneous. Indeed, their suggestion that the linguistic performance of the preschool child requires "intensive training" (1971, p. 188) is the *opposite* of one of the few claims to which virtually all language-acquisition researchers would assent. . . .

Lastly, it may be worth observing that the potential personal rewards of the ape projects have been substantial and emotional commitment commensurately high—the first person or team to give language to another species would certainly attain scientific immortality.

⁓⦿⁓

. . . In describing their aspirations for Washoe, the first of the modern ape language pupils, the Gardners expressed pessimism about a direct assault on the question "Can an ape talk?" and . . . adopted instead an unabashedly behavioristic goal: "We wanted to develop behavior that could be called conversation" (1969, p. 665). And critics . . . have maintained that Washoe and her peers, though they may have simulated conversation, acquired neither a human language nor something crucially like one, but rather a system of habits that are crude facsimiles of the features of language.

Refuting the claim that apes have the ability to learn a language logically entails proving that they do *not* have it. This [selection] has not succeeded in doing something that cannot be achieved: proving that something does not exist. The relevant refutable claim, rather, is that one or more of the animals featured in these pages learned a language. Refuting this unequivocally, however, presupposes a set of definitive criteria for language and a demonstration that at least one of them was not met by each of the animals in question. . . . [S]uch criteria do not yet exist, either for adult forms or for children's forms of language. So it is not possible in principle to show that no ape *could* learn a language, and it is not possible in practice to show that none *has* learned a language. . . .

The ape-language experiments confirmed what students dating back at least as far as the gestalt psychologist Wolfgang Kohler have repeatedly demonstrated, which is that apes are highly intelligent creatures, probably second only to us, on measures of human intelligence. We may wonder how the evolutionary process engendered such a powerful mentality in the midst of the African rain forests, asking, like Humphrey (1976), of what use "conditional oddity discrimination" is to an ape in the jungle. But the cognitive prowess of the apes is a fact regardless of our inability to account for it.

That the apes, too, are reflexive and capable of impressively abstract mentation suggests that at least modest versions of these faculties arose before the ancestral hominoid lineage diversified into the African apes on the one hand and us on the other. Consider a modest assertion: a capacity for culture requires at least ape-level powers of abstraction. And a case could be made for self-awareness, too, as prerequisite to culture. To the extent that Freud's understanding of humanity's cultural creations as "immortality projects" is sound, an ego is presupposed. If the capacity for language, too, had arisen prior to that last hominoid divergence, then linguistics might have been a branch of comparative psychology, the ape-language experiments would never have been conceived, and this [selection] would have been about something else, say patterns of interspecies marriage. But, for that matter, had language arisen prior to the split that produced them and us—had we all spoken the same language—there might not have been a them and an us.

POSTSCRIPT

Can Apes Learn Language?

The two sides on the issue of ape-language ability remain widely separated. At the heart of the issue are several questions about (1) the biological nature of human beings and their nearest primate relatives; (2) the character of language and cognition, particularly among children who are just beginning to acquire language; and (3) the best and most unbiased methods for investigating ape-language abilities.

One of the strongest critics of the ape-language experiments is the cognitive psychologist Steven Pinker, who outlines his arguments in his book *The Language Instinct* (HarperCollins, 1994). Pinker argues that ape trainers have inadvertently used very subtle conditioning to train their primates. The sequences of symbols produced by even the most talented of the apes are far simpler than normal children's linguistic abilities. His view is that Savage-Rumbaugh and other trainers have overinterpreted the primate symbolic sequences and ignored numerous random "utterances." Chimps and bonobos may be clever animals, he concedes, but their cleverness is conditioned along the lines that Skinner had proposed; it is not linguistic behavior as understood by Chomsky and most linguists. If true, Pinker's criticism suggests that all of the ape-language projects have been failures, and at best trainers have tricked themselves into believing that apes can use symbols in linguistic ways.

Do the ape-language experiments introduce bias by interpreting symbolic strings too broadly and ambiguously? Are detractors of these experiments themselves biased, refusing to believe that apes are capable of any human-like linguistic or cognitive processes? And even if these experiments do not demonstrate an ability to use symbols in ways that precisely parallel child language use, can they not tell us a great deal about general patterns of cognition relevant to both humans and primates?

If Pinker is correct that humans use a different part of the brain for language than do apes when making natural vocalizations, then the efforts to demonstrate language ability in even the brightest of the great apes may ultimately be unsuccessful. Nevertheless, as Wallman and Savage-Rumbaugh suggest, however primitive apes' use of symbols may be, researchers may still learn a great deal about certain kinds of cognitive processes. If research does convincingly show that apes have some kind of language capability, there is still much to be learned about ape cognition in several of the areas that Savage-Rumbaugh has suggested.

Such advances are possible only if ape-language researchers can develop research methods that are completely free from bias and inadvertent human conditioning of their ape subjects. While Savage-Rumbaugh and the other researchers have tried to minimize the possibility of conditioning on their subject animals, as Pinker suggests, the context of the training makes it difficult to exclude the possibility of conditioning.

Up to now none of the ape-language projects have been able to tell us much, if anything, about ape communication in natural settings because all of the projects were conducted in laboratory settings. Even though no languagelike communication has been identified among wild chimps or bonobos, there is still much to be learned about how these species communicate. Such studies, particularly if they can be linked to the ape-language experiments, may have a great deal to offer about primate cognition, and they may ultimately offer insights about the process of language acquisition in human children.

For a discussion of Washoe and other early ape-language projects, see R. Allen Gardner and Beatrice T. Gardner's essay "Communication With a Young Chimpanzee: Washoe's Vocabulary," in Rémy Chauvin, ed., *Modèles Animaux du Comportement Humain* (Centre National de la Recherche Scientifique), Herbert S. Terrace's *Nim* (Knopf, 1979), and David Premack and Ann Premack's *The Mind of an Ape* (W. W. Norton, 1983). On Kanzi, see Savage-Rumbaugh and Roger Lewin's *Kanzi: The Ape at the Brink of the Human Mind* (Wiley, 1994). On child language acquisition, see Pinker's *Language Learnability and Language Development* (Harvard University Press, 1984). For Skinner's original behavorist model of language learning, see his *Verbal Behavior* (Appleton-Century-Crofts, 1957) and Chomsky's critique *Syntactic Structures* (Mouton, 1957). Students may also enjoy Pinker's most recent analysis of what defines language in *Words and Rules: The Ingredients of Language* (Basic Books, 1999). For recent views about the state of ape-language experiments, see Savage-Rumbaugh, Stuart G. Shaker, and Talbot J. Taylor's *Apes, Language, and the Human Mind* (Oxford University Press, 1998), Barbara J. King, ed., *The Origins of Language: What Nonhuman Primates Can Tell Us* (SAR Press, 1999), and Barbara J. King's *The Information Continuum: Evolution of Social Information Transfer in Monkeys, Apes, and Hominids* (SAR Press, 1994).

ISSUE 7

Should Anthropologists and Linguists Be Concerned About Losing Endangered Languages?

YES: Ken Hale, from "Endangered Languages," *Language* (March 1992)

NO: Peter Ladefoged, from "Another View of Endangered Languages," *Language* (December 1992)

ISSUE SUMMARY

YES: Linguist Ken Hale contends that the loss of endangered languages represents a major tragedy for humanity, because each language that goes extinct reduces the world's linguistic diversity. The pace of extinctions has increased over the past century, mostly because government policies routinely encourage language loss. While linguists have a responsibility for recording and documenting endangered languages, they also have a role to play in influencing government policies that can encourage retention of these minority languages.

NO: Linguist Peter Ladefoged accepts the fact that endangered languages are disappearing, but feels that the position taken by Ken Hale and his colleagues is unacceptably paternalistic. He contends that while it is a good thing to study linguistic diversity, the people who speak endangered languages have just as much right to participate in their nation's affairs as anyone else, even if it means their children will learn the metropolitan language, not the endangered language.

$\mathbf{A}$pproximately 6,000 languages are spoken around the world. Some—such as English, French, German, Spanish, Russian, Hindi, Mandarin, Indonesian, and Tagalog—are spoken by millions of people, but about half of the world's languages are spoken by very small numbers of people in remote places with difficult environments. Many of these languages have fewer than 100 speakers.

Linguist Michael Krauss has estimated that 3,000 languages will become extinct by the end of the twenty-first century. Linguists and linguistic anthropologists have come to refer to these as "endangered languages," comparing them to natural species that are at the brink of extinction.

Languages can become extinct in a number of ways. Whole communities of Native Americans perished from introduced diseases for which they had no resistance, and their languages disappeared with them. In many more cases, Native children were sent to boarding schools where speaking their native language was forbidden and its use punished. Later, these young people were no longer fluent in their native language and did not teach it to their children. After a generation or so, these languages have come close to extinction.

Today, most communities around the world where endangered languages are spoken are not themselves dying out. They may even have large numbers of young people, but rather than use their parents' mother tongue, which feels backward and unsophisticated, they prefer to use the national language or some other important language used in commerce, in schools, or in films and music. In some cases, young people use a neighboring language that seems exciting and sophisticated. In such cases, it is not so much that the societies are dying out, but the young people are attracted to languages that have a higher status politically, economically, or socially.

Linguists like Ken Hale and Peter Ladefoged have spent more than 30 years studying obscure languages in remote corners of the world. In this issue, they acknowledge that the loss of another language means that linguists in the future will have less linguistic diversity to study. Where they differ from one another is whether linguists have any right to interfere with the linguistic preferences of the youth in these communities.

Hale argues that when people lose their language, they lose part of their cultural heritage. He thinks that linguists and anthropologists should encourage the revival of endangered languages. The youth are often attracted to the language and culture expressed in the dominant community's popular culture. For him, scholars should confront government policies that encourage young people in rural and undeveloped areas to abandon their native languages.

Ladefoged acknowledges that people lose some of their cultural heritage when they lose their language, but he argues that the attitudes of the speakers of endangered languages usually vary. He feels that scholars who are trying to convince them to continue to teach their children and actively use their language in daily life may be working against the interests of the people. In many cases, tribal people are excluded from the mainstream society because they use a different language. How can it be right to urge them not to participate in the mainstream society, with its jobs and consumer goods?

In these selections, consider who has the responsibility for maintaining these endangered languages. Does any researcher have the right to tell people what language to speak? Do indigenous people have a duty to preserve their languages? Does language really play a key role in cultural identity, as many anthropologists have argued?

YES ↩

Ken Hale

Endangered Languages

On Endangered Languages and the Safeguarding of Diversity

Like most people who have done linguistic field work for thirty years or so, I have worked on languages which are now extinct, eight of them in my case, and I have studied, and continue to study, many languages which are seriously imperiled. My experience is far from unusual, and the testimony of field workers alone would amply illustrate the extent of language loss in the world of the present era.

It is reasonable, I suppose, to ask what difference it makes. On the one hand, one might say, language loss has been a reality throughout history; and on the other, the loss of a language is of no great moment either for science or for human intellectual life.

I think, personally, that these ideas are wrong and that language loss is a serious matter. Or, more accurately, it is part of a process which is itself very serious.

From what I have been able to learn, . . . language loss in the modern period is of a different character, in its extent and in its implications [from the past]. It is part of a much larger process of LOSS OF CULTURAL AND INTELLECTUAL DIVERSITY in which politically dominant languages and cultures simply overwhelm indigenous local languages and cultures, placing them in a condition which can only be described as embattled. The process is not unrelated to the simultaneous loss of diversity in the zoological and botanical worlds. An ecological analogy is not altogether inappropriate. We understand to some extent the dangers inherent in the loss of biological diversity on this earth. It is correct to ask, I think, whether there are also dangers inherent in the loss of linguistic diversity.

This and other aspects of language endangerment in these times are addressed [here].

We have not attempted here to be truly representative either geographically or topically. Instead, we attempt to represent as forcefully as we can TWO facets of the situation of language endangerment—namely, (1) the reality of language loss and decline as a condition of the modern world and (2) the response to language imperilment on the part of various entities, e.g., above all,

From *Language*, vol. 68, no. 1, March 1992, pp. excerpts from 1–3, 35–38, 40–41. Copyright © 1992 by Linguistic Society of America. Reprinted by permission.

the communities directly affected by language loss. Our examples come from North and Central America.

MICHAEL KRAUSS was given the daunting task of preparing the first essay, a report on the realities of language loss for the world as a whole. This is our sole attempt to present a global perspective on the matter. Although, as Krauss notes, it is impossible now to be completely accurate in assessing the language situation in the world, it is clear that language extinction has reached an extraordinary level in recent times and that the outlook for an impressive percentage of the world's surviving languages is very poor.

These indications are certainly not heartening. But it is important, we feel, to counterpoise these realities with another, more encouraging reality—that of the great energy, courage, good sense, and optimism which many endangered language communities and allied support organizations are bringing to the formidable challenge of ensuring in this era a position of strength and dignity for their linguistic and cultural wealth. . . .

A local response to perceived language endangerment is exemplified . . . in the essay by LUCILLE WATAHOMIGIE and AKIRA YAMAMOTO, which describes the Hualapai Bilingual/Bicultural Education Program, of Peach Springs, Arizona, recognized as one of the very best in the country. The essay goes on to describe the manner in which this local community program played a central role in the development of regional and national movements affecting Native American languages and their speakers—specifically, the creation of the American Indian Languages Development Institute and the formulation and passage of the Native American Languages Act.

It happens occasionally that a responsible government, responding to the legitimate demands of its indigenous and ethnic populations, accepts as a proper part of its program the establishment of instruments and institutions designed to promote the development and use of the local languages under its authority. . . .

[Finally], I present an example of the kind of material that we can expect to lose with the loss of a language. I have chosen an example involving language and the expression of intellectual life, to emphasize the fact that the loss of a language is part of the more general loss being suffered by the world, the loss of diversity in all things.

⚜

Language Endangerment and the Human Value of Linguistic Diversity

Linguists typically celebrate the tension that plays between two realities of human linguistic knowledge, universality and diversity. But linguistic diversity is not something whose future can be taken for granted. Many local languages and cultures find themselves in great peril in this era, a fact well documented elsewhere in this collection.

In the following paragraphs I will be concerned with the idea that linguistic diversity is important to human intellectual life—not only in the context of scientific linguistic inquiry, but also in relation to the class of human activities belonging to the realms of culture and art.

From the perspective of linguistic science, arguments for safeguarding the world's linguistic diversity require no special discussion in this journal. Suppose English were the only language available as a basis for the study of general human grammatical competence. We know enough about the latter to be able to say now that we could learn a great deal about it from English alone. But we also know enough about linguistic diversity to know that we would miss an enormous amount.

If English were the only language, we could learn a lot about the fundamental principles of grammar, but we could only guess at the nature of that which can vary, except to the extent that this is evident from the varieties of English itself. And this would amount to missing an important point of human linguistic competence. By itself, English would supply a mere hint of the complexity of the system of principles and parameters. . . .

The notion that the world's linguistic diversity is a precious resource does not derive solely from linguistic science, of course. Language is much more than grammar. The term 'language' embraces a wide range of human competences and capacities, and it is not clear that it makes sense to think of it as a single entity.

Of supreme significance in relation to linguistic diversity, and to local languages in particular, is the simple truth that language—in the general, multifaceted sense—embodies the intellectual wealth of the people who use it. A language and the intellectual productions of its speakers are often inseparable, in fact. Some forms of verbal art—verse, song, or chant—depend crucially on morphological and phonological, even syntactic, properties of the language in which it is formed. In such cases the art could not exist without the language, quite literally. Even where the dependency is not so organic as this, an intellectual tradition may be so thoroughly a part of a people's linguistic ethnography as to be, in effect, inseparable from the language.

In this circumstance, there is a certain tragedy for the human purpose. The loss of local languages, and of the cultural systems that they express, has meant irretrievable loss of diverse and interesting intellectual wealth, the priceless products of human mental industry. The process of language loss is ongoing. Many linguistic field workers have had, and will continue to have, the experience of bearing witness to the loss, for all time, of a language and of the cultural products which the language served to express for the intellectual nourishment of its speakers.

In the remainder of this essay, I would like to describe one such product of a people's intellectual work. This is a tradition whose decline and virtual disappearance I witnessed in the course of field work in Australia. It was the treasure of a small group of Australian Aboriginal people, the Lardil, living on Mornington Island in North Queensland.

While working on the syntax and lexicon of Lardil in 1960, I heard of the existence of an auxiliary language, called Damin, which some initiated men in the community could still use. Most men could not, since the mission administrating Mornington Island during the early decades of this century had forbidden the practice of initiation many years earlier, and it was in the context of initiation that Damin was learned. Only men initiated before the mission was established had had the opportunity to learn Damin, and only a few of those men were still living in 1960.

I was not able to work on Damin until 1967. An anthropologist working with the Lardil people sent me a tape of Damin while I was working in another community farther south. When I heard the tape, I knew that Damin was something very special, so I arranged to visit Mornington Island again. The feature of Damin that first caught my attention was its phonology. It departs drastically from the phonology of Lardil, and it has sounds in it which do not exist in any other Australian language. For example, it has click consonants, otherwise found only in Africa—in the Khoisan languages, for example, and in the Nguni languages of the Bantu family, languages with no historical connection to Lardil. The use of clicks in Damin developed locally. Damin has the appearance of an invented language, and it is attributed, in fact, to a legendary figure named Kalthad (Yellow Trevally). If it was invented, then it is a clever invention, indeed, because it is almost unheard of for an invented language to depart radically from the phonological constraints of the ordinary language of the inventor. The impression that Damin is an invention is strengthened by the fact that it not only has sounds absent elsewhere in Australia, but it also has sounds found nowhere else in the world—as true phonological segments, that is. These include an ingressive voiceless lateral and a labia-velar lingual ejective.

Although its sound system is spectacular, the extraordinary genius of Damin is to be found in its lexicon. In its original purpose, Damin was an 'auxiliary language', in the sense that it was used in place of Lardil when this was necessary for ritual reasons. An idea of its nature can be gained from a consideration of how it was learned and used. According to the accounts of surviving Demiinkurlda, or 'Damin-possessors', as they were called, Damin was learned by novices in the advanced phase of men's initiation. Men who went through this stage were called Warama, and in theory only Warama learned Damin. In practice, however, since it was used in public, many people who were not Warama, both men and women, had passive knowledge of it. Its purpose, apart from the intellectual pleasure it gave, was to serve as a vehicle of communication between Warama and all individuals involved in their initiation. The use of ordinary Lardil with these people was forbidden, until they had been repaid the ritual debt owed to them by the Warama as a result of initiation. Damin is a lexicon, not an entire language. The rule in using Damin correctly is this: each lexical item of Lardil must be replaced by a Damin item, the inflectional morphology and syntax of Lardil remains intact. . . .

While inflectional and derivational morphology is the same for Lardil and Damin, the lexicon is totally different. Thus, each noun, verb, or pronoun in the Lardil of 1 matches a distinct item in Damin. It is the nature of this replacement lexicon which is extraordinary. It is constructed in such a way that, in principle, it can be learned in one day. In practice, it is said, learning

Daniin took place over a longer period, though one could, in fact, learn it in a day. The lexicon can be learned in one day, yet, in combination with Lardil syntax and morphology, it can be used to express virtually any idea. How can a lexicon be SMALL enough to learn in one day and, at the same time, be RICH enough to express all ideas? A moment's reflection on this question can only inspire admiration, in my judgment.

The answer, of course, is abstractness. The Damin lexicon cannot be rich in the usual sense of having large numbers of lexical items denoting concepts of great specificity (like the ordinary Lardil or English vocabulary, for example). Rather, the richness of Damin is of a different sort, the opposite of this in fact. Damin lexical items are abstract names for logically cohesive families of concepts. The richness of Damin resides in the semantic breadth of its lexical items, permitting a small inventory (less than 200 items) to accommodate the same range of concepts as does the much larger ordinary vocabulary (of unknown size). . . .

The Damin lexicon must achieve a balance between abstraction and expressive power, since it must satisfy two essentially contradictory requirements. It must be such that it can be learned quickly and, at the same time, it must be such that it can be used, in cooperation with Lardil inflectional morphology and syntax, to express any idea which Lardil itself can be used to express. It cannot be TOO abstract, therefore.

The Damin kinship terminology exemplifies this point well. The system has five terms. . . . This amounts to a massive reduction from the Lardil kinship terminology, which, like most Australian systems, is very large. There is a mystery in the reduction, though, since the logic of the classificatory kinship system would lead one to expect an even number, say four. But while this would be appropriately abstract, it would require merger of one of the most important kinship distinctions in Lardil society, that between second-cross cousins . . . the class that includes the preferred marriage partners, and first-cross cousins . . ., the class of alternant marriage partners. The Damin terminology strikes the optimal balance between abstraction and expressive power.

It is clear from what little we know of Damin that it involves a sophisticated semantic analysis of the lexical resources of Lardil. The system of abstractions lays bare aspects of lexical semantic structure to a degree which, quite possibly, is not achieved by any other system of analysis that attempts to accommodate an ENTIRE vocabulary.

The last fluent user of Damin passed away several years ago. The destruction of this intellectual treasure was carried out, for the most part, by people who were not aware of its existence, coming as they did from a culture in which wealth is physical and visible. Damin was not visible for them, and as far as they were concerned, the Lardil people had no wealth, apart from their land.

We cannot say that the Damin tradition is utterly lost to the Lardil people. However, it is all but gone, since revival of [it] would be from recorded sources; and if revival were to be attempted, a NEW Damin tradition would be initiated, necessarily, since the cultural context of the original tradition is irrecoverable—there are no survivors of that period. The development of a new

Damin tradition is not a bad thing, of course; in fact it would be an exciting thing. But the old Damin tradition is effectively lost. And the destruction of this tradition must be ranked as a disaster, comparable to the destruction of any human treasure.

It is perhaps of little use simply to bemoan the loss of a treasure. The example of Damin is offered as an instance of the nature of things that have been lost and of what can be lost if linguistic and cultural diversity disappears. On the other hand, the safeguarding of linguistic and cultural diversity does not guarantee the perpetuation of existing traditions of intellectual endeavor, of course. In fact, a living tradition implies change. And it is precisely the development of new traditions which is most consonant with the human purpose. And it is precisely where local languages are viable that new traditions develop. Thus, for example, in the Southwest of the United States, beside the continuing traditions of sung verse, a new tradition of poetry is developing, in Papago, Pima, Yaqui, Navajo, and Hualapai, for example, in the context of the growing use of the written form of these languages (encouraged by such institutions as AILDI, described elsewhere in this collection).

If the foregoing discussion is at all reasonable, then certain things follow. While it is good and commendable to record and document fading traditions, and in some cases this is absolutely necessary to avert total loss of cultural wealth, the greater goal must be that of safeguarding diversity in the world of people. For that is the circumstance in which diverse and interesting intellectual traditions can grow. Consider again the case of Damin. We have a small record of that auxiliary language, enough to appreciate its worth. But we have no idea what it would have become, how it would have changed, or, most important, what kind of role it might have played in Lardil intellectual life in this or the next decade. It might have disappeared, of course. That would have been their business. But it might have led to something even greater. We will never know, since the necessary condition has not existed—namely, an environment safe for cultural diversity which would have permitted the Lardil people to learn and use Damin into the next century.

Peter Ladefoged

Another View of Endangered Languages

Language seldom publishes opinion pieces, such as that of Hale, Krauss, Watahomigie, Yamamoto, Craig, Jeanne, & England 1992 on endangered languages. I have nothing but praise for the work that these linguists do. But language preservation and maintenance is a multifaceted topic on which different opinions are possible. The views expressed in these papers are contrary to those held by many responsible linguists, and would not be appropriate in some of the African countries in which I have worked in the last few years. Tanzania, for example, is a country which is striving for unity, and the spreading of Swahili is regarded as a major force in this endeavor. Tribalism is seen as a threat to the development of the nation, and it would not be acting responsibly to do anything which might seem, at least superficially, to aid in its preservation.

Hale et al. (1992) write from the perspective of linguists who have worked in particular cultures; but the attitudes of the speakers of the languages that they describe are far from universal. As they indicate, in many communities the language is regarded as sacred—literally God-given. Linguists working in such communities should obviously respect the opinions of the speakers, and honor their wishes. The speakers are giving access to something that is sacred to them, and it should be treasured accordingly. But not everyone holds this view. The half a dozen speakers of Angami (Tibeto-Burman) with whom I worked earlier this year had a different attitude. They regarded it as an intellectually valid pursuit for me to take an interest in their language. Admittedly, they were all high school or college educated students who had a similar intellectual interest in my language. They might therefore be regarded as part of an elite, with views that were only those of the elite. But I do not think this is so. The profane, as opposed to sacred, view of language is widely shared, even among those who are certainly not part of the socio-economically elite. Many of the people with whom I have worked in undeveloped parts of India and Africa regard being a language consultant as just another job, and a reasonably high status one at that. They have no problem with satisfying my intellectual curiosity. They in no way regard their work as prostituting something that is holy. Instead they are pleased with the honored status of being teachers. Furthermore, it pays better than alternative occupations, such as picking tea or digging yams, and it is much less hard work.

Even among those for whom language is a vital part of the sacred way of life, the attitude towards linguists is not always that outlined in Hale et al. 1992. The Toda, speakers of a Dravidian language in the Nilgiri Hills of Southern India, have a series of songs which are an important part of their religious life. They eagerly welcome linguists who wish to assist them in recording their language. They also realize that with less than 1,000 speakers they are unlikely to remain a distinct entity. Many of the younger people want to honor their ancestors, but also to be part of a modern India. They have accepted that, in their view, the cost of doing this is giving up the use of their language in their daily life. Surely, this is a view to which they are entitled, and it would not be the action of a responsible linguist to persuade them to do otherwise. In the circumstances of my fieldwork it would also have been somewhat hypocritical. I was working with an Indian colleague who has decided to forego the use of his and his wife's native language in their own home, so that their child could be brought up as a native language speaker of English. This choice, and any choices that the Toda might make, are clearly their prerogatives.

So now let me challenge directly the assumption of these papers that different languages, and even different cultures, always ought to be preserved. It is paternalistic of linguists to assume that they know what is best for the community. One can be a responsible linguist and yet regard the loss of a particular language, or even a whole group of languages, as far from a 'catastrophic destruction' (Hale et al. 1992:7). Statements such as 'just as the extinction of any animal species diminishes our world, so does the extinction of any language' (Hale et al. 1992:8) are appeals to our emotions, not to our reason. The case for studying endangered languages is very strong on linguistic grounds. It is often enormously strong on humanitarian grounds as well. But it would be self-serving of linguists to pretend that this is always the case. We must be wary of arguments based on political considerations. Of course I am no more in favor of genocide or repression of minorities than I am of people dying of tuberculosis or starving through ignorance. We should always be sensitive to the concerns of the people whose language we are studying. But we should not assume that we know what is best for them.

We may also note that human societies are not like animal species. The world is remarkably resilient in the preservation of diversity; different cultures are always dying while new ones arise. They may not be based on ethnicity or language, but the differences remain. Societies will always produce subgroups as varied as computer nerds, valley girls, and drug pushers, who think and behave in different ways. In the popular view the world is becoming more homogeneous, but that may be because we are not seeing the new differences that are arising. Consider two groups of Bushmen, the Zhu|oãsi and the !Xóõ, who speak mutually unintelligible languages belonging to different subgroups of the Khoisan family, but otherwise behave in very similar ways. Are these two groups more culturally diverse than Appalachian coal-miners, Iowa farmers, and Beverly Hills lawyers? As a linguist, I am of course saddened by the vast amount of linguistic and cultural knowledge that is disappearing, and I am delighted that the National Science Foundation has sponsored our UCLA research, in which we try to record for posterity the phonetic structures of some of the languages that will not be around much longer. But it is not for me to assess the virtues of programs for language preservation versus those of competitive programs for tuberculosis eradication, which may also need government funds.

In this changing world, the task of the linguist is to layout the facts concerning a given linguistic situation. The approach that I would advocate is exemplified in our study of language use and teaching in Uganda. With the full coöperation of the then (more or less) duly elected government (this was immediately before the time of Idi Amin), we assembled data on the linguistic situation. We tried to determine the linguistic similarities and mutual intelligibility of some of the major languages spoken in Uganda (about 16 Bantu, 5 Western Nilotic, 4 Eastern Nilotic, 2 Central Sudanic, and 4 non-Ugandan). We found that about 39% of the people could hold a conversation in Luganda (the largest single language), 35% in Swahili, and 21% in English. We noted that Radio Uganda put out programs in 16 Ugandan languages (some of them mutually intelligible), plus Swahili and English, and that there were literacy campaigns in 20 languages. Six Ugandan languages were used in schools. We summarized all our data so that the government could assess the linguistic situation. We did not try to determine the costs of making changes or of maintaining the *status quo*, in either monetary or human terms. It would have been presumptuous of us to weigh the loss of a language against the burdens facing Uganda. We tried to behave like responsible linguists with professional detachment.

Last summer I was working on Dahalo, a rapidly dying Cushitic language, spoken by a few hundred people in a rural district of Kenya. I asked one of our consultants whether his teen-aged sons spoke Dahalo. 'No,' he said. 'They can still hear it, but they cannot speak it. They speak only Swahili.' He was smiling when he said it, and did not seem to regret it. He was proud that his sons had been to school, and knew things that he did not. Who am I to say that he was wrong?

Reference

Hale, Ken; Michael Krauss; Lucille J. Watahomigie; Akira Y. Yamamoto; Colette Craig; Laverne Masayesva Jeanne; and Nora C. England. 1992. Endangered languages. Lg. 68.1–42.

POSTSCRIPT

Should Anthropologists and Linguists Be Concerned About Losing Endangered Languages?

Both of these linguists have spent their careers studying obscure languages, many of which have few surviving speakers and which are considered endangered languages. Neither wants to encourage any of these languages to go extinct, yet they take very different approaches to the question of whether linguists and linguistic anthropologists should be concerned about languages dying out.

Ken Hale argues that the extinction of languages is very similar to the loss of natural species of animals, because it robs humanity of part of its natural diversity. Each language offers us a better sense about what is linguistically possible for human beings. Hale argues that in recent decades language loss is largely due to government policies that make it desirable for indigenous people to abandon their languages in favor of important national or regional ones. The key measure of language endangerment is the number of children who speak the vernacular language, because if children do not speak the language it is unlikely that the language will be passed on to their descendants. For these younger people, popular culture has a compelling attraction. There can be little doubt that popular culture attracts adolescents to view the national or regional language associated with music, videos, films, and the like as exciting, while their parent's vernacular seems old fashioned out of step with modern times.

Peter Ladefoged agrees with Hale about the general attractiveness of modern life, employment, and popular culture. He acknowledges that it may be sad for linguists to see the object of their studies disappear as children and adolescents learn national or regional languages rather than their traditional vernacular. But he contends that no matter how unpleasant it may be for linguists, scholars have an obligation to recognize that people in most communities around the world want jobs, consumer goods, and participation in modern national life. It is paternalistic for researchers to attempt to decide for their subjects and informants whether they can participate in modern life.

Over the last decade or so, studying what communities that speak endangered languages are doing has become a topic of great interest for social researchers. Nancy Dorian's book *Language Death* (University of Pennsylvania Press, 1980) was one of the earliest; her paper "A Response to Ladefoged's Other View of Endangered Languages" (*Language* 69(3):575–579,

1993) supports Hale's point of view. Other informative texts would include Robert H. Robins and Eugenius M. Uhlenbeck's edited collection *Endangered Language* (Berg, 1991) and Lenore A. Grenoble and Lindsay J. Whaley's edited volume *Endangered Languages: Language Loss and Community Response* (Cambridge University Press, 1998).

Internet References . . .

Cultural Materialism

The Cultural Materialism Web site, created by Dr. M. D. Murphy of the University of Alabama, features an explanation of cultural materialism, a summary of the history of cultural materialism, and a list of pertinent scholars. This site also gives links to other relevant Web sites.

```
http://www.as.ua.edu/ant/Faculty/murphy/
              cultmat.htm
```

Margaret Mead's Anthropological Work

This site, created by the American Museum of Natural History, explores Margaret Mead's life and provides a history of her anthropological work. It also includes links to articles that discuss Mead's influence on anthropology.

```
http://www.amnh.org/exhibitions/expeditions/
treasure_fossil/Treasures/Margaret_Mead/mead.html
```

The following site has Margaret Mead's biography with lots of details.

```
http://www.interculturalstudies.org/IIS/Mead/
               index.html
```

This site considers Margaret Mead's centennial and its significance.

```
http://www.interculturalstudies.org/IIS/Mead/
            2001centennial.html
```

The !Kung of the Kalahari Desert

The !Kung of the Kalahari Desert Web site contains general information about this group of people who are now called the Ju/'hoansi by most scholars.

```
http://www.ucc.uconn.edu/~epsadm03/Kung.html
```

Collisions of Religions and Violence: Redux

Collisions of Religions and Violence: Redux is a Web site that contains a special issue of the journal *Cross Currents* and deals specifically with the question of whether or not conflict and violence emerge from immutable religious and ethnic differences.

```
http://www.crosscurrents.org/violencespecial.htm
```

Cultural Anthropology

*C*ultural *anthropologists study the culture and society of living communities. Like other anthropologists, cultural anthropologists are concerned with developing and testing models about the human condition and the range of human possibilities, such as whether gender inequality or violence are inevitable in human societies. Some anthropologists have asked whether the lives of small hunting-gathering bands resemble the lifeways of early human groups with similar technologies. Other anthropologists have asked about the strength of other people's religious beliefs. But at the heart of anthropological debate today is whether anthropology should model itself on the natural sciences or whether anthropologists should see their role more as interpreters of human cultures.*

- Should Cultural Anthropology Stop Trying to Model Itself on Sciences?
- Was Margaret Mead's Fieldwork on Samoan Adolescents Fundamentally Flawed?
- Do Native Peoples Today Invent Their Traditions?
- Do Men Dominate Women in All Societies?
- Is Gay Marriage Natural?
- Does the Natural-Supernatural Distinction Exist in All Cultures?
- Are San Hunter-Gatherers Basically Pastoralists Who Have Lost Their Herds?
- Do Some Illnesses Exist Only Among Members of a Particular Culture?
- Is Ethnic Conflict Inevitable?

ISSUE 8

Should Cultural Anthropology Stop Trying to Model Itself on Sciences?

YES: Clifford Geertz, from *The Interpretation of Cultures: Selected Essays* (Basic Books, 1973)

NO: Robert L. Carneiro, from "Godzilla Meets New Age Anthropology: Facing the Postmodernist Challenge to a Science of Culture," *EUROPÉA* (1995)

ISSUE SUMMARY

YES: Cultural anthropologist Clifford Geertz views anthropology as a science of interpretation, and he argues that anthropology should never model itself on the natural sciences. He believes that anthropology's goal should be to generate deeper interpretations of cultural phenomena, using what he calls "thick description," rather than attempting to prove or disprove scientific laws.

NO: Cultural anthropologist Robert Carneiro argues that anthropology has always been and should continue to be a science that attempts to explain sociocultural phenomena in terms of causes and effects rather than merely interpret them. He criticizes Geertz's cultural interpretations as arbitrary and immune to disconfirmation.

For more than a century, anthropologists have viewed their discipline as a science of humankind or of culture. But anthropologists disagree about what being a science should mean. At issue is the question: Just what kind of science is anthropology?

Nineteenth- and early-twentieth-century anthropologists generally viewed anthropology as one of the natural sciences, and most early theorists—such as Edward Tylor, James Fraser, and Lewis Henry Morgan—saw anthropology as an extension of biology. Like biology, anthropology is a comparative discipline. Early anthropologists were also attracted to the theory of natural selection of naturalist Charles Darwin. But for anthropologists, evolution meant explaining how one social form or type of society developed into another.

In the 1920s, most anthropologists abandoned evolutionary models as speculative and racist (white Europeans were always pictured as occupying the most "advanced" stage of cultural evolution). After the Second World War, Leslie White proposed a unilineal evolutionary model, arguing that cultural evolution could be explained in terms of how much energy people could capture with their technology. Julian Steward proposed a multilinear model, suggesting that cultures could be explained as adaptations to particular environments (now the theory of cultural ecology, a model popular among many prehistoric archaeologists). In the 1960s, Marvin Harris combined cultural ecology and neo-Marxian ideas into a new paradigm he called "cultural materialism." Harris and Carneiro believe that anthropology's goal should be to explain the existence and characteristics of cultural features by means of verifiable laws, like those used in other scientific fields.

In the 1920s, some anthropologists became more interested in what people thought than in what they did. Their definitions of culture emphasized shared beliefs and feelings more than behaviors (see Issue 3). This trend developed with the modern method of ethnographic fieldwork, which requires researchers to immerse themselves for a year or more in another society to learn the local language and engage in "participant observation." In the words of Bronislaw Malinowski, one objective of fieldwork is to grasp the "native's point of view." Geertz's "interpretive anthropology" grew out of this interest in cultural differences in thought worlds.

Geertz believes that it is futile to seek scientific laws to explain human behavior. Instead, he argues that anthropologists should produce interpretations of cultures in the form of "thick descriptions" that reveal the cultural meanings of what they have observed, heard, and experienced in the field. Thus, for Geertz, anthropology should be a science of interpretation rather than explanation.

Carneiro responds that anthropology should try to *explain* sociocultural phenomena, not merely interpret what people think about them, just as natural scientists seek to explain the phenomena they study. He argues that human thought and behavior are part of the external world and that they are subject to laws of cause and effect like other natural phenomena. He rejects Geertz's form of cultural interpretation as art rather than science. He saves his strongest criticism for the "postmodern" anthropologists, who take Geertz's interpretive anthropology to the next step, even of denying that a single objective reality exists.

These selections pose several questions that lie at the heart of all sociocultural anthropology. Should anthropologists try to explain the existence and characteristics of sociocultural phenomena, or should they merely seek to translate and make sense of other people's cultural beliefs and practices? Must we choose between these alternatives, or is anthropology broad enough to hold both of these perspectives and others as well? More specifically, to what extent is social action like a text? How can we know what interpretation of a practice is the correct one?

YES ⤹

Clifford Geertz

Thick Description: Toward an Interpretive Theory of Culture

I

[Here I argue] for a narrowed, specialized, and, so I imagine, theoretically more powerful concept of culture to replace E. B. Tylor's famous "most complex whole," which, its originative power not denied, seems to me to have reached the point where it obscures a good deal more than it reveals.

The conceptual morass into which the Tylorean kind of *pot-au-feu* theorizing about culture can lead, is evident in what is still one of the better general introductions to anthropology, Clyde Kluckhohn's *Mirror for Man*. In some twenty-seven pages of his chapter on the concept, Kluckhohn managed to define culture in turn as: (1) "the total way of life of a people"; (2) "the social legacy the individual acquires from his group"; (3) "a way of thinking, feeling, and believing"; (4) "an abstraction from behavior"; (5) a theory on the part of the anthropologist about the way in which a group of people in fact behave; (6) a "storehouse of pooled learning"; (7) "a set of standardized orientations to recurrent problems"; (8) "learned behavior"; (9) a mechanism for the normative regulation of behavior; (10) "a set of techniques for adjusting both to the external environment and to other men"; (11) "a precipitate of history"; and turning, perhaps in desperation, to similes, as a map, as a sieve, and as a matrix. In the face of this sort of theoretical diffusion, even a somewhat constricted and not entirely standard concept of culture, which is at least internally coherent and, more important, which has a definable argument to make is (as, to be fair, Kluckhohn himself keenly realized) an improvement. Eclecticism is self-defeating not because there is only one direction in which it is useful to move, but because there are so many: it is necessary to choose.

The concept of culture I espouse . . . is essentially a semiotic one. Believing, with [German sociologist and political economist] Max Weber, that man is an animal suspended in webs of significance he himself has spun, I take culture to be those webs, and the analysis of it to be therefore not an experimental science in search of law but an interpretive one in search of meaning. It is explication I am after, construing social expressions on their surface enigmatical. But this pronouncement, a doctrine in a clause, demands itself some explication.

II

. . . [I]f you want to understand what a science is, you should look in the first instance not at its theories or its findings, and certainly not at what its apologists say about it; you should look at what the practitioners of it do.

In anthropology, or anyway social anthropology, what the practitioners do is ethnography [the study of human cultures]. And it is in understanding what ethnography is, or more exactly *what doing ethnography is,* that a start can be made toward grasping what anthropological analysis amounts to as a form of knowledge. This, it must immediately be said, is not a matter of methods. From one point of view, that of the textbook, doing ethnography is establishing rapport, selecting informants, transcribing texts, taking genealogies, mapping fields, keeping a diary, and so on. But it is not these things, techniques and received procedures, that define the enterprise. What defines it is the kind of intellectual effort it is: an elaborate venture in, to borrow a notion from [British philosopher] Gilbert Ryle, "thick description."

Ryle's discussion of "thick description" appears in two recent essays of his (now reprinted in the second volume of his *Collected Papers*) addressed to the general question of what, as he puts it, *"Le Penseur"* is doing: "Thinking and Reflecting" and "The Thinking of Thoughts." Consider, he says, two boys rapidly contracting the eyelids of their right eyes. In one, this is an involuntary twitch; in the other, a conspiratorial signal to a friend. The two movements are, as movements, identical; from an I-am-a-camera, "phenomentalistic" observation of them alone, one could not tell which was twitch and which was wink, or indeed whether both or either was twitch or wink. Yet the difference, however unphotographable, between a twitch or wink is vast; as anyone unfortunate enough to have had the first taken for the second knows. The winker is communicating, and indeed communicating in a quite precise and special way: (1) deliberately, (2) to someone in particular, (3) to impart a particular message, (4) according to a socially established code, and (5) without cognizance of the rest of the company. As Ryle points out, the winker has now done two things, contracted his eyelids and winked, while the twitcher has done only one, contracted his eyelids. Contracting your eyelids on purpose when there exists a public code in which so doing counts as a conspiratorial signal *is* winking. That's all there is to it: a speck of behavior, a fleck of culture, and—*voilà!*—a gesture.

That, however, is just the beginning. Suppose, he continues, there is a third boy, who, "to give malicious amusement to his cronies," parodies the first boy's wink, as amateurish, clumsy, obvious, and so on. He, of course, does this in the same way the second boy winked and the first twitched: by contracting his right eyelids. Only this boy is neither winking nor twitching, he is parodying someone else's, as he takes it, laughable, attempt at winking. Here, too, a socially established code exists (he will "wink" laboriously, overobviously, perhaps adding a grimace—the usual artifices of the clown); and so also does a message. Only now it is not conspiracy but ridicule that is in the air. If the others think he is actually winking, his whole project misfires as completely, though with somewhat different results, as if they think he is twitching. One can go further: uncertain of his mimicking abilities, the would-be satirist may practice at home before the mirror, in which case he is not twitching, winking, or parodying, but rehearsing; though so far as what a camera, a radical behaviorist, or a believer in protocol sentences would record he is just rapidly contracting his right eyelids like all the others. Complexities are possible, if not practically without end, at least logically so. The original winker might, for example, actually have been fake-winking, say, to mislead outsiders into imagining there was a conspiracy afoot when there in fact was not, in which case our descriptions of what the parodist is parodying and the rehearser rehearsing of course shift accordingly. But the point is that between what Ryle calls the "thin description" of what the rehearser (parodist, winker, twitcher . . .) is doing ("rapidly contracting his right eyelids") and the "thick description" of what he is doing ("practicing a burlesque of a friend faking a wink to deceive an innocent into thinking a conspiracy is in motion") lies the object of ethnography: a stratified hierarchy of meaningful structures in terms of which twitches, winks, fake-winks, parodies, rehearsals of parodies are produced, perceived, and interpreted, and without which they would not (not even the zero-form twitches, which, *as a cultural category,* are as much nonwinks as winks are nontwitches) in fact exist, no matter what anyone did or didn't do with his eyelids.

Like so many of the little stories Oxford philosophers like to make up for themselves, all this winking, fake-winking, burlesque-fake-winking, rehearsed-burlesque-fake-winking, may seem a bit artificial.

. . . In finished anthropological writings, . . . this fact—that what we call our data are really our own constructions of other people's constructions of what they and their compatriots are up to—is obscured because most of what we need to comprehend a particular event, ritual, custom, idea, or whatever is insinuated as background information before the thing itself is directly examined. . . . There is nothing particularly wrong with this, and it is in any case inevitable. But it does lead to a view of anthropological research as rather more of an observational and rather less of an interpretive activity than it really is. Right down at the factual base, the hard rock, insofar as there is any, of the whole enterprise, we are already explicating: and worse, explicating explications. Winks upon winks upon winks.

. . . The point for now is only that ethnography is thick description. What the ethnographer is in fact faced with—except when (as, of course, he must do) he is pursuing the more automatized routines of data collection—is a multiplicity of complex conceptual structures, many of them superimposed upon or knotted into one another, which are at once strange, irregular, and inexplicit, and which he must contrive somehow first to grasp and then to render. And this is true at the most down-to-earth, jungle field work levels of his activity: interviewing informants, observing rituals, eliciting kin terms, tracing property lines, censusing households . . . writing his journal. Doing ethnography is like trying to read (in the sense of "construct a reading of") a manuscript—foreign, faded, full of ellipses, incoherencies, suspicious emendations, and tendentious commentaries, but written not in conventionalized graphs of sound but in transient examples of shaped behavior.

III

Culture, this acted document, thus is public, like a burlesqued wink or a mock sheep raid. Though ideational, it does not exist in someone's head; though unphysical, it is not an occult entity. The interminable, because unterminable, debate within anthropology as to whether culture is "subjective" or "objective," together with the mutual exchange of intellectual insults ("idealist!"—"materialist!"; "mentalist!"—"behaviorist!"; "impressionist!"—"positivist!") which accompanies it, is wholly misconceived. Once human behavior is seen as (most of the time; there *are* true twitches) symbolic action—action which, like phonation in speech, pigment in painting, line in writing, or sonance in music, signifies—the question as to whether culture is patterned conduct or a frame of mind, or even the two somehow mixed together, loses sense. The thing to ask about a burlesqued wink or a mock sheep raid is not what their ontological status is. It is the same as that of rocks on the one hand and dreams on the other—they are things of this world. The thing to ask is what their import is: what it is, ridicule or challenge, irony or anger, snobbery or pride, that, in their occurrence and through their agency, is getting said.

This may seem like an obvious truth, but there are a number of ways to obscure it. One is to imagine that culture is a self-contained "super-organic" reality with forces and purposes of its own; that is, to reify it. Another is to claim that it consists in the brute pattern of behavioral events we observe in fact to occur in some identifiable community or other; that is, to reduce it. But though both these confusions still exist, and doubtless will be always with us, the main source of theoretical muddlement in contemporary anthropology is a view which developed in reaction to them and is right now very widely held—namely, that, to quote [anthropologist] Ward Goodenough, perhaps its leading proponent, "culture [is located] in the minds and hearts of men."

Variously called ethnoscience, componential analysis, or cognitive anthropology (a terminological wavering which reflects a deeper uncertainty), this school of thought holds that culture is composed of psychological structures by means of which individuals or groups of individuals guide their behavior. "A society's culture," to quote Goodenough again, this time in a passage which has become the *locus classicus* of the whole movement, "consists of whatever it is one has to know or believe in order to operate in a manner acceptable to its members." And from this view of what culture is follows a view, equally assured, of what describing it is—the writing out of systematic rules, an ethnographic algorithm, which, if followed, would make it possible so to operate, to pass (physical appearance aside) for a native. In such a way, extreme subjectivism is married to extreme formalism, with the expected result: an explosion of debate as to whether particular analyses (which come in the form of taxonomies, paradigms, tables, trees, and other ingenuities) reflect what the natives "really" think or are merely clever simulations, logically equivalent but substantively different, of what they think.

As, on first glance, this approach may look close enough to the one being developed here to be mistaken for it, it is useful to be explicit as to what divides them. If, leaving our winks and sheep behind for the moment, we take, say, a Beethoven quartet as an, admittedly rather special but, for these purposes, nicely illustrative, sample of culture, no one would, I think, identify it with its score, with the skills and knowledge needed to play it, with the understanding of it possessed by its performers or auditors, nor, to take care, *en passant,* of the reductionists and reifiers, with a particular performance of it or with some mysterious entity transcending material existence. The "no one" is perhaps too strong here, for there are always incorrigibles. But that a Beethoven quartet is a temporarily developed tonal structure, a coherent sequence of modeled sound—in a word, music—and not anybody's knowledge of or belief about anything, including how to play it, is a proposition to which most people are, upon reflection, likely to assent.

To play the violin it is necessary to possess certain habits, skills, knowledge, and talents, to be in the mood to play, and (as the old joke goes) to have a violin. But violin playing is neither the habits, skills, knowledge, and so on, nor the mood, nor (the notion believers in "material culture" apparently embrace) the violin. To make a trade pact in Morocco, you have to do certain things in certain ways (among others, cut, while chanting Quranic Arabic, the throat of a lamb before the assembled, undeformed, adult male members of your tribe) and to be possessed of certain psychological characteristics (among others, a desire for distant things). But a trade pact is neither the throat cutting nor the desire. . . .

Culture is public because meaning is. You can't wink (or burlesque one) without knowing what counts as winking or how, physically, to contract your eyelids, and you can't conduct a sheep raid (or mimic one) without knowing what it is to steal a sheep and how practically to go about it. But to draw from such truths the conclusion that knowing how to wink is winking and knowing how to steal a sheep is sheep raiding is to betray as deep a confusion as, taking thin descriptions for thick, to identify winking with eyelid contractions or sheep raiding with chasing woolly animals out of pastures. The cognitivist fallacy—that culture consists (to quote another spokesman for the movement, [anthropologist] Stephen Tyler) of "mental phenomena which can [he means "should"]—be analyzed by formal methods similar to those of mathematics and logic"—is as destructive of an effective use of the concept as are the behaviorist and idealist fallacies to which it is a misdrawn correction. Perhaps, as its errors are more sophisticated and its distortions subtler, it is even more so.

The generalized attack on privacy theories of meaning is, since early [Edmund] Husserl and late [Ludwig] Wittgenstein, so much a part of modern thought that it need not be developed once more here. What is necessary is to see to it that the news of it reaches anthropology; and in particular that it is made clear that to say that culture consists of socially established structures of meaning in terms of which people do such things as signal conspiracies and join them or perceive insults and answer them, is no more to say that it is a psychological phenomenon, a characteristic of someone's mind, personality, cognitive structure, or whatever, than to say that Tantrism, genetics, the progressive form of the verb, the classification of wines, the Common Law, or the notion of "a conditional curse" . . . is. What, in a place like Morocco, most prevents those of us who grew up winking other winks or attending other sheep from grasping what people are up to is not ignorance as to how cognition works . . . as a lack of familiarity with the imaginative universe within which their acts are signs. . . .

IV

. . . [T]he aim of anthropology is the enlargement of the universe of human discourse. That is not, of course, its only aim—instruction, amusement, practical counsel, moral advance, and the discovery of natural order in human behavior are others; nor is anthropology the only discipline which pursues it. But it is an aim to which a semiotic concept of culture is peculiarly well adapted. As interworked systems of construable signs (what, ignoring provincial usages, I would call symbols), culture is not a power, something to which social events, behaviors, institutions, or processes can be causally attributed; it is a context, something within which they can be intelligibly—that is, thickly—described. . . .

In short, anthropological writings are themselves interpretations, and second and third order ones to boot. (By definition, only a "native" makes first order ones: it's *his* culture.) They are, thus, fictions; fictions, in the sense that they are "something made," "something fashioned"—the original meaning of *fictiō*—not that they are false, unfactual, or merely "as if" thought experiments. . . .

V

Now, this proposition, that it is not in our interest to bleach human behavior of the very properties that interest us before we begin to examine it, has sometimes been escalated into a larger claim: namely, that as it is only those properties that interest us, we need not attend, save cursorily, to behavior at all. Culture is most effectively treated, the argument goes, purely as a symbolic system (the catch phrase is, "in its own terms"), by isolating its elements, specifying the internal relationships among those elements, and then characterizing the whole system in some general way—according to the core symbols around which it is organized, the underlying structures of which it is a surface expression, or the ideological principles upon which it is based. Though a distinct improvement over "learned behavior" and "mental phenomena" notions of what culture is, and the source of some of the most powerful theoretical ideas in contemporary anthropology, this hermetical approach to things seems to me to run the danger (and increasingly to have been overtaken by it) of locking cultural analysis away from its proper object, the informed logic of actual life. There is little profit in extricating a concept from the defects of psychologism only to plunge it immediately into those of schematicism.

Behavior must be attended to, and with some exactness, because it is through the flow of behavior—or, more precisely, social action—that cultural forms find articulation. They find it as well, of course, in various sorts of artifacts, and various states of consciousness; but these draw their meaning from the role they play (Wittgenstein would say their "use") in an ongoing pattern of life, not from any intrinsic relationships they bear to one another. . . .

A further implication of this is that coherence cannot be the major test of validity for a cultural description. Cultural systems must have a minimal degree of coherence, else we would not call them systems; and, by observation, they normally have a great deal more. But there is nothing so coherent as a paranoid's delusion or a swindler's story. The force of our interpretations cannot rest, as they are now so often made to do, on the tightness with which they hold together, or the assurance with which they are argued. Nothing has done more, I think, to discredit cultural analysis than the construction of impeccable depictions of formal order in whose actual existence nobody can quite believe.

If anthropological interpretation is constructing a reading of what happens, then to divorce it from what happens—from what, in this time or that place, specific people say, what they do, what is done to them, from the whole vast business of the world—is to divorce it from its applications and render it vacant. A good interpretation of anything—a poem, a person, a history, a ritual, an institution, a society—takes us into the heart of that of which it is the interpretation. When it does not do that, but leads us instead somewhere else—into an admiration of its own elegance, of its author's cleverness, or of the beauties of Euclidean order—it may have its intrinsic charms; but it is something else than what the task at hand—figuring out what all that rigamarole with the sheep is about—calls for. . . .

The ethnographer "inscribes" social discourse; *he writes it down*. In so doing, he turns it from a passing event, which exists only in its own moment of occurrence, into an account, which exists in its inscriptions and can be reconsulted. . . .

The situation is even more delicate, because, as already noted, what we inscribe (or try to) is not raw social discourse, to which, because, save very marginally or very specially, we are not actors, we do not have direct access, but only that small part of it which our informants can lead us into understanding. . . .

VI

So, there are three characteristics of ethnographic description: it is interpretive; what it is interpretive of is the flow of social discourse; and the interpreting involved consists in trying to rescue the "said" of such discourse from its perishing occasions and fix it in perusable terms. The *kula* is gone or altered; but, for better or worse, *The Argonauts of the Western Pacific* remains. But there is, in addition, a fourth characteristic of such description, at least as I practice it: it is microscopic.

This is not to say that there are no large-scale anthropological interpretations of whole societies, civilizations, world events, and so on. Indeed, it is such extension of our analyses to wider contexts that, along with their theoretical implications, recommends them to general attention and justifies our constructing them. . . .

It is merely to say that the anthropologist characteristically approaches such broader interpretations and more abstract analyses from the direction of exceedingly extended acquaintances with extremely small matters. He confronts the same grand realities that others—historians, economists, political scientists, sociologists—confront in more fateful settings: Power, Change, Faith, Oppression, Work, Passion, Authority, Beauty, Violence, Love, Prestige; but he confronts them in contexts obscure enough . . . to take the capital letters off them. These all-too-human constancies, "those big words that make us all afraid," take a homely form in such homely contexts. But that is exactly the advantage. There are enough profundities in the world already.

Yet, the problem of how to get from a collection of ethnographic miniatures— . . . an assortment of remarks and anecdotes—to wall-sized culturescapes of the nation, the epoch, the continent, or the civilization is not so easily passed over with vague allusions to the virtues of concreteness and the down-to-earth mind. For a science born in Indian tribes, Pacific islands, and African lineages and subsequently seized with grander ambitions, this has come to be a major methodological problem, and for the most part a badly handled one. The models that anthropologists have themselves worked out to justify their moving from local truths to general visions have been, in fact, as responsible for undermining the effort as anything their critics—sociologists obsessed with sample sizes, psychologists with measures, or economists with aggregates—have been able to devise against them.

Of these, the two main ones have been: the Jonesville-is-the-USA "microcosmic" model; and the Easter-Island-is-a-testing-case "natural experiment" model. Either heaven in a grain of sand, or the farther shores of possibility.

The Jonesville-is-America writ small (or America-is-Jonesville writ large) fallacy is so obviously one that the only thing that needs explanation is how people have managed to believe it and expected others to believe it. The notion that one can find the essence of national societies, civilizations, great religions, or whatever summed up and simplified in so-called "typical" small towns and villages is palpable nonsense. What one finds in small towns and villages is (alas) small-town or village life. If localized, microscopic studies were really dependent for their greater relevance upon such a premise—that they captured the great world in the little—they wouldn't have any relevance.

But, of course, they are not. The locus of study is not the object of study. Anthropologists don't study villages (tribes, towns, neighborhoods . . .); they study *in* villages. You can study different things in different places, and some things—for example, what colonial domination does to established frames of moral expectation—you can best study in confined localities. But that doesn't make the place what it is you are studying. . . .

The "natural laboratory" notion has been equally pernicious, not only because the analogy is false—what kind of a laboratory is it where *none* of the parameters are manipulable?—but because it leads to a notion that the data derived from ethnographic studies are purer, or more fundamental, or more solid, or less conditioned (the most favored word is "elementary") than those derived from other sorts of social inquiry. The great natural variation of cultural forms is, of course, not only anthropology's great (and wasting) resource, but the ground of its deepest theoretical dilemma: how is such variation to be squared with the biological unity of the human species? But it is not, even metaphorically, experimental variation, because the context in which it occurs varies along with it, and it is not possible (though there are those who try) to isolate the y's from x's to write a proper function. . . .

The methodological problem which the microscopic nature of ethnography presents is both real and critical. But it is not to be resolved by regarding a remote locality as the world in a teacup or as the sociological equivalent of a cloud chamber. It is to be resolved—or, anyway, decently kept at bay—by realizing that social actions are comments on more than themselves; that where an interpretation comes from does not determine where it can be impelled to go. Small facts speak to large issues, winks to epistemology, or sheep raids to revolution, because they are made to.

VII

There is an Indian story—at least I heard it as an Indian story—about an Englishman who, having been told that the world rested on a platform which rested on the back of an elephant which rested in turn on the back of a turtle, asked (perhaps he was an ethnographer; it is the way they behave), what did the turtle rest on? Another turtle. And that turtle? "Ah, Sahib, after that it is turtles all the way down."

. . . Cultural analysis is intrinsically incomplete. And, worse than that, the more deeply it goes the less complete it is. It is a strange science whose most telling assertions are its most tremulously based, in which to get somewhere with the matter at hand is to intensify the suspicion, both your own and that of others, that you are not quite getting it right. But that, along with plaguing subtle people with obtuse questions, is what being an ethnographer is like.

There are a number of ways to escape this—turning culture into folklore and collecting it, turning it into traits and counting it, turning it into institutions and classifying it, turning it into structures and toying with it. But they *are* escapes. The fact is that to commit oneself to a semiotic concept of culture and an interpretive approach to the study of it is to commit oneself to a view of ethnographic assertion as, to borrow W. B. Gallie's by now famous phrase, "essentially contestable." Anthropology, or at least interpretive anthropology, is a science whose progress is marked less by a perfection of consensus than by a refinement of debate. What gets better is the precision with which we vex each other. . . .

My own position in the midst of all this has been to try to resist subjectivism on the one hand and cabbalism on the other, to try to keep the analysis of symbolic forms as closely tied as I could to concrete social events and occasions, the public world of common life, and to organize it in such a way that the connections between theoretical formulations and descriptive interpretations were unobscured by appeals to dark sciences. I have never been impressed by the argument that, as complete objectivity is impossible in these matters (as, of course, it is), one might as well let one's sentiments run loose.

As [economist] Robert Solow has remarked, that is like saying that as a perfectly aseptic environment is impossible, one might as well conduct surgery in a sewer. Nor, on the other hand, have I been impressed with claims that structural linguistics, computer engineering, or some other advanced form of thought is going to enable us to understand men without knowing them. Nothing will discredit a semiotic approach to culture more quickly than allowing it to drift into a combination of intuitionism and alchemy, no matter how elegantly the intuitions are expressed or how modern the alchemy is made to look.

The danger that cultural analysis, in search of all-too-deep-lying turtles, will lose touch with the hard surfaces of life—with the political, economic, stratificatory realities within which men are everywhere contained—and with the biological and physical necessities on which those surfaces rest, is an ever-present one. The only defense against it, and against, thus, turning cultural analysis into a kind of sociological aestheticism, is to train such analysis on such realities and such necessities in the first place. It is thus that I have written about nationalism, about violence, about identity, about human nature, about legitimacy, about revolution, about ethnicity, about urbanization, about status, about death, about time, and most of all about particular attempts by particular peoples to place these things in some sort of comprehensible, meaningful frame.

To look at the symbolic dimensions of social action—art, religion, ideology, science, law, morality, common sense—is not to turn away from the existential dilemmas of life for some empyrean realm of de-emotionalized forms; it is to plunge into the midst of them. The essential vocation of interpretive anthropology is not to answer our deepest questions, but to make available to us answers that others . . . have given, and thus to include them in the consultable record of what man has said.

Robert L. Carneiro

NO

Godzilla Meets New Age Anthropology: Facing the Postmodernist Challenge to a Science of Culture

As we strive to understand nature, do we seek truth or solace?

Stephen Jay Gould

When I began working on the first incarnation of this paper, years ago, the greatest threat to a science of culture, it seemed to me, came from those anthropologists who considered themselves humanists. Today, though, the picture has changed radically. A much greater threat now comes from that large, amorphous host who march under the banner of postmodernism. Compared to the old-fashioned humanists, the threat they pose is as the Black Plague to the chicken pox. So it is against *them* that my major battle will be waged. By comparison, my engagement with traditional humanists will be but a preliminary skirmish.

Nonetheless, let me begin with the humanists, for, in their distaste for a science of culture, both humanists and postmodernists have much in common. If not genetically related, the two have at least sprouted from the same seedbed.

The antagonism between humanism and science is not only deep, but old. Almost two centuries ago the poet John Keats was provoked to cry "A Confusion on Newton!". Why? Because Newton had shown the rainbow to be caused by the refraction of light through raindrops, and *that*, for Keats, destroyed the wonder of it all. . . .

More recently, Joseph Wood Krutch has argued that "the experience of living is the thing which . . . has the greatest value, and . . . all the social sciences which tend to manipulate and regularize and unify human conduct result in a general lowering of the intensity of the experience . . . and . . . therefore, from my standpoint, they are bad."

Finally, E. E. Cummings expressed his contempt for science in this short verse:

> While you and I have lips and voices which,
> are for kissing and to sing with
> who cares if some oneeyed son of a bitch
> invents an instrument to measure spring with?

From EUROPÆA, 1995, I–1. Copyright © 1995 by EUROPÆA. Reprinted by permission.

That scientists and humanists should be antagonists is thus nothing new or unusual. What *is* anomalous is that within something calling itself a science, there should be a large nucleus of persons who reject the ways of science and profess to practice anthropology as a humanity.

Since science vs. humanism is such a major issue, let us look at its philosophical basis. Part of this basis is the distinction between science and art, a distinction which Leslie White has expressed very nicely:

> Science is one of two basic ways of dealing with experience. The other is art. . . . The purpose of science and art is one: to render experience intelligible. . . . But although working toward the same goal, science and art approach it from opposite directions. Science deals with particulars in terms of universals: Uncle Tom disappears in the mass of Negro slaves. Art deals with universals in terms of particulars: the whole gamut of Negro slavery confronts us in the person of Uncle Tom. Art and science thus grasp a common experience, or reality, (but) by opposite poles.

White's distinction strikes me as valid. At bottom, humanists do look at the world as artists. But there is more to it than that. Humanists are not content merely to *contemplate* their subject; they also *celebrate* it. If you doubt this, just look inside the front cover of the *Anthropology and Humanism Quarterly*, a new journal published by our Association. There you will read that humanistic anthropology "celebrates" the fact that "human reality" is something that "we creative primates construct".

Now, celebration is all well and good, but it is not part of science. No physicist "celebrates" acceleration, and no chemist "celebrates" carbon tetrachloride. This is simply not a function of science. Our job, as scientists, is not to celebrate, but to *explain*, to *account for.* That's what makes us scientists. Let a poet enrapture himself over a lily, admiring the symmetry of its petals, the delicacy of its stamens, and let him sigh over the subtle fragrance of its nectar, but let him not try to pass himself off as a botanist! . . .

Let us not think, though, that by asserting that humanists do not do science, we are puncturing their balloon. You cannot puncture what was never inflated to begin with, and the fact is that the humanists in our ranks do not *claim* to be doing science. On the contrary, they cheerfully admit that they are *not*. But they aren't content with this. They go on to assert that *we* cannot do science, social science, either. Indeed, many of them claim that social science *cannot* be done.

Clifford Geertz, the leading literary humanist in anthropology, finds those of us who consider ourselves social scientists "ignorant and pretentious usurpers of the mission of the humanities". So the gauntlet has been thrown down. Well, if Geertz says there can't be a social science, why not? Only two possibilities exist: either we cannot do it because it is intrinsically undoable, or, if it is theoretically possible, we cannot do it because, in practice, it is too difficult.

Let us look at each possibility in turn. To begin with, why should a science of culture be inherently impossible? The answer is, only if the things and events it studies are not subject to cause and effect. So then we must ask, is human behavior subject to strict causality? Not if there is free will.

No one has put the matter more concisely than the 19th century British historian James Anthony Froude:

> When natural causes are liable to be set aside and neutralized by what is called volition, the word Science is out of place. If it is free to a man to choose what he will do or not do, there is no adequate science of him. . . .

This is not the place to attempt a formal refutation of free will. Instead, I would like to try to convince the humanists among you that determinism is not such a bad thing after all. In fact, I would argue that when you look at it deeply enough, free will turns out to be rather uncongenial to the artist. Let me present my case.

First, though, some background. Several years ago, to help us with an exhibit at the museum in which I work, we hired an artist from San Francisco. During the course of his work, I became well acquainted with him, and in one of our conversations, the subject of free will came up. As you might expect, he and I were on opposite sides of the fence on this issue. We argued about it, but neither of us made much headway in convincing the other. His work completed, the artist returned to San Francisco, but we continued to correspond. And in one of my letters, I presented an argument which I hoped might persuade him to abandon free will and embrace determinism. Here is what I wrote:

> *Dear ***,*
>
> *It is my contention that whenever an artist creates, he is never acting outside the stream of causation. What he engenders, no matter how novel, is never fortuitous. It is neither totally unforeseen nor unaccountable. It is, in fact, the product of lots of things swirling around in his psyche, conscious and unconscious. And—here's the kicker—I would argue that, from the artist's point of view, determinism, seen in this light, is better than free will! Genuine free will implies that, whatever you produce is entirely unconstrained by anything that went before. But if that were true, your creation would be completely out of your hands, entirely at the mercy of chance.*
>
> *And how could such a state of affairs possibly be satisfying to an artist? Isn't it much more congenial for you to think of your art as a summation and expression of everything that has gone into you, than for it to be unconnected and unrelated to you? Let's face it, free will—real free will—is completely deper-sonalizing and dehumanizing. It would work like a purely mechanical game of chance, in which you weren't even allowed to hold the dice. Surely the deter-minism I offer you, which puts you and your life experiences at the very heart of your artistic creation, should be much more congenial.*
>
> *Sincerely,*

Now, if free will is merely an illusion, if human behavior is indeed strictly determined, there is no reason why, in principle, there cannot be a science of human behavior, a science of culture. Some humanists may grudgingly concede this, but then raise another objection: Whatever the case may be in *principle*, they say, in *practice*, human behavior is simply too complex for any genuine regularities, let alone any laws, to be teased out of it.

But is complexity of behavior solely a problem for the anthropologist? Not at all. The phenomena of physics are intricate and complex too. Of the thousands of leaves on a tree, no two fall to earth exactly the same way. Yet physics was able to see past the unique and erratic behavior of each fluttering leaf, and to formulate a general law of falling bodies. Could it be, then, that the anthropological humanist has given up finding any underlying laws in human behavior because he has not looked for them hard enough? When he triumphantly proclaims the impossibility of formulating any cultural laws, could he merely be making a virtue out of his own shortcomings? Could this, then, be nothing more than a case of the tailless fox preaching taillessness?

Having thus warded off the humanists, we come now to the main event: the challenge to the science of culture posed by postmodern anthropology. Humanism was a straightforward, innocent adversary. Postmodernism is anything *but*. Sometimes it appears quite amorphous, but at other times it has the head of a hydra and the arms of a squid. Nor is this only my opinion. C. Richard King, a not unsympathetic observer of the movement, has said that postmodernism "lacks a single, unitary definition . . . It appears to be, at once, everything and nothing." . . .

[W]hatever else postmodernism might aspire to be, it is, at bottom, one more manifestation of the old, familiar prejudice against science. Thus, in her book, *Postmodernism and the Social Sciences*, Pauline Rosenau tells us that the postmodernist "questions the validity of modern science and the notion of objective knowledge". Moreover, postmodernism's headlong retreat from science goes further than humanism's ever did. Not only does it disdain science, it declares science to be dead.

Although postmodernism has challenged anthropology on all fronts, its main attack has been leveled at ethnography. To give the devil his due, postmodernists have had a valid point to make here. Ethnographers have traditionally tended to round things off, to smooth things up. Their monographs often present a single "authoritative" statement of a particular custom or belief, as if that were all there was to it. Yet anyone who has ever done fieldwork knows that informants' versions of a custom or belief often vary all over the map. Thus, presenting only one version *masks* the actual complexity. This foreshortening of reality, though, is not done to deceive. It is done for practical reasons. Were a monograph to include 16 different versions of every custom and belief, it might be more "real," but would also become so cumbersome and wearying as to vitiate the effort. So ethnographers generally round off their accounts to the first decimal place, so to speak, and present a kind of "official" version.

But what does this "official" version of a culture really represent?, ask the critics of traditional ethnography. Is it the opinion of one's best-liked informant? Or the most reliable one? Is it the response of one informant or of several? And if several, and if their range of responses has been "averaged," then what is this "average" that gets printed in the monograph—the mean, the median, or the mode?

Postmodern critics contend that ethnography should stress the many "voices" that may be raised in a primitive society. It is certainly true that there may well be many such "voices," even in a small native village, and that most of them usually remain unheard. That, in itself, is an objective fact, and deserves to be duly noted. But to *dwell* on the myriad voices of informants—indeed, to make a *career* out of it—seems to me to attenuate and trivialize the craft of ethnography.

Yet this has become a dominant theme in postmodern anthropology. With full-throated voice, postmodernists proclaim that there is not *one* reality, but *multiple* ones. The trouble is, though, that as realities are multiplied, they are also divided; as they become more numerous, they become correspondingly smaller. And, there being more and more of them, facts now count for less and less, and so reality becomes progressively diluted and rarified. And it is but a small step from this to saying that there is *no* reality at all! And once *that* assertion has been made, the wheels come off the wagon.

⋙◉⋘

Let us look at this dissolution of reality a little more closely. Postmodern ethnography likes to call itself "dialogical". It puts a high premium on the *dialogue* that takes place between ethnographer and informant. James Clifford says that in the new ethnography "monophonic authority is questioned", and in its stead "dialogism and polyphony are recognized as modes of textual production". And Stephen Tyler, another leading voice in the movement, holds that postmodern ethnography "emphasizes the cooperative and collaborative nature of the ethnographic situation in contrast to the ideology of the transcendant observer". But Tyler goes a step further, claiming that the postmodern ethnographer "rejects the ideology of 'observer-observed', there being nothing observed and no one who is observer". If this is literally true, one is left to wonder, with Richard King, whether "an anthropology which dismisses the distinctions between self and other . . . is possible or even imaginable?".

Setting that question aside, we come to the matter of "truth". Consider the following dilemma. If "truth" is a statement about reality, but reality has already been bargained away, where does that leave truth? "In cultural studies", says Clifford, "we can no longer know the whole truth, or even claim to approach it". But if the search for truth, the traditional objective of science, is left lying in the dust, what happens to science itself? The answer is inescapable. If, as Clifford says, "Cultures are not scientific 'objects', the science of culture loses its subject matter, and with it, its identity and even its very existence. . . .

With ethnographic facts now having but a tenuous reality, they are being reassigned a place in the domain of literature, namely, fiction. Clifford puts his seal of approval on this change in the following words: "Ethnographic writings can properly be called fictions in the sense of 'something made or fashioned'. . . . But it is important to preserve the meaning not merely of making, but also of making up, of inventing things not actually real". So there we are, in the Land of Diggledy Dan.

❧

Any serious study of literature naturally involves the use of *texts*. And texts have become a focus of postmodern ethnography. According to Geertz's oft-quoted remark, culture itself is "an ensemble of texts, themselves ensembles, which the anthropologist strains to read over the shoulder of those to whom they properly belong". So the new ethnographer's field notes become his texts, and he proceeds to deal with them accordingly.

Yet, the more texts are scrutinized, the more they seem to proliferate, spawning *subtexts*. Now, teasing subtexts from a main text is surely slippery business, but it's also a lot of fun. It's a game *any*one can play, and *every*one can win, because there are no rules. There is no correct interpretation, no right answer. Any answer is as good as any other. . . .

Another offshoot of literary ethnography is narrative. Its practitioners focus on *stories* rather than customs. These "stories" started out as biographies, the life histories of one's informants. But it wasn't long before biography turned into *auto*biography, and the subject of one's research became, not one's informants, but oneself. As James Clifford put it, "With the 'fieldwork account' the rhetoric of experienced objectivity yields to that of the autobiography and the ironic selfportrait. The ethnographer, a character in a fiction, is at center stage". . . .

Practiced with fervor, this form of postmodern ethnography becomes supremely self-centered. The ethnographer focuses, not on what he is observing, but on what he *feels* about what he is observing! He is, in effect, watching the patient, but taking his own pulse! Thus, he has become more important than his subject matter. Or rather, he has turned himself *into* his own subject matter. So, by sleight-of-hand, ethnography has become autobiography. . . .

Needless to say, all of this is the very antithesis of science. The cornerstone of science has always been the premise that there is a real world out there, independent of our individual existences. And it is *this* world that, as scientists—as *anthropologists*—we should be studying. If anyone still doggedly prefers to contemplate his own navel, fine. But let him call his contemplation by a different name than anthropology. . . .

❧

I find it quite ironic that persons so concerned with "meaning" as postmodern ethnographers claim to be, should show so little regard for the process of *conveying* meaning, namely, communication. Yet, "meaning" is certainly what they profess to be after. Listen to Clifford Geertz:

> Believing . . . that man is an animal suspended in webs of significance he himself has spun, I take culture to be those webs, and the analysis of it to

be therefore not an empirical science in search of law but an interpretive one in search of meaning.

Beware of those "webs of significance"! From them we have much to fear. The new ethnographer, like a spider, draws forth from his spinaret, threads of infinite subtlety, and with them, creates his own webs which, like those of the spider, are not only delicate, but sticky. And in them, he entraps his prey, holding it fast while he sucks out its meaning. Then, perhaps, he will discard the eviscerated carcass, leaving it to the old-fashioned ethnographer to find whatever vestige of structure and substance may be left in it.

Confronted with a choice between substance and meaning, it is perfectly clear that Geertz will take meaning any day. For him, nothing is what it *is*. It is what it *means*. The famous Balinese cockfight, for example, becomes, at his hands—and here I quote Geertz directly—"image", "fiction", "a model", "a metaphor". So far does he give flight to his fancies in this regard that even his fellow postmodernist, Vincent Crapanzano, feels it necessary to bring him to heel. Thus, Crapanzano says sharply, "Cockfights are surely cockfights for the Balinese—and not images, fictions, models, and metaphors". Indeed, Geertz's rendition of Balinese cockfights so disturbs Crapanzano that he characterizes it as "constructions of constructions of constructions", a simple, bloody fight between two roosters transmogrified into Cloud Cuckooland! . . .

⋅⦿⋅

In the frontal attack of postmodernism on anthropology, one major casualty has been . . . *ethnology*. So *fixated* are postmodernists at the level of ethnography, that they have failed to fulfill ethnography's traditional obligation to ethnology. From its earliest days, ethnography has always been the handmaiden of ethnology. It quarried and dressed the stones which ethnology then used to erect its larger stuctures. For it is here, in ethnology, that broad theories are built and generalizations crafted; where the major questions of anthropology are asked and answered. *Here* it is that we debate the origin of clans, the invention of agriculture, the function of crosscousin marriage, the role of age grades, the rise of chiefdoms, and the development of states. What have postmodernists contributed to the solution of these great problems? Nothing. Has anyone even *heard* of a postmodernist theory of the origin of the state? Alas, what will happen to such questions in an age of postmodern anthropology?

The new ethnographers are not, however, unaware that they're sidestepping these issues. George Marcus, for example, notes that "because of modern ethnography's commitment to social criticism, . . . it has rarely been directed to answering macrosociological questions about the causes of events or the constitution of major systems and processes". The new ethnographer, then, is like a mason so enamored of the peculiarities of each brick, that he turns them over in his hands, carefully studying them, but cannot bring himself to arrange them into some larger structure. He is a mason who has neglected to apply for his architect's license. And why not? Because he doubts that major edifices can ever be built anyway.

But it gets worse. Not only does the new ethnographer refuse to start building himself, he would deny the *ethnologist* a building permit too. He is not content to say what *he* can't do, he also tells us what *we* can't do. And why can't we? Because—among other things—the tools we choose to employ are defective. They are tools of our own devising—"hegemonic concepts"— rather than the simple adzes and digging sticks of our informants. And, Stephen Tyler tells us, "postmodern ethnography . . . seeks . . . to avoid grounding itself in the theoretical and commonsense categories of . . . Western tradition".

Were we to follow Tyler's injunction, though, we would be severely hamstrung. Consider this example. I regard the proportion of waking time that a society spends on subsistence to be of fundamental importance in determining the general level of its culture. Accordingly, I have tried to ascertain this figure for the Kuikuru of central Brazil during the course of my field work among them. However, not being a concept the Kuikuru themselves would be likely to think of, Tyler would rule such a calculation out of court as a "hegemonic Western category". Carried to this extreme, cultural relativism surely cuts us off at the knees. . . .

                                       c⁄◉¬

As we noted earlier, postmodernists are rather ambivalent about truth. At times, they assert there is no such thing; but at other times they tell us there are a thousand different truths. Where on earth does that leave us?

Needless to say, one can define truth any way one feels like. If one wants to define it as that which it is impossible to attain, fine. That takes care of the matter, once and for all. But what *good* does that do? It merely evades an important issue. Here's what I suggest instead. Truth need not be regarded as some mystical, vaporous essence; a holy grail to be sought for but never found. Truth can simply be defined as an *agreement* or *correspondence* between a proposition and something in the external world. As such, it becomes quite possible to attain it. In fact, it is, and has always been, the stated goal of science.

Another notion I rebel against is that truth, if allowed to exist at all, is at best tenuous and protean, and that anyone's "truth" is just as valid as anyone else's. The implications of this view for an ethnographer working in the field are jolting, to say the least. It implies that he should be satisfied with whatever answer he gets to a question, and not try to ferret out the "truest" truth he can. . . .

Is this really where we want to be? Suppose, for example, that Napoleon Chagnon had accepted at face value the genealogies first given to him by the Yanomamö as being as good as any other, and let it go at that. By eschewing verification he would, according to Tyler, have been following good, postmodernist procedure. But he would also have been sorely deceived, because, as he found out months later, the Yanomamö had purposely and systematically lied to him. Now, can any postmodernist seriously hold that the spurious genealogies Chagnon first obtained were just as good, just as true, just as valid, as the ones he got later? . . .

⌘

I have often been struck by the fact that there is no such thing as postmodern chemistry, or postmodern geology. Why not? To begin with, no serious science would be foolish enough to define itself out of existence. Nor could it afford to spend so much of its time dabbling in hairsplitting and pettifogging. No real science would devote itself so wholeheartedly to the inconsequential. To be sure, all the sciences have their many tiny facts, but these are gathered, not for their own sake, but to serve some larger purpose. And this purpose is to formulate a series of overarching propositions that seek to explain ever larger segments of nature. And are these aims not all we really need? . . .

So, what is to happen? What can we expect in the future? Despite my previous lamentations, I am not altogether worried; at least not in the long run. Why? Because I'm a firm believer in the principle of natural selection, and natural selection works on ideas just as it does on organisms. In the realm of ideas, as everywhere else, it's the payoff that counts. Ultimately, any intellectual movement will be judged by its results. If it produces nothing tangible, substantial, or enlightening, it will fall by the wayside, just as so many intellectual fads have before it. Thus I am ready to predict that postmodernism, like phrenology, prohibition, and free silver, will quietly fade away, and center stage will once more be occupied by less scintillating but more productive forms of inquiry. . . .

POSTSCRIPT

Should Cultural Anthropology Stop Trying to Model Itself on Sciences?

Cultural anthropology is often viewed as a big tent capable of embracing many diverse points of view, as the selections by Geertz and Carneiro suggest. Many anthropologists easily slip back and forth between humanistic and scientific approaches, depending on the type of problem they are trying to solve. For example, one might use an interpretive approach to analyze a religious ritual and a scientific approach to work out the effects of globalization on a people's economy. But true partisans of the two paradigms, such as Geertz and Carneiro, would point out that the approaches are based on fundamentally incompatible epistemologies, totally different conceptions of what knowledge is and how we can get at it.

Geertz believes that it is futile to seek natural laws of human thought and behavior and that any positivist, nomothetic anthropology leaves out what is most important to understand, namely, the meanings and significance of social action to the people themselves. To Geertz, the job of the anthropologist is to decipher the meanings of social behaviors as if they were manuscripts in an obscure foreign language. Elsewhere he says, "The culture of a people is an ensemble of texts, themselves ensembles, which the anthropologist strains to read over the shoulders of those to whom they properly belong" (*The Interpretation of Cultures*, Basic Books, 1973, p. 452). Carneiro, on the other hand, considers anthropology's job to be explaining why human ideas and actions take the form they do. He is committed to the notion that forms of culture have causes, some within the culture itself and others—like the natural environment—external to it. He is best known for creating the "circumscription theory" of the origin of the state, which suggests that state forms of social organization (social hierachy, centralized political systems, geographical boundaries, etc.) arise when the population of a society increases, but there are geographical or social barriers preventing the people from merely spreading out while retaining a less complex form of political organization. Such problems, he would argue, cannot be solved by humanistic approaches like interpretive anthropology.

While Geertz is an ardent champion of humanistic anthropology, he is not the harshest critic of anthropology as a law-based science. A number of so-called postmodern scholars—such as James Clifford, George Marcus, and Edward Tylor—have been much more vocal in their attacks on positivism in anthropology. They have urged anthropology to become a self-reflective social science, practicing what has been termed "critical theory." For these scholars, anthropologists should seek the implicit, underlying assumptions and motivations of the anthropologists who have produced what passes for anthropological knowledge. They have borrowed methods from literary criticism to "deconstruct" many classic ethnographic monographs, revealing the rhetorical techniques used by the authors to convince readers of the veracity of their accounts. Opponents have suggested that critical theorists are more concerned with studying the culture of anthropology than with understanding anthropology's traditional subject matter. Postmodernists have offered suggestions on how to improve the writing of ethnography, but do not offer any substitute for the kinds of explanations of sociocultural phenomena that natural science-minded anthropologists aim to produce.

Marvin Harris's cultural materialist approach, incorporating cultural evolution and environmental adaptation, is probably the most widely used scientific paradigm in anthropology. Carneiro uses this approach. Another scientific approach taken by some anthropologists (as well as biologists and psychologists) is "sociobiology." Sociobiologists argue that humans, like all animals, are genetically programmed to respond in certain ways, and cultural practices are just an external manifestation of inner biological drives. For an example of a sociobiological explanation, see the selection by Napoleon Chagnon in Issue 11.

Geertz's *The Interpretation of Cultures* (Basic Books, 1973), for which this selection was written, is the most coherent statement outlining the breadth and scope of an interpretive anthropology. It contains what is probably his best-known interpretive essay, "Deep Play: Notes on the Balinese Cockfight." Students should also consult his *Local Knowledge: Further Essays in Interpretive Anthropology* (Basic Books, 1983) and *Works and Lives: The Anthropologist as Author* (Stanford University Press, 1988). Michael Fisher's review essay "Interpretive Anthropology," *Reviews in Anthropology* (vol. 4, no. 4, 1977) offers a useful overview.

Important essays from a critical or postmodern perspective are contained in two edited volumes: George E. Marcus and Michael M.J. Fisher's *Anthropology as Cultural Critique: An Experimental Moment in the Human Sciences* (University of Chicago Press, 1986) and James Clifford and George E. Marcus's *Writing Culture: The Poetics and Politics of Anthropology* (University of California Press, 1986).

Recent books by Robert Carneiro include *The Muse of History and the Science of Culture* (Kluwer Academic/Plenum, 2000) and *Evolutionism in Cultural Anthropology: A Critical History* (Westview, 2003). A summary of his circumscription theory of state formation can be found in the article, "A Theory of the Origin of the State," *Science* (vol. 169, 1970). For an extended treatment of Harris's views, see his *Cultural Materialism: The Struggle for a Science of Culture* (Random House, 1979).

ISSUE 9

Was Margaret Mead's Fieldwork on Samoan Adolescents Fundamentally Flawed?

YES: Derek Freeman, from *Margaret Mead and Samoa: The Making and Unmaking of an Anthropological Myth* (Harvard University Press, 1983)

NO: Lowell D. Holmes and Ellen Rhoads Holmes, from *Samoan Village: Then and Now,* 2d ed. (Harcourt Brace Jovanovich College Publishers, 1992)

ISSUE SUMMARY

YES: Social anthropologist Derek Freeman argues that Margaret Mead was wrong when she stated that Samoan adolescents had sexual freedom. He contends that Mead went to Samoa determined to prove anthropologist Franz Boas's cultural determinist agenda and states that Mead was so eager to believe in Samoan sexual freedom that she was consistently the victim of a hoax perpetrated by Samoan girls and young women who enjoyed tricking her.

NO: Cultural anthropologists Lowell D. Holmes and Ellen Rhoads Holmes contend that Margaret Mead had a very solid understanding of Samoan culture in general. During a restudy of Mead's research, they came to many of the same conclusions that Mead had reached about Samoan sexuality and adolescent experiences. Mead's description of Samoan culture exaggerates the amount of sexual freedom and the degree to which adolescence in Samoa is carefree but these differences, they argue, can be explained in terms of changes in Samoan culture since 1925 and in terms of Mead's relatively unsophisticated research methods as compared with field methods used today.

In 1925 a student of anthropologist Franz Boas named Margaret Mead set off for a nine-month study of adolescent women in Samoa. At only 23 years old, Mead was just barely beyond adolescence herself. Concerned about Mead's safety in a remote and distant place, Boas arranged for her to stay with an

American family. Here she could live in a European-style house and her physical safety would be ensured. For the next several months she studied the culture and lives of young Samoan women by visiting their village.

On her return to New York in 1925, she wrote up her dissertation for Boas, revising this volume for publication in 1928. She titled the book *Coming of Age in Samoa: A Psychological Study of Primitive Youth for Western Civilization.* Mead concluded that because Samoan culture was so much more relaxed about sexuality than Western culture, Samoan adolescents had a much more tranquil transition from childhood to adulthood than was observed in America and other Western countries. *Coming of Age in Samoa* was an immediate best-seller and it earned Mead renown as a scientist.

In 1983 Derek Freeman published his book entitled *Margaret Mead and Samoa: The Making and Unmaking of an Anthropological Myth* (Harvard University Press), an excerpt of which is provided as the Yes-side selection. Freeman argues that Mead was so eager to find support for her model that she blatantly biased her Samoan fieldwork findings and in effect falsified her data.

Freeman had worked in Western Samoa from 1940 to 1943, returning for further fieldwork from 1965 to 1967. During his research he found evidence that challenges some of Mead's published field data as well as a number of her conclusions regarding Samoan adolescence. He contends that his findings call into question Mead's entire project. He also contends that Mead's young Samoan informants perpetrated a hoax on her by making up stories about their promiscuity.

Freeman's selection is countered by a selection written by Lowell D. Holmes and Ellen Rhoads Holmes, who, in the 1950s, had conducted a restudy of the same community that Mead had visited. Holmes and Holmes had expressly intended to test the reliability and validity of Mead's findings. They conclude that while Mead's characterizations of Samoans are in some ways exaggerated, the characterizations are by no means fundamentally wrong.

These selections allow us to ask a number of questions about Mead's research: Did Mead unintentionally exaggerate her findings about sexual freedom? Or did she intentionally falsify her field data, specifically so that she could support Boas's model of cultural determinism? Could Mead's excesses be explained as the consequence of her being a youthful and inexperienced field researcher? Or can differences between Mead's findings and those of the selection authors be explained in other ways?

These selections raise a number of questions about the replicability of anthropological fieldwork, as well. Is it possible to conduct a systematic restudy of another anthropologist's field subjects? Can an anthropologist working in another village or on another island reliably challenge the findings of another anthropologist?

This issue also raises questions about the adequacy of Freeman's ethnographic data and his conclusions. Did Freeman also have biases that fundamentally affect his conclusions and should encourage us to challenge his assertions? Do either Mead or Freeman provide data that could resolve the nature-nurture question?

YES ↩

Margaret Mead and Samoa

Preface

By far the most widely known of Margaret Mead's numerous books is *Coming of Age in Samoa,* based on fieldwork on which she embarked in 1925 at the instigation of Franz Boas, her professor at Columbia University. Boas had sent the 23-year-old Mead to Samoa to study adolescence, and she returned with a startling conclusion. Adolescence was known in America and Europe as a time of emotional stresses and conflicts. If, Mead argued, these problems were caused by the biological processes of maturation, then they would necessarily be found in all human societies. But in Samoa, she reported, life was easy and casual, and adolescence was the easiest and most pleasant time of life. Thus in anthropological terms, according to Mead, Samoa was a "negative instance"—and the existence of this one counterexample demonstrated that the disturbances associated with adolescence in the United States and elsewhere had cultural and not biological causes. In the controversy between the adherents of biological determinism and those of cultural determinism, a controversy that was at its height in the 1920s, Mead's negative instance appeared to be a triumphant outcome for believers in the sovereignty of culture.

When *Coming of Age in Samoa* was published in 1928 it attracted immense attention, and its apparently conclusive finding swiftly entered anthropological lore as a jewel of a case. Since that time Mead's finding has been recounted in scores of textbooks, and through the vast popularity of *Coming of Age in Samoa,* the best-selling of all anthropological books, it has influenced the thinking of millions of people throughout the world. It is with the critical examination of this very widely accepted conclusion that I am concerned [here].

Scientific knowledge, as Karl Popper has shown, is principally advanced through the conscious adoption of "the critical method of error elimination." In other words, within science, propositions and theories are systematically tested by attempts to refute them, and they remain acceptable only as long as they withstand these attempts at refutation. In Popper's view, "in so far as a scientific statement speaks about reality it must be falsifiable," and rational criticism entails the testing of any particular statement in terms of its correspondence with the facts. Mead's classing of Samoa as a negative instance obviously depends on the adequacy of the account of Samoan culture on which it is based. It is

From *The Making and Unmaking of an Anthropological Myth,* 1983, pp. xi–xviii, 281–293. Copyright © 1983 by Harvard University Press. Reprinted by permission.

thus very much a scientific proposition, for it is fully open to testing against the relevant empirical evidence.

While the systematic testing of the conclusions of a science is always desirable, this testing is plainly imperative when serious doubts have been expressed about some particular finding. Students of Samoan culture have long voiced such doubts about Mead's findings of 1928. . . . I adduce detailed empirical evidence to demonstrate that Mead's account of Samoan culture and character is fundamentally in error. I would emphasize that I am not intent on constructing an alternative ethnography of Samoa. Rather, the evidence I shall present has the specific purpose of scientifically refuting the proposition that Samoa is a negative instance by demonstrating that the depictions on which Mead based this assertion are, in varying degree, mistaken.

In undertaking this refutation I shall limit my scrutiny to those sections of Mead's writings which have stemmed from, or refer to, her researches on Samoa. My concern, moreover, is with the scientific import of these actual researches and *not* with Margaret Mead personally, or with any aspect of her ideas or activities that lies beyond the ambit of her writings on Samoa. I would emphasize also that I hold in high regard many of the personal achievements of Margaret Mead, Franz Boas, and the other individuals certain of whose assertions and ideas I necessarily must question in the pages that follow.

. . . When I reached Western Samoa in April 1940, I was very much a cultural determinist. *Coming of Age in Samoa* had been unreservedly commended to me by [Ernest] Beaglehole, and my credence in Mead's findings was complete.

After two years of study, during which I came to know all the islands of Western Samoa, I could speak Samoan well enough to converse in the company of chiefs with the punctilio that Samoan etiquette demands, and the time had come to select a local polity for intensive investigation. My choice was Sa'anapu, a settlement of 400 inhabitants on the south coast of Upolu. On my first visit to Sa'anapu I had become friendly with Lauvi Vainu'u, a senior talking chief. . . . I was to become his adopted son. From that time onward I lived as one of the Lauvi family whenever I was in Sa'anapu.

In my early work I had, in my unquestioning acceptance of Mead's writings, tended to dismiss all evidence that ran counter to her findings. By the end of 1942, however, it had become apparent to me that much of what she had written about the inhabitants of Manu'a in eastern Samoa did not apply to the people of western Samoa. After I had been assured by Samoans who had lived in Manu'a that life there was essentially the same as in the western islands, I realized that I would have to make one of the objectives of my research the systematic testing of Mead's depiction of Samoan culture.

Soon after I returned to Sa'anapu its chiefs forgathered one morning at Lauvi's house to confer on me one of the chiefly titles of their polity. I was thus able to attend all *fono,* or chiefly assemblies, as of right, and I soon came to be accepted by the community at large. From this time onward I was in an exceptionally favorable position to pursue my researches into the realities of Samoan life.

By the time I left Samoa in November 1943 I knew that I would one day face the responsibility of writing a refutation of Mead's Samoan findings.

This would involve much research into the history of early Samoa. This task I began in 1945 in the manuscript holdings of the Mitchell Library in Sydney and later continued in England, where I thoroughly studied the Samoan archives of the London Missionary Society.

During 1946–1948, while studying anthropology at the University of London, I wrote a dissertation on Samoan social organization. . . . There then came, however, the opportunity to spend some years among the Iban of Borneo. With this diversion, . . . the continuation of my Samoan researches was long delayed.

I finally returned to Western Samoa, accompanied by my wife and daughters, at the end of 1965. Sa'anapu, now linked Apia by road, was once again my center of research. The chiefs of Sa'anapu immediately recognized the title they had conferred on me in 1943, and I became once again an active member of the Sa'anapu *fono*. My family and I remained in Samoa for just over two years, making frequent visits elsewhere in the district to which Sa'anapu belongs, as also to numerous other parts of the archipelago, from Saua in the east to Falealupo in the west.

Many educated Samoans, especially those who had attended college in New Zealand, had become familiar with Mead's writings about their culture. A number of them entreated me, as an anthropologist, to correct her mistaken depiction of the Samoan ethos. Accordingly, early in 1966 I set about the systematic examination of the entire range of Mead's writings on Samoa, seeking to test her assertions by detailed investigation of the particulars of the behavior or custom to which they referred. . . .

[I]n 1967 organized a formal traveling party to [the island of] Ta'ū. We visitors were received as long-lost kinsmen, and in the company of chiefs from both Ta'ū and Sa'anapu I was able to review all those facets of Mead's depiction of Samoa which were then still at issue. In Ta'ū I also recorded the testimony of men and women who remembered the period to which Mead's writings refer. In many instances these recollections were vivid and specific; as one of my informants remarked, the happenings of the mid 1920s were still fresh in their memories.

As my inquiries progressed it became evident that my critical scrutiny of Mead's conclusions would have to extend to the anthropological paradigm of which *Coming of Age in Samoa* was a part. . . .

My researches were not completed until 1981, when I finally gained access to the archives of the High Court of American Samoa for the 1920s. Thus my refutation of Mead's depiction of Samoa appears some years after her death. In November 1964, however, when Dr. Mead visited the Australian National University, I informed her very fully, during a long private conversation, of the empirical basis of my disagreement with her depiction of Samoa. From that time onward we were in correspondence, and in August 1978, upon its first completion, I offered to send her an early draft of my refutation of the conclusions she had reached in *Coming of Age in Samoa*. I received no reply to this offer before Dr. Mead's death in November of that year.

In September 1981 I returned to Western Samoa with the specific purpose of submitting a draft of [my] book to the critical scrutiny of Samoan scholars. . . . In the course of the refutation of Mead's misleading account of their culture, which many Samoans encouraged me to undertake, I have had to deal realistically with the darker side of Samoan life. During my visit of 1981 I found among contemporary Samoans both a mature appreciation of the need to face these realities and a clear-headed pride in the virtues and strengths of the Samoan way of life. . . .

Mead's Misconstruing of Samoa

. . . [The] notion that cultural determinism was absolute was "so obvious" to Mead that . . . she also avowed it in *Coming of Age in Samoa,* in respect of adolescent behavior.

That this doctrine of the absoluteness of cultural determinism should have seemed "so obvious" to Mead is understandable. Anthropology, when she began its study in 1922, was dominated by Boas' "compelling idea," as Leslie Spier has called it, of "the complete moulding of every human expression—inner thought and external behavior—by social conditioning," and by the time she left for Samoa in 1925 she had become a fervent devotee of the notion that human behavior could be explained in purely cultural terms. Further, although by the time of Mead's recruitment to its ranks cultural anthropology had achieved its independence, it had done so at the cost of becoming an ideology that, in an actively unscientific way, sought totally to exclude biology from the explanation of human behavior. Thus as, [Alfred] Kroeber declared, "the important thing about anthropology is not the science but an attitude of mind"—an attitude of mind, that is, committed to the doctrine of culture as a superorganic entity which incessantly shapes human behavior, "conditioning all responses." It was of this attitude of mind that Mead became a leading proponent, with (as Marvin Harris has observed) her anthropological mission, set for her by Boas, being to defeat the notion of a "panhuman hereditary human nature." She pursued this objective by tirelessly stressing, in publication after publication, "the absence of maturational regularities."

In her own account of this mission, Mead describes it as a battle which she and other Boasians had had to fight with the whole battery at their command, using the most fantastic and startling examples they could muster. It is thus evident that her writings during this period, about Samoa as about other South Seas cultures, had the explicit aim of confuting biological explanations of human behavior and vindicating the doctrines of the Boasian school. By 1939 this battle, according to Mead, had been won. . . .

For Mead's readers in North America and elsewhere in the Western world, there could be no more plausible location for the idyllic society of which she wrote than in the South Seas, a region that since the days of Bougainville has figured in the fantasies of Europeans and Americans as a place of preternatural contentment and sensual delight. So, as Mead reports, her announcement in 1925 that she was going to Samoa caused the same breathless stir as if she had been "setting off for heaven." Indeed, there were many in the 1920s, according to Mead, who longed to go to the South Sea islands "to escape to a kind of divine nothingness in which life would be reduced to the simplest physical terms, to sunshine and the moving shadows of palm trees, to bronze-bodied girls and bronze-bodied boys, food for the asking, no work to do, no obligations to meet."

. . . How did the young Margaret Mead come so to miscronstrue ethos and ethnography of Samoa? The fervency of her belief in cultural determinism and her tendency to view the South Seas as an earthly paradise go some way in accounting for what happened, but manifestly more was involved.

The Ph.D. topic that Boas assigned to Mead was the comparative study of canoe-building, house-building, and tattooing in the Polynesian culture area. During 1924 she gathered information on these activities from the available literature on the Hawaiians, the Marquesans, the Maori, the Tahitians, and the Samoans. These doctoral studies did not have any direct relevance to the quite separate problem of adolescence in Samoa that Boas set her in 1925, and, indeed, the fact that her reading was mainly on Eastern rather than Western Polynesia concealed from her the marked extent to which the traditional culture and values of Samoa differ from those of Tahiti. Again, during the spring of 1925 she had little time for systematic preparation for her Samoan researches. Indeed, the counsel she received from Boas about these researches prior to her departure for Pago Pago lasted, she tells us, for only half an hour. During this brief meeting Boas' principal instruction was that she should concentrate on the problem he had set her and not waste time doing ethnography. Accordingly, when in the second week of November 1925 Mead reached Manu'a, she at once launched into the study of adolescence without first acquiring, either by observation or from inquiry with adult informants, a thorough understanding of the traditional values and customs of the Manu'ans. This, without doubt, was an ill-advised way to proceed, for it meant that Mead was in no position to check the statements of the girls she was studying against a well-informed knowledge of the fa'aSamoa [Samoan way of life].

It is also evident that Mead greatly underestimated the complexity of the culture, society, history, and psychology of the people among whom she was to study adolescence. Samoan society, so Mead would have it, is "very simple," and Samoan culture "uncomplex." . . .

As any one who cares to consult Augustin Krämer's *Die Samoa-Inseln,* Robert Louis Stevenson's *A Footnote to History,* or J. W. Davidson's *Samoa mo Samoa* will quickly discover, Samoan society and culture are by no means simple and uncomplex; they are marked by particularities, intricacies, and subtleties quite as daunting as those which face students of Europe and Asia. Indeed, the fa'aSamoa is so sinuously complex that, as Stevenson's step-daughter, Isobel Strong, once remarked, "one may live long in Samoa without understanding the whys and wherefores." Mead, however, spent not even a few months on the systematic study of Manu'a before launching upon the study of adolescence immediately upon her arrival in Ta'ū in accordance with Boas' instructions. Thus, she has noted that while on her later field trips she had "the more satisfactory task of learning the culture first and only afterwards working on a special problem" in Samoa this was "not necessary."

. . . Another problem was that of being able to communicate adequately with the people she was to study. Mead had arrived in Pago Pago without any knowledge of the Samoan language. . . . In this situation Mead was plainly at some hazard pursuing her inquiries in Manu'a, for Samoans, when diverted by the stumbling efforts of outsiders to speak their demanding language, are inclined not to take them seriously.

Mead, then, began her inquiries with her girl informants with a far from perfect command of the vernacular, and without systematic prior investigation of Manu'an society and values. Added to this, she elected to live not in a Samoan household but with the handful of expatriate Americans who were the local representatives of the naval government of American Samoa, from which in 1925 many Manu'ans were radically disaffected. . . . Of the immense advantage that an ethnographer gains by living among the people whose values and behavior he is intent on understanding there can be not the slightest doubt. Mead, however, within six weeks of her arrival in Pago Pago, and before she had spent any time actually staying in a traditional household, had come to feel that the food she would have to eat would be too starchy, and the conditions of living she would have to endure too nerve-racking to make residence with a Samoan family bearable. In Ta'ū, she told Boas, she would be able to live "in a white household" and yet be in the midst of one of the villages from which she would be drawing her adolescent subjects. This arrangement to live not in a Samoan household but with the Holt family in their European-style house, which was also the location of the government radio station and medical dispensary, decisively determined the form her researches were to take.

According to Mead her residence in these government quarters furnished her with an absolutely essential neutral base from which she could study all of the individuals in the surrounding village while at the same time remaining "aloof from native feuds and lines of demarcation." Against this exiguous advantage she was, however, depriving herself of the close contacts that speedily develop in Samoa between an ethnographer and the members of the extended family in which he or she lives. Such contacts are essential for the gaining of a thorough understanding of the Samoan language and, most important of all, for the independent verification, by the continuous observation of actual behavior, of the statements being derived from informants. Thus, by living with the Holts, Mead was trapping herself in a situation in which she was forced to rely not on observations of the behavior of Samoans as they lived their lives beyond the precincts of the government station on Ta'ū, but on such hearsay information as she was able to extract from her adolescent subjects. . . .

It is evident then that although, as Mead records, she could "wander freely about the village or go on fishing trips or stop at a house where a woman was weaving" when she was away from the dispensary, her account of adolescence in Samoa was, in the main, derived from the young informants who came to talk with her away from their homes in the villages of Lumā, Si'ufaga, and Faleasao. So, as Mead states, for these three villages, from which all her adolescent informants were drawn, she saw the life that went on "through the eyes" of the group of girls on the details of whose lives she was concentrating. This situation is of crucial significance for the assessment of Mead's researches in Manu'a, for we are clearly faced with the question of the extent to which the lens she fashioned from what she was being told by her adolescent informants and through which she saw Samoan life was a true and accurate lens.

. . . [M]any of the assertions appearing in Mead's depiction of Samoa are fundamentally in error, and some of them preposterously false. How are we to account for the presence of errors of this magnitude? Some Samoans who have read *Coming of Age in Samoa* react, as Shore reports, with anger and the insistence "that Mead lied." This, however, is an interpretation that I have no hesitation in dismissing. The succession of prefaces to *Coming of Age* in Samoa published by Mead in 1949, 1953, 1961, and 1973 indicate clearly, in my judgment, that she did give genuine credence to the view of Samoan life with which she returned to New York in 1926. Moreover, in the 1969 edition of *Social Organization of Manu'a* she freely conceded that there was a serious problem in reconciling the "contradictions" between her own depiction of Samoa and that contained in "other records of historical and contemporary behavior." . . .

Mead's depiction of Samoan culture, as I have shown, is marked by major errors, and her account of the sexual behavior of Samoans by a mind-boggling contradiction, for she asserts that the Samoans have a culture in which female virginity is very highly valued, with a virginity-testing cere-mony being "theoretically observed at weddings of all ranks," while at the same time adolescence among females is regarded as a period "appropriate for love-making," with promiscuity before marriage being both permitted and "expected." And, indeed, she actually describes the Samoans as making the "demand" that a female should be "both receptive to the advances of many lovers and yet capable of showing the tokens of virginity at marriage." Some-thing, it becomes plain at this juncture, is emphatically amiss, for surely no human population could be so cognitively disoriented as to conduct their lives in such a schizophrenic way. Nor are the Samoans remotely like this, for . . . they are, in fact, a people who traditionally value virginity highly and so disapprove of premarital promiscuity as to exercise a strict surveillance over the comings and goings of adolescent girls. That these values and this regime were in force in Manu'a in the mid 1920s is, furthermore, clearly estab-lished by the testimony of the Manu'ans themselves who, when I discussed this period with those who well remembered it, confirmed that the fa'aSamoa in these matters was operative then as it was both before and after Mead's brief sojourn in Ta'ū. What then can have been the source of Mead's erroneous statement that in Samoa there is great premarital freedom, with promiscuity before marriage among adolescent girls, being both permitted and expected?

The explanation most consistently advanced by the Samoans themselves for the magnitude of the errors in her depiction of their culture and in partic-ular of their sexual morality is, as [Eleanor Ruth] Gerber has reported, "that Mead's informants must have been telling lies in order to tease her." Those Samoans who offer this explanation, which I have heard in Manu'a as well as in other parts of Samoa, are referring to the behavior called *tau fa'ase'e*, to which Samoans are much prone. *Fa'ase'e* (literally "to cause to slip") means "to dupe," as in the example given by Milner, *"e fa'ase'e gofie le teine,* the girl is easily duped"; and the phrase *tau fa'ase'e* refers to the action of deliberately duping someone, a pastime that greatly appeals to the Samoans as a respite from the severities of their authoritarian society.

Because of their strict morality, Samoans show a decided reluctance to discuss sexual matters with outsiders or those in authority, a reticence that is especially marked among female adolescents. Thus, Holmes reports that when he and his wife lived in Manu'a and Tutuila in 1954 "it was never possible to obtain details of sexual experience from unmarried informants, though several of these people were constant companions and part of the household." Further, as Lauifi Ili, Holmes's principal assistant, observes, when it comes to imparting information about sexual activities, Samoan girls are "very close-mouthed and ashamed." Yet it was precisely information of this kind that Mead, a liberated young American newly arrived from New York and resident in the government station at Ta'ū, sought to extract from the adolescent girls she had been sent to study. And when she persisted in this unprecedented probing of a highly embarrassing topic, it is likely that these girls resorted, as Gerber's Samoan informants have averred, to *tau fa'ase'e*, regaling their inquisitor with counterfeit tales of casual love under the palm trees.

This, then, is the explanation that Samoans give for the highly inaccurate portrayal of their sexual morality in Mead's writings. It is an explanation that accounts for how it was that this erroneous portrayal came to be made, as well as for Mead's sincere credence in the account she has given in *Coming of Age in Samoa*, for she was indeed reporting what she had been told by her adolescent informants. The Manu'ans emphasize, however, that the girls who, they claim, plied Mead with these counterfeit tales were only amusing themselves, and had no inkling that their tales would ever find their way into a book.

While we cannot, in the absence of detailed corroborative evidence [but see addendum following], be sure about the truth of this Samoan claim that Mead was mischievously duped by her adolescent informants, we can be certain that she did return to New York in 1926 with tales running directly counter to all other ethnographic accounts of Samoa, from which she constructed her picture of Manu'a as a paradise of free love, and of Samoa as a negative instance, which, so she claimed, validated Boasian doctrine. It was this negative instance that she duly presented to Boas as the ideologically gratifying result of her inquiries in Manu'a. . . .

We are thus confronted in the case of Margaret Mead's Samoan researches with an instructive example of how, as evidence is sought to substantiate a cherished doctrine, the deeply held beliefs of those involved may lead them unwittingly into error. The danger of such an outcome is inherent, it would seem, in the very process of belief formation. . . .

In the case of Mead's Samoan researches, certainly, there is the clearest evidence that it was her deeply convinced belief in the doctrine of extreme cultural determinism, for which she was prepared to fight with the whole battery at her command, that led her to construct an account of Samoa that appeared to substantiate this very doctrine. There is, however, conclusive empirical evidence to demonstrate that Samoa, in numerous respects, is not at all as Mead depicted it to be.

A crucial issue that arises from this historic case for the discipline of anthropology, which has tended to accept the reports of ethnographers as entirely empirical statements, is the extent to which other ethnographic accounts may have been distorted by doctrinal convictions, as well as the methodological question of how such distortion can best be avoided. These are no small problems. I would merely comment that as we look back on Mead's Samoan researches we are able to appreciate anew the wisdom of Karl Popper's admonition that in both science and scholarship it is, above all else, indefatigable rational criticism of our suppositions that is of decisive importance, for such criticism by "bringing out our mistakes . . . makes us understand the difficulties of the problem we are trying to solve," and so saves us from the allure of the "obvious truth" of received doctrine.

Addendum: New Evidence of the Hoaxing of Margaret Mead

In my book *The Fateful Hoaxing of Margaret Mead* (1998) there is an account, based on the sworn testimony of Fa'apua'a, of how Margaret Mead in March of 1926 on the island of Ofu in American Samoa was hoaxed about the sexual mores of the Samoans by her two Samoan traveling companions, Fa'apua'a and Fofoa.

I [have recently discovered] direct evidence, from Mead's own papers, that Margaret Mead was indeed taken in by the "whispered confidences" (as she called them) of Fa'apua'a and Fofoa. This incontrovertible historical evidence finally brings to closure the long-running controversy over Margaret Mead's Samoan fieldwork. . . .

The crucially important direct evidence in question is contained in a little known book entitled *All True! The Record of Actual Adventures That Have Happened To Ten Women of Today* that was published in New York in 1931 by Brewer, Warren and Putnam. The "adventure" by Dr. Margaret Mead is entitled "Life as a Samoan Girl". It begins with a wistful reference to "the group of reverend scientists" who in 1925 sent her to study (Mead, 1925) "the problem of which phenomena of adolescence are culturally and which physiologically determined" among the adolescent girls of Samoa, with "no very clear idea" of how she was "to do this." It ends with an account of her journey to the islands of Ofu and Olosega in March of 1926 with the "two Samoan girls," as she calls them, Fa'apua'a and Fofoa. In fact, Fa'apua'a and Fofoa were both twenty-four years of age and slightly older than Dr. Mead herself. Dr. Mead continues her account of her visit to the islands of Ofu and Olosega with Fa'apua'a and Fofoa by stating: "In all things I had behaved as a Samoan, for only so, only by losing my identity, as far as possible, had I been able to become acquainted with the Samoan girls receive their whispered confidences and learn at the same time the answer to the scientists' questions."

This account, by Mead herself, is fully confirmed by the sworn testimony of Fa'apua'a (cf. Freeman, 1998, Chapter 11). It can be found on p. 141 of the second and paperback edition (1999) of my book *The Fateful Hoaxing of Margaret*

Mead: A historical analysis of her Samoan research. It is definitive historical evidence that establishes that Martin Orans is in outright error in asserting (1996:92) that it is "demonstrably false that Mead was taken in by Fa'apua'a and Fofoa." It is also evidence that establishes that *Coming of Age in Samoa,* far from being a "scientific classic" (as Mead herself supposed) is, in certain vitally significant respects (as in its dream-like second chapter), a work of anthropological fiction.

References

Freeman, Derek, 1999, *The Fateful Hoaxing of Margaret Mead,* Boulder: Westview, 2nd edition.

Mead, Margaret, 1925, Plan of Research Submitted to the National Research Council of the U.S.A. (Archives of the National Academy of Sciences).

Mead, Margaret, 1928, *Coming of Age in Samoa.* New York: Morrow.

Mead, Margaret, 1931, "Life as a Samoan Girl," in *All True! The Record of Actual Adventures That Happened to Ten Women of Today.* New York: Brewer, Warren and Putnam.

Orans, Martin, 1996, *Not Even Wrong: Margaret Mead, Derek Freeman and the Samoans,* Novato: Chandler and Sharp.

Lowell D. Holmes and
Ellen Rhoads Holmes

NO

Samoan Character and the Academic World

On January 31, 1983, the *New York Times* carried a front-page article, the headline of which read, "New Samoa Book Challenges Margaret Mead's Conclusions." The book that precipitated this somewhat unexpected turn of events was *Margaret Mead and Samoa: The Making and Unmaking of an Anthropological Myth* by Derek Freeman, an emeritus professor of anthropology at Australian National University in Canberra. This work, which some claim set off the most heated controversy in sociocultural anthropology in one hundred years, is described by its author as a "refutation of Mead's misleading account" of Samoan culture and personality as presented in her 1928 ethnography, *Coming of Age in Samoa.*

The *New York Times* article was of special interest to me because, in 1954, I had conducted a year-long methodological restudy of the Mead data under attack. I had lived in Ta'ū village, where Mead had worked twenty-nine years earlier, and had used many of her informants in a systematic and detailed evaluation of every observation and interpretation she had made about the lifestyle of the people in that Samoan village. A methodological restudy, incidentally, involves a second anthropologist going into the field with the *express purpose* of testing the reliability and validity of the findings of a former investigator. This restudy is made in order to establish what kinds of errors of data collection or interpretation might have been made by certain kinds of people, in certain kinds of field research situations, researching certain kinds of problems. For example, Margaret Mead was a twenty-three-year-old woman investigating a male-dominated society that venerates age. She was a student of Franz Boas and, therefore, went equipped with a particular theoretical frame of reference. She was also on her first field trip—at a time when research methods were crude. My task in this methodological restudy was not only to analyze how my findings might be different from hers (if that would be the case), but I would also attempt to speculate on how differences in the status of the investigators (for example, sex, age, family situation, education) and other personal factors might affect the collection and interpretation of data.

My critique of Margaret Mead's study was presented in my doctoral dissertation, *The Restudy of Manu'an Culture. A Problem in Methodology,* which by 1983 had been collecting dust on a Northwestern University library shelf for some twenty-seven years. I was therefore eager to obtain a copy of Freeman's new evaluation of Mead's work from its publisher, Harvard University Press. In reading the book this is what I found.

In *Margaret Mead and Samoa: The Making and Unmaking of an Anthropological Myth* (1983), Derek Freeman argues that Mead perpetuated a hoax comparable in consequence to that of Piltdown Man when, in 1928, she described Samoa as a paradise where competition, sexual inhibition, and guilt were virtually absent. Refusing to believe that adolescents in all societies inevitably experience emotional crises—storm and stress—because of biological changes associated with puberty (as hypothesized in *Adolescence* in 1904 by psychologist G. Stanley Hall), Mead set out to discover a society where the passage to adulthood was smooth and without trauma. She described such a society in *Coming of Age in Samoa*. In delineating this "negative instance" (which challenged Hall's theory of universal adolescent rebellion and strife), Margaret Mead had in effect established that nurture (culture) is more critical than nature (biology) in accounting for adolescent maturation behavior in the human species. Derek Freeman, on the other hand, rejects the idea that human behavior is largely shaped by culture and believes that Mead and her mentor, Franz Boas (commonly called the "Father of American Anthropology"), were guilty of *totally* ignoring the influence of biological heredity. He believes that Mead's "negative instance" results entirely from faulty data collection and that Mead's Samoan findings have led anthropology, psychology, and education down the primrose path of pseudoscience. Freeman's book, therefore, is an attempt to set the record straight through his own, more accurate, observations of Samoa and Samoans—although his observations of Samoan behavior were in another village, on another island, in another country, and fourteen years later.

Freeman's main theoretical approach in this evaluation of Mead's work derives from the German philosopher of science, Karl Popper, who maintains that science should be deductive, not inductive, and that progress in scientific research should consist essentially of attempts to refute established theories. Thus, Derek Freeman is out to destroy the credibility of what he interprets as the "absolute cultural determinism" to be found in the work of Margaret Mead as well as in much of the work of Boas and his other students. This claim is, of course, spurious, as any student of American anthropological theory knows. For example, in Melville J. Herskovits' biography of Franz Boas, we find the statement that, because of his "rounded view of the problem Boas could perceive so clearly the fallacy of the eugenicist theory, which held the destiny of men to be determined by biological endowment, with little regard for the learned, cultural determinants of behavior." By the same token, he "refused to accept the counter-dogma that man is born with a completely blank slate, on which can be written whatever is willed. He saw both innate endowment and learning—or, as it was called popularly, heredity and environment—as significant factors in the making of the mature individual" (1953:28). Herskovits also points out that "numerous examples can be found, in reports on the various studies he conducted, of how skillfully Boas was able to weave cultural and biological factors into a single fabric" (*Ibid.*).

Marvin Harris concurs: "American anthropology has always been concerned with the relationships between nature (in the guise of habitat and genic programming) and culture (in the guise of traditions encoded in the brain, not in the genes). Neither Boas nor his students ever denied that *Homo sapiens* has a species-specific nature" (1983:26). In his book, *The Rise of Anthropological Theory,* Harris writes, "Boas systematically rejected almost every conceivable form of cultural determinism" (1968:283).

Evaluation of the Mead Data

My restudy experience in Ta'ū village in 1954 led me to conclude that Margaret Mead often overgeneralized; that, in many cases, we interpreted data differently; and that, because of her age and sex, some avenues of investigation apparently were closed to her—particularly those having to do with the more formal aspects of village political organization and ceremonial life. However, her overall characterization of the nature and dynamics of the culture were, in my judgment, quite valid and her contention that it was easier to come of age in Samoa than in America in 1925–1926 was undoubtedly correct. In spite of the greater possibilities for error in a pioneer study, Mead's age (only 23), her sex (in a male-dominated society), and her inexperience, I believe the reliability and validity of the Ta'ū village research is remarkably high.

I look upon an ethnographic account as a kind of map to be used in finding one's way about in a culture—in comprehending and anticipating behavior. Mead's account never left me lost or bewildered in my interactions with Samoan islanders, but I also felt that if one were to come to a decision about the comparative difficulties of coming of age in Samoa and the United States, it would be necessary to know something about what life was like for adolescents in America in 1925–1926. Joseph Folsom's book, *The Family,* published in 1934, but researched about the time Mead was writing *Coming of Age in Samoa,* provided that information. Folsom describes the social environment in which children came of age at that time as follows:

> Children are disciplined and trained with the ideal of absolute obedience to parents. Corporal punishment is used, ideally in cold blood. . . . All sexual behavior on the part of children is prevented by all means at the parents' disposal. . . . For the sake of prevention it has been usual to cultivate in the child, especially the girl, an attitude of horror or disgust toward all aspects of sex. . . . Premarital intercourse is immoral though not abhorrent. . . . Violations are supposedly prevented by the supervision of the girl's parents. . . . Illegitimate children are socially stigmatized. . . . The chief stigma falls upon the unmarried mother, because she has broken an important sex taboo (1934:10–25). . . .

While Freeman contends that Mead was absolutely wrong about nearly everything (partly, he maintains, because the teenage girls she used as informants consistently lied to her), I found discrepancies mainly in such areas as the degree of sexual freedom Samoan young people enjoy, the competitive nature of the society, the aggressiveness of Samoan behavior, and the degree of genuine affection and commitment between lovers and spouses.

I saw Samoan culture as considerably more competitive than Mead, although I never considered it as inflexible or aggressive as Freeman does. I observed a great preoccupation with status, power, and prestige among men of rank and, on more than one occasion, was present at fierce verbal duels between Talking Chiefs trying to enhance their own prestige and, incidentally, that of their village. . . .

I also found that Samoan culture was not as simple as Margaret Mead claimed, nor was Ta'ū village the paradise she would have us believe. She often romanticized, overgeneralized, and, on some occasions, took literary license in her descriptions of Samoan lifeways. For example, her very dramatic chapter, "A Day in Samoa," crowds typical activities (some of which occur only at particular times of the year) into a typical day and thereby presents a village scene that was much more vibrant, bustling, and picturesque than I ever encountered in any twenty-four hour period. Mead's chapter is good prose, but is it good anthropology? . . .

I also did not agree with Mead on the degree of sexual freedom supposedly enjoyed by her informants, but I believe her characterization comes closer to the truth than that of Freeman. Samoans have a very natural and healthy attitude toward sex. Judging by the number of illegitimate children in Ta'ū village when I was there and by the fact that divorce frequently involved claims of adultery, I would conclude that, while Samoans are far from promiscuous, they are not the puritanical prudes Freeman paints them to be. However, I must admit that it was difficult to investigate anything of a sexual nature, primarily because of pressure from the London Missionary Society church. Even today, older Samoans seem more distressed over Mead's claims that they are sexually active than Freeman's claims that they are aggressive with strong passions, even psychopathological tendencies. I would assume, however, that Mead was better able to identify with, and therefore establish rapport with, adolescents and young adults on issues of sexuality than either I (at age 29—married with a wife and child) or Freeman, ten years my senior.

Freeman maintains that Mead imposed her own liberated ideas of sexuality onto the Samoans and that her teenage informants consistently lied to her about these matters solely out of mischief. He has recently made contact with one of Mead's informants, Fa'apua'a Fa'amu, who lived in Fitiuta while Mead was working in Ta'ū village. Freeman believes this informant when she says that she consistently lied to Mead (while also identifying her as a good friend), but Freeman does not seem to consider the possibility that she may be lying to him. The possibility of Mead's informants being successful at such long-term deception is simply not credible considering the fact that Mead was an extremely intelligent, well-trained Ph.D. who constantly cross-checked her data with many informants. Anyone who has studied her field notes in the Library of Congress, as I have, must be impressed with her savvy and sophistication.

I must also disagree with Mead's statements that all love affairs are casual and fleeting, and no one plays for very heavy emotional stakes. Custom dictates that displays of affection between spouses and between lovers not take place in public. However, expressions of love and affection were often observed in the families of my informants. . . .

Although I differed with Margaret Mead on many interpretations, the most important fact that emerged from my methodological restudy of her Samoan research is that, without doubt, Samoan adolescents have a less difficult time negotiating the transition from childhood to adulthood than American adolescents. . . .

Critique of the Freeman Refutation

My objections to Derek Freeman's picture of Samoa are much more substantial than to the picture presented by Margaret Mead. Basically, I question Freeman's objectivity and believe he is guilty of an age-old temptation in science, which was recognized as early as 1787 by Thomas Jefferson—no slouch of a scientist himself. In a letter to his friend Charles Thomson, Jefferson wrote, "The moment a person forms a theory, his imagination sees, in every object, only the traits which favor that theory" (Martin 1952:33).

Not only does Freeman ignore counterevidence, he also ignores time and space and assumes that it is legitimate to assess data obtained by Mead in Manu'a in 1925–1926 in terms of the data he collected in Western Samoa in the 1940s, 1960s, and 1980s.

Time differences.   Freeman plays down the fact that Mead did her study of Ta'ū village in the Manu'a Island group of American Samoa fourteen years before he arrived as a teacher (not as an anthropologist) in Western Samoa and that he did not return to Samoa with the express purpose of refuting Mead's study until forty-three years after her visit. Minimizing this time gap, he arbitrarily states that "there is no . . . reason to suppose that Samoan society and behavior changed in any fundamental way during the fourteen years between 1926, the year of the completion of Mead's inquiries, and 1940, when I began my own observation of Samoan behavior" (1983:120).

However, Freeman did not visit Ta'ū village, the site of Mead's research, until 1968. Having established to his satisfaction that there had been few changes in Samoan culture during this long period of time, Freeman went on to state that he would "draw on evidence of my own research in the 1940s, the years 1965 to 1968, and 1981" (1983:120). I might add that he would draw upon historical sources, some of which go back as far as the early eighteenth century, to prove his points. My own analysis of Samoan cultural change, as published in *Ta'ū, Stability and Change in a Samoan Village* (1958), indicates, however, that while there was relative stability in the culture from 1850 to 1925 and from 1925 to 1954, change definitely did take place, particularly in the twentieth century. There is absolutely no basis for Freeman's dealing with Samoa as though it existed in a totally static condition despite its long history of contact with explorers, whalers, missionaries, colonial officials and bureaucrats, entrepreneurs, anthropologists, and, more recently, educators with Western-style curricula and television networks.

Place differences.   It also must be kept in mind that Sa'anapu (where Freeman observed Samoan culture) is not Ta'ū village (where Mead did her study). They are different villages, on different islands, in different countries, and there are great historical and political differences between the island of Upolu in Western Samoa and Ta'ū island in the isolated Manu'a Group of American Samoa. Western Samoa has experienced a long and often oppressive history of colonialism under Germany and New Zealand, while the Manu'a Group and American Samoa in general have been spared this. The U.S. Navy administration (1900–1951) exerted little influence outside the Pago Pago Bay area on the island of Tutuila, and the Department of the Interior, which took over from the Navy, has been an ethnocentric—but still benevolent—force in the political history of the territory. While Sa'anapu is on the opposite side of Upolu from Apia, it has daily bus communication with that port town, with all of its banks, supermarkets, department stores, theaters, bookstores, and nightclubs. Cash cropping has always been more important in Western Samoa than in American Samoa, and today, the economies of the two Samoas are vastly different. . . . On five separate research trips to Manu'a, I have never witnessed a single physical assault or serious argument that threatened to get out of hand. However, urban centers such as Apia in Western Samoa and Pago Pago in American Samoa have a very different character. As early as 1962, there were delinquency problems in the Pago Pago Bay area involving drunkenness, burglary, assaults, and rapes. Young people who migrate to urban areas such as Pago Pago and Apia are no longer under the close supervision and control of their *matai* [chief of the family] and often behave in very nontraditional ways. It is difficult, indeed, to make a blanket statement that all villages in Samoa are the same and that all behavior within the two Samoas is comparable. I have studied several villages during my thirty-seven-year contact with Samoa, and I find each unique in numerous, social, ceremonial, economic, and political respects.

Freeman's subjective use of literature.   A serious scientist considers all the literature relating to his or her research problem. One does not select data that supportive and ignore that which is not. Freeman violates that principle repeatedly. . . . When [Ronald Rose's book, *South Seas Magic* (1959)] can be used to corroborate or advance Freeman's position, he is quoted; however, where Rose's statements concerning Samoan sexual behavior run contrary to Freeman's claims, and fall in line with Mead's observations, his work is ignored. For example, while Freeman insists that Samoans are puritanical and sexually inhibited, Rose writes that "sexual adventures begin at an early age. Although virginity is prized, it is insisted on only with the taupo. . . . If a girl hasn't had a succession of lovers by the time she is seventeen or eighteen, she feels she is 'on the shelf' and becomes the laughing stock among her companions" (1959:61).

    With regard to the matter that Freeman believes was Mead's spurious example of a "negative instance"—a culture where coming of age is relatively less stressful—Rose writes (but understandably is not quoted by Freeman) as follows:

> Mental disturbances, stresses and conflicts occur at puberty but, as might be expected. these are not quite as common as in our society where taboos associated with sex abound (*Ibid.*: 164).

One can question the objectivity of a scientist who describes Samoans as "an unusually bellicose people" (1983:157) and attempts to substantiate the claim with citations from the eighteenth century, but fails to quote the favorable impressions of the very first European to come in contact with Samoan islanders from the village of Ta'ū, the very village Mead studied. In 1722, Commodore Jacob Roggeveen anchored his vessel off the village of Ta'ū and allowed a number of the islanders to come aboard. After a two-hour visit, the Commodore wrote in his log:

> They appeared to be a good people, lively in their manner of conversing, gentle in their deportment towards each other, and in their manners nothing was perceived of the savage. . . . It must be acknowledged that this was the nation the most civilized and honest of any that we had seen among the Islands of the South Sea. They were charmed with our arrival amongst them, and received us as divinities. And when they saw us preparing to depart, they testified much regret (Bumey 1816:576).

Rather than quote Roggeveen, Freeman chooses to discuss, as an example of Samoan bellicosity, the La Perouse expedition's visitation at Tutuila in 1787 that ended in tragedy. It is true that Samoans in the village of A'asu attacked a shore party, killing several crew members, but what Freeman fails to mention is that the attack occurred only after crew members punished a Samoan for pilfering by hanging him by his thumbs from the top of the longboat mast. . . .

It also should be noted that the eminent writer, Robert Louis Stevenson, who lived among Samoans the last four years of his life, recorded in his chronicle of Samoan events, *A Footnote to History,* that Samoans were "easy, merry, and pleasure loving; the gayest, though by no means the most capable or the most beautiful of Polynesians" (1892:148) and that their religious sentiment toward conflict was "peace at any price" (*Ibid.*: 147).

Observers contemporary with Mead in Samoa also record descriptions of Samoan chararacter that do not square with Freeman's allegations or his citations from early literature. For example, William Green, the principal of the government school in American Samoa in the 1920s writes:

> Personal combats and fist fights are rather rare today. I believe there has been no murder case in American Samoa since our flag was raised in 1900. Natives will suffer indignities for a long time before resorting to a fight but they remain good fighters. Boxing contests are held occasionally. . . . Respect for elders and magistrates has, I suppose, tended to discourage frequent combats. Life is easy, and one's habitual tendencies and desires are seldom blocked (1924:134).

Professional Reactions

. . . It is questionable whether any anthropology book to date has created such a media circus or produced such a media hero as *Margaret Mead and Samoa, The Making and Unmaking of an Anthropological Myth.* It is also doubtful whether any academic press ever mounted such a campaign of Madison Avenue hype to market a book as did Harvard University Press. The early reviews of the book and feature articles about the controversy were primarily penned by journalists and tended to be highly supportive of Freeman's critique, but once the anthropologists began evaluating the Freeman book, the tide took a definite turn. George Marcus of Rice University called the book a "work of great mischief," the mischief being that Freeman was attempting to reestablish "the importance of biological factors in explanations of human behavior" (1983:2). . . . Marvin Harris observed in his review that Freeman "seems obsessed with the notion that to discredit Mead's Samoan material is to discredit any social scientist who holds that 'nurture' is a more important determinant of the differences and similarities in human social life than nature" (1983:26).

It is only fair to point out that Derek Freeman had, and continues to have, a cadre of anthropological supporters, mostly in Europe and Australia, and the Samoans are mixed in their support of Mead or Freeman. . . .

Like most American anthropologists, and a few scholarly Samoans, we believe the Freeman book has done a disservice to Samoans and to the memory of Margaret Mead. *Margaret Mead and Samoa* is not an objective analysis of Mead's work in Manu'a, but an admitted refutation aimed at discrediting not only Margaret Mead, but Franz Boas and American cultural anthropology in general. Anthropology has often been referred to as a "soft science" throughout much of this rhubarb over Samoa and nature/nurture. It is little wonder, since Freeman's diatribe, published by a supposedly scholarly press, has been accepted by the media, by a select group of anthropologists, and by a number of distinguished ethologists and sociobiologists as legitimate anthropology. Margaret Mead would have loved to have debated the issues with Derek Freeman, but unfortunately, the book was not published while she was alive. It would have been great sport and good for the science of anthropology. As a friend wrote immediately after the publication of Freeman's book, "Whatever else she was, Margaret was a feisty old gal and would have put up a spirited defense which would quickly have turned into a snotty offense." We would have put our money on the plump little lady with the no-nonsense attitude and the compulsion to "get on with it."

References

Burney, James. 1816. *A chronological history of the voyages and discoveries in the South Seas or Pacific Ocean.* London: Luke Hansard and Sons.

Folsom, Joseph K. 1934. *The family: Its sociology and psychiatry.* New York: J. Wiley and Sons.

Freeman, Derek. 1983. *Margaret Mead and Samoa: The making and unmaking of an anthropological myth.* Cambridge, MA: Harvard University Press.

Green, William M. 1924. "Social traits of Samoans." *Journal of Applied Sociology* 9:129–135.

Hall, G. Stanley. 1904. *Adolescence: Its psychology and its relations to physiology, anthropology, sociology, sex, crime, religion and education.* New York: D. Appleton and Company.

Harris, Marvin. 1968. *The rise of anthropological theory.* New York: Thomas Y. Crowell Company.

——. 1983. "The sleep-crawling question." *Psychology Today* May:24–27.

Herskovits, Melville J. 1953. *Franz Boas.* New York: Charles Scribner's Sons.

Holmes, Lowell D. 1958. *Ta'ū: Stability and change in a Samoan village.* Reprint No. 7, Wellington, New Zealand: Polynesian Society.

Marcus, George, 1983. "One man's Mead." *New York Times Book Review* March 27, 1983:2–3, 22–23.

Martin, Edwin T. 1952. *Thomas Jefferson: Scientist.* New York: Henry Schuman.

Rose, Ronald. 1959. *South Seas magic.* London: Hale.

Stevenson, Robert Louis. 1892. *Vailima papers and A footnote to history.* New York: Charles Scribner's Sons.

POSTSCRIPT

Was Margaret Mead's Fieldwork on Samoan Adolescents Fundamentally Flawed?

The response to Freeman's *Margaret Mead and Samoa* was quite extraordinary and included books, journal articles, editorials, and conference papers. Special sessions at the annual meetings of the American Anthropological Association were devoted exclusively to the Mead-Freeman debate. The first reaction was largely defensive. But as the initial shock of Freeman's assertions wore off, scholars began to address some of the specific points of criticism. A representative sample of these would include Lowell D. Holmes's *Quest for the Real Samoa: The Mead/Freeman Controversy and Beyond* (Bergin and Garvey, 1987) and Hiram Caton's edited volume, *The Samoa Reader: Anthropologists Take Stock* (University Press of America, 1990).

A number of scholars have pointed out that Samoan life has changed significantly since Mead's fieldwork. The Christian Church now exerts a much stronger pressure over the very same women that Mead had interviewed. Another point is that Mead's informants themselves have become much more puritanical as old women than they were as girls. These women now have reputations of social propriety to uphold that would not have concerned them in their youth. Can we believe that they had the same views so many years ago?

In the 1980s Freeman returned to Ta'u with an Australian documentary film crew, specifically to interview some of Mead's now elderly informants. When asked what they had told Mead 60 years earlier, the women stated that they fibbed continuously and explained that it is a cherished Samoan custom to trick people in these ways. Freeman and the film crew take such statements as incontrovertible evidence that Mead was hoaxed. But if it is Samoan custom to trick others, how can Freeman and his film crew be certain that they are not victims of a similar hoax?

Another Samoa specialist, Martin Orans, approaches the controversy in his book *Not Even Wrong: Margaret Mead, Derek Freeman, and the Samoans* (Chandler & Sharp, 1996). Orans contends that neither Mead nor Freeman framed their research questions about cultural determinism in ways that can be tested. Arguing that anthropologists must frame their conclusions as testable hypotheses, Orans asserts that Mead and Freeman are so vague that neither makes their case, and both are so ambiguous that they are "not even wrong." But if Orans is correct, how can anthropologists frame the nature-versus-nurture debate in more specific and testable ways in specific field settings?

ISSUE 10

Do Native Peoples Today Invent Their Traditions?

YES: Roger M. Keesing, from "Creating the Past: Custom and Identity in the Contemporary Pacific," *The Contemporary Pacific* (Spring/Fall 1989)

NO: Haunani-Kay Trask, from "Natives and Anthropologists: The Colonial Struggle," *The Contemporary Pacific* (Spring 1991)

ISSUE SUMMARY

YES: Cultural anthropologist Roger M. Keesing argues that what native peoples in the Pacific now accept as "traditional culture" is largely an invented and idealized vision of their past. He contends that such fictional images emerge because native peoples are largely unfamiliar with what life was really like in pre-Western times and because such imagery distinguishes native communities from dominant Western culture.

NO: Hawaiian activist and scholar Haunani-Kay Trask asserts that Keesing's critique is fundamentally flawed because he only uses Western documents—and native peoples have oral traditions, genealogies, and other historical sources that are not reflected in Western historical documents. Anthropologists like Keesing, she maintains, are trying to hold on to their privileged position as experts in the face of growing numbers of educated native scholars.

In 1983 Eric Hobsbawm and Terence Ranger published a collection of essays entitled *The Invention of Tradition* (Cambridge University Press). For many anthropologists trained in a structural-functionalist style of research, this volume was striking because it suggested two points that seemed to fly in the face of many cherished anthropological ideas. First, they argued that traditions in all societies change as a response to the political, economic, and social needs of the community. Second, they contended that the "historical" traditions societies celebrated were often invented in the recent past as a way of distinguishing one indigenous group from a dominant one. By 1983 most anthropologists had accepted the axiom that all societies change over time.

Culture and social institutions may work to inhibit changes and keep society functioning as it had in the previous generation, but innovations inevitably occurred. What made Hobsbawm and Ranger's book so important was that it used several Western examples to demonstrate that even in Western countries with rich historical documentation, institutions such as Scottish tartans could become routinized and accepted as a traditional and essential marker of Scottish ethnicity, even though the custom had existed for barely a century. They argued that the idea that tartans had ancient origins was particularly appealing to the Scots because it distinguished them from the dominant English culture that had long oppressed them.

In the following selection, Roger M. Keesing builds on Hobsbawm and Ranger's argument by turning his attention to the "invention of tradition" in Pacific countries. Throughout the Pacific, people now accept as historical traditions and customs practices that could only have emerged following the invasion and conquest of their islands by Western people. Keesing contends that because colonial intrusion has been so comprehensive, Pacific islanders know almost nothing about what their precolonial societies were really like. As a result, islanders have grasped onto certain idealized images of their past as themes and motifs to celebrate the distinctiveness of their cultures from dominant Western society. These idealized and largely fictional images have great political power for oppressed people, and they have often become a rallying point for various social movements. Nevertheless, concludes Keesing, these images of Pacific traditions find little support in historical documents and should largely be understood as modern mythmaking for the political ends of modern Pacific elites.

Hawaiian activist Haunani-Kay Trask attempts to turn Keesing's argument on its head by suggesting that Keesing's assertions about the "inventions" of Hawaiian traditions are yet another example of colonialism, racism, and white presumptions of superiority. She contends that Keesing only accepts Western historical sources, completely ignoring oral tradition, local mythologies, genealogies, and even rituals. Historical documents were biased by Western culture, argues Trask, and often represented an inaccurate understanding of native culture and social institutions. She questions whether or not white anthropologists have a privileged view of native customs, suggesting that most of Keesing's claims are racist attempts to further belittle native understanding and appreciation of the past.

Do native peoples or Western anthropologists have a better understanding of the native past? Have native traditions changed as much as Keesing would have us believe? Have these changes been the direct result of Western colonialism or have native peoples been active agents in such changes? Are Western historical sources biased and inaccurate when describing native practices? Are native oral traditions today accurate and authentic visions of traditional ways of life? Is there an authentic cultural tradition in any society, or, as Keesing suggests, are there different traditions for chiefs and for commoners, for men and for women? And, finally, are these "traditions" powerful as tools to fight oppression?

YES ⤶

Roger M. Keesing

Creating the Past: Custom and Identity in the Contemporary Pacific

Across the Pacific, from Hawai'i to New Zealand, in New Caledonia, Aboriginal Australia, Vanuatu, the Solomon Islands, and Papua New Guinea, Pacific peoples are creating pasts, myths of ancestral ways of life that serve as powerful political symbols. In the rhetoric of postcolonial nationalism (and sometimes separatism) and the struggles of indigenous Fourth World peoples, now minorities in their own homelands, visions of the past are being created and evoked.

Scholars of Pacific cultures and history who are sympathetic to these political struggles and quests for identity are in a curious and contradiction-ridden position in relation to these emerging ideologies of the past. The ancestral ways of life being evoked rhetorically may bear little relation to those documented historically, recorded ethnographically, and reconstructed archaeologically—yet their symbolic power and political force are undeniable.

Perhaps it does not matter whether the pasts being recreated and invoked are mythical or "real," in the sense of representing closely what actual people did in actual times and places. Political symbols radically condense and simplify "reality," and are to some extent devoid of content: that is how and why they work. Perhaps it matters only whether such political ideologies are used for just causes, whether they are instruments of liberation or of oppression. In the contemporary Pacific they are being used both to recapture just rights and to deny them. The question is less simple than that.

The process of recapturing the past, of reconstructing, of questioning Western scholarship—historical and anthropological—is important and essential. My intention is neither to defend established versions of the past from a standpoint of vested scholarly interest, nor to debunk emerging political myths by comparing them to actual pasts to which I claim privileged access. Rather, in showing contradictions in this process of political mythmaking and in showing how in many ways the contemporary discourses of cultural identity derive from Western discourses, I seek to promote a more genuinely radical stance in relation to both the more distant and the more recent past—and to Western domination, of minds as well as societies.

The discourse of identity, legitimacy, and historical origins—the political mythmaking of our time—is not as different from the political mythmaking of the pre-European Pacific as it might seem.

The "invention of tradition" has been extensively explored in recent years . . . , in relation to theoretical issues of ideology and representation, questions of political economy (such as the invention and evocation of a symbolically constructed Scottish Highlands culture, replete with woollen kilts from British mills as well as bagpipes . . . , and the dynamics of national-identity construction in postcolonial nation states. These phenomena have not been extensively explored for the Pacific. Nonetheless, they have occurred in other times and places and are going on at present in other settings. Contemporary Malaysia, where a mythic "Malay culture," a conflation of indigenous (but heavily Indianized) court traditions and Islam, is being used to persecute and disenfranchise Chinese and Indian minorities and indigenous ethnic groups, is a case in point.

Modern Mythmaking in the Pacific

Before I turn to some of the important theoretical issues raised by contemporary movements and ideologies of cultural identity, let me sketch briefly the range of phenomena I am concerned with.

Beginning with ideologies of *kastom* in contemporary Melanesia, I will illustrate four variants, or levels, mainly with reference to the Solomon Islands. These phenomena have counterparts in Vanuatu and Papua New Guinea.

First, at a national and regional level, are rhetorical appeals to "The Melanesian Way," and idealizations of custom (most often emanating from a Westernized elite). In Vanuatu in particular, the ideologies and charters of the postcolonial state enshrine customary law and institutions.

Second, are ritualized celebrations of custom in the form of the arts—music, dance, "traditional" dress—as dramatically enacted in art festivals, tourist events, and rituals of state.

Third, the rhetoric of custom is invoked with reference to a particular region or island or province within a postcolonial state. This may take the form of competition for state resources and political power, regional separatism, or even secessionist demands. . . . In the emergence of Papua New Guinea, secessionist claims by North Solomons and East New Britain were cast partly in terms of customary unity. . . .

Fourth, if the field of view is narrowed to particular language groups, particularly on islands like Malaita (or Tanna) where the commitment to "traditional" culture remains strong, we find ideologies of *kastom* used to resolve the contradictions between ancestral ways and Christianity. As Burt has documented, the Kwara'ae of central Malaita have produced origin myths that trace their ancestors back to wandering tribes of Israelites and codify ancestral rules in the style of Biblical commandments. The creation of mythical customs has been encouraged and even demanded by institutions of the postcolonial state that empower and legitimize "paramount chiefs" or other "traditional" leaders: contemporary Melanesia is now filled with "paramount chiefs" in areas that in precolonial times had no systems of chiefly authority or hereditary rank. . . .

In Australia, idealized representations of the pre-European past are used to proclaim Aboriginal identity and the attachment of indigenous peoples to the land, and are being deployed in environmentalist as well as Aboriginal political struggles. In New Zealand, increasingly powerful and successful Maori political movements incorporate idealized and mythicized versions of a precolonial Golden Age, the mystical wisdom of Aotearoa.

Hawai'i and New Caledonia exhibit further variants on the themes of Fourth World political struggle, with idealized representations of precolonial society deployed to assert common identity and to advance and legitimate political demands. In the Hawaiian case, a cultural tradition largely destroyed many decades ago must be reconstituted, reclaimed, revived, reinvented. A denial that so much has been destroyed and lost is achieved by political mythology and the sanctification of what survives, however, altered its forms. In New Caledonia, the issues are not simply the desperate struggle for political power and freedom from colonial oppression, but also the creation of both common bonds and common cultural identity among peoples whose ancestors were deeply divided, culturally and linguistically, into warring tribes speaking mutually unintelligible languages.

Some Theoretical Themes

These discourses of cultural identity in the contemporary Pacific, although they depict the precolonial past and claim to produce countercolonial images, are in many ways derived from Western ideologies.

. . . [C]ontemporary Third World (and Fourth World) representations of their own cultures have been shaped by colonial domination and the perception of Western culture through a less direct reactive process, a dialectic in which elements of indigenous culture are selected and valorized (at the levels of both ideology and practice) as *counters to* or *commentaries on* the intrusive and dominant colonial culture. That is, colonized peoples have distanced themselves from (as well as modeling their conceptual structures on) the culture of domination, selecting and shaping and celebrating the elements of their own traditions that most strikingly differentiate them from Europeans.

. . . Pacific Island elites, and Aboriginal Australians, Maori, and Hawaiians in a position to gain leadership roles and become ideologues, have been heavily exposed, through the educational process, to Western ideologies that idealize primitivity and the wisdom and ecological reverence of those who live close to Nature. Idealizations of the precolonial past in the contemporary Pacific have often been derivatives of Western critiques of modern technology and progress; ironically, those in the Pacific who in their rhetorical moments espouse these idealized views of the past are mainly (in their political actions and life-styles) hell-bent on technology, progress, materialism, and "development."

In the process of objectification, a culture is (at the level of ideology) imagined to consist of "traditional" music, dances, costumes, or artifacts.

Periodically performing or exhibiting these fetishized representations of their cultures, the elites of the new Pacific ritually affirm (to themselves, the tourists, the village voters) that the ancestral cultural heritage lives on.

. . . [A]ssertions of identity based on idealizations of the ancestral past draw heavily on anthropological concepts—particularly ideas about "culture"— as they have entered Western popular thought. It is ironic that cultural nationalist rhetoric often depicts anthropologists as villains who appropriate and exploit, although that anti-anthropological rhetoric is itself squarely shaped by anthropology's concepts and categories. . . .

European scholars are implicated in a more direct way in some of the misrepresentations of ancestral cultures. Some of the classic accounts and generalizations about the cultures of Polynesia and Melanesia by expatriate scholars—to which Islanders have been exposed through books and other media—are misleading. Western scholars' own misrenderings and stereotypes have fed back into contemporary (mis)representations of the Pacific past.

In questioning the political myths of our time, I am not defending the authority of anthropological representations of the Pacific past, or the hegemonic position of scholarly discourse in relation to the aspirations of indigenous peoples to recapture their own pasts. The past . . . is contested ground. I am urging that in contesting it, Pacific Islanders be more relentlessly radical and skeptical—not that they relinquish it to the "experts." (We who claim expertise, too, can well reflect on the politics and epistemology of our privileged authority.)

Finally (and critically), if I seem to imply a gulf between the authenticity of actual precolonial societies and cultures and the inauthenticity of the mythic pasts now being invented in the Pacific, such a characterization in fact perpetuates some of anthropology's own myths. The present political contexts in which talk of custom and ancestral ways goes on are of course very different from precolonial contexts. Nonetheless, such mystification is inherent in political processes, in all times and places. Spurious pasts and false histories were being promulgated in the Pacific long before Europeans arrived, as warrior leaders draped veils of legitimacy over acts of conquest, as leaders sought to validate, reinforce, [and] institutionalize, . . . and as factions battled for dominance. Ironically, then, the "true" and "authentic" cultures of the Pacific past, overlain and distorted by today's political myths, represent, in part at least, cumulations of the political myths of the ancestors.

In Pacific communities on the eve of European invasion, there were multiple "realities"—for commoners and for chiefs, for men and for women, for young and for old, for free persons and for captives or slaves, for victors and for vanquished. Genealogies, cosmologies, rituals were themselves contested spheres. The "authentic" past was never a simple, unambiguous reality. The social worlds of the Pacific prior to European invasion were, like the worlds of the present, multifaceted and complex.

Moreover, however the past may be constructed as a symbol, and however critical it may be for historically dominated peoples to recapture this ground, a people's cultural heritage poses a challenge to radical questioning. We are all to some degree prisoners of "real" pasts as they survive into the present—in the form of patriarchal values and institutions, of patterns of thought, of structures of power. A deeply radical discourse (one that questions basic assumptions) would aspire to liberate us from pasts, both those of our ancestors and those of (colonial or other) domination, as well as to use them as political symbols.

Let me develop these arguments. . . .

The Fetishization of "Culture"

Not only in the Pacific are dramatizations and ritual enactments of cultural traditions being celebrated—in the form of dress, music, dance, handicrafts— while actual cultural traditions are vanishing. The two processes—the celebration of fossilized or fetishized cultures and the destruction of cultures as ways of life and thought—are going on in the Soviet Union, eastern Europe, and China and also in the Andean states, Brazil, Malaysia, and Indonesia. Perhaps it is an essential element in the process of nation building, where populations are ethnically diverse. Most often, a dominant national population imposes its language and cultural tradition on minority groups while appearing to value and preserve minority cultures: they are preserved like specimens in jars. . . . What greater alienation than watching those who dominate and rule you perform symbolically central elements of your cultural heritage: selling *your* culture?

What makes the Pacific distinctive here is the way, particularly in the Melanesian countries, the specimens in the jars are the cultures those with political power have themselves left behind. Members of the Westernized elites are likely to be separated by gulfs of life experience and education from village communities where they have never lived: their ancestral cultures are symbols rather than experienced realities. Bringing the specimens out of the jars on special occasions—cultural festivals, rituals of state—is a denial of alienation at a personal level, and a denial that cultural traditions are being eroded and destroyed in the village hinterlands. . . .

By the same logic, the "cultures" so commoditized and packaged can be sold to tourists. I have commented elsewhere on the way this commoditization shapes Pacific cultures to fit Western fantasies:

> Mass tourism and the media have created a new Pacific in which what is left or reconstructed from the ruins of cultural destruction of earlier decades is commoditized and packaged as exoticism for the tourists. The Pacific [is] Fantasy Land for Europe and the United States (and now for Japan) . . . to be symbolically constructed—and consumed by a consumerist society, to serve its pleasures and needs.
>
> The commoditization of their cultures has left tens of thousands of Pacific Islanders as aliens in their own lands, reduced to tawdry commercialized representations of their ancestors, histories and cultures. Beneath the veneer of fantasy, the Islanders are pauperized in village hinterlands or themselves commoditized as menial employees. Serving the comforts as well as the fantasies of rich tourists, they are constrained to smile and "be happy," because that is part of their symbolic image.

We need only think of tourism in Fiji. There, at least, the elements of culture enacted for tourists represent a version, if an edited and Christianized one (no strangling of widows in the hotel dining rooms), of a past that actually existed. The representations of "Hawaiian culture" for tourists, with hula dances, ukuleles, and pineapples, illustrate that where there is a gulf between historical realities and the expectations of tourists, the fantasies will be packaged and sold.

Invented Pasts and Anthropology

The objectification of a way of life, the reification of the customs of ancestors into a symbol to which a political stance is taken—whether of rejection or idealization—is not new in the Pacific, and is not confined to Islanders who have learned the Western concept of "culture." The so-called Vailala Madness of the Gulf Division of Papua in 1919, where villagers destroyed cult objects in a wave of iconoclasm, and proclaimed their rejection of the ways of ancestors who had withheld material riches from them, is but one example. Other classic "cargo cults" echoed the same theme.

The political stances being taken toward the ways of the ancestors in the contemporary Pacific reflect some of the same mechanisms. When massively confronted with an engulfing or technologically dominating force—whether early colonial invaders or more recently the world capitalist system and late-twentieth-century technology and wealth—one is led to take an objectified, externalized view of one's way of life that would hardly be possible if one were simply *living* it. Land, and spiritual connection to it, *could not* have, other than in a context of invasion and displacement and alienation, the ideological significance it acquires in such a context.

The ideologies of our time, unlike cargo cult ideologies, are phrased in terms of "culture" and other anthropological concepts, as they have passed into Western popular thought and intellectual discourse. This is hardly surprising, given the educational experiences of Pacific Island leaders, but it is problematic nonetheless, because the concepts that have been borrowed oversimplify in ways that have bedeviled anthropology for decades. First, "culture" represents a reification. A complex system of ideas and customs, attributed a false concreteness, is turned into a causal agent. Cultures are viewed as doing things, causing things to happen (or not happen).

In the framework of functionalist anthropology, societies and cultures have been attributed a spurious coherence and integration and portrayed in a timeless equilibrium. The timelessness and integration of the ideologically constructed Pacific pasts represent in part a projection of anthropology's own conceptual simplifications into contemporary political myths.

. . . Pacific Island peoples asserting their identity and their continuity with the past are led to seek, characterize, and proclaim an "essence" that has endured despite a century or more of change and Westernization.

In a different and older anthropological tradition—one that lives on in anthropology museums, hence is represented in the contemporary Pacific—a culture is metonymically represented by its material artifacts. This museological tradition, which has old roots in the nineteenth-century folklorism of Europe, has fed as well into the discourse on cultural identity, as I have noted. From it derives the view that in preserving the material forms and performance genres of a people, one preserves their culture.

In borrowing from anthropological discourse, ideologies of cultural identity in the contemporary Pacific have not only acquired conceptual over-simplifications but have incorporated some empirical distortions and mis-interpretations for which anthropologists (and other European scholars) are ultimately responsible.

It is not that Aboriginal or Maori activists, or contemporary Samoans or Trobriand Islanders, are uncritical in their acceptance of what anthropologists have written about them. In Aboriginal struggles for land rights, for example, one of the battles has been waged against orthodox views, deriving ultimately from Radcliffe-Brown, of the patrilineality of local territorial groups—views incorporated into federal land rights legislation. The ironies and contradic-tions of Aboriginal peoples being denied rights they believe are culturally legitimate on grounds that they do not fit an anthropological model have chilling implications for those of us who would claim privileged authority for our "expertise" or *our* constructions of the past.

There is a further twist of irony when scholarly interpretations that may be faulty, or at least misleadingly oversimplified or overgeneralized, have been incorporated by Pacific Islanders into their conceptions of their own pasts. Let me illustrate with the concept of *mana* in Oceanic religion. . . . When I was at the University of South Pacific in 1984 and spoke on *mana*, I discovered that Polynesian students and faculty had been articulating an ideology of a common Polynesian cultural heritage and identity in which *mana* was central. Yet, as I pointed out, in many languages in Western Polynesia *mana* is used as a noun only to describe thunder, lightning, or other meteorological phenomena. Where *mana is* used as a noun to refer to spiritual power, in a number of Polynesian languages, it seems to be a sec-ondary usage, less common than its usage as a stative verb ('be effective', 'be potent', 'be sacred').

Mana in the sense it has acquired in anthropology seems centrally important only in a few languages of eastern Polynesia, notably Maori and Hawaiian. . . .

The imputation of mystical wisdom to Polynesians (who in the process were distinguished from their dark-skinned, savage, cannibal neighbors to the west) has roots in European theories of race. The construction of the Polyne-sians in European thought, a process going back to the early explorers, has been brilliantly examined by Bernard Smith. Most striking has been the con-struction of Maori culture in European imagination. . . . The cosmic philoso-phy of the Maori, the mystical worldview, is as much a European as a Polynesian creation. Even though contemporary Maori ideologues attempt to discredit some aspects of the representation of Maori culture by Western scholars, the counterrepresentation advanced as authentic seems deeply infused by early Western romanticizations of the Maori. . . .

Political Mythology and Cultural "Authenticity": A Wider View

So far, I have implied that there is a wide gulf between the authentic past—the real ways of life that prevailed in the Pacific on the eve of European invasion—and the representations of the past in contemporary ideologies of cultural identity. This gulf requires a closer look.

. . . My point is . . . that the real past was itself highly political. Pacific societies, in pre-European times, were far from stable and static . . . : they were, as the archaeological record makes very clear, marked by political expansions and contractions, regional systems, warfare, trade—and change. Anthropological models have by and large failed to capture the dynamics of cultural production and change. Cultures are often imagined to be like coral reefs, the gradual accumulation of countless "polyps." . . . To the contrary, . . . cultural production is a highly political process. The symbolic material of cultures—rules imputed to ancestors, rituals, myths—serves ideological ends, reinforcing the power of some, the subordination of others.

From such a viewpoint, the authentic ancestral cultures of the past begin to appear in a different light. The rituals, the myths, the ideologies of hierarchy and the sanctity of chiefs, served political purposes. Conquering chiefs—or their priestly retinues—invented genealogies connecting them to the gods, and discrediting fallen rivals. Those individuals or classes acquiring sufficient political power to control symbolic production could bend cultural rules and roles to their own ends, reinforcing and legitimating their power. (The old Polynesian process whereby ascendant chiefly factions produce and impose versions of the past that legitimate their ascendancy in cosmic and genealogical terms has clearly continued into the latter twentieth century, notably in Tonga.) "Ancestral cultures" themselves represented legitimations of political power and aspirations; cultures were contested spheres. In this sense, the political myths of the contemporary Pacific that refashion the past to advance the interests of the present are not so different from the political myths of the past, dutifully recorded by the early ethnographers.

There are political contexts where it is important for an idealized vision of the past to be used as counter to the present: to the world capitalist system as it incorporates poor Third World countries on its margins as primary producers and consumers; to mindless materialism, disintegration of bonds of kinship and community, narcissistic individualism, destruction of environments for short-term profit. There is a place for pastoral visions, in the West and in the Pacific.

And there is certainly a place for discourses of resistance cast in terms of cultural identity. For Fourth World indigenous minorities in the Pacific—Maori, Aboriginal Australians, Kanaks, Hawaiians—a reverence for what survives of the cultural past (however altered its forms), and for a lost heritage, is a necessary counterpoint to deep anger over the generations of destruction.

But such ideologies become self-delusory if they are not interspersed with visions of "real" pasts that cast into relief not simply their idealized virtues, but their cracks of contradictions. . . . European scholars of the Pacific have been complicit in legitimating and producing male-oriented and elitist representations of societies that were themselves male- and (in many cases) elite-dominated. A critical skepticism with regard to pasts and power, and a critical deconstruction of conceptualizations of "a culture" that hide and neutralize subaltern voices and perspectives, should, I think, dialectically confront idealizations of the past. I am encouraged by the emergence, in the last several years, of critical writings in this vein by Pacific Islanders, including Epeli Hau'ofa and a number of feminist critics.

This is not the time to leave the past to the "experts," whether of the present generation or their predecessors. . . .

A more radical Pacific discourse would also be more deeply self-reflexive about the hegemonic force of Western education, of Christianity (an integral part of the colonial-imperialist project), of Western pastoral myths as appropriations of Otherness. . . .

A similar self-reflexivity is a continuing challenge for scholars working in the Pacific. Both the political implications and epistemology of our projects and representations are deeply problematic. The frame of certainty that surrounds scholarly expertise—like mythical history—is less solid than it seems: it dissolves in the right mixture of astute skepticism and self-reflexivity. But specialists on the Pacific do not best serve the interests of a less hegemonic scholarship or best support the political struggles of decolonizing and internally colonized Pacific peoples by suspending their critical judgment or maintaining silence—whether out of liberal guilt or political commitment—regarding mythic pasts evoked in cultural nationalist rhetoric. Our constructions of real pasts are not sacrosanct, but they are important elements in a continuing dialogue and dialectic.

Haunani-Kay Trask **NO**

Natives and Anthropologists:
The Colonial Struggle

As a Hawaiian, a long-time outspoken defender of my people's claim to nationhood, a scholar, and a Native who knows her history and people, I found Roger Keesing's article . . . a gem of academic colonialism. Knowing oldfashioned racism too crude to defend but bitterly clinging to his sense of white superiority, Keesing plows the complaining path of the unappreciated missionary who, when confronted by ungrateful, decolonizing Natives, thinly veils his hurt and anger by the high road of lamentation: Alas, poor, bedeviled Natives "invent" their culture in reaction to colonialism, and all in the service of grimy politics!

Keesing's peevishness has a predictably familiar target: Native nationalists—from Australia and New Zealand through the Solomons and New Caledonia to Hawai'i. The problem? These disillusioned souls idealize their pasts for the purpose of political mythmaking in the present. Worse, they are so unoriginal (and, by implication, unfamiliar with what Keesing calls their "real" pasts) as to concoct their myths out of Western categories and values despite their virulent opposition to same. Thus the romanticization of pre-European Native pasts (the "Golden Age" allegedly claimed by the Maori); the assertion of a common Native identity (eg, Fijian "culture"); the "ideology" of land as spiritually significant (supposedly argued by Hawaiians, Solomon Islanders, Kanaks, and Aborigines). The gospel, according to Keesing, is that these claims are "invented." To be specific, there never was a "Golden Age," a common identity, or a spiritual attachment to the land.

Proof? Keesing supplies none, either on the charge that Native nationalists have made such claims or that their claims are false. He merely asserts fabrication then proceeds to belabor, through the mumbo jumbo of academic "discourse," the crying need for Natives (and academics) to face "our" pasts with "skepticism," while pursuing a "critical deconstruction of conceptualizations" to achieve "dialectical confrontation." The final intention should be to "liberate us" from our pasts.

Well, my answer to Keesing has been said by modern-day Natives to would-be White Fathers many times: What do you mean "us," white man?

Among Hawaiians, people like Keesing are described as *maha'oi haole*, that is, rude, intrusive white people who go where they do not belong. In Keesing's case, his factual errors, cultural and political ignorance, and dismissive

From *The Contemporary Pacific*, Spring 1991, pp. 159–166. Copyright © 1991 by University of Hawaii Press. Reprinted by permission.

attitude qualify him perfectly as *maha'oi*. Unlike Keesing; I cannot speak for other Natives. But regarding Hawaiian nationalists, Keesing neither knows whereof he speaks, nor given his *maha'oi* attitude, does he care.

Example.   Keesing only cites works by *haole* academics on the current situation in Hawai'i. Obviously, he hasn't bothered to read our Native nationalists and scholars, including those, like myself, who have been very critical of these same *haole* academics. Indeed, most of his comments on Hawaiian nationalists come from one problematic and contested article (contested by Natives, that is) by anthropologist Jocelyn Linnekin, hardly a sound evidentiary base for sweeping claims that we invent our past.

Beyond his poverty of sources, there is Keesing's willful ignorance of solid evidence from Native forms of history—genealogy—which reveal that in pre-*haole* Hawai'i our people looked on land as a mother, enjoyed a familial relationship with her and other living things, and practiced an economically wise, spiritually based ethic of caring for the land, called *mālama 'āina*.

Contrary to Linnekin's claims, and Keesing's uncritical acceptance of them, the value of *mālama 'āina* has been "documented historically," and "recorded ethnographically," (as Keesing might learn if he read Native sources), two of the criteria Keesing cites as central to any judgment of the accuracy of "ancestral ways of life being evoked rhetorically" by Native nationalists today.[1] If Natives must be held to Keesing's criteria, why should he be allowed to escape them?

The answer is that Keesing, with many Western academics, shares a common assumption: Natives don't know very much, even about their own lifeways, thus there is no need to read them. (The only "real" sources are *haole* sources, hegemony recognizing and reinforcing hegemony).

Keesing's racism is exposed here. Not only has he refused to read what we Native nationalists write and say, he has refused to look at our sources of knowledge. But then, Keesing believes, Natives are so colonized, why bother?

Example.   Keesing has also failed to distinguish between what Hawaiian nationalists say about our ways of life and what the mammoth tourist industry advertises "Hawaiian culture" to be, including "hula dances, ukuleles, and pineapples." Because he is totally ignorant of modern Hawaiian resistance, he is also totally ignorant of the Native criticism of the tourist industry, including the myth of happy Natives waiting to share their "culture" with tourists. In fact, after years of Native resistance to tourism, the churches in Hawai'i (with the push of Native nationalists and international ecumenical groups) sponsored a conference on the impact of tourism on Hawaiian people and culture in 1989. At that conference, Hawaiians from each of our major islands spoke eloquently of tourism's damage to Hawaiian sites, dance, language, economics, land, and way of life. The declaration issued from that conference listed ways to halt this damage, including a ban on all resorts in Hawaiian communities. Keesing should be reading this kind of primary evidence if he wants to learn what Hawaiian nationalists think about tourism and our culture.

Example.   Keesing claims that Native nationalists hark back to an "authentic," "simple, unambiguous reality," when, in fact, "there were multiple 'realities'— for commoners and chiefs, for men and for women . . ." in cultures where "genealogies, cosmologies, rituals were themselves contested spheres."

As usual, the critical reader finds not a single reference here to a single Native nationalist statement. More *haole* sources follow, especially Keesing on Keesing. But where are the Natives?

In the dark, naturally.

The truth is that Keesing has made a false charge. Those of us in the current Hawaiian nationalist movement know that genealogies are claimed and contested all the time. Some of the chiefly lineages have legal claims on lands taken by the United States government at the American annexation of Hawai'i in 1898, which means that genealogies have an impact beyond the Hawaiian community. Cosmologies are also contested, with nationalists citing and arguing over accuracy and preferability.[2]

Finally, at the Center for Hawaiian Studies—which generates nationalist positions, sponsors nationalist conferences, and teaches the historical background and political substance of nationalist arguments—students are required to take a course on genealogies.

Given Roger Keesing's shameless claims about us Hawaiian nationalists, I invite him to take this course, or any other offered at our center. We Natives might teach him something.

Example.   Keesing asserts that "cultural nationalist rhetoric often depicts anthropologists as villains who appropriate and exploit." In a note, he adds that anthropologists are "imagined to be appropriating and profiting from other people's cultures. . . ."

In Hawai'i, contract work is a major source of funding for archaeologists and anthropologists. These people are hired by investors and state or private institutions to survey areas and deem them ready for use. In highly controversial cases regarding removal of Hawaiian bones and destruction of Hawaiian temple and house sites, many archaeologists and anthropologists have argued *for* development and *against* preservation while receiving substantial sums of money. At its worst, these controversies have exposed the racist paternalism of anthropologists who pit (in their own words) *emotional* Hawaiians who try to stop disinterment and development against *scientific* anthropologists who try to increase the store of (Western) knowledge.

Of course, these *haole* anthropologists would be outraged were we Hawaiians to dig up *their* relatives for osteological analysis, search for evidence of tuberculosis and other diseases, and, not coincidentally, get paid handsomely for our troubles. To my knowledge, no anthropologist has ever dug up missionary bones, despite their plentiful presence. Nor has any haole "expert" ever argued that missionary skeletons should be subjected to osteological analysis, despite historical evidence that missionaries did bring certain diseases to Hawai'i. White colonialism in Hawai'i ensures that it is the colonizers who determine disinterment. Since we are the colonized, we have no power to disinter the bones of the colonizer. Thus, Native remains are dug up and studied. Missionary and explorer remains are sacrosanct.

Apart from contract work, anthropologists make academic careers and employment off Native cultures. Keesing may not think this is "profiting," but anthropologists who secure tenure by studying, publishing, and lecturing about Native peoples are clearly "profiting" through a guaranteed lifetime income. Of course, Keesing is disingenuous, at best. He knows as well as Native nationalists that anthropologists without Natives are like entomologists without insects.

For Hawaiians, anthropologists in general (and Keesing in particular) are part of the colonizing horde because they seek to take away from us the power to define who and what we are, and how we should behave politically and culturally.[3] This theft testifies to the stranglehold of colonialism and explains why self-identity by Natives elicits such strenuous and sometimes vicious denials by members of the dominant culture.

These denials are made in order to undermine the legitimacy of Native nationalists by attacking their motives in asserting their values and institutions. But motivation is laid bare through the struggle for cultural expression. Nationalists offer explanations at every turn: in writing, in public forums, in acts of resistance. To Natives, the burst of creative outpouring that accompanies cultural nationalism is self-explanatory: a choice has been made for things Native over things non-Native. Politically, the choice is one of decolonization.

The direct links between mental and political decolonization are clearly observable to representatives of the dominant culture, like Keesing, who find their status as "experts" on Natives suddenly repudiated by Natives themselves. This is why thinking and acting like a native is a highly politicized reality, one filled with intimate oppositions and psychological tensions. But it is not Natives who create politicization. *That* was begun at the moment of colonization.

In the Hawaiian case, the "invention" criticism has been thrown into the public arena precisely at a time when Hawaiian cultural and political assertion has been both vigorous and strong willed. Since 1970, Hawaiians have been organizing for land rights, including claims to restitution for the American overthrow of our government in 1893 and for forced annexation in 1898. Two decades of struggle have resulted in the contemporary push for Hawaiian sovereignty, with arguments ranging from complete secession to legally incorporated land-based units managed by Hawaiians, to a "nation-within-a-nation" government akin to Native American Indian nations. The US government has issued two reports on the status of Hawaiian trust lands, which encompass nearly half the State of Hawai'i. And finally, a quasi-governmental agency—the Office of Hawaiian Affairs—was created in 1978, partly in response to Hawaiian demands.

This kind of political activity has been accompanied by a flourishing of Hawaiian dance, a move for Hawaiian language immersion schools, and a larger public sensitivity to the destructive Western relationship to the land compared to the indigenous Hawaiian way of caring for the land.

Non-Native response to this Hawaiian resistance has varied from humor, through mild denial that any wrong has been committed against the Hawaiian people and government, to organized counteraction, especially from threat-ened agencies and actors who hold power over Hawaiian resources. Indeed, representatives of the dominant culture—from historians and anthropologists to bureaucrats and politicians—are quick to feel and perceive danger because, in the colonial context, all Native cultural resistance is political: it challenges hegemony, including that of people like Keesing who claim to encourage a more "radical stance" toward our past by liberating us from it.

But Keesing obviously knows nothing about Hawaiians. He has failed to distinguish land claims from cultural resurgence, although both have nationalist origins. And he has little or no background regarding the theft of Hawaiian domain and dominion by the American government in the nine-teenth century. Given this kind of ignorance of both our recent and distant past, Keesing would do better to take a "radical" look at the racism and arro-gance of *his* culture which originated anthropology and its "search for the primitive."

As for nationalist Hawaiians, we know our future lies in the ways of our ancestors, not in the colonial world of *haole* experts. Our efforts at "libera-tion" are directed against the colonizers, whether they be political agencies, like the American government, or academics, like Keesing himself. We do not need, nor do we want to be "liberated" from our past because it is the source of our understanding of the cosmos and of our *mana*.

In our language, the past (*ka wā mamua*) is the time in front or before; the future (*ka wā mahope*) is the time that comes after. In the words of one of our best living Native historians, Lilikalā Kame'eleihiwa (whom Keesing did not read), "The Hawaiian stands firmly in the present, with his back to the future, and his eyes fixed upon the past, seeking historical answers for present-day dilemmas. Such an orientation is to the Hawaiian an eminently practical one, for the future is always unknown whereas the past is rich in glory and knowledge."

Notes

1. In her article, Linnekin writes, "For Hawai'i, 'traditional' properly refers to the precontact era, before Cook's arrival in 1778." But later on the same page, she admits that "tradition is fluid . . ." Despite this confusion she criticizes Hawaiians for a "reconstruction of traditional Hawaiian society" in the present.

   But what constitutes "tradition" to a people is ever-changing. Culture is not static, nor is it frozen in objectified moments in time. Without doubt, Hawaiians were transformed drastically and irreparably after contact, but remnants of earlier lifeways, including values and symbols, have persisted. One of these values is the Hawaiian responsibility to care for the land, to make it flourish, called *mālama 'āina* or *aloha 'āina*. To Linnekin, this value has been invented by modern Hawaiians to protest degradation of the land by developers, the military, and others. What Linnekin has missed here—partly because she has an incomplete grasp of "traditional" values but also because she doesn't understand and thus misapprehends Hawaiian cultural nationalism—is simply this: the Hawaiian relationship to land has persisted into the present. What has changed is ownership and use of the land (from collective use by Hawaiians for subsistence to private use by whites and other non-Natives for profit). Asserting the Hawaiian relationship in this changed context results in politicization. Thus, Hawaiians assert a "traditional" relationship to the land *not* for political ends, as Linnekin (and Keesing) argue, but because they continue to believe in the cultural value of caring for the land. That land use is now contested makes such a belief political. This distinction is crucial because the Hawaiian cultural motivation reveals the persistence of traditional values, the very thing Linnekin (and Keesing) allege modern Hawaiians to have "invented."

2.   In Hawai'i the Kawananakoa line contests the loss of governance, since they were heirs to the throne at the time of the American military-backed overthrow of Hawaiian Queen Lili'uokalani. The Salazar family lays claim to part of the Crown lands for similar reasons. Regarding land issues, the Ka'awa family occupied Makapu'u Point in 1988 in protest over its current use. Their argument revolved around their claim to ownership because of their genealogical connection to the Kamehameha line. Among nationalist organizations, 'Ohana o Hawai'i, led by Peggy Ha'o Ross, argues claims to leadership based on genealogy. These examples illustrate the continuity of genealogy as profoundly significant to Hawaiians in establishing mana and, thus, the power to command recognition and leadership. Keesing obviously knows nothing about any of these families or their claims.

3.   The United States government defines Native Hawaiians as those with 50 percent or more Hawaiian blood quantum. Those with less than 50 percent Hawaiian blood are not considered to be "Native" and are thus not entitled to lands and monies set aside for 50 percent bloods. Hawaiians are the only human beings in the State of Hawai'i who are categorized by blood quantum, rather like Blacks in South Africa.

While bureaucrats are happily dividing up who is and is not Native, the substance of *what* constitutes things Hawaiian is constantly asserted by anthropologists against Native nationalists. Of course, the claim to knowledge by anthropologists is their academic training applied to the field. Native nationalists' claim to knowledge is their life experience as Natives.

The problem is more serious than epistemology, however. In a colonial world, the work of anthropologists and other Western-trained "experts" is used to disparage and exploit Natives. What Linnekin or Keesing or any other anthropologist writes about Hawaiians has more potential power than what Hawaiians write about themselves. Proof of this rests in the use of Linnekin's argument by the US Navy that Hawaiian nationalists have invented the sacred meaning of Kaho'olawe Island (which the US Navy has controlled and bombed since the Second World War) because nationalists need a "political and cultural symbol of protest" in the modern period. Here, the connection between anthropology and the colonial enterprise is explicit. When Natives accuse Western scholars of exploiting them, they have in mind the exact kind of situation I am describing. In fact, the Navy's study was done by an anthropologist who, of course, cited fellow anthropologists, including Linnekin, to argue that the Hawaiian assertion of love and sacredness regarding Kaho'olawe was "fakery." Far from overstating their case, Native nationalists acutely comprehend the structure of their oppression, including that perpetuated by anthropologists.

POSTSCRIPT

Do Native Peoples Today Invent Their Traditions?

Building on Hobsbawm and Ranger's notion of the "invention of traditon," Keesing makes the case that in most—if not all—Pacific societies, the history and cultural traditions that are regarded as authentic are substantially different from the events and practices that actually occurred. In his mind, there can also be little doubt that controlling what is accepted as tradition has become politically important. How does Trask's concern over professional bias impact Keesing's other arguments? What criteria would Trask suggest as a substitute as a way of judging which practices are authentic traditions and which are modern innovations?

Many other anthropologists have addressed the question of the invention of tradition. In Hawaii, the best-known work is by Jocelyn Linnekin, especially her 1983 essay "Defining Tradition: Variations on the Hawaiian Identity," *American Ethnologist* (vol. 10) and her book *Children of the Land* (Rutgers University Press, 1985). See also Trask's review of the latter in the *Hawaiian Journal of History* (vol. 20, 1986).

Questions about the invention of traditions have become important in North America as well. In 1997 Brian D. Haley and Larry R. Wilcoxon published an essay in *Current Anthropology* (vol. 38) entitled "Anthropology and the Making of Chumash Tradition." They argued that anthropologists and environmentalists had encouraged Chumash Indians to exaggerate claims that a site proposed for industrial development was traditionally sacred. The following year, archaeologist John McVey Erlandson published a reply to Haley and Wilcoxon in *Current Anthropology* (vol. 39). Like Keesing, Erlandson drew on historical (white American) sources to defend his position that the site was held to be sacred.

Another anthropologist, Alan Hanson, wrote a similar but more focused argument about the invention of tradition among the Maori of New Zealand in "The Making of the Maori: Culture Invention and Its Logic," *American Anthropologist* (vol. 91, no. 4, 1989). This essay prompted a vigorous and at times hostile debate within New Zealand, and at one point some Maori threatened to censure the American Anthropological Association because of this article, which some considered racist and anti-Maori. Stephen Webster discusses this topic in light of the so-called Maori renaissance, a revival of Maori cultural values within the modern bicultural state of New Zealand in his book, *Patrons of Maori Culture: Power, Theory and Ideology in the Maori Renaissance* (University of Otago Press, 1998).

ISSUE 11

Do Men Dominate Women in All Societies?

YES: **Steven Goldberg**, from "Is Patriarchy Inevitable?" *National Review* (November 11, 1996)

NO: **Kirk M. Endicott and Karen L. Endicott,** from *The Headman Was a Woman: The Gender Egalitarian Batek of Malaysia* (Waveland Press, 2008)

ISSUE SUMMARY

YES: Sociologist Steven Goldberg contends that in all societies men occupy most high positions in hierarchical organizations and most high-status roles, and they also tend to dominate women in interpersonal relations. This is because men's hormones cause them to compete more strongly than women for status and dominance.

NO: Cultural anthropologists Kirk and Karen Endicott argue that among the Batek people of Malaysia gender roles are not rigidly distinguished. Even the headman of the foraging band in which they lived was a woman. Batek women and men have autonomy and similar access to possessions. They contend that Batek social and cultural treatment of the two sexes is remarkably egalitarian.

$\mathbf{I}$n most of the world's societies, men hold the majority of leadership positions in public organizations, from government bodies to corporations and religious institutions. In families, husbands usually serve as heads of households and as primary breadwinners, while wives take responsibility for children and domestic activities within the household. Is the predominance of men in these public areas of family life universal and inevitable, a product of our human nature, or is it a cultural fact that might vary or be absent under different cultural conditions? Is it even possible for any human society to be sexually egalitarian? Are there any societies where men and women are equally valued and have equal access to possessions, power, and prestige?

Some nineteenth-century cultural evolutionists, including J. J. Bachofen and J. F. MacLellan, postulated that the patriarchal societies known from history had been preceded by a matriarchal stage of evolution in which women held the dominant social roles in society. Today, nearly all anthropologists doubt that any matriarchal societies ever existed. Some societies trace descent through women, matrilineally, and in these societies women play a more prominent public role than in patrilineal societies, where descent is traced from father to children.

European societies have never been either matrilineal or matriarchal; they are examples of societies that are firmly patriarchal. Most Europeans and Americans have long considered this state of affairs both natural and God-given.

The anthropology of women arising in the 1970s challenged claims that the subordination of women was either natural or inevitable. Feminists took up the rallying cry, "Biology is not destiny." They argued that women could do anything that society permitted them to do, and that patriarchal society, like any other social institution, could be changed.

Some feminist anthropologists considered male dominance to be universal, but attributed it to universal cultural, not biological, causes. The groundbreaking volume *Women, Culture, and Society,* edited by Michelle Rosaldo and Louise Lamphere (Stanford University Press, 1974), presents some possible cultural reasons for universal male dominance. Rosaldo and Lamphere propose that all societies distinguish between "domestic" and "public" domains; women are associated with the domestic domain, with the home and raising children, while men are active in the public domain, where they have opportunities to obtain wealth, power, and ties with other men.

Some anthropologists contend that sexually egalitarian societies once existed (e.g., Eleanor Leacock's "Women's Status in Egalitarian Society: Implications for Social Evolution," *Current Anthropology* [vol. 19, 1978]). They attribute the scarcity of such societies today to historical circumstances, especially the spread of European patriarchal culture to the rest of the world.

Here, Steven Goldberg presents a biological explanation for male dominance, contending that males have more of the hormones that cause individuals to strive for dominance than women do. Thus, regardless of cultural variations, men will occupy most of the high-status and high-ranking positions in any society. Biologically, men are also best suited to be dominant in interpersonal relations with women.

In their selection, Kirk and Karen Endicott present evidence that the Batek of Malaysia are an example of a gender egalitarian society. Males and females participate in most of the same daily activities, and both men and women are involved with children and domestic affairs. There are no high-status roles in this society, but the headman of the hunter-gatherer band with whom the Endicotts lived was a woman, not a man. For the authors, the Batek case challenges authors like Goldberg who assert that men are dominant in all societies.

While reading these selections, ask yourself whether or not the Batek case actually contradicts Goldberg's assertion that all societies are male dominated. Would a single egalitarian society disprove Goldberg's thesis? If you accept Goldberg's contention that males have an innate tendency toward domination, can you think of any cultural arrangements that might neutralize male superiority, or at least keep it in check?

YES

Steven Goldberg

Is Patriarchy Inevitable?

In five hundred years the world, in all likelihood, will have become homogenized. The thousands of varied societies and their dramatically differing methods of socialization, cohesion, family, religion, economy, and politics will have given way to a universal culture. Fortunately, cultural anthropologists have preserved much of our present diversity, which may keep our descendants from too hastily allowing their natural human ego- and ethno-centricity to conclude that theirs is the only way to manage a society.

However, the anthropological sword is two-edged. While diversity is certainly apparent from anthropological investigations, it is also clear that there are realities which manifest themselves no matter what the varied forms of the aforementioned institutions. Because these universal realities cut across cultural lines, they are crucial to our understanding of what society *by its nature* is and, perhaps, of what human beings are. It is important, then, that we ask why, when societies differ as much as do those of the Ituri Pygmy, the Jivaro, the American, the Japanese, and a thousand others, some institutions are universal.

It is always the case that the universal institution serves some need rooted in the deepest nature of human beings. In some cases the explanation of universality is obvious (e.g., why every society has methods of food gathering). But there are other universalities which are apparent, though without any obvious explanation. Of the thousands of societies on which we have any evidence stronger than myth (a form of evidence that would have us believe in cyclopes), there is no evidence that there has ever been a society failing to exhibit three institutions:

1. Primary hierarchies always filled primarily by men. A Queen Victoria or a Golda Meir is always an exception and is always surrounded by a government of men. Indeed, the constraints of royal lineage may produce more female societal leaders than does democracy—there were more female heads of state in the first two-thirds of the sixteenth century than there were in the first two-thirds of the twentieth.

2. The highest status roles are male. There are societies in which the women do most of the important economic work and rear the children, while the men seem mostly to hang loose. But, in such societies, hanging loose is given

From *The National Review*, November 11, 1996, pp. 32, 34–36. Copyright © 1996 by National Review, Inc., 215 Lexington Avenue, New York, NY 10016. Reprinted by permission.

higher status than any non-maternal role primarily served by women. No doubt this is partly due to the fact that the males hold the positions of power. However, it is also likely that high-status roles are male not primarily because they are male (ditch-digging is male and low status), but because they are high status. The high status roles are male because they possess—for whatever socially determined reason in whichever specific society—high status. This high status exerts a more powerful influence on males than it does on females. As a result, males are more willing to sacrifice life's other rewards for status dominance than are females.

In their *Not in Our Genes*, Richard Lewontin, Leon Kamin, and Stephen Rose—who, along with Stephen Jay Gould are the best-known defenders of the view that emphasizes the role of environment and de-emphasizes that of heredity—attempt to find fault with my work by pointing out that most family doctors in the Soviet Union are women. However, they acknowledge that in the Soviet Union "family doctoring [had] lower status than in the United States."

Which is precisely the point. No one doubts that women can be doctors. The question is why doctors (or weavers, or load bearers, etc.) are primarily women only when being a doctor is given lower status than are certain roles played mostly by men—and furthermore, why, even when this is the case (as in Russia) the upper hierarchical positions relevant to that specific area are held by men.

3. Dominance in male-female relationships is always associated with males.   "Male dominance" refers to the feeling, of both men and women, that the male is dominant and that the woman must "get around" the male to attain power. Social attitudes may be concordant or discordant with the reality of male dominance. In our own society there was a time when the man's "taking the lead" was positively valued by most women (as 30s' movies attest); today such a view is purportedly detested by many. But attitudes toward male-dominance behavior are causally unimportant to the reality they judge—and are not much more likely to eliminate the reality than would a social dislike of men's being taller be able to eliminate men's being taller.

⋅❦⋅

Over the past twenty years, I have consulted every original ethnographic work invoked to demonstrate an exception to these societal universalities. Twenty years ago many textbooks spoke cavalierly of "matriarchies" and "Amazons" and pretended that Margaret Mead had claimed to find a society in which sex roles were reversed. Today no serious anthropologist is willing to claim that any specific society has ever been an exception.

It is often claimed that "modern technology renders the physiological differentiation irrelevant." However, there is not a scintilla of evidence that modernization alters the basic "motivational" factors sufficiently to cast doubt on the continued existence of the universals I discuss. The economic needs of modern society probably do set a lower limit on the status of women;

no modern society could give women the low status they receive in some non-modern societies. But modernization probably also sets an upper limit; no modern society is likely to give women the status given to the maternal roles in some other matrilineal societies.

Scandinavian nations, which have long had government agencies devoted to equalizing women's position, are often cited by social scientists as demonstrating modernization's ability to override patriarchy. In fact, however, Norway has 454 municipal councils; 443 are chaired by men. On the Supreme Court, city courts, appellate courts, and in Parliament, there are between five and nine times as many men as there are women. In Sweden, according to government documents, men dominate "senior positions in employer and employee organizations as well as in political and other associations" and only 5 of 82 directors of government agencies, 9 of 83 chairpersons of agency boards, and 9 per cent of judges are women.

One may, of course, hope that all this changes, but one cannot invoke any evidence implying that it will.

Of course, there are those who simply try to assert away the evidence. Lewontin *et al.* write, "Cross cultural universals appear to lie more in the eye of the beholder than in the social reality that is being observed." In fact, with reference to the universalities mentioned above, they do not. If these universals were merely "in the eye of the beholder," the authors would merely have to specify a society in which there was a hierarchy in which males did not predominate and the case would be closed.

The answer to the question of why an institution is universal clearly must be parsimonious. It will not do to ascribe causation of a universal institution to capitalism or Christianity or modernization, because many hundreds of societies lacked these, but not the universal institutions. If the causal explanation is to be at all persuasive, it must invoke some factor present in every society from the most primitive to the most modern. (Invoking the male's physical strength advantage does meet the requirement of parsimony, but does not counter the evidence of the central importance of neuro-endocrinological psycho-physiological factors.)

When sociologists are forced to acknowledge the universals, they nearly always invoke "socialization" as explanation. But this explanation faces two serious problems. First, it does not explain anything, but merely forces us to ask another question: *Why* does socialization of men and women always work in the same direction? Second, the explanation implicitly assumes that the social environment of expectations and norms acts as an *independent* variable capable of acting as counterpoise to the physiological constituents that make us male and female.

In individual cases, of course, anything can happen.

Even when a causation is nearly entirely hereditary, there are many exceptions (as tall women demonstrate). Priests choose to be celibate, but this does not cast doubt on the physiological basis of the "sex drive." To be sure, there is also feedback from the environmental to the physiological, so that association of physical strength with males results in more males lifting weights. However, in principle, a society could find itself with women who were physically stronger than men if women lifted weights throughout their lives and men remained sedentary.

But, in real life, this can't happen because the social environment is a *dependent* variable whose limits are set by our physiological construction. In real life we all observe a male's dominance tendency that is rooted in physiological differences between males and females and, because values and attitudes are not of primary causal importance here, we develop expectations concordant with the male–female behavioral differences.

Most of the discussion of sex differences has emphasized the neuroendocrinological differentiation of males and females and the cognitive and behavioral differentiation this engenders. This is because there is an enormous amount of evidence demonstrating the role of hormones in fetally differentiating the male and female central nervous systems, CNS response to the potentiating properties of certain hormones, and the thoughts and actions of males and females.

There is not room here for detailed discussion of the neuro-endocrinological mechanism underlying dominance behavior. But a useful analogy is iron and magnet. Iron does not have a "drive" or a "need" to find a magnet, but when there is a magnet in the area, iron, as a result of the very way it is built, tends to react in a certain way. Likewise, the physiological natures of males and females predispose them to have different hierarchies of response to various environmental cues. There is no response that only one sex has; the difference between men and women is the relative strengths of different responses. Males react more readily to hierarchical competitiveness than do females; females react more readily to the needs of an infant-in-distress. Norms and socialization do not cause this difference, but reflect it and make concrete a specific society's specific methods for manifesting the response. (Cleaning a rifle and preparing Spaghetti-Os are not instinctive abilities).

The iron–magnet analogy makes clear the role of social environment. Were there to be a society without hierarchy, status, values, or interdependence of the sexes, there would be no environmental cue to elicit the differentiated, physiologically rooted responses we discuss. But it is difficult to imagine such a society and, indeed, there has never been such a society.

Even if we had no neuro-endocrinological evidence at all, the anthropological evidence alone would be sufficient to force us to posit a mechanism of sexual psycho-physiological differentiation and to predict its discovery. We do, however, possess the neuro-endocrinological evidence and the anthropological evidence permits us to specify the institutional effects—the limits of societal variation that the neuro-endocrinological engenders.

For thousands of years, everyone, save perhaps some social scientists and others ideologically opposed to the idea, have known perfectly well that men and women differ in the physiological factors that underlie masculine and feminine thought and behavior. They may not have known the words to describe the linkage of physiology with thought and behavior, but they knew the linkage was there. (I recently read a comment of a woman in Pennsylvania: "They keep telling us that men and women are the way they are because of what they've been taught, but you can go a hundred miles in any direction and not find a single person who really believes that.") And even the most feminist parent, once she has children, can't help but notice that it is nearly impossible to get small boys to play with dolls not named "Killer Joe, the Marauding Exterminator," or at least with trucks—big trucks.

❧

None of this is to deny tremendous variation on the level of roles. Even in our own society, in just a century the role of secretary changed from virtually solely male to virtually solely female. With the exception of roles associated with child nurturance, political leadership, warfare, security, and crime, virtually every specific role is male in some societies and female in others. No one doubts that the women who exhibit the dominance behavior usually exhibited by men encounter discrimination. But the question remains: why is dominance behavior usually exhibited by *men*?

The implication of all this depends on context. Clearly the correctness or incorrectness of the theory I present is important to an understanding of human behavior and society. But to the individual man or woman, on the other hand, the universals are largely irrelevant. The woman who wishes to become President has a sufficient number of real-life equivalents to know that there is not a constraint rendering impossible a female head of state. But there is no more reason for such a woman to deny that the motivation to rule is more often associated with male physiology than there is for the six-foot woman to pretend that women are as tall as men.

Kirk M. Endicott and
Karen L. Endicott

→ **NO**

Understanding Batek Egalitarianism

The Batek were remarkably egalitarian in the social and cultural treatment of the sexes. This was so as recently as 2004, despite economic changes due to government-sponsored development projects. There was no area of Batek culture or social life in which men controlled women or subjected them to asymmetrical systems of evaluation. Batek concepts of males and females recognized the physical differences between the sexes without imposing evaluative or symbolic significance on them. In daily social life, men and women had equal control over themselves and an equal voice in the affairs of the camp-group. Men and women were equal partners in marriage: the choice of spouse was left to the individuals involved, husbands and wives cooperated economically but were not exclusively dependent upon each other, decision making was a shared responsibility, and divorce could be initiated by either spouse. The political system did not favor men over women except in the headmanship system imposed by outsiders. In the economic sphere, males and females had equal access to the sharing network, which included the foods brought in by both men and women. Neither sex was prohibited from participating in any activity, except for the prohibition among a few Aring River people in 1990 against women doing blowpipe hunting and men weaving pandanus. The contributions by each sex to the food supply differed between 1975–76 and 1990, but in both periods both sexes contributed to the material well-being of the group, and neither sex group thought it was being exploited by the other. Socialization to gender roles occurred without coercion or preferential treatment of either sex.

In this chapter we attempt to bring out the features of Batek culture and circumstances that fostered their gender egalitarianism. We think of these features as leveling mechanisms that prevented the rise of male dominance, for we accept the premise that in societies in which there is competition for control, males are at an advantage because of their greater physical strength and their freedom from childbearing and nursing. We do not mean to imply that the conditions enabling the Batek to be gender egalitarian are the only conditions that could do so. Gardner argues that a number of different combinations of cultural and natural circumstances can lead to individual autonomy—which we see as a key feature of gender equality—in hunting and gathering societies.

The Bases of Batek Gender Egalitarianism

We define . . . a gender egalitarian society as one in which neither sex has overall control over the other or greater cultural value than the other. Control can be based in the economic system (e.g., the ability to withhold a resource necessary for survival), the system of authority (authority may be vested in such areas as political offices, kinship relationships, and religious ideologies), and in direct force. With these possible bases of control in mind, let us turn to a consideration of how the Batek prevented men from gaining control over women.

Economic Security

We believe that the key economic reason Batek men did not dominate Batek women is that no woman was dependent on a specific man—such as a father, husband, brother, or son—for survival. Women were economically secure, surviving through their own foraging efforts and through direct participation in the camp-wide food-sharing network. In 1975–76 most of the staple foods in the Batek diet, including rice and flour obtained in trade, could be procured by both men and women using skills, knowledge, and tools that were readily available to all. No rights of exclusive ownership over resources restricted women's access to any foods or other necessities, and the flexible division of labor permitted them to harvest any resources they came upon. Women also had full rights in the food-sharing network, and they retained these rights even when men obtained most of the food, as was the case in 1990. By contributing to and drawing from the food-sharing network, women could usually be certain of getting some food—including the foods ordinarily obtained by men, such as honey and arboreal game—even when they were ill or when their own food-getting efforts failed. Thus, the economic security of Batek women was based on their being able to depend upon the group as a whole in addition to their own efforts. Although Batek women—and men—could survive by their own efforts alone for limited periods of time, they were not economically *independent* like Hadza and Paliyan women, who gathered most of their own food and shared little even with their husbands.

Because Batek women were economically secure, women could withdraw from unsatisfactory marriages without suffering economic hardship. Both in 1975–76 and in 1990 we saw divorced women with children living happily for extended periods without remarrying, even when they had persistent suitors.

Some scholars have claimed that external trade and other economic processes that involve a delay between when the work is done and when the reward is received undermine the autonomy and equality of women in hunting and gathering societies. Leacock argues, following Engels, that when hunter-gatherers begin to produce commodities for trade, in addition to goods for consumption, families become isolated from each other, and women come to depend on their husbands and sons for survival, rather than on the group as a whole. Woodburn contends that "delayed-return" economic processes, which include collecting goods for trade, enmesh women in a system of binding commitments that place them under the authority of men.

Why, then, hasn't trade led to male dominance among the Batek? The answer is certainly not that trade is a recent innovation; there is good reason to suppose that the ancestors of the Batek have traded forest produce to horticulturalists for cultivated foods and other goods for the last 3000–4000 years, and commercial trade goes back at least to the 1930s. Rather, the reason seems to be that the Batek practiced trade in ways that were compatible with the general conditions ensuring women's economic security. Among the Batek, both men and women could and did collect and trade forest produce in 1975–76, although men generally spent more time at it than women. Trade in forest produce was just one of several sources of food for the Batek, and it was compatible with the other forms of food getting they practiced and with their general nomadic, egalitarian way of life. Most importantly, they shared all food obtained by trade just as they shared all food obtained directly from the forest. Thus, women benefited from external trade in the same way as men.

Dispersed Authority

Another characteristic of Batek society that seems to have inhibited the development of male dominance was the broad dispersal of authority. What little authority existed was spread among all adult men and women and consisted mainly of the authority to govern oneself and one's young children. Leadership was based on persuasion; there was no possibility of coercion. In these circumstances it was the qualities of the individual—including eloquence, intelligence, and tact—that determined what, if any, influence a person had over others. Group decisions were usually based on open discussion, and individuals had the right to ignore the consensus and follow their own desires. Batek ethics promoted extreme respect for personal freedom, constrained only by a general obligation to help others—as exemplified by the food-sharing requirement. Men, women, and children could all express their ideas and wishes and act on them as they saw fit.

Nonviolence

Another feature of Batek culture that seems to have inhibited male dominance was their suppression of all physical aggression. Like the horticultural Semai Orang Asli, who also appear to be gender egalitarian, the Batek abhorred violence and claimed that they would abandon anyone who was habitually aggressive. They regarded violent behavior as a sign of madness. They were usually successful at defusing potential violence through their methods of conflict resolution, and they took great pains to teach their children to avoid all aggressive behavior. Because no aggression was tolerated, Batek women were safe from coercion based on physical force or the threat of physical force.

Is Batek Culture a Result of Encapsulation?

The conditions we have identified as making gender egalitarianism possible among the Batek are largely cultural. Some scholars would go further to the question of why the Batek culture took the form it did in the first place. Why were Batek nomadic forager-traders and why were they organized in a fashion that permitted egalitarian relations between the sexes?

A number of scholars have argued that basic cultural features of some contemporary foraging peoples—including egalitarian gender relations where they exist—result from the societies being "encapsulated," surrounded and politically dominated by more numerous and powerful people. The Batek and other Semang could be categorized as encapsulated because they are surrounded by Malays. The encapsulation theory implies that egalitarian relations in foraging societies are an "abnormal" social condition and did not exist before the societies came under the influence of more powerful neighbors. Although the various proponents of the theory agree that the influence of the surrounding society shapes the culture of the foraging group, they do not agree on exactly how this takes place.

In an early formulation of this idea, Gardner describes the foraging Paliyan of India as being extremely individualistic, noncompetitive, nonviolent, noncooperative (to the point of not even sharing food with spouses), independent, and egalitarian even between the sexes. They show little emotion for others, and they hold idiosyncratic rather than shared views about the world. He postulates that these characteristics are due to the Paliyan having been subjected to centuries of abuse, threats, exploitation, and contempt from surrounding peoples. He argues that the relative helplessness of the Paliyan "made withdrawal or subservience more realistic than attempts at retaliation" and that their repression of aggressive impulses led to their particular cultural characteristics. He claims that a whole category of similarly surrounded and subordinate foragers ("refugee gathering peoples") share similar characteristics.

Testart defines a category of hunter-gatherers as *chasseurs-cueilleurs enclaves*, "enclaved hunter-gatherers," who are surrounded by more numerous and powerful farmers or herders with whom they trade. He says that the political domination of the outsiders promotes nomadism among the foragers: they keep moving to escape their tormentors. The foragers are egalitarian, he asserts, because continuous exploitation in trade equally impoverishes all of them. Woodburn also examines the relations between foragers and surrounding peoples. He asks: "Have their sharing and egalitarian leveling mechanisms developed in opposition to domination by outsiders? Have we here a sort of moral oppositional solidarity of low-status groups, akin to the egalitarian solidarity manifest in some working-class or millenarian movements?" Some writers have argued that the cultures of most if not all contemporary foraging peoples are predominantly shaped by their position in the larger surrounding society. The cultural characteristics of a people such as the Ju/'hoansi of southern Africa, they contend, are determined by their position as an impoverished rural proletariat in the class-stratified societies of Botswana and Namibia.

Could it be that the Batek were gender egalitarian because they were encapsulated by Malays? We think the answer is no. In fact, Malays could never have exercised real control over Semang as long as the latter were nomadic, economically self-sufficient, and had a vast empty forest to hide in. Even before Malay villages were removed from the Lebir watershed, local Malays were far from numerous enough or well-organized enough to have politically dominated the Batek. In recent years the Malaysian government, with all the resources of a modern nation-state, has been unable to exercise control over them. And the Batek never depended on trade with Malays for their survival, so trade with Malays was voluntary for both parties. If Batek had been coerced or abused by traders, they could have moved to remote areas or to areas near more congenial Malay villagers.

However, the Batek case does support Testart's claim that abuse or the potential for abuse by a more numerous and powerful people may reinforce the nomadism of some foraging groups. Frequent movement was probably the most effective defense the Semang had against the slave raiding that went on in some areas into this century. But the Batek economy also required nomadism, and there is no reason to suppose that they would have—or could have—settled down had there been no threat from Malays. Most Batek remained nomadic as recently as 1990, even though slave raiding ceased in the 1920s.

The Batek culture did not show the kinds of distortions and gaps that would suggest that they were merely a subdivision of the larger surrounding society, like some of the Indian foraging groups that appear to be occupational subcastes of forest produce collectors within Hindu society. The Batek had a strong sense of unity and a complete and distinctive culture, including a separate language, religion, and way of life. They considered Malays to be the archetypical "outsiders" with whom they often contrasted themselves. There is no reason to doubt that the Batek could have existed as an independent society with much the same form of culture before the Malays came on the scene.

In our opinion the most plausible reason that the Batek were nomadic forager-traders, with a culture supporting egalitarian relations between the sexes—and the reason that most closely resembles the Batek's own views of why they live the way they do—is that they were filling an ecological and social niche that provided them with a relatively secure and satisfying way of life, one that had some advantages over swidden horticulture, the main alternative possibility in their environment. For example, foraging was a more reliable way of getting food than farming in the deep forest, where birds, monkeys, wild pigs, elephants, and crop diseases could easily destroy the results of an entire season's labors. As Benjamin argues, the Semang are probably the descendants of the Hoabinhians who, after the advent of agriculture in the Malay Peninsula, opted to pursue a way of life based on nomadic foraging combined with trade with their farming neighbors. Until the arrival of the Malays in the interior in the last few hundred years, those neighbors were mainly Senoi Orang Asli, the descendants of other Hoabinhians who opted to concentrate on horticulture. Both groups became skilled specialists who shared the fruits of their respective modes of adaptation by means of trade. Pursuing complementary ways of life reduced the possibility of intergroup friction that could have arisen had they been competing for the same resources. No doubt there have been individual crossings back and forth across the Senoi–Semang boundary, especially when intermarriage has been involved, but the two ways of life have nevertheless remained distinct into the twenty-first century. As we have shown in this book, egalitarian relations between the sexes were an integral feature of the foraging-trading mode of adaptation the ancestors of the Batek chose.

POSTSCRIPT

Do Men Dominate Women in All Societies?

In these two selections, Goldberg and the Endicotts disagree on how to interpret cultural facts. Goldberg contends that all societies are dominated by males, while the Endicotts present a case that seems to be gender egalitarian. The Endicotts argue that three features of Batek society lead directly to gender equality. Batek men do not dominate Batek women because no woman is dependent on any particular man for survival, political authority is widely dispersed, and aggression is suppressed. Goldberg would disagree, asserting that because of our distinctive human biology all societies exhibit some form of male domination. Of course, he has never observed the Batek and argues largely on theoretical grounds.

The authors of the two selections also disagree on what types of forces, cultural and biological, determine relations between the sexes and how men and women interact interpersonally. For Goldberg, it is the presence of certain hormones in males that have conditioned them to be competitive, assertive, and dominating. For the Endicotts, gender equality emerges from a complex interplay of local cultural factors. Every woman can forage and hunt for her own food as well as for food to feed her children. Every Batek man, woman, and child shares with all others in the community, creating a egalitarian ethos in nearly every aspect of social life. Another key feature of Batek society is their nonviolent approach to life, something that is much less common in societies with complex economies and social hierarchies. For the Endicotts, if male hormones and biology played a role in Batek life, these have been overshadowed by the need to share, the social requirement to be noncompetitive, and avoidance of violence.

During the last 30 years, anthropologists have conducted many studies that have focused specifically on gender roles and indigenous ideas about gender in specific societies. The most provocative of these studies have been in non-Western and tribal societies, usually the kinds of societies we might describe as small-scale or preindustrial societies. The general finding of these studies is that gender relations are much more complicated and variable than scholars thought in the early days of feminist anthropology. For example, as among the Batek, a number of studies have shown that not all societies make a simple distinction between domestic and public domains, associate women exclusively with a domestic domain, or evaluate activities outside the home as superior to those inside it. Scholars have also realized that analytical concepts like "male dominance" and the "status of women" are too crude to describe the range of variation found in all human societies. They have attempted to break up these categories into several different components that can be identified and measured in more systematic ways in ethnographic field studies.

The question of whether or not males are dominant in a particular society is not as clear-cut as it may once have seemed. Among the Batek, the two genders seem to be about as equal as one could imagine men and women to be. But part of this egalitarianism can be explained by the fact that as hunter-gatherers, the Batek have few material possessions and no social hierarchy or stratification as we find it in most agricultural and industrial societies. In sedentary societies where individuals and families can amass larger quantities of material possessions, the situation is more complex. For example, in her book *Fruit of the Motherland: Gender in an Egalitarian Society* (Columbia University Press, 1993), anthropologist Maria Lepowski has argued that the Vanatinai of Papua New Guinea are sexually egalitarian. Compared to many other New Guinea societies, the Vanatinai show status differences between the genders that are indeed quite modest. If we listen to the ways men talk about women and their social position in society in this community, they seem to have a level of gender equality that is hard to find in other societies. But as a horticultural and fishing community, the Vanatinai do have modest forms of social ranking, and men tend to take on more of the elevated social positions than do women. In many other small-scale societies like the Vanatinai, anthropologists have shown that women and men may have similar amounts of influence over daily life, but the cultural ideology (or at least men's ideology) portrays women as inferior to men, just as it portrays the things women do as less important than what men do. In some other cases men's and women's spheres of activity and control are separate and independent. Some societies have competing ideologies, in which both men and women portray their gender as superior. And some societies, such as the Hua of Papua New Guinea, have multiple ideologies, which simultaneously present women as inferior, superior, and equal to men (see Anna Meigs's book *Food, Sex, and Pollution: A New Guinea Religion* [Rutgers University Press, 1984]). Despite these complications, it may still be useful to describe or refer to a culture as "gender egalitarian," as the Endicotts do in the case of the Batek and Lepowski does of the Vanatinai. Goldberg, of course, would say that such societies do not exist.

A readable introduction to feminist anthropology is Henrietta Moore's book *Feminism and Anthropology* (University of Minnesota Press, 1988). An interesting collection of articles showing variations in male-female relations is Peggy Sanday and Ruth Goodenough's edited volume *Beyond the Second Sex: New Directions in the Anthropology of Gender* (University of Pennsylvania Press, 1990). For a discussion of gender equality and inequality among hunter-gatherers, see Karen L. Endicott's article "Gender Relations in Hunter-Gatherer Societies," in *The Cambridge Encyclopedia of Hunters and Gatherers,* Richard B. Lee and Richard Daly, eds. (Cambridge University Press, 1999).

For a full explication of Goldberg's theory of innate male dominance, see his book *Why Men Rule, A Theory of Male Dominance* (Open Court, 1999). Other works that argue for a biological basis for male dominance include

Lionel Tiger's book *Men in Groups* (Holt, Rinehart & Winston, 1969); Lionel Tiger and Robin Fox's book *The Imperial Animal* (Holt, Rinehart & Winston, 1971); Robert Wright's article "Feminists Meet Mr. Darwin," *The New Republic* (November 28, 1994); and Barbara Smuts's article "The Evolutionary Origins of Patriarchy," in *Human Nature* (6:1–32, 1995). For a more general survey of the anthropological literature on hormones and gender, see Carol M. Worthman's "Hormones, Sex, and Gender," in *Annual Review of Anthropology* (24:593–616, 1995).

ISSUE 12

Is Gay Marriage Natural?

YES: Linda S. Stone, from "Gay Marriage and Anthropology," *Anthropology News* (May 2004)

NO: Peter Wood, from "The Marriage Debate Goes Multicultural: Anthropologists Jump In—And Distort the History of Their Field," *National Review Online*, `http://www.nationalreview.com/comment/wood200504260810.asp` (April 2005)

ISSUE SUMMARY

YES: Anthropologist Linda S. Stone argues that anthropologists have traditionally sought to discover and describe the range of variation among the world's cultures. A definition of marriage that covers this institution in all human societies has been futile. Institutions that resemble marriage in Western countries confer birth rights, sexual access, residence, and other rights, but no set of these rights covers "marriage" in all societies. She views gay marriage in Western Europe, Canada, and Massachusetts as simply another example of the wide variation found in human societies.

NO: Anthropologist Peter Wood argues that 150 years of ethnographic studies of kinship have demonstrated that in the vast majority of human societies marriage consists of a union between a man and a woman. Claims by anthropologists that suggest otherwise are misleading by focusing on a handful of exceptional cases in exotic places. Such cases do not demonstrate that gay marriage has ever been an established way of organizing families in non-Western societies. Gay marriage, he argues, is a novel institution, not merely a minor variation among the diverse forms of marriage that have been observed in the ethnographic record.

On May 17, 2004, the Massachusetts Supreme Court ruled that it was unconstitutional for the state to deny a gay couple the right to marry when it allowed heterosexual couples to do so. This ruling brought the issue of gay marriage to the heart of American politics as conservative groups lobbied for amendments to the Massachusetts and U.S. constitution that would define marriage as a union between one man and one woman. The debate over gay marriage has been a hot political issue for candidates and voters ever since. At the heart of this debate is the question of whether gay marriage is a natural social institution.

Some religious organizations view gay sexual relations as unnatural, immoral, and sinful, gay and lesbian activist groups have argued that denying them the right to marry prevents gay partners from participating in medical decision-making, hospital visitation, inheritance, rights to custody over children, and a variety of other rights that are routine for married spouses. Thus, the issue of gay marriage touches on issues that involve religious, moral, legal, financial, and social aspects of the institution of marriage.

At its heart anthropology, unlike many other social sciences, tries to avoid being ethnocentric, passing judgment on what other societies do. We call this cultural relativism, where anthropologists try to look at cultures in terms of their own cultural assumptions. From studies of hundreds of different cultures around the world anthropologists have also tried to assess what social institutions, practices, and social forms are universal and which are less common institutions, practices, and social forms that make up the broad panorama of human variation. This tension between human universals and the range of variation in social institutions is at the heart of this issue about whether gay marriage is natural or not.

Linda S. Stone argues that anthropologists have studied the world's diverse kinship systems for more than a century. During the 1950s anthropologists turned to the question of what is universal about marriage in all human societies. Polygamy (marriage of one man to several women) is banned in Western societies, but historically it was common in most societies. But was polyandry (the marriage of one women to several men) also a form of marriage? Pointing to the range of variation in marriage practices, as well as their legal, sexual, and residential implications, Stone concludes that while gay marriage is somewhat different from what anthropologists have observed in other societies, it nevertheless falls within the range of expectable variation in this institution.

Peter Wood tackles the question from a different perspective. Rather than defining marriage by the full range of marriage-like practices around the world, he looks to the most typical examples of marriage. For Wood what people in some remote part of the Third World do has no relation to what should be happening in the United States. Before recent legislation homosexual marriage was exceedingly rare, never the basis of a "viable social order." For him heterosexual marriage was found in nearly every human society and was always its "pivotal institution." In exotic locales not all marriage practices are identical to our own, but he sees documenting these cases as examples of butterfly collecting. These extraordinary examples prove his point that gay marriage is not within the traditional range of human marriage practices, but an innovative experiment in modern Western societies.

In reading these selections think about the different social functions that the institution of marriage organizes for Americans. How do some of these exotic examples of marriage fail to provide for some of these functions? How do these authors use ethnographic data to support their perspectives on the naturalness of gay marriage? How do they understand the goal of anthropological inquiry differently?

YES ⬅

Linda S. Stone

Gay Marriage and Anthropology

Politicians and the public in the US today are raising a question once pursued by anthropologists in the 1950s, namely, what should we mean by marriage? The politically charged issue concerns whether or not a constitutional definition of marriage can exclude same-sex couples. With over a century of experience in the study of kinship and marriage worldwide, anthropology can offer perspectives on this debate that may be of interest to our students or the general public.

Can Marriage Be Defined?

Many politicians claim that those advocating gay and lesbian marriage are trying to *re*define marriage. But what anthropologists have learned is that from a global, cross-cultural perspective, "marriage" is in the first place extremely difficult, some would say impossible, to define. One anthropologist, Edmund Leach tried to define marriage in his 1955 article "Polyandry, Inheritance and the Definition of Marriage" published in *MAN*. Leach quickly gave up this task, concluding that no definition could cover all the varied institutions that anthropologists regularly consider as marriage. Rejecting Leach's conclusion, Kathleen Gough attempted to define marriage cross-culturally in 1959 as an institution conferring full "birth status rights" to children (*The Nayars and the Definition of Marriage. Royal Anthropological Institute of Great Britain and Ireland* 89:23–34). Gough's definition of marriage was convoluted—notable, in her own words, for its "inevitably clumsy phraseology"—since it covered monogamy, polygyny, polyandry and same-sex marriage. But most important, its core feature—conferring of birth status rights on children—does not hold up cross-culturally.

It is true that virtually every society in the world has an institution that is very tempting to label as "marriage," but these institutions simply do not share common characteristics. Marriage in most societies establishes the legitimacy or status rights of children, but this is not the case, for example, among the Navajo where children born to a woman, married or not, become full legitimate members of her matriclan and suffer no disadvantages. "Marriage" around the world most often involves heterosexual unions, but there are important exceptions to this. There are cases of legitimate same-sex marriages

From *Anthropology News*, vol. 45, no. 5, May 2004, pp. 10–11. Copyright © 2004 by the American Anthropological Association. Reprinted by permission.

as, for example, woman-woman marriage among the Nuer and some other African groups. Here, a barren woman divorces her husband, takes another woman as her wife, and arranges for a surrogate to impregnate this woman. Any children from this arrangement become members of the barren woman's natal patrilineage and refer to the barren woman as their father. Among some Native American groups, males who preferred to live as women (*berdache*) adopted the names and clothing of women and often became wives of other men.

Marriage usually involves sexual relationships between spouses. Yet this was not true of Nuer woman-woman marriages and we find in European history cases of "celibate marriages" among early Christians. Often spouses are co-resident but very often this is not the case. A separate residence of husbands in "men's houses," away from their wives and children, has been common in many places. Among the polyandrous/polygynous Nayar of India, wives and husbands remained in their own natal groups with husbands periodically "visiting" their wives and with children raised by their mothers and mothers' brothers. Indeed the only feature of marriages that is apparently universal is that they will create affinal (in-law) relationships, or alliances, a fact that Lévi-Strauss and others considered to lie behind the origin of human marriage. But even here, affinal relationships are themselves quite varied in their nature and importance across societies. Thus, in terms of child legitimacy, sex of spouses, sexual activity, residence and so on, what we see around the world in terms of marriage is most notable for its variation.

Variation and Change

Anthropologists have accounted for this variation in a number of ways, looking to economic, ecological, demographic and historical processes. For example, polyandry, especially in Himalayan regions, is now well understood as in part related to the benefits of low population growth in areas of scarce environmental resources (Nancy Levine, *The Dynamics of Polyandry*, 1981). On a broader scale, Jack Goody has contributed to our understanding of marriage variations by drawing comparisons between Eurasian monogamy (with dowry) and sub Saharan African polygyny (with bridewealth). His work, published in *Production and Reproduction* (1976), has shown important connections that marriage forms have with agricultural practices, the development (or lack of development) of socioeconomic classes, marriage payments and patterns of property inheritance throughout the history of Africa and Eurasia.

Anthropological studies of kinship and marriage can also provide an understanding that within any society, marriage and the family will change over time. Whereas in the US legal marriages have been traditionally monogamous unions between a woman and a man, the nature of marriage, the domestic economy, husband-wife relationships, parent-child relationships, family structure and household structure have seen considerable transformation since the 1700s (Stephanie Coontz, *The Social Origins of Private Life*, 1988). Relevant transformations of marriage and the family have been in particular occurring in the US since the 1960s. Here we have seen rising rates of divorce, resulting in greater numbers of single-parent households. A rise in remarriage following divorce has additionally brought about the growth of so-called blended families, consisting of various combinations of step-parents, step-children and step-siblings. Many US children today are raised in two separate households, where one or both may consist of a previous parent and a newer set of step-relations.

The development of New Reproductive Technologies (such as, surrogate motherhood, in-vitro fertilization, frozen embryos) meanwhile has conceptually fragmented motherhood. We can today distinguish a birth mother from a genetic mother from a legal mother; all three "mothers" may be one, two or even three separate women. By contrast, fatherhood, once considered "uncertain" compared with motherhood, can now be made certain, one way or another, through DNA testing.

From Biology to Choice

Perhaps the most profound change of all, and one undoubtedly linked with the above transformations of kinship and the family, is a perceptible change in the cultural construction of kinship in the US. An earlier emphasis on kinship as based on biological connection (what David Schneider termed "shared biogenetic substance" in *American Kinship*, 1980), is giving way to a new conception of kinship as a relation based on personal choice and commitment (Linda Stone, Introduction, Contemporary Directions in Kinship, *Kinship and Family*, 2004). The US is in many respects culturally embracing a wider variety of family forms and an expanded construction of kinship through choice and self-definition as much as through biology.

It is within these new dimensions of family variation and choice as a basis of kinship that, I think, we can best view the movement for legalization of same-sex marriage. From an anthropological perspective that focuses on the whole of humanity, what same-sex couples seeking legal marriage in the US are trying to do is not to redefine marriage. They are seeking legal recognition in the US for doing what people around the world have always done, that is to construct marriage for themselves.

Peter Wood

→ **NO**

The Marriage Debate Goes Multicultural

Last year the executive board of the American Anthropological Association (AAA) joined the controversy over gay marriage by issuing a statement that declared

> The results of more than a century of anthropological research on households, kinship relationships, and families, across cultures and through time, provide no support whatsoever for the view that either civilization or viable social orders depend upon marriage as an exclusively heterosexual institution.

Ideologically, I suppose this is what one has come to expect from the AAA: a reflexive affirmation of leftist pieties. But still, it is surprising to see a professional organization propound such a breathless lie. As an AAA member for some 25 years, I am embarrassed.

In fact, some 150 years of systematic inquiry by anthropologists leaves little doubt that heterosexual marriage is found in nearly every human society and almost always as a pivotal institution. Homosexual marriage outside contemporary Western societies is exceedingly rare and never the basis of "viable social order."

Since the executive board cites the history of anthropological research, let's oblige. An upstate New York lawyer, Lewis Henry Morgan (1818–1881), published the first modern systematic ethnography in 1851. Morgan's *League of the Ho-De'-No-Sau-Nee, Iroquois* offered an admiring account of how the Seneca and the other Iroquois tribes had built up an entire Indian confederacy based on extensions of their ideas of kinship and family. Anthropology has covered a lot of ground in the 154 years since, but Morgan's insight remained central during most of that time.

Morgan, though largely unknown outside anthropology, was one of America's greatest 19th-century scholars. He virtually invented the study of kinship; published a massive worldwide comparison of kinship terminologies; mounted his own expedition to visit the Indian nations east of the Rockies; and in his spare time published an exceptional natural history book, *The American Beaver*. In the United States, by historical mischance, anthropology came to be dominated by the German immigrant Franz Boas (1858–1942) and his numerous students, including Margaret Mead, who emphasized the particularity of individual cultures. (It was, in fact, Boas who first added the "s" to culture: a small addition that continues to exact a large cost.) But while Boas and his students were busy popularizing cultural relativism in the U.S., Morgan's stature was growing in Europe. His methods were taken up by both British and French anthropologists, who emphasized the bases of social order common to all societies.

The rift between American and European anthropology never completely healed, especially as the Morgan-inspired European approach proved far more intellectually powerful. At mid-century, for example, an American anthropologist, George Peter Murdock (1897–1985), launched a blistering attack on the British social anthropologists of his day, but to no avail. To the contrary, many American anthropologists began to take a more serious interest in kinship and marriage.

But the old Boasian preference for viewing each culture separately never died out, and it made a grand re-entrance in 1984. That year American anthropologist David Schneider (1918–1995), known for his studies of matrilineal and American kinship, was suddenly overwhelmed by doubt. Schneider's *A Critique of the Study of Kinship* accused anthropologists of projecting Western ideas of kinship everywhere they looked and thus failing to discern the actual, local definitions of how people relate to one another. The arguments in Schneider's *Critique* are not all that impressive, but they landed like a match in dry tinder. The study of kinship had grown baroquely complicated and was beset by arid scholastic debates. Schneider's essay gave an excuse to anthropologists who were already eager to move on.

Postmodernism was in the air, and so were exciting political ideologies including feminism and gender studies. Suddenly anthropology was ablaze with repudiations of the idea that the family, kinship, and marriage were the organizing ideas of human society.

Eradicating the central concept of an intellectual discipline, however, is not that easy. Anthropology departments proceeded by eliminating courses in kinship. Where the forest of kinship studies once stood, now grew the gardens of women's studies, and soon gender studies. Anthropologists who began their careers studying kinship redefined themselves as specialists on "inequality." The perspective that kinship holds a society together made way for the perspective that, at bottom, societies are "contested sites," where men and women strive against each other, the powerful oppress the weak, and the weak seek ways to subvert their oppressors.

In the last few years, the study of kinship has made a modest comeback in anthropology. Partly this is the product of young anthropologists with little or no training in kinship who go off to do fieldwork and discover themselves ignorant of the basics. But kinship studies are also heating up because anthropologists committed to feminist and gender studies have realized that to connect their ideological advocacy with the real world they too need to study kinship. Without a hint of embarrassment they have therefore announced the re-birth of the field they spent the last 20 years deconstructing. The new field is distinguished from the old as *critical* kinship studies, implying I suppose

that Morgan and the five or six generations that followed him were practitioners of *credulous* kinship studies.

For an instance of the new critical kinship studies at work, consider the
forum, "Are Men Missing?" in the newest issue of the journal *The American
Ethnologist*. The lead article, "Wedding Bell Blues," is by Evelyn Blackwood,
an anthropologist at Purdue University. She complains that anthropologists have
assumed "heteronormative marriage" as "a foundational model for human
society" and thereby treated "matrifocal families" as a weak alternative. Once
we get rid of underlying "constructs" of "masculine domination," we are free
to see the alternatives. Blackwood's principal example is a group in Western
Sumatra, the Minangkabau, for whom descent is reckoned through women, a
man moves upon marriage to his mother-in-law's household, and women hold
both real estate and political clout.

The Minangkabau situation indeed looks favorable to women, but it
does not exactly look like a challenge to the idea that men and women marry
to form key social units. But Blackwood says otherwise: "I found that the
normative model of conjugal relations is absent. In this particular case,
intergenerational ties through women, rather than heterosexual conjugal
bonds, are constitutive of households and kin groups." Translation: Marriage happens among the Minangkabau, but it doesn't have any genuinely
important consequences.

The non-anthropologist who reaches this point may well ask, "So what?"
Does it matter how a small ethnic group in Western Sumatra arranges its
household affairs? Do the Minangkabau matrifocal households have any bearing on whether the United States should legalize gay marriage?

Obviously these are not the terms in which the debate is going to play
out in Congress and in the states. But it would be a mistake to underestimate
the degree to which these seemingly arcane academic disputes play into the
larger debate. Last April, John Borneman, an anthropologist at Princeton, and
Laurie Kain Hart, an anthropologist at Haverford College, published an essay
in the *Washington Post* purporting to find in the history of anthropology a
mandate for gay marriage: "Does marriage have to be heterosexual? The
human record tells us otherwise." As proof, they cite a well-known East
African case, in which a woman pays the brideprice of another woman and
officially claims her as a "wife." The trouble is that this "marriage" is only a
legal fiction, not a lesbian coupling. Borneman and Hart clearly knew that,
but buried the explanation in an opaque observation that "This role of wife is
above all social, and not contingent on her sexual relations."

Borneman is also among the contributors to the *American Ethnologist*
forum, and he commences his essay by telling how his *Washington Post* article
resulted in an invitation to appear on *Nightline*, which was unfortunately can-
celled at the last minute.

So offering reckless distortions of the ethnographic record in support of
gay marriage may indeed feed into the national debate. Neither the *Washington
Post* nor *Nightline* is likely to factcheck East African marriage customs. And I
would not be much surprised to see the Minangkabau matrifocal family
cropping up in future mainstream-media pronouncements to the effect that

"marriage" is just one of a myriad of cultural forms, and is of no essential significance. Some tribes shrink heads; some drink reindeer milk; some marry. All is flux.

In her article, Evelyn Blackwood takes a moment to congratulate John Borneman for using "insights from queer theory to destabilize the dualism of married-unmarried." This is the typically obtuse jargon of contemporary anthropology, but surely Blackwood has it right. Borneman aims to knock (heterosexual) marriage out of its "privileged place in the replication of our present social order." But he is one among many anthropologists engaged in this ideologically motivated demolition disguised as social science.

The difficulty they face is that the factual record is overwhelmingly against them. That is why Blackman, among others, are straining after ethnographic gnats and propounding tendentious interpretations of gnat anatomy.

I don't know whether the editors of the *American Ethnologist* (published by the AAA) or the AAA's executive board really think that "The results of more than a century of anthropological research . . . provide no support whatsoever" for the importance of marriage as "an exclusively heterosexual institution." Maybe they are so trapped in contemporary ideology that this strange assertion seems plausible to them; or maybe this is just an attempt to throw dust in the eyes of opponents of gay marriage who might think (correctly) that the anthropological record *does* lend support to the view that heterosexual marriage is very likely a foundational human institution. Perhaps it is best to assume good faith, even though that implies dismal scholarship.

In any case, what the anthropological record really shows is that a society's decisions about marriage are among its most consequential. Political regimes and economic systems are, deep down, the results of particular ways of organizing families. Until Scandinavia and the Low Countries, Canada, and Massachusetts began their experiments with gay marriage, humanity appears to have steered away from this particular option. Possibly gay marriage will be a step forward for humanity; but it is a step into the dark. Civilization as we have known it, even on the western coast of Sumatra, has depended until now on exclusive heterosexual marriage.

POSTSCRIPT

Is Gay Marriage Natural?

Both of these selections intend to support one or the other side in the gay marriage debate. They do so by considering ethnographic data. Linda Stone uses extreme ethnographic examples that differ most from what we think of as marriage. She uses these examples to show that the domestic institutions most analogous to Western marriage practices do not deal with all the social, economic, sexual, and residential functions that we might expect in Western societies. In the U.S., for example, we expect a married couple to live in the same house and look after the children, household duties, and relations with neighbors either jointly or with each partner having complementary responsibilities. But in many New Guinea societies men live in longhouses with other men, while their wives live with their daughters and young sons in separate houses that the husbands have built for their wives. Tension between husbands and wives may run quite high, so that men spend very little time in the company of their wives. And in some New Guinea societies like that discussed by Gilbert Herdt in his book *The Sambia: Ritual, Sexuality, and Change in Papua New Guinea* (Thomson Wadsworth, 2006), men routinely have sexual relations with other men as part of male initiation rituals, even though these homosexual relations do not prevent them from have sex with their wives. These patterns do not correspond very closely to American expectations of marriage, yet in their local cultures each of these practices is considered normal.

For Stone such examples show how hard it is to find any definition of marriage that will fit analogous institutions in all societies. But even without a solid definition, she does not abandon the notion that there is some form of domestic relation in every society. Rather she sees it as evidence that the institution is a very broad one, in which each society uses marriage for its own local functions.

Peter Wood takes precisely the opposite view, arguing that what anthropologists like Stone are doing is butterfly collecting. Such examples of peculiar marriage practices are exotic and mentioned not because they constitute the typical form of marriage, but because they are indeed exceptional. Homosexual marriage, he argues, was not the fundamental basis for any society and has only recently become a common social form in a handful of Western societies. If Nuer women took wives, it was not for sex. For this reason, Wood contends that homosexual marriage is a totally novel institution. Perhaps it will become an institution practiced by many more societies, but at present it is an innovative institution. Anthropological claims that it is a traditional human institution are for him simply a misreading of the evidence to support a political agenda.

Other scholars have argued that because marriage has always been an extremely varied institution, gay marriage as practiced in some European countries, Canada, and Massachusetts, while somewhat innovative, is not so far from ethnographic examples as to be especially remarkable. Certainly the case of the Nayar and the Toda, in which women have multiple husbands and even sanctioned lovers, is much further from the more common monogamous form of marriage than modern gay marriage.

Some of the forms of marriage that are most challenging to Eurocentric definitions of marriage are found in matrilineal societies, where rights pass through women from one generation to another. The best collection of studies is *Matrilineal Kinship*, edited by David Schneider and Kathleen Gough (University of California Press, 1961).

Ellen Lewin discusses why gay and lesbian people find the right to marry so important (http://www.aaanet.org/press/an/0405if-comm3.htm). For a collection of comparative studies of different kinds of masculinities, see Andrea Cornwall and Nancy Lindisfarne's edited volume *Dislocating Masculinity: Comparative Ethnographies* (Routledge, 1994).

Peter Wood expands his view that anthropology has focused on exceptional cases rather than general trends in his book *Diversity: The Invention of a Concept* (Encounter Books, 2004).

ISSUE 13

Does the Natural–Supernatural Distinction Exist in All Cultures?

YES: Roger Ivar Lohmann, from "The Supernatural Is Everywhere: Defining Qualities of Religion in Melanesia and Beyond," *Anthropological Forum* (November 2003)

NO: Frederick (Fritz) P. Lampe, from "Creating a Second-Storey Woman: Introduced Delineation Between Natural and Supernatural in Melanesia," *Anthropological Forum* (November 2003)

ISSUE SUMMARY

YES: Cultural anthropologist Roger Ivar Lohmann argues that a supernaturalistic worldview or cosmology is at the heart of virtually all religions. For him, the supernatural is a concept that exists everywhere, although it is expressed differently in each society. For him, supernaturalism attributes volition to things that do not have it. He argues that the supernatural is also a part of Western people's daily experience in much the same ways that it is the experience of the Papua New Guineans with whom he worked.

NO: Lutheran pastor and anthropological researcher Frederick (Fritz) P. Lampe argues that "supernatural" is a problematic and inappropriate term like the term "primitive." If we accept the term "supernatural," it is all too easy to become ethnocentric and assume that anything supernatural is unreal and therefore false. He considers a case at the University of Technology in Papua New Guinea to show how use of the term "supernatural" allows us to miss out on how Papua New Guineans actually understand the world in logical, rational, and naturalistic terms that Westerners would generally see as illogical, irrational, and supernaturalistic.

Making sense of other people's religions has been an interest of anthropology from the beginning of the discipline. In his book *Primitive Culture* (J. Murray, 1871), Sir Edward B. Tylor offered the first anthropological definition of religion: the belief in spiritual beings. Since the age of enlightenment in the eighteenth century, scientists had adopted the view that all phenomena could be explained in rational, naturalistic terms. Thus, for Tylor, the belief in ghosts, spirits, demons, demigods, and gods was evidence of irrational thought and misunderstanding of the natural world. He reasoned that people in all societies had dreams, but primitive people mistakenly interpreted these dreams as reality and the characters in them as spiritual beings.

Similarly, Bronislaw Malinowski had distinguished between science on the one hand and magic and religion on the other in his book *Magic, Science, and Religion* (Beacon, 1948). In 1966, American anthropologists Anthony F. C. Wallace defined religion as "beliefs and rituals concerned with supernatural beings, forces, and powers."

Despite these definitions, there is no necessary reason why the notion that there is a distinction between the natural and the supernatural should be present in all societies. Whether people in all societies accept this distinction is an empirical question.

This issue is about whether all societies actually do believe in the supernatural as a category of reality distinct and separate from the natural world. Both essays were presented as part of a panel that was addressing an issue raised by anthropologist Morton Klass in his book *Ordered Universes* (Westview, 1995). Klass, who argued that the use of the term "supernatural" is problematic in many of the same ways that the terms "primitive" and "race" are.

Anthropologist Roger Ivar Lohmann argues that the core of the supernatural is attributing volition to things that do not have it. For him, this is the central feature of religious thinking in all societies around the world. He distinguishes the supernatural as a concept that can be observed empirically in all societies, although its particular cultural expression will vary quite widely in the diverse cultures around the world. For him, attributing volition to things that cannot have volition or to things that do not exist is at the heart of the supernatural. Thus, the supernatural is not limited to spirits, gods, or ghosts, but can also include "luck," "karma," or "the mystical."

Lutheran Pastor Frederick (Fritz) P. Lampe was chaplain at the University of Technology in Papua New Guinea for four years in the 1980s. He draws upon these experiences to challenge whether these Papua New Guineans are using supernatural thinking in responding to such issues as traditional notions of the polluting quality of female menstrual blood for men. For Europeans, the idea that menstrual blood is dangerous is self-evidently wrong; therefore, it is classified as a supernatural idea. But Lampe shows that these New Guinean ideas are based on a naturalistic worldview, not a supernaturalistic one.

In reading these essays, consider how each author understands what is meant by "the supernatural." Do the cases mentioned by Lohmann demonstrate that the supernatural concept is present in every society? What about our own society? Does Lampe's case study actually demonstrate that the supernatural is not a salient part of the worldview he discusses? If it did, would this finding dismiss Lohmann's claim about universality? Even if in one or another case "the supernatural" is not a salient concept, would we necessarily want to abandon the concept as we have the term "primitive?"

YES ↵

Roger Ivar Lohmann

The Supernatural Is Everywhere: Defining Qualities of Religion in Melanesia and Beyond

Supernaturalism depicts conscious will or volition as the ultimate cause of phenomena. Supernaturalistic cosmologies are at the heart of virtually all religions. All humans seem to sense a supernatural realm, yet we are unable to detect it scientifically. It is an imagined dimension where volition can exist without brains, and control the physical world. I argue that the concept of 'supernatural' is necessary both to describe particular worldviews accurately, and to understand spirit belief and religion as ubiquitous in human experience.

In conceptualising the supernatural, it is very important at the outset to distinguish between the etic perspectives of scientific observers and the emic views of cultural participants. The supernatural can be viewed as a universal assumption among humans, or as the unique spiritual reality of a given culture. The supernatural is in this regard like sex, which, like all realms of common human experience, is modelled differently in different traditions to produce different gender systems. The distinction between sex and gender is necessary to understand the relationship between objective physicality and cultural models of the physically real. For the same reason that we need to distinguish etic and emic perspectives on reproductive capacity, we need to separate etic and emic definitions of 'supernatural'. As a technical term in anthropology, 'supernatural' serves best as an etic concept describing a universal human experience that is elaborated differently in different traditions.

I define the etic category of supernatural as a ubiquitous mental model that depicts one or more sentient, volitional agencies that are independent of a biological substrate and understood to be the ultimate cause of elements of physical reality. Individual cultural models of the supernatural, like the various forms of gender, are distinctive in different societies. Ethnographers should describe these differences carefully. Some anthropologists, however, argue that the spiritual worlds posited by different peoples are so distinctive that generalising about them with terms like 'supernatural' is inaccurate. I make the case to the contrary that, whereas there is indeed much variation in the spiritualities of different peoples, they are all similar enough to one another

From *Anthropological Forum*, vol. 13, no. 2, 2003, pp. 175–180, 181–154. Copyright © 2003 by Taylor & Francis Journals. Reprinted by permission. References omitted.

that we can recognise virtually all of them as variants of a common human tendency to assume that a supernatural world exists. For example, many Melanesian peoples model the supernatural world as a hidden realm existing inside the material world. While Melanesians typically consider the supernatural to be immanent, some other peoples model the supernatural as being separate from its creation.

People everywhere learn that volition can find expression in physical phenomena, because they routinely experience and witness human creativity. For example, when a man desires a house, his volition brings about the construction of a house. One might call the mental model of this sort of agentive causation the 'volition schema.' Supernaturalism is the extension of the volition schema to phenomena that do not in fact result from will and choice, like the origin of the world. Belief in an afterlife, to give another example, results from extending the volition schema to the dead, who are no longer volitional, to explain our ongoing memories of them.

'Supernatural' is a venerable term in anthropology. However, some criticise it as ethnocentric or misleading, because many peoples do not think spiritual powers are separate from the 'natural' world. Moreover, they point out that, in its etic sense, the term implies that only the natural is real, while the supernatural is not, which does not represent the view of those who believe in a spirit world. These critiques do not demonstrate a problem with the category of 'supernatural'; rather, they point to the dangers of conflating various etic and emic *definitions* of the supernatural. When these are distinguished, the supernatural concept both clarifies a scientific position on a major source of religious behaviour and improves our ability to understand religious worldviews. The supernatural, as I define it, is a real phenomenon with physical causes and effects, which people model differently from one culture to the next. I suggest that all people can distinguish supernaturalistic ideas from naturalistic ones, though they may not find the distinction salient. The distinction is expressed using various idioms, including transcendent vs. tangible, real vs. illusory, sacred vs. profane, living vs. lifeless, ethereal vs. material, and, as I suggest is widespread in Melanesia, hidden vs. exposed, and inside vs. outside.

Critiques of 'supernatural'

Critics of the supernatural concept have two basic arguments. First, they say that it implies condescension toward credulous believers in non-existent beings. Second, they argue that by using the term we erroneously assume that all religions share the West Asian assumption, found in Judaism, Christianity, and Islam, that the natural world is separate from a supernatural creator. These are valid critiques of certain ways of using the term 'supernatural', but they do not damn its usefulness when employed with respect, precision, and a distinction between etic and emic.

To see that this is so, consider an eloquent critique by Morton Klass. Klass points out the similarity between a farmer's offering to the deceased first owner of a field and his rent payment to an absentee landlord. Why, he asks, should we classify the former as supernatural and the latter as natural, when both the first owner and the landlord are invisible and ostensibly require compensation? To do so, he says, merely underlines our disbelief in the efficacy of the offering, and ethnocentrically smears our understanding of the farmer's worldview.

I do not think that seeking an etic explanation requires one to disregard or disrespect the emic one. Nor do we distort the emic perspective by asserting that the farmer can distinguish between dealings with spirits and people. Klass, however, does us a service by emphasising that this distinction may not be salient to the believer, and this should be described in the ethnography.

Having made an analogy with sex above, I consider one with language. In the same way as the pan-human cognitive capability for language is expressed locally as specific languages, and individually as speech, supernaturalism is expressed in local variants as religions, and individually as spirituality. The thousands of different languages all represent one kind of cognitive and behavioural capacity made possible by our neurological apparatus for language. Just as one can distinguish linguistic thought from purely image-based thought, one can likewise distinguish supernaturalism from naturalism. This is so even though both occur simultaneously, mix freely, and may be conflated in ethnopsychologies.

The disregard of Klass's farmer for a distinction that an anthropologist would notice is analogous to a native speaker's inattention to the difference between a voiced and an unvoiced consonant in a language in which this distinction does not carry meaning. Anyone can be made aware of the objective (phonetic) difference between the two sounds, and, for linguists, attention to phonetics is vital. Likewise, for practical purposes, the farmer may not think about the difference between an offering to a dead person and a payment to a living one, but he could make that distinction were it relevant to his task. For anthropologists, it is central to ours. Different peoples emphasise or de-emphasise the distinction between supernatural and natural causation, or mark it in different ways, and critics of the fuzzy use of the concept rightly bring this to our attention.

[Anthropologist Benson] Saler observes that anthropologists often use the term 'supernatural' without defining what they mean, possibly to appear respectful of local beliefs that they in fact consider erroneous. I concur with his view that, if by 'supernatural beings' we mean imaginary ones, we should go ahead and say so. One can openly disagree with others without disrespecting their views. During my fieldwork among the Asabano, a Papua New Guinea people who are enthusiastic Christians, I truthfully told them that I do not believe that Christianity or other religions are true, but that I am nevertheless interested in why they have found them convincing. We had a very amicable and productive exchange of views. Of course, we often disagree with the peoples among whom we work—we are culturally different. Mutual respect and friendship across cultural boundaries are possible, as any anthropologist knows. Cultural relativism serves well as a method to understand another's point of view, but, if used to limit our ability to make comparisons, generalisations, and scientific advances, it closes the mind it has only just opened.

Supernaturalism and the imagination

Granted our right to draw etic conclusions from studies of emic experiences, the question remains as to whether the supernatural is really a product of the human mind. There appears to be little controversy that the imagination is heavily engaged in religious life, but are supernatural worlds made up? [James] Lett declares that, though many anthropologists are loath to admit it, we already know all religious beliefs to be false because they are not based on rationality or objectivity. I am in sympathy with his conclusion about the objective truth of religious beliefs; however, to write supernaturalism off as mere irrationality strikes me as unrealistic. Greenfield shows that, depending on people's knowledge, supernaturalism can offer a reasonable account for cures, and may actually help effect them. A community of believers can agree because they share experiences grounded in similarly biased perception, leading them to see what they expect to see.

Like naturalism, supernaturalism is normally based on rationally structured models of experiential evidence. Supernaturalism is distinctive in that it is based on extended, serious productions of what [Michele] Stephen calls the 'autonomous imagination', imagined realities that we do not recognise as our own inventions. The autonomous imagination, working with the volition schema, produces experiences of and belief in supernatural realms, as revealed in anthropological studies of dreaming. Supernaturalism builds wondrous mental models that could not result only from irrationality and subjectivity gone wild; religions have too much in common for that.

Some anthropologists have referred to spirits as non-empirical beings. Relationships with supernatural beings are central to religion, but these beings are not non-empirical; they are imaginary. The distinction is important, for while the imagination's creations need not accurately *portray* the reality that exists outside of the cogitating brain, they are *themselves* empirical phenomena in that human mental and motor behaviour can be studied scientifically.

Spirit beings are mental models of reality to which the imagination has granted volition. Spirits resemble the objectively real, but are clearly different. We cannot show our friends a spirit the way we can show them a rock. We cannot photograph spirits. Of course, showing a rock and saying it is *really* a spirit allows the listener to create a mental image partially based on the rock; but the imagination must also be invoked to give the rock life. Supernaturalistic models make scientific sense when we see them as arising from the imagination. This is why supernatural beings are often harder to see or touch, act at variance with our everyday knowledge of physics, and are so relevant to human fears and desires.

In so far as volition is a characteristic of humans, and spirits are imagined and related to as though they were people, anthropomorphism is a necessary component of supernatural models, but not all anthropomorphism is supernaturalistic. Non-supernaturalistic anthropomorphism recognises human-like qualities in the exterior or current form of an object that can be directly perceived with the senses, such as a bottle resembling a man in form or function. It includes playful, consciously metaphorical, and surface attributions of human-like qualities to the non-human. However, if one understands the anthropomorphised bottle to have sentience or to have been the result of an extra-biological volition, then one is engaging in supernaturalism. Supernatural anthropomorphism is long-lasting and serious (like the earnest belief among the Asabano that tree spirits are responsible for deaths), rather than brief mis-apprehensions (such as mistaking a sack for a person), or playful, purposeful fantasy anthropomorphism (like advertisements that endow products, such as Mr Clean cleanser, with human qualities).

Animism, however, defined as attributing spirits (foundational sentient agency) to materials, is by definition the stuff of supernaturalism. More depersonalised notions of mysterious power and meaning, known as *mana*, luck, or animatism—or reverence for persons, places, and things because of their history or symbolic significance . . . are not necessarily supernatural. There is a fine line between thinking that one is lucky because of personal circumstances, and attributing one's frequent success to a caring or powerful spirit. Likewise, a place can seem mystical because it evokes strong memories or feelings, with or without the additional notion that this indicates some kind of spiritual presence. Most of us probably cross the border between naturalism and supernaturalism several times each day.

The scientific theory that the supernatural is a natural product of the imagination is supported by the fact that spiritual experiences occur more easily in states of consciousness that allow the autonomous imagination greater play, such as trance and dreams. They also seem more plausible when socially supported: if everyone in the village says that witches are responsible for unfortunate events, witches come to seem very real indeed, as Evans-Pritchard discovered. The weight of tradition grants supernatural beings a veneer of objective reality. A community of believers can see the same spirit, not because it exists as an external being, but because all have similar imaginative hardware and tendencies, and shared instructions on what to picture.

The universality of spiritual experience indeed reveals that there is objective truth to the supernatural. That truth, however, is that the 'spirits' are found *inside* all our heads and not outside any of them. In the same way, all of us experience and can verify with one another that the earth appears to be flat, so it was not unreasonable when people made the jump to conclude that the earth is flat. This conclusion is wrong, of course, as an etic glance from above can show. The more distant perspective and the greater, but never perfect or absolute, objectivity it affords make it plainly visible that the universal experience of flatness, like that of supernaturalism, does reveal a more objective truth, and the truth is not what it first appeared. . . .

Recognising the Supernatural in Melanesia

Melanesians are sometimes characterised as lacking a supernatural concept (e.g., see Lampe). They are not alone in this. In this issue, White argues that supernaturalism can appear and disappear in the history of groups; Shorter notes that others do not divide the world into a supernatural/natural dichotomy; and Aragon points out that some peoples have imminent spiritualities and lack a transcendent supernaturalism in which events are understood to be miraculous. All these authors question the universality of the supernatural on an emic level, and therefore question its status as an etic category. It should be clear from my argument so far that I disagree with these positions in so far as they are using a definition of 'supernatural' similar to my own. I agree with Aragon that the notion of a miracle does not jibe with monistic worldviews but, as her paper makes very clear, even monists habitually apply the volition schema to nonliving things. The Tobaku do not perceive the spirits as miraculously breaking natural laws when they make the land fertile, but, in envisioning the land's fertility as coming from its spirit 'owners', they are attributing volition to something that does not, to the best current scientific knowledge, have it. Thus, by my definition of 'supernatural', Sulawesi highlanders are supernaturalists, but by Aragon's they are not. I prefer my own definition because it captures a universal human propensity that manifests itself within a range of variation.

I am clearly a lumper, while some of my colleagues are splitters, when it comes to categorising spiritual behaviours. To support my position that some lumping (as well as a clear definition) is called for in the case of supernaturalism, I wish to demonstrate that, even in a place that has been considered free of supernaturalism by excellent ethnographers, we can identify versions of the etic supernaturalism that I am at pains to argue exists. It is valuable to examine the bases on which claims of supernatural-free cultures are made. [Peter] Lawrence and [Mervin] Meggitt, for example, rightly note an interpenetration of spiritual and physical among Melanesian peoples. Elaborating, [Peter] Lawrence correctly states that 'gods, spirits, and totems were regarded as a real, if not always visible, part of the ordinary physical environment . . . described as more powerful than men but always as corporeal, taking human, animal, or insect form at will'. Based on these characteristics of Melanesian religions, he further describes them as lacking a concept of the supernatural. Yet what he is actually documenting is a conception of supernatural beings as not necessarily separate or ethereal, *not* a lack of supernaturalism per se. Then, somewhat contradictorily, he refers to these rather solid Melanesian spirits as 'non-empirical'.

Many Melanesian peoples believe that spirits can take physical form (*bodi devel* in Tok Pisin) rather than merely inhabiting an object. Kaluli, for example, consider birds to be dead people. Melanesians understand at least some spirits to be tangible and visible, so supernatural beings (volitional entities that are independent of brains and cause physical phenomena) *do* appear in their cosmologies. Stephen observes that Melanesian belief in physical spirits contradicts characterisations of Melanesian spirit beings as either non-empirical or unseen. Both believers and outsiders can verify birds' existence; it is the *significance* of physical phenomena that is disputed. To Kaluli, birds are really the dead, in spite of outer appearances. Interpreting birds as an expression of deceased human volition is supernaturalism. Ethnographers, unable to see the volition, but only its supposed physical manifestation, might conclude that the spirits themselves are non-empirical or unseen. However, even human volition originating in biochemical processes is not visible with the naked eye; only our skins and behaviours are.

Stephen reports that the Mekeo believe in a disembodied 'hidden self', perceived to leave the body in dreams. While avoiding the terms 'supernatural' and 'natural', Stephen identifies the main idiom in which Melanesians express the dichotomy: hidden vs. external realms. This accords closely with a large Melanesianist literature emphasising the religious role of secrecy and disclosure. To say something is hidden is not to say that it is invisible, ethereal, or non-empirical. A hidden thing, though usually obscured, can appear on occasion. The Asabano described certain beings and powers as hidden. Forest sprites, for example, called *wobuno* ('wild ones'), are alternatively called *balebaleno* ('those who hide'). Traditional Asabano religious knowledge was secret by definition. *Walemaw* means simultaneously secret and sacred. Asabano also believe the dead can become birds who may appear or hide. As reported widely in Melanesia, some Asabano felt at first contact that Whites were spirits: they had great technological and productive powers like the ancestors, and had been hidden until then.

Associated with the idea of hidden in Melanesia is the notion that interiors are more powerful and genuine than exteriors. Ngaing, for example, associate Whites with supernatural power because of their idea that interiors are light, while exteriors are dark. Ngaing discovered in dreams that the land of the Whites is really inside their own land. Inside themselves, they discover, they are white. I recorded an Asabano dream narrative in which the dreamer pulled down a zipper to reveal white skin underneath: an indication of what will happen in the afterlife. This interest in obscured interiors as the locus of the supernatural also resonates with widespread gender separation in Melanesia. Thus, men retain and fan their supernatural powers by isolating and hiding themselves, their rituals, and their sacra from women—a concern with 'purity' that makes sense when seen as an effort to maximise contact with hidden, supernatural interiors. The Telefol male's sacred net bag, for example, is covered with feathers to conceal the human bone sacra secreted inside from the profaning and withering female gaze.

While Melanesian worlds of inside and outside, of hidden and exposed, are deeply intertwined, they are nevertheless distinguished one from the other. Melanesians do not conceive of the distinction as non-empirical vs. empirical, or necessarily as ethereal vs. material or transcendental vs. immanent. Rather, they model the supernatural as a living inside truth, cause, and potential that, like the supernatural envisioned by transcendentalist Christians, is a volition that makes things happen, but is not always visible. Melanesians definitely recognise the supernatural as distinct from the natural, as I have defined the terms.

Conclusion

The natural/supernatural distinction is necessary for understanding religions, from both etic and emic points of view. From a scientific etic perspective, the distinction is between a physically perceived universe of ultimately non-volitional origins (the natural realm) and an imagined universe depicted as having ultimately volitional origins (the supernatural realm). The refined etic category 'supernatural' defines what ideal typical religions refer to, which all peoples, even those with an immanent spirituality, can recognise, but model differently.

All humans can use the volition schema to think about things. Scientists studying consciousness have to do the opposite and apply physical-chemical schemas to human minds in order to understand how physical matter can give rise to volition. You might find some of those same scientists believing in an afterlife. Klass's farmer, too, knows physical cause and effect: that rain must fall on his crops if they are to grow. He may also think that the ultimate reason the rain falls is because the guardian spirit of the field is pleased with his offering. The supernatural is real, but it is also imaginary, and, while prayer may move spiritual mountains, only work can move physical ones.

Supernaturalism attributes volition to things that do not have it; in this sense it is a kind of cognitive 'dirt'. [Mary] Douglas defines dirt as matter 'out of place', and explains the human fascination with purity as an effort to remove what cannot be placed into our categories. Similarly, the supernatural is *volition* out of place, and this in no small measure accounts for the human fascination with the anomalous idea of spirits. People strive to clean up dirt in order to make their environment 'conform to an idea'. In the realm of religion, however, they accomplish this same parity between ideal and physical worlds by projecting the supernatural—imagined volition out of place—onto the physical world.

Frederick P. Lampe

NO

Creating a Second-Storey Woman: Introduced Delineation Between Natural and Supernatural in Melanesia

Words matter. The use of the term 'supernatural' to describe social activities related to the ethereal maintains a dichotomy that may not be appropriate at this stage in the history of anthropology. I join Morton Klass in suggesting that the time has come to set aside the term 'supernatural', as we have other seemingly descriptive terms like 'race' and 'primitive'. Our continued distinction between natural and supernatural is problematic in that it is relatively easy to succumb to the temptation of labelling natural as real and supernatural as unreal.

In the 1980s, I spent 4 years as the Lutheran chaplain in and around the University of Technology in Lae, Papua New Guinea. The University of Technology, Unitech, was, at that point, one of two government-funded, degree-granting universities in Papua New Guinea. This paper considers the classificatory term 'supernatural' as it relates to men, women and housing at Unitech. The case in point involves the security arrangements for female students, the considered power of vaginal secretions, and the Enlightenment-driven, unilineal, evolutionary schema that contextualises economic and social development in Melanesia. Assuming there to be no natural reason to do otherwise, student living arrangements were organised by administrators without regard, or perhaps in spite of, social taboos prohibiting such things.

The question before us is the descriptive classification 'supernatural'. My argument suggests that on a macro-scale the propensity for anthropologists to impose imprecise distinctions, such as between natural and supernatural, for the sake of classificatory (etic) evaluation is akin to the colonial disregard for social practices and traditions. I contend that its continued use perpetuates an unhealthy power differential between researcher and subject. The use of supernatural retains elements of the colonial legacy that may not be particularly helpful or accurate.

The exploration, colonisation, and conversion of Melanesia by Europeans brought a highly segmented worldview into conflict with a largely cohesive collection of ideas about reality. The European propensity to distinguish between

From *Anthropological Forum*, vol. 13, no. 2, 2003, pp. 167–173, omit references. Copyright © 2003 by Taylor & Francis Journals. Reprinted by permission. www.tandf.co.uk/journals

profane and sacred spheres effected a dichotomous differentiation between 'natural' and 'supernatural' in Melanesia. Current higher education in Papua New Guinea reflects this distinction. Melanesian university students participate in a highly differentiated academic context representing a distinct and artificial social experience. An undifferentiated coalition of symbolic elements, with no distinction between supernatural and natural, is forced to contend with a highly differentiated system based upon a post-Enlightenment model of education.

I assume two things: the first is that the Enlightenment is the intellectual and cultural context for those who came to Papua New Guinea as colonisers; the second is that there is power associated with the sexual fluids of women within Melanesian society.

These two frame the subsequent structure for issues that surrounded student housing in the 1980s. The University's housing arrangements, like the intellectual climate of the Enlightenment, effected an artificial ordering of being. The culturally constructed explanation of women's power effects an unauthentic sense of what it means to be human in Melanesia. I join Shorter in this collection, suggesting that as interpreters of culture we must be cautious in our ethnographic reporting, so that we do not perpetuate power differentials through the use of distinctions that are no longer helpful or beneficial. The context of European contact and colonisation and the ontological nature of women vis-à-vis men force a false dichotomy between natural and supernatural. Klass (emphasis in original) observes the following regarding 'supernatural':

> that there is on the one hand a natural—real—universe, and on the other hand there are notions about aspects of the universe that are situated outside the natural and real and are therefore labeled supernatural by the person who *knows* what belongs in which category.

It must be noted that this analysis relies upon a very broad use of the term 'supernatural'. In *Miriam-Webster's collegiate dictionary*, Nature is defined, first, as 'the inherent character or basic constitution of a person or thing' and, second, 'as a creative controlling force in the universe', but neither of these really gets at what this debate is fundamentally about. The second definition of 'natural' states: 'a: being in accordance with or determined by nature b: having or constituting a classification based on features existing in nature'. 'Super' connotes something that is above or beyond. Thus, 'supernatural' refers to something above or beyond that which is a classification of features existing in nature. By using the term to distinguish one thing from another, we separate that which is united in the minds of those with whom we work. This separation is natural in the minds and socio-cultural experience of Europeans but not, perhaps, in the experience of others, specifically Melanesians.

As [Morton] Klass and [Maxine] Weisgrau, [Bengt] Sundkler and [Christopher] Steed and others have argued, the complex of symbols used by social groups was in constant flux. [Deborah] Gewertz and [Fred] Errington, [Donald] Tuzin, [Andrew] Lattas and others documented this creative reflexivity in their recent work in Melanesia. Thus, the introduction of a natural/supernatural dichotomy is one of many imported material and social elements that included technology, ideology and social practice. To suggest that colonial incursion and influence represent a new phenomenon would discount precolonial experience in Melanesia. Change is not the point. Rather, it is the ways in which Melanesians think about themselves, and organise and categorise their universe. What is at issue here is the representation by social scientists of the Melanesian experience. Klass and Weisgrau note: 'One of the most serious problems in the comparative study of religion is the ultimate tendency to impose values and categories deriving from the anthropologist's culture upon the one being studied.' This is at the core of my argument against applying a macro-level classificatory term for the sake of etic clarity.

The colonial context

The Enlightenment played a significant role in the relationship that developed between Melanesians and Europeans. Rationality was a dominant ideology underlying colonial attitudes up to and through 1975 Independence in Papua New Guinea as the country negotiated nationhood and economic development. In its pure form, Reason demanded dissociation from spirits, magic, and polluting elements that were inextricably interwoven in the cultural complex of Melanesia.

Significant European contact on the eastern half of New Guinea began in the mid-nineteenth century. The distinctions between sacred and profane, supernatural and natural, religious and pagan, permeated life among the colonisers. The rationalised dissection of what had previously been undifferentiated meant that, in the minds of colonisers, a clear order of natural facts existed. Understanding what happened in European colonies such as the Territories of Papua and New Guinea is as much about those who came expecting, facilitating and forcing change as it is about the people who lived there. John and Jean Comaroff have reflected on this as it relates to South Africa.

The symbolic systems of Melanesia were under significant pressure to adapt to this incursion. The ways in which food was produced, illness explained, healing facilitated, rites of passage practised, death explained, origins identified, and differences understood existed in a mass of cultural peculiarities. Spirits existed, power was recognised, and social organisation was regulated. There was no distinction between the natural and the supernatural. The ontological nature of men and women in society was defined within this complex social structure. Each ethnic group had a distinct social construction of gender, creating fluid yet distinct references about what it meant to be a man or woman. These ontological constructions reflect distinct ideas about human relationships, the world of spirits and power.

Women of power in Melanesia

One cannot speak of a trans-Melanesian understanding of adult gendered relationships. Yet areas in which male cults were active include respect for the power of the menstrual fluid of women, although the specificity of taboos surrounding female body fluid varies. [Polly] Wiessner and [Akii] Tumu suggest that 'the idea that contact with menstruating females and menstrual blood is harmful to men is widespread throughout the highlands'. General prohibitions are linked to space and time. The preparation or handling of food, physical contact and specific sexual relations between men and girls once they have begun menses appear to be highly regulated. [Terence] Hays and [Patricia] Hays describe the Kwaasi initiation rite among the Ndumba as a time of realisation:

> It is only when a girl becomes a kwaasi that she discovers the extent of men's vulnerability and, because of it, the threat she represents to all. In the seclusion house and in subsequent life, a maturing woman learns that no man is immune to the forces she possesses. From the moment her menstrual blood begins to flow, the new responsibilities attendant upon being the custodian of a lethal weapon are placed squarely upon the initiate's shoulders.

When a woman is menstruating, she retires to the menstrual hut to protect the community. [Philip] Newman and [David] Boyd note that the initiation of Awa women includes warnings to:

> watch where they walk and sit and to be particularly careful in the handling and preparation of food. Menstrual blood is especially dangerous, they are told, and when the signs of a menstrual period appear, they must immediately go to the menstrual hut, [and] remain there until the flow stops.

The consequences of women ignoring these precautions include incapacitation and death for the men: the bones weaken, muscles atrophy and the body withers. Precautions include prohibition of food handling by women in menses, separate and distinct living arrangements, separated sleeping quarters or spaces, spatial orientation including physically higher male position (walking across slopes, within buildings, on ladders, elevations, and so on) and care of waste fluid.

[Mary] Douglas's hypothesis of inter-related symbolic systems of particular societies suggests that, in the case of women's sexual fluids, there appears to be a relationship between prohibitions and the structure of the wider society. More recently, [Thomas] Buckley and [Alma] Gottlieb suggest that menstrual prohibitions reflect the power of women over and against the danger they offer to society. Menstrual rules bring with them social arrangements that are desirable as well as problematic. [Marla] Powers proposes that, when individual rites (seclusion, for example) are taken in isolation 'rather than as a part of the dynamic whole', the result is 'misinterpretation'. Ritual seclusion thus must be viewed within the entire complex of the female life cycle—birth to menarche to death—all associated with creative birth power.

University practicalities and cosmological constructions

The University's distinction between natural and supernatural, as embodied in housing arrangements, fostered an artificial systematic ordering of being and social order in Melanesia.

The University of Technology was founded in 1967, eight years before Independence. In the late 1980s, the faculty was largely expatriate, but the administration and support staff were Papua New Guinean. Unitech served the professional needs of a country that was then, and is now, emerging in global networks of economic trade and resource development. The training of engineers and professionals to work with national and transnational corporations with interests in gold, copper, silver, natural gas, timber, oil and fisheries was the central University mission.

In its early years, the student body was exclusively male. As a part of nation building, Papua New Guinea instituted countrywide educational opportunities for both boys and girls. The goal was to train Papua New Guinean professionals in the technical skills necessary to develop the country socially, politically and economically. These highly trained graduates were ultimately to replace imported expatriates. The student body was composed of men and women from much of Oceania. A Higher School Certificate from a National High School, awarded upon successful completion of Grade 12, was a prerequisite for entry.

Students who attended the University of Technology did so at the invitation of the PNG Department of Education. Papua New Guinea has, along with many former British colonies, adopted a national examination system in which a student's ability to continue beyond Grade 6 is determined through testing. In this land of over 700 languages, English is the language of education.

Female students at Unitech presented a security dilemma for the institution. With a student body that was predominantly male, there was an interest in protecting female students from attack or sexual assault. To this effect, female students were housed on the second floor of two cinderblock dormitories in 1986. Window bars and cyclone-fenced gates secured with heavy chains and padlocks secured these women each night. First-year male students were housed beneath their female counterparts.

The folklore of the campus indicated that this housing arrangement was intentional—upper-division students refused to be housed beneath women; first-year students did not have a choice. Informal interviews I conducted with first-year male students brought to light discomfort at living beneath women. In some cases, these students would sleep on the floor of upper-class male compatriots' dormitories for the duration of the year rather than stay in their own rooms. Upper-division students would regale others with stories about the lengths to which they and current students would go to avoid their housing assignments. Glee was evident in noting the consternation of newly arrived male students who discovered their dormitory arrangements. Upon the successful completion of their first year, male students then moved out to lodge-style dormitories on the outer perimeter of the campus.

The solution to women's security in the late 1980s included ignoring customary cautions regarding the power of highly charged female sexual fluids, and subjecting first-year male students to potential danger. Science, nature, and reason became the primary criteria for distinguishing between things considered to be true.

The dilemma of position

[Edward] Tylor speaks of the ritual practices and beliefs of the 'primitive' as parts of systems that are 'devised by human reason', in other words, of 'natural religions' as those that exist 'without supernatural aid or revelation'. He includes Christianity in this analysis. Belief systems are formed as part of a rational system of thought to make sense of the human place in the cosmos. This position appears to be at the heart of our dialogue here. To follow Tylor suggests that outsiders are able to explain what really occurs in religious systems (etic) vis-à-vis the explanations of participants (emic). In doing so, however, we risk denigrating that which is very real for the actors. At issue is power. In spite of an enlightened postmodern anthropological sensitivity to cultural contexts, distinctive phenomena, reflective positioning, and comparative inclinations, we have not moved far beyond Tylor. [Russell] McCutcheon notes that 'the Enlightenment provides the foundation of a strong outsider position in the study of religion', and goes on to suggest that the study of religion, rooted in the Enlightenment, 'consists in submitting the irrational aspects of human behavior to rational analysis'. Irrationality and rationality, however, exist only within the 'enlightened' etic perspective.

This differential analysis of an integrated system suggests that the human desire for synthesis is mistaken:

> [The Enlightenment's approach] has gone by such names as the scientific or the naturalistic study of religion. By 'naturalistic' one does not mean that this approach is more natural but simply that it presumes from the outset that religion is not *sui generis*, not a special case. Instead, it presumes that when religious people claim to have had supernatural experiences that defy rational explanation they are mistaken in some way.

In the attempt to synthesise the dichotomous relationship between natural and supernatural, European scholars seized upon ritual activity and accompanying mythological construction to define, organise and arrange their cosmos. The study of this language and activity is a recent project. As [Jonathan Z.] Smith (emphasis in original) notes: 'Simply put, the *academic study of religion is a child of the Enlightenment*'.

The issue of power is clearly present in this conversation as it relates to the category of supernatural. By continuing to use 'supernatural' as a classificatory term we perpetuate a false and imposed distinction. While the scientific minds thought they had solved the problem of providing security for arriving female students (their arrival being a significant step in itself), we anthropologists must avoid the temptation to shortcut cultural complexities by creating classifications that are imprecise and alien to the people with whom we work. The natural and supernatural are part of a cultural composite. In the case of housing and higher education in Papua New Guinea, the differentiation may only exist in our own minds.

The histories of both Melanesians and Europeans bring together ideas, practices, and constructions about what it means to be human. Such is the case with descriptive classificatory language that is introduced from without. As anthropologists, we may well be stuck with the awkward yet appropriate obligation of recognising and honouring the complex synthesis of human experience. By avoiding the use of a classificatory schema that perpetuates the positivist tendencies of the Enlightenment, we open the door for honest dialogue about the continual evolution of social experience. The indigenisation of the modern experience can, as a result, proceed with reflective analysis on the part of both insiders and outsiders, using common symbolic imagery that honours the whole.

POSTSCRIPT

Does the Natural–Supernatural Distinction Exist in All Cultures?

Beginning in the late 1960s, many anthropologists challenged the use of many Western terms such as "primitive," "savages," and "barbarism" on the grounds that such terms were pejorative, and that they were based on an ethnocentric bias that prevented anthropologists from understanding other cultures. By the mid-1970s, some anthropologists suggested that even basic categories like kinship, politics, law, art, and religion had to be reexamined because they were based on the fundamental categories of Western societies that were not present in non-Western languages. The argument was that just because we find kinship, politics, or religion in America, there is no reason to believe that in radically different societies such as those in Africa, the Amazon, or New Guinea that people understand or view their societies in these terms. Indeed, several of these abstract categories such as "art," "kinship," and "religion" have no indigenous terms in many societies.

Other anthropologists have challenged this view arguing that whether peoples actually have words for kinship, religion, politics, or law, these are nevertheless useful concepts for analysis and interpretation of non-Western societies. According to this view, these concepts are categories that provide a descriptive language for documenting and analyzing how individual societies operate and how different societies vary from one another. This perspective acknowledges that "kinship," "religion," "law," "politics," "art," and "the economy" are modeled on Western social and cultural practices and do not always represent indigenous categories. But in this view, these criticisms do not limit an anthropologist from understanding the relevant indigenous categories and how they may differ from our own.

The anthropologist Morton Klass (1928–2001) raised this question in his book *Ordered Universes: Approaches to the Anthropology of Religion* (Westview, 1995). He likened the term "supernatural" to the term "race," because it implied a phenomenal reality that simply was not present in the empirical, observable data. In the case of "race," there is no question that physical differences clearly exist from one part of the world to another. But human biological variation is much more complex than most Americans assume it to be, and there is actually more variation within the so-called races than between any two races. The handful of features Americans have come to associate with "race" are some of the least important differences among human populations. In a similar way, the existence of the supernatural is imposed by Western culture, and as Klass suggests, this notion has its roots in the age of enlightenment beginning in the 1700s.

Frederick (Fritz) Lampe, who is a Lutheran pastor, suggests that when considering the Papua New Guineans he knows, Klass's view is correct. This is particularly striking given the fact that he is himself a religious man. He acknowledges that New Guineans have beliefs that Lohmann would consider "supernatural," but they do not distinguish the natural and the supernatural as distinct categories of experience or belief.

Roger Ivar Lohmann professes not to be religious, and yet he claims to see the supernatural in all of the Papua New Guinean societies he has encountered. Moreover, Lohmann suggests that even nonreligious Americans may adopt supernatural thinking on a daily basis as they impute conscious motives to non-conscious things. For him, this is the heart of the supernatural. He feels that all societies are consciously aware that supernatural things are similar to natural ones, but are nevertheless different in fundamental ways.

The debate between Lohmann and Lampe appeared in a special issue of the journal *Anthropological Forum* (vol. 13, no. 2, 2003), edited by Lohmann, and including eight other essays that take slightly different positions from these two. Although this is one of the first debates discussing whether the supernatural is a universal human category, others have been discussing similar issues for a number of years. Several of the essays in Morton Klass and Maxine K. Weisgrau's edited volume *Across the Boundaries of Belief* (Westview, 1999) addresses these concerns. Earlier discussions of these topics would include Pascal Boyer's book *The Naturalness of Religious Ideas: A Cognitive Theory of Religion* (University of California Press, 1994), Stewart Guthrie's *Faces in the Clouds: A New Theory of Religion* (Oxford University Press, 1993), and John S. Kennedy's *The New Anthropomorphism* (Cambridge University Press, 1992). Nurit Bird-David's article "'Animism' Revisited: Personhood, Environment, and Relational Epistemology," *Current Anthropology* (vol. 40 supplement, February 1999, pp. S67–S91) and comments about this essay offer some other thoughts.

ISSUE 14

Are San Hunter-Gatherers Basically Pastoralists Who Have Lost Their Herds?

YES: James R. Denbow and Edwin N. Wilmsen, from "Advent and Course of Pastoralism in the Kalahari," *Science* (December 19, 1986)

NO: Richard B. Lee, from *The Dobe Ju/'hoansi*, 3rd ed. (Wadsworth Thomson Learning, 2003)

ISSUE SUMMARY

YES: Archaeologists James R. Denbow and Edwin N. Wilmsen argue that the San of the Kalahari Desert in southern Africa have been involved in pastoralism, agriculture, and regional trade networks since at least A.D. 800. They imply that the San, who were hunting and gathering in the twentieth century, were descendants of pastoralists who lost their herds due to subjugation by outsiders, drought, and livestock disease.

NO: Cultural anthropologist Richard B. Lee counters that evidence from oral history, archaeology, and ethnohistory shows that the Ju/'hoansi group of San living in the isolated Nyae Nyae-Dobe area of the Kalahari Desert were autonomous hunter-gatherers until the twentieth century. Although they carried on some trade with outsiders before then, it had minimal impact on their culture.

$\mathbf{C}$an hunter-gatherers (also called "foragers") be economically self-sufficient and politically autonomous even when in contact with more powerful food-producing peoples? This is the basic question behind the "Great Kalahari Debate," which is illustrated by the following selections.

Even in the late nineteenth century, hunting-and-gathering peoples living outside the disruptive influence of complex societies and colonialism were scarce. By then most Native American hunter-gatherers were on reservations or incorporated into the fur trade, and others, like the Veddas of Sri Lanka, had been absorbed and transformed by the dominant societies that surrounded them. The most striking exception was the Australian Aborigines, who were still nomadic hunter-gatherers using stone tools at the time of European contact. Aborigines became the model of the earliest stage of cultural evolution as discussed by Emile Durkheim in *The Elementary Forms of the Religious Life* (George Allen and Unwin Ltd., 1915) and Sigmund Freud in *Totem and Taboo* (Moffat, Yard, 1918). By the 1950s, however, most Aborigines, too, had been settled on ranches, missions, or government settlements, and their cultures had been radically disrupted. Anthropologists' waning hopes of studying other "pristine" foragers were suddenly raised when an American family, the Marshalls, found and studied a group of Ju/'hoansi (!Kung) San living by independent foraging in the Kalahari Desert of Southwest Africa (now Namibia). Lorna Marshall's scholarly articles (later collected in her book *The !Kung of Nyae Nyae* [Harvard University Press, 1976]), her daughter Elizabeth Marshall Thomas's popular book *The Harmless People* (Knopf, 1959) and her son John's films (e.g., *The Hunters*) attracted great attention to the San.

In 1963 then–graduate student Richard B. Lee went to northwestern Bechuanaland (now Botswana) in search of an independent foraging San group. He found such a group in the Ju/'hoansi at Dobe waterhole. Although he recognized that they interacted with Bantu-speaking herding people in the region, his research focused on their adaptation to the natural environment. His findings led to a radically new image of the San and, eventually, of foragers in general. Once thought to live in a precarious struggle for survival, he found that the Ju/'hoansi actually needed to work less than 22 hours a week to get an adequate amount of food. The key to their success was their dependence on plant foods, mostly gathered by women, rather than meat, and the emphasis placed on food sharing.

By the early 1970s, however, some anthropologists had begun to question the popular image of San as isolated people with a continuous history of independent foraging since preagricultural times. In their selection, James R. Denbow and Edwin N. Wilmsen make the case that the Kalahari San have long participated in the regional economy and political system. They argue that the Ju/'hoansi and other inhabitants of the Kalahari Desert were agropastoralists (farmer-herders) and commodity traders until the late nineteenth century, when dominating outsiders, drying climate, and livestock diseases caused some of them to lose their herds and revert (temporarily) to full-time foraging.

Richard B. Lee responds that some San groups—such as the Ju/'hoansi of the Nyae Nyae-Dobe area—were quite isolated from outsiders until the late nineteenth century, when Europeans and Bantu-speaking Africans began to make occasional journeys into their homeland. Thus, his research suggests that foraging societies can live in contact with food-producers without being economically or politically subjugated by them.

This debate raises a number of important questions. Can small-scale, politically weak societies have economic and political ties with powerful outsiders without being dominated and fundamentally changed? Can one generalize from one case like the Dobe Ju/'hoansi to other foraging peoples? If foragers were herders or farmers in the past, can they still tell us something about the hunting-and-gathering way of life before the advent of agriculture?

YES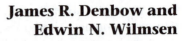

James R. Denbow and
Edwin N. Wilmsen

Advent and Course of Pastoralism in the Kalahari

It has long been thought that farming and herding were comparatively recent introductions into the Kalahari and that it has been a preserve of foraging "Bushmen" for thousands of years. Agropastoral Bantu-speakers were thought to have entered this region only within the last two centuries. However, fully developed pastoralism and metallurgy are now shown to have been established in the Kalahari from A.D. 500, with extensive grain agriculture and intracontinental trade added by A.D. 800. Archeological, linguistic, and historical evidence delineates the continuation of mixed economies in the region into the present. Consequences of this revised view for anthropological theory and for policy planning concerning contemporary Kalahari peoples are indicated.

When the principal ethnographic studies of southern African peoples, then called "Bushmen" (*1*), were undertaken in the 1950's and 1960's, very little was known of their prehistory or of the history of their association with herding and farming peoples; a similar lack of historic depth characterized earlier southern Bantu studies (*2*). At the time, it was universally assumed that Bantu-speaking farming-herding peoples had intruded into the Kalahari no more than two or three centuries ago. The region was presumed to have been peopled previously only by San-speaking foragers who had, until then, remained isolated from external influences.

Before the mid-1970's, only two systematic archeological investigations had been carried out in Botswana, an area approximately the size of Texas (575,000 square kilometers); only one attempt had been made to integrate the history of relations among hunting and herding Kalahari peoples. In addition, the climatic history of the Kalahari and its potential influence on local economies was entirely unknown. Likewise, linguistic studies, with their implications for revealing the history of social interaction and diversification in the region, were in their infancy. The assumption that pastoralism and social heterogeneity in the Kalahari were very recently introduced appeared to be correct.

Current work in archeology, geology, linguistics, and anthropology renders that assumption untenable. Since 1975, excavations have been carried out at 34 archeological sites in Botswana as well as at other sites in Zimbabwe and Namibia. Seventy-nine radiocarbon dates now delineate the chronology of

From *Science*, vol. 234, December 19, 1986, pp. 1509–1514. Copyright © 1986 by American Association for the Advancement of Science. Reproduced with permission from AAAS. www.sciencemag.org

domesticated food production in Botswana during the past 2000 years. These investigations indicate that cattle (*Bos taurus*) and ovicaprids were introduced along with ceramics into the northern Kalahari in the final centuries B.C. and first centuries A.D. Slightly later, grain cultivation and metallurgy were part of the economic repertoire of Early Iron Age (EIA) pastoralists in the region. By the ninth century, these peoples were engaged in trade networks that brought exotic goods such as glass beads and marine shells from the Indian Ocean into the Kalahari.

Geologic evidence suggests that significantly higher rainfall may have created an environment that encouraged the initial establishment of pastoral economies in the region. Linguistic evidence points to the diversification of Khoisan and southern Bantu languages coincident with this agropastoral expansion. Archival sources from the 18th and 19th centuries as well as oral histories document varying conjunctions of pastoralism and foraging in the economies of both Khoisan and Bantu-speakers that existed in precolonial time and characterize the region to this day. These sources also confirm the continued involvement of these peoples in ancient intracontinental trade networks that were not dominated by European colonial merchants until the second half of the 19th century. As a result of these studies, relations among hunters and herders in the Kalahari are shown to be both of longer duration and more integrated than has been thought.

The Context of Initial Pastoralism

Excavations of Late Stone Age (LSA) sites in the Kalahari reveal forager subsistence patterns differing from those recorded ethnographically among San in the region. Brooks and Helgren report that, in at least some LSA sites in the Makgadikgadi Pans area, fish and other aquatic resources complemented land animals in the subsistence of foragers between 4000 and 2000 years ago. At Lotshitshi, on the southeastern edge of the Okavango Delta, a LSA stratum dating within this period was found to contain fish, bullfrogs, and turtles along with large land mammals. Reconnaissance in the Makgadikgadi complex located over 50 additional LSA sites; two of these include small quantities of Bambata ceramics in their assemblages; eight others contain somewhat later EIA Gokomere or Kumadzulo pottery types. At Bambata Cave, in Zimbabwe, ceramics with remains of domesticated sheep are dated tentatively as early as the second century B.C. Maunatlala, in eastern Botswana, has ceramics and pole-and-clay hut remains at the end of the fourth century A.D.

The middle LSA level of Lotshitshi dates in the third century A.D. Faunal remains from this component indicate a broadly based economy including cattle (*B. taurus*) along with zebra, wildebeest, duiker, warthog, smaller game, and fish. Ceramics from this site are too fragmented for accurate identification, but their thin, charcoal-tempered fabric and finely incised decoration are compatible with Bambata types. Farther westward, in Namibia, ceramics (not Bambata ware) were present before A.D. 400 at Mirabib (with domestic sheep) and Falls Rock. Of the sites mentioned thus far, only Maunatlala has yielded evidence of metal use.

Radiocarbon dates placing sheep, and possibly cattle, but not metal, as far south as the Cape of Good Hope in the first century A.D. have been available for some years, consequently, a gap in data existed between these very early pastoralist manifestations in the far south and older centers north of the Okavango and Zambezi Rivers. The early pastoralist sites in the Kalahari and its margins begin to fill that gap. Consistent association of ceramics and domestic animals with LSA assemblages and their early dates indicate that pastoralist elements were introduced from the north into indigenous foraging economies here before the currently documented beginning of the Iron Age in southern Africa.

Recently acquired geomorphological evidence for fluctuating climates in the region has implications for these changes in LSA economies. At the Cwihaba caverns in western Ngamiland, periodically more humid climatic conditions are indicated by episodes of rapid sinter formation. In order to account for these episodes, Cooke suggests that rainfall in western Ngamiland reached 300 percent of the present annual mean between 2500 and 2000 years ago and again around 750 years ago. In general, these dates parallel those obtained for the sequence of beach levels found around the Makgadikgadi, Ngami, and Mababe basins where a number of higher lake levels with intervening regressions are indicated between 3000 and 1500 years ago.

Although it cannot be assumed that these high lake levels were caused solely by increased rainfall, Shaw argues for generally wetter conditions over the delta at dates congruent with those of Cwihaba. He estimates that rainfall over the Okavango increased between 160 and 225 percent. Under such a regime, many currently ephemeral pans and springs would also have contained more constant supplies of available water. Brain and Brain found evidence, in the form of microfaunal proportions, for episodes of climatic amelioration between about 4000 and 500 years ago at Mirabib in Namibia. Thus, several independent studies indicate higher rainfall during the millennium embracing the initial spread of agropastoral economies through the region 2500 to 1500 years ago.

In recent years, studies of Khoe (Central Khoisan) languages have proliferated in the Kalahari; all lead to an estimate that Khoe diversification in this region began about 2000 years ago. Vossen finds words for cattle and milking with apparent Proto-Khoe roots in the Khoe languages of north central Botswana. Köhler finds such words, along with a Khoe crop vocabulary, among the Kxoe (Khoe-speakers of northern Namibia). Both conclude that pastoralism must have been familiar to these peoples for a long time.

Ehret also argues that the basic separation of Khoi and Central Khoisan languages took place in the Botswana-Angola border region shortly after 500 B.C. He proposed further, from lexical evidence, that the basic pastoralist vocabulary of southern Bantu is derived through a Khoisan intermediary in this area, implying that these Bantu-speakers, but not others farther north, acquired cattle and sheep from Khoisan-speaking peoples. Pfouts suggests diversification of the Bantu languages of Namibia and southern Angola beginning about 1500 to 2000 years ago, whereas Ehret and Kinsman specifically place diversification of Proto-southeast Bantu in the EIA of this time frame.

These authors suggest that economic factors contributed to this process of linguistic differentiation; their conclusions are compatible with the archeological evidence regarding initiation of pastoralism and socioeconomic heterogeneity in southern Africa. Elphick reconstructs historical data to reach a similar conclusion.

The Early Iron Age

The western sandveld.   The presence of Iron Age agropastoral communities in the Kalahari by the middle of the first millennium is now attested for Ngamiland as well as for eastern Botswana. At Tsodilo Hills, in the sandveld, 70 kilometers west of the Okavango, extensive excavations have uncovered settlements that span the period from the 6th to the 11th centuries A.D. Ceramics from the earliest (A.D. 550–730) of these sites, Divuyu, indicate that it belongs to an EIA variant, the distribution of which appears to extend northward into Angola. There are no close parallels in known EIA assemblages to the south, either in Zimbabwe or South Africa. Common decoration motifs consist of multiple parallel bands of combstamping separated by spaces that are either blank or filled-in with incised motifs. Divuyu ceramics are charcoal tempered but have substantial inclusions of calcrete.

A wide variety of iron and copper implements and ornaments were recovered from Divuyu but only a single stone tool. The presence of slag and bloomery waste indicates that metal working took place on the site. An amorphous scatter of friable burned clay fragments with stick impressions marks the probable location of a pole-and-clay hut. Fragments of perforated ceramic strainers indicate that salt was extracted from local sources. Unidentified marine shells provide firm evidence for coastal links, possibly through Angolan sites. Local trade with peoples of the Okavango system is indicated by the presence of fish bones and river mollusk shells (*Unio* sp. or *Aspartharin* sp.). Domesticated ovicaprids made up a large portion of the diet at Divuyu; domesticated *Bos* was rare. Large quantities of carbonized mongongo nut shells (*Ricinodendron rautanenii*) attest to the importance of foraging in the economy.

In the second Iron Age site at Tsodilo, Nqoma, a lower stratum contains Divuyu ceramics contemporary with the final dates at Divuyu itself. The major components at Nqoma stratigraphically overlie this material and are dated in the ninth and tenth centuries. Ceramics from these later components are uniformly charcoal tempered with few inclusions of other materials; decoration is most often applied as bands of interlocking triangles or in pendent triangles filled with hatching, combstamping, or linear punctuating. False-relief chevron designs occur frequently. Only a few dated sites are presently available for comparison. We see affinities with Sioma, in southwestern Zambia, and Dundo, in northeastern Angola, dated to the sixth through eighth centuries in the range of Divuyu and the beginning of Nqoma occupations at Tsodilo, but systematic ceramic comparisons of these sites have yet to be undertaken. Nqoma ceramics are similar to those from the ninth century site at Kapako on the Okavango River in Namibia; charcoal-tempered ceramics have been dated to the same period far out in the sandveld at NxaiNxai and are found in adjacent parts of Botswana and Namibia.

Evidence for metal working is attested at Nqoma by the presence of tuyeres as well as slag and bloom. Iron and copper ornaments are common and include finely made chains and necklaces with alternating links of copper and iron as well as bracelets with designs sometimes preserved by rust and oxidation. Moderate numbers of stone tools of LSA types are present. Dense areas of burned clay with pole and stick impressions mark the locations of substantial house structures.

Cattle (*Bos taurus*) were paramount in the pastoral economy of Nqoma; preliminary analysis suggests they outnumber ovicaprids by a factor of 2. Bifid thoracic vertebrae indicate that at least some of these cattle were of a hump-backed variety. Carbonized seeds of sorghum (*Sorghum bicolor* caffra), pearl millet (*Pennisetum americannum* thyphoides), and perhaps melons (*Cucurbita* sp.) provide direct evidence for cultivation. Remains of wild game along with carbonized mongongo nuts and *Grewia* seeds indicate that foraging continued to form an important part of the diet of this Iron Age population. Fish bones and river mollusk shells document continuing trade connections with the Okavango to the north and east.

Many glass beads and marine shells, primarily cowrie, along with worked ivory, one piece in the shape of a conus shell, provide evidence that Nqoma was an important local center in an intracontinental trade network extending to the Indian Ocean in the ninth century.

The river systems.   Although the origins of the EIA communities at Tsodilo point consistently northward to Angola, contemporary agropastoralist sites on the eastern margins of the Okavango Delta as well as on the Chobe River belong firmly within the Kumadzulo-Dambwa complex documented by Vogel for the Victoria Falls area. This complex forms a regional facies of the widespread Gokomere tradition of western Zimbabwe and northeastern Botswana. Kumadzulo-Dambwa complex ceramics and small clay figurines of hump-backed cattle were found at the eighth century site of Serondela, on the Chobe River, and cattle bones along with LSA lithics and similar ceramics were recovered at Hippo Tooth on the Botletle River dating to the early ninth century. At the island site of Qugana, in the eastern delta, the same ceramic complex with burned, reed-impressed clay hut remains dates to the eighth century; as yet, no domestic fauna have been recovered from this site.

Matlhapaneng, on the southeastern Okavango, is an extensive site dated between the late seventh and tenth centuries, contemporary with the Nqoma sequence at Tsodilo. Ceramics are charcoal tempered with Kumadzulo-Dambwa decoration motifs. Pole-and-clay structures, iron, copper, and ivory ornaments, slag, and bloomery waste mark this as a fully formed EIA community. LSA stone tools are also present. Although this site is not as rich as Nqoma, long-distance trade connections are attested by the presence of cowrie shells and glass beads. Carbonized remains of sorghum (*S. bicolor* caffra), millet (*P. americanum* typhoides), and cow peas (*Vigna unguiculata*) provide evidence for agriculture; cattle and ovicaprids dominate faunal remains. Foraging was important here as it was at Tsodilo; carbonized marula (*Sclerocarya caffra*) and *Grewin* seeds are present and wild animal remains are common.

The eastern hardveld.   Similar developments took place simultaneously in the eastern hardveld where thick kraal dung deposits vitrified by burning have been found at more than 200 sites, indicating that large herds were kept in the region. The same EIA suite of materials already described is present, although ceramics are of Gokomere-Zhizo types with affinities eastward to Zimbabwe and northern Transvaal. East coast trade, documented by glass beads and marine shells, is dated in the late first millennium at a number of these sites as well as at contemporary sites in Zimbabwe and the Transvaal.

Major chiefdoms developed along this eastern margin of the Kalahari at the end of the first millennium, marking a transition to later centralized state development. A tripartite hierarchy of settlement size and complexity is discernible at this time. Large towns of approximately 100,000 square meters, Toutswe, K2, and Mapungubwe, dominated extensive hinterlands containing smaller villages and many small hamlets. Rulers of these chiefdoms succeeded in controlling the Indian Ocean trade into the Kalahari; it is possible that a system supplying valued goods in tribute to these chiefdoms from the western sandveld was instituted at this time, displacing previous exchange relations in which foreign imports as well as local exports had circulated widely.

Supporting evidence for changes in social relations of economic production is found in a comparison of age distributions of cattle and ovicaprid remains at the middle-order sites, Nqoma, Matlhapaneng and Taukome, with those at the capital towns, Mapungubwe and K2. At the first set of sites, a bimodal culling pattern is found similar to that of present-day cattle posts in Botswana, where slaughter is highest in nonreproductive age classes. Such a strategy conserves breeding stock and emphasizes rates of herd growth rather than meat production. Producers and consumers of herd products at these sites probably belonged to the same local social units.

In contrast, at Mapungubwe and K2, both primary centers, the majority of cattle slaughtered were in prime age classes; offtake appears not to have followed the conservative strategy found at the secondary sites. In other studies, this form of distribution has been associated with differential social stratification among occupants of a site. This appears to be the most plausible explanation for the contrasting culling patterns observed in our study. Elites at primary centers appear to have been selective consumers of prime rather than very old animals, many of which would have been produced elsewhere.

The Kalahari in the Second Millennium

These eastern Kalahari chiefdoms collapsed around the beginning of the 13th century. Great Zimbabwe emerged at this time, supplanting the political role played earlier at Toutswe, K2, and Mapungubwe. The extent of this new hegemony is indicated by stone-walled Zimbabwe-Khami outposts found far out in the Kalahari on the margins of the Makgadikgadi Pans. Control of trade became the prerogative of this kingdom. The final component at Toutswe

(A.D. 1500) is devoid of exotic goods and no long-distance trade items have been recovered from two rock shelters, Qomqoisi and Depression, excavated at Tsodilo and dated to the 16th and 17th centuries, nor in an upper stratum at Lotshitshi, which, though undated, probably falls in this period.

Glass beads reappear at Xaro in Ngamiland at the beginning of the 17th century. These and cowrie shells are abundant at the 18th century site, Kgwebe, as well as in a probably contemporary (though not yet dated) upper stratum at Nqoma. Portuguese, through their Atlantic trade into the Kongo and Angola, were the probable source of these beads, which reached the interior along trade routes that had functioned since the Early Iron Age. Many of the first Europeans to enter the region from the Cape record that this trade in Portuguese goods was active south of the Orange River and to the east at least as far as the Zambezi by the 18th century. Native peoples including San-speakers, not Portuguese themselves, are specified in these records as the interior agents of this trade.

Archival records as well as oral histories testify to the importance of pastoralism throughout the Kalahari long before Europeans arrived. Every European who first observed the region from the 18th century on reports the presence of peoples of different languages, appearance, and group designation—Bantu and Khoissan—everywhere they went. Virtually every one of these Europeans remarks on the importance of pastoralism in all parts of the region and on the involvement of San-speakers in herding; several specifically mention San owners of livestock. Indeed, the herds of subsequently subjugated peoples were one inducement for Tswana expansion into Ngamiland in 1795. So rich in cattle was the northwestern Kalahari that 12,000 head were exported annually from it alone to the Cape during the 1860's through the 1880's, while unknown but apparently large numbers of interior cattle had been supplied to the Atlantic trade since the late 18th century.

In addition to cattle, 100,000 pounds of ivory along with many bales of ostrich feathers and hides are recorded to have been exported annually from the region as a whole during those decades in exchange for guns, tobacco, sugar, coffee, tea, cloth, beads, and other European goods. These were newly developed markets, but the trade networks they followed were continuations of Iron Age systems. Both Khoisan- and Bantu-speakers are reliably recorded by many observers to have been thoroughly involved in production for precolonial regional exchange networks. When first seen by Europeans in the 19th century, the copper mines and salt pans of northern Namibia were exclusively under San control; 50 to 60 tons of ore were estimated to be taken annually from those mines and traded to Bantu smiths. Trade routes were linked to wider subcontinental networks. Salt, manufactured into loaves, was traded far into the interior and is reported to have been at least as important an exchange commodity as copper.

In extension of this economic activity, San are credited with producing the bulk of ivory and ostrich feathers exported through Bantu and Nama middlemen during the 19th century. Relations of production and exchange were thus not strictly bounded by ethnic or linguistic divisions but cut across them. More than anything else, it is this negotiable lattice of relations among peoples and production that characterizes the last two millennia in the Kalahari.

Discussion

We have summarized a large body of data pertaining to prehistoric and historic economies of Kalahari peoples, and those surrounding them, which has been accumulated by a number of investigators. . . . We have concentrated on the early introduction and subsequent local transformations of agropastoralism in the region because these have been the least known aspects of those economies. Pastoralism has been treated in the ethnographies cited at the beginning of this article as if its history in and adjacent to the Kalahari has been recent and separate from that of indigenous foraging. A guiding assumption of these anthropological studies was that 20th-century foraging there is a way of life that has remained unchanged for millennia. Practitioners of these segregated economies have been rather strictly supposed to have had distinct ethnic and racial origins, in contact only for the last two centuries or less. This position can no longer be supported.

Many problems remain to be investigated. Much of the central Kalahari is unexplored archeologically, and the extent to which Iron Age pastoralism penetrated this area is unknown. A hiatus exists in our knowledge of the entire region between the 12th and 16th centuries. While large centralized states with many satellite communities flourished in the east, few if any sites are presently known for this period in the entire western half of southern Africa, with some possible exceptions at the Cape. Drier conditions may have led to shifts in settlement size and location, making detection of sites in the Kalahari difficult under present conditions. A reasonable hypothesis posits a concentration of population along the river systems and permanent springs leaving less densely peopled the drier hinterland, where foraging may have waxed and waned in accordance with changing environmental and regional economic conditions, particularly after European influence penetrated the region. It is unlikely that herders withdrew entirely from the sandveld; more likely, they at least continued to exploit seasonal surface water and grazing. At present, there is no evidence either to support or refute these propositions.

All of the peoples of the Kalahari during the past two millennia have been linked by extensive social and economic networks; thus, during this period of time, the Kalahari was never the isolated refuge of foragers it has been thought to be. It was the vastly intensified extraction of commoditized animal products in the colonial period, abetted by a drying climatic trend and stock diseases, especially rinderpest, which killed 75 percent of all cattle and antelope in southern Africa at the end of the 19th century, that combined to pauperzie the region. These forces became factors leading to increased labor migration to the newly opened South African mines. In the process, the dues and privileges of earlier native states became increasingly translated into private family fortunes of a colonially favored aristocracy, while previously flexible relations among Khoisan and Bantu-speakers were transformed into ethnic categories defined by criteria of race, language, and economic class. The resultant divisions gave, to anthropological observers in the 20th century, the false impression of a Kalahari eternally empty, its peoples long segregated and isolated from each other.

An unresolved problem concerns the presence of Bantu-speakers in the western half of the subcontinent, a presence that now appears to have been more pervasive and much earlier than previously assumed. There is no doubt that the introduction of EIA economies from central Africa brought with it a complex interdigitation of people south of the Zambezi-Okavango-Cunene Rivers. In the eastern half of the subcontinent, it is well established that Iron Age Bantu agropastoralists gained a dominant position over indigenous foragers and pastoralists, ultimately subjugating, absorbing, or eliminating them. This did not happen in the west where, in fact, Khoi-speaking (Nama) herders dominated a large part of the area when first encountered by Europeans. It has been thought that a major reason for this difference lay in the short history of association of these peoples in the west. The perceived isolating severity of the Kalahari environment has been seen as a primary factor protecting San foragers from Bantu pastoralist domination. Neither supposition finds support in the research reported here.

This research has profound implications for understanding relations among contemporary southern African peoples. In particular, those relegated to the ethnographic categories "Bushman" and "hunter-gatherers" are seen to have a history radically different from that hitherto assumed. It is clear that, rather than being static, uniform relics of an ancient way of life, San societies and cultures have undergone transformations in the past 2000 years that have varied in place and time in association with local economic and political alterations involving a variety of peoples.

Two important consequences flow from this new understanding. The first forces reevaluation of models of social evolution based on assumptions brought to the anthropological study of these peoples. At the very least, ethnographic analogies formulated on modern San "foragers" and applied to studies of evolving social forms must be modified to take into account the millennia-long association of these peoples with both pastoralism and Bantu-speakers. Following on this, and more immediately important, is the need to bring the results of this research into the arena of policy planning. In this arena, San are routinely dismissed as rootless "nomads," without legitimate claim to full participation in modern national politics because they are conceived to be unprepared by history to cope with complex decisions involving economic and political alternatives. That this is no more true of them than of any other peoples should be clear in even this brief account of their recent past.

Notes

1.   Etymologies of the terms "Bushmen" and "San" are debated; a long-standing derogatory connotation is acknowledged for the first of these, but San, as also "Bantu," has acquired segregating racial and ethnic overtones. To avoid such

implications, we use Khoisan and Bantu as adjectives to designate speakers of two different language families, retaining San only where necessary to specify peoples so labeled in ethnographies. We use Setswana spelling, in which c and x represent the front clicks and q the back clicks of Khoisan words.

2. L. Marshall, *The !Kung of NyaeNyae* (Harvard Univ. Press, Cambridge, MA, 1976); R. Lee, *The !Kung San* (Harvard Univ. Press, Cambridge, MA, 1979); J. Tanaka, *The San* (Univ of Tokyo Press, Tokyo, 1980); G. Silberbauer, *Hunter and Habitat in the Central Kalahari Desert* (Cambridge Univ. Press, Cambridge, 1981); I. Schapera, *The Bantu-Speaking Tribes of Southern Africa* (Routledge, London, 1937); W. Hammond-Tooke, Ed., *The Bantu-Speaking Peoples of Southern Africa* (Routledge, London, 1974).

Richard B. Lee

The Kalahari Debate: Ju/'hoan Images of the Colonial Encounter

The Kalahari Debate, also known as Kalahari revisionism, sprung up in the late 1980s and early 1990s, and has been a topic of discussion among anthropologists ever since. What is at stake in the Kalahari Debate is the question of who the San peoples are historically—autonomous foragers or dependent serfs. The position taken [here] is that the Ju/'hoansi of the Dobe area, despite recent changes, show an unbroken history as independent hunters and gatherers that can be traced back far into the past. The "revisionists" argue that the Nyae Nyae and Dobe area Ju/'hoansi have been bound into regional trade networks and dominated by distant power holders for centuries. In this view they were not even hunters in the past but cattle-keepers, or servants of cattle people, raising the possibility that the Ju/'hoansi's unique cultural features of sharing and egalitarianism come not from their hunting and gathering traditions, but rather from being outcasts, at the bottom of a social hierarchy.

Curiously, until recently, neither the revisionists or their opponents had bothered to systematically ask the Ju people themselves for their views of their own history. How do the Ju/'hoansi interpret their past and how does that picture square with the evidence from archaeology and history? . . .

Beginning in 1986–1987 when the revisionist debate began to heat up, I started to ask Botswana Ju elders focused questions about the time they refer to as n//a k'aishe or "first time." The goal was to elicit collective memories of their pre-colonial past, a time we could date historically to the pre-1870s. Subsequently I returned for two more periods of interviewing, in 1995 and 1997, with informants from the Nyae Nyae and Cho/ana areas of Namibia. Now there are five major areas of Ju settlement represented in the oral history accounts. In this discussion, I will draw on three bodies of evidence on the Nyae Nyae-Dobe area Ju/'hoansi: their own oral histories, archaeology, and ethnohistory. . . .

Oral Histories

During my fieldwork in the Dobe area starting in the 1960s, the Ju/'hoansi were acutely aware that they were living under the gaze and control of the Tawana chiefdom and, beyond it, the British colonial authority. However in

speaking of the area's past, Ju/'hoansi informants spoke of their own autonomy in the nineteenth century as a given: they were foragers who lived
entirely on their own without agriculture or domesticated animals.

The existence of many Later Stone Age archeological sites in the Dobe
area with thousands of stone artifacts and debris supports this view. But left
unexplained is the presence on these same sites of small quantities of pottery
and iron, indicating Iron Age presence or contact with Iron Age cultures. The
Ju/'hoansi themselves explain the presence of these goods in terms of their
long-standing trade relations with riverine peoples. On the other hand, Kalahari revisionists have argued that these archeological traces are proof positive
of domination of the Dobe area by Iron Age peoples and the incorporation of
the Ju/'hoansi into a regional polity. Wilmsen has further argued that people
labeled Bushmen had raised cattle in centuries past:

> [I]n this century . . . an overwhelming majority of peoples so labeled have
> pursued a substantially pastoral way of life in symbiosis with, employed
> by, or enserfed to Bantu-speaking cattle owners . . . this is equally true of
> earlier centuries.

Remarkably, in all the voluminous writings on the Kalahari Debate . . . ,
neither side had systematically investigated how the Ju/'hoansi themselves
articulate their own history.

An Interview With Kumsa N≠whin

Kumsa n≠whin, a 70-year-old Dobe man, was a former tribal policeman and
famous healer I interviewed in 1987. I began by asking him if long ago his
ancestors had lived with cattle.

"No," he replied. "My father's father saw them for the first time. My
father's father's father did not know them. The first non-San to come to the
region were Europeans, not Blacks. We worked for them, got money and
obtained our first cattle from the Tswana with that money. The Whites first
came to !Kubi [south of Dobe], killed elephants and pulled their teeth [i.e.,
ivory]. In the old days the Ju/'hoansi also killed elephants with spears for the
meat. At least 15 men were required for a hunt. They dumped the tusks [they
didn't have a use for them].

"The Whites came by ≠dwa-/twe [lit. "giraffe-horse" [i.e., camels]. The
Whites had no cattle, they had horses and camels. 'Janny' came from the
south. Another one made a well at Qangwa [also called Lewisfontein]. My
father said 'Oh, can water come out of there?' They used metal tools but not
engines. This well is not used today. They spoke Burusi [Afrikaans]."

I asked, "Before the Whites came did you know 'Ju sa jo' [Black people]
here?" His response was unequivocal: "No. We only knew ourselves. Ju/'hoansi
exclusively."

"But when the Blacks did come, who was first?"

"The first Black was Mutibele, a Tswana, and his older brother,
Mokgomphata. They came from the east following the paths made by the

Whites going in the opposite direction. They were shown the waterholes by Ju/'hoansi including my father/Twi. They were shown the killing sites of the elephants, where the bones lay, the sites where Whites killed. And they said 'Oh, the Whites have already got the n!ore [territory] from us.' Then [Mutibele's] father claimed the land and all the Ju/'hoansi on it, but he deceived us."

"How did he deceive you? When the Tswana claims he is master of you all, do you agree?"

"If he was the master, he didn't give us anything, neither clothes nor pots, or even one calf. The Europeans had given the Ju/'hoansi guns. When the Tswana saw this they decided to give guns to other Ju/'hoansi, so that they could hunt eland and giraffe."

Later in the conversation I explored the nature of San-Black interactions in the precolonial period. What had they received from the Blacks?

"When I was young," Kumsa replied, "we had no iron pots. We used the clay pots of the Goba. We couldn't make them ourselves."

"Then how do you account for the fact that there are many potsherds on old Ju/'hoansi sites around here?"

"Our fathers' fathers and their fathers' fathers got them from the Gobas. They would trade for them with skins. The Gobas didn't come up here. They stayed where they were [on the rivers] and we went to them. This went on for a very long time [so that is why there are so many potsherds]."

"We [always] got two things from them: iron and pots. If you go to Danega today you will find the right earth. But the Gobas didn't come here. We always went to them."

⋅⟨◉⟩⋅

Kumsa's statements are congruent with a model of autonomy. Others had also made the point that a long-standing trade existed with riverine peoples *in which the Ju did the travelling*. It would be hard to argue that the Blacks could dominate the Dobe area without any physical presence, but I suppose it is not impossible. The trading trips made by the Ju to the east and elsewhere would certainly account for the presence of Iron Age materials on the Dobe area sites. In fact Polly Wiessner has argued that the levels of iron and pottery found on Dobe area Later Stone Age (LSA) sites can be accounted for by *hxaro* trade, a traditional form of delayed exchange still practiced by the Ju/'hoansi that historically has been a vehicle for long-distance trade.

One suggestive point was Kumsa's intriguing statement that the precolonial Ju hunted elephant but discarded the tusks; remarkable because it indicates that the Dobe Ju/'hoansi were hunting elephant for subsistence and were not part of a mercantile *or* a tributary network, since in either case elephant ivory would have been a prime valuable item.

Also interesting is Kumsa's rather dismissive view of the Tswana as overlords. For Kumsa the criterion for being a chief [lit. in San, "wealth-person"] is giving away in this context, not exercising power *per se*. The Europeans were chiefs because they gave guns, the Tswana were "deceivers" because in Kumsa's terms they claimed chiefly status but gave nothing.

A !Goshe Commentary on the Early Days of Contact

/Ti!kai-n!a, aged 80 at the time of the interview (1987), and /Ti!kai-tsau ("tooth") age 63, were two of the leading men of !Goshe, 16 kilometers east of Qangwa, and the easternmost and most economically "progressive" of the Dobe area villages. !Goshe is the jumping-off point for travel to the east, and the village has kept Tswana cattle since the 1910s. With their strong ties to the east where most Blacks reside, !Goshe people, by reason of history and geography, are the most attuned to links to "Iron Age" peoples.

"Certain Europeans in Gaborone," I began, "argue that long ago you Ju/'hoansi, [that is] your fathers' fathers' fathers' fathers had cattle. Do you agree?"

"No! Not a bit!" was the younger /Ti!kai's emphatic answer. "Long ago our fathers' fathers' fathers' fathers, the only meat *they* had was what they could shoot with arrows. We only got cows from the Tswana."

I persisted. "But when you dig holes deep down beneath where you live, you find pieces of pottery. Where did they come from?"

"Oh those pots were our own work!" replied the elder /Ti!kai. "Our ancestors made them. They would put them on the fire and cook with them. But since we got iron pots from you Europeans we lost the knowledge of pottery making."

Shifting the topic, I asked, "What about iron?"

"We got that from the Mbukushu," said /Ti!kai. "But we learned how to work it ourselves. . . . You stick it in the fire, heat it up, and hammer it. . . . We did it ourselves. We saw how the Gobas did it and we learned from them."

"Where did you get the iron itself from?"

Their answer surprised me. "The Europeans," said /Ti!kai. "The Tswana and Gobas didn't have it. They also got it from the Europeans."

I had to disagree. "But," I said, "in the oldest abandoned villages of the Gobas, iron is there. Long before the Europeans came."

At this point the older /Ti!kai intervened. "Yes! /Tontah is right. Long ago the Mbukushu had the pieces of iron that they worked."

The younger /Ti!kai turned to the older and asked, incredulously, "Well, where did they get the iron from?"

Matter-of-factly, the older man replied, "From the earth."

Much discussion followed on this point. The younger man was unconvinced that the Gobas had iron before the Europeans, but old /Ti!kai stuck to his story.

Shifting topic again, I asked, "Long long ago, did your fathers' fathers' fathers' fathers practice //hara [farming]?"

There was no disagreement on this point. "No, we didn't. We just ate the food that we collected from the bush."

The older /Ti!kai added, "When I was a boy we had learned about //hara from the Tswanas. They showed us how [to do it]."

The !Goshe interviews corroborate the account of Kumsa on the absence of cattle and agriculture before the twentieth-century arrival of the Tswana. They add detail on Ju/'hoan understandings of the history of pottery and iron use. In the first case they spoke of Ju manufacture of pottery, whereas other informants spoke of it as only imported. In the second case there was an intriguing difference of opinion. There was agreement that iron was imported from the Gobas but only in the recent past, but some believed that iron was so recent that the Gobas only obtained iron *after* the arrival of the Europeans, a view that we were to encounter elsewhere.

N!ae and /Kunta at Cho/ana

Another round of oral history interviews took place in 1995 at Cho/ana, a former Ju/'hoan waterhole, 65 kilometers northwest of Dobe, now located in Namibia's Kaudom Game Reserve. The informants were N!ae and her husband /Kunta (/Tontah) one of my namesakes. Cho/ana has long been known to historians as a meeting point for Ju/'hoansi from several regions. It was a convenient water hole for Ju/'hoan parties engaged in *hxaro* trade to meet.

In tracing the earliest history of the place, /Kunta saw the original owners as Ju/'hoansi, not Blacks or any other ethnic group. In the beginning, asserted /Kunta, only Ju/'hoansi lived here; there were no Gobas. Ju people would come from Nyae Nyae and from the north, to do *hxaro* here. It was a waterhole that always held water. People from the South (Nyae Nyae) would bring /*do* (ostrich eggshell beads). People from the North brought /*an* (glass beads). In /Kunta's words, "*Hxaro* brought them together."

A point of emphasis in our interviews was the question of whether the Gobas made trips to the interior to trade or to make their presence felt. /Kunta was emphatic: "No, [they didn't come to us] we went to them. We saw pots on their fires and wanted them, so they gave us some."

"And what did you give them in return?"

"We gave Gobas /*do* in exchange for pots."

The interior Ju/'hoansis' proximity to Iron Age peoples on their periphery and the use of iron as a marker of Iron Age overlordship has been a particular point of emphasis for the revisionists. I was anxious to hear /Kunta and N!ae's views of the pre-colonial use of iron and its source.

"Did your ancestors have *!ga* (iron)?"

"Are you joking? We didn't know *!ga*. If we needed arrows we used ≠*dwa* (giraffe) or *n!n* (eland) bones."

"Who gave Ju/'hoansi the iron?"

"We visited north and east and saw this wonderful stuff for arrows and knives; we asked Gobas for it and got some. It was very valuable; when others saw it their hearts were sad because they didn't have it; they wanted it so badly they would even fight other Ju for it. Parties went north to seek it; Gobas gave it to them in exchange for steenbok and duiker skins and other things."

"Where did Goba get iron from?"

Without hesitation /Kunta replied, "From the European."

"Are you saying that before Europeans came Gobas had no iron?"

"Yes, they had no iron."

⟡

It is interesting that informants see iron coming ultimately from Europeans; they saw the appearance of iron and Europeans in their areas as so close in time that iron was associated with Europeans. While it is true that the amount of iron on Nyae Nyae-Dobe LSA sites is miniscule, it is striking that the long history of Iron Age occupation on their periphery, for example at the Tsodilo Hills with radiocarbon dates as early as 500 A.D., doesn't have much resonance with the Ju/'hoansi informants. When they did obtain iron from the Gobas, it was clearly an item of trade and not a marker of overlordship. In any event the very (post-European) regency of the trade in iron challenges the revisionist view of a deep antiquity of Ju/'hoan subservience.

Discussion

In all interviews there was repeated insistence that no Gobas or any other Blacks occupied their area or even visited prior to the late nineteenth century; several spoke of the Gobas' preference for staying on the river and avoiding the dry interior. All these accounts illuminate the pragmatic and matter-of-fact approach of Dobe and Nyae Nyae area people to questions of history. These, after all, are questions of the most general nature and the accounts agree closely, not only about the autonomy of the area from outside domination but also about the absence of cattle and agriculture in pre-colonial times (though not of pottery and iron). There are interesting divergences of opinion on whether pottery was imported or locally made, and on whether the Gobas had iron before the Europeans. Taken together these accounts along with others . . . constitute a fair representation of mid and late twentieth-century Ju/'hoan views of their forebearers' nineteenth-century history of autonomy.

One other indication of the Ju sense of their history is the largely positive self-image of their past. They see themselves as actors, not victims, and this contrasts with the negative self-imagery expressed by other San people, (such as Hai//om or Nharo views of their present and past).

Archaeological Tie-ins

The oral history interviews in both 1995 and 1997 accompanied archaeological excavation, designed to link archaeology with the knowledge that was part of the living tradition of the Ju/'hoansi. Professor Andrew Smith of the University of Cape Town started excavating a rich Later Stone Age archaeological site at Cho/ana, which provided a continual stimulus for oral history as new and interesting materials came to light in the excavations. The Ju informants' comments provided a valuable adjunct to the archaeological work (and vice versa). They identified plant remains, made tentative suggestions regarding fragmentary bone materials, and provided a social context in which the material could be interpreted. For example, the elders described a kind of white glass bead as one of the earliest of the European trade goods obtained through intermediaries to the north. A few days after the interview, precisely such a bead was found in a sealed level in association with an LSA industry.

But the most stunning confirmation of the direct late nineteenth-century encounter between people with advanced stone-working skills and colonialists was a piece of bottle glass (mouth and neck) showing signs of delicate micro-retouching that the South African Later Stone Age is famous for. This gave a further indication of the persistence of LSA stone-working techniques into the colonial contact period.

The oral history's insistence on the absence of cattle and Blacks in the interior was confirmed by the complete lack in the archaeological record of the presence of domesticated animals or of non-Ju/'hoan people in the area prior to the latter part of the nineteenth century. . . .

Colonial Constructions of the Ju/'hoansi

Turning to the third body of evidence, what light do ethnohistoric documents shed on these Ju accounts of their own past? Do they support or contradict Ju accounts of relative autonomy? In general, the few historical accounts we do have support the Ju/'hoansi view of autonomy. . . .

One of the earliest detailed accounts of the Nyae Nyae-Dobe Ju/'hoansi comes relatively late when Hauptman Müller, a German colonial officer, traveled through the Nyae Nyae area in 1911. Müller offers some unusually detailed observations on the situation of the Nyae Nyae-Dobe area Ju/'hoansi some 30 years after colonial trade had been established. In Müller's account (1912) the area remained remote and inaccessible. His visit was the first to the interior from the west in five years.

Most telling is Müller's ethnographic description of the bushman inhabitants of this stretch of land he calls "virginal" [jungfräulich]. He depicts their state as "noch uberuhrt von aller Zivilisation, in alter Ursprunglichkeit" [still untouched by all civilization in their old pristine state]. He reports with amusement how European objects such as matches and mirrors were unknown to them, as well as the camels of his troopers, which startled them and caused the women to grab their children and scatter into the bush. However, he did find them using such things as wooden bowls, glass and iron beads, cooper rings, and "Ovambo knives," all obtained through trade with Black neighbors.

Of particular interest is Müller's descriptions of the Bushman themselves. In his account they were well nourished and relatively tall, thanks to an ample diet of meat (hunted with bone-tipped arrows) and a variety of wild plants. There is no mention in Müller's account of any resident cattle or Bantu-speaking overlords, though BaTswana were visiting the area during his stay. For Müller the association of the Nyae Nyae Bushmen with the BaTswana was not ancient; it was of recent date and was based on trade and assistance rendered at the latters' hunting expeditions. The Bushmen were rewarded with gifts for their services and the relationship with the hunter/herders is described as equitable and friendly:

> The Bushmen seem, however, to be good friends with the BaTswanas. When I asked a Bushman if it didn't bother him that the BaTswanas were killing off so much game every year he said "Yes, but we are getting presents!" . . .

Müller's is one of the earliest accounts to be based on actual reports of what he observed, as distinguished from second-hand accounts at a distance.

And the preceding short quotation is among the very first to cite the actual words of a Ju/'hoan person.

౼◉౽

To sum up this section, both German and Ju/'hoan testimony are consistent and mutually supportive. The detail presented by Müller and the others (such as Hans Schinz and James Chapman) attests to five propositions that accord closely with statements made by the Ju/'hoansi themselves:

1. The relative isolation of the Nyae Nyae-Dobe area from the West and the low volume of European traffic, 1880–1911
2. The absence of cattle in pre-colonial Ju subsistence
3. The absence of Bantu overlords or tributary relations
4. The relatively favorable terms of trade between Blacks and San
5. The relatively good foraging subsistence base and nutritional status of the San

These lines of evidence argue the case that the views of the Ju/'hoansi about their historical autonomy are not sharply at odds with the ethnohistoric sources.

Hunter-Gatherer Discourse and Agrarian Discourse

Both the Ju oral histories and the German and other historical texts are cultural constructions, and yet, how are we to account for the correspondences between these two bodies of evidence? Why do they corroborate one another? To argue that both are careful fabrications still leaves open the question of why they agree so closely. One would have to invoke conspiracy or coincidence, in either case a tough sell. Surely it would be more reasonable to assume that they agree because they are describing the same reality. If Kumsa's, the two /Ti!kai's, N!ae and /Kunta's and others' collective accounts of the Ju/'hoansi autonomous past gibe so closely with those of European eyewitnesses such as Müller, then on what grounds rests the view of the historic Ju/'hoansi as enserfed pastoralists? And why has this view gained such currency in anthropological circles?

A more fruitful approach to understanding the recent debates is to attempt to place them in the context of the intellectual currents of the late twentieth century. How does the current conjuncture shape our perceptions of the situation of indigenous "others"?

Obviously, by the 1990s, the processes affecting the Dobe Ju/'hoansi had brought them to becoming clients, laborers, and rural proletarians, subject to and dependent on regional and world economies. Their current predicament is well understood by recourse to theories arising from political economy, dependency theory, or colonial discourse. Current theorizing is much weaker, however, in understanding the antecedent conditions. Part of the inability of contemporary theory to encompass hunters and gatherers as historical subjects is the lack of attention to the *differences* between discourses about hunters and gatherers and the discourses concerning agrarian societies and the emerging world system.

In agrarian discourse the presence of structures of domination are taken as given; it is the *forms* of domination and the modes of exploitation and surplus extraction that are problematic. In the literature on the agrarian societies of the Third World, stratification, class and class struggle, patriarchy, accumulation, and immiseration constitute the basic descriptive and analytical vocabulary.

In hunter-gatherer discourse it is not the forms and modes of domination that are at issue; rather the prior question to be asked is whether domination is *present*. I have been struck by the eagerness of otherwise competent analysts to gloss over, sidestep, or ignore this question.

There is no great mystery about what separates hunter-gatherer from agrarian societies. The former usually live lightly on the land at low densities; they can move and still survive, an escape route not available to sedentary farmers. The latter, with high densities and fixed assets, can no longer reproduce themselves outside the system, and are rendered far more vulnerable to domination.

In the recent debate some analysts seem to have taken the world systems/ political economy position so literally that every culture is seen as nothing more than the sum total of its external relations. But surely there is more to a culture than its links of trade, tribute, domination, and subordination. There is the internal dynamic of the means by which a social group reproduces itself ecologically, socially, and in terms of its collective consciousness. . . .

An historically informed ethnography can offer an alternative to the totalizing discourses of world systems theory. The unself-conscious sense of their own nineteenth- and early twentieth-century autonomy expressed by Ju/'hoan hunter-gatherers and its corroboration by contemporaneous colonial observers is one example of how these powerful assumptions can be challenged. They bear testimony that in the not very distant past other ways of being were possible.

That said, autonomy should not be taken as an article of faith, nor is it an all-or-nothing proposition. It is, or should be, an empirical question, and each society may exhibit a complex array of more or less autonomy at stages in its history. Even in agrarian societies spaces are opened up, however small, for the expression of autonomous thought and behavior. Thus it need not be the exclusive preserve of non-hierarchical or noncolonized societies. . . .

With reference to the latter though, a final point: What is desperately needed is to theorize the communal mode of production and its accompanying world view. Without it there is a theoretical vacuum filled far too facilely by imputing capitalist relations of production, bourgeois subjectivity, or "culture of poverty" frameworks to hunter-gatherer peoples.

POSTSCRIPT

Are San Hunter-Gatherers Basically Pastoralists Who Have Lost Their Herds?

These selections express two radically different worldviews. Denbow and Wilmsen's view—which has been called the "revisionist" view—emphasizes the interconnectedness of societies and the tendency for powerful polities to exert control over their less powerful neighbors. On the other hand, Lee's view—called the "traditionalist" view—emphasizes the people's adaptation to their natural environment and sees their relations with outsiders as variable, depending on local circumstances. Most anthropologists recognize that all cultures are influenced by local conditions and by the larger social environment, including, to some extent, the entire "world system." The question is, How much weight should one give to these two types of influence?

The disagreement between these scholars and their supporters is not merely a matter of theoretical emphasis. They also disagree about the facts and their proper interpretation. In subsequent publications Wilmsen and Lee, in particular, have argued over such matters as the precise locations of groups and trade routes mentioned in travelers' journals and whether or not the presence of cattle bones, for example, in an archaeological site indicates trade or outside domination. For elaboration of Wilmsen and Denbow's views see "Paradigmatic History of San-Speaking Peoples and Current Attempts at Revision," *Current Anthropology* (vol. 31, no. 5, 1990) and Wilmsen's book *Land Filled With Flies: A Political Economy of the Kalahari* (University of Chicago Press, 1989). For Lee's critique of these sources see his and Mathias Guenther's "Problems in Kalahari Historical Ethnography and the Tolerance of Error," *History in Africa* (vol. 20, 1993) and "Oxen or Onions? The Search for Trade (and Truth) in the Kalahari," *Current Anthropology* (vol. 32, 1991).

The literature on the San is voluminous. Alan Barnard's book *Hunters and Herders of Southern Africa: A Comparative Ethnography of the Khoisan Peoples* (Cambridge University Press, 1992) is an excellent overview of the various San and Khoi (formerly called "Hottentot") peoples. Important expressions of the revisionist view include Carmel Schrire's article "An Inquiry Into the Evolutionary Status and Apparent Identity of San Hunter-Gatherers," *Human Ecology* (vol. 8, no. 1, 1980) and her chapter entitled "Wild Surmises on Savage Thoughts," in her edited volume *Past and Present in Hunter-Gatherer Studies* (Academic Press, 1984). A crucial source on the history of the San is Robert Gordon's *The Bushman Myth: The Making of a Namibian Underclass* (Westview Press, 1992). Works supporting the traditionalist view include Susan Kent's "The Current Forager Controversy: Real vs. Ideal Views of Hunter-Gatherers," *Man* [n.s.] (vol. 27, 1992).

ISSUE 15

Do Some Illnesses Exist Only Among Members of a Particular Culture?

YES: Sangun Suwanlert, from *"Phii Pob:* Spirit Possession in Rural Thailand," in William Lebra, ed., *Culture-Bound Syndromes, Ethnopsychiatry, and Alternate Therapies,* vol. 4 of *Mental Health Research in Asia and the Pacific* (The University of Hawaii Press, 1976)

NO: Robert A. Hahn, from *Sickness and Healing: An Anthropological Perspective* (Yale University Press, 1995)

ISSUE SUMMARY

YES: Physician Sangun Suwanlert from Thailand asks whether or not one particular illness he observed in northern Thai villages, called *phii pob,* corresponds to Western diagnostic categories or is restricted to Thailand. After documenting how this condition does not fit standard psychiatric diagnoses, he concludes that *phii pob* is indeed a "culture-bound syndrome" that can only occur among people who share rural Thai cultural values and beliefs.

NO: Medical anthropologist Robert A. Hahn counters that the very idea of the so-called culture-bound syndrome is flawed. He contends that culture-bound syndromes are reductionist explanations for certain complex illness conditions—that is, explanations that reduce complex phenomena to a single variable. Hahn suggests that such conditions are like any illness condition; they are not so much peculiar diseases but distinctive local cultural expressions of much more common illness conditions that can be found in any culture.

For most of a century, anthropologists have observed that people in many tribal societies suffer from peculiar health complaints that seemed to occur only among members of particular cultures. Most of these illnesses were psychiatric in nature, including various kinds of "wild man" behaviors, such as *amok* in Malaysia, the *witiko* (or *windigo*) psychosis of the Ojibwa, the "Arctic hysterias" of some Eskimo and Siberian groups, startle reactions like *latah* in Indonesia and Malaysia, and various panic reactions found among certain Australian aboriginal groups. In some Australian tribes, observers have reported that people have died of no apparent physiological cause after learning that they were victims of sorcery performed against them by an enemy. These diverse conditions appeared quite different from mental illnesses observed in Western countries, and some seemed to have physiological symptoms that were not seen in industrial countries. Such cases raised the possibility that some illnesses might be rooted in a specific culture or even caused by aspects of the cultures themselves. Thus, the idea of the culture-bound syndrome was born.

For medical anthropologists, these culture-bound syndromes seemed to define a special niche in the medical world where anthropologists could contribute valuable insights that physicians, psychologists, and psychiatrists could not provide. Most anthropologists accepted the premise that anthropology could offer few new insights about such conditions like pneumonia, malaria, gastrointestinal diseases, and cancer. But if psychological conditions in different cultures were profoundly shaped by culture or even caused by aspects of a particular culture, then anthropology seemed to have a special role to play in medicine.

For these medical anthropologists, the question that confronted them was, How different are these syndromes from Western psychiatric conditions and neuroses? How can such different symptomatologies be explained? How do the details of local cultural traditions actually influence the symptoms of a particular condition, or alternatively, how does culture actually cause such illnesses?

These are some of the questions that Sangun Suwanlert addresses in the following selection. He focuses attention on a particular syndrome called *phii pob,* which he observed in northern Thailand. Rural Thai explain *phii pob* as a kind of spirit possession, which most typically affects married women. Symptoms of possession include numbness of limbs, falling down (sometimes with convulsions), rigid limbs, clenched fists, and sometimes shaking. While each of these symptoms has been observed in Western cultural contexts, the specific configuration observed in Thailand does not readily map onto any specific Western diagnosis. Suwanlert concludes that *phii pob* represents a syndrome that is culture-bound and can only emerge among rural Thai.

Robert A. Hahn challenges the very notion that any specific syndrome is so closely linked to any particular culture that it would justify the label "culture-bound syndrome." All illnesses, he argues, are shaped by the local cultures in which they occur. These illnesses would include psychological and psychiatric conditions as well as those we ordinarily assume to be strictly physiological, such as infections, diabetes, chronic pain, and so on. Thus, for Hahn, *phii pob, amok,* Arctic hysteria, and the *witiko* psychosis are merely distinctive local symptomatic expressions of conditions that are found in industrialized nations.

YES

Sangun Suwanlert

Phii Pob: Spirit Possession in Rural Thailand

In Thailand, as in all other countries, there are many people who seem to believe in spirits and ghosts. The Thais refer to the spirits and ghosts in general as *phii*. From my experience in treating psychiatric patients, I have found that the patients and their relatives are very much concerned with spirits and ghosts. *Phii* (evil spirit) possession is often found to be a basic cause in mental disease, both functional and organic, and we can divide them into three types:

- Ghosts of the dead: *phii* of grandparents, father, mother, ancestors, or spirits of important and respected people.
- Spirits of sacred things, not emanating from human beings.
- Spirits of the living, such as *phii pong, phii pob, phii ka,* and *phii krasu.*

My paper will be on the spirits of the living, the third type, or *phii pob,* with special emphasis on the psychiatric study of the *phii pob*. The first two kinds of *phii* mentioned above, those that originate from the dead and sacred things, are found to possess people more often than the third kind. . . .

Phii pob . . . is a common spirit in the northeast, north, and some provinces of the central plain of Thailand. Some say that *phii pob* is nonsubstantial; that nobody can definitely describe its shape. Some say that it is in the shape of a black dog; others say it is shaped more like a monkey. . . .

Phii pob originates in a living person, conceals itself in the body of that person, who is called the originating host, and comes and goes at any time. There are three ways in which a person can become a source of *phii pob:* it may originate in the person himself; he may inherit it from his ancestors; or he may possess an object said to bring good fortune to its owner, and the *phii pob* dwelling in this object may transfer itself to the owner.

Origination within the host. *Phii pob* seems to originate in people who study magic arts and spells, such as the spell for prosperous trading, the spell enabling one to talk cleverly, and the magical love arts, to make a person desire sexual intercourse with the opposite sex or to make one's sexual organs attractive. After a person completes his study, he becomes a teacher in his special field of magic. Almost every teacher of magic observes certain restrictions against doing certain things. . . . These restrictions may proscribe eating certain kinds of food, accepting fees for treatment and teaching, or going underneath a clothesline. As time passes and such a person forgets these restrictions, the *phii pob* originates automatically within him, although the host may not be aware of it. Since it is believed that the *phii pob* hiding within a person can leave the body of that person to possess another, the new possessed host can discover and make known who the originating host of the *phii pob* is. Usually a person hosts only one *phii pob* of the same sex as himself, but many informants confirm that it is possible for a person to host many and possess both males and females.

Inherited from the host's ancestors.   Although the host grows old and eventually dies, the *phii pob* does not. It goes on hiding in the children of the host, usually the eldest child of the same sex; that is, the father's *phii pob* will transfer to the eldest son and the mother's to the eldest daughter. If the host has no children, the *phii pob* will hide in a close relative and is called *pob chue.*

Origination in objects.   One can become host of *phii pob* by possessing commodities such as *wan krachai* and *wan phii pob,* a tuberous plant, or *see poeng sanei,* a wax charm, which are said to bring good fortune to the possessor. Some believe that *phii pob* dwell in these things and may transfer themselves to the owner.

A person will be possessed by a *phii pob* when he has had an argument with its host, but this is not necessarily the only time. A person or animal can be possessed in four ways:

1. Possession can occur in time of sickness, causing complications, during menopause or at the age of involution, or during the transition from adolescence to adulthood. It is believed that the spirit will eat away at the viscera (kidney, intestines, liver, et cetera) until the individual finally dies.
2. A *phii pob* can possess a boy or a girl under ten years of age and make the child talk irrelevantly. It is believed that most children thus possessed will eventually die.
3. Large domestic animals such as cows, buffalo, and horses can be possessed and die suddenly.
4. A *phii pob* can enter people who have had no previous symptoms, generally women between the ages of 18 and 40, men, less frequently. The possessed host will usually identify the originating host; this is called *ook pak* ("to speak out") in Northeastern Thai.

The Study

At various times from 1967 to 1971, I conducted a study of *phii pob* possession in north and northeast Thailand. My research had the following aims:

- To study the nature of *phii pob* in the upper regions of Thailand, where people believe that *phii pob* is the cause of some illness.

- To study the relationship between the possession syndrome and the environment, the local culture, and the reaction of the people toward this syndrome.
- To determine whether this is a psychiatric syndrome and, if so, how to classify it.
- To study folk treatment for the possessed host and originating host.

This paper reports on sixty-two cases of possessed hosts; six cases of originating hosts; and ten cases of possessed hosts whose *phii pob* refused to leave them. . . .

Symptoms of Possession

The earliest sign of the onset of possession is a numbness of limbs, followed by falling, with or without convulsions. Most who are possessed become unconscious; some become rigid, clench their fists, and must be forced to lie down or sit. After being in this condition for a while, some can answer questions, although somewhat confusedly. There are five categories of symptoms that appear after a person has been possessed:

1. Making noises like *"phii,"* shouting out, screaming, weeping.
2. Tensing, clenched fists, or short spasms.
3. Shaking following spasms, (not in all cases).
4. Timidity or shyness, manifested by an inability to speak to or face others. Sometimes facial expressions are similar to those of the originating host.
5. Identifying or speaking out the host's name (*ook pak*).

The fifth is the most important symptom, for it reveals not only the host's name but also the purpose of the possession, whether it is good or bad and whether it is merely passing through the village. Whether this symptom appears depends largely on the ability of the shaman; if he is skillful, he will have the victim talking relevantly.

Possessed Host: Case Illustrations

For illustration, I would like to describe the two cases of possession occurring at the health station that I was able to observe from the onset. . . .

Case 1.   A young, unmarried girl, 16 years of age, a Buddhist, with a primary-school education, from the Amnatcharoen District, and of low economic status was admitted to the Class I health station complaining of abdominal pain in the umbilical region. A physical examination revealed no abnormality, and she was referred to me for observation.

In an interview with the girl's mother, it was learned that, although she was very cooperative, the mother knew very little about her daughter because since the age of two the girl had been under her grandmother's care and had lived in another district. When the mother was in her sixth month of pregnancy, the girl's father left home and never returned. After the birth of the child, the mother struggled to make a living for both of them; when the girl was two, the mother remarried, and the child was sent off to her grandmother's. At the age of 15 the girl went to Bangkok with relatives and worked as a servant for six months, but she was unable to cope with her job so went back to live with her mother and stepfather.

Two days after witnessing her drunken stepfather slap her mother during an argument, the girl was possessed by a *phii pob*. The possession, according to the mother, lasted for about an hour. The originating host seemed to be one of the stepfather's friends who lived in the next village, because during possession the girl's general bearing was masculine when she described the kind of husband her stepfather was and when she threatened him with punishment by his ancestors' spirits.

The patient, with decorative cotton strings tied around her neck and wrists, was an attractive girl with sad eyes and a low, soft manner of speaking. During the interview she repeatedly said, "I don't know what my problem is, but I'm anxious about it." Crying, she complained of severe abdominal pain while continually asking her stepfather to do things for her.

The second night after being admitted, about 11:00 P.M., the patient was again possessed by a *phii pob*. When I went to the ward, the relatives, fearful of her falling off the bed, had her lying on the floor, and her mother was massaging her legs. I spoke to her but there was no recognition on her part. However, when she heard me, she sat up immediately in a cross-legged position. Her face became flushed and her eyes widened but did not focus. She raised her hand and said coherently, "I'm Mr. —— (stepfather's friend). I was angry when I heard that my friend did something wrong in the village. I'm here for a visit only." The mother cried out, "Please, go." "No," replied the girl. To the other relatives' suggestion of calling a shaman, the possessed girl answered, "I don't care." Then a relative asked, "Why don't you? This is a government office." (It is a common belief that *phii pob* are afraid of government offices.) The reply was, "I want my friend to behave. I want to let him know that if he doesn't, the ancestors' spirits will break his neck." After the stepfather promised that he would behave, the other relatives asked many questions; an hour later the spirit departed via the mouth, without the help of a shaman.

The patient was treated for ten days with a mild tranquilizer and superficial psychotherapy. She was discharged when she stopped complaining of abdominal pain, and she returned home to her grandmother.

Case 2. A 32-year-old Buddhist woman, wife of a peasant, with a primary-school education, and of low-income status, was admitted to the health station because of manifest muscle twitching in both arms, insomnia, and loss of appetite. A physical examination did not reveal any abnormality.

According to her husband, they had been married for several years. Before their marriage he had been a bachelor and she a divorcée with no children. About a year before admission, the wife was informed that the husband had had a long talk with a girl. Subsequently she began to nag, asking about his relationship with the girl. The more he denied, the more she nagged. A few days later the woman was possessed twice in one day. Ten days before her hospitalization, the husband went to see the girl in question on a business matter. When the wife learned of it she became hysterical, swore at her husband, cried, and ultimately fell into depression. Two days later the muscles in her arms began to twitch.

I visited the patient an hour every morning during her hospitalization because she was on a mild tranquilizer and superficial psychotherapy under my care. Whenever I started talking to her, her husband had to hold on to her arms to prevent them from twitching. Although the patient was pale, she looked younger than her years. She seemed to understand me well enough to make me think that she was not confused. However, she often said, "I'm quite worried about my future."

On the fourth night after admission, she became possessed by a female *phii pob.* The spirit claimed that it had come for a visit and asked the husband how things were going at home and how he had been behaving lately. Approximately fifteen minutes later the patient became silent and fell into depression, indicating that the spirit had departed. After ten days at the health station, the patient felt much better and the muscle twitching disappeared; she was discharged.

I consider the two cases cited above simple cases, but only when the precipitating cause of possession is taken into consideration. The cause was a kind of wish-fulfillment for people living in a noncomplex society. . . .

Originating Hosts

Case 1. Mrs. S., age 65, was from Amphur Wapee Patum, Mahasarakam Province. She looked slightly younger than her age, was dressed neatly in a long-sleeved blouse and a local type of skirt and wore the Northeastern type of earrings. Throughout the interview she sat properly and was very cooperative.

According to her, about five years ago in 1963, one of her sons who was working at Amphur Barn Pai in Kohnkaen Province befriended a man who had fallen off a car and broken his leg. The man had run out of money and wanted to sell a box containing a small image of Buddha on one side and a closely knitted gold fabric on the other. The man wanted 100 baht (US$5) for it but took the 20 baht offered. The man told him to take good care of it since it was valuable. When her son returned home, he placed the object on the shelf for worship. About a month later Mrs. S. began to have headaches and insomnia, so she consulted a shaman. He advised her that the object was the cause of the ailment and to get rid of it. One neighbor suggested that she throw it away but another asked for it so she gave it to the latter. Her headaches and insomnia soon disappeared.

After she disposed of the object in 1967, three of her neighbors, girls aged 14–15, were entered by *phii pob.* All of them claimed that it was a *phii pob* from Mrs. S. Mrs. S. felt very uneasy and asked the head of the village to find an expert who could expel the *phii pob* from her. She was referred to someone and paid over 1,000 baht (US$50) for his service. Because she feared that she might not be completely cured, she continued to receive a treatment of "holy water" at least once a month.

When asked how she felt after the shaman had beaten her with a stick and the *phii pob* had supposedly left, although the neighbors still accused her of being a *phii pob*, Mrs. S. said that she felt no pain nor anything else but shame and worry. She did not want to see anybody. She was worried about her seven sons who would have to bear the accusation for a long time. This is why she made her way to Wat Dhat Panom for the expulsion of *phii pob* from her. The person she consulted told her that if she would gather together a small Buddhist image, holy thread, and a fallen fragment of a pagoda, she would be protected from *phii pob*. She replied that she had spent all her money and could not purchase the necessary articles. I bought and gave them to her, and it seemed to lift up her spirits.

Case 2. A 36-year-old man, Mr. B., married and living in Amphur Boor Kaw, Kalasinthu Province, came to Wat Dhat Panom to have *phii pob* driven out of his body. He was told that he had two *phii pob,* both in the shape of monkeys, perched on his shoulder. In our interview, Mr. B. reported that about five years before, when he was unmarried, he bought a wax charm to attract women and make them fall in love with him. He did not think much more about it until he discovered that his *phii pob* was going around possessing the neighborhood women.

When asked how he felt when the *phii pob* left his body to enter into another, he said that he trembled with no apparent cause, but did not feel anything leave his body. He was not concerned that his neighbors would do any harm to him. Whenever he thought about it, he said, he felt sad and worried, but he strongly denied having any illness.

I then asked him about his wife's and children's reaction to his being called the host. He said they were all ashamed and worried about it, especially when one of his children overheard the villagers talking about him.

About a month before he came for treatment at Wat Pra Dhat, someone in the village became possessed again. At that time a villager fired a shot into the sky, and Mr. B. began to fear for his life. Until then, he was sad and worried about the situation he was in, but he never thought anyone would do him any harm. (The probable reason for this was that he had a relative in a monastery who was highly respected by the villagers.) After this incident, he was unable to sleep well and often dreamed of monkeys and black dogs. Finally he decided to seek help at Wat Pra Dhat since the two spirit doctors who had treated him did not help him feel better.

I studied the symptoms of depression in the six cases of originating hosts to see whether illness such as depression existed in the distant villages. A questionnaire based on Cleghorn and Curtis' depression study was used. Results suggested that the patients came for treatment out of worry over bodily harm that they might receive and out of depression manifested by the symptoms such as sadness, insomnia, and loss of appetite. These symptoms lead one to conclude that villagers do become depressed and try to avoid other people when they are accused of being a *phii pob*. . . .

Villagers' Attitude toward *Phii Pob*

Belief in spirits has become a part of village tradition. The spirits, both good and bad, are perceived as superhuman beings, so good spirits are worshipped or respected and the bad ones are driven away as quickly as possible. The modernization introduced by education and communication has not changed these beliefs much. The villagers justify their belief in spirits by declaring that it is not harmful to anyone.

Actually there are three groups of people with respect to belief in spirits. (1) Nonbelievers include persons who have had some training in Buddhism, those who have been educated in cities or towns, and those whose families were troubled by spirits and have become good Buddhists. (2) Partial believers usually have a little more formal education than the average villager and often talk about true and false spirit possession and have tried to prove it. (3) Full believers include those who have lived only in the village, those who have experienced spirit possession, and those persuaded by others to believe in spirits. In actual number there are more full believers than nonbelievers and partial believers put together.

One may conclude that *phii pob* are considered suprahuman but bad spirits that should not be dwelling inside a human being. The method of driving out the bad spirit is either by physical punishment, beating the possessed with a cane, or by luring the bad spirits with the good because if the spirit is in a person too long the person can die or become mentally ill (*phii ba'*). Once a person's spirit has been expelled, he is considered cured and can continue to live in the village without prejudice. . . .

Analysis

Possessed host group 1.   Working in the health station and in the villages, I was soon able to recognize a person who had been possessed by a *phii pob*. A possessed woman was usually distinguished in her beauty, dramatic in manner, and charmingly seductive. It was common to see her with cotton strings tied around her neck and wrists. While being interviewed, I noted, the possessed hosts were sensitive and easily stimulated, quick-tempered, self-centered, and susceptible to suggestions. These characteristics may be classified as belonging to a "hysterical personality," which is generally found more in women than in men. Perhaps this could be one of the reasons for the predominance of women among the 50 possessed hosts whom I studied in 1967. Fully 96 per cent of them were women, and only 4 per cent were men; 38 per cent were 21–30 years old; 76 per cent were married. They may have had problems before being possessed. It seems that the mechanism of *phii pob* possession is a socially accepted way of solving social and internal conflicts.

The feeling of numbness prior to possession experienced by 42 per cent of the possessed was, I feel, a result of emotional tension rather than malnutrition, because most of the possessed hosts were physically healthy (see Table 1). After exhibiting other symptoms, such as depression and visual and auditory hallucinations, they went through a state of which they had no recollection.

Table 1

Pre- and Post-Possession Symptoms (ranked by frequency)

Pre-Possession Symptoms (frequency rate = 42-2)*	Post-Possession Symptoms (frequency rate = 41-2)**
1. Felt numbness throughout the body and limbs.	1. Felt quite well.
2. Felt like crying.	2. Felt aches and pains all over the body.
3. Felt dizzy.	3. Felt weary.
4. Had vision of round shapes.	4. Became frightened and worried.
5. Felt sick at heart.	5. Developed insomnia.
6. Had headaches and chills.	6. Felt heart palpitations.
7. Had vision of a monkey.	7. Became groggy and befuddled.
8. Had vision of a man.	
9. Had vision of a dog or a cat.	
10. Heard voices calling.	
11. Felt stiffness in chest.	
12. Had vision of a chicken.	
13. Heard a dog barking.	
14. None.	

*Some symptoms appeared in combination, e.g., numbness and having vision of a monkey, but here they are listed separately.
**Most of the possessed could not remember what they said or did while being possessed, but some felt pains as though beaten with a cane, although very vaguely. Their gestures were similar to those of the originating host.

This syndrome should without question be considered psychiatric, although there was not much content to their hallucination. Mainly they saw round objects, monkeys, cats, men, or dogs, suggesting toxic psychosis. But the symptom that makes it different from toxic psychosis is the state of trance, during which the patients could talk relevantly.

While being possessed, the patients seemed to take on a "double personality" for a short period, not more than an hour (see Table 2). At this time the possessed seemed to be in a state of trance as if hypnotized, which I would classify as "dissociative reaction". *Phii pob* possession may be a type of hysteria, but I feel that it is a kind of "dissociative reaction" that occurs only in specific Thai cultural groups but has not yet been geographically localized or classified, unlike *amok* or *latah*.

An originating host is considered a clever person who practices many kinds of spells and is respected by the villagers. Because he is considered a clever person, the possessed identifies with the host and does not feel that any harm will come about. Identification is said to be an important mental mechanism in hysteria and it occurs in people who have had a previous relationship with each other. Characterization appears to be on the conscious level.

The villagers feel that *phii pob* possession is a genuine occurrence—everyone in my investigation believed in it. They might be smiling and giggling, but when asked about *phii pob,* their facial expression at once becomes

Table 2

Characteristics of Possession Episode (Group 1, 1957: N = 50)

Characteristic	Number	Percent
Duration:		
Momentary	13	26
1 hour	16	32
2 hours	7	14
3 hours	5	10
8 hours	2	4
48 hours	1	2
Undetermined	6	12
Departure Point:		
Unknown	16	32
Mouth (vomiting)	9	18
Bladder (urinating)	7	14
Another part of the body	18	36
Number of times Possessed:		
1	22	44
2	6	12
3	10	20
>3	12	24

solemn. They also believe that the *phii pob* or the hosts have their central location in Baan Chyak, Tambon Nacik, which perhaps accounts for the fact that more patients come from south of Amnat Charoen than from north of it.

Possessed host group 2. Group 2 includes ten possessed hosts, whose *phii pob* refused to depart after 48 hours, whom I studied in 1969–1971. After receiving treatment at the hospital for about a week, these persons felt much better. In their case, the diagnosis might be hysterical psychosis and the mechanism of *phii pob* is more complicated and difficult to generalize than for group 1.

Originating hosts. It was very difficult to get information from originating hosts at the beginning of the study, because I presumed that my clients would resent inquiries from a total stranger. In addition, there were always others around when I conducted the interviews, and I felt that harm might result. However, through the cooperation of the Buddhist monks, I was able to interview six originating hosts (*phii pob*).

Through the interviews it was established that one could become a *phii pob* by three means: through inheritance, incantation study, and possession of "sacred" things. Although the *phii pob* accepted the causes, they could not see how the spirits in their bodies could go and possess others. They admitted to worrying and feeling depressed and ashamed about what had happened, but they had no other feelings or reactions.

Being a *phii pob* seemed to last from one to five years. All of those affected earnestly sought to expel the spirits in them. I felt that the only time the villagers noticed that one of them was a *phii pob* was when the *pob* possessed another and "spoke." On the other hand, such identification could have been a vindictive fabrication. Once identified, though, the only way out for the accused was to announce that he was going to have treatments to expel the *phii pob*.

Judging from the six cases I studied, the mental health of the accused was poor, affecting the immediate family members and other relatives. I often wonder what was the basic cause of the one case where the healing process was completed and the *phii pob* was supposedly buried only to have the woman go and dig it up. Was it the power over others that she enjoyed, or was she really overpowered by the spirits, as claimed? These questions still remain unanswered.

Some people are sympathetic toward *phii pob* but will not live under the same roof with them and will try to exile them. Tolo Village in Roi-Et Province seemed to accept the exiles; no one in that village seemed possessed, although the majority of the villagers were known to be *phii pobs*.

Phii pob possession is both good and bad. It may be a socially acceptable way of solving social and interpersonal conflicts. On the other hand, it is quite simple for a person to falsely accuse another of being *phii pob*, with disastrous consequences. Usually the only way out for the accused is to admit that he is a *phii pob* and to promise to undergo treatment to drive out the spirit, or move to another place. I believe that public reaction profoundly affects a person's mental health.

Conclusion

. . . Sixty-two cases of possessed hosts were studied in the villages of two provinces in Northeast Thailand; ten were admitted by relatives for treatment at Srithunya Hospital, Nondhaburi, because shamans could not drive the spirits off.

With group 1, 50 cases studied in 1967, *phii pob* possession occurred in the village, and the duration of possession was momentary to 48 hours. After the spirit was driven off, the possessed hosts became their former selves and felt quite well. The personalities of hosts who were repeatedly possessed were hysterical, precipitating various kinds of causes for illness. During the period of possession, the symptoms were similar to hysterical trance or a dissociative phenomenon. The diagnosis might be a hysterical neurosis that occurs only in specific Thai cultural groups. It seemed that the mechanism of *phii pob* possession was a socially accepted way of solving social and internal conflicts.

Group 2, studied in 1969–1971, comprised ten cases of *phii pob* who refused to depart from their possessed hosts within 48 hours. The possessed hosts were brought into the psychiatric hospital as psychotics. After receiving treatment for about a week, they felt much better. The diagnosis might be hysterical psychosis. The mechanism of *phii pob* possession for this group is more complicated than for group 1. . . .

Robert A. Hahn

➡ **NO**

Culture-Bound Syndromes Unbound

One of the jumpers while sitting in his chair with a knife in his hand was told to throw it, and he threw it quickly, so that it stuck in a beam opposite; at the same time he repeated the order to throw it, with cry or utterance of alarm resembling that of hysteria or epilepsy. He also threw away his pipe when filling it with tobacco when he was slapped upon the shoulder. . . . They [the jumpers] could not help repeating the word or sound that came from the person that ordered them any more than they could help striking, dropping, throwing, jumping, or starting; all of these phenomena were indeed but parts of the general condition known as jumping. . . . All of the jumpers agree that it tires them to be jumped and they dread it, but they were constantly annoyed by their companions.

— "Jumpers," Moosehead Lake, Maine, described by Beard

E. A. B. at the time of the event was 20 years old, unmarried, the third of four siblings and an Iban. At the time he ran amok he had been uprooted from his normal surrounding, a longhouse in one of the upper reaches of the Batang Lupar river. He was working in an oil drilling camp, approximately 200 miles from home with no direct communication. One night, while living on a barge near the camp, he grabbed a knife and slashed five of his fellow workers, three Malay and two Chinese.

— A man with *amok* in Malaysia, described [by] Schmidt

A man, about age 45, with wife and children, took a second wife. Afraid of the first wife's jealousy, he tried to keep the new relationship secret, but in time the second marriage became known. One evening, he came home tired and fatigued. He got the shivers, broke out in a cold sweat, and felt that his penis was shrinking. At his cry for help, the neighbors came running. Only men helped him. One man tightly held the patient's penis while another went for a sanro, a native healer. The sanro performed one ritual and after a while the anxiety disappeared, ending the day's attack.

— An Indonesian man with *koro*, reported [by] Chabot

Observers of seemingly strange behavior have distinguished a variety of behavioral syndromes that, because of their apparent uniqueness and fit to local cultural conditions, are described as culture-bound. The observers of such behavior have most often been from Western settings, the behavior observed principally in non-Western ones. In this [selection], I examine the logic by which the generic diagnostic label "culture-bound syndrome" is ascribed to some conditions and not to others. I claim that the idea of culture-bound syndromes is a conceptual mistake, confusing rather than clarifying our understanding of the role of culture in sickness and fostering a false dichotomy of events and the disciplines in which they are studied. All conditions of sickness are affected in many ways, and none is exhaustively determined by its cultural setting. Physiology, medicine, psychology, and anthropology are complementary rather than contrary and exclusive; all are relevant and necessary to the comprehensive understanding of human phenomena of sickness and healing. . . .

The very notion of a culture-bound syndrome indicates a form of reductionism—the explanation of a given phenomenon by a single principle or body of knowledge. Other explanatory principles are thus denied relevance. Reductionists may claim that they have fully explained a culture-bound syndrome and that, in consequence, this phenomenon falls exclusively within their domain of inquiry. This mistaken effort is apparent in versions of anthropology as well as in Western medicine, psychiatry, psychoanalysis, and psychology. I argue that such claims fragment human function and its study into falsely opposed divisions.

Although anthropologists may believe that they have established a firm position by appropriating culture-bound syndromes to their own domain of explanation, their claims are at once excessive and too modest, claiming too much for culture-bound syndromes and too little for the diseases staked out by Biomedicine. I argue that full explanation requires an opening of the inner sanctum of Biomedicine to anthropological review and a concomitant recognition of pervasive physiological constraint in the workings of culture. Humans are bound by their cultures—but not rigidly. Nor is culture the only binding principle; body, mind, society, and the broader environment also bind. An exploration of culture-bound syndromes thus reaches the variety of forms of sickness and the range of human disciplinary approaches.

To assess the notion of culture-bound syndrome, I briefly define *syndrome* and *culture* and suggest how syndromes might be *bound* by culture. I distinguish three ways in which culture-bound syndromes have been understood. . . . I propose that we discard the misleading concept of culture-bound syndrome in favor of a broader study of the role of human mind, physiology, culture, and society in pathology and its relief.

Syndromes, Cultures, and Binds

A *syndrome* (from the Latin "things that run together") is a group of conditions, generally pathological, that may be physical and/or mental, signs and/or symptoms, and that is thought to constitute a discrete entity. One syndrome, AIDS (acquired immunodeficiency syndrome), has gained recent attention; it is defined by a complex set of signs and symptoms that has evolved with changing knowledge as well as political-economic circumstances. Numerous other syndromes are named in Biomedicine, some after their discoverer, others after their symptoms. Syndromes are distinguished from other events that co-occur in that their co-occurrence is thought to be not simply coincidental; a syndrome is a part of a unifying phenomenon—for example, a recognized biological process. The constituents of a syndrome may reflect a group of similar causes. What makes AIDS a syndrome is the acquisition of a specific virus, the human immunodeficiency virus, which causes a range of outcomes constituting AIDS.

The specificity with which a syndrome is defined will substantially affect what can validly be said about it—its distribution by nation and ethnic group, and other characteristics. . . .

A culture, in the anthropological sense, is the set of beliefs, rules of behavior, and customary behaviors maintained, practiced, and transmitted in a given society. Different cultures may be found in a society as a whole or in its segments—for example, in its ethnic groups or social classes.

A syndrome may be regarded as culture-bound if particular cultural conditions are *necessary* for the occurrence of that syndrome; thus the culture-bound syndrome is thought not to occur in the absence of these cultural conditions. Some analysts of culture-bound syndromes may regard specific cultural conditions as *sufficient* for the syndrome's occurrence; in this view, no conditions other than these cultural ones (for example, other cultural conditions or noncultural ones) are necessary to provoke the occurrence of the culture-bound syndrome.

A Hypothetical Ethnography of the Diagnosis Culture-Bound Syndrome

Some of the dilemmas inherent in the notion of culture-bound syndrome are apparent in the ethnographic sources of this diagnosis. The history of specific terms and interpretations of these conditions is most often lost in the memories and notes of colonial settlers. Winzeler provides a rare historical account of the development of notions of latah. Edwards formulates the history of another condition, koro, its multiple names, and purported cases; as in the example of koro described at the outset of this [selection], a person who experiences koro is usually under great stress or anxiety, suffers a retraction of the genitals, and may fear death.

In general, we may guess that the application of the generic label culturebound syndrome and of terms for specific conditions, such as latah, and "wildman behavior," occurs in a sequence approximating the following:

1. Observers, most often trained in Western medicine, psychiatry, or psychoanalysis, or in anthropology or psychology, visit a foreign setting or an ethnic setting at home. Most often, ethnic settings are those that differ in their culture from the observers' own. Most often, though not always, the observers are white Americans or Europeans.
2. The observers notice behavior that seems strange (that is, unusual by their standards of normality) and indicative of deviance and disturbance. According to their interpretive bent, the observers are

likely to take the observed behavior as pathological in some way—medically, psychiatrically, psychodynamically, behaviorally, and so on. Yet they may not know how to diagnose this pathology since it does not fit the familiar criteria of Western nosology. The culture-bound syndromes were early described as "exotic," a term that may tell us more about its users than about its intended referent.

3. The people among whom the strange behavior occur may offer a solution to the diagnostic dilemma. They may distinguish and label the observed behavior, although recognition of such labels in an unfamiliar setting is problematic. A response to an observer's question (such as, "What and I observing, and what is it called?"), which perhaps is not well understood, may not truly indicate what nevertheless comes to be accepted as an indigenous label for the observed condition. Vallee, for example, suggests that the term for one such condition, *pibloqtoq* (also referred to as "Arctic hysteria"), is the fabrication of early explorers rather than a usual term of Eskimo usage. . . .

4. The observers return home with their prized possession: a new syndrome that, because it seems to be found only in the cultural setting from which they have returned, is labeled culture-bound. Culture-bound syndromes are residual; they are conditions that do not fit the nosological scheme of a Western observer. Rather than questioning the completeness or validity of the Western nosology, the new syndrome is set apart as an oddity from another culture.

5. The observers now face the ambiguous challenge of showing how this culture-bound syndrome actually fits into their own explanatory paradigm. The dilemma here is that, as the phenomenon is encompassed by the observers' explanatory system, it may lose its uniqueness and become a version of the broader phenomenon. Explanatory gain may be culture-specific loss. Analysts of culture-bound syndromes have attempted to keep their syndrome while reducing it also, by showing how social, cultural, and psychological conditions—general elements of their own scheme—are so distinctively configured in the local scene as to make this particular syndrome unlikely to occur elsewhere. Their reductions combine the universal principles of their own discipline—for example, the learning theories of psychology—with the unique cultural peculiarities of the local setting—for example, the specifics of who teaches, what is taught, and how. The local fit and indigenous label appear to give these conditions an immunity from spreading elsewhere; they may *look* like the "xyz" syndrome found elsewhere, but they are really different.

6. Having established a new condition, often distinguished by an ascribed indigenous term, the "discoverer" of this syndrome (or other observers) may then find further instances of similar conditions in new settings, applying the established term, but now crossing cultural boundaries. Amok is the most notorious condition to be exported. . . .

Understanding Culture-Bound Syndromes

Three alternative understandings of culture-bound phenomena are plausible. One may be described as "exclusionist," the other two as "inclusionist." I refer to one inclusionist position as "nature-culture continuum," to the second as "multiple-aspect."

The exclusionist interpretation of culture-bound syndromes is suggested by the phrase "culture-bound syndrome" itself. The phrase implies or assumes that some conditions are culture-bound and others are not. Conditions that are not culture-bound may be regarded as culture-free, culture-blind; perhaps they are thought of as nature-, physiology-, or materiality-bound. In the exclusionist view, that a condition falls in one-half of this divide implies that it does not fall in the other, and vice versa. Latah and amok are culture-bound syndromes; measles and lung cancer are not. This division is held to correspond to disciplinary divisions as well, so that culture-bound syndromes are the concern of anthropological and/or psychological or psychiatric expertise and culture-free syndromes are the subject of medical or physiological examination.

Kenny provides an excellent example of the exclusionist position in his analysis of latah. In Kenny's work, some conditions are regarded as clearly culture-bound and others as clearly universal (though universal conditions may be differently interpreted in different settings).

> Measles or smallpox, for example, are clearly identifiable disease entities, but receive very different cultural interpretations. Is this also true for "latah," "amok," and other ostensibly culture-bound syndromes? In short, are latahlike startle responses better considered [quoting Simons 1980] as the "exploitation of a neurophysiological potential," *or* are they themselves more plausibly considered as the outcome of social *rather than* biological factors? (emphasis added)

Kenny's "or" and "rather than" are exclusive connections. "Disease entities" are regarded as universal phenomena, the results of biological factors; culture-bound syndromes, in contrast, are not diseaselike and result from social factors. Kenny claims that cultural patterns "fully explain" latah; it would thus seem that biological explanation has no room. . . .

Kenny believes the "true" nature of latah to be dramaturgic, an arena he believes unrelated or exclusive of human biology. . . . Kenny writes: "If this is the case, then the latah performance is taken out of the province of biomedical reductionism and is seen in what I take to be its true light—as theater." Kenny here replaces biomedical reductionism with theatrical reductionism.

Psychologist John Carr's interpretation of another Southeast Asian condition, amok, represents a version of the exclusionist position distinct from Kenny's. Though Carr writes that some syndromes are culture-bound, he goes on to formulate a plausible interpretation of amok behavior based on a theory of learning from Western psychology. Carr applies universal principles to the Malay setting, asserting that amok is a learned behavior response to a highly ambiguous yet demanding culture situation. Langness claims that similar cultural conditions—"contradictory demands and discontinuities"—account for "wildman behavior" in New Guinea.

Yet although Carr relates this culture-bound syndrome to universal principles of learning, like Kenny, he explicitly dissociates it from universal processes of disease, as formulated in Biomedicine: "The notion that culture-bound syndromes share underlying common disease forms is rejected. Instead, the ethno-behavioral model postulates that culture-bound syndromes consist of culturally specific behavioral repertoires legitimated by culturally sanctioned norms and concepts, but with both behavior and norms acquired in accordance with basic principles of human learning universal to all cultures."

Using notions of disease and illness developed by Kleinman, Carr associates culture-bound syndromes with illness behavior, which, "as distinct from the disease process, is always culturally determined." He concludes that a culture-bound syndrome is "a distinct repertoire of behaviors that (1) have evolved as the result of a social learning process in which the conceptual and value systems, and the social structural forms that mediate their effects, have served to define the conditions under which such behavior is an appropriate response, and (2) have been legitimated within the indigenous system as *illness* primarily in terms of extreme deviation from the behavioral norm as defined by preeminent culturally-specific conceptual dimensions governing social behavior."

This description of culture-bound syndromes parallels Kleinman's distinction between disease and illness and corresponds to disciplines appropriate to each [as seen in Table 3].

Carr notes, however, that culture-bound syndromes "may be precipitated by any number of etiological factors, among them physical, as well as socio-cultural determinants." Thus, the basic cause of amok is thought to be psychological; the particular elements that are psychologically incorporated are culturally specific, and given this established syndrome, a number of precipitants, including physical ones, may elicit this behavior. Carr regards diseases as phenomena that appear universally, in "inviolate" form, and that are the legitimate concern of medicine and psychiatry, whereas illnesses are "always culturally determined" and are thus the legitimate concern of psychology and anthropology. . . .

The inclusionist nature-culture continuum position maintains that all human events, including the supposed culture-bound ones, have cultural *and* biological *and* cognitive *and* psychodynamic aspects, though some events are more profoundly shaped by one of these aspects than by others. Thus, although no conditions are exclusively culture-bound or culture-free, some

Table 3

Explanatory Principle

	Culture	Nature
Condition	Culture-bound syndrome Illness	Culture-free syndrome Disease
Discipline	Psychology Anthropology	Physiology Medicine Psychiatry

may be largely culturally shaped and others principally determined by universal physiology. In this conception, the notion of culture-bound syndrome remains a valid one. An example of the nature-culture continuum position is the work of Leighton and Murphy:

> So far as the total process in the development of psychiatric disorder is concerned, it would seem best to assume that heredity, biological, and psychological factors are all three engaged. To claim dominance for one, or for any subarea within one, *as a matter of general theory,* is to express a linear conception of cause and effect which is out of keeping with what we know about all the processes in the world around us. More germane is an approach to the topic that aims to discover and map out the interrelated factors and the nature of their interrelationships.

The recommendation that the relative importance of heredity, biology, and psychology cannot be theoretically determined in advance but must be empirically analyzed suggests that these factors may have more or less weight for different sicknesses.

The continuum understanding would make the extent to which a condition is culture-bound a matter of degree. It might be possible, at least theoretically, to quantify the proportions in which different factors contribute to given outcome conditions. Measles might occupy the natural, physiological end of this spectrum, the culture-bound syndromes the other; it is not clear what sorts of conditions might fall between—perhaps depression and alcoholism. . . .

Anthropological Queries and Logical Doubts . . .

Defining Syndromes: Category and Context

The prevailing view of culture-bound syndromes is that these behaviors are distinctive of their cultural circumstances. Taken to its extreme, this view has implications that make scientific comparison impossible. All phenomena and events are unique, each differentiable from all others by some or, more likely, by many characteristics: each screw produced in a factory, every case of depression and tuberculosis, every episode of latah. The variations of each occurrence of a phenomenon are explicable, though perhaps not by current knowledge, in terms of the context of that occurrence. Indeed, such explanation is what we mean by "context"—a phenomenon's context is its circumstance, its environment. It is the explanatory power of a phenomenon rather than its simple physical contiguity that constitutes the context of something to be explained. Because one phenomenon is significant in the explanation of another, however, does not bind the two to the exclusion of other explanatory principles. Occurrences of latah may well be different in large and small communities, as manifested by older and younger performers, by one person and another, even by an individual person at different times or in different circumstances. Do we then talk of community-bound, age-bound, person-bound, person-time-circumstance-bound syndromes?

By contextualizing in this way, we end up with a list of occurrences-for-persons-at-times-in-circumstances, and so on, ad infinitum. . . .

In Search of the Whole: Interpretive and Causal Explanation

The exclusionist claim that some behavioral complexes are culture-bound and that others are not, and that the latter fit into some universal scheme, suggests that the culture-bound phenomena are so distinctive that they are beyond comparison. The explanation of such phenomena, exclusionists assume, connects them with other local phenomena and patterns of meaning, rather than with phenomena and patterns elsewhere. This perspective parallels one of two radically different positions that divide anthropology as well as literary studies, historiography, and psychology: interpretive and causal. Culture-bound syndromes provide a perfect example of the interpretive school, since they are thought to be explicable only by their local context.

According to the interpretive understanding, a position also called hermeneutic and phenomenological and sometimes associated with the philosopher Ludwig Wittgenstein, social and cultural phenomena are fully explained when they are shown to fit with their local phenomena in a system that "makes sense." In this view, questions about the causes of the phenomena of interest are regarded as misconceived or tangential. Thus, Kenny objects to attempts to explain culture-bound syndromes by universal, causal principles: "These medical or pseudo-medical labels evoke the notion that there is some kind of causal process underlying *latah*. The interpreters of *latah* seek to identify factors in the life experience of the victim which make her condition inevitable." It is implied that no kind of causality underlies latah. In a more general vein, Geertz writes, "Believing, with Max Weber, that man is an animal suspended in webs or significance he himself has spun, I take culture to be those webs, and the analysis of it to be therefore not an experimental science in search of law but an interpretive one in search of meaning."

Although it is obvious that anthropology is not an experimental science, Geertz goes further to assert that a search for law, presumably causal, excludes a search for interpretation. Interpretation is deemed appropriate only in the study of the workings of culture. Thus Geertz distinguishes blinks, which may be causally analyzed by science, from winks, which are intentional acts shaped by cultural systems to be analyzed by an interpretation of meaning in society and the circumstances of the winker. Yet, at some level, human biology is the mechanism of winks and may be involved in their motivation as well, and blinks, too, may express a symbolic meaning; these two forms of eye movement are not as distinctive as Geertz claims them to be.

. . . [I]f comprehensive explanation rests with those who perform an action, we become ensnared in webs of meaning that lead logically to solipsism [a theory holding that the self can know nothing but its own modifications and that the self is the only existent thing]. If local phenomena and labels for them can be understood only in terms of other local phenomena and their labels, then research across localities, as in much of anthropology, becomes impossible. Anthropologists may pursue their own tales, but not those of others.

Anthropology, Sibling Disciplines, and the Spectrum of Sickness

A conceptual and theoretical solution to the troubles of the exclusionist position might be founded in four principles:

1. A cross-cultural theory of sickness should begin, though not necessarily end, with the indigenous and personal understandings of the sufferer. Forms of suffering that do not fit the Biomedical mold will not be excluded as culture-bound. Patients at home will not be rejected as superstitious or as "crocks" because they fail to fall into Biomedical diagnostics. Pathology would be defined by the experience of the patient rather than by principles that seem a priori universal because they work fairly well among some groups at home and because they can be significantly explained by physiology, also apparently universal. Although a person may be (asymptomatically) unaware of the conditions that might later affect his or her well-being, still the state of well-being itself, and thus the sources of threat to it, are defined by the thought world of the patient him- or herself.

2. Interpreting a human act or syndrome—that is, showing its fit to the understandings and to the local circumstances in which it occurs— may be necessary, but it is not sufficient for full understanding. Minimally, an explanation that some phenomenon occurs in one place because of such-and-such conditions must also show that it does not occur elsewhere, where these conditions are not met. Comparison is a necessity and requires the development of comparative categories so that we may say that this is found here but not there, and that that is found there but not here. Even interpretation itself requires comparative categories; without them, the terms of one language and culture (say, the interpreter's) could not apply to those of another; translation would be impossible; and interpretation could thus be made only in local terms and only for local consumption. Exclusionism, by insisting on the exclusive local fit of all cultural phenomena, thereby precludes comparison; indeed it precludes communication across cultural boundaries.

   The difficulties of causal explanation are notorious, though perhaps better recognized than the hazards of interpretation. Nevertheless causal explanation, however systematic and nonlinear, must be pursued. In this way a universal scheme will come to take local meaning into account.

3. The course of human events is inevitably many-leveled, so that neither our disciplines—such as anthropology, physiology, psychology— nor their central concepts—culture, biochemical exchanges, human experience—can exclusively appropriate any event. That is, human events are not simply cultural or psychological, but inevitably bear these aspects and others.

4. . . . [T]here are several ways in which the organization and culture of societies affect their processes of pathogenesis and healing. Societies inform their members about how the world is divided up and put together. With regard to pathogenic and healthful processes I have recommended three forms of understanding: *disease* models, *illness* models, and *disorder* models. Societies also engage in the production of sickness because of the ways in which they organize cultural beliefs and social relations. Carr's psychosocial analysis of amok illustrates the pathogenic powers of the social environment.

Such a sociocultural framework applies not only to conditions that are obviously affected, but to the purportedly hard-core diseases as well. The Biomedical model has obscured rather than enlightened such effects. Yet the history of tuberculosis, as brilliantly portrayed by René and Jean Dubos forty years ago, illustrates sociocultural effects in this condition whose biological characteristics appear to be clearly defined. The variety and power of ideology in tuberculosis-like conditions in European society are visible in a great range of attitudes toward this former (and reemerging) "captain of the men of death," its victims sometimes believed to manifest intensified creative powers as they were "consumed." Ideologies continue to be modified. The Duboses suggest that the term *tuberculosis,* already bearing a denotation not directly indicative of contemporary etiological conceptions, could be modified to fit current knowledge. The bacterium itself was then being shown to be neither necessary nor sufficient to the symptomatic complex that we call tuberculosis. The Duboses insisted on the causative importance of the host's sociocultural and natural environment. They also noted that though psychological factors were likely to be of importance, their extent and workings were unknown. A great variety of remedial efforts have also followed beliefs about this condition and about the broader order of social life. Tubercular patients have been revered and isolated, placed in dry climates and wet ones, required to rest and to exercise exhaustively.

Culture, nature, and the human mind between play central roles in diseases commonly thought of in terms of microorganisms and toxins as well as in apparently strange behavioral complexes. Only an inclusionist framework can encompass the range of pathological (and healthy) forms.

Culture-bound syndromes constitute an important frontier between anthropology, Biomedicine, and the medical systems of other societies. Built in premises different from our own, they challenge our standard divisions of things. In striking fashion they have reminded us that our own forms of sickness and of reacting to events do not cover the spectrum of the humanly possible. A comprehensive theory of human reactions and pathology must take them into account.

I have argued that the exclusionist understanding of culture-bound syndromes, implicit in the term, yet not intended by early proponents, distorts the role of culture and of physiology in human affairs. It claims too much of culture at the margin of our nosological scheme and too little of culture at medicine's core. Medical professionals, anthropologists, and others have conspired in a false division of labor. False divisions obstruct understanding. The abandonment of the erroneous category, culture-bound syndrome, might serve to redirect our attention to the formulation of a theory of human sickness in which culture, psychology, and physiology were regarded as mutually relevant across cultural and nosological boundaries.

POSTSCRIPT

Do Some Illnesses Exist Only Among Members of a Particular Culture?

In discussing *phii pob,* Suwanlert accepts this condition as a medical problem that he believes occurs only among rural Thai people. As he outlines the syndrome, he links its occurrence to cultural factors specific to rural communities in transition that are not found in industrial societies. He does not find any systematic correspondence between *phii pob* and psychological diagnoses in the West, and thus he concludes that *phii pob* is a culture-bound syndrome. Hahn, in contrast, steps back from the details of specific conditions described as culture-bound syndromes to ask what they all have in common rather than focus simply on one condition like *phii pob.* He asks, In what sense can these syndromes be seen as distinct from Western diagnostic categories? Hahn concludes that authors like Suwanlert have typically reduced what must be complex illness experiences to a single set of cultural factors. He concludes that there are no culture-bound syndromes; all illness conditions are rooted in the biology and psychology of individual patients but shaped by the cultures in which they live. Thus, culture plays no more important role in *phii pob* than in malaria, pneumonia, cancer, or depression.

Suwanlert and Hahn differ on whether or not conditions like *phii pob* are really so different that they cannot be explained as manifestations or local cultural expressions of more common psychological problems. Suwanlert argues that *phii pob* is unlike anything described in the standard reference manual, *Diagnostic and Statistical Manual of Mental Disorders (DSM-IV),* (American Psychiatric Association, 1994). Hahn contends that the symptoms associated with conditions such as *phii pob* are typically so vague and ambiguous that they only seem to not fit *DSM-IV.* In this instance, patients with *phii pob* may have any subset of the symptoms that include numbness, falling down, convulsions, tensing, clenched fists, short spasms, timidity, and a distinctive kind of vocalizations. None of these symptoms by itself is sufficient to define the condition as *phii pob,* and no particular set of these symptoms are required for the case to be defined as spirit possession.

A similar issue concerns whether or not we could actually compare culture-bound syndromes if they genuinely were bound to particular cultures. Hahn argues that if they were truly culture-bound, comparisons among different kinds of hysterias, wild man behaviors, startle reactions, spirit possessions, and the like would be impossible. Such syndromes would have no common basis for comparison since it is the distinctive cultures, not something in the bodies and psyches of patients, that are causing the conditions.

Hahn suggests that comparison among different conditions, such as the comparison Suwanlert provides in his selection, would be impossible.

Ronald C. Simons and Charles C. Hughes edited *The Culture-Bound Syndromes: Folk Illnesses of Psychiatric and Anthropological Interest* (D. Reidel, 1985), which surveys the various syndromes and attempts to sort them into general patterns. This volume has an exhaustive bibliography of primary sources about most of the documented conditions that have been labeled as culture-bound syndromes. Although Simons and Hughes accept the premise of the culture-bound syndrome, they conclude that some conditions probably should not be considered culture-bound, while others, such as Arctic hysteria, *amok,* and *latah,* probably should be accepted as legitimate culture-bound syndromes. Despite the fact that this volume accepts some culture-bound syndromes as distinctive, Hughes challenges the suitability of using this terminology, since many of the conditions can be related to conditions described in the *DSM-IV.*

Suwanlert's selection comes from one of the first collections to document many of the culture-bound syndromes: *Culture-Bound Syndromes, Ethnopsychiatry, and Alternate Therapies,* William P. Lebra, ed. (University Press of Hawaii, 1976). The collection contains detailed discussions of *latah, amok, witiko* psychosis, Arctic hysteria, and other syndromes mentioned here. Another volume of interest to psychological anthropologists and students interested in the relationship between culture and mental health is *Cultural Conceptions of Mental Health and Therapy,* edited by Anthony J. Marsella and Geoffrey M. White (D. Reidel, 1982). For a good discussion of *latah,* see Robert L. Winzeler's *Latah in Southeast Asia: The History and Ethnography of a Culture-Bound Syndrome* (Cambridge University Press, 1995).

ISSUE 16

Is Ethnic Conflict Inevitable?

YES: Sudhir Kakar, from "Some Unconscious Aspects of Ethnic Violence in India," in Veena Das, ed., *Mirrors of Violence: Communities, Riots, and Survivors in South Asia* (Oxford University Press, 1990)

NO: Anthony Oberschall, from "The Manipulation of Ethnicity: From Ethnic Cooperation to Violence and War in Yugoslavia," *Ethnic and Racial Studies* (November 2000)

ISSUE SUMMARY

YES: Indian social researcher Sudhir Kakar analyzes the origins of ethnic conflict from a psychological perspective to argue that ethnic differences are deeply held distinctions that from time to time will inevitably erupt as ethnic conflicts. He maintains that anxiety arises from preconscious fears about cultural differences. In his view, no amount of education or politically correct behavior will eradicate these fears and anxieties about people of differing ethnic backgrounds.

NO: American sociologist Anthony Oberschall considers the ethnic conflicts that have recently emerged in Bosnia and contends that primordial ethnic attachments are insufficient to explain the sudden emergence of violence among Bosnian ethnic groups. He adopts a complex explanation for this violence, identifying circumstances in which fears and anxieties were manipulated by politicians for self-serving ends. It was only in the context of these manipulations that ethnic violence could have erupted, concludes Oberschall.

Since the 1960s anthropologists and other social scientists have debated the causes, origins, and necessary conditions for ethnic differences to erupt into ethnic violence. Such discussions have built on an older debate about the origins of ethnicity. In the earlier debate, two key positions emerged. The first is the *primordialist* view, in which ethnic attachments and sentiments emerge from the fact of being members of the same cultural community. Although cultural in origin, the primordialists see kinship, language, and customary practices as the source of ethnic identity and social bonds between people of the same ethnicity. Ethnicity in this view is something one is born with, or at least born into, because it develops as one learns kinship, language, and culture. A second position, often called the *circumstantialist* perspective, was developed by the Norwegian anthropologist Fredrik Barth in his book *Ethnic Groups and Social Boundaries* (Little, Brown, 1969). For Barth, a person's ethnicity is neither fixed nor a natural condition of his or her birth. One's ethnicity could be (and often was) manipulated under different circumstances. By dressing differently, by learning a different language, and by intermarriage, people in many ethnic groups within a generation or two could become members of another ethnic group and have a different ethnic identity. Later, if it became advantageous to be members of the first ethnic group, these same people could acknowledge their past and become members of the first group.

The following selections shift the ethnicity debate to the problem of whether or not ethnic conflict is inevitable. Sudhir Kakar uses a psychological approach to develop a primordialist argument to explain the frequent and almost continual problems of ethnic violence in India. For Kakar, ethnic sentiments and attachments emerge from deep psychological concerns at the unconscious or even preconscious level. He contends that psychologically there are primordial differences between Indians of different ethnic backgrounds, and such differences lead to conflicts over access to resources, jobs, and the like.

Anthony Oberschall considers possible explanations for the sudden appearance of ethnic conflict in the former Yugoslavia. He acknowledges that the primordialist variables of kinship, religion, and language may play some role in explaining why Serbs, Croats, and Bosnian Muslims behaved as they did once ethnic conflict broke out. Traditional animosities existed for centuries in the Balkans, and they reemerged suddenly after 50 years of peace and cooperation. But such variables cannot explain why these groups started fighting with one another in the first place, says Oberschall, after nearly half a century of living together peacefully, regularly socializing, and even intermarrying with one another; such ties as kinship, language, and religion do not explain why tensions flared up or why neighbors suddenly tried to eliminate people of other ethnic backgrounds from their towns and villages. Drawing on a complex pattern of circumstantial variables, Oberschall develops a circumstantialist model, arguing that politicians were manipulating local sentiments for their own ends. In the context of great uncertainty and crisis, people of all ethnic backgrounds bought into the anxieties suggested by their different leaders.

What leads people to hate people of different ethnic backgrounds? Is it deeply held fears of cultural differences? Or does conflict emerge because individuals fear losing what they have worked hard to obtain? How could people in Yugoslavia live together harmoniously for 50 years and then suddenly participate in the "ethnic cleansing" of their neighborhoods? Could the willingness to commit such acts of violence against neighbors have been suppressed for half a century by a strong central government? What is the source of this kind of group hatred, since differences in skin color and physical features are largely not present in either the Indian or Yugoslavian cases?

YES ⤶

Some Unconscious Aspects of Ethnic Violence in India

The need to integrate social and psychological theory in the analysis of cultural conflicts, i.e. conflicts between ethnic and religious groups, has long been felt while its absence has been equally long deplored. Though everyone agrees on the theoretical questions involved—how do these conflicts originate, develop, and get resolved; how do they result in violent aggression—a general agreement on the answers or even on how to get these answers moves further and further away.

A large part of the problem in the study of these questions lies with the nature of and the crisis within the social sciences. The declining fortunes of logical positivism, hastened in the last twenty years by the widespread circulation and absorption of the views of such thinkers as Gadamer, Habermas, Derrida, Ricouer and Foucault, has led to a plethora of new models in the sciences of man and society. The dominant model of yesteryears—social science as social physics—is now only one among several clamouring for allegiance and adherents. It incorporates only one view among many on the nature of social reality and of social science knowledge. Anthropology, sociology, political science, psychology and even economics are all becoming more pluralistic and scattering into frameworks. In such a situation, the calls for a general theory of ethnic violence or indeed (as Clifford Geertz has remarked) of anything *social,* sound increasingly hollow, and the claims to have one science seem megalomaniacal. Thus, without taking recourse to other disciplines and even ignoring the grand theories of human aggression in psychology itself— those of animal ethology, sociology, Freudian Thanatos and so on—I would like to present some limited 'local knowledge' observations on ethnic violence in India from a psychoanalytic perspective.

In the manner of a clinician, let me begin with the concrete data on which I base my observations on the first question, namely the origins of ethnic conflict. The data for these observations, and those which follow, come from diverse sources: spirit possession in north India, dreams of psychotherapy patients, eavesdropping on group discussions at the Golden Temple complex in July 1984, and finally, personal participation in large religious assemblies.

The Other in Ethnic Conflict

Some years ago, while studying the phenomenon of possession by spirits in rural north India, I was struck by a curious fact. In a very large number of cases, 15 out of 28, the *bhuta* or malignant spirit possessing Hindu men and women turned out to be a Muslim. When, during the healing ritual, the patient went into a trance and the spirit started expressing its wishes, these wishes invariably turned out to be those which would have been horrifying to the patient's conscious self. In one case, the Muslim spirit possessing an elderly Brahmin priest vigorously insisted on eating kababs. The five women surrounding the man who had engaged the *bhuta* in conversation were distinctly disheartened that he had turned out to be a *Sayyad* and one of them lamented: 'These Mussulmans! They have ruined our *dharma* but they are so strong they can withstand our gods.' In another case, the *bhuta* inhabiting a young married woman not only expressed derogatory sentiments towards her 'lord and master' but also openly stated its intentions of bringing the mother-in-law to a violent and preferably bloody end.

Possession by a Muslim *bhuta,* then, seemed to reflect the afflicted person's desperate efforts to convince himself and others that his hunger for forbidden foods and uncontrolled rage towards those who should be loved and respected, as well as all other imagined transgressions and sins of the heart, belonged to the Muslim destroyer of taboos and were furthest away from his 'good' Hindu self. In that Muslim *bhutas* were universally considered to be the strongest, vilest, the most malignant and the most stubborn of the evil spirits, the Muslim seemed to symbolize the alien and the demonic in the unconscious part of the Hindu mind.

The division of humans into mutually exclusive group identities of tribe, nation, caste, religion and class thus seems to serve two important psychological functions. The first is to increase the feeling of well being in the narcissistic realm by locating one's own group at the centre of the universe, superior to others. The shared grandiose self, maintained by legends, myths and rituals, seems to demand a concomitant conviction that other groups are inferior.

India has not been exempt from this universal rule. Whatever idealizing tendencies we might have in viewing our past history, it is difficult to deny that every social group in its tales, ritual and other literature, has sought to portray itself nearer to a purer, divine state while denigrating and banishing others to the periphery. It is also undeniable that sharing a common ego-ideal and giving one's own group a super-individual significance can inspire valued human attributes of loyalty and heroic self-sacrifice. All this is familiar to students of culture and need not detain us further here.

For the psychoanalyst it is the second function of division into ethnic groups, namely the need to have other groups as containers for one's disavowed aspects, which is of greater significance. These disavowed aspects, or the demonic spirits, take birth during that period of our childhood when the child, made conscious of good and bad, right and wrong, begins to divide himself into two parts, one that is the judge and the other that is being judged.

The unacceptable, condemned parts of the self are projected outside, the projective processes being primitive attempts to relieve pain by externalizing it. The expelled parts of the self are then attached to various beings—animals and human—as well as to whole castes, ethnic and religious communities. This early split within our nature, which gives us a future license to view and treat others as if they were no better than the worst in ourselves, is normally completed by the time the child is six to seven years old. The earliest defenses for dealing with the unacceptable aspects of the self—namely their denial, the splitting from awareness and projection onto another group—require the active participation of the members of the child's group-parents and other adults who must support such a denial and projection. They are shared group defenses. The family and extended group of a Hindu upper-caste child, for instance, not only provides him with its myths and rituals which increase his sense of group cohesion and of narcissism in belonging to such an exalted entity, but also help him in elaborating and fleshing out his demonology of other ethnic and religious groups. The *purana* of the Muslim demon, for instance, as elaborated by many Hindu groups, has nothing to do with Sufi saints, the prophet's sayings or the more profound sentiments of Islam. Instead, its stories are of rape and pillage by the legions of Ghazni and Timur as well as other more local accounts of Muslim mayhem.

The Muslim demon is, so to say, the traditional container of Hindu conflicts over aggressive impulses. It is the transgressor of deeply-held taboos, especially over the expression of physical violence. Recent events in Punjab, I am afraid, are creating yet another demon in the Hindu psyche of north India. Over the last few years, tales of [Sikh militant leader] Bhindranwale's dark malevolence and the lore of murderous terrorists has led to a number of reported dreams from patients where Sikhs have appeared as symbols of the patient's own aggressive and sadistic superego. A group of Sikhs with raised swords chasing a patient who has broken into an old woman's shop, a Nihang stabbing a man repeatedly with a spear on the street while another patient as a frightened child looks down upon the scene from an upstairs window—these are two of many such dream images. Leaving aside the role played by these images in the patients' individual dramas, the projection of the feared aggressive parts of the self on the figure of the Sikh is an unhappy portent for the future relationship between the two communities. The fantasy of being overwhelmed by the frightening aggressive strength of the Sikhs can, in periods of upheaval and danger—when widespread regression in ego takes place and the touch with reality is weakened—lead to psychotic delusions about Sikh intentions.

Sikh Militancy

Until this point I have used some psychoanalytic, especially Kleinian, concepts of splitting and projective identification to understand data that bears on the question of ethnic conflict. More specifically, I have outlined the origins of certain pre-conscious attitudes of Hindus towards Muslims and Sikhs. These attitudes reflect the psychological needs of the child, and the adult, to split off his bad impulses, especially those relating to violence, and to attach them to other communities, a process supported and reinforced by other members of the group. Let me now use another set of analytical concepts of group identity and narcissism, narcissistic hurt and rage, to understand the phenomenon of Sikh militancy. To avoid any misunderstanding let me state at the outset that I am primarily talking about the militant Sikh youth of Punjab, not of all Sikh youths, and certainly not of the Sikh community as a whole. Also, the word narcissism in psychoanalysis is not used in a pejorative sense but, together with sexuality and aggression, as the third major and fundamental motivational factor in human beings which is concerned with the maintenance of self-esteem. The data for these observations comes from being an observer of heated and anguished discussions among randomly formed groups which were being spontaneously held all over the Golden Temple complex in Amritsar, five weeks after Operation Blue Star.* said elsewhere, the aftermath of Blue Star, which heightened the awareness of their cultural identity among many Sikhs, also brought out in relief one of its less conscious aspects. I have called it the Khalsa warrior element of Sikh identity which, at least since the tenth guru and at least among the Jats, has expressed itself in images of 'lifting up the sword' against the 'oppression of a tyrannical ruler', and whose associated legends only countenance two possible outcomes—complete victory (*fateh*) or martyrdom (*shaheedi*) of those engaged in the battle. The surrounding society has of course reinforced this identity element over the years by its constant talk of Sikh martial process and valour. The Sikh youth's acceptance of these projections of heroic militancy made by the Hindu can lead to his overestimation of this aspect of his identity as he comes to feel that it is his very essence. All other qualities which may compromise heroic militancy, such as yearnings for passivity, softness and patience, will tend to be denied, split off and projected onto other, despised groups. The damage done to the Akal Takht—as much a symbol of corporate militancy as of religious piety—reinforced the two M's— militance and martyrdom—the inner counterparts of the well-known five K's which constitute the outer markers of the Khalsa warrior identity. The exaggerated value placed on martyrdom is hard to understand for Hindus since oppressors in *their* mythology—the Hindu equivalent of Sikh legendary history— tended to be destroyed by divine intervention rather than by the sacrifice of martyrs.

The army action was then a hurt to Sihk religious sentiments in a very different way from the sense in which a Hindu understands the term. It was an affront to group narcissism, to a shared grandiose self. The consequent feelings were of narcissistic hurt and rage. This was brought home to me again and again as I listened to groups of anguished men and women in front of the ruins of the Akal Takht. Most men stood in attitudes of sullen defeat, scorned and derided by the women with such sentences as 'Where is the starch in your moustache now?'

---

* [Operation 'Blue Star' was the code name for the army action to clear the Golden Temple of Sikh militants in June 1984, in which Bhindranwale died. The operation resulted in extensive damage to the sacred site.—Ed.]

Given the collective need for the preservation of this core of the group identity, the Golden Temple action automatically completed a circle of associations. The army action to clear Akal Takht from desperadoes became an attack on the Sikh nation by a tyrannical 'Delhi durbar'. It was seen as an assault designed to wipe out all its traces, its *nishan*—since this is how it was in the past. The Sikhs killed in the attack were now defenders of the faith and martyrs—since this too is a pattern from the past. The encounter was viewed as a momentous battle, an oppressive empire's defeat of the forces of the Khalsa. The relatively heavy army losses are not a consequence of its restraint but a testimony to the fighting qualities of the Khalsa warrior. Paradoxically, the terrorist losses were exaggerated to simultaneously show the overwhelming strength of the army and the Khalsa readiness to die in martyrdom when victory is not possible.

Bhindranwale, in dramatically exemplifying the two M's of militancy and martyrdom, has touched deep chords. His status with much of the Sikh youth today is very near that of an eleventh guru. Initially, Bhindranwale may have been one of many *sants,* though more militant than most, who dot the countryside in Punjab. What began the process of his elevation was his successful defiance of the government—echoes, again of Sikh history, of defiant gurus contesting state authority. In setting the date and terms of his arrest ('*Santji* gave arrest', and not 'He was arrested', is how the people at the Temple complex put it), and predicting the day of his release, Bhindranwale began to be transformed from a mortal preacher to a 'realized' saint with miraculous powers. (And the reputation of being able to work miracles is, we know, essential for those aspiring to enter the portals of gurudom in all religious traditions.) His 'martyrdom' has now cemented the transformation and made his elevation into the Sikh militant pantheon irreversible. The tortures and murders in the Temple complex or outside are no longer his responsibility, being seen as the doings of deluded associates, acts of which Santji was, of course, unaware.

It is obvious that after the army action there was a threat to the cultural identity of at least a section of the Jat Sikh youth. This led to regressive transformations in the narcissistic realm, where reality is interpreted only as a balm to narcissistic hurt and as a coolant for narcissistic rage. It needs to be asked what precisely constituted this threat. I would tend to see the threat to the Jat Sikh group identity as part of a universal modernizing process to which many groups all over the world have been and continue to be exposed. This group though has preferred to change a social-psychological issue into a political one. The cultural decay and spiritual disintegration talked of in the Anandpur resolution are then viewed as an aspect of majority-minority relations rather than as an existential condition brought on by the workings of a historical fate. A feeling of inner threat is projected outside as oppression, a conflict around tradition and modernity as a conflict around power.

Narcissistic rage, then, is the core of the militancy of Sikh youth and Sikh terrorism. As Kohut says about this rage: 'The need for revenge, for righting a wrong, for undoing a hurt by whatever means, and a deeply anchored, unrelating compulsion in the pursuit of all these aims, gives no rest to those who have suffered a narcissistic injury.' For the analyst, this becomes paramount in the understanding of youthful militancy, the foreground, while political, social and other issues recede into the background.

Let me now make a few observations on the question of ethnic conflict resulting in violent aggression, i.e on mob violence. My data for these remarks is, paradoxically, personal participation in largely peaceful and loving groups engaged in religious and spiritual endeavours. Yet many of the psychological processes are common to the two kinds of groups. Both emotionally charged religious assemblies and mobs on the rampage bring out in relief the vulnerability of human individual ego functions confronted with the power of group processes. In the face of these, the 'integrity', 'autonomy', and 'independence' of the ego seem to be wishful illusions and hypothetical constructs. Mobs, more than religious congregations, provide striking examples of the massive inducement, by group processes, of individuals towards a new identity and behaviour of the sort that would ordinarily be repudiated by a great majority of the individuals so induced. They illustrate, more clearly than in any other comparable social situation, the evanescence of rational thought, the fragility of internalized behavioural controls, values, and moral and ethical standards.

The most immediate experience in being part of a crowd is the sensual pounding received in the press of other bodies. At first there may be a sense of unease as the body, the container of our individuality and the demarcator of our boundaries in space, is sharply wrenched away from its habitual way of experiencing others. For, as we grow up, the touch of others, once so deliberately courted and responded to with delight, increasingly becomes a problem. Coming from a loved one, touch is deliciously welcomed; with strangers, on the other hand, there is an involuntary shrinking of the body, their touch taking on the menacing air of invasion by the other.

But once the fear of touch disappears in the fierce press of other bodies and the individual lets himself become a part of the crowd's density, the original apprehension is transformed into an expansiveness that stretches to include others. Distances and differences—of class, status, age, caste hierarchy— disappear in an exhilarating feeling that individual boundaries can indeed be transcended and were perhaps illusory in the first place. Of course, touch is only one of the sensual stimuli that hammers at the gate of individual identity. Other excitations, channelled through vision, hearing and smell, are also very much involved. In addition, there are exchanges of body heat, muscle tension and body rhythms which take place in a crowd. In short, the crowd's assault on the sense of individuality, its invitation to transcend one's individual boundaries and its offer of a freedom from personal doubts and anxieties is well nigh irresistible.

The need and search for 'self-transcending' experience, to lose one's self in the group, suspend judgement and reality-testing, is, I believe, the primary motivational factor in both religious assembly and violent mob, even though the stated purpose is spiritual uplift in one and mayhem and murder in the other. Self-transcendence, rooted in the blurring of our body image, not only opens us to the influx of the divine but also heightens our receptivity to the demonic. The surge of love also washes away the defences against the emergence of archaic hates. In psychoanalytic terms, regression in the body image is simultaneous with regression in the superego system. Whether the ego reacts to this regression in a disintegrated fashion with panic that manifests itself (in a mob) in senseless rage and destructive acts—or in a release of love encompassing the group and the world outside—depends on the structure provided to the group. Without the rituals which make tradition palpable and thus extend the group in time by giving assurances of continuity to the beleaguered ego, and without the permanent visibility of leaders whose presence is marked by conspicuous external insignia and who replace the benign and loving functions of the superego, religious crowds can easily turn into marauding mobs. Transcending individuality by merging into a group can generate heroic self-sacrifice but also unimaginable brutality. To get out of one's skin in a devotional assembly is also at the same time to have less regard for saving it in a mob.

Some Implications

The implications of my remark, I know, are not too comforting. The need for communities, our own to take care of our narcissistic needs and of others to serve as recipients for our hostility and destructiveness, are perhaps built into our very ground-plan as human beings. Well meaning educative efforts in classrooms or in national integration seminars are for the most part too late and too little in that they are misdirected. They are too late since most of the evidence indicates that the communal imagination is well entrenched by the time a child enters school. They are misdirected in that they never frankly address the collective—and mostly preconscious—fears and wishes of the various communities. Demons do not much care for 'correct' interpretations of religious texts by scholars, nor are they amenable to humanist pleas of reason to change into good and loving beings. All we can do is accept their existence but reduce their potential for causing actual physical violence and destruction. The routes to this goal, the strategies for struggle with our own inner devils, are many. One strategy strives for the dissolution of small group identities into even large entities. Sikhs and Hindus in Punjab can move towards a group identity around 'Punjabiyyat', in which case the despised demon shifts outside to the *Purubia* or the *Madrasi*. One can go on to progressively larger identities of the nationalist Indian whose *bete-noire* can then be the Pakistani or the Chinese. One can envisage even larger groupings, for instance of the 'Third World', where the sense of narcissistic well being provided by this particular community needs a demonic West as the threatening aggressor.

A second strategy is, in a certain sense, to go the opposite way. By this I mean less the encouragement of various ethnic identities than in ensuring that all manifestations of ethnic group action—assemblies, demonstrations, processions—are given as much religious structure as possible in order to prevent the breakout of archaic hate. Vedic chants and Koranic prayers, *mahants, pujaris* and *mullahs* in their full regalia and conspicuous by their presence, are fully encouraged to be in the forefront of religious processions and demonstrations. Traditional religious standards, flags and other symbols are liberally used to bind the religious assemblies.

Yet another strategy (and let me note that none of these are exclusive) is to concentrate all efforts at the containment of the communal demon on the dominant community. We know that the belief of the dominant party in a relationship often becomes a self-fulfilling prophecy, involuntarily changing the very consciousness of the weaker partner. In India the Hindu image of himself and of other communities is apt to be incorporated in the self image of non-Hindu minorities. Even when consciously accepted, the denigrating part of the image is likely to be a source of intensive unconscious rage in other communities. Their rage is stored up over a period of time, till it explodes in all its violent manifestations whenever historical circumstances sanction such eruptions.

Anthony Oberschall

NO

The Manipulation of Ethnicity: From Ethnic Cooperation to Violence and War in Yugoslavia

Four views on ethnicity and ethnic violence are common. In the 'primordial' view, ethnic attachments and identities are a cultural given and a natural affinity, like kinship sentiments. They have an overpowering emotional and non-rational quality. Applied to the former Yugoslavia, the primordialist believes that despite seemingly cooperative relations between nationalities in Yugoslavia, mistrust, enmity, even hatred were just below the surface, as had long been true in the Balkans. Triggered by fierce competition for political power during the breakup of Yugoslavia and driven by the uncertainties over state boundaries and minority status, these enmities and hatreds, fuelled by fear and retribution, turned neighbour against neighbour, and district against district, in an expanding spiral of aggression and reprisals. Although the primordial account sounds plausible, and it is true that politicians activated and manipulated latent nationalism and ethnic fears, some evidence contradicts it. Ethnic cleansing was more commonly militias and military against civilians than neighbour against neighbour. In seventeen assaults against villages during the ethnic cleansing of Prijedor district in Bosnia in May/June 1992, we found that the aggressors wore military and paramilitary uniforms and insignia. In fourteen assaults, the survivors did not recognize any of the aggressors, who did not bother to wear masks or disguises. These 'weekend warriors' from central Serbia openly bivouacked at the Prijedor police station. The primordial theory omits the fact that ethnic hatreds can subside as a consequence of statecraft and living together. [President Charles] de Gaulle and [Chancellor Konrad] Adenauer managed to reconcile the French and German people. Why no lasting conciliation in Yugoslavia after forty years of ethnic peace?

In the second, 'instrumentalist' view, ethnic sentiments and loyalties are manipulated by political leaders and intellectuals for political ends, such as state creation. For Yugoslavia, the instrumentalist explanation highlights Serb nationalists' goal of a Greater Serbia, and a similar Croat nationalism. Ethnic cleansing resulted from a historical longing by Serbs in Croatia at first backed moderate nationalists, for a Greater Serbia, with deep cultural roots. [Slobodan] Milosevic and Serb nationalists tried to implement it when the opportunity arose in the late 1980s and early 1990s. Greater Serbia required ethnic cleansing of non-Serbs from areas inhabited by a majority of Serbs and the corridors linking Serb population clusters. Although there is evidence that ethnic cleansing was a state policy, orchestrated by the highest authorities in Serbia and the Bosnian Serb leadership, this explanation ignores that many Bosnian Serbs did not want secession, that many Serbs in Croatia at first backed moderate nationalists, and that many Serbs evaded the draft. The instrumentalist view assumes an ethnic consensus that initially does not exist. But if many were reluctant to wage war and to participate in ethnic cleansing, how did ethnic extremists prevail over these moderates?

The third 'constructionist' view of ethnicity and ethnic conflict was originally formulated by [Leo] Kuper. It supplements the insights of the primordial and of the instrumentalist views. Religion or ethnicity are very real social facts, but in ordinary times they are only one of several roles and identities that matter. There is a great deal of variance in a population on ethnic attachments and identities. In the words of [Juan J.] Linz and [Alfred] Stepan 'political identities are less primordial and fixed than contingent and changing. They are amenable to being constructed or eroded by political institutions and political choices'. The constructionist view offers insights but is incomplete. How are nationality and ethnicity constructed and eroded by political mobilization and mass media propaganda?

A fourth model of ethnic violence centres on state breakdown, anarchy, and the security dilemma that such conditions pose to ethnic groups who engage in defensive arming to protect their lives and property against ethnic rivals, which then stimulates arming by other ethnic groups like an arms race between states. The driving motivations are not ethnic hatreds but fear and insecurity. In the Yugoslav crisis Michael Ignatieff puts it thus:

> Once the Yugoslav communist state began to split into its constituent national particles the key question soon became: will the local Croat policeman protect me if I am a Serb? Will I keep my job in the soap factory if my new boss is a Serb or a Muslim? The answer to this question was no, because no state remained to enforce the old ethnic bargain.

There is a security dilemma in ethnic conflict, but why so much ethnic violence without state breakdown? Can insecurity and fear be spread by propaganda even when daily experience contradicts the allegations of ethnic hostility and threat? Can the powerful fear the weak?

Building on the four views and mindful of [Rogers] Brubaker and [David] Laitin's criteria for a satisfactory theory of ethnic violence, I use the idea of latent nationalism at the grass roots, and show how it was activated; I highlight ethnic manipulation by political leaders, and explain why manipulation was successful; I take into account the variance in ethnic identities and analyse why extremists prevailed over moderates; I focus on the security dilemma and ethnic fears and insecurity, and show how fears and insecurity grew from lies and propaganda. To this arsenal of concepts and models for generating the dynamics of ethnicization and collective violence, I add 'cognitive frames'.

Combining all, I seek to explain how forty years of cooperative ethnic relations ended with collective violence and war.

Prijedor: A Case-Study

To get a sense of what is to be explained about ethnic conflict and violence at the grass roots, consider the Prijedor district in Northwest Bosnia where major ethnic violence took place in the spring of 1992. In the 1991 Census, Prijedor district was 42.5 percent Serb and 44 percent Muslim. It was surrounded by districts that had either a slight Serb majority or were close to even, as Prijedor was. Prijedor Serbs were not an isolated Serb minority island surrounded by a sea of Muslims and Croats.

There had been no Serb complaints of mistreatment, discrimination, or intimidation in Prijedor by non-Serbs, or vice versa. On the contrary, as a bewildered Muslim refugee from Prijedor stated,

> In Prijedor there were no conflicts between nationalities. We didn't make the distinctions. My colleague at work was an Orthodox Serb, we worked together. When we were children we went to the Orthodox church or the mosque together . . . I don't understand. Before there were never any problems between us. We lived together. My sister is married to a Serb, and a brother of my wife is married to a Croat.

According to the [United Nations] Bassiouni Report, Serbs held the leading positions in Prijedor in 1991, as they had done for decades. . . . In the 1991 elections, the predominantly Muslim SDA [Party of Democratic Union in Bosnia] won thirty seats; the Serb SDS [Serbian Democratic Party] twenty-eight, and thirty-two went to other parties. The Muslims refrained from taking over a number of leading posts to which their electoral victory entitled them because they believed in power-sharing. Even so, the SDS blocked the work of the Prijodor Assembly and organized a parallel governance for Serbs, in alliance with the SDS leaders in nearby Banja Luka. In Bosnia as a whole, the Serbs shared political power and controlled the most important military forces.

As in other towns and cities in Bosnia, the SDS in Prijedor organized a successful Serb plebiscite for Greater Serbia. A parallel Serb governance, called the 'Crisis Committee', secretly created an armed force of Serbs with weapons obtained from Serbia. Serb crisis committees were also formed among Serbs in some of Prijedor district's towns and villages. On the night of 29 April 1992, without any provocation or a shot being fired, 1,775 well-armed Serbs seized the city of Prijedor in a *coup d'état*. By this time the Prijedor local government had completely lost power to various Serb groups. Paramilitaries had seized the radio and television transmitters and cut off all but Serb transmissions. The Serb *coup d'état* in Prijedor is similar to what happened elsewhere in Northern Bosnia.

Non-Serb leaders were arrested and shortly afterwards disappeared, presumed executed. The Muslim police and other officials were fired from their posts. Schools closed; the newspaper ceased publication, and a Serb paper was started. Non-Serbs were harassed, intimidated, fired from their jobs. Amid incessant house searches, weapons, mostly hunting guns, belonging to non-Serbs, were rounded up. After the attempt on 30 May by the Patriotic League of Croats and Muslims—an armed formation of 150 fighters—to retake the old city, many non-Serb inhabitants were arrested and sent to the infamous Omarskca camp. At Omarska, prisoners were tortured, brutalized, starved and killed. The guards were rural Serbs from nearby villages; the interrogators were Prijedor police inspectors. . . . People were rounded up and some were executed: those shot were Muslim leaders whose names appeared on a list. Atrocities took place elsewhere in the district.

Several observations should be made about the events in Prijedor. Muslims and Serbs had lived in peace before the conflict erupted. The Serbs were neither a numerical minority, nor discriminated against. They not only had a share of power, but they had the biggest share, and they were well armed. Why, then, did Serbs fear their fellow citizens in Prijedor? A cartoon from this period expresses the puzzle well. It shows a bearded Serb paramilitary, armed to the teeth, with guns, hand-granades, ammunition belts, knives, waving a machine gun, looking worried, and yelling at the top of his voice, 'I am being threatened!' There was no anarchy, no state breakdown in Prijedor. The Serbs used the police and military of a functioning government to subdue the non-Serbs. Serbs may have been apprehensive about their future in an independent Bosnia, but even in Bosnia they had a big presence—numerical, military, political, economic. There was no spontaneous violence initiated by Serb civilians against non-Serbs, nor vice-versa. Instead, there was a highly organized, secretly prepared *coup d'état,* like the 1917 Bolshevik seizure of power in Russia. . . . As in the Russian revolution with the Soviets, the Serb parallel government was not only an instrument for seizing power from non-Serbs but of stripping the moderate Serbs of any influence and authority.

What was the reaction of ordinary Serbs to these events? Though there is no information on Prijedor itself, one can learn from what observers recorded in nearby Banja Luka. Peter Maas reports that a Serb lawyer there estimated that 30 percent of Serbs oppose such things [ethnic cleansing], 60 percent agree or are confused and go along with the 10 percent who 'have the guns and control the television tower'. . . . An armed, organized 10 percent who control mass communications can have its way when the majority supports it overtly or tacitly or is confused, and when the opposition is unorganized, divided, and scared. One has to explain how it was that 60 percent were supportive of or confused on ethnic cleansing, since their support and quiescence were necessary for the success of the extremist 10 percent.

Was Violent Conflict Inevitable?

In a multinational state such as Yugoslavia, nationality will be a salient dimension of political contention, and there will be leaders and intellectuals with a nationalist ideology and agenda. The Yugoslav constitution and its political institutions were delicately balanced and crafted to deal with nationality.

A nationalist challenge would inevitably zero in on stateness, minority rights and power-sharing: if accepted boundaries of political units are renegotiated or remade, who decides which peoples and territories belong to new and old political entities? Will all peoples in the new units be equal citizens for governance, or will majority ethnonational affiliation become the admission ticket for full citizenship?

Once unleashed, nationalism in Yugoslavia set on a collision course the two largest nationalities, the Serbs and the Croats. With a quarter of Serbs living outside Serbia; a centralized Yugoslav state was a guarantor of Serb security. For Croats and their history of opposition to Hapsburg rule, a decentralized state and weak federation meant control of their own destinies, unencumbered by inefficient state agencies and enterprises staffed and controlled by Serbs. Nevertheless, nationality issues could have been sorted out with democratic institutions in a confederation, with collective rights for minorities, and with systems of political representation in elections and collective decision rules in assemblies that would protect minority voice and favour coalitions rather than majority domination. With these reforms, nationalist leaders would have found it difficult to rally the citizenry to their cause.

In a country with great differences in economic development and standards of living between the Republics, there will be disagreements over economic policies, taxation, transfer, subsidies across regions, and abandoning socialism for a market economy. All Republics had experienced dramatic economic gains since World War II. Yugoslavia was not beyond economic repair.

As in other communist states in the late 1980s, the Yugoslav communist leaders wanted to remain in power. Some reprogrammed as reform communists, and hoped to move into European-style social democracy. Others chose ethnonationalism as the issue that would carry them to power and create a new principle of legitimacy for the post-communist regime. Moderate nationalists stood for conciliation among nationalities; extremists were willing to pursue their goals with force and violence. The defeat of the moderates was not inevitable. Why did xenophobic nationalism resonate with the citizenry? How is it that when the media unleashed the war of words and symbols before the war of bullets, so many believed the exaggerations, distortions and fabrications that belied their personal experiences?

Ethnic Relations Before the Crisis

Survey research on ethnic relations in mid-1990 found that in a national sample of 4,232 Yugoslavs, only 17 percent believed that the country would break up into separate states, and 62 percent reported that the 'Yugoslav' affiliation was very or quite important for them. On ethnonational relations, in workplaces, 36 percent characterized them as 'good', 28 percent as 'satisfactory', and only 6 percent said 'bad' and 'very bad'. For ethnonational relations in neighborhoods, 57 percent answered 'good', 28 percent 'satisfactory', and only 12 percent chose 'bad' and 'very bad'. For the majority of Yuogoslavs, on the eve of the Yugoslav wars, nationalist contention in the public arena did not translate into hostile interpersonal ethnic relations. . . .

Ignatieff is puzzled, 'What is difficult to understand about the Balkan tragedy is how . . . nationalist lies ever managed to take root in the soil of shared village existence. . . . In order for war to occur, nationalists had to convince neighbors and friends that in reality they had been massacring each other since time immemorial.'

The Manipulation of Ethnicity

For explaining ethnic manipulation one needs the concept of a cognitive frame. A cognitive frame is a mental structure which situates and connects events, people and groups into a meaningful narrative in which the social world that one inhabits makes sense and can be communicated and shared with others. Yugoslavs experienced ethnic relations through two frames: a normal frame and a crisis frame. People possessed both frames in their minds: in peaceful times the crisis frame was dormant, and in crisis and war the normal frame was suppressed. Both frames were anchored in private and family experiences, in culture and in public life. In the normal frame, which prevailed in [Josip Broz] Tito's Yugoslavia, ethnic relations were cooperative and neighbourly. Colleagues and workers, schoolmates and teammates transacted routinely across nationality. Some did not even know or bother to know another's nationality. Intermarriage was accepted. Holidays were spent in each others' Republics. Except in Kosovo, the normal frame prevailed for most Yugoslavs throughout the 1980s.

The crisis frame was grounded in the experiences and memories of the Balkan wars, the first and second world wars—and other wars before that. In these crises, civilians were not distinguished from combatants. Old people, children, women, priests were not spared. Atrocities, massacres, torture, ethnic cleansing, a scorched-earth policy were the rule. Everyone was held collectively responsible for their nationality and religion, and became a target of revenge and reprisals. . . .

Tito had wanted to eradicate the crisis frame, but it simmered in the memories of older people, the families of victims, intellectuals and religious leaders. Milosevic, Tudjman and other nationalists did not invent the crisis frame; they activated and amplified it. . . .

If the normal frame prevailed in the 1980s as shown by . . . survey findings, how did nationalists activate and amplify the crisis frame after decades of dormancy? The emotion that poisons ethnic relations is fear: fear of extinction as a group, fear of assimilation, fear of domination by another group, fear for one's life and property, fear of being a victim once more. After fear comes hate. The threatening others are demonized and dehumanized. The means of awakening and spreading such fears in Yugoslavia were through the newsmedia, politics, education, popular culture, literature, history and the arts.

The crisis frame in Yugoslavia was first resurrected by Serb intellectuals over the plight of the Kosovo Serbs. . . .

Fear of extinction was spread with highly inflated figures on the ethnic killings in World War II. . . .

In my interview with a Serb refugee one can trace how the atrocities discourse switched on the crisis frame: 'We were afraid because nationalists revived the memory of World War II atrocities . . . nationalist graffiti on walls awakened fears of past memories; it was a sign that minorities [Serbs in Croatia] would not be respected and safe'.

Fears of domination, oppression and demographic shrinkage were roused by the incessant rape and genocide discourse. . . .

Ordinary people echo the intellectuals' and the media crisis discourse. . . . Peter Maas asks a Serb refugee couple why they had fled their village. Their answer: Muslims planned to take over, a list of names had been drawn up, Serb women were to be assigned to Muslim harems after the men had been killed. They had heard about it on the radio; the Serb military had uncovered the plan. The journalist probes: 'Did any Muslims in the village ever harm you?' They reply, 'Oh no, our relations with the Muslims in the village were always good, they were decent people'. In the minds of the Serb couple, the crisis frame had eclipsed the normal frame. What under peaceful circumstances were totally implausible events—young women become sexual slaves in harems for breeding janissaries; a fifteenth- and sixteenth-century style Turkish/Islamic invasion of Europe—become credible narratives of ethnic annihilation and domination within the crisis frame.

Fear and the crisis frame provided opportunities for nationalists to mobilize a huge ethnic constituency, get themselves elected to office, and organize aggressive actions against moderates and other ethnics. . . .

Populist nationalism worked. The Vojvodina and Montenegro party leaderships resigned and were replaced by Milosevic loyalists. Abolishing the autonomous provinces of Kosovo and Vojvodina precipitated a constitutional crisis. . . . The nationality balance in Yugoslav politics was thus disturbed. Serbia gained control of over half the votes in all federal bodies and institutions. Slovenes and Croats reacted with their own nationalism.

There was grass-roots resistance to nationalism and to activation of the crisis frame. A content analysis of news stories in *Oslobodjenje* for 1990 indicates that municipalities, youth and veterans' organizations, and trade unions repeatedly protested against ethnic polarization and hatreds. . . . Important as this opposition was, it was countered by the spread of populist nationalism. *Oslobodjenje* in 1990 is full of affirmations of national symbols and identities: the renaming of localities; the reburial of bones of atrocity victims from World War II; nationalist graffiti on churches, mosques, monuments and in cemeteries; fights over flags, ethnic insults, nationalist songs, ethnic vandalism. To many, these were signs that normal times were sliding into crisis, and the authorities had lost control.

Mass communications and propaganda research help to explain why ethnic manipulation worked and why the crisis frame eclipsed the normal frame. First, . . . fear arousing appeals, originating in a threat, were powerful and effective in changing opinion and belief. Furthermore, the most important reaction to fear is removing the source of threat, precisely what nationalists were promising to do in Yugoslavia. Second, studies of propaganda routinely find that repetition is the single most effective technique of persuasion. It does not matter how big the lie is, so long as it keeps being repeated.

Third, much of what we know is vicarious knowledge and not based on personal experience. We accept the truths of authorities and experts whom we respect and who have socially recognized positions and titles. Who could really tell or check how many Serbs had been massacred by Ustasha? Fourth, outright falsehoods were common and intentional. According to a media analyst, 'In Serbia and Croatia, TV fabricated and shamelessly circulated war crime stories . . . the same victims would be identified on Zagreb screens as Croat, on Belgrade screens as Serb'. . . .

Fifth, mass communications studies of the two-step flow of communication show that in ordinary circumstances crude propaganda from 'patriotic journalism' is discounted because people are exposed to a variety of broadcast messages and because they check media messages against the beliefs and opinions in their social milieus in interpersonal relationships and conversations. Ethnic crisis politics breaks down the two-step flow. . . .

Nationalists Win the 1990 Elections

Second only to the mass media wars for the revival of the crisis frame were the 1990 elections. Every town and city experienced the founding of political parties, often at a huge rally in a public building or a sports stadium, during which speaker after speaker gave vent to exaggerated nationalist rhetoric and hostile pronouncements and attacks against other nationalities. . . .

Nationalists persuaded voters not to 'split the ethnic vote' but to vote as a bloc for the nationalists because the other nationalities would bloc-vote and gain power. Bloc-voting became a self-fulfilling prophecy. . . . The politicians elected were more nationalist than their voters. . . .

Repression of Minorities and Moderates

The demise of the moderates was due to a combination of electoral defeats, loss of credibility about being effective in a crisis, and intimidation and threats from extremists. . . .

The nationalist winners purged their ethnic opponents and moderates of their own nationality from party and state positions. The targets were sent anonymous threat letters, were fired from their jobs, forced into military service, charged with treason, subversion and plotting armed rebellion, and subject to office and house searches for weapons, radio transmitters and 'subversive' literature. . . . In a Bosnian example reported by [Tadeusz] Mazowiecki, 'According to a witness [from Bosanska Dubica], the elected authorities who were moderates and who tried to prevent acts of violence were dismissed or replaced by Serbian extremists'.

Other methods were cruder. . . . Ordinary people could not escape ethnic polarization. In an interview a Serb taxi driver explained: 'No one wanted the coming war, but if I don't fight, someone from my side [Serb] will kill me, and if my Muslim friends don't fight, other Muslims will kill them'.

The overthrow of moderates by extremists or radicals is well known in the great revolutions: Girondins were overthrown by the Jacobins in the French revolution and all groups were overthrown by the Bolsheviks in the Russian revolution. The means of seizing power are similar. The radicals create parallel governance to the state and come to exercise *de facto* authority in many institutions, and militias and mutineers execute a *coup d'état*. Then the remaining moderates are purged. It happens in ethnic violence as well. It did so in the mixed ethnic districts of Croatia and Bosnia, and it happened in Prijedor.

Militias Take Over

Militias and paramilitaries roamed far and wide and perpetrated ethnic cleansing, massacres, atrocities and other war crimes, as in the Prijedor district. . . .

Militiamen were not necessarily fanatics filled with hatred to start with. [Tim] Judah described how a Serb militiaman got recruited by his peers from the local SDS who pressured him for weeks: 'We've all got to take up arms, or we'll disappear from here'. He had Muslim and Croat friends. Would they protect him against extremists of all nationalities? Not likely, if it got violent. So he 'took out a gun'. Peer pressure, fear, not only of Muslims but of extremist Serbs who might finger him as a 'traitor', were the major reasons for joining a militia. Some of these men were unemployed and expected a job in the coming Serb government as militia or police.

Once the young man 'took out a gun' he became encapsulated in a quasimilitary unit subject to peer solidarity and ethnic loyalty. He was trained in weapons and indoctrinated with the beliefs and norms of the crisis frame about other ethnics:

a. **Collective guilt:** 'They' act in unison; children grow into adults; women give birth to future warriors; even old people stab you from behind; 'they' will never change.
b. **Revenge and retaliation:** 'They' massacred 'us' in the past, and are about to do it again, in fact they have already started. A setting of scores is justified; an eye for an eye.
c. **Deterrence/first strike:** Disable them before they strike, which is what they are about to do, despite appearances, because they are secretive and treacherous.
d. **Danger/survival:** These are extraordinary times, one's entire nationality is threatened, and extreme measures are justified.
e. **Legitimacy:** Ordinary people and militias are justified in taking extreme measures because the constituted authorities have not come to the defence of our people.

These are the rationalization and the justifying norms for unrestrained, collective, ethnic violence. Other motives for collective violence were economic gain, peer pressure and lack of accountability. From being an ordinary man in normal times the militiaman changed into being a killer at crisis times.

The Bassiouni report (UN Security Council 1994) counted eighty-three paramilitaries in Bosnia alone operating between June 1991 and late 1993, fifty-three for Serbs, with an estimated 20,000–40,000 members, thirteen for Croats, with 12,000–20,000, and fourteen for Bosniac, with 4,000–6,000 men. In view of 700,000 Bosnian Serb men aged fifteen to thirty-five, militiamen were 10–20 percent of the Serb men of military age in Bosnia. Ten to 20 percent of adult males in militias, added to the military and police, are more than enough for death and destruction against civilians on a massive scale.

Conclusion

My account is not a narrative of events but an analytic explanation for the breakup of Yugoslavia amid collective violence. . . . On the eve of the wars, Yugoslavs reported cooperative interpersonal ethnic relations and opposed a breakup of the state. Nationalist leaders succeeded in manipulating ethnicity by spreading fear, insecurity and hatred, which advanced their political agenda of separate national states.

To explain their success I draw on elements from the primordialist, instrumentalist and constructionist views on ethnicity and on the theory of ethnic violence originating in fear and insecurity. To these I add the concept of a cognitive frame which clarifies élite-grass-roots linkage and ethnic manipulation. Nationalism, ethnic identity and attachment alone, however intense, do not explain grass-roots ethnic actions. Yugoslavs possessed two frames on ethnic relations: a cooperative frame for normal, peaceful times, as in the decades of the fifties to the eighties. They also possessed a dormant crisis frame anchored in family history and collective memory of wars, ethnic atrocities and brutality. Threats and lies that were implausible and dismissed in the normal frame could resonate when the crisis frame was switched on: they became persuasive, were believed, and inspired fear.

In the waning days of Communism, nationalists activated the crisis frame on ethnicity by playing on fears of ethnic annihilation and oppression in the mass media, in popular culture, in social movements, and in election campaigns. Élite crisis discourse resonated at the grass roots, made for ethnic polarization, and got nationalists elected. Once in office, nationalists suppressed and purged both moderates in their own ethnic group and other ethnics. They organized militias who perpetrated acts of extreme violence against innocent civilians. They conducted war according to the crisis script. Without the tacit, overt or confused support of the majority, the nationalist leaders could not have escalated ethnic rivalry and conflict into massive collective violence.

POSTSCRIPT

Is Ethnic Conflict Inevitable?

Although Kakar's argument draws heavily on psychology, he clearly adopts a primordialist perspective that ethnic differences are inherently threatening; such differences lead to tension and will ultimately emerge as conflict. Individuals may keep their fears and anxieties in check for a time, but preconscious fears and anxiety will eventually emerge. For Kakar, no amount of education or politically correct training will eliminate these anxieties or permanently overcome them.

Oberschall's argument accepts the reality of primordialist variables such as kinship, language, and religion as more important than did Barth in his original formulation of the circumstantialist perspective. But for Oberschall, such variables must be triggered by circumstantialist factors before they can be aroused. The Balkans case is a particularly apt one, as ethnicity in Bosnia is largely based on religious differences. All three "ethnic" communities have emerged from essentially the same pool of genetic material. The language spoken by all three groups is essentially the same language, often called Serbo-Croatian by linguists, though the Serbs use a Cyrillic alphabet and the Croats use a Roman one. The main "ethnic" differences emerge from their three different religions: Eastern Orthodox, Roman Catholic, and Islam. Religious differences in Bosnia correspond to traditional political alliances, but, as in the conflict in Northern Ireland, they are not fundamentally based on significant biological or linguistic differences. In Bosnia, unlike Northern Ireland, people of all three ethnicities had lived and worked side by side; they socialized together and had even intermarried. The primordialist variables are, in Oberschall's view, insufficient to trigger the ethnic violence and brutality that erupted in Bosnia. Ethnic violence, massacres, and ethnic cleansing could only have emerged if people in the towns and villages were manipulated into fearing their neighbors, concludes Oberschall.

Anthropologists and sociologists have long recognized that racial and ethnic tensions in the United States and other countries are linked to issues about access to jobs, land, resources, and opportunities. But it is not clear whether or not such circumstantialist variables are sufficient to explain why social conflict so often allows ethnic affiliations to become so central.

For further reading on genocide and ethnic cleansing, see Alexander L. Hinton's edited volume *Annihilating Difference: The Anthropology of Genocide* (University of California Press, 2002). For another view on ethnic conflict in India, see Ashutosh Varshney's *Ethnic Conflict and Civic Life: Hindus and Muslims in India* (Yale University Press, 2002). For a recent perspective about ethnicity, see André Burguière and Raymond Grew's edited volume *The Construction of*

Minorities: Cases for Comparison Across Time and Around the World (University of Michigan Press, 2001). For more circumstantialist discussions of ethnic conflict, see Jack Eller's *From Culture to Ethnicity to Conflict* (University of Michigan Press, 1999) and *The Myth of "Ethnic Conflict": Politics, Economics, and "Cultural" Violence,* edited by Beverly Crawford and Ronnie D. Lipschutz (International Area Studies, University of California at Berkeley, 1998).

Internet References . . .

American Anthropological Association Code of Ethics

Created by the American Anthropological Association, the largest organization of anthropologists in the world, this American Anthropological Association Code of Ethics Web site provides a code of ethics for its members and a handbook on ethical issues faced by anthropologists.

http://www.aaanet.org/committees/ethics/
ethcode.html

Kennewick Man

This site contains an article on the controversy following the discovery of the bones of a 8,400-year-old man, now called Kennewick Man. The article discusses whether the bones, which do not appear to be Native American, should be protected under the Native American Graves Protection and Repatriation Act (NAGPRA) and therefore be reburied. Links are provided to previous articles, which give further information from both sides of the debate on Kennewick Man.

http://www.archaeology.org/9701/etc/
specialreport.html

The Yanomamö

Created by Brian Schwimmer, the first Yanomamö (also spelled *Yanomami*) Web site listed explores intergroup relations, alliances, and the role of warfare among the Yanomamö. The next two Web sites provide links to photos of the Yanomamö and pages that deal with aspects of change in these communities.

http://www.umanitoba.ca/faculties/arts/anthropology/
tutor/case_studies/yanomamo/

http://www.geocities.com/Athens/Academy/9118/
yanomami.html

http://www.trinity.wa.edu.au/plduffyrc/subjects/
sose/geography/respop/yano.htm

Exhibitions at the Smithsonian: National Museum of the American Indian

This Web site of the National Museum of the American Indian was created by the Smithsonian Institution and provides images of current and recent exhibits about Native American art and society. The links provided on this site allow students to evaluate how this museum represents the Native American community.

http://www.nmai.si.edu/subpage.cfm?subpage=
exhibitions&second=online

Ethics in Anthropology

*T*he ethical treatment of other peoples has come to play an increasingly important role in contemporary anthropology. Ethical issues directly affect how cultural anthropologists should treat their living human subjects. But similar issues also affect archaeologists and biological anthropologists because the artifacts of past communities often represent the ancestors of living communities. Here the interests of anthropologists and native peoples diverge, and we ask whether such bones should be reburied to respect the dead or if they should be studied for science. Similarly, we may ask what the ethical responsibilites of Western anthropologists should be when they find certain cultural practices abhorrent or unjust. Should anthropologists work to change these practices? All of these issues raise questions about how involved anthropologists should become with the peoples with whom they work. Should anthropologists take a passive, objective, and even scientific position or should they use what they know to support or change these native communities?

- Should the Remains of Prehistoric Native Americans Be Reburied Rather Than Studied?

- Did Napolean Chagnon's Research Methods and Publications Harm the Yanomami Indians?

- Do Museums Misrepresent Ethnic Communities Around the World?

ISSUE 17

Should the Remains of Prehistoric Native Americans Be Reburied Rather Than Studied?

YES: James Riding In, from "Repatriation: A Pawnee's Perspective," *American Indian Quarterly* (Spring 1996)

NO: Clement W. Meighan, from "Some Scholars' Views on Reburial," *American Antiquity* (October 1992)

ISSUE SUMMARY

YES: Assistant professor of justice studies and member of the Pawnee tribe James Riding In argues that holding Native American skeletons in museums and other repositories represents a sacrilege against Native American dead and, thus, all Indian remains should be reburied.

NO: Professor of anthropology and archaeologist Clement W. Meighan believes that archaeologists have a moral and professional obligation to the archaeological data with which they work. Such data are held in the public good and must be protected from destruction, he concludes.

From the beginning, the relationship between Native Americans and anthropologists in the United States has been an uncertain one, ranging from mutually cooperative to overtly hostile in which Native Americans deeply mistrust anthropologists and feel that Native American culture is exploited.

Native American activists have invoked concerns about religious freedom, arguing that the excavation of bones is a desecration, a violation of native rights, and a sacrilege against Native American religion. These individuals and organizations demanded the immediate return and reburial of all Native American skeletons currently held in public museums and other repositories. They objected both to the exhibition of the remains and to research on remains by physical anthropologists. Many Native Americans have pointed out that the same museums that exhibit Native American skeletons do not simultaneously display the bones of white Americans.

Responding to the concerns of Native Americans, in 1990 the U.S. Congress enacted the Native American Graves Protection and Registration Act (NAGPRA), which mandates that all public collections of Native American remains must be returned to relatives or descendants for reburial. The return of bones and material culture has come to be called "repatriation."

James Riding In, himself a Pawnee, argues that anthropologists and archaeologists have consistently desecrated graves by excavating and studying the bones of Native Americans. He begins his discussion by outlining the history of many public museum collections of Native American skulls. Many of these, he maintains, were war dead from the Indian Wars of the 1870s, and they should have been reburied on the spot. Riding In says that Native Americans believe that the bodies of the dead must be reunited with "Mother Earth."

Clement W. Meighan counters that the debate over what should be done with bones from archaeological excavations is a conflict between science and religion. In the case of very early prehistoric sites, there is usually no evidence that links living tribes inhabiting the surrounding areas with the early community; many of these groups would either be unrelated to living tribal members or might even be the remains of enemy groups.

For Meighan the requirements of science must be defended, and the unraveling of humankind's prehistory in the New World is of public interest to all Americans, whether Native or not. He contends that the public's right to know about the past is important, and any reburial of archaeological material represents the destruction of scientific data that can never be recovered. Arguing that political motives are at the heart of Native American claims to religious interest in archaeological remains, Meighan views reburial as an attempt to censor archaeological and anthropological findings that conflict with Native American legends and myths.

Although NAGPRA has been the official law of the land for a decade, there remain many contentious concerns about just which bones should be repatriated and how they should be treated both legally and professionally. Riding In and Meighan raise a number of questions about the interests of science and Native American religions. Are Native American religious beliefs more important than those of secular scientists? Do archaeologists desecrate Native American sacred sites whenever they excavate? Should the religious concerns of one ethnic or cultural community override either the professional concerns of another group or the intellectual rights of the general public? Who should control information about the past? Who should control depictions of any ethnic group's past?

YES ⤶

James Riding In

Repatriation: A Pawnee's Perspective

My opposition to scientific grave looting developed partially through the birth of the American Indian repatriation movement during the late 1960s. Like other American Indians of the time (and now), I viewed archaeology as an oppressive and sacrilegious profession that claimed ownership over many of our deceased relatives, suppressed our religious freedom, and denied our ancestors a lasting burial. My first encounter with an archaeologist occurred at a party in New Mexico in the late 1970s. After hearing him rant incessantly about the knowledge he had obtained by studying Indian remains, burial offerings, and cemeteries, I suggested that if he wanted to serve Indians he should spend his time excavating latrines and leave the graves alone. Of course, he took umbrage at the tone of my suggestion, and broke off the conversation. While studying history at the University of California, Los Angeles [UCLA] in the mid-1980s, I became committed to pursuing the goals of the repatriation movement, which was gaining momentum. Like other reburial proponents, I advocated the reburial of all Indian remains warehoused across the nation in museums, universities, and federal agencies. I also promoted the extension or enactment of laws to protect Indian cemeteries from grave looters, including archaeologists.

While working to elevate the consciousness of the UCLA campus about the troubled relationship between archaeologists and Indians, a few of us, including students, staff, faculty, and community members, took advantage of opportunities to engage in dialogue with the anti-repatriation forces. During these exchanges, tempers on both sides often flared. Basically, the archaeologists were functioning on metaphysical and intellectual planes that differed from ours. We saw their professional activities as sacrilege and destructive, while they professed a legal and scientific right to study Indian remains and burial goods. We wanted the university to voluntarily return the human remains in its collections to the next-of-kin for proper reburial. They desired to protect excavation, research, and curatorial practices. Asserting profound respect for Indian concerns, beliefs, and values, members of the archaeology group offered a host of patronizing excuses for refusing to endorse our calls for repatriation. In this sense, the UCLA struggle mirrored the conflict over human remains ensuing throughout much of the country. In 1989, as the UCLA battle ensued, I accepted an offer to assist the Pawnee government in its efforts as a sovereign nation to reclaim the remains of its ancestors held at the

Smithsonian Institution. Being a citizen of this small and impoverished nation of Indians, I welcomed the opportunity to join other Pawnee activists in the repatriation quest. Earlier that year, Congress had enacted a repatriation bill that provided a legal mechanism for Indian governments to reclaim ancestral remains and burial offerings held at the Smithsonian.

Despite the law, obdurate Smithsonian personnel sought to frustrate Indian repatriation efforts with such tactics as stonewalling, deceit, and misinformation. Although Smithsonian personnel claimed that the true identities of six skulls classified as Pawnee could not be positively established, subsequent research on my part uncovered a preponderance of evidence confirming the authenticity of the accession records. This research also showed that, after U.S. soldiers and Kansas settlers had massacred a party of Pawnee men who had been recently discharged from the U.S. army, a Fort Harker surgeon had collected some of the victims' skulls in compliance with army policy and shipped them to the Army Medical Museum for craniometric study.

Since that report, I have written articles, given presentations, and, in conjunction with others, conducted research on behalf of Pawnee repatriation initiatives at Chicago's Field Museum of Natural History. I also have written a report from information found in the Native American Graves Protection and Repatriation Act (NAGPRA) summary letters showing the location of additional Pawnee remains, sacred objects, objects of cultural patrimony, and cultural artifacts.

This essay offers some of my views concerning the reburial aspect of the repatriation struggle. It seeks to show the intellectual and spiritual foundations behind the movement as a means for understanding the complexity of the controversy. It also attempts to demonstrate how repatriation advocates managed to effect discriminatory laws and practices. Finally, it conveys a message that, although old attitudes continue to function within the archaeology and museum communities, a concerted effort brought to bear by people who espouse cooperative relations is in place to bring Indian spiritual beliefs in conformity with non-Indian secular values.

At another level, I write with the intent of creating awareness about a pressing need to disestablish racial, institutional, and societal barriers that impede this country's movement toward a place that celebrates cultural diversity as a cherished and indispensable component of its social, political, and economic fabric. Despite the tone of skepticism, caution, and pessimism found within this study, I envision a society where people can interact freely, respecting one another without regard to race, color, ethnicity, or religious creed. Before this dream becomes a reality, however, America has to find ways to dissolve its racial, gender, cultural, and class barriers.

Pawnee Beliefs, Critical Scholarship, and Oppression

The acts committed against deceased Indians have had profound, even harmful, effects on the living. Therefore, as an activist and historian, I have had to develop a conceptual framework for giving meaning and order to the conflict.

The foundation of my perspective concerning repatriation is derived from a combination of cultural, personal, and academic experiences. An understanding of Pawnee religious and philosophical beliefs about death, gained through oral tradition, dreams, and research, informs my view that repatriation is a social justice movement, supported by native spirituality and sovereignty, committed to the amelioration of the twin evils of oppression and scientific racism. Yet, I am neither a religious fundamentalist nor a left- or right-wing reactionary. Concerning repatriation, I simply advocate that American Indians receive what virtually every other group of Americans enjoys; that is, the right to religious freedom and a lasting burial.

My training as critical scholar provides another cornerstone of my beliefs about the nature of "imperial archaeology." My writings cast the legacy of scientific body snatching within the realm of oppression. Oppression occurs when a set or sets of individuals within the dominant population behave in ways that infringe on the beliefs, cultures, and political structures of other groups of people. Acts of stealing bodies, infringing on spirituality, and resisting repatriation efforts represent classic examples of oppression.

Although exposed to years of secular interpretations about the nature of the world and the significance of archaeology for understanding the past through formal Euroamerican education, I have continued to accept Pawnee beliefs about the afterlife. To adopt any other perspective regarding this matter would deny my cultural heritage. I cannot reconcile archaeology with tradition because of the secular orientation of the former as well as its intrusive practices. Unlike archaeologists who see Native remains as specimens for study, my people view the bodies of deceased loved ones as representing human life with sacred qualities. Death merely marks the passage of the human spirit to another state of being. In a 1988 statement, then Pawnee President Lawrence Goodfox Jr. expressed a common perspective stressing the negative consequences of grave desecration on our dead: "When our people die and go on to the spirit world, sacred rituals and ceremonies are performed. We believe that if the body is disturbed, the spirit becomes restless and cannot be at peace."

Wandering spirits often beset the living with psychological and health problems. Since time immemorial, Pawnees have ceremoniously buried our dead within Mother Earth. Disinterment can occur only for a compelling religious reason. Equally critical to our perspective are cultural norms that stressed that those who tampered with the dead did so with profane, evil, or demented intentions. From this vantage point, the study of stolen remains constitutes abominable acts of sacrilege, desecration, and depravity. But racist attitudes, complete with such axioms as "The only good Indian is a dead Indian," have long conditioned white society to view Indians (as other nonwhites) as intellectually inferior subhumans who lacked a right to equal treatment under legal and moral codes. Complicating matters, value judgments about the alleged superiority of the white race became interlocked with scientific thought, leading to the development of oppressive practices and policies.

Consequently, orgies of grave looting occurred without remorse. After the Pawnees removed from Nebraska to Oklahoma during the 1870s, local settlers, followed by amateur and professional archaeologists, looted virtually every Pawnee cemetery they could find, taking remains and burial offerings. Much of the "booty" was placed in an array of institutions including the Nebraska State Historical Society (NSHS) and the Smithsonian Institution.

We have a right to be angry at those who dug our dead from the ground, those who established and maintained curatorial policies, and those who denied our repatriation requests. Last year, my elderly grandmother chastised white society in her typically reserved, but direct fashion for its treatment of our dead. After pointing to an Oklahoma bluff where many Pawnee relatives are buried, she declared, "It is not right, that they dug up all of those bodies in Nebraska." What she referred to can be labeled a spiritual holocaust. When anyone denies us our fundamental human rights, we cannot sit idly by and wait for America to reform itself. It will never happen. We have a duty not only to ourselves, but also to our relatives, our unborn generations, and our ancestors to act. Concerning repatriation, we had no choice but to work for retrieval of our ancestral remains for proper reburial and for legislation that provided penalties for those who disrupted the graves of our relatives.

Yet our initiatives sought redress in a peaceful manner. In 1988, Lawrence Goodfox expressed our goals, declaring "All we want is [the] reburial of the remains of our ancestors and to let them finally rest in peace and for all people in Nebraska to refrain from, forever, any excavation of any Native American graves or burial sites." In our view, reburying the disturbed spirits within Mother Earth equalizes the imbalance between the spiritual and physical worlds caused by the desecration.

National Challenges to Imperial Archaeology and Oppression

The Pawnee reburial struggle occurred within the context of a worldwide indigenous movement. What beset my people had affected Natives everywhere. In this country, few Indian nations escaped the piercing blades of the archaeologists' shovels or the slashes of the headhunters' knives. These operations infringed on Indian beliefs, burial rights, and sovereignty. The notion that this type of research had validity was so ingrained in the psyche of many non-Indians that rarely did anyone question the morality, ethics, or legality of these practices; that is, until the repatriation movement surfaced in the late 1960s. This movement stands on a paramount footing with the valiant struggles of African-Americans for civil rights and women for equality. Taking a leading role during the early stages of the repatriation movement, organizations such as the American Indian Movement (AIM), International Indian Treaty Council, and American Indians Against Desecration (AIAD) expressed in dramatic fashion Indian concerns about the excesses of archaeology and oppression. Committed to the causes of reburying all disinterred Indians and stopping grave disruptions, these groups often employed confrontational strategies. Near Welch, Minnesota, in 1972, for example, AIM members risked arrest by disturbing a dig site. In addition to burning field notes and tools, they confiscated unearthed artifacts and exposed photographic film. Throughout the 1970s and 1980s, AIAD challenged the human remains collections and curatorial policies of government agencies, museums, and universities. As time progressed, many college campuses saw a dramatic increase in tensions between Indians and archaeologists. These actions catapulted the repatriation movement into the consciousness of sympathetic politicians, newspaper editors, and members of the general public. Increased knowledge of the issues subsequently spawned unprecedented levels of non-Indian backing of repatriation.

As the 1980s progressed, more conciliatory Indians, often coming from the professions of law and politics, surfaced as leading figures in the movement. Unlike the universal reburial advocates, these moderates tended to see compromise as the most expedient means available to acquire the desired legislation. They often sought a balance between scientific study of Native remains and the need for Indians to gain religious, burial, and repatriation rights under the law. Organizations such as the National Congress of American Indians and the Native American Rights Fund espoused the moderate cause. Realizing that public sentiments increasingly favored the Indians' views, some archaeologists and museum administrators endorsed compromise as a means of cutting their losses and saving face. With common ground beneath their feet, individuals and organizations waged a series of intense political battles at the state and federal levels.

With moderates in control, reform transpired relatively swiftly. By 1992, more than thirty states had placed laws on the books extending protection to Indian cemeteries, including several with repatriation provisions. Congress passed two pieces of legislation, the National Museum of the American Indian Act in 1989 and NAGPRA the following year. Collectively, these national laws provided Indian nations a means to obtain human remains linked to them by a "preponderance of evidence" and associated funerary offerings held by institutions that received federal funding. NAGPRA also provides penalties for individuals convicted of trafficking in human remains.

Ongoing Reburial Initiatives

With legal avenues now open for Indian governments to reclaim stolen ancestral remains and associated burial objects, some of the old repressive policies fell by the wayside. The change enabled relatives to begin the task of reclaiming stolen bodies and grave offerings for reburial. Collectively, Indian nations thus far have interred thousands of stolen remains. To date (summer 1995), the Pawnees alone have placed nearly a thousand bodies back in Mother Earth. The total number of recovered bodies will surely reach the tens of thousands within a few years.

Reinterment ceremonies, along with funeral feasts, evoke a gamut of emotional expressions ranging from sorrow to joy. When conducting reburials, people rejoice at the fact that the repatriated remains are finally being returned to Mother Earth, but, like modern funerals, an air of sadness pervades the ceremonies. In particular, reinterring the remains of young children causes grieving and weeping. Mourning is part of the healing process in that reburials seek to restore harmony between the living and dead by putting restless spirits to rest. At another level, reburials bring closure to bitterly contested struggles.

Future Concerns

Legislation emanating from the repatriation movement has changed the customary ways that archaeologists and museums operate. Most notably, Indian governments now have established a sovereign right to reclaim the bodies of their ancestors from offending museums, universities, and federal agencies. In this capacity, they have the power to grant and deny access to their dead. Additionally, the new laws make face-to-face interaction routine between museums and Indian nations in certain repatriation matters. Several observers have proclaimed that the common ground signals the dawning of a new era of cooperative relations between Indians and museums. Despite changing attitudes and practices, it is too soon to assess the long-term ramifications of the reburial controversy. Six problematic areas cause me concern about the future of repatriation:

First, the laws do not provide for the reinterment of ancient, unclaimed, or unidentified remains. In other words, the fate of tens of thousands of bodies, along with associated funerary offerings, is uncertain. Will those with authority take steps to provide for a proper reburial for these bodies or will they allow the continuance of old practices and policies?

Second, the absence of legislation and aggressive enforcement of burial protection laws in some states may send a message that grave looting can resume without fear of arrest, prosecution, or punishment.

Third, NAGPRA's graves protection stipulations apply only to federal lands and entities that receive federal funding. In states without both progressive reburial legislation and a substantial Indian populace, large-scale acts of grave desecration may continue. . . .

Fourth, and perhaps most significant a pervasive attitude among elements of the archaeology and museum communities keeps repressive and archaic ideas alive. In fact, members of these groups have consistently disavowed any wrongdoing by themselves and their predecessors. Rather, some present their work to the public as neutral, impartial, and objective interpretations of distant Native American cultures. To counter claims that the digging and study is disrespectful, others assert that taking remains for study shows respect for Indian people and culture. In a twisted logic, still others insist that they are the "true spiritual descendants of the original Indians and the contemporary Indians [are] foreigners who had no right to complain about their activities." Like most other repatriation advocates, I reject these pleas as condescending and duplicitous acts of misguided people and lost souls. . . .

Anti-repatriation advocates echoed a common refrain. They viewed their pursuits as being under attack by narrow-minded and anti-intellectual radicals who sought to destroy archaeology. Equating repatriation with book burning, some alarmists often charged falsely that Indians would not rest until they had stripped museums and universities of their Indian collections.

These strategies contain elements of self-delusion, arrogance, and racism. A tacit message found in these paternalistic defenses of imperial archaeology was that Indians must, for their own good, learn to respect the work of archaeology. Equally disturbing is the notion that Indians need archaeology. However, the exact opposite is true. Beneath the self-serving rhetoric lay a deceptive ambiance of cultural imperialism that masked the stark reality of how archaeology and museums infringed on Indian religion and burial rights.

Fifth, imperial archaeologists have had substantial levels of support from real and pretend Indians. The phenomena of co-optation and self-interest reverberates loudly here. Usually found working in museums, universities, and government agencies, some of these individuals claim a heritage complete with a Cherokee princess, but they embrace the secular views and values of Western science. Others belonging to this camp clearly have significant amounts of Indian blood, but they rely heavily on the goodwill of their non-Indian colleagues to promote and maintain their careers. Non-institutional advocacy surfaced from some grassroots Indians. At meetings, conferences, and confrontations, archaeologists rarely failed to produce a reservation Indian or two who spoke passionately against reburial in an effort to convince the public and policy makers that Native communities lacked unanimity on the subject. Whatever their motive, degree of Indian blood, or cultural orientation, their willingness to endorse oppressive archaeological practices marks a radical departure from traditional Indian philosophy.

Collectively, "wannabes" and misguided Indians may be able to damage reburial efforts. As the movement pushed for national repatriation legislation in the late 1980s, we found them sitting on committees convened by anthropology and museum associations that issued reports condemning repatriation. In a worst-case scenario, NAGPRA and other committees stacked with them and imperial archaeologists could conceivably frustrate or undermine repatriation requests.

Finally, it seems that archaeologists have launched a campaign to convince the public, tribal leaders, and others that skeletal investigations are necessary for a variety of reasons. According to a recent *Chronicle of Higher Education* article, "More and more of those kinds of opportunities will occur, many scholars agree, when researchers learn to persuade American Indians and others that skeletal remains and artifacts represent something other than a publication toward a faculty member's promotion and tenure." In other words, we are seeing archaeologists adopt less abrasive tactics to get their hands on our dead. Succumbing to subtle pressure, aimed at convincing us to accept a secular view of the dead as research objects, will erode a cherished part of our belief systems and cultures. In any event, some Indian nations have allowed the creation of archaeology programs on their reservations.

Clearly, the repatriation movement has won some major victories, but the war is unfinished. United States history teaches the lesson that individuals who face the threat of losing a privileged status often will devise rationalizations and strategies to resist change. Southern slave owners, for example, argued against abolitionism by making the outlandish claim that involuntary servitude was a benevolent institution that saved millions of blacks from the savagery of Africa. Historians repeated this claim well into the twentieth century.

It is conceivable that at some point someone will challenge the constitutionality of NAGPRA. If this occurs, will the courts respect Indian beliefs and burial rights? America's long history concerning issues of Indian religious freedom and political rights makes the possibility of a legal suit a scary thought. The Supreme Court has occasionally protected Indian sovereignty, as well as hunting, fishing, and water rights, but it also has incorporated such imperialistic notions as the doctrine of discovery and the plenary power doctrine into U.S. law. Its decisions also have eroded the power of Indian self-government by allowing the imposition of federal jurisdiction over certain crimes committed on Indian lands.

In recent years, conservative justices appointed by President Ronald Reagan have endangered Indian religious freedom. In *Lyng v. Northwest Indian Cemetery Protective Association* (108 S. Ct. 1319 (1988)) Justice Sandra Day O'Connor wrote the majority decision stating that the U.S. government had the right to build a road through an area on federal lands sacred to Yurok, Karok, and Tolowa Indians even if such a construction project would destroy the ability of those people to worship. In *Employment Division Department of Human Resources of Oregon v. Smith* (110 S. Ct. 1595 (1990)) the court held that a state could abridge expressions of religious freedom if the state had a compelling reason to do so. In this case, the court paved the way for states to deprive Native American Church (NAC) members of the right to use peyote in connection with their worship. Fortunately, in 1994, Congress addressed the religious crisis caused by the court by enacting a law that sanctioned peyote use for NAC services.

History demonstrates that promises made by white America to help Indians have not always materialized. The administrative branch of the federal government has entered into 371 treaties with Indian nations and systematically violated each of them. The legislative record is another cause of concern. The Indian Reorganization Act of 1934 authorized Indian nations to restructure themselves politically but only in accordance with models and terms acceptable to Department of Interior officials. During the 1970s, Congress declared that Indian government could exercise more powers of self-government. Federal bureaucratic controls over Indian governments, however, actually became more stringent, if not suffocating, in this era. During that decade, Congress also enacted the American Indian Religious Freedom Act of 1978 in a half-hearted effort to encourage federal agencies to accommodate customary Indian worship practices at off-reservation sites. The act provided virtually no protection because federal agencies and the Supreme Court, as we have seen, have followed a tradition that sees nothing wrong with suppressing Indian religious freedom. Although Indians are pursing a legislative remedy to resolve these problems, Congress has yet to enact a true religious freedom law for them.

Conclusion

Facing overwhelming odds, the repatriation movement has achieved many noteworthy successes. United States society, including a growing number of sympathetic archaeologists and museum curators, has finally recognized that Indians are not disappearing, and that Indians are entitled to burial rights and religious freedom. Nevertheless, under the new repatriation laws, many non-Indian entities still "legally" hold thousands of Indians remains and burial offerings. With many archaeologists and museum curators committed to upholding oppressive operational principles, values, and beliefs, the fate of these bodies remains in question. Moreover, others, perhaps best described as wolves in sheeps' clothing, are seeking to gain our cooperation, a euphemism meaning the delivery of another blow to our revered philosophies about the dead.

Given the durability of imperialist archaeology and the new approaches being used to gain access to the remains of our beloved ancestors, we must remain vigilant and monitor their operations. Protecting our dead must remain a moral and spiritual obligation we cannot callously abandon for we cannot allow further erosions of our beliefs and traditions. Thus a need still exists for maintaining the cultural traditions that inspired the repatriation movement.

Clement W. Meighan

 NO

Some Scholars' Views on Reburial

[T]here is something inherently distasteful and unseemly in secreting either the fruits or seeds of scientific endeavors.

— Judge Bruce S. Jenkins

Destruction of archaelogical collections through the demands for reburial presents a serious conflict between religion and science. Archaeologists should not deal with these matters by "compromise" alone, but must sustain their rights and duties as scholars.

The above quotation is from a court case having nothing to do with archaeology, yet if we believe that archaeology is a scientific endeavor we must agree that this statement applies to archaeology as well as medicine, chemistry, or other fields of scholarship. The recent increased attention given to the ethics of scientists and scientific organizations, with news accounts almost weekly in such journals as *Science,* requires archaeologists to examine their basic assumptions about the nature of science and their obligations to scholarship. This is brought forward most forcefully in the debate over the past 20 years about the problems of reburial of archaeological and museum collections.

The discussion by Goldstein and Kintigh (1990) is a valiant effort to unravel some of the strands of conflict inherent in the controversy over the destruction of museum collections in the name of Indian religious beliefs. They seek some sort of middle ground in which scholarly and ethnic concerns can coexist in a constructive way. However, in view of the massive losses of scientific data now legislated by the federal government and some of the states, it needs to be made clear that many archaeologists do not agree with some aspects of the philosophical position taken by Goldstein and Kintigh. In particular, their statement that "We must change the way we do business" (Goldstein and Kintigh 1990:589) is not justified, particularly since their suggestions for change involve the abandonment of scholarly imperatives and the adoption of an "ethical" position that accepts the right of nonscholars to demand the destruction of archaeological evidence and the concealment of archaeological data. Of course, changes in the way archaeology is done will inevitably take place, for both internal (professional) and external (social/legal) reasons. This does not mean that the basic rules of scholarly obligations to one's data should change as well.

From *American Antiquity*, vol. 57, no. 4, October 1992, pp. 704–710. Copyright © 1992 by Society for American Archaeology. Reprinted by permission.

Goldstein and Kintigh fall into the anthropological trap of cultural relativism. In asserting that we must balance our concerns for knowledge with "our professional ethic of cultural relativism," they argue that our values are not the only values or ethics, but only one legitimate belief system. The implication is that all belief systems are of equal legitimacy, therefore one cannot make a clear commitment to any particular values as a guide to action. However, most individuals do make a commitment to the values that will guide their personal action. Recognizing that other people may have other values does not mean that one must accept those values or compromise his/her own ethical standards. Indeed, the dictionary has a word for believing one way and acting another—it is "hypocrisy."

Those who affiliate with organized groups, whether the Church of the Rising Light or the Society for American Archaeology (SAA), supposedly accept the beliefs and goals of the organization as stated in their by-laws or scriptures. The SAA, as an organization dedicated to scholarly research in archaeology, is bound by the general rules of scholarship that require *honest reporting and preservation of the evidence.* If the research data are subject to censorship, how can there be honest reporting? If the evidence (collections) is not preserved, who can challenge the statements of the researcher? Who can check for misinterpretations, inaccuracies, or bias? Once the collection is destroyed, we have only an affidavit from the researcher; we can believe it or not, but there is no way that additional investigation or new laboratory techniques can be applied to the collection to gain a better understanding of the evidence. The astounding new methods for medical and genetic research on ancient populations require a piece of the bone—pictures and notes won't do. Similarly, laboratory advances in dating and determining the source of artifact materials require that the relevant objects be available for study. Since we commonly proclaim that archaeological collections are unique and irreplaceable, how can we ever justify the conscious and acquiescent destruction of our data?

The suggestion of Goldstein and Kintigh that we balance our own values with the professional ethic of cultural relativism by "compromise and mutual respect" is not realistic. Many archaeologists are not going to compromise away their most fundamental scholarly beliefs. Similarly, many Indian activists are not going to compromise away their beliefs (however unsupported by evidence) that every Indian bone of the past 12,000 years belongs to one of their ancestors. There are some instances in which compromise and mutual respect have led to satisfactory results for both sides; there are many more instances in which these valued qualities have been insufficient to prevent or postpone destruction of important archaeological finds.

Those who want to do away with archaeology and archaeological collections are of course entitled to their beliefs, and they are also entitled to use whatever political and legal machinery they can to bring about their stated goals. Originally, the goals were modest, but they have escalated every year since this discussion began more than 20 years ago, as reviewed by me in an earlier article (Meighan 1984). The present-day goals have repeatedly been made clear. For example, Christopher Quayle, an attorney for the Three Affiliated Tribes, stated in *Harpers* (Preston 1989:68–69): "It's conceivable that some time in the not-so-distant future there won't be a single Indian skeleton in any museum in the country. We're going to put them out of business." The "them" refers in this statement to physical anthropologists, but it is also extended to archaeologists. For example, the recent agreement between state officials in West Virginia and a committee representing Indian viewpoints (a committee which, incidentally, includes non-Indians) states that everything in an ongoing study of a 2,000-year-old Adena mound must be given up for reburial within a year—"everything" includes not only the bones of the mythical "ancestors" of the claimants, but also all the artifacts, the chipping waste, the food refuse, the pollen samples, the soil samples, and whatever else may be removed for purposes of scientific study. While the tax-payers are expected to pay for a 1.8-million-dollar excavation on the grounds that it is in the public interest for archaeological data to be preserved, *nothing* of the tangible archaeological evidence is to be preserved. Meanwhile, Indian activists are paid to "monitor" the excavation, and they were given the right to censor the final report and prevent any objectionable photographs or data from appearing.

If there is any doubt about the goals of the anti-archaeology contingent, consider the case of Dr. David Van Horn, charged with a felony in California for conducting an environmental impact study required by law, and being honest enough to report what he found in the site, including some small bits of cremated bone, which required hours of study by physical anthropologists to identify as human. Is the reporting of a legally mandated salvage excavation a felony? It can be in California, and there are many who would like to make archaeology a crime throughout the United States. Archaeologists who accept these situations or treat them as merely local concerns (apparently the position of most scholarly organizations including the SAA), have not just compromised, they have abandoned scholarly ethics in favor of being "respectful and sensitive" to nonscholars and anti-intellectuals. When the current round of controversy is over, this loss of scientific integrity will be heavily condemned.

So there are some situations in which compromise is not necessarily the best approach, and this is one of them. Archaeologists may well be legislated out of business, and museums may well lose all their American Indian collections, and indeed the Indians have been far more successful than the archaeologists in the political arena. Many archaeologists believe, however, that this should not occur with the happy connivance of the scholarly profession of archaeology. Over 600 of them are members of the American Committee for Preservation of Archaeological Collections (ACPAC), which has argued for over 10 years that archaeology is a legitimate, moral, and even useful profession, and that collections that were legally made should remain in museums as an important part of the heritage of the nation. Bahn may have had this group in mind in his news report on the "first international congress on the reburial of human remains," in his reference to "the extremists, who unfortunately did not attend the congress to put the case for rejecting the whole notion of reburial." Who are these extremists? Neither ACPAC nor any individual known to me has stated that no reburial of any kind should take place; everyone agrees that bones of known relatives should be returned to demonstrable descendants. The disagreement is over remains to which no living person can demonstrate any relationship. Museum materials 5,000 years old are claimed by people who imagine themselves to be somehow related to the collections in question, but such a belief has no basis in evidence and is mysticism. Indeed, it is not unlikely that Indians who have acquired such collections for reburial are venerating the bones of alien groups and traditional enemies rather than distant relatives.

If the present attacks on archaeological data were happening in engineering, medicine, or chemistry, they would not be accepted by the general public since destruction or concealment of the facts in those areas of scientific knowledge can lead to disastrous results for many living people. The general lack of public concern about the attack on archaeology arises from the perception that archaeological conclusions really do not matter—if someone's reconstruction of the ancient past is ridiculous or unsupported by evidence, who cares? It will not affect the daily lives of anyone now alive, no matter what we believe about what happened thousands of years ago. However, the principles of scholarship and scientific evidence are the same in all scholarly research, including archaeology and anthropology, and credibility of conclusions is an essential consideration for any field of scholarship, whether or not there are immediate practical effects of the conclusions that are reached.

In one of the polemics put forward by Indian spokesmen in the student newspaper at the University of California (Los Angeles), those of us on the archaeological faculty were accused of participating in an activity that was comparable to the "killing fields of Cambodia." Even allowing for the juvenile rhetoric characteristic of student newspapers, I was dumbfounded at such a statement. How could I harm any person who had already been dead for thousands of years? How could anything that my studies did with the bones of these ancient people harm any living person? The condemnation seems extreme for a "crime" that is merely a failure to invite mythical descendants to control my research and destroy museum collections held in the public interest. When issues of respect and sensitivity are raised, it needs to be pointed out that these work both ways.

Some Legal Issues: Constitutional Requirements

The first amendment states that Congress shall make no laws respecting an establishment of religion. Most state constitutions have similar clauses; that of California says the state will *never* pass such laws. Yet California, other states, and the federal government have numerous laws on the books that are specifically written to favor aboriginal tribal religious beliefs and compel others to act in accordance with them. Religious infringement also occurs when archaeologists are excluded from evaluating claims regarding repatriation because they do not hold particular religious beliefs. Until these statutes are challenged and overturned, they remain an opening for other groups to seek similar legislation making their religious beliefs enforceable by law. Creationists, for example, have been trying for over 60 years to outlaw the teaching of evolution because it is in conflict with their religious tenets.

That there is a science vs. religion aspect is clear in the religious justification for the claiming of bones and "sacred" artifacts, as well as the proclamation of many activists that archaeologists and museums are committing sacrilege in obtaining, storing, and studying archaeological remains. I discuss bone worship elsewhere (Meighan 1990). Tonetti (1990) provides a case study of the situation in Ohio, documenting the religious roots of the anti-archaeology movement. He also reports a survey of Ohio legislators that reveals a frightening ignorance of science in general and archaeology in particular: "As Zimmerman so dramatically stated in his op ed piece in the Columbus Dispatch, he does not want the General Assembly making law dealing with science issues when over 75% do not know what his 5 year old son has known for years—that dinosaurs and humans did not coexist" (Zimmerman [1989], as quoted in Tonetti [1990:22]; recent news reports state that some Indians are now claiming dinosaur bones recovered by paleontologists).

Some Legal Issues: Cultural-Resource Laws

There is a serious conflict between the laws mandating return and destruction of archaeological material (not just bones but also artifacts and anything deemed "ceremonial" by the claimants), and those laws mandating cultural-resource management and the study and conservation of archaeological sites and remains. The Van Horn case previously mentioned put Van Horn in the position of doing an environmental-impact report required by law, only to find himself spending thousands of dollars defending himself against a felony charge for violating laws based on Indian religious beliefs about cremated bones. The judge agreed with defense witnesses that there was no basis for a trial, but the state made its point that archaeologists will be heavily punished if "Indians" request it, regardless of the validity of their complaint.

The legal dichotomy between science and religion as it pertains to archaeology may be related, as Goldstein and Kintigh (1990:589) point out, to the fact that public perception does not include Indian history as part of the history of the United States, even though they recognize that public policy and law include the non-European past as an integral part of the history of the nation. That part of American history that is Indian history is largely the contribution of archaeology; *all* of it prior to 1492 is the contribution of archaeology. This has been recognized and supported by the government since the Antiquities Act of 1906, and it is the basis for all the environmental-impact laws dealing with archaeological remains.

Many opponents of archaeological-resource laws believe that since archaeology has no effect on public health or safety, it ought to be excluded from environmental impact laws. They are given considerable ammunition by laws that state that it is in the public interest to spend a lot of money to get archaeological materials, and then state that such materials are not worth preservation but are to be reburied as soon as possible after they are dug up, in some cases within a few days or weeks of the fieldwork. Further, the belief that archaeology belongs to Indians removes it from the heritage of all of the citizens and makes it less likely that the public will be interested in supporting

activities not seen to be in the broad public interest. In these times of stringent budgets, it is hard enough to convince the taxpayers that they should
finance archaeological excavations without having to convince them that they
should also finance the reburial of the items recovered.

There are major negative results for archaeology in the present situation
where not only the federal government, but states, counties, cities, and a plethora
of political agencies believe that they should pass regulations controlling archaeological research. These laws and regulations conflict with one another and vary
from jurisdiction to jurisdiction. In some states the conduct of archaeological
research is a risky business. The smart archaeologist in California does not find
certain things. If they are found, they are either thrown away or not mentioned in
his/her reports. Field classes are also careful not to expose students or teachers to
criminal charges, meaning that students in those classes will never expose a burial
or deal with any "controversial" finds. Chipping waste is still a safe area for study.

This chilling effect on research is creating an underground archaeology
of ill-trained students, dishonest researchers, and intimidated teachers who
are afraid to show a picture of a burial to their classes, let alone an actual
human bone. Students, who are often more perceptive than their professors,
rapidly catch on and change their major or move their archaeological interests
to parts of the world where they will be allowed to practice their scholarly
profession. There is an increasing loss to American archaeology, and of course
to the Indians whose history is dependent on it.

Some Museum Issues

A negative effect of the ongoing shift to tribalism and the right of anyone to
claim anything in museums is already happening. In the past, most of the support for museums came from private donors, who contributed not only money
but collections. Donors of collections had the tacit (and sometimes written)
agreement that their materials would be preserved in the public interest. Who
would contribute anything to a museum if they thought the museum was
going to give their material away for reburial or destruction? When even Stanford University and other respected repositories of scientific collections decide
that their first obligation is to whatever Indian claimant comes along, the
donor who wants his/her material *preserved* will seek a repository in a state or
country that is dedicated to that aim. It is a paradox that the National Park Service is busily developing new standards of curation for government collections
at the same time the new National Museum of the American Indian is declaring that it will not keep anything that Indian claimants declare that they want.

Reviewers of this article believe that only a very small part of archaeological collections will be taken away from museums and archaeologists. This
is a pious hope in view of the escalation of claims previously noted, reaching the
apex in the West Virginia case in which *everything* recovered by archaeologists
is to be given up for reburial. There are numerous cases in which archaeologists
or museum employees have given up entire collections rather than negotiate
with Indian claimants; for example, one prominent California case (the Encino
excavation) included reburial of a number of dog skeletons, not required by

any statute. It is true that the Smithsonian and some other museums now have committees to evaluate claims against their collections; perhaps these will protect scholarly and public interests, but it remains to be seen whether they can withstand the political pressures brought to bear. While I am sure that not all collections will entirely disappear, under current legislation all physical remains, all mortuary associations, and all items claimed to have religious or ceremonial significance are at risk—these are the major sources of information in many archaeological studies. When claimants can get museum specimens merely by using the word "sacred," it should be apparent that anything can be claimed by someone. It does happen, it has happened, and scholars can only hope that it will not happen in the future.

Conclusions

When scholarly classes in United States archaeology and ethnology are no longer taught in academic departments (they are diminishing rapidly), when the existing collections have been selectively destroyed or concealed, and when all new field archaeology in the United States is a political exercise rather than a scientific investigation, will the world be a better place? Certainly the leadership in archaeological research, which has been characteristic of the last 50 years of American archaeology, will be lost, and it will be left to other nations to make future advances in archaeological methods, techniques, and scholarly investigations into the ancient past.

One reviewer of this paper commented that I am engaged in a "futile attempt to resurrect a bankrupt status quo." In this view, not only can nothing be done to improve the present situation, but nothing *should* be done, and we should all meekly accept the regulations, limitations, and restrictions of academic freedom that are brought forward by politicians and pressure groups. For the last 20 years, those who have attempted to change these restrictions in favor of scholarly ethics and the preservation of collections have been dismissed as a small group of outmoded discontents who cannot adapt to a changing world. This is a mistake; I may represent a minority view, but it is not confined to a small number and is growing rapidly as archaeologists see more and more of their basic data destroyed through reburial. ACPAC's 600 members (in 44 states) include a sizeable fraction of the leading archaeologists in the United States as well as physical anthropologists, museum workers, and yes, Indians.

I am, however, triggered by the accusation that my comments lead to nothing but intransigence to offer a few suggestions for action other than "compromise," which so far has mostly meant giving in to political demands. My suggestions:

1. Archaeologists negotiating with Indians or other groups should make an effort to be sure that *all* factions of the affected group are heard, not merely the group of activists who are first in the door. Many archaeologists have been doing this for years, and nearly all of us can report that we had little difficulty in finding Indians who would work with us in a mutually agreeable and often rewarding

relationship that respected Indian interests but at the same time preserved the archaeological collections. Unfortunately, numerous instances can be cited of savage personal attacks on those Indians who agreed to share the archaeologists' task, with attempts to force the archaeologist to use other consultants and claims that the one chosen was not a real Indian (see an example in Tonetti [1990:21]). When money is involved, this is probably inevitable. However, there is no reason for archaeologists to be controlled by enemies of their discipline when they can work with friends. The existence of Indian physical anthropologists, archaeologists, and museum workers, as well as the increasing number of Indian-owned museums with scientific objectives and high standards of curation, should offer opportunities for real collaboration that do not require the destruction of evidence nor the censorship of scientific reporting.

2. Professional organizations should work to amend the legislation dealing with archaeology to get a time cut-off inserted: Remains older than a certain age should not be subject to reburial. The present laws, which ignore time and assume that everything, regardless of age, is directly related to living people, are not scientifically valid, and the scientific organizations are in a position to make this clear, if necessary in court. The recent reburial of an Idaho skeleton dated at 10,600 years ago should never have happened, but as reported by the State Historic Preservation Office of that state, Idaho law requires *no* demonstration of any relationship between Indians and archaeological remains.

3. Professional organizations should point out the disagreements between "preservation" laws and "religion" laws and should try to strengthen the former and eliminate the conflicts. If they are unable to resolve the issue by negotiation, they should support court cases that address the matter.

4. If scholarly organizations are unwilling or unable to make a clear statement of their position with respect to the giving up of archaeological collections and data, it is left to the individual archaeologist to decide his or her own professional ethics in this matter. A clear review of the moral issues is given by Del Bene (1990). This should be considered, particularly by young archaeologists entering the profession, so that they are consciously aware of the decisions they are making and the consequences for their professional future.

References

Del Bene, T.A. 1990. Take the Moral Ground: An Essay on the "Reburial" Issue. *West Virginia Archeologist* 42(2):11–19.

Goldstein, L., and K. Kintigh. 1990. Ethics and the Reburial Controversy. *American Antiquity* 55:585–591.

Meighan, C.W. 1984. Archaeology: Science or Sacrilege? In *Ethics and Values in Archaeology,* edited by E.L. Green, pp. 203–233. Free Press, New York.

1990. Bone Worship. *West Virginia Archeologist* 42(2):40–43.

Preston, D.J. 1989. Skeletons in Our Museums' Closets. *Harpers.* February: 66–75.

Tonetti, A.C. 1990. Ghost Dancing in the Nineties: Research, Reburial and Resurrection Among the Dead in Ohio. *West Virginia Archeologist* 42(2):20–22.

POSTSCRIPT

Should the Remains of Prehistoric Native Americans Be Reburied Rather Than Studied?

Since these two selections were written, many Native American groups have requested the return of human remains from museums, and these bones have been reburied. Other groups have expressed little interest in recovering the remains of ancestors or skeletons excavated from their lands because they do not share the same cultural beliefs as those expressed by Riding In. A number of museum curators and archaeologists have taken a much more tempered and conciliatory approach to dealing with these issues than the position expressed by Meighan.

Such possibilities suggest that there are a variety of alternative approaches to the issue of reburial besides the diametrically opposed positions expressed here. Many groups, both from museums and universities, have urged compromise. A number of Native American groups have also tried to find ways to accommodate anthropological interests without sacrificing their own rights. Several contentious issues remain. What should be done with the remains of prehistoric Native Americans who have no known living descendants or cultural groups? Should the religious beliefs of one group of Native Americans stand for the rights of all groups? Should modern Native American communities have rights to rebury any human remains found on their lands? What should happen to the remains of the very earliest settlers in North America who are unlikely to be biologically related to modern tribes?

One recent incident arose in 1996 when a prehistoric skeleton was found along the banks of the Columbia River near Kennewick, Washington. Kennewick Man, as this individual has been called, appears to have lived 9,000 years ago and has been the center of an intense academic, political, and legal debate.

At first the bones were thought to be a white settler's, but carbon-14 dating suggests a much earlier date, which has ruled out ancestry from some early-nineteenth-century settler. When forensic anthropologist James Chatters examined the bones he concluded that the bones were Caucasoid rather than Native American. If true, such a finding would require a revision of North American prehistory. Although archaeologists wanted to examine these bones more carefully, local Native American groups claimed the right to rebury this individual, and the courts have generally supported their motions. These legal wranglings have led some archaeologists to complain that the Native Americans simply want to rebury the evidence that Europeans may have reached the New World at some early prehistoric period and may have predated the arrival of Native American groups coming from Asia. Evidence that Kennewick Man is Caucasoid is slim at best, but without examination by physical anthropologists we will never know.

For a discussion of the Kennewick Man debate, see David Hurst Thomas's recent *Skull Wars: Kennewick Man, Archeology, and the Battle for Native American Identity* (Basic Books, 2000). Other sources on this controversy include Douglas Preston's "The Lost Man: Umatilla Indians' Plan to Rebury 9,300 Year Old Kennewick Man With Caucasoid Features," *The New Yorker* (June 16, 1997) and two articles in *Archaeology,* "A Battle Over Bones: Ancestry of Kennewick Man" (January/February 1997) and "Kennewick Update: Nondestructive Lab Tests on Controversial Skeleton to Begin" (November/December 1998).

For an excellent summary of anthropological interest in Native American remains, see Robert Bieder's *A Brief Historical Survey of the Expropriation of American Indian Remains* (Native American Rights Fund, 1990). J. C. Rose, T. J. Green, and V. D. Green's "NAGPRA Is Forever: Osteology and the Repatriation of Skeletons," *Annual Review of Anthropology* (vol. 25, 1996) provides a useful summary of NAGPRA.

Riding In has also explored the issue of repatriation and the imperialist nature of archaeology in "Without Ethics and Morality: A Historical Overview of Imperial Archaeology and American Indians," *Arizona State Law Journal* (vol. 24, Spring 1992).

Several essays in Karen D. Vitelli, ed., *Archaeological Ethics* (Altamira Press, 1996) are relevant to this debate. For an example of a more moderate approach that urges compromise, see Lynne Goldstein and Keith Kintigh's "Ethnics and the Reburial Controversy," *American Antiquity* (vol. 55, 1990).

ISSUE 18

Did Napoleon Chagnon's Research Methods and Publications Harm the Yanomami Indians?

YES: Terence Turner, from *The Yanomami and the Ethics of Anthropological Practice* (Cornell University Latin American Studies Program, 2001)

NO: Edward H. Hagen, Michael E. Price, and John Tooby, from *Preliminary Report,* http://www.anth.ucsb.edu/ucsbpreliminaryreport.pdf (Department of Anthropology, University of California Santa Barbara, 2001)

ISSUE SUMMARY

YES: Anthropologist Terence Turner contends that journalist Patrick Tierney's book *Darkness in El Dorado* accurately depicts how anthropologist Napoleon Chagnon's research among the Yanomami Indians caused conflict between groups and how Chagnon's portrayal of the Yanomami as extremely violent aided gold miners trying to take over Yanomami land.

NO: Anthropologists Edward Hagen, Michael Price, and John Tooby counter that Tierney systematically distorts Chagnon's views on Yanomami violence and exaggerates the amount of disruption caused by Chagnon's activities compared to those of others such as missionaries and gold miners.

In September 2000 a startling message flew around the e-mail lists of the world's anthropologists. It was a letter from Cornell University anthropologist Terry Turner and University of Hawaii anthropologist Leslie Sponsel to the president and president-elect of the American Anthropological Association (AAA), with copies to a few other officers, warning them of the imminent publication of a book that they said would "affect the American Anthropological profession as a whole in the eyes of the public, and arouse intense indignation and calls for action among members of the Association." The book in question, which they had read in galley proofs, was Patrick Tierney's *Darkness* *in El Dorado: How Scientists and Journalists Devastated the Amazon* (W.W. Norton and Company, 2000). The letter summarized some of Tierney's charges that medical researcher James Neel, anthropologist Napoleon Chagnon, and others seriously harmed the Yanomami Indians of Venezuela, even causing a measles epidemic that killed hundreds.

The leaking of the letter and the subsequent publication of an article by Tierney in *The New Yorker* caused great excitement at the annual meeting of the AAA in San Francisco in mid-November 2000. Discussion climaxed at a panel discussion that filled a double ballroom at the Hilton Hotel with several thousand anthropologists and media representatives from around the world. The panel included Tierney, anthropologist William Irons (representing Chagnon, who declined to attend), and experts on the history of science, epidemiology, and South American Indians. (Neel could not defend himself, as he had died earlier that year.) Numerous members of the audience also spoke. During and after the meeting a consensus developed that Tierney was wrong in his claim that the measles epidemic in 1968 was caused by Neel's and Chagnon's inoculations, since measles vaccines are incapable of causing the actual disease. However, Tierney's accusations that Chagnon had treated the Yanomami in an unethical manner during his research and had distorted his findings were not so easily dismissed. Later, the Executive Board of the AAA established a task force to examine the allegations in Tierney's book. The 300-page Task Force Final Report was completed on May 18, 2002 and is now posted on the AAA Web site.

Why would a book about researchers' treatment of a small Amazonian tribe have caused such an uproar? The reason is that, due to the enormous sales of Chagnon's book *The Yanomamö* (now in its fifth edition) and the prizewinning films he made with Timothy Asch, the Yanomami (as most scholars spell their name) are probably the world's best-known tribal people and Chagnon one of the most famous ethnographers since Margaret Mead. Chagnon's use of his Yanomami data to support his sociobiological explanation of human behavior has also had influence outside anthropology (for example, in evolutionary psychology). The idea that the most aggressive men win the most wives and have the most children, thus passing their aggressive genes on to future generations more abundantly than the peaceful genes of their nonaggressive brethren, is a cornerstone of the popular view that humans are innately violent (see Issue 2). Thus, Tierney's attack on Chagnon's credibility sent shock waves through the scholarly community.

In this selection, Turner argues that Tierney is correct in claiming that Chagnon failed to object when gold miners used his portrayal of the Yanomami as violent to hinder the establishment of a Yanomami reserve in Brazil, that Chagnon manipulated his demographic data to support his hypothesis that more violent Yanomami men have more wives and children than less violent ones, and that his fieldwork practices caused conflict between Yanomami groups. Hagen, Price, and Tooby counter that Tierney deliberately misrepresents evidence in claiming that Chagnon violated Yanomami taboos in his fieldwork and that he manipulated his data to support his claim that killers have more offspring than nonkillers.

340

Terence Turner

The Yanomami and the Ethics of Anthropological Practice

Controversy over the mistreatment of the Yanomami, an indigenous people of Venezuela and northern Brazil, by scientific researchers and anthropologists had smoldered for over a decade before it burst into flame [in 2001] with the publication of Patrick Tierney's *Darkness in El Dorado*. The controversy over the issues raised in the book, and more broadly over what has been done to the Yanomami by anthropologists and other researchers, confronts the discipline of anthropology, as represented by its professional society, the American Anthropological Association, and several universities and learned societies with which some of the principals in the case were connected, with ethically fraught issues. How these issues are dealt may well set significant precedents for the ethical and scientific standards of the institutions and professions involved, particularly in regard to the responsibilities of professional associations for the conduct of their members, and of researchers in the field for their human subjects. . . .

My work as head of the AAA Special Commission to Investigate the Situation of the Brazilian Yanomami in 1990–91 was the original reason for my involvement in Yanomami affairs. Together with subsequent work with NGOs and anthropologists engaged in the struggle to support and defend the Yanomami, it remains the basis of my appraisal of much of Tierney's account of Chagnon's activities among the Yanomami, including his attacks on Yanomami-support NGOs and Yanomami leaders. I was appointed to head the Special AAA Commission on the Brazilian Yanomami by the then President of the AAA, Annette Weiner, on the basis of my work as an activist with Brazilian indigenous groups and indigenous support NGOs and my personal acquaintance, based on long-standing cooperation, with many actors and groups involved in the Yanomami struggle. My mission was to report back to the President and Executive Board of the Association on what if any action the Association should take on behalf of the Yanomami of Brazil. The context of this unusual appointment was the desperate, and at the time apparently losing battle to save the huge Yanomami Reserve. After a ten year struggle led by the Brazilian NGO, the CCPY (Committee to Create a Yanomami Park), the area had been studied, surveyed and tentatively demarcated by an official Brazilian governmental team, only to be invaded by 40,000 illegal gold miners in 1988. . . .

My investigation of the situation created by the multiple Yanomami crises of 1988 to 1991 for the AAA involved me in new or renewed contacts with

Brazilian NGO workers, indigenous rights activists, medical doctors and health workers from governmental and private agencies, personnel of FUNAI, missionaries, progressive journalists, lawyers, politicians, and anthropologists (including officers of the Brazilian Anthropological Association, ABA). These encounters and consultations, together with further contacts and collaborations on subsequent visits to Brazil, comprise the basis of my published responses to Chagnon's unfounded calumnies against NGOs, Missions and the Yanomami leader Davi Kopenawa at the time of the gold miners' invasions and the campaign to dissolve the Yanomami Reserve from 1988 to 1991, his untruthful statements on the responsibility of the Salesians and the Yanomami themselves for the massacre at Haximu in December 1993, and his renewed diatribes against Davi Kopenawa at the 1994 AAA Meetings and on more recent occasions. They are also the basis of my evaluation of Tierney's account of the same events in his book, which I find substantially correct. . . .

The great majority of contemporary researchers who have worked with the Yanomami, or who have studied the effects of Chagnon's representations of the Yanomami in both Brazil and Venezuela, have critically challenged many of Chagnon's ethnographic and theoretical claims, his methods and actions in the field, and a number of his statements in popular media. . . .

The interdependence of ethical and empirical issues is unavoidable in dealing with Chagnon's work, in which factual claims of Yanomami aggressiveness and the link between killing and reproductive success are adduced, explicitly or implicitly, as "scientific" evidence for the sorts of statements he has made in the media that have been decried on ethical grounds. The issue becomes even more complex when one confronts the criticisms of Chagnon's data and analysis summarized and extended by Tierney. These criticisms, notably in Tierney's Chapter 10 that deals with Chagnon's 1988 article in *Science,* seriously imply the manipulation and withholding of data to support unsound but theoretically and ideologically desired conclusions. . . .

I will organize my discussion under five general headings [excerpt: from two are included here], designating general types of ethically problematic behavior, comprising representative instances from Tierney's text that seem to me to be sufficiently well documented and analyzed, and/or attested from other sources, to be considered "well founded". . . .

I. Statements and Silences by Chagnon Damaging to the Yanomami

I.A. Statements About "Fierceness" or Violent Aggressiveness as a Dominant Feature of Yanomami Society, and Silences (Failure to Speak Out Against Misuses of These Statements Damaging to the Yanomami)

Chagnon stood by virtually without demur during the drive to dismantle the Brazilian Yanomami reserve in 1988–92, while politicians, military leaders and journalists allied with mining interests employed his portrayal of the

Yanomami as ferocious savages involved in chronic warfare over women, to justify the dismemberment of Yanomami territory. Their argument ran that Yanomami communities needed for their own safety to be isolated from one another by "corridors" of open land, which would incidentally be accessible to gold miners. Chagnon's refusal to disown this use of his work in Brazilian media, where it might have had some effect, became understood by both sides in the struggle over the Yanomami reserve from 1988 to 1992 as a statement by omission in support of the miners and their political allies. This had a serious enough impact that the Brazilian Anthropological Association formally appealed to the American Anthropological Association in 1989 demanding that the U.S. Association investigate the ethics of its member's tacit support of those who were exploiting his statements. The American Association failed to take action, and this failure has come back to haunt it. . . .

The issue, as the Brazilian Association's new statement forcefully put it, is not simply that third parties exploited Chagnon's statements and silences for their own purposes. Anthropological researchers, its statement acknowledges, have an obligation to speak the truth about their research findings, and cannot control the uses to which others may put their findings. They do, however, have an ethical responsibility to speak out against the misuse of their findings by third parties, especially when such misuse directly damages the people referred to and most especially when these people were the subjects of the anthropologist's research. . . .

I.B. Repeated and Untruthful Attacks on NGOs, Anthropological Activists and Yanomami Leaders

I.B.1. Attacks on NGOs, Anthropological Activists

. . . Tierney . . . accurately reports Chagnon's shocking charge "that the very people who posed as defenders of the Indians were actually destroying them". This was Chagnon's allegation, which he repeated in the *Times Literary Supplement* and the *New York Times,* that the medical clinics and outreach programs instituted by missionaries and NGOs were not actually helping but rather "killing" the Indians ("killing by kindness", in his words. Although primarily directed against the Salesians in Venezuela, this allegation was phrased so as implicitly to include missions and secular NGOs in Brazil. He further asserted that the Salesian missionaries, as well as unnamed Protestant missionaries at Mucajaí, were promoting warfare among Yanomami villages by giving or selling shotguns to the Indians on their mission stations. Yanomami leaders like Davi Kopenawa, he claimed, were not authentic leaders but "pawns" or "parrots", mindlessly repeating what their NGO and missionary manipulators told them to say. . . .

I.B.3. Chagnon's Attacks on Yanomami Leaders: (1) Davi Kopenawa

Chagnon has publicly charged on several occasions, beginning in the late 1980's and early 1990's, that the Brazilian Yanomami leader Davi Kopenawa was a mere "parrot" of NGOs, mouthing lines he was fed by the do-gooder organizations that supposedly kept him as a useful symbol for self-serving fund-raising campaigns (again, he never cited specific statements or texts). Davi Kopenawa was a major asset in these struggles, as virtually the only Yanomami leader capable of speaking out for Yanomami interests in the Brazilian and international political arenas, who at the same time commanded genuine support among the Yanomami of his own and other communities. Kopenawa was and remains the most important spokesman for the Brazilian Yanomami: he is a dynamic, effective, and independent person and leader. Chagnon's gratuitous and untruthful attacks damaged (or were clearly intended to damage) him. Chagnon is still at it: A CNN TV crew that interviewed Chagnon in November 2000 was startled to hear him call Kopenawa "a cigar store Indian"). . . .

I.C. Ethnographic Misrepresentation as an Ethical Issue

Tierney analyzes a number of Chagnon's texts and statements that appear to involve possible manipulations of statistical data to support theoretical conclusions that would otherwise not follow, and the use of the same kinds of manipulations to implicate political enemies in causing the deaths of (or, in Chagnon's blunter term, "killing") Yanomami. Cases of the first kind may be considered to constitute a grey area between incorrect statistical analysis and deliberate manipulation. There seems little doubt, however, about the ethics of the much graver charges in the second category. . . .

Chagnon's article, "Life Histories, Blood revenge, and warfare in a tribal population", published in *Science* in 1988, has been taken by his critics and sociobiological supporters alike as the quintessential formulation of his theoretical claim that violent competition (fierceness) among males is driven by competition for sexual access to females, and that success in this competition, as measured by killing other men, therefore leads to increased reproductive success. Sociobiologists seized upon the Yanomami, as represented by Chagnon, as living examples of the evolutionary past of the race: the most direct links between the human present and the supposed primate heritage of Alpha male-centered harems and dominance hierarchies. . . . Tierney correctly points out that this notoriety, and the central misconception on which it was based, was overtly cultivated by Chagnon in public statements such as his presidential address to the Human Behavior and Evolutionary Society:

> I demonstrated that Yanomamo men in my 25 year study who had participated in the killing of other men had approximately three times as many children and more than two times as many wives as men their own ages who had not.

As Tierney also correctly says, this statement is thoroughly false. . . .

Tierney, relying partly on Lizot, somewhat more on Albert and most heavily on Ferguson, and contributing some findings of his own, provides a reasonably accurate summary of the criticisms of Chagnon's analysis. He reviews three fundamental criticisms of Chagnon's statistical manipulation of his data. Firstly, Chagnon's statistical comparison of the number of wives and children of "killers" (defined as "unokai", on the basis of their having undergone the ritual of purification for those who have participated in the killing of a person, *unokaimou*) to those of non-killers has been criticized as skewed by his inclusion of a large number of young men between 20–25 and 25–30 as members of the statistically relevant population. Very few Yanomami men of this age had killed anyone and almost none had wives or children. The result was to inflate the relative advantage of the killers, almost all of whom were older men, some over 30 and most over 40. When killers were compared with men of their own age-bracket, "the reproductive success of killers was not nearly as impressive—ranging between 40 to 67 percent, a fraction of the 208 percent advantage that Chagnon had broadcast to the press". In other words, age was a factor that accounted for much of the variation, and Chagnon had not taken it properly into account.

Another variable Chagnon left out of account, according to critics like Ferguson and Albert, was headman status (and the additional, partly overlapping status of shaman). In his 1988 paper, he simply classed all headmen as killers, "*unokai*", but as Tierney says, that is a confusion of categories. Most Yanomami headmen have several wives, because of their status as headmen rather than their status as "killers" ("*unokai*", in Chagnon's translation). Headman status, like age, is thus another variable that must be recognized as accounting for a significant part of the contrast in number of wives and children between men in the killers category and non-killers. Yet another important variable, explicitly excluded by Chagnon in his text, was the death of fathers. For reasons he did not explain, Chagnon excluded the children of dead fathers from his initial analysis. This turns out to have been a strategic point for his whole argument about reproductive success. According to Chagnon and other Yanomami ethnographers, successful killers become themselves the main targets of vengeance raids, and are highly likely to be killed in the midst of their reproductive years. As Brian Ferguson had been the first to point out, if this likelihood of killers to have their reproductive careers cut short were taken into account, the supposed reproductive advantage of killers might actually disappear to become negative. . . .

Tierney also raises a series of questions about manipulations of statistically strategic bits of data. Two young men in their twenties were listed in Chagnon's 1997 *Yanomamo Interactive* CD on The Ax Fight as having four and five children respectively. This was far more than the other men in their age category, and these two men had been identified as violent participants in the ax fight shown in the CD. Tierney checked Chagnon's original census and found that Mohesiwa was listed as born in 1938 and Ruwamowa in 1939, thus making them 33 and 32, respectively, rather than 24 and 27, as Chagnon now claimed, at the time of filming. Tierney "found no other mistakes in the census transfer. And if these were mistakes, they were statistically perfect ones"— as they seemed to show the greater reproductive success of violent men in contrast to their supposed age-mates in the under-30 categories.

There was also the case of the five young men Chagnon listed as killers in the under 25 age group, all of whom had wives. When challenged by Albert, however, Chagnon removed them to the 30-plus category, remarking that since the Yanomami do not count past three, the estimation of age is necessarily approximate. Their removal substantially altered the statistical predominance of killers as husbands and fathers in their age category. In sum, as Tierney remarks, "Minute manipulations in each age category could easily skew all the results"—and apparently had done so in the cases in question. . . .

Tierney also pointed out that although Chagnon had given the impression in his *Science* article that the three raids he described involved communities that were still living in a relatively traditional way, unaffected by the presence of missionaries and government agents that had led to the decline or suppression of warfare in other areas of Yanomami country, this was not the case. Chagnon had identified the villages in his article only by number, which Lizot had complained made them impossible to match up with any known (named) Yanomami communities. Tierney succeeded in identifying 9 of the 12 villages involved, showing that they were the same ones where he had done most of his fieldwork. . . .

Once identified and connected by Tierney to their known historical contexts, the three raids described in abstract terms in the *Science* article assumed different meanings. Pinning down the actual identities and locations of the villages showed that they were actually situated in an area of heavy contact with Venezuelan society and missionary influence. No longer abstract instances of violent competition for reproductive success, in an indigenous world whose essential patterns of warfare had not yet been affected by alien presences such as missionaries or anthropologists, they now appeared as significantly affected by Chagnon's own presence and activities. Chagnon himself, it transpired, had "filmed, transported, and coordinated" two of the three raiding parties over part of the distance to their targets. . . .

I.C. False Accusations Against Missions and NGO's of "killing" Yanomami or Otherwise Being Responsible for Raising Their Death Rate

In an OpEd column in the New York Times of October 1993, Chagnon claimed that Yanomami were dying at missionary posts with medical facilities at four times the rate obtaining in "remote" villages. This was supposedly based on statistics Chagnon had collected and was the key data he cited in support of his shocking allegation that the Salesian missionaries were "killing the Yanomami with kindness". Tierney notes that this has become "one of the most frequently quoted statements in the Yanomami controversy," but shows that it is actually a misleading effect obtained by switching statistical data between categories of the study. He explains,

> Chagnon divided the villages in three categories of mission contact: "remote", "intermediate", and "maximum". The villages with maximum [mission] contact had a thirty percent *lower* mortality rate than remote groups, while the "intermediate" villages suffered four times as many deaths as the missions. Chagnon's data thus confirmed what all other researchers have found, but in the NYT Chagnon converted the "intermediate" villages

into "missions", which they are not. . . There is no doubt that the debate about mission mortality has been based on misinformation.

Tierney accurately chronicles Chagnon's attempt to spin the tragic episode of the massacre of twelve Yanomami from the village of Haximu by Brazilian gold miners in July 1993 into a series of spurious charges against the Yanomami from the village of Paapiu for being partly responsible for the massacre and the Salesian missionaries for trying to cover it up. The "cover up", in Chagnon's version, chiefly consisted in a campaign by the missionaries to block his "investigation" of the massacre, in order to prevent him from discovering and disclosing their role in "killing the Yanomami by kindness" at their mission stations (see preceding section). This was tantamount to accusing the Salesians of being accessories after the fact to mass murder.

Chagnon claimed he had the right to investigate the murders as a member of a Venezuelan Presidential Commission on Yanomami affairs. With his ally Brewer-Carias, Chagnon had in fact been appointed to a commission to supervise the projected Yanomami Biosphere Reserve by the transitional President who succeeded Carlos Andres-Perez after the latter's impeachment. This commission, however, lacked any specific investigative powers relevant to the massacre. An unprecedented national outcry, with massive street demonstrations and protests against Brewer's and Chagnon's appointments, specifically including their declared intention to conduct an investigation of the massacre, followed the announcement of these appointments. This historically unprecedented wave of opposition led the President to appoint a different commission specifically to investigate the massacre. The intent was clearly to remove Chagnon and Brewer from any connection with the Haximu investigation, and it was so understood by the Venezuelan media and public, although the President did not get around to formally dissolving the Brewer-Chagnon commission until later. . . . Chagnon, accompanied by Brewer, nevertheless attempted to go to Haximu to "investigate", regardless of the fact that the new Presidential investigating commission was already en route to the spot, and they lacked the necessary authorization to go to the area, let alone to conduct an investigation. When they landed at the village airstrip, two miles from the massacre site, they were summarily ordered to leave by the judge who headed the legitimate investigative commission. She gave Brewer and Chagnon a choice: get out of Haximu immediately or face arrest. The air force pilot who had flown them to the spot sided with the judge. He flew Chagnon straight to Caracas, confiscated his notes and told him to get out of Venezuela within twenty-four hours. Chagnon did so. . . .

Another of Chagnon's attempts to implicate missionaries in fomenting Yanomami killings by distributing shotguns was his attack, in the fourth edition of his book, on the Protestant Missionaries of the Evangelical Mission of Amazonia, supposedly stationed at Mucajaí. Tierney shows that this account is a fictional pastiche, combining aspects of the geography, personnel and history of the distant, and long-abandoned, mission station of Surucucu with those of Mucajaí, and adding elements of fantasy and distorted and displaced versions of actual actions. Indians lugging a washing machine over the mountain by the mission station at Surucucu becomes a single Missionary carrying a refrigerator on his back over a non-existent mountain at Mucajaí. The refusal of missionaries at Surucucu to sell shotguns to the Indians, and their abandonment of the mission post there rather than be obliged to do so, becomes the provision of shotguns by the Mucajaí missionaries to the Yanomami, their guilt supposedly redoubled by their subsequent refusal to inquire if the guns they had provided had been those used in an attack on a "remote" village (Chagnon suggests that if they found out that the guns they had provided had been the ones used, they would have to confiscate them, which would have made the Yanomami forsake the mission. As Tierney reports, everyone with any knowledge of these events, including the missionaries in question and others familiar with the different posts and mission families Chagnon had conflated, denounces Chagnon's account as fictional. . . .

II. Field Methods Disruptive of Yanomami Society

Drawing heavily on the writings of Brian Ferguson and his own data, Tierney documents charges that Chagnon's methods of obtaining the names of dead relatives, by exploiting enmities between factions and hostile communities, and above all by giving massive amounts of steel goods as presents, destabilized Yanomami communities and inter-communal relations, giving rise to conflicts, raids and wars. He also documents that Chagnon took a limited part in raids by transporting raiding parties in his motor launch. The issues here centrally involve the scale of operations and the time-pressure under which Chagnon was obliged to collect his pedigree data. Whether working for James Neel or on his own, his commitment to surveying the maximum possible numbers of villages in relatively minimal periods of time precluded normal anthropological methods of building rapport and finding culturally appropriate ways of obtaining culturally taboo information that have been used successfully by other anthropologists who have worked among the Yanomami. This forced him to resort to bullying and intimidation, including shooting off firearms and performing shamanic rituals of magical child-killing. It also led him to resort to bribery on a massive scale, using huge amounts of steel tools, pots, etc. These hoards of otherwise rare and highly valued items became foci of conflict between rival factions and villages, which on a number of documented occasions led to raids and wars in which people were killed.

As his work continued over the years, Chagnon, rather than modifying his modus operandi to diminish its destabilizing effects, continued to raise the ante, becoming a player in the regional system of conflicts and the struggle for dominance that were set off in part by quarrels over the wealth he brought with him. There began to be wars between "Chagnon's" village, containing Yanomami dependent on him for steel goods, and villages associated with other sources of goods, such as the anthropologist Lizot, and the independent Yanomami cooperative SUYAO. All of this, Tierney, Ferguson, Albert, and others have argued, represented a massive disruption of Yanomami social peace consequent upon Chagnon's field methods. If so, it may be considered to constitute a violation of clause III.A.2 of the AAA

Code of Ethics: "Anthropological researchers must do everything in their power to ensure that their research does not harm the safety, dignity, or privacy of the people with whom they work. . .".

The sheer scale of Chagnon's operations thus came to constitute a sui generis factor with ethical effects and implications not anticipated by the existing AAA Code of Ethics. Over a period of thirty years, according to anthropologist Brian Ferguson and others familiar with the political and historical aspects of his research, Chagnon has used methods to extract culturally sensitive data and biological specimens from Yanomami that have involved the violation of Yanomami cultural norms and caused dissension, and occasionally conflict, between communities and between factions of the same community. These conflicts, according to Ferguson, seconded by Tierney, have sometimes led to the breakup of communities and to inter-village raiding. Chagnon's tactics reportedly included giving large amounts of steel tools, the most esteemed presents, to certain villages or factions, thus inevitably destabilizing relations with non-recipients groups. The[se] also included, by his own account, deliberately lying to a village or faction that he had obtained the taboo names of their dead relatives from another village or faction, thus arousing anger and resentment that he could exploit to get the village or faction in question to give up the names of the deceased ancestors of the other group. After Chagnon got his data and departed, the villagers were left with bitter resentments that could aggravate existing tensions and provoke open conflicts. Chagnon seems also to have employed bullying and intimidation, brandishing weapons and shooting off firearms to make the Yanomami (who are usually the opposite of "fierce" in relations with non-Yanomami such as Venezuelans and Euro-North Americans) willing to give him information, if only to get rid of him.

The effectiveness of these tactics owed much to Chagnon's dramatic exploitation of the great discrepancy between his resources of wealth and power and those of the Yanomami as leverage to extract information, without regard to the ways this disrupted the social relations, stability and political peace of the communities of the people among whom he worked. The main authority for these allegations are the writings and public statements of Chagnon himself. One does not need to be a "left wing academic" or an "anti-science culturologist" to agree that these tactics raise questions of research ethics. . . .

IV.B. What Is to Be Done?

I believe that we as anthropologists owe it to the Yanomami, and to ourselves, to speak the truth publicly about what has been done to the Yanomami. In this sense, the role of the Association and its Task Force may be compared to that of truth commissions in places like South Africa or Guatemala: not to punish individuals, but to make principled public statements about what has been done, by whom, and in what ways the actions and statements in question may have violated the collective ethical standards of the profession. . . .

Anthropology as a discipline and as a profession can learn valuable lessons from analyzing what went wrong in Neel's and Chagnon's work, and why.

I have suggested that a common thread connecting the ethical problems of both researchers is that concern with large-scale data collection under high time pressure, exacerbated in some cases by the institutional pressures of big scientific research projects, led both to make inadequate allowance for ethical and cultural standards, and in some cases, the social and physical well-being of the individual persons and communities comprising their subject populations. For anthropology, the lesson is that the pursuit of large amounts of quantitative data in abstraction from the cultural and social forms of life of the local people may become an end in itself that leads researchers to lose sight of or ignore the social standards and needs of the people they study. Such data, no matter how scientifically valuable, must never be pursued to the point of disruption of local social relations and cultural standards, or allowed to take priority over the well being of persons and communities. . . .

Edward H. Hagen, Michael E. Price,
and John Tooby

 NO

Preliminary Report

Introduction

As we will begin to show in this report, *Darkness in El Dorado* is essentially a work of fiction. Its author, Patrick Tierney, has very selectively quoted hundreds of sources in order to, first, caricature anthropologist Napoleon Chagnon's work on the Yanomamö, and second, to discredit what he claims is "Chagnon's ethnographic image of the ferocious Yanomami" by instead portraying them as meek, peaceful, helpless, and, ultimately, victims of Chagnon himself. Tierney's creative use of primary sources in this venture begins almost immediately. After a brief introductory chapter, Tierney wastes little time attempting to undermine Chagnon's portrayal of Yanomamö males as relatively healthy and frequently engaged in war:

> Before going into the jungle, I had read and admired The Fierce People. So it was surprising to see that the Yanomami—so terrifying and "burly" in Chagnon's text—were, in fact, among the tiniest, scrawniest people in the world. Adults averaged four feet seven inches in height, and children had among the lowest weight-height ratios on the planet.

References are supposed to support, not refute, the claims one is making. Tierney's reference above cites a relatively short paper by Rebecca Holmes on Yanomamö health. Although the paper does confirm the widely known fact that Yanomamö are short, it does not support one of Tierney's major themes: that Chagnon has exaggerated the frequency of Yanomamö warfare. What Tierney fails to mention here or anywhere else in his book is what Holmes says in her paper about Yanomamö war:

> Raids resulting in serious wounds and death occur *several times a year* in spite of missionary pressure to restrict warfare. About 20 warriors from Parima A, a two-day walk through the jungle from Parima B, raided one of the settlements in Parima B during our fieldwork. There were no injuries, although a study of the nurse's recent medical records indicates that these raids not uncommonly result in wounds from poison arrows. (Holmes 1985, p. 249; emphasis added).

Tierney cites Holmes' paper four times but he fails to mention her evidence on war and violence on any of these occasions, evidence which is directly relevant to one of the major themes of his book. This failure is obviously deliberate. . . .

Preliminary Evaluation of Chapter 3

Naming the Dead

Tierney, in Chapter 3 (The Napoleonic Wars) and elsewhere in his book, fingers Chagnon's method of obtaining accurate genealogies as a source of conflict between individuals and villages, and, more generally, as an affront to Yanomamö dignity (Chagnon's recent statement on this issue can be found in Appendix XIV). What we will show below is that Tierney's account is substantially undermined by the very sources he cites.

First, however, it may be useful to note that most societies, including the US, have a 'name taboo.' In the US, for example, it is not wrong to mention one person's first name or nickname to another person who does not know it, but it is often considered rude to *use* the nickname or first name of someone if you do not know them well. For example, even if Judith Smith's friends call her 'Judy', she might be offended if a stranger used that name instead of 'Judith' or Ms. Smith. How many news articles on *Darkness* have referred to 'Pat' or even 'Patrick' instead of 'Patrick Tierney' or 'Mr. Tierney'? None. In professional contexts, it is also rude to use someone's first name instead of their title and last name (e.g., Dr. Smith). In court rooms, we do not even use the judge's name, but instead address him or her as 'your honor' even though it is perfectly OK to know the judge's name, or ask someone what his or her name is. So, Americans have a rather elaborate name taboo.

The Yanomamö 'name taboo' is quite similar to the American 'name taboo.' Names are *not* 'scared [*sic*] secrets' (almost everyone knows them, in fact), but their *use* in particular social contexts is considered rude and insulting, just as, for Americans, *knowing* someone's first name or nickname is not insulting or wrong, but the *use* of nicknames and first names is rude and insulting in certain social contexts. (For the Yanomamö, the improper use of names is much more insulting than for Americans, however.) Here is Chagnon explaining the name taboo:

> The taboo is maintained even for the living, for one mark of prestige is the courtesy others show you by not using your name publicly. This is particularly true for men, who are much more competitive for status than women in this culture, and it is fascinating to watch boys grow into young men, demanding to be called either by a kinship term in public, or by a teknonymous reference such as 'brother of Himotoma' (see Glossary). The more effective they are at getting others to avoid using their names, the more public acknowledgment there is that they are of high esteem and social standing. Helena Valero, a Brazilian woman who was captured as a child by a Yanomamö raiding party, was married for many years to a Yanomamö headman before she discovered what his name was. The sanctions behind the taboo are more complex than just this, for they involve a combination of fear, respect, admiration, political deference, and honor.

The Yanomamö were understandably concerned that if the stranger in their midst (Chagnon) learned their names, he might *use* them disrespectfully. Chagnon *never* did this. Chagnon *always* addressed individuals in the proper manner, and he never intentionally used names disrespectfully (nor does Tierney present any evidence that Chagnon used names disrespectfully). Chagnon always used the Yanomamö equivalent of 'Judith' when that was appropriate, 'Ms. Smith' when that was appropriate, and 'Your Honor' when that was appropriate. Because he was struggling with a foreign culture, Chagnon occasionally but *unintentionally* offended individuals. Unlike academics, the Yanomamö are forgiving; they knew his missteps were accidental, and took no lasting offence.

Chagnon also found that it was easier to obtain a person's name from non-kin or enemies. In the US, Judith Smith's friends might be reluctant to reveal Judith's nickname to a stranger—not because *knowing* the nickname is taboo, but because its improper *use* might offend their friend—but people who were not close friends of Judith's would feel no such reluctance, nor would they violate any taboo by revealing the nickname. The same applies to the Yanomamö—asking non-kin and enemies about names is *not* taboo (remember, these names are widely known, and there is no taboo against outsiders knowing these names).

Contrary to Tierney's claims, Chagnon did *not* play enemies or villages off one another to obtain names. Notice that in Tierney's account of Chagnon's method, these claims have no supporting citations:

> Chagnon found himself in a difficult predicament, having to collect gene-alogical trees going back several generations. This was frustrating for him because the Yanomami do not speak personal names out loud. And the names of the dead are the most taboo subject in their culture.
>
> "To name the dead, among the Yanomami, is a grave insult, a motive of division, fights, and wars," wrote the Salesian Juan Finkers, who has lived among the Yanomami villages on the Mavaca River for twenty-five years.
>
> Chagnon found out that the Yanomami "were unable to understand why a complete stranger should want to possess such knowledge [of per-sonal names] unless it were for harmful magical purposes." So Chagnon had to parcel out "gifts" in exchange for these names. [Anthropologists have 'to parcel out gifts' for most interviews with most informants on most topics. Giving gifts in exchange for extensive genealogical informa-tion is common practice in anthropology] One Yanomami man threatened to kill Chagnon when he mentioned a relative who had recently died. Oth-ers lied to him and set him back five months with phony genealogies [both these events are discussed in detail by Chagnon]. But he kept doggedly pur-suing his goal.
>
> Finally, he invented a system, as ingenious as it was divisive [no cita-tion], to get around the name taboo [Chagnon was not trying to 'get around the name taboo,' a claim that makes no sense ('getting around the name taboo' would entail *using* names disrespectfully—something he never did, nor had any desire to do). Chagnon was trying, not only to get information necessary to his research, but also to integrate himself into

Yanomamö society by learning what was common knowledge: everyone's name, including those of ancestors]. Within groups, he sought out "informants who might be considered 'aberrant' or 'abnormal,' outcasts in their own society," people he could bribe and isolate more easily. These pariahs resented other members of society, so they more willingly betrayed sacred secrets [names are not 'sacred secrets'—they are public knowledge] at others' expense and for their own profit. [son-in-laws doing bride service— who are therefore not living with their kin—are a common example of what Tierney terms 'pariahs'] He resorted to "tactics such as 'bribing' children when their elders were not around, or capitalizing on animosities between individuals." [using children as informants is, again, common practice among anthropologists—usually because they have the patience for the all the tedious questions that anthropologists ask]

Chagnon was most successful at gathering data, however, when he started playing one village off against another. "I began traveling to other villages to check the genealogies, picking villages that were on strained terms with the people about whom I wanted information. I would then return to my base camp and check with local informants the accuracy of the new information. If the informants became angry when I mentioned the new names I acquired from the unfriendly group, I was almost certain that the information was accurate." [see below for the material that Tierney has omitted from this quote]

When one group became angry on hearing that Chagnon had gotten their names, he covered for his real informants but gave the name of another village nearby as the source of betrayal [no citation]. It showed the kind of dilemmas Chagnon's work posed. In spite of the ugly scenes he both witnessed and created, Chagnon concluded, "There is, in fact, no better way to get an accurate, reliable start on genealogy than to collect it from the enemies."

His divide-and-conquer information gathering exacerbated individual animosities [no citation], sparking mutual accusations of betrayal [no citation]. Nevertheless, Chagnon had become a prized political asset of the group with whom he was living, the Bisaasi-teri.

As usual, Tierney deliberately omits critical evidence that readers need to fairly evaluate his accusations and insinuations. With the exception of the quote from the Salesian missionary Juan Finkers, all of the cited information in the above quote comes from Chagnon's publications.

Tierney also conveniently fails to mention that Kaobawa, a Yanomamö headman, *demanded* that Chagnon learn the truth, even though he knew that would involve Chagnon learning the names of his dead kinsmen:

[Kaobawa's] knowledge of details was almost encyclopedic, his memory almost photographic. More than that, he was enthusiastic about making sure I learned the truth, and he encouraged me, indeed, *demanded* that I learn all details I might otherwise have ignored. . . . With the information provided by Kaobawa, and Rerebawa [another informant], I made enormous gains in understanding village interrelationships based on common ancestors and political histories and became lifelong friends with both. And both men knew that I had to learn about his recently deceased kin from the other one. It was one of those quiet understandings we all had but none of us could mention.

This information is in Chagnon's popular monograph, *Yanomamö* (which Tierney cites numerous times).

When Chagnon began his fieldwork with a Yanomamö village in the sixties, the Yanomamö did not know why Chagnon wanted to know their names, and were understandably quite reluctant to reveal this information to an outsider who might use it disrespectfully. Chagnon recounts the humorous and ingenious tactics the villagers used to deceive him about their real names during his initial stint in the field, and his own equally ingenious method of penetrating this deception by getting the information from other Yanomamö in enemy villages (see Appendix XIII for the monograph excerpt). Indeed, this is one of the major flaws in Tierney's account: he conveniently fails to mention that the methods that Chagnon discusses are those he used during the first six months or so of his fieldwork, before the Yanomamö had come to trust that Chagnon was not going to use the information disrespectfully. That Chagnon made strenuous attempts to avoid offending anyone while collecting names is clear from sentences that immediately follow those Tierney chooses to cite (material in bold not cited by Tierney):

I began traveling to other villages to check the genealogies, picking villages that were on strained terms with the people about whom I wanted information. I would then return to my base camp and check with local informants the accuracy of the new information. If the informants became angry when I mentioned the new names I acquired from the unfriendly group, I was almost certain that the information was accurate. **For this kind of checking I had to use informants whose genealogies I knew rather well: they had to be distantly enough related to the dead person that they would not go into a rage when I mentioned the name, but not so remotely related that they would be uncertain of the accuracy of the information. Thus, I had to make a list of names that I dared not use in the presence of each and every informant. Despite the precautions, I occasionally hit a name that put the informant into a rage, such as that of a dead brother or sister that other informants had not reported. This always terminated the day's work with that informant, for he would be too touchy to continue any further, and I would be reluctant to take a chance on a accidentally discovering another dead kinsman so soon after the first.**

These were always unpleasant experiences, and occasionally dangerous ones, depending on the temperament of the informant.

Chagnon stresses his efforts to avoid mentioning the names of the dead to close kin in all five editions of his monograph, yet Tierney *deliberately* fails to mention this. . . .

However history may judge Chagnon's method of obtaining accurate genealogies (Native North Americans rely heavily on accurate genealogies in laying claim to valuable government benefits, etc.) it is important to properly represent what he did. Tierney instead deliberately omits key evidence that would allow the reader to evaluate his claims and improperly characterizes names as "sacred secrets" of the Yanomamö as a group; instead, their public *use* reflects the status and respect accorded to particular individuals. Using the same sources cited by Tierney, it is clear that Chagnon never used names disrespectfully, and soon came to be trusted on this matter by the Yanomamö. . . .

Detailed Evaluation of Chapter 10: To Murder and to Multiply

Brief Introduction

Chapter 10 of *Darkness in El Dorado* by Patrick Tierney is an extended attack on a well-known 1988 paper published by Chagnon in *Science* entitled "Life Histories, Blood Revenge, and Warfare in a Tribal Population." In this paper, Chagnon argues that warfare among the Yanomamö is characterized by blood revenge: an attack on one group by another prompts a retaliatory attack, which itself prompts retaliation, *ad infinitum.* In other words, Yanomamö war is quite similar to the patterns of conflict we see in the Balkans, the Middle East, Africa—anywhere ethnic groups come into armed conflict. In order to understand this pattern among the Yanomamö (and thus, perhaps, every-where else), Chagnon presents data which suggest that successful Yanomamö warriors (unokai—men who have killed) are rewarded for their bravery and success. Among the Yanomamö, these rewards take the form of wives. Chagnon showed that unokai have more wives, and consequently more offspring, than non-unokai. Chagnon argued that if, over evolutionary time, cultural success lead [sic] to reproductive success, individuals would be selected to strive for cultural success. He further argued that cultural success is often achieved by engaging in successful military actions against enemies. Perhaps, then, the cycles of violence suffered by countless groups worldwide are driven, in part, by men who seek status and prestige by successfully attacking enemies.

This entire thesis has been assailed by Chagnon's critics, and Tierney hopes to bury it by demonstrating that Chagnon's research was shoddy, dishonest, and contradicted by other studies. In fact, whether or not Chagnon's theory is correct, *many* studies have demonstrated that, in small-scale societies, cultural success does lead to reproductive success, that cultural success is frequently associated with military success, and conflicts are often caused by conflicts over women. Tierney reviews almost none of these studies, and when he does, he omits key evidence that supports Chagnon's thesis.

Before we begin our analysis of Tierney's efforts in this chapter, we note that people often misconstrue Chagnon's work to mean that the Yanomamö are exceptionally violent, unlike other groups. Nothing could be further from the truth. In fact, we now know that most non-state societies have (or had) high rates of violence compared to state societies. Chagnon was one of the first to document in detail the profound impact of intergroup violence on a non-state society. . . .

Chagnon has also famously claimed that Yanomamö wars often start with conflicts over women. Tierney implies or states several times that this is either unimportant, "secondary," or a fabrication of Chagnon's. For example:

> Yet the popular image of the Yanomami waging war for women persisted. Chagnon deftly *created it* by repeatedly claiming that men went on raids, captured women, and raped them at will afterward.

If Chagnon had created this image, then there should be no independent reports of Yanomamö raiding for women, and there should especially be no such reports predating Chagnon's. There are, however, many accounts of Yanomamö raiding for women that predate Chagnon's, accounts that place more emphasis on wife-capture than Chagnon does (Chagnon has stated several times that it is often not the principle [sic] motivation for a raid). . . .

Selective Omission of Data Which Support Chagnon's Findings

Claim   Tierney argues against Chagnon's claim that warriorship and reproductive success are correlated in tribal societies, citing a study of the Waorani:

> Among the Waorani of the Ecuadorian Amazon, a tribe with the world's highest known rate of attrition of war, every known male has killed at least once. But warriors who killed more than twice were more than twice as likely to be killed themselves—and their wives were killed at three times the rate of other, more peaceful men. Most prolific killers lost their wives and had to remarry—which made it look as if they had more wives if they survived.

Misrepresentation   Here, Tierney omits important information which supports the validity of Chagnon's result. Tierney refers to a recent ethnography of the Waorani in which the authors actually went out and collected the data to test Chagnon's model. The problem was, since all Waorani males had participated in a killing, they could not separate killers from non-killers. Instead they categorized men based on how many killings they had participated in: 1–5, 6–10, and 11+. Then they compared the numbers of wives and offspring among men in each of these categories. They found that killers of 1–5 people averaged 1.35 wives and 4.37 offspring, killers of 6–10 people averaged 2.00 wives and 6.08 offspring, and killers of 11+ people averaged 2.25 wives and 8.25 offspring. Thus, these data are highly consistent with those of Chagnon. The Robarcheks have essentially replicated Chagnon's finding, although they have a different interpretation of this result. They go on to present data showing that more prolific killers are more likely to get killed themselves and to lose a wife to violence; the latter are the only data that Tierney chooses to report. Tierney thus omits what is both the crux of the Robarcheks' study, and also the most useful element for evaluating the reliability of Chagnon's result: the successful replication of that result. . . .

Insinuates That Chagnon Dishonestly Confounded
Unokais and Headmen

Claim   Tierney insinuates that Chagnon dishonestly includes headmen, in addition to unokais, in his sample and that the presence of headmen somehow skewed his results:

> "In his *Science* piece all headmen were also included as "killers," a confusion of categories; when the headmen were factored out, the study's statistical significance in one of its major age categories collapsed, Chagnon admitted. He would not say which category it was. . . . Again, Chagnon maintained a tenacious silence in the face of public challenge, this time by the anthropologist Brian Ferguson."

Misrepresentation   Chagnon does indeed include headmen in his sample of unokais, but only because these headmen are unokai, as Chagnon states clearly: "All headmen in this study are unokai." Tierney seems to suggest that Chagnon includes some headmen that he knows not to be unokai. Brian Ferguson, in *American Ethnologist,* did challenge Chagnon's inclusion of headmen in his study, saying that since headmen usually have more wives and children, and since all headmen in the study were unokai, the inclusion of headmen might increase the correlation between unokainess and reproductive success. Ferguson's point is actually misguided: the fact that all headmen were unokai is highly consistent with Chagnon's theory that in tribal societies "cultural success leads to biological success," i.e. good warriorship leads to high social status, which in turn leads to high reproductive success, and it is absurd to suggest that the presence of unokai headmen somehow contradicts a theory which it in fact strongly supports. Nevertheless, in a piece entitled "Response to Ferguson" which immediately followed Ferguson's challenge in the same issue of *American Ethnologist,* Chagnon agreed to reanalyze the data with headmen removed. Even with headmen removed, unokais (compared to non-unokais) had significantly more offspring in all four age categories, and more wives in three of four age categories ($ps < .05$). In one age category (ages 31–40), the difference between unokai and non-unokai wives was just barely not significant ($p = .07$). The statistical "collapse" to which Tierney refers is apparently the fact that $p = .07$ rather than $<.05$ for the 31–40 category, an extremely minor discrepancy misleadingly referred to as a "collapse." And there was no "tenacious silence" by Chagnon with regard to which age category was affected by the removal of headmen: Chagnon states clearly in his *American Ethnologist* piece that the category is "31–40." Tierney is clearly aware of this article (he cites it and it appears in his bibliography), so it is odd that he seems to overlook it here. . . .

Misrepresents Chagnon's Explanation for Unokai Reproductive Success

Claim   Tierney suggests that Chagnon claims that the link between killing and reproductive success is due solely to the fact that Yanomamö killers are more successful in abducting women in raids. Tierney notes that this link is "tenuous" because only a "low" number of women are actually abducted in raids:

> Nor was there anything but the most tenuous connection between killing, raiding, and the capture of women. The number of women captured in the warfare of the Yanomami is low, despite their reputation. . . . Yet the popular image of the Yanomami waging war for women persisted. Chagnon deftly created it by repeatedly claiming that men went on raids, captured women, and raped them at will afterwards.

Misrepresentation   In fact, Chagnon has stated repeatedly that when he says the Yanomamö "fight over women," he does not mean that they usually initiate raids for the purpose of abducting women. He simply means that most conflicts begin as some kind of sexual dispute, and he makes this clear in the target article: "most fights begin over sexual issues: infidelity and suspicion of infidelity, attempts to seduce another man's wife, sexual jealousy, forcible appropriation of women from visiting groups, failure to give a promised girl in marriage, and (rarely) rape." On the same page he is clear that most wars are perpetuated by revenge, not the desire to abduct women: "The most common explanation given for raids (warfare) is revenge for a previous killing, and the most common explanation for the initial cause of the fighting is 'women'." In his famous ethnography—cited extensively by Tierney—Chagnon says "although few raids are initiated solely with the intention of capturing women, this is always a desired side benefit" and "Generally, however, the desire to abduct women does not lead to the initiation of hostilities between groups that have no history of mutual raiding in the past." Tierney completely ignores that Chagnon downplays the significance of abduction as a motivation to raid and then claims that Chagnon "deftly created" the image of the Yanomamö waging war in order to abduct women.

Further, by concentrating exclusively on abduction as the only explanation for the high reproductive success of unokais, Tierney ignores what Chagnon claims might be "the most promising avenue of investigation to account for the high reproductive success of unokais," the fact that "cultural success leads to biological success." Chagnon explains that unokais, because of their prowess and willingness to take risks in military matters, are regarded as more valuable allies than non-unokais: "in short, military achievements are valued and associated with high esteem." This high status of unokais makes them more attractive as mates. In a published response to criticism about the target article, Chagnon goes into even greater detail about how unokai status makes men more attractive as mates.

Why Has Tierney Been So Dishonest?

To conclude our preliminary report, we ask the obvious question, "Why has Tierney been so dishonest?" The short answer is, we don't know. We offer the following two speculations [one included here]—but we must stress that these are only speculations, speculations we ourselves find less than satisfying. . . .

The field of anthropology has been riven for at least the last two decades by a debate between 'scientifically oriented' anthropologists and 'humanistically oriented' anthropologists. The former tend to believe that there is an objective human reality and that scientific methods will help us discover it. The latter tend to believe that realities are relative, and socially or culturally constructed, and they are often extremely skeptical and critical of Western science. The debate between these two camps has frequently been so bitter that it has caused prominent anthropology departments, like Stanford's, to split in two. The debate is not confined to anthropology. It is widespread in the humanities and social sciences, and has come to be known as the Science Wars.

Tierney clearly hoped to successfully indict two of the most famous scientists to work with indigenous people in the Amazon, Chagnon and Neel, with serious crimes and breaches of ethics, and thus strike a blow against scientific, and particularly evolutionary, anthropology. For students and others, we provide our perspective on this issue, and how it may account, in part, for Tierney's dishonesty.

There are three fundamental aspects of Chagnon's career that place him at ground zero in the debate between 'scientific' anthropologists and 'humanistic' anthropologists. First, Chagnon has been a staunch and vocal proponent and practitioner of scientific anthropology, one whose books and films are widely assigned in anthropology courses around the world. Second, and even more galling to 'humanistically' oriented anthropologists (and disconcerting to many 'scientific' anthropologists as well) is Chagnon's use of sociobiological theory. Sociobiology is a set of theories and general principles about animal social behavior that derive from Darwin's theory of evolution by natural selection. Although biologists were excited by the sociobiological theories that appeared in the 1960's and 1970's, there was an immediate outcry by some biologists (e.g., Stephen J. Gould) and many social scientists when E. O. Wilson suggested that sociobiology might be useful for understanding *human* social behavior. It was 'obvious' to both sides in the sociobiology debate that the other side was motivated entirely by politics. In the ensuing war of words between supporters and critics of sociobiology, the field became stigmatized. Few social scientists are willing to use the theory, and even the many biologists employing sociobiology in their study of non-human animals avoid mentioning the word 'sociobiology.' Despite this, sociobiology is a standard part of the theoretical toolkit used by biologists in virtually every biology department in the world. It is, without doubt, the theory most widely used to study and understand the social behavior of all (non-human) living things. The world's most prestigious scientific journals, Science and Nature, routinely publish research articles using sociobiology, and hundreds of research articles using sociobiology are published every year in major biology journals. Applying sociobiology to humans, however, remains strictly taboo. Chagnon has openly violated this taboo by interpreting his data in light of sociobiological theories.

Finally, Chagnon has focused his career on one of the most contentious issues in anthropology: violence and aggression in small-scale, 'primitive' societies. Critiquing Western culture has been a popular topic in anthropology since the 1920's. (In fact, a widely used cultural anthropology text is titled *Anthropology as Cultural Critique.*) In order to critique Western culture, anthropologists often feel they must find non-Western cultures that do things better. Because violence and aggression in Western societies are well deserving of critique, anthropologists hoped to discover societies with little aggression or violence that could serve as examples of a better way of living. Chagnon, by contrast, argues that violence and aggression are common in most non-Western societies—even small-scale societies like the Yanomamö—and that violence and aggression are probably part of human nature. This has infuriated the many anthropologists who prefer practicing anthropology as cultural critique. The favorite alternative to Chagnon's interpretation of Yanomamö war is that of Brian Ferguson. Ferguson, unsurprisingly, blames Yanomamö war on the influence of Western culture.

By taking aim at Chagnon, Tierney has charged into the middle of this debate on the side of the humanists against the scientists, particularly against the tiny minority who apply Darwinian theory to people. The subtitle of his book is "How Scientists and Journalists Devastated the Amazon." The very first words in the book, in the frontpiece, are from Daniel Dennett: "It is important to recognize that Darwinism has always had an unfortunate power to attract the most unwelcome enthusiasts—demagogues and psychopaths and misanthropes and other abusers of Darwin's dangerous idea." (Although Tierney doesn't mention it, Dennett is actually a strong advocate of Darwinian approaches to social science, and has written in defense of Chagnon.) And much of the book is a muddled attempt to attack Chagnon's sociobiological approach to Yanomamö warfare. Tierney constantly inserts comments like "Chagnon picked up where Social Darwinists left off" (Ch. 2), and he is even willing to make unsupported accusations of murder: "the incredible faith the sociobiologists had in their theories was admirable. Like the old Marxist missionaries, these zealots of biological determinism sacrificed everything—including the lives of their subjects—to spread their gospel." (Ch. 2).

Maybe Tierney thought that if he could destroy Chagnon, arch-enemy of many humanistic anthropologists and culture critics, he would be a hero in the Science Wars. And maybe he really thought a victory in the Science Wars would help the Amazon and its peoples. But the Amazon is not being devastated by scientists. Or journalists. Or sociobiologists. It is being devastated by logging, mining, road building, and slash-and-burn farming by the region's burgeoning population. Character assassination will do precisely nothing to change this.

POSTSCRIPT

Did Napoleon Chagnon's Research Methods and Publications Harm the Yanomami Indians?

Turner agrees with journalist Patrick Tierney that Chagnon callously refused to disavow the image he created of the Yanomami as violent when gold miners and their supporters used that image against them. He also blames Chagnon for manipulating his data to contend that Yanomami are genetically programmed to be violent, due to violent males having more children than nonviolent ones, and for actually causing violence by his gift giving and violations of taboos. Hagen, Price, and Tooby retort that Tierney systematically selects and distorts his evidence to portray Chagnon in the worst possible light, and they argue that the amount of harm Chagnon did to the Yanomami pales compared to that caused by missionaries, gold miners, and other intruders into their territory.

This controversy exposed a deep rift in the anthropological community. The rift has been variously defined as between those who see anthropology as a science and those who consider it a humanistic discipline, between sociobiologists and cultural determinists, and, at the basest level, between scholars who personally like or dislike Neel and Chagnon. The battle lines are sharply drawn, and few anthropologists have remained neutral. The antagonists are pulling no punches in their charges and countercharges.

The El Dorado Task Force of the American Anthropological Association (AAA), which investigated Tierney's accusations, concluded, among other things, that Neel and his associates should be praised, not condemned, for vaccinating Yanomami against measles, an action that "unquestionably . . . saved many lives" (see the Final Report on the AAA Web site at http://www.aaanet. org). However, it criticized Chagnon on ethical and professional grounds for working with a group of wealthy and corrupt Venezuelans to gain access to the Yanomami in 1990, despite having been denied a research permit by the Venezuelan government. It also criticized him for misrepresenting the Yanomami as the "fierce people," a view used by others to justify violence against them, and for not correcting that image or supporting their human rights. Not surprisingly, the report has been criticized by Chagnon's supporters as too harsh and by his enemies as too lenient.

This controversy has generated a huge literature in a short time, the speed being due in large part to the widespread use of the Internet. The literature includes articles and book reviews in newspapers, popular magazines, and scholarly newsletters and journals; radio programs; and numerous documents and opinions posted on Web sites. The most comprehensive and balanced guide to sources is the Web site of Douglas Hume, a graduate student at the University of Connecticut (http://members.aol.com/archeodog/darkness_in_el_dorado/index.htm). It includes a comprehensive bibliography of materials published from September 2000 to the present and links to relevant Web sites and documents. The Web site for Public Anthropology (http://www.publicanthropology.org) contains papers from a round table discussion among several scholars with varying points of view. The Department of Anthropology at the University of California at Santa Barbara Web site (http://www.anth.ucsb.edu/chagnon.html) provides a number of documents and statements supporting Chagnon. The paperback edition of Tierney's book contains an eleven-page postscript responding to his critics. Other printed publications include the *Current Anthropology* Forum entitled "Reflections on Darkness in El Dorado," which presents comments by six scholars (*Current Anthropology,* vol. 42, no. 2, pp. 265–76, 2001). A relevant earlier source is Leslie Sponsel's article "Yanomami: An Arena of Conflict and Aggression in the Amazon" (*Aggressive Behavior,* vol. 24, no. 2, pp. 97–122, 1998).

ISSUE 19

Do Museums Misrepresent Ethnic Communities Around the World?

YES: James Clifford, from *The Predicament of Culture: Twentieth-Century Ethnography, Literature, and Art* (Harvard University Press, 1988)

NO: Denis Dutton, from "Mythologies of Tribal Art," *African Arts* (Summer 1995)

ISSUE SUMMARY

YES: Postmodernist anthropologist James Clifford argues that the very act of removing objects from their ethnographic contexts distorts the meaning of objects held in museums. He contends that whether these objects are displayed in art museums or anthropological museums, exhibitions misrepresent ethnic communities by omitting important aspects of contemporary life, especially involvement with the colonial or Western world.

NO: Anthropologist Denis Dutton asserts that no exhibition can provide a complete context for ethnographic objects, but that does not mean that museum exhibitions are fundamentally flawed. Dutton suggests that postmodernists misunderstand traditional approaches to interpreting museum collections, and what they offer as a replacement actually minimizes what we can understand of ethnic communities from museum collections.

In the late nineteenth and early twentieth centuries, museums were a major focus of anthropological research. In the United States, for example, until after the First World War more anthropologists were employed in museums than in universities. By 1940 cultural anthropologists had largely moved out of museums as they focused on intensive fieldwork. This change was directly related to a shift in paradigms from cultural evolution to functionalism, which happened in the 1920s and 1930s.

As anthropologists later began to focus on functional questions about how societies and their institutions worked, museum collections became increasingly unimportant. Many anthropologists believed that differences in the bindings of stone axes have little to say about how marriages were contracted or how clans were linked together; objects cannot explain how leadership worked or what role religious ideas might have had in maintaining social order.

The following selections deal with the question of how museums should exhibit and interpret ethnographic collections that were obtained during the "museum period" of anthropology. Both authors are critical of certain exhibitions, particularly art historian William Rubin's "Primitivism" show from 1984, and both feel that a good exhibition should contextualize museum objects historically. But the authors differ profoundly in their approach to the study of museum objects.

James Clifford surveys several different kinds of museum exhibits in New York and asks, Do any of them do justice to the peoples who made and used these objects? For Clifford, objects and the cultures from which they come have histories. He questions how much of these histories are present in the several exhibitions he visited. By definition, each and every non-Western object in a Western museum has been removed from its original ethnographic context, a process often referred to as "decontextualization."

Clifford explains in his selection how museums offer a "representation" of tribal peoples as if these societies were timeless and without history. By focusing on particular features of tribal culture, each exhibition makes statements about the relationship between modern Americans and "primitive" peoples. For him, these are fundamentally misleading representations.

Denis Dutton accepts that exhibitions such as those discussed by Clifford are inevitably incomplete, but the lack of a full context does not completely invalidate the exercise of exhibiting objects from tribal societies. He argues that Clifford and the other postmodernist critics of museum exhibitions go too far in their criticisms and that they, too, have an agenda that is itself misleading. Referring to this postmodernist agenda as a "new mythology" about tribal art, Dutton contends that the new mythologists have exaggerated their interpretations of museum exhibitions.

Dutton argues that museums can never offer complete representations of ethnic communities; but this does not mean that exhibitions cannot be both informative and enlightening even if they are incomplete. He asserts that Clifford's analysis leads us away from any understanding of museum objects; instead Clifford prefers to present his understandings of the culture through museum curators in our own modern culture. For Dutton, the goal should be to discover the meanings and significance of objects from the point of view of their original communities, and such meanings will never emerge from critiques of museum exhibitions like Clifford's.

How serious are the inevitable distortions of a museum exhibit? Does the omission of the current historical and global economic context misinform the public? How much context can a museum exhibition realistically provide? If such misrepresentations do occur, would it be better not to exhibit "primitive" art at all? What solutions to the problem of distortion do Clifford and Dutton propose?

YES

James Clifford

Histories of the Tribal
and the Modern

> During the winter of 1984–85 one could encounter tribal objects in an unusual number of locations around New York City. This [selection] surveys a half-dozen, focusing on the most controversial: the major exhibition held at the Museum of Modern Art (MOMA), "'Primitivism' in 20th Century Art: Affinity of the Tribal and the Modern." The . . . "ethnographic present" is late December 1984.

The "tribal" objects gathered on West Fifty-third Street have been around. They are travelers—some arriving from folklore and ethnographic museums in Europe, others from art galleries and private collections. They have traveled first class to the Museum of Modern Art, elaborately crated and insured for important sums. Previous accommodations have been less luxurious: some were stolen, others "purchased" for a song by colonial administrators, travelers, anthropologists, missionaries, sailors in African ports. These non-Western objects have been by turns curiosities, ethnographic specimens, major art creations. After 1900 they began to turn up in European flea markets, thereafter moving between avant-garde studios and collectors' apartments. Some came to rest in the unheated basements or "laboratories" of anthropology museums, surrounded by objects made in the same region of the world. Others encountered odd fellow travelers, lighted and labeled in strange display cases. Now on West Fifty-third Street they intermingle with works by European masters—Picasso, Giacometti, Brancusi, and others. A three-dimensional Eskimo mask with twelve arms and a number of holes hangs beside a canvas on which Joan Miró has painted colored shapes. The people in New York look at the two objects and see that they are alike.

Travelers tell different stories in different places, and on West Fifty-third Street an origin story of modernism is featured. Around 1910 Picasso and his cohort suddenly, intuitively recognize that "primitive" objects are in fact powerful "art." They collect, imitate, and are affected by these objects. Their own work, even when not directly influenced, seems oddly reminiscent of non-Western forms. The modern and the primitive converse across the centuries and continents. At the Museum of Modern Art an exact history is told featuring individual artists and objects, their encounters in specific studios at precise

From *The Predicament of Culture, Twentieth Century Ethnography, Literature, and Art*, April, 1988, pp. 189–193, 195–207. Copyright © 1988 by Art In America. Reprinted by permission.

moments. Photographs document the crucial influences of non-Western arti-facts on the pioneer modernists. This focused story is surrounded and infused with another—a loose allegory of relationship centering on the word *affinity*. The word is a kinship term, suggesting a deeper or more natural relationship than mere resemblance or juxtaposition. It connotes a common quality or essence joining the tribal to the modern. A Family of Art is brought together, global, diverse, richly inventive, and miraculously unified, for every object displayed on West Fifty-third Street looks modern.

The exhibition at MOMA is historical and didactic. It is complemented by a comprehensive, scholarly catalogue, which includes divergent views of its topic and in which the show's organizers, William Rubin and Kirk Varnedoe, argue at length its underlying premises. One of the virtues of an exhibition that blatantly makes a case or tells a story is that it encourages debate and makes possible the suggestion of other stories. Thus in what follows different histories of the tribal and the modern will be proposed in response to the sharply focused history on display at the Museum of Modern Art. But before that history can be seen for what it is, however—a specific story that excludes other stories—the universalizing allegory of affinity must be cleared away.

This allegory, the story of the Modernist Family of Art, is not rigorously argued at MOMA. (That would require some explicit form of either an arche-typal or structural analysis.) The allegory is, rather, built into the exhibition's form, featured suggestively in its publicity, left uncontradicted, repetitiously asserted—"Affinity of the Tribal and the Modern." The allegory has a hero, whose virtuoso work, an exhibit caption tells us, contains more affinities with the tribal than that of any other pioneer modernist. These affinities "measure the depth of Picasso's grasp of the informing principles of tribal sculpture, and reflect his profound identity of spirit with the tribal peoples." Modernism is thus presented as a search for "informing principles" that transcend culture, politics, and history. Beneath this generous umbrella the tribal is modern and the modern more richly, more diversely human.

⋅⟨◉⟩⋅

The power of the affinity idea is such (it becomes almost self-evident in the MOMA juxtapositions) that it is worth reviewing the major objections to it. Anthropologists, long familiar with the issue of cultural diffusion versus inde-pendent invention, are not likely to find anything special in the similarities between selected tribal and modern objects. An established principle of anthro-pological comparative method asserts that the greater the range of cultures, the more likely one is to find similar traits. MOMA's sample is very large, embracing African, Oceanian, North American, and Arctic "tribal" groups. A second principle, that of the "limitation of possibilities," recognizes that invention, while highly diverse, is not infinite. The human body, for example, with its two eyes, four limbs, bilateral arrangement of features, front and back, and so on, will be represented and stylized in a limited number of ways. There is thus a priori no reason to claim evidence for affinity (rather than mere resemblance or coincidence) because an exhibition of tribal works that seem impressively "modern" in style can be gathered. An equally striking collection could be made demonstrating sharp dissimilarities between tribal and modern objects.

The qualities most often said to link these objects are their "conceptualism" and "abstraction" (but a very long and ultimately incoherent list of shared traits, including "magic," "ritualism," "environmentalism," use of "natural" materials, and so on, can be derived from the show and especially from its catalogue). Actually the tribal and modern artifacts are similar only in that they do *not* feature the pictorial illusionism or sculptural naturalism that came to dominate Western European art after the Renaissance. Abstraction and conceptualism are, of course, pervasive in the arts of the non-Western World. To say that they share with modernism a rejection of certain naturalist projects is not to show anything like an affinity. Indeed the "tribalism" selected in the exhibition to resemble modernism is itself a construction designed to accomplish the task of resemblance. Ife and Benin sculptures, highly naturalistic in style, are excluded from the "tribal" and placed in a somewhat arbitrary category of "court" society (which does not, however, include large chieftainships). Moreover, pre-Columbian works, though they have a place in the catalogue, are largely omitted from the exhibition. One can question other selections and exclusions that result in a collection of only "modern"-looking tribal objects. Why, for example, are there relatively few "impure" objects constructed from the debris of colonial culture contacts? And is there not an overall bias toward clean, abstract forms as against rough or crude work?

The "Affinities" room of the exhibition is an intriguing but entirely problematic exercise in formal mix-and-match. The short introductory text begins well: "AFFINITIES presents a group of tribal objects notable for their appeal to modern taste." Indeed this is all that can rigorously be said of the objects in this room. The text continues, however, "Selected pairings of modern and tribal objects demonstrate common denominators of these arts that are independent of direct influence." The phrase *common denominators* implies something more systematic than intriguing resemblance. What can it possibly mean? . . . The affinity idea itself is wide-ranging and promiscuous, as are allusions to universal human capacities retrieved in the encounter between modern and tribal or invocations of the expansive human mind—the healthy capacity of modernist consciousness to question its limits and engage otherness.

. . . The affinities shown at MOMA are all on modernist terms. The great modernist "pioneers" (and their museum) are shown promoting formerly despised tribal "fetishes" or mere ethnographic "specimens" to the status of high art and in the process discovering new dimensions of their ("our") creative potential. The capacity of art to transcend its cultural and historical context is asserted repeatedly. . . .

At West Fifth-third Street modernist primitivism is a going Western concern. . . .

Indeed an unintended effect of the exhibition's comprehensive catalogue is to show once and for all the incoherence of the modern Rorschach of "the primitive." . . . [T]he catalogue succeeds in demonstrating not any essential affinity between tribal and modern or even a coherent modernist attitude toward the primitive but rather the restless desire and power of the modern West to collect the world.

⚜

. . . If we ignore the "Affinities" room at MOMA, however, and focus on the "serious" historical part of the exhibition, new critical questions emerge. What is excluded by the specific focus of the history? Isn't this factual narration still infused with the affinity allegory, since it is cast as a story of creative genius recognizing the greatness of tribal works, discovering common artistic "informing principles"? Could the story of this intercultural encounter be told differently? It is worth making the effort to extract another story from the materials in the exhibition—a history not of redemption or of discovery but of reclassification. This other history assumes that "art" is not universal but is a changing Western cultural category. The fact that rather abruptly, in the space of a few decades, a large class of non-Western artifacts came to be redefined as art is a taxonomic shift that requires critical historical discussion, not celebration. That this construction of a generous category of art pitched at a global scale occurred just as the planet's tribal peoples came massively under European political, economic, and evangelical dominion cannot be irrelevant. But there is no room for such complexities at the MOMA show. Obviously the modernist appropriation of tribal productions as art is not simply imperialist. The project involves too many strong critiques of colonialist, evolutionist assumptions. As we shall see, though, the scope and underlying logic of the "discovery" of tribal art reproduces hegemonic Western assumptions rooted in the colonial and neocolonial epoch.

Picasso, Léger, Apollinaire, and many others came to recognize the elemental, "magical" power of African sculptures in a period of growing *négrophilie,* a context that would see the irruption onto the European scene of other evocative black figures: the jazzman, the boxer (Al Brown), the *sauvage* Josephine Baker. To tell the history of modernism's recognition of African "art" in this broader context would raise ambiguous and disturbing questions about aesthetic appropriation of non-Western others, issues of race, gender, and power. This other story is largely invisible at MOMA. . . . Overall one would be hard pressed to deduce from the exhibition that all the enthusiasm for things *nègre,* for the "magic" of African art, had anything to do with race. Art in this focused history has no essential link with coded perceptions of black bodies—their vitalism, rhythm, magic, erotic power, etc.—as seen by whites. The modernism represented here is concerned only with artistic invention, a positive category separable from a negative primitivism of the irrational, the savage, the base, the flight from civilization.

A different historical focus might bring a photograph of Josephine Baker into the vicinity of the African statues that were exciting the Parisian avant-garde in the 1910s and 1920s; but such a juxtaposition would be unthinkable in the MOMA history, for it evokes different affinities from those contributing to the category of great art. The black body in Paris of the twenties was an ideological artifact. Archaic Africa (which came to Paris by way of the future—that is,

America) was sexed, gendered, and invested with "magic" in specific ways. Standard poses adopted by "La Bakaire," like Léger's designs and costumes, evoked a recognizable "Africanity"—the naked form emphasizing pelvis and buttocks, a segmented stylization suggesting a strangely mechanical vitality. The inclusion of so ideologically loaded a form as the body of Josephine Baker among the figures classified as art on West Fifty-third Street would suggest a different account of modernist primitivism, a different analysis of the category *nègre* in *l'art nègre* and an exploration of the "taste" that was something more than just a backdrop for the discovery of tribal art in the opening decades of this century.

Such a focus would treat art as a category defined and redefined in specific historical contexts and relations of power. . . .

Since 1900 non-Western objects have generally been classified as either primitive art *or* ethnographic specimens. Before the modernist revolution associated with Picasso and the simultaneous rise of cultural anthropology associated with Boas and Malinowski, these objects were differently sorted—as antiquities, exotic curiosities, orientalia, the remains of early man, and so on. With the emergence of twentieth-century modernism and anthropology figures formerly called "fetishes" (to take just one class of object) became works either of "sculpture" or of "material culture." The distinction between the aesthetic and the anthropological was soon institutionally reinforced. In art galleries non-Western objects were displayed for their formal and aesthetic qualities; in ethnographic museums they were represented in a "cultural" context. In the latter an African statue was a ritual object belonging to a distinct group; it was displayed in ways that elucidated its use, symbolism, and function. The institutionalized distinction between aesthetic and anthropological discourses took form during the years documented at MOMA, years that saw the complementary discovery of primitive "art" and of an anthropological concept of culture." . . .

Cultural background is not essential to correct aesthetic appreciation and analysis: good art, the masterpiece, is universally recognizable. The pioneer modernists themselves knew little or nothing of these objects' ethnographic meaning. What was good enough for Picasso is good enough for MOMA. Indeed an ignorance of cultural context seems almost a precondition for artistic appreciation. In this object system a tribal piece is detached from one milieu in order to circulate freely in another, a world of art—of museums, markets, and connoisseurship.

Since the early years of modernism and cultural anthropology non-Western objects have found a "home" either within the discourses and institutions of art or within those of anthropology. . . . Both discourses assume a primitive world in need of preservation, redemption, and representation. The concrete, inventive existence of tribal cultures and artists is suppressed in the process of either constituting authentic, "traditional" worlds or appreciating their products in the timeless category of "art."

e·⊙·ɔ

Nothing on West Fifty-third Street suggests that good tribal art is being produced in the 1980s. The non-Western artifacts on display are located either in a vague past (reminiscent of the label "nineteenth-twentieth century" that accompanies African and Oceanian pieces in the Metropolitan Museum's Rockefeller Wing) or in a purely conceptual space defined by "primitive" qualities: magic, ritualism, closeness to nature, mythic or cosmological aims. In this relegation of the tribal or primitive to either a vanishing past or an ahistorical, conceptual present, modernist appreciation reproduces common ethnographic categories.

The same structure can be seen in the Hall of Pacific Peoples, dedicated to Margaret Mead, at the American Museum of Natural History. This new permanent hall is a superbly refurbished anthropological stopping place for non-Western objects. In *Rotunda* (December 1984), the museum's publication, an article announcing the installation contains the following paragraph:

> Margaret Mead once referred to the cultures of Pacific peoples as "a world that once was and now is no more." Prior to her death in 1978 she approved the basic plans for the new *Hall of Pacific Peoples.* (p. 1)

We are offered treasures saved from a destructive history, relics of a vanishing world. Visitors to the installation (and especially members of *present* Pacific cultures) may find a "world that is no more" more appropriately evoked in two charming display cases just outside the hall. It is the world of a dated anthropology. Here one finds a neatly typed page of notes from Mead's much-disputed Samoan research, a picture of the fieldworker interacting "closely" with Melanesians (she is carrying a child on her back), a box of brightly colored discs and triangles once used for psychological testing, a copy of Mead's column in *Redbook*. In the Hall of Pacific Peoples artifacts suggesting change and syncretism are set apart in a small display entitled "Culture Contact." It is noted that Western influence and indigenous response have been active in the Pacific since the eighteenth century. Yet few signs of this involvement appear anywhere else in the large hall, despite the fact that many of the objects were made in the past 150 years in situations of contact, and despite the fact that the museum's ethnographic explanations reflect quite recent research on the cultures of the Pacific. The historical contacts and impurities that are part of ethnographic work—and that may signal the life, not the death, of societies—are systematically excluded.

The tenses of the hall's explanatory captions are revealing. A recent color photograph of a Samoan *kava* ceremony is accompanied by the words: "STATUS and RANK were [sic] important features of Samoan society," a statement that will seem strange to anyone who knows how important they remain in Samoa today. Elsewhere in the hall a black-and-white photograph of an Australian Arunta woman and child, taken around 1900 by the pioneer ethnographers Spencer and Gillen, is captioned in the *present* tense. Aboriginals apparently must always inhabit a mythic time. Many other examples of temporal incoherence could be cited—old Sepik objects described in the present, recent Trobriand photos labeled in the past, and so forth.

The point is not simply that the image of Samoan *kava* drinking and status society presented here is a distortion or that in most of the Hall of Pacific

Peoples history has been airbrushed out. (No Samoan men at the *kava* ceremony are wearing wristwatches; Trobriand face painting is shown without noting that it is worn at cricket matches.) Beyond such questions of accuracy is an issue of systematic ideological coding. To locate "tribal" peoples in a nonhistorical time and ourselves in a different, historical time is clearly tendentious and no longer credible (Fabian 1983). This recognition throws doubt on the perception of a vanishing tribal world, rescued, made valuable and meaningful, either as ethnographic "culture" or as primitive/modern "art." . . .

At the Hall of Pacific Peoples or the Rockefeller Wing the actual ongoing-life and "impure" inventions of tribal peoples are erased in the name of cultural or artistic "authenticity." Similarly at MOMA the production of tribal "art" is entirely in the past. Turning up in the flea markets and museums of late nineteenth-century Europe, these objects are destined to be aesthetically redeemed, given new value in the object system of a generous modernism.

⋅◦⊙◦⋅

The story retold at MOMA, the struggle to gain recognition for tribal art, for its capacity "like all great art . . . to show images of man that transcend the particular lives and times of their creators," is taken for granted at another stopping place for tribal travelers in Manhattan, the Center for African Art on East Sixty-eighth Street. Susan Vogel, the executive director, proclaims in her introduction to the catalogue of its inaugural exhibition, "African Masterpieces from the Musee de l'Homme," that the "aesthetic-anthropological debate" has been resolved. It is now widely accepted that "ethnographic specimens" can be distinguished from "works of art" and that within the latter category a limited number of "masterpieces" are to be found. Vogel correctly notes that the aesthetic recognition of tribal objects depends on changes in Western taste. For example it took the work of Francis Bacon, Lucas Samaras, and others to make it possible to exhibit as art "rough and horrifying [African] works as well as refined and lyrical ones." Once recognized, though, art is apparently art. Thus the selection at the Center is made on aesthetic criteria alone. A prominent placard affirms that the ability of these objects "to transcend the limitations of time and place, to speak to us across time and culture . . . places them among the highest points of human achievement. It is as works of art that we regard them here and as a testament to the greatness of their creators."

There could be no clearer statement of one side of the aesthetic anthropological "debate" (or better, *system*). On the other (anthropological) side, across town, the Hall of Pacific Peoples presents collective rather than individual productions—the work of "cultures." At the American Museum of Natural History ethnographic exhibits have come increasingly to resemble art shows. Indeed the Hall of Pacific Peoples represents the latest in aestheticized scientism. Objects are displayed in ways that highlight their formal properties. . . . While these artistically displayed artifacts are scientifically explained, an older, functionalist attempt to present an integrated picture of specific societies or culture areas is no longer seriously pursued. There is an almost dadaist quality to the labels on eight cases devoted to Australian aboriginal society (I cite the complete series in order): "CEREMONY, SPIRIT FIGURE, MAGICIANS AND SORCERERS, SACRED ART, SPEAR THROWERS, STONE AXES AND KNIVES, WOMEN, BOOMERANGS." Elsewhere the hall's pieces of culture have been recontextualized within a new cybernetic, anthropological discourse. For instance flutes and stringed instruments are captioned: "MUSIC is a system of organized sound in man's [sic] aural environment" or nearby: "COMMUNICATION is an important function of organized sound."

In the anthropological Hall of Pacific Peoples non-Western objects still have primarily scientific value. They are in addition beautiful. Conversely, at the Center for African Art artifacts are essentially defined as "masterpieces," their makers as great artists. The discourse of connoisseurship reigns. Yet once the story of art told at MOMA becomes dogma, it is possible to reintroduce and co-opt the discourse of ethnography. At the Center tribal contexts and functions are described along with individual histories of the objects on display. Now firmly classified as masterpieces, African objects escape the vague, ahistorical location of the "tribal" or the "primitive." The catalogue, a sort of *catalogue raisonné,* discusses each work intensively. The category of the masterpiece individuates: the pieces on display are not typical; some are one of a kind. The famous Fon god of war or the Abomey shark-man lend themselves to precise histories of individual creation and appropriation in visible colonial situations. Captions specify *which* Griaule expedition to West Africa in the 1930s acquired each Dogon statue. . . . We learn in the catalogue that a superb Bamileke mother and child was carved by an artist named Kwayep, that the statue was bought by the colonial administrator and anthropologist Henri Labouret from King N'Jike. While tribal names predominate at MOMA, the Rockefeller Wing, and the American Museum of Natural History, here personal names make their appearance.

In the "African Masterpieces" catalogue we learn of an ethnographer's excitement on finding a Dogon hermaphrodite figure that would later become famous. The letter recording this excitement, written by Denise Paulme in 1935, serves as evidence of the aesthetic concerns of many early ethnographic collectors. These individuals, we are told, could intuitively distinguish masterpieces from mere art or ethnographic specimens. (Actually many of the individual ethnographers behind the Musée de l'Homme collection, such as Paulme, Michel Leiris, Marcel Griaule, and André Schaeffner, were friends and collaborators of the same "pioneer modernist" artists who, in the story told at MOMA, constructed the category of primitive art. Thus the intuitive aesthetic sense in question is the product of a historically specific milieu.) The "African Masterpieces" catalogue insists that the founders of the Musée de l'Homme were art connoisseurs, that this great anthropological museum never treated all its contents as "ethnographic specimens." The Musee de l'Homme was and is secretly an art museum. The taxonomic split between art and artifact is thus healed, at least for self-evident "masterpieces," entirely in terms of the aesthetic code. Art is art in any museum. . . .

The non-Western objects that excited Picasso, Derain, and Léger broke into the realm of official Western art from outside. They were quickly integrated, recognized as masterpieces, given homes within an anthropological-aesthetic object system. By now this process has been sufficiently celebrated. We need exhibitions that question the boundaries of art and of the art world, an influx of truly indigestible "outside" artifacts. The relations of power whereby one portion of humanity can select, value, and collect the pure products of others need to be criticized and transformed. This is no small task. In the meantime one can at least imagine shows that feature the impure, "inauthentic" productions of past and present tribal life; exhibitions radically heterogeneous in their global mix of styles; exhibitions that locate themselves in specific multicultural junctures; exhibitions in which nature remains "unnatural"; exhibitions whose principles of incorporation are openly questionable. The following would be my contribution to a different show on "affinities of the tribal and the postmodern." I offer just the first paragraph from Barbara Tedlock's superb description of the Zuni Shalako ceremony, a festival that is only part of a complex, living tradition.

> Imagine a small western New Mexican village, its snow-lit streets lined with white Mercedes, quarter-ton pickups and Dodge vans. Villagers wrapped in black blankets and flowered shawls are standing next to visitors in blue velveteen blouses with rows of dime buttons and voluminous satin skirts. Their men are in black Stetson silver-banded hats, pressed jeans, Tony Lama boots and multicolored Pendleton blankets. Strangers dressed in dayglo orange, pink and green ski jackets, stocking caps, hiking boots and mittens. All crowded together they are looking into newly constructed houses illuminated by bare light bulbs dangling from raw rafters edged with Woolworth's red fabric and flowered blue print calico. Cinderblock and plasterboard white walls are layered with striped serapes, Chimayó blankets, Navajo rugs, flowered fringed embroidered shawls, black silk from Mexico and purple, red and blue rayon from Czechoslovakia. Rows of Hopi cotton dance kilts and rain sashes; Isleta woven red and green belts; Navajo and Zuni silver concha belts and black mantas covered with silver brooches set with carved lapidary, rainbow mosaic, channel inlay, turquoise needlepoint, pink agate, alabaster, black cannel coal and bakelite from old '78s, coral, abalone shell, mother-of-pearl and horned oyster hang from poles suspended from the ceiling. Mule and white-tailed deer trophy-heads wearing squash-blossom, coral and chunk-turquoise necklaces are hammered up around the room over rearing buckskins above Arabian tapestries of Martin Luther King and the Kennedy brothers, The Last Supper, a herd of sheep with a haloed herder, horses, peacocks.

Denis Dutton

Mythologies of Tribal Art

Forty years ago Roland Barthes defined a mythology as those "falsely obvious" ideas which an age so takes for granted that it is unaware of its own belief. An example of what he means can be seen in his 1957 critique of Edward Steichen's celebrated photographic assemblage "The Family of Man." Barthes declares that the myth this exhibition promotes first seems to stress exoticism, projecting a Babel of human diversity over the globe. From this picture of diversity, however, a pluralistic humanism "is magically produced: man is born, works, laughs and dies everywhere in the same way. . . ." The implicit mythological background of the show postulates "a human essence."

Barthes is exactly on target about the philosophic intentions of "The Family of Man." In his introduction to the published version of the exhibition, Steichen had written that the show was "conceived as a mirror of the universal elements and emotions in the everydayness of life—as a mirror of the essential oneness of mankind throughout the world." Such juxtapositions as that which places Nina Leen's *Life* magazine image of an American farm family next to a family in Bechuanaland (now Botswana), photographed by another *Life* photographer, Nat Farbman, are therefore meant to convey the idea that despite all differences of exterior form, of cultural surface, the underlying nature of all families and peoples is essentially the same. This position is what Barthes views as the sentimentalized mythology of "classic humanism," and he contrasts it with his own "progressive humanism," which must try "constantly to scour nature, its 'laws' and its 'limits' in order to discover History there, and at last to establish Nature itself as historical." While classic humanism regards the American and African families as embodying, beneath culture and skin color, abiding natural relationships of kin and affection, progressive humanism would insist that these bourgeois conceptions of the natural are themselves historically determined. Barthes claims that such imperialistic juxtapositions ignore the political and economic roots of diversity.

Although "The Family of Man" had a potently relevant message for the generation that had witnessed the genocidal horrors of the Second World War, it was also worth paying attention to Barthes's claim that Steichen's collection, for all its antiracism and humanist charms, conveyed an implicit illusion of equality of power among the cultures it portrayed. It is now two generations later, however, and critics who accept the importance of exposing cultural mythologies and covert ideologies have new work to do. One area of criticism

From *African Arts*, vol. 28, no. 3, Summer 1995, pp. 32–41. Copyright © 1995 by Denis Dutton. Reprinted by permission.

that especially stands in need of fresh examination is the shell-pocked field where battles have raged over the status and understanding of ethnographic arts. Barthes's reaction to MOMA's "The Family of Man" is particularly pertinent in this regard, because much of what he says adumbrates reactions to another exhibition, " 'Primitivism' in 20th Century Art," which took place over a quarter of a century later in that same museum. That show displayed side-by-side images of Africa and Europe, not photographs of people, but works of art. And it too was denounced as complacently positing, without regard to cultural difference, a specious universalism—aesthetic instead of moral.

But a sea change in academic thinking separates Barthes's critique of "The Family of Man" from the more strident critics of the "Primitivism" show. In the middle 1950s, Barthes was nearly alone in his dissent against a much loved and widely praised exhibition. The generation of critics who questioned (or denounced) "Primitivism" represented a manner of thinking that had become a virtual academic fashion. Some of these later critics were arguing from a set of ideas that had themselves come to embody a virtual mythology in precisely the Barthesian sense. Their views presuppose and constitute, in point of fact, a New Mythology of tribal arts—a prevailing set of presuppositions, prejudices, and articles of political and philosophical faith which govern many discussions of these arts and their relations to European criticism, art, and aesthetics. A contemporary Africanist art historian [Sidney Kasfir] for example, writes in a recent *African Arts* article on the authenticity of African masks and carvings: "That from an African perspective, these objects are *not* art in the current Western sense is too well known to discuss here." The phrase "too well known to discuss here" is symptomatic of a mythology. Barthes claimed his intention to unmask "the mystification which transforms petit-bourgeois culture into universal nature." Today we should be just as willing to deal with those mystifications that transform prevailing conventions of academic culture into validated truth.

This vigorous New Mythology of tribal arts takes on its life against the backdrop of what it posits as the Old Mythology. As with other ideologies, the New Mythology would no more describe its precepts as "mythology" than would the Old: both operate according to the familiar adage "Your views are so much mythology; mine speak the truth." Nevertheless, much contemporary theorizing and criticism about tribal arts are founded on a complacent acceptance of a substrate of givens and unsupported hypotheses which constitute the central tenets of the New Mythology. To be sure, not all of the theses are false. On the other hand, not all of the beliefs the New Mythologists stigmatize as Old Mythology are false either. Independent, critical thinkers should want to choose the component ideas of these mythologies that are worth rejecting, preserving, or reviving.

Providing a disinterested assessment of these ideas is not easy in the present ideologically charged and factious atmosphere. This indeed is part of the problem: so many contemporary theorists of tribal arts posit enemies who have it all wrong, in contrast to themselves, who have it right. This lack of any generosity whatsoever toward one's perceived (or invented) opposition increasingly stultifies writing in this area. The New Mythology finds itself expressed by a wide range of writers, including, for example, the more vociferous critics of the "Primitivism" show such as Thomas McEvilley and Hal Foster; James Clifford in his treatment of museums and ethnographic art; Arnold Krupat in *Ethnocriticism;* Sidney Kasfir in her article "African Art and Authenticity," published in this journal; Sally Price in *Primitive Art in Civilized Places;* Marianna Torgovnick in *Gone Primitive;* and Christopher B. Steiner in *African Art in Transit.*

Mythologies, Old and New

There are actually two phases of the Old Mythology to which these writers tend to react. What I will call *premodernist* or *colonialist* Old Mythology includes the elements of nineteenth-century imperialism—racism, contempt for "childish" artifacts, and regard for "primitive" art as representing a lower evolutionary stage of human development, with missionaries burning "fetishes" and the wholesale looting of indigenous art, as in Benin. The later, more enlightened, *modernist* Old Mythology, exemplified by such figures as Picasso, Roger Fry, and the "Primitivism" exhibition itself, is, from a New Mythological perspective, perhaps even more insidious, because while it pretends to valorize these arts, it perpetuates acts of imperialism, appropriation, and ethnocentric insensitivity toward Third World peoples—all in the name of enlightened, magnanimous liberalism. The grounds for my three-fold distinction—between premodernist/ colonialist Old Mythology, modernist Old Mythology, and the New Mythology— can be usefully developed in terms of the following key ideas. Again, some of these notions included within these mythologies are entirely valid, some constitute half-truths, and some are plainly false; no one of these sets of ideas has a monopoly on truth.

> *(1) According to the premodernist Old Mythology, at least as the New Mythology likes to imagine it, tribal artifacts weren't works of art at all, but merely "fetishes," "idols," "fertility symbols," "ancestor figures," and the like, which colonialists collected as they might botanical specimens. The later, post-Picasso modernist version of the Old Mythology insists, on the contrary, that they are works of art, embodying universal aesthetic values.*

Curiously, the New Mythology frequently sides with the colonialist Old Mythology by aggressively questioning the status of tribal artifacts as works of art: in the New Mythological view, the Old Mythology at least acknowledged difference. This convergence of opinion, however, is complicated. Philistine colonialists often regarded artifacts as demonstrating little skill and no sense of form: the colonialists were applying nineteenth-century European aesthetic criteria to genres of work they did not begin to comprehend, and so were reluctant to call them "art." The New Mythologists' reluctance to identify tribal artifact genres as "art" is based on the notion that this would be hegemonic or imperialistic. Such reluctance is frequently supported by unthinking repetition of the folk legend that pretechnological peoples have no art because they have no word that refers to what Europeans call "art." Patrick R. McNaughton recognizes another aspect of this New Mythologists' doctrine and has stressed the importance of challenging it, "because so many scholars still recite what has become a kind of maxim asserted by outsiders about Africans, that they unlike us treat what we call art as a functional part of life" rather than something for aesthetic contemplation.

> *(2) The Old Mythology essentialized the primitive, subsuming the endless variety of tribal cultures under a few crude stereotypes.*

The New Mythology, on the other hand, while eager to recognize the diverse and frequently unique characteristics that distinguish tribal societies, essentializes "the West," creating, in an inversion of Edward Said's familiar formulation, a kind of Occidentalism. Thus, in the example cited earlier, Kasfir qualifies her discussion of authenticity with the remark that the artifacts in question should not be considered art "in the current Western sense." The quaintness of this last phrase should not go unnoticed: among Praxiteles, Donatello, Rembrandt, Judy Chicago, Duchamp, and Koons—not to mention the myriad genres of European folk craft and popular art—there is no "current Western sense" of art, but various, radically different, and rival senses of the concept, each partially implicated in competing social practices and theories of art. In fact, in its crudity, the very phrase "the West" is the New Mythologists' answer to "the Primitive" as that term might have been used a century ago. The latter was a lazy and misleading way of lumping together such cultures as Hopi, Sepik, Benin, and !Kung—even Aztec, in some understandings of "primitive." In the New Mythology, "the West" refers to twelfth-century French villages, horror movies, the Industrial Revolution, the theology of St. Augustine, New Zealand public education, the international banking system, modern toy retailing, medieval concepts of disease, Thanksgiving dinner, electronic mail, Gregorian chants, Linnaean botany, napalm, the Chopin études, and bar codes—as though the values and ideologies found therein can be the subject of useful generalization. The New Mythology replaces one set of stereotypes with another set, equally banal.

> *(3) In the Old Mythology, precontact tribal societies were seen as largely isolated, unchanging, coherent, and unbroken in their cultural tradition. Colonialism was supposed to have destroyed their structure and belief base. Their Golden Age of aesthetic and cultural achievement, and hence authenticity, predates European contact. Postcolonial culture and artifacts are culturally "inauthentic."*

The New Mythology asserts to the contrary that these societies never were isolated, were not necessarily "unified" or "coherent," and underwent profound breaks in their traditions before European contact. The Old Mythology's "people without a history" view was a convenient colonialist construction. The New Mythology responds to claims of "inauthenticity" by variously claiming (a) indigenous belief systems were not destroyed but only occulted during the colonial period, and are now coming again into flower; (b) what is truly authentic is now found in the process of mutual appropriation by indigenous and colonial cultures; and in any event, (c) authentic cultural values must always be defined by the people who hold them: therefore, whatever indigenous people claim as authentic is, *ipso facto*, authentic, whether traditional, postcolonial, or merely imported.

Old and New Mythologists for the most part agree that small-scale indigenous societies have been permanently altered or obliterated by the encounter with the West's political systems, media, missionaries, technology, commerce, wage labor, and so forth. New Mythologists, however, are especially keen to emphasize that this has involved imperialist domination and exploitation. What is awkward for them is the fact that less desirable elements of culture change have been enthusiastically (and voluntarily) embraced by many indigenous peoples: cigarettes, soft drinks, movies, pop music, and Jack Daniels. By stressing that tribal cultures were always borrowing and in a state of flux, the New Mythology places in benign perspective the obliteration (or active abandonment) of traditional indigenous values: all cultures, it seems, are in the process of being altered by history.

> *(4) The Old Mythology, especially in its colonial form, held it unproblematic that traders or travelers might buy or barter for artifacts. Alternatively, artifacts might be accepted as gifts. None of this disturbs their meanings in the Old Mythology, and if anything the native should be thankful for receiving payment for the work before the termites got to it.*

The New Mythology sees buying, selling, and trading as essentially Western concepts. Even to accept these objects as gifts is to become, as Kasfir puts it, implicated in "the web of conflicting interests that surround them." There is hence no "noninterventionist" way of obtaining these artifacts, since somewhere in the scheme power relations will obtrude, leading to the exploitation of the indigenous maker or owner of the object. In other words, the native always gets cheated. The New Mythology seems to impute to precontact tribal societies a premercantile edenic state, as though trade and barter (not to mention theft or conquest) of ritual or other valuable artifacts did not occur among these peoples until Europeans came along.

> *(5) The only reason to collect primitive artifacts, according to premodernist Old Mythology, was as curiosities, examples perhaps of an early stage of Social Darwinist development: they were to be placed in a cabinet alongside fossils and tropical insects. After Picasso & Co., the Old Mythology proclaimed that primitive art embodied the aesthetic sensibilities found in all art, and therefore was as much worth collecting as Constables or Utamaros, and for precisely the same reasons.*

The New Mythology displays an oddly ambivalent attitude toward collecting. On the one hand, collecting is persistently disparaged, for instance as a "hegemonic activity, an act of appropriation . . . a largely colonial enterprise . . . the logical outcome of a social-evolutionary view of the Other." McEvilley speaks of "captured" tribal objects, a trope suggesting they exist in Western collections as prisoners or slaves. Given the reprehensible nature of collecting, one would expect New Mythologists to demand that the trade in ethnographic art cease, but I have not encountered any such suggestions (except, of course, for the criminal trade in looted antiquities). Even those writers who take moral satisfaction from criticizing collecting appear themselves to have "captured" the occasional artifact.

(6) On puritanical grounds the Old Mythology often forbade taking pleasure in works of tribal art: the sexual element in carvings offended missionary and nineteenth-century colonial sensibilities. In New Zealand, as elsewhere, genitals were hacked off Maori figures, and some overtly sexual carvings were simply burned, lest prurient pleasure be aroused.

The New Mythology replaces this attitude with a new and asexual form of puritanism. Enjoyment of any sort derived from the experience of ethnographic art is considered a cultural mistake at best, a form of visual imperialism at worst: "the colonialist gaze." Angst-ridden New Mythologists are reluctant to record appreciation or enthusiastic emotional reactions to artifacts. Thus Torgovnick heaps contempt on Roger Fry, among many others, for his "insensitive" and "racist" readings in praise of African art, but she never provides, in her own voice, nonracist, sensitive readings to instruct us on how to do it right. Nicholas Thomas is simply bemused: of the museums crammed with indigenous artifacts—"carved bowls, clubs, spears, baskets, pots," etc.—he honestly admits that "I have never understood why people want to look at such things (although I often look at them myself)." Christopher B. Steiner makes the bizarre claim that the objects are valued by Westerners as a way to "celebrate" the loss of the utility they had in their original cultural contexts. Other New Mythologists, such as James Clifford and James Boon (whose article title "Why Museums Make Me Sad" is clear enough), write about ethnographic arts with such a brooding sense of guilt about the historical treatment of conquered cultures that no sense of joy or love for the art is ever allowed to emerge.

(7) Colonialist Old Mythology held that though primitive cultures were to some degree capable of adopting Western technologies and manufactured articles, they could not possibly understand Western culture. In fact, having no adequate comparative perspective, the primitives could not even fully understand their own cultures. Their simple little societies were, however, transparent to the educated, sophisticated Westerner.

The New Mythology, on the contrary, contends that it is the "educated" West which fails to grasp the vast subtleties offered by these cultures, ranging from ethnobotany and folk medicines to spiritual wisdom. Instead, the West ethnocentrically imposes on them its own categories, such as "individual," "religion," or "work of art," when in actuality these concepts have no place in the cultural landscape of the Other. In the matter of borrowing, the New Mythology holds that indigenous artists are, in its preferred parlance, free to appropriate from European culture, infusing their new work with "transformed meanings," fresh associations given to foreign elements introduced into a new cultural context. The reverse—Europeans borrowing from indigenous arts—is to be discouraged. This inversion of the Old Mythology means that an innovative Sepik dancer who incorporates cigarette wrappers in an elaborate headdress is participating in an exciting fusion of cultures, while a Swedish office-worker who wears a New Guinea dog-tooth necklace is implicated in hegemonic, colonialist appropriation.

As a frontispiece for *Gone Primitive,* Torgovnick presents a heavily ironic, not to say sneering, painting (by Ed Rihacek) of a stylish European woman wearing sunglasses and sitting before a zebra skin, surrounded by a collection of "primitive art." In his derisory essay on the "Primitivism" exhibition, Clifford reproduces a 1929 photograph of Mrs. Pierre Loeb, seated in her Paris apartment filled with Melanesian and African carvings. Clifford labels this as an "appropriation" which was "not included in the 'Primitivism' Show" (a curious observation inasmuch as this very photograph appears in the show's catalogue). Both of these images suggest a kind of disapproval of European cultural appropriation that it would be unthinkable to direct toward their cultural inversion—for example, the 1970s posed village photograph Susan Vogel has published showing a Côte d'Ivoire man seated before a wrinkled, painted backdrop of an airplane, a cassette radio proudly displayed on his lap.

(8) The Old Mythology at its colonialist worst posited an ethnocentric aesthetic absolutism: advanced, naturalistic European art forms were seen, especially because of their naturalism, as demonstrating a higher stage in the evolution of art. Modernist Old Mythology retained the idea of universal aesthetic standards, but argued that tribal arts fully met these criteria for excellence, which were formalist rather than naturalistic.

In rejecting both these positions, some New Mythologists urge the abandonment of any idea of transcultural aesthetic criteria (which would be implicitly imperialistic) in favor of complete aesthetic relativism. McEvilley imputes to Kant an epistemology which "tacitly supported the violent progress of 19th- and 20th-century imperialisms" and which justified a view of the Western aesthetic sense as superior to that of non-Western cultures. The New Mythology owes its aesthetic relativism entirely to the climate of poststructural thought rather than to any empirical study of ethnographic and other world arts.

(9) More generally, both colonialist and modernist Old Mythologies imply or presuppose an epistemic realism: they both presume to describe the actual, existent characteristics of tribal societies and their arts.

Under the influence of poststructuralism, the New Mythology often presupposes various forms of constructivism, the idea that categories of human existence are constituted entirely by our own mental activity: we "invent" or "construct" the "primitive," tribal "art," "religion," and so on. The knots into which theorists become tied in trying to introduce such poststructural rhetoric into the study of indigenous arts is illustrated by Barbara Kirshenblatt-Gimblett who writes: "Ethnographic artifacts are objects of ethnography.

They are artifacts created by ethnographers. Objects become ethnographic by virtue of being defined, segmented, detached, and carried away by ethnographers." From her first sentence, a dictionary definition, Kirshenblatt-Gimblett deduces a constructivist howler: the trivial fact that ethnographers define the ethnographic status of artifacts does not entail that *they create the artifacts.* Nor do they create the artifacts' meanings; it is the people being studied who determine that, and this awkward reality gets obviously in the way of attempts by New Mythologists to relativize cultural knowledge and meaning. Constructivism is a strong force among New Mythologists most influenced by literary theory, and is less persistent among those who come from a background of academic anthropology. Despite their tendency to toy with the jargon of literary theory, anthropologists generally acquire a robust respect for the independent existence and integrity of the peoples they study.

> *(10) Finally, premodernist Old Mythology, especially in its Victorian colonialist guises, preached the superiority of Western culture. It proposed to bring moral enlightenment to people it viewed as savages, mainly through Christianity, but also with science and modern medicine. In this, it stands starkly apart from modernist Old Mythology, and even from some eighteenth-century explorers of the South Pacific, who claimed that the moral sense and intellectual capacities of "primitive man" were at least equal to those of Europeans.*

The air of smug moral superiority has returned with a vengeance with the arrival of the New Mythology, whose champions patronize, censure, and jeer at any Old Mythology text they find wanting. The New Mythology of tribal arts displays a sense of righteous certitude that would fit the most zealous Victorian missionary.

At Play in the Fields of the Text

In some respects, the New Mythology's frequent borrowing from poststructuralism and the general intellectual climate of postmodernism is healthy and appropriate. For example, the approach to tribal arts must necessarily involve "blurred genres" and fused disciplines, bringing together ethnography, art history, philosophical aesthetics, and general cultural, including literary, criticism. This is fully in the poststructural/postmodern spirit, as is calling into question the peculiarly European distinction between the so-called fine arts and the popular and folk arts and crafts, which normally has no clear application in understanding tribal arts. But there are other aspects of poststructuralism which sit uneasily with the study of tribal arts.

One such notion is the pervasive poststructuralist attack on the authority of the artist or author in aesthetic interpretation. Barthes, whose thinking was again seminal in this regard, proclaimed the death of the god-author, along with the end of the ideologies of objectivity and truth, insisting that the meaning of a literary text is a critical construction instead of a discovered fact. In the theory of literature and the practice of criticism, such constructivist ideas have had their uses, liberating criticism from traditional demands to invoke authorial intention as a validating principle for critical interpretation.

However, the poststructural abandonment of the notion that texts contain meanings placed there by their authors (which it is criticism's job to determine) is only possible in a cultural landscape in which there is enough prior agreement on meanings to allow criticism to become thus freely creative. The poststructural death of the author could only take hold in literary theory because there was already in place an extensive tradition of interpretation of, say, *Madame Bovary* or *Moby Dick*. These novels enjoy a canonical status as works of literary art: they observe the conventions of established genres and were written in European languages by recognized literary artists. The cultural conditions that form the context of their creation and reception are solid enough to enable a generation of critics—notably Barthes, Foucault, and Derrida, but also the New Critics of the Anglo-American world—to declare the hypothetical death of the author and advocate a liberated, creative criticism of *jouissance*.

But do these doctrines and strategies of contemporary theory provide useful models for the critical ethnography of indigenous arts? Hardly. Poststructuralism's image of the free-spirited critic at play in textual fields goes counter to one of the most strongly held (indeed, in my opinion, indispensable) principles of the New Mythology: respect for the autonomous existence of tribal artists, including respect for their intentions and cultural values. Declaring the death of the (European) author may be jolly sport for jaded literary theorists, but an analogous ideological death of the tribal artist is not nearly so welcome in the New Mythology, nor should it be in any anthropology department. The study of tribal arts—indeed, all non-Western arts—cannot presuppose a sufficiently stable, shared background understanding against which one might declare artists' intentions irrelevant or passé. Moreover, the New Mythology gains its sense of identity by pitting itself against what it takes to be the Old Mythology's ethnocentric disregard not only for the intentions of tribal artists but for their very names as well. (Price calls this "the anonymization of Primitive Art," and it was a major complaint lodged against the "'Primitivism' in 20th Century Art" exhibition. If such ethnocentrism is not to be actively encouraged, the tribal artist's interpretations *must* enjoy special status, defining in the first instance the object of study. In order to respect the cultures and people from which tribal works of art are drawn, the New Mythology must treat indigenous intentions—ascertained or, where unavailable, at least postulated—as constituting the beginning of all interpretation, if not its exhaustive or validating end.

This deep conflict between doctrines of the New Mythology and the poststructuralism it seems so eager to appropriate keeps breaking out despite efforts to paper it over. McEvilley and Clifford enthusiastically adopt the discourse of constructivism, so long as they are talking about how "we," or "the West," or the "omniscient" curatorial mind, construct the generalized primitive, but New Mythologists are not nearly so keen to revert to constructivist parlance when it comes to discussing the actual meanings of works of tribal art. Thus Kasfir asks, "Who creates meaning for African art?," where "for" indicates "on behalf of," implying that Western collectors and exhibitors make a meaning for African art to satisfy the Western eye and mind.

This, however, avoids the more obvious wording of the question "Who creates the meaning *of* African art?" If there is any answer at all to this question, it must begin with the artists and cultures that produce the art. The West can "construct" in the poststructuralist manner to its heart's content, but its understandings will always be about the indigenous constructions of the cultures from which African works derive. It is indigenous intentions, values, descriptions, and constructions which must be awarded theoretical primacy. If an African carving is intended by its maker to embody a spirit, and that is an ascertainable fact about it, then any ethnography that constructs its meaning in contradiction to that fact is false. Of course, ethnography need not culminate with indigenous meanings and intentions, any more than literary criticism comes to an end when an author's intended meaning for a work of fiction has been determined. But ethnography has no choice except to begin with indigenous meanings, which it does not construct, but discovers.

POSTSCRIPT

Do Museums Misrepresent Ethnic Communities Around the World?

Clifford, like many critical theorists, is deeply suspicious of all representations of others. Dutton, in contrast, seems to question both the motives and the logic of this suspicion. He is especially critical of Clifford's lack of historical accuracy when describing the goals and motivations of museums and their curators. Are Clifford's postmodernist conclusions guilty of misrepresenting the museum world in ways that parallel his critique of particular exhibits? Does Dutton's critique of the postmodernists solve the historical problems that are present in both museums and the writings of their critics? Is there a middle ground that would allow for exhibitions with more sensitive context?

Clifford has also dealt with museum exhibits in his book *Routes: Travel and Translation in the Late Twentieth Century* (Harvard University Press, 1997). Related approaches to the problem of representation in museums include Sally Price's *Primitive Art in Civilized Places* (University of Chicago Press, 1989) and Shelly Errington's *The Death of Authentic Primitive Art and Other Tales of Progress* (University of California Press, 1998).

Nicholas Thomas's *Entangled Objects: Exchange, Material Culture and Colonialism in the Pacific* (Harvard University Press, 1991) considers the problem of representation among ethnographic objects in the Pacific. Enid Schildkraut and Curtis A. Keim's *The Scramble for Art in Central Africa* (Cambridge University Press, 1998), Ruth B. Phillips and Christopher B. Steiner's *Unpacking Culture: Art and Commodity in Colonial and Post Colonial Worlds* (University of California Press, 1999), and Michael O'Hanlon and Robert L. Welsch's *Hunting the Gatherers: Ethnographic Collectors, Agents, and Agency in Melanesia* (Berghahn, 2000) provide examples of the rich historical context of museum collections of the sort Dutton seeks.

Both Clifford and Dutton build their arguments on the premise that objects have complex histories, an idea that was originally developed in slightly different ways by anthropological historian George W. Stocking, Jr.'s *Objects and Others: Essays on Museums and Material Culture* (University of Wisconsin Press, 1985) and by anthropologist Arjun Appadurai's *The Social Life of Things: Commodities in Cultural Perspective* (Cambridge University Press, 1986). Both books make two crucial points: objects have histories, and the meanings of objects change when the objects themselves move from one context to another. Also, both argue that objects can take on many different meanings depending on context and viewpoint. Together these books have redefined museological studies and transformed what had been an anthropological backwater into a thriving specialization within the discipline.

Contributors to This Volume

EDITORS

KIRK M. ENDICOTT is a professor and the chairman of the Department of Anthropology at Dartmouth College. He received a B.A. in anthropology from Reed College in 1965, a Ph.D. in anthropology from Harvard University in 1974, and a D.Phil. in social anthropology from the University of Oxford in 1976. He has repeatedly conducted field research among the Batek people of Malaysia. He is the author of *An Analysis of Malay Magic* (Clarendon Press, 1970) and *Batek Negrito Religion: The World-view and Rituals of a Hunting and Gathering People of Peninsular Malaysia* (Clarendon Press, 1979), and is coauthor, with Robert K. Dentan, Alberto G. Gomez, and M. Barry Hooker, of *Malaysia and the "Original People": A Case Study of the Impact of Development on Indigenous Peoples* (Allyn and Bacon, 1997).

ROBERT L. WELSCH is a visiting professor of anthropology at Dartmouth College and adjunct curator of anthropology at The Field Museum in Chicago. He received a B.A. in anthropology from Northwestern University in 1972, an M.A. in anthropology from the University of Washington in 1976, and a Ph.D. from the same department in 1982. He has conducted field research among the Ningerum people of Papua New Guinea, the Mandar people of South Sulawesi, Indonesia, and the diverse peoples of the Sepik Coast of Papua New Guinea. He is the author of *An American Anthropologist in Melanesia* (University of Hawaii Press, 1998) and coeditor, with Michael O'Hanlon, of *Hunting the Gatherers: Ethnographic Collectors, Agents, and Agency in Melanesia* (Berghahn Publishers, 2000).

AUTHORS

BRIAN R. BILLMAN is an associate professor of anthropology at the University of North Carolina. His research has focused on the prehistory of Peru and the American Southwest. His publications include *Settlement Pattern Studies in the Americas: Fifty Years Since Virú* (Smithsonian Institution Press, 1999), which he coauthored with Gary M. Feinman.

BRUCE BRADLEY is a senior lecturer in the Department of Archaeology at the University of Exeter. He has published widely on Paleoindians, flaked stone technologies, and the American Southwest.

ROBERT L. CARNEIRO is a cultural anthropologist and a curator of anthropology at the American Museum of Natural History in New York. He has conducted field research in Brazil, Peru, and Venezuela, focusing on cultural evolution and political evolution. He is the author of many books and articles, including *Evolutionism in Cultural Anthropology: A Critical History* (Westview, 2003).

JAMES CLIFFORD is a professor of the history of consciousness at the University of California at Santa Cruz. He has written many books and articles about postmodern anthropology, including *Routes: Travel and Translation in the Late Twentieth Century* (Harvard University Press, 1997).

JAMES R. DENBOW is an associate professor of anthropology at the University of Texas at Austin. He has conducted field research in southern Africa and was curator of archaeology at The National Museum of Botswana.

KURT E. DONGOSKE is a tribal archaeologist working in the Cultural Preservation Office of the Hopi Tribe. He is coauthor, with Mark S. Aldenderfer, of *Working Together: Native Americans and Archaeologists* (Society for American Archaeology, 2000).

DENIS DUTTON is associate professor of art theory in the School of Fine Arts at the University of Canterbury at Christchurch, New Zealand. He is a specialist on aesthetics and tribal art and is the author of *The Forger's Art: Forgery and the Philosophy of Art* (University of California Press, 1983).

KAREN L. ENDICOTT is director of communications at the Thayer School of Engineering at Dartmouth College. She was trained as a cultural anthropologist and conducted field research among the Batek of Malaysia.

T. J. FERGUSON is a consultant with Heritage Resource Management Consultants in Tucson, Arizona. He is the author of many articles and books, including *Historic Zuni Architecture and Society* (University of Arizona Press, 1996).

STUART FIEDEL is an archaeologist working with John Milner Associates in Alexandria, Virginia. He is the author of many books and papers, including *Prehistory of the Americas,* 2nd ed. (Cambridge University Press, 1992).

DEREK FREEMAN (1916–2001) was an emeritus professor of anthropology at the Research School of Pacific and Asian Studies at the Australian National University. He conducted field research among the Iban of Borneo and the Samoans of western Samoa. He is author of many books and articles, including *The Fateful Hoaxing of Margaret Mead* (Penguin, 1999).

CLIFFORD GEERTZ (1923–2006) was a professor at the Institute for Advanced Study in Princeton, New Jersey. He has conducted field research in Indonesia and Morocco. He is the author of *Works and Lives: The Anthropologist as Author* (Stanford University Press, 1988) and many other books.

GEORGE W. GILL is a professor of anthropology at the University of Wyoming. He is a biological and forensic anthropologist and has examined human skeletons from Mexico, Peru, Easter Island, and the Great Plains.

STEVEN GOLDBERG is a professor of sociology at City University of New York. He has written many books and journal articles, including *Why Men Rule: A Theory of Male Dominance* (Open Court, 1993).

DONALD K. GRAYSON is a professor of anthropology at the University of Washington (Seattle). He is a specialist on prehistoric environments and has excavated many early sites in the Great Basin and in other western states. He is author of *The Desert's Past: A Natural Prehistory of the Great Basin* (Smithsonian Institution Press, 1993) and many other books.

EDWARD H. HAGEN is an anthropologist in the Institute for Theoretical Biology at Humboldt University in Berlin. His research has focused on evolutionary approaches to depression. He has published several articles about biosocial science and sociobiology.

ROBERT A. HAHN is an epidemiologist with the Centers for Disease Control and Prevention and an adjunct professor of anthropology at Emory University. He has published many articles and books on various topics in medical anthropology, including *Anthropology in Public Health: Bridging Differences in Culture and Society* (Oxford University Press, 1999).

KEN HALE (1934–2001) was an emeritus professor of linguistics at Massachusetts Institute of Technology. He has studied languages from most parts of the world and is the author of many books and articles, including *The Green Book of Language Revitalization Practice* (Academic, 2001), which he coedited with Leanne Hinton.

GARY HAYNES is a professor of anthropology at the University of Nevada at Reno. His research has focused on Paleoindians, the peopling of the New World, and North American large mammals. He is author of *The Early Settlement of North America: The Clovis Era* (Cambridge University Press, 2002).

ELLEN RHOADS HOLMES has conducted field research in Samoa. She is coauthor, with her husband Lowell D. Holmes, of *Samoan Village: Then and Now* (Harcourt Brace, 1992) and *Other Cultures, Elder Years: An Introduction to Cultural Gerontology* (Sage, 1995).

LOWELL D. HOLMES is an emeritus professor of anthropology at Wichita State University. He has conducted field research in Samoa and in contemporary America. He is the author of many articles and books, including *Quest for the Real Samoa* (Bergin & Garvey, 1986).

SUDHIR KAKAR is widely known as the father of Indian psychoanalysis and has practiced for many years in New Delhi. He has been a visiting professor of psychology at the University of Chicago and is currently a senior fellow at the Center for the Study of World Religions at Harvard University. His books include *The Colors of Violence: Cultural Identities, Religion and Conflict* (University of Chicago Press, 1996).

ROGER M. KEESING (1935–1993) was a professor of anthropology at McGill University. He is best known for his research among the Kwaio people of Malaita in the Solomon Islands and published four books and many articles about them, including *Custom and Confrontation: The Kwaio Struggle for Cultural Autonomy* (University of Chicago Press, 1992).

PETER LADEFOGED is a professor of linguistics at the University of California at Los Angeles who specializes in the sound systems of the world's languages. He has studied the sound systems of endangered languages around the world, and is author of many books and articles including *Vowels and Consonants: An Introduction to the Sounds of Languages* (Blackwell, 2004) and *The Sounds of the World's Languages* (Blackwell, 1996).

PATRICIA M. LAMBERT is an associate professor of anthropology at Utah State University. Her research focuses on a variety of topics in North American bioarchaeology. She edited *Bioarchaeological Studies of Life in the Age of Agriculture: A View from the Southeast* (University of Alabama Press, 2000).

FREDERICK (FRITZ) P. LAMPE is the Lutheran chaplain at Syracuse University, where he is also affiliated with the department of anthropology. He spent four years as a Lutheran missionary and chaplain at the University of Technology (Unitech) in Lae, Papua New Guinea.

RICHARD B. LEE is a professor of anthropology and chair of the African Studies Programme at the University of Toronto. He is best known for his research among the San peoples of the Kalahari Desert. He is senior editor of *The Cambridge Encyclopedia of Hunters and Gatherers* (Cambridge University Press, 1999).

BANKS L. LEONARD is an archaeological consultant with Soils Systems, Inc. in Phoenix, Arizona. He has coauthored a number of articles and book chapters about Southwestern prehistory.

ROGER IVAR LOHMANN is a professor of anthropology at Trent University, Oshawa, Ontario. He conducted research concerning the anthropology of religion among the Asabano of Papua New Guinea. He was editor of *Dream Travelers: Sleep Experiences and Culture in the Western Pacific* (Palgrave Macmillan, 2003).

DEBRA L. MARTIN is a professor of biological anthropology at Hampshire College. Her research has focused on skeletal biology and bioarchaeology in North America. She is the author of many articles and books, as well as coeditor of *Harmony and Discord: Bioarchaeology of the La Plata Valley* (Museum of New Mexico Press, 2001).

CLEMENT W. MEIGHAN (1925–1997) was a professor of anthropology at the University of California at Los Angeles (UCLA) and for many years director of UCLA's Archaeological Survey. He excavated numerous archaeological sites in California and Mesoamerica. He was coauthor of *Chronologies in New World Archaeology* (Academic Press, 1978).

DAVID J. MELTZER is a professor of prehistory at Southern Methodist University. He has excavated numerous sites in search of archaeological evidence of early Paleoindians. He is author of *Folsom: New Archaeological Investigations of a Classic Paleoindian Bison Kill* (University of California Press, 2006) and many other books.

ANTHONY OBERSCHALL is professor of sociology at the University of North Carolina at Chapel Hill. He has written many books and articles dealing with social conflict, including *Social Movements: Ideologies, Interests, and Identities* (Transaction Books, 1993).

DALE PETERSON is a professor at Tufts University. He is the author, with Jane Goodall, of *Visions of Caliban: On Chimpanzees and People* (Houghton Mifflin, 1993) and, with Richard Wrangham, of *Demonic of Males: Apes and the Origins of Human Violence* (Houghton Mifflin, 1996).

MICHAEL E. PRICE is an anthropologist and postdoctoral fellow at the University of Indiana, formerly a graduate student at the University of California at Santa Barbara. He has published several articles about biosocial science and sociobiology.

JAMES RIDING IN is an associate professor of Justice Studies and American Indian Studies at Arizona State University. A historian by training, he is also a member of the Pawnee tribe.

E. S. SAVAGE-RUMBAUGH is a professor of biology at Georgia State University. She is the author of many articles and books about apes and their capacity for language, including *Ape Language: From Conditioned Response to Symbol* (Columbia University Press, 1986).

DENNIS STANFORD is a curator of archaeology at the Department of Anthropology at the National Museum of Natural History of the Smithsonian Institution. He has conducted excavations in the Arctic and High Plains.

LINDA S. STONE is professor emeritus of anthropology at Washington State University. She has conducted field research in Nepal and on issues related to gender in the United States. She is the author of *Kinship and Gender* (Westview, 2005) and many other books.

LAWRENCE GUY STRAUS is a professor of anthropology at the University of New Mexico. His research has focused on Old World adaptations during the Pleistocene. He is the author of *Iberia before the Iberians: The Stone Age Prehistory of Cantabrian Spain* (University of New Mexico Press, 1996) and many other books.

ROBERT W. SUSSMAN is professor of physical anthropology at Washington University in St. Louis and was recently editor of *American Anthropologist*. He is the author of many articles and books, and editor of *The Biological Basis of Human Behavior: A Critical Review*, 2nd ed. (Prentice Hall, 1999).

SANGUN SUWANLERT was a physician and psychiatrist at Srithunya Hospital in Nondhaburi, Thailand. His research has focused on the use of psychotropic drugs and other psychological phenomena in Thailand, about which he has published several articles in English.

JOHN TOOBY is a professor of anthropology at the University of California at Santa Barbara (UCSB) and codirector of UCSB's Center for Evolutionary Psychology. He is a specialist on the evolution of hominid behavior and cognition. He is coeditor of *The Adapted Mind: Evolutionary Psychology and the Generation of Culture* (Oxford University Press, 1992).

HAUNANI-KAY TRASK is a professor of Hawaiian studies at the University of Hawai'i at Manoa. She is a well-known native Hawaiian activist with Ka Lahui Hawai'i, one of several organizations advocating native Hawaiian sovereignty. She is the author of *From a Native Daughter: Colonialism and Sovereignty in Hawai'i,* rev. ed. (University of Hawai'i Press, 1999).

TERENCE TURNER is a professor of anthropology at Cornell University. He is best known for his research among the Kayapo of the Amazon. His current research focuses on, among other topics, ethics and human rights. He has published many articles and book chapters about the Kayapo.

JOEL WALLMAN is a program officer at the Harry Frank Guggenheim Foundation in New York. In recent years he has studied aggression and linguistic ability. He is the author of *Aping Language* (Cambridge University Press, 1992).

EDWIN N. WILMSEN is a research fellow at the University of Texas at Austin. He has conducted research in Botswana and is the author of *Land Filled With Flies: A Political Economy of the Kalahari* (University of Chicago Press, 1989).

PETER WOOD is an anthropologist who is currently executive director of the National Association of Scholars. Formerly he taught anthropology at Boston University and at King's College in New York City. He is the author of *Diversity: The Invention of a Concept* (Encounter Books, 2003) and *A Bee on the Mouth: Anger in America Today* (Encounter Books, 2006).

RICHARD WRANGHAM is a professor of anthropology at Harvard University. He studies primate behavior and ecology and evolutionary biology. He is the author, with Dale Peterson, of *Demonic Males: Apes and the Origins of Human Violence* (Houghton Mifflin, 1996).